The Praeger International Collection on Addictions

THE PRAEGER INTERNATIONAL COLLECTION ON ADDICTIONS

Volume 2
Psychobiological Profiles

Edited by Angela Browne-Miller

Praeger Perspectives
Abnormal Psychology
Thomas G. Plante, Series Editor

Westport, Connecticut
London

Library of Congress Cataloging-in-Publication Data

The Praeger international collection on addictions / edited by Angela Browne-Miller.
    v. cm. — (Abnormal psychology, ISSN 1554–2238)
    Includes index.
    Contents: v. 1. Faces of addiction, then and now—v. 2. Psychobiological
profiles—v. 3. Characteristics and treatment perspectives—v. 4. Behavioral
addictions from concept to compulsion.
        ISBN 978–0–275–99605–5 (set : alk. paper)—ISBN 978–0–275–99607–9
(v.1 : alk. paper)—ISBN 978–0–275–99609–3 (v.2 : alk. paper)—
ISBN 978–0–275–99611–6 (v.3 : alk. paper)—ISBN 978–0–275–99613–0
(v.4 : alk. paper)   1. Substance abuse.   2. Alcoholism.   3. Compulsive
behavior.   4. Addicts.   I. Browne Miller, Angela, 1952–
    HV4998.P72   2009
    616.86—dc22   2008051468

British Library Cataloguing in Publication Data is available.

Library of Congress Catalog Card Number: 2008051468
ISBN: 978–0–275–99605–5 (set)
        978–0–275–99607–9 (Vol. 1)
        978–0–275–99609–3 (Vol. 2)
        978–0–275–99611–6 (Vol. 3)
        978–0–275–99613–0 (Vol. 4)
ISSN: 1554–2238

First published in 2009

Praeger Publishers, 88 Post Road West, Westport, CT 06881
An imprint of Greenwood Publishing Group, Inc.
www.praeger.com

Printed in the United States of America

The paper used in this book complies with the
Permanent Paper Standard issued by the National
Information Standards Organization (Z39.48–1984).

10 9 8 7 6 5 4 3 2 1

Contents

Contents

PART II: BODIES

PART III: PSYCHOBIOLOGIES

Series Foreword

Tragically, most people across the globe have either struggled with a health- and relationship-damaging addiction or know someone who has. Addictions, broadly defined, have touched the lives of the majority of people in multiple cultures and locations. For centuries, numerous people have suffered with their addictions to alcohol and drugs as well as with other addictions, with often devastating outcomes. Sadly, important relationships, jobs and careers, and many lives have been lost due to the destructive power of addiction. These tragedies not only occur for those who suffer from addiction, but for their loved ones, coworkers, and community members, and for innocent victims who are perhaps in the wrong place at the wrong time when an addiction-related accident, crime, or violence occurs. The enormous cost of addiction in health care, traffic accidents, crime, violence, loss of workplace productivity, and broken families is too large to quantify. The global spread and success of organizations such as Alcoholics Anonymous (as well as related organizations such as Narcotics Anonymous, Sexoholics Anonymous, and Overeaters Anonymous) is a testament to the numerous people trying to recover from their addictions. Sadly, for every person seeking help for his addiction problem, there are likely to be many more people who never do. Clearly we need help to better understand, evaluate, treat, and cope with those who suffer from addictions.

In this remarkable four-volume set, *The Praeger International Collection on Addictions*, Angela Browne-Miller, PhD, DSW, MPH, has assembled an all-star and diverse team of leading experts from across the globe to provide a state-of-the-art understanding of the various facets of addiction. Each chapter is written in a manner that is suitable for professionals working in the field as well as educated lay readers and those who either struggle with addictions or live or work with someone who does. What is especially remarkable about the four-volume set is its emphasis on addiction from around the globe, examining multicultural and international issues in addiction, as well as its coverage of so many multifaceted aspects of diverse addictions. For example, it certainly makes sense to cover fully addiction topics such as alcohol abuse and illegal drug use of, say, cocaine and heroin, yet chapters are also offered that examine addictions to caffeine, Internet pornography, work, television, intimate relationship abuse, and shopping. The chapters highlight biological, psychological, social, spiritual, and public health perspectives, with chapter authors who are psychologists, psychiatrists, other physicians, nurses, social workers, counselors, clergy, and other professionals. Dr. Browne-Miller is uniquely qualified to assemble this project as she is someone who has worked in the field of addiction for many years and has training in a unique blend of both the policy and the clinical sides of psychology, social work, education and public health.

The set is complete, state of the art, and highly informative and engaging. There is something for everyone interested in the field of addiction for professional or personal reasons. It is hoped that professionals and lay readers will greatly benefit from this important work and, in doing so, will find a way to improve the lives of those touched by addiction. It is my hope that both research and practice in the field of addiction will be greatly improved thanks to this set. The lives of those who either struggle with addiction or live with those who do will ultimately be improved thanks in part to this critical series. I am grateful to Dr. Browne-Miller and her assembled contributors for providing us all with such important and high-quality volumes that are now available to the public and professional communities. If only one life is saved or improved thanks to this set, it will be a great success in my view; yet I expect that many lives will ultimately be saved or greatly improved thanks to *The Praeger International Collection on Addictions.*

Thomas G. Plante, PhD, ABPP
Santa Clara University and Stanford University School of Medicine,
Praeger Series Editor, Abnormal Psychology

Preface

Angela Browne-Miller, PhD, DSW, MPH

Welcome to *The Praeger International Collection on Addictions*, addressing the insidious, pervasive, worldwide problem of human addiction. Addiction is clearly a global issue, touching every population, every nation, and every age group, people from all walks of life everywhere, directly or indirectly. Indeed, we are talking about an affliction of epic and epidemic proportions. We cannot look away. This is the health of the human species we are talking about.

The World Health Organization (WHO, 2008, p. 1) reports that "psychoactive substance use poses a significant threat to the health, social and economic fabric of families, communities and nations. The extent of worldwide psychoactive substance use is estimated at 2 billion alcohol users, 1.3 billion smokers and 185 million drug users" (p. 1). The WHO has estimated there to be at least 76.3 million persons with alcohol use disorders worldwide, and at least 15.3 million persons with drug use disorders worldwide. Alcohol use and abuse as well as the use and abuse of other psychoactive substances contributes to substantial individual and public health costs. Alcohol is but one substance playing a major role in this global addiction epidemic, but clearly there are many others, despite efforts to prevent new addictions and addicts, and to contain world drug markets (UN, 2008, p. 7).

For example, cocaine shares the stage with other abused drugs. Its prevalence is estimated to be up to 3 percent of the population in developing countries, with severe medical, psychological, social, and economic consequences including, but not limited to, the spread of infectious diseases (e.g., AIDS, hepatitis, and tuberculosis), plus crime, violence, and neonatal drug exposure.

Amphetamine-type stimulant (ATP) abuse is more widespread than cocaine abuse in at least 20 countries. Methamphetamine is presumed to lead in ATP addiction rates, with massive meth epidemics affecting several whole countries and entire regions of others. Social and public health costs of methamphetamine production and use via smoking, sniffing, inhaling, and injecting are staggering and growing in many regions. Additionally, there has been a global increase in the production, transportation, and use of opioids, especially heroin, with worldwide heroin production doubling or even tripling since the mid-1980s. Global estimates are that 13.5 million persons consume opioids, with 9.5 million of these being heroin users who face health risks including hepatitis, HIV, and death. And cocaine, meth, and heroin are just one piece of the picture.

The hotly debated drug cannabis—or the *Cannabis* family of drugs with the euphoric tetrahydrocannabinols, or THCs, including marijuana and hashish preparations—is said to be the most widely abused drug. Research is now suggesting the risk for acute health effects of long-term, chronic cannabis use, including potential impairment of cognitive development, learning, memory, recall, attention, and coordination. (Certainly the presence and extent of long-term effects of casual, of regular and of chronic use are as yet not entirely ascertained.) Both casual use of marijuana and medical use of forms of what is termed medical marijuana (e.g., dronabinol sold as Marinol, the cannabidiols, or CBDs) are subsets of all forms of cannabis use. There are legitimate therapeutic uses of this substance, and these uses make it all the more difficult to regulate marijuana drugs fairly and effectively.

We have here, and in the use of any psychoactive medication for therapeutic purposes, a gray area in which illicit and licit use overlap and can confuse many adult and youth consumers, researchers, and policy makers, among others. In the emergence (or reemergence in history, some will argue) of cannabis as medicine, we have a model for asking which, if any, abused substances may, and perhaps should, be repurposed for medicinal or treatment purposes, and how this is best done against the backdrop of the global addiction epidemic.

Regarding marijuana, we are confronted with the age-at-first-use issue, which suggests that early onset of regular cannabis use may affect not only the academic and social performance of children and teens, but also their future susceptibility to addictions. It was in the 1960s that the hotly debated label "gateway drug" was applied to marijuana, perhaps to scare off its use, and only in the decades since have we understood better what this might actually mean to us. It may not be that marijuana provides the training wheels for drug addiction, but rather that it may serve as an indicator of future use of the same or other drugs. Of course, today, with so many young people having access, and taking advantage of their access, to the whole range of psychoactive substances, the question of which drug might be a gateway to which other drug dissolves into the fury of the countless addiction conundrums of our constantly changing times.

There is always a new, or rediscovery of an old, addiction on the horizon. There is also always a new (or rediscovered) psychoactive substance for exploratory, research, and perhaps even treatment purposes emerging (or re-emerging). Labeling all of these substances as addictive right out the gate may or may not serve science or even humanity itself. How can we be certain the approach we take will be a constructive one? With new legal (where licensed for development and experimentation) and illegal (where not being utilized under protection of law) so-called designer drugs emerging at a staggering rate, we must admit that we cannot know what is coming, nor whether the new compound will be addictive, or popular, or of medicinal value, or even accessible. We can only imagine what the brave new world of chemistry will continue to bring and whether any benefits can be made available without accompanying risks and detriments.

Moreover, the desire to explore and achieve various altered states of consciousness in religious, spiritual, ritual, and perhaps even treatment settings, is unfolding into debates about rights (Browne-Miller, 1989, pp. 258–260). When there is no demonstrated risk to self or others, we have to ask ourselves whether this right should be protected, especially in circumstances of traditional uses for religious purposes. Again, this dilemma arises against the backdrop of the global and runaway epidemic of substance addiction. How do we balance pressures from opposite directions (freedom protecting the right to use versus control to stop injury and costs of using), when these pressures are not balancing themselves?

Also against the backdrop of global addiction levels, is the massive level of addiction to legal drugs, many of which are heavily marketed to consumers. The legal drug tobacco is said to be the substance causing the most damage globally, with at least one-third of the global population smoking. While smoking rates may be dropping in some countries, the reverse is true globally. As just one of its effects, smoking accounts for some 90 percent of all lung cancer in men and 70 percent of all lung cancer in women. And yet tobacco use is overwhelmingly viewed as being "the single most avoidable cause of disease, disability and death" in the United States (CDC, 2008, p. 2).

And perhaps nothing here has touched so many lives as the regularly consumed, legal drug caffeine, perhaps because coffee drinking is considered so very normal and acceptable, even necessary, in everyday life. However, we must ask whether there is a level of caffeine use that is abuse—or perhaps self-abuse. Surely we do not want to throw caffeine use onto this list of substance abuses and addictions. Still, a collection on addiction would not be complete without at least touching on this matter, and therefore we do address caffeine herein.

And then there are also the addictions to prescription drugs (such as Vicodin, Percocet, OxyContin, and Darvon), which we find increasing rapidly and already a worldwide phenomenon, with the most commonly abused prescription drugs being opiates. The U.S. National Institute of Mental Health characterizes prescription drug addiction as the second most common illegal use of drugs in the United States, second only to marijuana.

We must also note that unusual, virtually invisible psychoactive substances are working their way into our everyday lives. Household and workplace products contain many volatile substances, exposure to which can be not only damaging, but also intoxicating, and perhaps addicting. Although this domain of substance use and abuse is not specifically addressed herein, we must acknowledge the severe and perhaps largely unmeasured effects of this domain of even routine, legal substance use as well as unintentional and intentional abuse.

So as not to exclude nonsubstance addictions in this overview of addiction today, the fourth volume in this collection on addiction reminds us that work, television, shopping, food (with its particularly difficult-to-call-addiction nature), intimate partner relationship, gambling, Internet, and even pornography addictions make their marks in our lives, either indirectly or directly. These behavioral, nondrug addictions, which occur alone and co-occur with each other, also do co-occur with substance uses, abuses, and addictions. Every human being is in some way affected by the prevalence of behavioral addictions, either directly or indirectly. The study of behavioral addictions teaches us a great deal about addiction itself.

All this suggests the picture of an addiction-prone and largely chemically dependent human species. And this is just the tip of the iceberg. With this truly incomplete laundry list of human fallibilities—or better stated, perhaps, human *vulnerabilities*—this four-volume collection on addiction is truly that: a collection of perspectives, approaches, and findings. Each chapter is a snapshot of the work and thinking taking place in many fields of addiction. Contributors to this collection work with addiction on the various social, philosophical, psychological, spiritual, policy, political, economic, biological, and even cellular levels, all places where this thing we call "addiction" lives. Certainly this collection would have to comprise hundreds of volumes, rather than the four that it does, to address addiction in all its iterations.

Here we give voice to a diverse cross section of perspectives on addiction. This is in no way an exhaustive cross section (of either perspectives or addictions); rather, this collection suggests the diversity of perspectives, theories, practices, and types of addiction in the field—or better stated, *fields*—of addiction. The four volumes of this collection represent the voices of those who have graciously and even bravely stepped forward from their numerous countries and arenas of work to contribute their ideas, research, and experiences. Certainly there are many others out there, many other aspects of addiction, and many other drugs and objects of addiction not addressed in these volumes.

This work is divided into four volumes, with the first three addressing addictions to substances and the fourth addressing behaviors that show characteristics of addiction. Volume 1, *Faces of Addiction, Then and Now*, offers a sampling of the depth and breadth of addiction today and in the past; volume 2, *Psychobiological Profiles*, surveys some of the interlinked psychological and biological aspects of addiction; volume 3, *Characteristics and Treatment Perspectives*, samples the range of addiction treatment perspectives and approaches; and volume 4, *Behavioral Addictions from Concept to Compulsion*, gives the reader a glimpse of behavioral addictions other than substance addictions.

Readers will observe that the content of these volumes is indeed diverse and in no way represents any one view or theory of addiction. There are many other voices out there who must also be heard, and only in the interest of time and space are we stopping here, at these volumes. The content of these volumes in no way expresses the opinion of this editor, nor of this publisher, regarding what is right, best proven, or even most en vogue in the addiction world; rather, this *International Collection on Addictions* seeks a display of, a sampling of, the diversity of effort to quell the detrimental effects of addiction on individuals, families, communities, societies, economies, and international relations; on ecologies; and in fact, on the human population of planet Earth.

REFERENCES

Browne-Miller, Angela. (2008, reprint of 1989). Synaptic rights. In *Working dazed: Why drugs pervade the workplace and what can be done about it* (pp. 258–260). Houston, Texas: Questia Media. Also available at http://www.questia.com/library/book/working-dazed-why-drugs-pervade-the-workplace-and-what-can-be-done-about-it-by-angela-browne-miller.jsp

Centers for Disease Control (CDC). (2008). *Targeting tobacco use: The nation's leading cause of preventable death* (March 2008 revision). Atlanta, GA: U.S. Department of Health and Human Services, Centers for Disease Control and Prevention.

United Nations (UN). (2008). 2008 world drug report. UNODC (United Nations Office on Drug Control), Vienna, Austria: Vienna International Centre, Full report in English available at http://www.unodc.org/documents/wdr/WDR_2008/WDR_2008_eng_web.pdf

World Health Organization, Management of Substance Abuse, Facts and Figures. (2008). "The Global Burden," 2008, (Accessed 9-01-08), p. 1 http://www.who.int/substance_abuse/facts/global_burden/en/index.html. **See Also:** http://www.who.int/substance_abuse/facts/en/index.html

Introduction to Volume 2: Where Psychology and Biology Meet

Angela Browne-Miller, PhD, DSW, MPH

This is Volume 2 of *The Praeger International Collection on Addictions: Psychobiological Profiles*. Here we sample the array of understandings of addiction as we know it today. The intent is to share a sampling from a wide range of material, not to hone in on any one drug addiction, or any one mechanism of addiction, but rather to establish the multilevel (social, psychological, biological) omnipresence of addiction, its reality and dangers. As our scientific understanding of the psychological, neuropsychological, molecular, genetic, and related, even inextricably linked, bases of addictions and interacting conditions is rapidly increasing, there is hope that augmented and new approaches to addiction can turn the tide of this mounting global condition.

We begin "Part I: Issues" with chapter 1, "Addiction and Health Promotion," by Kathleen Bradbury-Golas, DNP, RN, APN, of the Richard Stockton College of New Jersey, in Pomona, New Jersey, United States, and also a nurse in private practice in New Jersey. Bradbury-Golas reminds us that substance abuse is harmful both directly and via the negative lifestyle behaviors that accompany it. Relapse prevention therapy and other treatments surely can decrease the conditions which would invite relapse. Primary care practitioners must recognize what is involved here, and collaborate with addiction specialists to achieve positive health outcomes. Clearly, collaborating or at least coordinating to treat and curb addiction is going to be more effective than working in isolation. This collaboration flows in both directions. Bradbury-Golas also notes that what is most hopeful in the primary prevention of addiction—treating it before it occurs—is the addiction vaccine. According to the U.S. National Institute on

Drug Addiction (NIDA), this vaccine is likely to be available within from one to 10 years. One vaccine in this genre is TA-CD, which prevents the cocaine metabolite from ever reaching the user's brain. Like any other vaccine, TA-CD causes the immune system to create antibodies that attach to cocaine molecules, which in turn are broken down by enzymes found in the bloodstream, with the result that both the desire for and the "pleasure" of cocaine use is prevented.

Next, in chapter 2, Ted Goldberg, PhD, at the department of Social Work at Stockholm University, Stockholm, Sweden, and also at the department of Caring Sciences and Sociology at the University of Gävle, in Gävle, Sweden, shares his insights into the process of "Becoming a Problematic Consumer of Narcotics." Based on studies in Stockholm, Sweden over a four-and-a-half-year period, Goldberg presents a four-stage life-history model indicating why drug use begins and continues. Goldberg applies a life development or life-history career model to explain what brought his subjects to, and led them to continue, their drug use. Discussion of the "future problematic consumer" of narcotic drugs includes a review of symptoms that precede first consumption of narcotics. Goldberg notes the "destructive life-project" he has seen in his subjects: "The problematic consumers of illicit substances I studied are extremely self-destructive people who lead lives that slope steeply toward extermination." Those self-destruction and self-extermination tendencies that may be present in drug addiction behavior warrant our direct attention. We must ask what these behaviors may be telling us about ourselves and about our species.

Ann N. Dapice, PhD, of T. K. Wolf, Inc., an American Indian-focused addiction treatment program in Tulsa, Oklahoma, United States, contributes chapter 3, "Adaptation and Addiction." Have we outlived the usefulness of once-essential survival traits? Do we therefore walk around with antiquated brains and nervous systems that are not adapting rapidly enough to our changing environments—or are we more than ever in need of these age old basic functions, such as the fight or flight response? Addiction is nothing new, and in a species scenario in which the environment may change more rapidly than we do, addiction, that enduring and self-exacerbating human behavior, persists. Dapice writes: "Food and tobacco are connected to other addictive substances in important evolutionary and physiological ways. Understanding the co-development of mammalian brains and ancient psychotropic plants, as well as the implications of ancient psychotropic substance abuse in altering mammalian brains, helps assess the causes and effects of addiction in today's world." Dapice also points out that some things can be used addictively by some people while not addictively by others.

Scott E. McClure, PhD, at the University of California San Diego, department of Psychiatry, Center for Criminality and Addiction Research, Training, and Application (CCARTA) in San Diego, California, United States, authors chapter 4, "Co-occurring Trauma and Substance Use Disorders with Criminal Offenders." McClure points out that individuals who have been abused physically and/or sexually, and those who have "criminally involved" families, have increased chances of being incarcerated and of being traumatized. Hence, post-traumatic stress disorder (PTSD) is common among this group. McClure also notes that the majority of persons in substance abuse treatment programs have experienced traumas, and that there is a significant overlap between "criminogenic" risk factors and those for substance abuse, trauma, and incarceration itself. McClure adds that: "Safety and coping should be the primary focus for individuals in corrections-based treatment. This is especially true for individuals with severe forms of PTSD and other co-occurring disorders who may decompensate upon addressing trauma symptoms. After clients have successfully developed skills to regulate emotions and cope with trauma symptoms without substance use, they may progress to processing the trauma through exposure therapy, and eventually shift their focus on reconnecting to a functional life."

Joan Mathews-Larson, PhD, LADC, and Mark K. Mathews, LADC, BCCR, both of the Health Recovery Center in Minneapolis, Minnesota, United States, add another aspect of addiction, in chapter 5, "The Role of Allergies in Addictions and Mental Illness." Mathews-Larson and Mathews bring together the sciences of human ecology (which says, among other things, that human behavior and mental health can be profoundly affected by substances in our environment) and orthomolecular medicine (which concentrates on particular vitamin and mineral molecules present in the human body to treat particular diseases). Mathews-Larson and Mathews say that both human ecology and orthomolecular medicine must be involved in addressing allergies that affect mental health to reduce inflammatory responses destabilizing the brain, and related tendencies toward addiction. Special attention to "delayed onset allergies" is important, as these allergies can produce numerous symptoms and affect every organ in the body. As Mathews-Larson and Mathews explain: "Unlike the quick response . . . immediate-onset allergy, [delayed onset] symptoms come on slowly—from two hours to several days. Ingesting allergy-provoking foods prompts the gradual formation of immune complexes until finally they overload the immune system's ability to clear them out. That's when symptoms are felt. Unfortunately, the time differential makes symptoms difficult to link to the foods that cause them. And because the initial response to allergy-provoking foods is often a pleasurable, endorphin-like effect, it becomes even more difficult to accept that they are a problem. In the end, a pattern, initiated and sustained by these foods, contributes to an addictive progression of disease." Here we have a model for the pathogenesis of alcoholism, proceeding the way delayed onset allergic reactions proceed: "Whether responding to alcohol, drugs, or allergy foods, allergic/addictive chemistry follows the same course because the body recognizes all these substances as toxins, and turns to the same system—the immune system—to clear them. It's when the toxic load exceeds the immune system's ability to clear it that inflammation begins its destructive process."

"Part II: Bodies" begins with consideration of something that is oft overlooked in discussions of addiction—the all-too-common effects of caffeine, the world's most popular psychoactive drug. Kyle M. Clayton, MS, and Paula Lundberg-Love, PhD, both of the University of Texas at Tyler (UTT), in Tyler, Texas, United States, address caffeine as addictive in chapter 6, "Caffeine: Pharmacology and Effects of the World's Most Popular Drug." In the United States, about 90 percent of all adults consume caffeine on a daily basis. Caffeine withdrawal brings on a range of symptoms, and caffeine use affects health in a number of ways. Caffeine intoxification, something most of us rarely think about in daily life, is indeed possible when the level of 250 mcgs is consumed, and doses of caffeine over 5 to 10 grams can be lethal.

Dirk Hanson, MA, of the blog, Addiction Inbox, and freelance science writer based in Ely, Minnesota, United States, offers another commonly overlooked aspect of addiction in terms of its potential severity and symptoms in chapter 7, "Marijuana Withdrawal: A Survey of Symptoms." With approximately 14 million Americans smoking marijuana regularly, we cannot avoid noting the presence of withdrawal symptoms among many heavy users. In fact, there is growing evidence that there is a "marijuana withdrawal syndrome" characterized by restlessness, anxiety, hostility, depression, sleeplessness, loss of appetite, and a mental state described as "inner unrest." (Additional withdrawal systems are being detected every day.) Clearly, marijuana withdrawal has gone unnoticed or less noticed as withdrawal from other substances is so much more severe, and better documented.

We then move into three chapters that delve into what is considered a "more serious" addiction, methamphetamine addiction. Mary F. Holley, MD, of Mothers Against Methamphetamine in northern Alabama, United States, and the Alabama State Attorney General's Methamphetamine Task Force, shares her look at "Marijuana Interaction with Methamphetamine Addiction" in chapter 8. Holley informs us that marijuana affects the brain in many of the same areas that methamphetamine does. Injury to the hippocampus and frontal lobes arising in heavy marijuana users can be amplified by use of methamphetamine. Holley refers to the endocannabinoid system here, noting that early use of marijuana can affect adolescent neurodevelopment, as can early meth use. Together, marijuana and meth set the stage for severe effects on development.

Herbert C. Covey, PhD, of the Adams County, Colorado, (United States) Social Services Department, and instructor at the College of Continuing Education, University of Colorado at Boulder, Colorado, United States, asks "What Is Methamphetamine and How and Why Is It Used?" in chapter 9. Covey explains that "Meth abusers typically take the drug early in the morning and in two- to four-hour intervals, similar to being on a medication. In contrast, cocaine abusers typically take the drug in the evening and take it over a period of several hours that resembles a recreational-use pattern. They typically continue using until all of the cocaine is gone." Covey reminds us that a certain amount of meth use, and meth addiction, is hidden while taking place right before our eyes: "Some meth addicts use at levels that allow them to maintain jobs, homes, some money, and at least the appearance of being in control."

In chapter 10, Kathryn M. Wells, MD, at the Kempe Center for the Prevention and Treatment of Child Abuse and Neglect and the Health Sciences Center, both at the University of Colorado at Denver, in Denver, Colorado, United States, reports on "The Short- and Long-Term Medical Effects of Methamphetamine on Children and Adults," which are marked and costly to individual lives and to societies, in fact, to entire nations—with global ramifications. She states, "Meth use and abuse in this country [United States] has far-reaching ramifications for not only the user but for society." Wells calls for "continued collaborative efforts" as these "are critical to advancements in understanding the medical effects of meth on the users and children who are exposed."

In a look at the dangers of "vapors," Jace Waguspack, BS, and Paula K. Lundberg-Love, PhD, at the University of Texas at Tyler (UTT), Tyler, Texas, United States, contribute their research in chapter 11, "Vapors May Be Dangerous If Inhaled: An Overview of Inhalants and Their Abuse." Waguspack and Lundberg-Love tell us that the word *inhalant* is used to describe a "heterogeneous group of chemicals that share a common route of administration," reporting that inhalant use is a "serious problem, particularly among young people. The incomplete knowledge of the mechanisms of action for some of these substances, combined with insufficient resources for the treatment of the abusers and the complexity of the issues surrounding inhalant abuse, make it difficult for these individuals to receive the help that they need."

This is followed by chapter 12, "The Effects and Abuse Potential of GHB: A Pervasive 'Club Drug,'" submitted by Bethany L. Waits, BA, at the University of Texas at Tyler (UTT), Tyler, Texas, United States, and Paula K. Lundberg-Love, PhD, also at UTT. Gamma-hydroxybutyrate (GHB) is a widely used drug—in its purest form, a white powdery substance soluble in water, sometimes found in tablet or a capsule form, sometimes injected into the bloodstream, and distributed, both legally and illegally, as a colorless, odorless, and tasteless solution. Use of GHB has undergone a marked increase since its discovery in the late 1960s. It affects the brain as Waits and Lundberg-Love explain: "Once ingested, GHB acts by depressing or downregulating the activity of the central nervous system (CNS), including the brain and the spinal cord, and its effects are similar to other CNS depressants such as alcohol and benzodiazepines (BZDs)." GHB offers an example of the novel drug model: "Although GHB was initially synthesized for use as an intravenous anesthetic for surgical procedures, it has since been marketed therapeutically as a dietary supplement, an anabolic agent, and a drug for the treatment of narcolepsy." Additionally, GHB has been studied for its relief of withdrawal symptoms, including those from alcohol. Against the backdrop of treatment uses of GHB is the disturbing undercurrent of illegal GHB abuse by adults and teens, and even children.

In chapter 13, "HIV and Addiction from an African Perspective: Making the Link," we have the work of Mary Theresa Webb, PhD, of the Global Outreach for Addiction Leadership and Learning (GOAL) Project based in Aliquippa, Pennsylvania, United States; also of the International Substance Abuse and Addiction Coalition (ISAAC) based in the UK; and of the OPORA Training Center in Moscow, Russia. ("Opora" is the Russian word for "support." Moscow based nongovernmental OPORA works with the Russian government to fight addiction, has trained over 3,000 people in addiction and Twelve-Step programs, and has implemented 60 recovery groups in 31 cities in Russia.) Webb writes this chapter with Donald Omonge, BA, of the Substance Abuse Recovery and HIV/AIDs (SARAH) Network, a Kenyan faith-based organization. Webb and Omonge advocate that it is essential that special programs be suited specifically to the African cultures and customs in order to effectively combat the spread of HIV/AIDS. They state that "implementing model programs specifically suited to African cultures and customs to combat the spread of HIV/AIDS must include training components that cross both disciplines (HIV/AIDS and alcohol and other drugs) [and] . . . must be geared to those within the culture who are most effective as change agents." Webb and Omonge also note that "unless GBV [gender-based violence] and rape of vulnerable women and children is curtailed through establishing shelters and a legal protection system, very little hope exists for curbing the spread of the HIV virus in Kenya as well as in other African countries." Also note that injected heroin was determined to be the major risk factor for the spread of HIV; however, now alcohol consumption has became a greater risk than injecting heroin.

And, finally, closing Part II of this volume, in chapter 14, "Drug Abuse–Related HIV/AIDS Epidemic in India: Situation and Responses," Atul

Ambekar, MD, and Meera Vaswani, PhD, at the National Drug Dependence Treatment Center, Department of Psychiatry, All India Institute of Medical Sciences, in New Delhi, Delhi, India, insist that we take heed of a serious aspect of HIV/AIDS in India: "The first case of HIV was detected in India in 1986. In the past two decades since then, the HIV epidemic continues to grow unabated in India." Yet, there is "still no generalized epidemic of HIV in India at the national level. . . . The national level data should, however, be interpreted with caution. India, being a vast and heterogeneous country, has a heterogeneous HIV situation. It has often been commented that there is not one, but many, simultaneous HIV epidemics currently spreading in India," Ambekar and Vaswani write. Certainly, there are harm-reduction services in India; however, they are not enough: "There is a visible and obvious gap in terms of the number of services available and the requirements of these services. Without a rapid scale-up in the number and the quality of the services, [it will be] very challenging to realize the goal of halting and reversing the HIV epidemic."

"Part III: Psychobiologies" moves deeper into various psychological and biological aspects of addition, beginning with chapter 15, "Alcohol Abuse: Impact on Vital Brain Functions and Societal Implications" by Mary Theresa Webb, PhD. In this chapter, Webb notes that the European Union countries and the United States have sounded the global alarm that we are destroying our brains as well as our bodies with the high level of alcohol use around the world. Webb reports on the damaging effects of alcohol on vital brain functions, and the related profound effects on the societal level. Webb notes that neuroimaging study data reveal an alarming increase in heavy alcohol use, with related risks in older adults of loss of cognitive abilities, increased risk of cardiovascular incidents, and dementia.

Chapter 16, "Addiction and Cognitive Control," contributed by Vicki W. Chanon, PhD, and Charlotte A. Boettiger, PhD, both at the Behavioral Neuroscience Program at the University of North Carolina at Chapel Hill in Chapel Hill, North Carolina, United States, characterizes substance use disorder as a neurobehavioral disorder, influenced by disruptions in the cognitive control functions of the brain. With the advent of cognitive neuroscience tools, we are now in a position to make great strides in understanding the brain mechanisms of addiction. Chanon and Boettiger detail the functions of cognitive control and explain that "addicts disproportionately direct their attentional resources toward stimuli associated with their abused substance," referring to "abnormalit[ies] in attentional allocation to drug cues in addicts." Further research along these lines can lead to new treatments, and effectiveness in these treatments, of substance abuse disorders. We have just begun to understand the effect of cognitive regulation on addiction etiologies.

Next, Giuseppe Carrà, MD, MSc, PhD, Consultant Psychiatrist and Research Fellow at the University College London, in London, England, and Sonia Johnson, MSc, MRCPsych, DM, Clinical Lecturer at the University College London, share their work on "Schizophrenia and Substance Misuse" in chapter 17. Comorbid substance abuse problems and schizophrenia or other severe psychoses are associated with poor treatment outcomes. The numbers of those affected by this dual condition are significant: U.S. data show that it may be as much as half of persons with schizophrenia who have co-occurring substance abuse disorders. There is a significant overlap between mental illness and substance abuse, one that insists we do not forget it lest we miss a major subpopulation of persons who are addicted.

Mary F. Holley, MD, of northern Alabama, United States, returns in chapter 18, with her look at the "Neural Basis for Methamphetamine Addiction—Rethinking the Definition of Dependence." As indicated by the title, Holley moves for the rethinking of the very definition of dependence. Motivated by her great concern regarding the high usage of methamphetamine and the severe consequences of this, Holley reminds us that low availability of treatment for meth addiction places the burden on the corrections system. Holley writes, "addiction is a brain disease and not merely a moral failure." Rethinking addiction to fully incorporate this perspective, this reality in fact, will shift the entire field of addiction.

This is followed by chapter 19, "Neurobiological Mechanisms and Cognitive Components of Addiction," written by Jorge Juárez, PhD, and Olga Inozemtseva, PhD, both at the Universidad de Guadalajara in Guadalajara, Jalisco, Mexico. Juárez and Inozemtseva note that the boundaries between the concept that addiction is a public health concern and the concept that it is a problem of inadequate social adaptation are blurry. Furthermore, the pleasure center of the brain, the mesolimbic-cortical system, is central in that several potentially addictive substances act upon it. To effectively address addiction, we must take all of this and more into account from a highly interdisciplinary perspective.

And Mary F. Holley, MD, speaks to us again, in chapter 20, with her report on "Fetal, Neonatal, and Early Childhood Effects of Prenatal Methamphetamine Exposure." Methamphetamine, unlike cocaine, is used by women in equal rates to men, and is far more toxic than cocaine, with a far more intense addiction, and a far more rapid disintegration of personal and family life. Children exposed to methamphetamine in utero are highly likely to show learning disabilities and neurologic dysfunction, which is indeed a public health disaster.

Emmanuel S. Onaivi, MSc, PhD, at William Patterson University in Wayne, New Jersey, United States, also of the U.S. National Institute of

Health (NIH), headquartered in Bethesda, Maryland, United States, writes on the "Endocannabinoid Hypothesis of Drug Addiction" in chapter 21. Onaivi argues that pharmacological treatment of drug addiction is disappointing for the most part, and that new approaches are very much needed. Onaivi tells us that, at least to some extent, misconceptions of addiction as a willpower and morality problem have receded, and recognitions that addiction is a brain disease have surfaced. However, misconceptions holding that dopamine is released in the brain's reward system with all drug use linger. Onaivi reports that many substances, or "agents" as they are also called, do not activate midbrain dopamine-mediated transmission and therefore this popularly applied marker (the dopamine marker) is no longer supporting the perception that drugs are merely activating the brain's reward system. Onaivi contends that in the central nervous system the role of marijuana-like substances produced by the human body, endocannabinoids, must be addressed.

Chapter 22, "Regulation of μ-Opioid Receptor Desensitization in Sensory Neurons," is contributed by Cui-Wei Xie, MD, PhD, at the Department of Psychiatry and Biobehavioral Sciences, David Geffen School of Medicine, and the Semel Institute for Neuroscience and Human Behavior, University of California Los Angeles (UCLA), Los Angeles, United States. Here, Xie calls for further study to "identify and characterize interactions between endogenous receptors in native neurons." Such research may reveal to us mechanisms of "control of opioid receptor signaling" facilitating the strength of "treatment of opiate tolerance and dependence." While most studies to date focus on systems where receptors are "overexpressed," Xie writes that "emerging evidence indicates that formation of hetero-oligomers [between receptors] permits cross regulation of receptor signaling and trafficking, which in some cases, leads to the development of cross desensitization." Such research is key to advancing the power and focus of the treatment of addiction on the cellular level.

Each of the contributors to this volume and the other volumes in the *Praeger International Collection on Addictions* is working on one of the many frontiers of modern addiction research and treatment. And all presented herein is surely just the tip of the iceberg, a sampling of what we know and what we think we know about how addictions work as these addictions feed this global epidemic we call *addiction*. The global picture is both one of grim need and one of unwavering hope. If somehow the goal of massive international collaboration to stop both addiction and the conditions it results in can be realized, perhaps hope will triumph.

Part I

ISSUES

Chapter 1

Addiction and Health Promotion

Kathleen Bradbury-Golas, DNP, RN, APN

Substance abuse interferes with a person's life purpose and interpersonal relationships. Health care researchers expect that the overuse of alcohol and illicit medications will impact upon society's health for decades. The impact of substance abuse, addiction, and relapse is far-reaching. Cardiovascular disease, stroke, cancer, human immunodeficiency virus (HIV)/acquired immunodeficiency syndrome (AIDS), hepatitis, and lung disease can all be affected by drug abuse (National Institute on Drug Abuse [NIDA], 2005). Some of these effects occur when drugs are used at high doses or after prolonged use; however, some may occur after just one use.

Substance abuse harms the body not only from the use of the substance itself but from the negative lifestyle behaviors in which the user participates. Poor nutrition, tobacco smoking, insomnia, and lack of exercise all impact on the physical well-being of a person. Pregnant drug users not only have poor self-care, they also bear lower birth weight and addicted babies who must go through withdrawal soon after birth. These negative lifestyle practices create an environment of continued addiction by decreasing the energy level and self-esteem of the abuser (Apovian, 2006). Recovery becomes almost impossible. If an addict manages to achieve a recovered state, he may believe that the other habits don't matter. For example, smokers who are in recovery believe that smoking cessation will threaten the other substance recovery. However, people are more likely to die of tobacco-related diseases than from alcohol-related problems (American Academy of Family Physicians, 2006).

To add to the problem, the 2005 Monitoring the Future and the Centers for Disease Control and Prevention's (CDC) Youth Risk Behavior Surveillance

System (YRBSS) found heroin use beginning as early as 8th grade. The 2005 YRBSS reported 2.4 percent of 8th- to 12th-grade students using heroin at least once in their lifetime. Early-age heroin use will not only complicate the physical and mental health of the individual, but can lead to lost time in the person's most productive years. They are at risk of their educations being interrupted or negatively affected, which in turn, may influence the ability to make necessary lifestyle changes later in life.

The user's obsession with substance use disrupts family life and creates a destructive pattern of a co-dependency within the family; family members supply the user with money to purchase the substance, thereby denying the problem. Families may split apart, either from separation or divorce due to spousal addiction or children being placed in foster care, group homes, or with other relatives due to parental addiction. Employed drug abusers are more likely to have occupational accidents, affecting either themselves or others. These accidents cost their employers two times more in medical and worker compensation claims than their drug-free workers (NIDA, 1999). About 70 percent of crime is drug related and the judicial system in several states has had to resort to drug court (Herbert & Shaw, 2007).

In order to maintain recovery, addicts not only have to resist the use of mood-altering substance(s) but return to a healthy physical state, repair interpersonal relationships, and develop some sense of peace or spirituality. To accomplish this, substance abusers move through a process in which decisions are made to not only initiate the behavior change but to maintain it (Bandura, 1986; Miller & Rollnick, 1991; Ritter, 2002). Many factors, such as increased self-efficacy and educational level, have been identified as important to the recovery process. Other factors, particularly depression, have been shown to increase the likelihood of relapse, preventing recovery from occurring (Compton, Cottler, Jacobs, Ben-Abdallah, & Spitznagel, 2003; Stein, Solomon, Herman, Anderson, & Miller, 2003; Subramaniam, Lewis, Stitzer, & Fishman, 2004). Research has not shown definitive evidence on what triggers relapse or what changes recovering abusers have made in their lives to decrease the incidence of relapse, thereby maintaining a healthy, productive life. Once recovering abusers have not used drugs, do they practice healthy lifestyle behaviors? No studies have focused on substance abusers health behaviors while in recovery.

RESEARCH FINDINGS

Maslow's theory of human motivation (1970) suggests that as persons experience higher levels of need satisfaction, there is less lower-level tension and they are motivated to make better decisions about health promotion. Much of the early research regarding health and illness used theoretical models that primarily centered on illness prevention, not health promotion. These prevention models include but are not limited to the Health Belief Model (Rosenstock, 1960), Theory of Reasoned Action and Planned Behavior (Ajzen, 1991), and the Relapse Prevention Model (Marlatt & Gordon, 1985).

Drug relapse prevention treatment models have long been based on social cognitive and behavioral theories that transition the addict through the withdrawal phase to identifying and preventing high-risk situations for relapse (Witkiewitz & Marlatt, 2004). All acknowledge self-efficacy as essential in behavior change. Self-efficacy is defined as the degree to which an individual feels confident and capable of performing a certain behavior in a specific situation (Bandura, 1977). Increased self-efficacy is a strong predictor of outcomes in all types of addictive behavior, including gambling (Sylvain, Ladouceur, & Boisvert, 1997), smoking, and drug use (Sklar, Annis, & Turner, 1999). Not only has self-efficacy been a major determinant in relapse prevention, it is also a key factor in maintaining any health-promoting behavior.

Therefore, once substance abusers stop using and have found the motivation to abstain, they not only begin altering their brain chemistry but build new identities (Spriggs, 2003; Wilcox & Erikson, 2004). With improved self-efficacy and relapse prevention skills, the substance abuser reaches a nonusing state, a chosen behavior change. This builds a firm foundation for future health behavior changes. However, presently, health promotion practices of substance users who are maintaining a substance-free lifestyle have not been described in the literature.

Though much of the research on health promotion has described various populations of interest, few studies have been done that utilized an intervention to achieve a behavior change. Nola Pender's revised Health Promotion Model (HPM) combines numerous constructs from expectancy-value and social cognitive theories within a nursing holistic perspective (Pender, Murdaugh, & Parsons, 2006). The model proposes a positive and humanistic definition of health and though disease is present, it is not the most important element. Once a person commits to the behavior change, his affect toward the behavior increases self-efficacy, which in turn, increases the likelihood of enacting the behavior. As the addict attains substance abstinence, his confidence to maintain the behavior increases, which in turn, gives the addict strength to continue the recovery state. Another proposition of the model states that as self-efficacy increases, the number of perceived barriers, such as the loss of a high and withdrawal symptoms, to a specific health behavior decreases. However, in the end, if addicts do not believe that they can succeed at quitting, they will relapse and continue to use. Measuring health promotion can be completed through use of the Health Promotion Lifestyle Profile II. This reliable and valid instrument includes the six subscales of health promotion: nutrition, physical activity, health responsibility, spirituality, interpersonal relations, and stress management. Much research utilizing this model has centered on adopting improved nutrition and physical activity into a healthy lifestyle.

Many other factors affect the adoption of health-promoting behavior, such as unavailability of primary prevention facilities (Wilson, 2005), obesity (Nies, Buddington, Cowan, & Hepworth, 1998), and internal motivation (Weitzel & Waller, 1990). Internal motivation and recovery engagement have been shown to be major determinants of relapse prevention (Brown, 2003; Zeldman, Ryan, & Fiscella, 2004). Internally motivated study participants had lower relapse rates and higher self-efficacy. Therefore, educational level and increased self-efficacy are the strongest predictors of health promotion in any population (Ahluwalia, Mack, & Mokdad, 2005; Gillis, 1993; Holloway & Watson, 2002; Kawabata, Cross, Nishioka, & Shimai, 1999; Kim, Jeon, Sok, & Kim, 2006; Martinelli, 1999a, 1999b; McCleary-Jones, 1996; Washington, 2001). In one of the few studies using intervention to change health behavior, Sorensen et al. (1998) conducted a WellWorks Study at one of four intervention centers that were participating in the Working Well Cooperative. After assessment for and education regarding weight management and smoking cessation, results showed that those who received ongoing education and assessment reduced their fat consumption significantly. However, smoking cessation was not statistically changed. The researchers found that health promotion programs are most effective among white-collar workers, verifying the previous research findings that education is a strong predictor of lifestyle behavior change.

Much research has been completed on the importance of interpersonal relationships and health. Social support has contributed to physical health by changing diet and exercise regimens, reducing smoking and alcohol use, promoting better sleep and adherence to medical regimens, thereby improving health (Cohen, Underwood, & Gottlieb, 2000). Berkman and Syme (1979) found during a nine-year period that those people who had no social or community ties were more likely to die of all causes than those who maintained family, friend, and community relationships. Allgower, Wardle, and Steptoe (2001) found that low social support was directly related to sedentary lifestyle, poor sleep, and risky behavior such as not wearing seatbelts and not using sunscreen. Numerous other studies have linked poor social support with excessive alcohol consumption, tobacco use, and drug use (Barnes, Reifman, Farrell, & Dintcheff, 2000; Fisher & Feldman, 1998; Shedler & Block, 1990). Other study results demonstrated that intrapersonal determinants accounted for 52 percent of drug use relapses and a person's perception of setting risk for relapse was the most important element in determining future relapse (Cummings, Gordon, & Marlatt, 1980; Walton, Reischl, & Ramanthan, 1995). Jackson's (2006) study found that depressive symptoms and perceived social support contributed significantly to the prediction of healthy nutritional practices, exercise, substance abuse, and adherence to medical regime in women but not in men.

Lastly, stress management and spirituality are an important part of wellness and are indispensable to maintaining health. Behavioral coping skills have a positive effect to manage work-related stress (Gardner, Rose, Mason, Tyler, & Cushway, 2005). Spirituality, or spiritual growth, is a component of health promoting self-care behavior, or health responsibility. It is a concept that has long been addressed as essential in chronic illness, quality of life and death. A study by Daaleman and Kaufman (2006) found that those participants who reported greater spirituality ($p < 0.01$) were more likely to report less symptoms of depression. Callaghan (2005) investigated the relationship between self-care behaviors and self-care efficacy and found that spiritual growth is significantly related to an adolescent's initiative and health responsibility. This is consistent to existing literature regarding the direction of similar associations with spirituality (National Institute of Mental Health, 2006).

Only one research study has explored health promotion and drug users. Branagan (2006) evaluated a nurse-led education program on preventing overdose among 23 methadone treatment clinics in Ireland. The education program consisted of leaflet and poster education promoting overdose prevention and how to deal with an overdose should it occur. The posters and leaflets were placed in high visual impact locations in 15 clinics in Ireland. A total of 200 questionnaires were distributed and 81 percent of the participants responded positively to reading the poster or leaflet. Of those who responded, 71 percent indicated that they would make changes in their lifestyles based on what they read in the leaflet and recommended that this information be distributed to other agencies that have contact with drug users, such as prisons, and general practice surgeries. Branagan showed positive response to the education; however, the study did not indicate any statistics on overdose knowledge prior to the education program. Being that 16–43 percent of opiate addicts in the United States suffer from multiple overdoses or die from suicide, most frequently the result of overdose, repetition of this educational endeavor may be worthwhile (Hickman et al., 2003; Pfab, Eyer, Jetzinger, & Zilker, 2006).

Regarding addiction, tobacco smoking has been the most extensively studied in relation to health. Smoking increases risks for multiple causes of illness and death, and studies show that 71 percent of those who use illicit drugs also smoke (Ritchie, Ahluwalia, Mosier, Nazir, & Ahluwalia, 1997). Tobacco smoking has been shown to increase mortality from other health-related ill-nesses and increase the number of risky lifestyle practices (U.S. Department of Health and Human Services [USDHHS], 2004a; Perkins et al., 1993). Positive relationships between self-efficacy and not initiating smoking, not increasing smoking, and environmental tobacco avoidance was evidenced by Martinelli (1999a, 1999b) and Kawabata et al. (1999). McCleary-Jones (1996) found that age, educational level, and income modified health-promoting practices in smok-ing and nonsmoking black women. This study found that educational level was the strongest predictor of practicing health promotion, a finding consistent with other studies (Lusk, Kerr, & Ronis, 1995; Foulds et al., 2006).

HEALTH PROMOTION INTERVENTIONS AND SUBSTANCE ABUSE

In January 2000, the U.S. Department of Health and Human Services launched Healthy People 2010, a comprehensive, nationwide health promo-tion and disease prevention agenda. The National Center for Health Statistics/ Centers for Disease Control and Prevention (CDC) quantified the cost of sub-stance abuse (i.e., smoking, illegal drug use, and alcohol) to the United States at more than $484 billion per year, treating such adverse effects as infectious diseases, crime, unintentional injuries, teenage pregnancies, and chronic psy-chiatric disorders (USDHHS, 2004b). Twenty-five percent of patients seen in primary care clinics have alcohol or drug disorders (Jones, Knutson, & Haines, 2003). Healthy People 2010 has proposed that opioid-dependent patients be able to receive treatment services and opiate antagonist medication (buprenor-phine) in outpatient settings, such as primary care offices. In addition, evidence is suggesting that access to primary care will improve not only general health but also drug abuse–related outcomes (Alba, Samet, & Saitz, 2004). The pos-sibility of improved outcomes has created Current Procedural Terminology (CPT) codes for the screening and counseling of alcohol or substance abuse in primary care offices (Hughes, 2008).

Recently, studies have examined common medical problems in patients who are recovering from chemical dependency. Alba et al. (2004) found that chemi-cally dependent individuals without primary care suffered from increased hospitalization, reported chronic medical conditions, and practiced unhealthy lifestyle choices. Friedmann, Zhang, Hendrickson, Stein, and Gerstein (2003) found that the availability of primary care services at onsite substance treatment programs significantly improved addiction severity at follow-up by 14 percent, but did not change the severity of medical outcome. Another alternative is to deliver behavior health services within primary care. In this type of treatment service, the primary care practitioner addresses the health care issues related to substance abuse whereas the behavioral health and/or addiction specialist services provide management of the substance abuse issues (Ernst, Miller, & Rollnick, 2007).

Substance abuse patients are returning to primary care follow-up sooner than the expected 90 days. With insurance restrictions, patients are often discharged from addiction specialty treatment centers within 7 days and are expected to be monitored for continued use and any other comorbid conditions by primary care providers. The first 90 days postaddictions specialty discharge is the highest risk period for relapse (National Clearinghouse Guidelines, 2005). It requires primary care health providers to be knowledgeable of when to contact the addiction specialist or mental health care provider, assessing the patient for signs of abuse or adherence to the recovery plan, monitoring for adverse effects of addiction-focused pharmacotherapy and consistent motivational support to maintain abstinence. It is imperative that primary care providers work with patients to become more engaged in their own health.

Additional demands are placed on the body while achieving or maintaining recovery. There is a need for more energy, improved psychological well-being, and stabilization of organ function. Proper nutrition supplies the body with the adequate building blocks by which the person can maintain proper health and fight off infection. For cocaine users, the loss of appetite and weight loss from overstimulation can lead to malnutrition; whereas marijuana increases appetite and many long-term users become overweight. Opiate abusers suffer from the constipation effects of the drug class. Diet recommendations include but are not limited to regular mealtimes, portioned low-fat nutritious meals, to prevent overeating and increased vitamins, protein, and fiber. Dehydration is common during recovery, therefore, encouraging adequate fluid intake is essential (Apovian, 2006).

Exercise not only improves mood and reduces mood swings, it adds the internal strength to deal with negative stressful states, which often are triggers that lead to lapses or relapses (Gross, 2006). Stress management techniques assist the substance abusers in preventing lapses and improve their interpersonal communication skills. These interventions create a circle of positive outcomes, thereby leading to a healthier lifestyle, both physiologically and psychosocially. As recovery progresses and the user improves health promotion activities, self-esteem and motivation increase to maintain substance recovery and health. However, the most important element of health promotion is for the person to avoid returning to substance use, before changing diet or quitting smoking.

Pharmacologic agents may assist in achieving recovery. Gamma–vinyl-GABA (Vigabartin) has shown positive effects in blocking the craving for cocaine. When combined with counseling, 30 percent of patients successfully kept off cocaine during a nine-week study (Interlandi, 2008). Another medication, Acamprosate calcium (Camparal), already on the market for alcoholism, has the potential to reduce cravings and help prevent relapses, though the effect is individual. Naltrexone extended release injectable suspension (Vivitrol) works on blocking the action of the alcohol directly, thereby blocking the feel-good effect. Nothing has been as successful as varenicline (Chantix) for nicotine addiction. Varenicline studies have shown that 44 percent of tobacco addicts were able to quit smoking after 12 weeks. However, none of these medications will work without extensive behavioral-cognitive group therapy and counseling and they are not to be a permanent part of the treatment regimen. These medications remain only tertiary prevention in the early phases of detoxification.

It is the potential of vaccines that is the most hopeful for primary prevention in addiction. Worldwide research is developing vaccines to inoculate people against addictive substances such as cocaine, heroin, and methamphetamine. The National Institute of Drug Abuse states that these vaccines may be available within 1 to 10 years. The most promising vaccine TA-CD, a vaccine for cocaine abuse, prevents the addictive substance from ever reaching the user's brain. It will work like any other vaccine. The immune system is prompted to create antibodies and when an individual takes cocaine the next time, the body mounts an automatic defense. Antibodies attach to the cocaine molecules, which are then broken down by enzymes in the bloodstream. This in turn eliminates the high and desire to have more cocaine (Hylton, 2008). Unfortunately, it has taken almost 10 years to develop this vaccine.

Research on depression as a factor contributing to addiction and relapse has been inconclusive in the literature. The question is not if the depression actually exists since co-occurrence of a mood disorder and substance abuse ranges from 42.6 to 60.3 percent in the United States (Grant, Stinson, & Dawson, 2004; Kessler et al., 1996). However, the question is really "Does depression cause substance abuse?" or "Does substance abuse cause a depressive state?" Depression has a greater impact on overall health than other chronic medical conditions. The underdiagnosis of co-occurring disorders affects clinical interventions, medications, and the psychosocial treatments that can improve patient outcomes, particularly relapse prevention and health promotion behaviors. Without detection and appropriate treatment, the physical and mental health of the individual fails.

Studies have shown that there is a relationship between substance abuse recovery and spirituality. Spirituality in recovery has been limited to the 12 Step–based spiritual practices, whereby a person accepts the existence of a higher power and develops faith, gratitude, and humility that govern the recovery process. Beyond this 12 Step method, however, other spiritual interventions, such as transcendental mediation and therapeutic touch, have been shown to have a significant positive effect on the recovery process, though not always at a significant level. Unfortunately, many of these studies were limited due to limited funding and allocated resources. Additional research in complementary spiritual practices is needed.

Harm-reduction strategies are presently very controversial in health philosophy, as they are misinterpreted as drug legalization tools. These approaches are to reduce the negative consequences of drug abuse to an individual or harm done to the addict's family or community. Sometimes these strategies ignore the needs of the individual addict as a trade-off for the betterment of the community at large. Needle-exchange programs' primary goal is to reduce the risk of spreading infectious diseases such as HIV/AIDS and hepatitis by taking infected needles out of circulation. Yet, these programs require local funds to operate and are not consistently available throughout the United States. Even the use of agonist medications for heroin addicts is not widely accepted practice, though research has shown that the use of these medications helps in restoring the individual to functionality in the family, at work, and in the community (Kosten, 2005). These strategies have been shown to be helpful in the adolescent age group through behavioral modification, which may eliminate substance use (Canadian Medical Association, 2008).

Patient care is affected by policy. Policy determines who gets what kind of care from whom and when (Mason, Leavitt, & Chaffee, 2007). A major role of the health care providers dealing with substance abusers is to recognize the needs of the client/patient and work toward attaining the resources required to provide high-quality patient care. Caring for the addicted and recovering patient in the outpatient primary care setting is a goal of Healthy People 2010. Discrimination has been shown to have a negative impact on both mental and physical health. Young, Subere, Ahern, and Galea (2005) found that discrimination was significantly associated with poor mental health, depression, and the number of chronic physical health conditions in illicit drug users. Negative emotional states and stress have been shown to have a direct effect on patterns of behavior that affect physical health. Yet, these underserved and misunderstood patients are most often treated negatively and inconsistently when compared to other widely publicized medical conditions, such as cardiovascular and pulmonary disease. Even pharmaceutical companies are reluctant to develop products for drug addicts.

With better health promotion, health care costs in future years could potentially decrease. In addition, earlier initiation of health promotion in the abusing population may assist those individuals in avoiding major disease complications and help in substance abuse recovery. However, the initiation of health promotion education and services is not often covered under insurance or Medicaid and requires money to enact. Discrimination due to drug use may limit available resources, access to social welfare, and compliance with medications and health care regimens (Young et al., 2005). Obtaining the financial resources for this endeavor would necessitate creating or changing policy at the insurance company, state, or federal level. Primary care and addictions specialty providers are empowered to make these changes occur. Grassroots lobbying efforts from the local to federal level enable these policies to come to fruition.

SUMMARY

Healthy lifestyle practices or behaviors have been defined by many groups, yet perception of health, benefits of a health-promoting behavior, and barriers to the behavior are all individual. The person must have the internal motivation and develop the self-efficacy or confidence to adopt the behavior change and then to maintain it. As addicts attain substance abstinence, their confidence to maintain the behavior increases which in turn gives the addict strength to continue the recovery state. Research has shown internal motivation and self-efficacy as the best predictors of behavior change, including relapse prevention and recovery from drug use. Other factors, such as perceptions of risk and control, also play crucial roles in the recovery process. Barriers to abstinence, such as craving, depression, and withdrawal symptoms, prevent many substance abusers from adopting a permanent lifestyle change. This in turn decreases their chance of life without multiple medical problems. Increasing participation in drug abuse treatment can decrease the spread of these diseases by reducing risky behaviors, such as sharing injection equipment and having unprotected sex.

Relapse prevention therapy, along with other adjunctive treatments, to reduce stress, improve nutrition, decrease depression and physical symptoms, increase the addicted person's emotional and spiritual states, energy level, and overall well-being (Brooks, 2006). With the rise of rapid three-day addiction detoxification programs in health care institutions, addicted individuals will be relying on primary care practitioners to address their addiction and other health needs. To maintain the recovery process, collaboration between primary care and addictions specialists is pivotal in evaluating and treating these patients to ensure positive health outcomes.

REFERENCES

Ahluwalia, I., Mack, K., & Mokdad, S. (2005). Changes in selected chronic disease-related risks and health conditions for nonpregnant women 18–44 years old. *Journal of Women's Health, 14*(5), 382–386.

Ajzen, I. (1991). The theory of planned behavior. *Organizational Behavior and Human Decision Processes, 50*, 179–211.

Alba, I., Samet, J., & Saitz, R. (2004). Burden of medical illness in drug- and alcohol-dependent persons without primary care. *American Journal on Addictions, 13*, 33–45.

Allgower, A., Wardle, J., & Steptoe, A. (2001). Depressive symptoms, social support and personal health behaviors in young men and women. *Health Psychology, 20*, 223–227.

American Academy of Family Physicians. (2006). *Smoking cessation in recovering alcoholics.* Retrieved April 4, 2008, from http://familydoctor.org/online/famocen/home/common/addictions/tobacco/269.printview

Apovian, C. (2006). Diet and substance abuse recovery. *Medical encyclopedia.* Retrieved April 4, 2008, from http://www.nim.nih.gov/medlineplus/ency/article/002149.htm

Bandura, A. (1977). Self efficacy: Toward a unifying theory of behavioral change. *Psychological Review, 84*(2), 191–215.

Bandura, A. (1986). *Social foundations of thought and action: A social cognitive theory.* Englewood Cliffs, NJ: Prentice Hall.

Barnes, G., Reifman, A., Farrell, M., & Dintcheff, B. (2000). The effects of parenting on the development of adolescent alcohol misuse: A six wave latent growth model. *Journal of Marriage and the Family, 62*, 175–186.

Berkman, L., & Syme, S. (1979). Social networks, host resistance and mortality: A nine year follow up study of Alameda County residents. *American Journal of Epidemiology, 109*, 186–204.

Branagan, O. (2006). Providing health education on accidental drug overdose. *Nursing Times, 102*(6), 32–33.

Brooks, A., Schwartz, G., Reece, K. and Nangle, G. (2006). The effect of *Johrei* healing on substance abuse recovery: A pilot study. *Journal of Alternative and Complementary Medicine, 12*(7), 625–631.

Brown, N. (2003). Relapsing, running and relieving: A model for high-risk behavior in recovery. *Journal of Addictions Nursing, 14*, 14–17.

Callaghan, D. (2005). The influence of spiritual growth on adolescents' initiative and responsibility for self-care. *Pediatric Nursing, 31*(2), 91–97.

Canadian Medical Association. (2008). Youth substance use and abuse: Challenges and strategies for identification and intervention. *Canadian Medical Association Journal, 178*(2), 145–148.

Cohen, S., Underwood, L., & Gottlieb, B. (2000). *Social support measurement and intervention.* London: Oxford University Press.

Compton, W., Cottler, L., Jacobs, J., Ben-Abdallah, A., & Spitznagel, E. (2003). The role of psychiatric disorders in predicting drug dependence treatment outcomes. *American Journal of Psychiatry, 160*(5), 890–895.

Cummings, C., Gordon, J., & Marlatt, G. (1980). Relapse strategies of prevention and prediction. In W. R. Miller (Ed.), *The addictive disorders: Treatment of alcoholism, drug abuse, smoking, and obesity.* New York: Pergamon.

Daaleman, T., & Kaufman, J. (2006). Spirituality and depressive symptoms in primary care outpatients. *Southern Medical Journal, 99*(12), 1340–1345.

Ernst, D., Miller, W., & Rollnick, S. (2007). Treating substance abuse in primary care: A demonstration project. *International Journal of Integrated Care, 7*(10), 1–8.

Fisher, L., & Feldman, S. (1998). Familial antecedents of young adult health risk behaviors: A longitudinal study. *Journal of Family Psychology, 12*, 66–80.

Foulds, J., Gandhi, K., Steinberg, M., Richardson, D., Williams, J., Burke, M., et al. (2006). Factors associated with quitting smoking at a tobacco dependence treatment clinic. *American Journal of Health Behavior, 30*(4), 400–412.

Friedmann, P., Zhang, Z., Hendrickson, J., Stein, M., & Gerstein, D. (2003). Effect of primary medical care on addiction and medical severity in substance abuse treatment programs. *Journal of General Internal Medicine, 18*, 1–8.

Gardner, B., Rose, J., Mason, O., Tyler, P., & Cushway, D. (2005). Cognitive therapy and behavioural coping in the management of work-related stress: An intervention study. *Work and Stress, 19*(2), 137–152.

Gillis, A. (1993). Determinants of a health-promoting lifestyle: An integrative review. *Journal of Advanced Nursing, 18*, 345–353.

Grant, B., Stinson, P., & Dawson, D. (2004). Prevalence and co-occurrence of substance user disorders and independent mood and anxiety disorders. *Archives of General Psychiatry, 61*, 807–816.

Gross, S. (2006). *Relapse prevention.* Retrieved April 24, 2008, from http://www.helphorizons.com/library/search_details.htm?id=77

Herbert, K., & Shaw, J. (2007, January 2). Drug courts are battling addictions behind crime. *Philadelphia Inquirer, 178*(216), pp. A1, A8.

Hickman, M., Carnwath, Z., Madden, P., Farrell, M., Rooney, C., Ashcroft, R., et al. (2003). Drug related mortality and fatal overdose risk: Pilot cohort study of heroin users recruited from specialist drug treatment sites in London. *Journal of Urban Health, 80*, 274–287.

Holloway, A., & Watson, H. (2002). Role of self efficacy and behaviour change. *International Journal of Nursing Practice, 8*, 106–115.

Hughes, C. (2008). CPT 2008: A glimpse of the future of family medicine. *Family practice management.* Retrieved April 17, 2008, from http://www.aafp.org/fpm

Hylton, H. (2008). *A drug to end drug addiction.* Retrieved April 12, 2008, from http://www.time.com/time/health/article/0,8599,1701864,00.html

Interlandi, J. (2008, March 3). What addicts need. *Newsweek*, 36–43.

Jackson, T. (2006). Relationships between perceived close social support and health practices within community samples of American women and men. *Journal of Psychology, 140*(3), 229–246.

Jones, E., Knutson, D., & Haines, D. (2003). Common problems in patients recovering from chemical dependency. *American Family Physician, 68*(10), 1971–1978.

Kawabata, T., Cross, D., Nishioka, N., & Shimai, S. (1999). Relationship between self-esteem and smoking behavior among Japanese early adolescents: Initial results from a three-year study. *Journal of School Health, 69*(7), 280–284.

Kessler, R., Nelson, C., McGonagle, K., Edlund, M., Frank, R., & Leaf, P. (1996). The epidemiology of co-occurring addictive and mental disorders: Implications for prevention and service utilization. *Annuals of Orthopsychiatry, 66*, 17–31.

Kim, S. Y., Jeon, E. Y., Sok, S., & Kim, K. B. (2006). Comparison of health-promoting behaviors of noninstitutionalized and institutionalized older adults in Korea. *Journal of Nursing Scholarship, 38*(1), 31–35.

Kosten, T. (2005). What are America's opportunities for harm reduction strategies in opiate dependence? *American Journal of Addictions, 14*, 307–310.

Lusk, S., Kerr, M., & Ronis, D. (1995). Health promoting lifestyles of blue-collar, skilled trade, and white-collar workers. *Nursing Research, 44*(1), 20–24.

Marlatt, G., & Gordon, J. (1985). *Relapse prevention: Maintenance strategies in the treatment of addictive behaviors.* New York: Guilford Press.

Martinelli, A. (1999a). An explanatory model of variables influencing health promotion behaviors in smoking and nonsmoking college students. *Public Health Nursing, 16*(4), 263–269.

Martinelli, A. (1999b). Testing a model of avoiding environmental tobacco smoke in young adults. *Image: Journal of Nursing Scholarship, 31*(3), 237–242.

Maslow, A. H. (1970). *Motivation and personality.* New York: Harper and Row.

Mason, D., Leavitt, J., & Chaffee, M. (2007). *Policy and politics in nursing and health care.* Philadelphia: Elsevier.

McCleary-Jones, V. (1996). Health promotion practices of smoking and non-smoking black women. *ABNF Journal, 7*(1), 7–10.

Miller, W. R., & Rollnick, S. (1991). *Motivational interviewing: Preparing people to change addictive behaviors.* New York: Guilford Press.

National Clearinghouse Guidelines. (2005). Medication-assisted treatment for opioid addiction in opioid treatment programs: Approaches to providing comprehensive care and maximizing patient retention. Retrieved April 24, 2008, from http://www.guideline.gov/summary/summary.aspx?doc_id=8352&nbr=004675&string=substance+AND+abuse

National Institute on Drug Abuse. (1999). *InfoFacts—Workplace trends.* Retrieved January 6, 2007, from www.nida.nih.gov/infofacts/workplace.html

National Institute on Drug Abuse. (2005). *InfoFacts—Hospital visits.* Retrieved January 6, 2007, from www.nida.nih.gov/infofacts/hospitalvisits.html

National Institute on Drug Abuse (NIDA) and University of Michigan. (2005). *Monitoring the future 2005: Data from in-school surveys of 8th, 10th and 12th grade students.* Retrieved January 23, 2007, from http://www.monitoringthefuture.org/pubs/monographs/overview2005.pdf

National Institute of Mental Health. (2006). *NIMH, the numbers count.* National Institutes of Health. Retrieved March 4, 2007, from http://nimh.nih.gov/public at/numbers.cfm

Nies, M., Buddington, C., Cowan, G., & Hepworth, J. (1998). Comparison of lifestyles among obese and nonobese African American and European American women in the community. *Nursing Research, 47*(4), 251–257.

Pender, N. J., Murdaugh, C. L., & Parsons, M. A. (2006). *Health promotion in nursing practice* (5th ed.). Upper Saddle River, NJ: Prentice Hall.

Perkins, K., Rohay, J., Meilahn, E., Wing, R., Matthews, K., & Kuller, L. (1993). Diet, alcohol, and physical activity as a function of smoking status in middle aged women. *Health Psychology, 12*(5), 410–415.

Pfab, R., Eyer, F., Jetzinger, E., & Zilker, T. (2006). Cause and motivation in cases of non-fatal drug overdoses in opiate addicts. *Clinical Toxicology, 44,* 255–259.

Ritchie, K., Ahluwalia, H., Mosier, M., Nazir, N., & Ahluwalia, J. (1997). A population-based study of cigarette smoking among illicit drug users in the United States. *Addiction, 97,* 861–869.

Ritter, A. J. (2002). Naltrexone in the treatment of heroin dependence: Relationship with depression and risk of overdose. *Australian and New Zealand Journal of Psychiatry, 36,* 224–228.

Rosenstock, I. (1960). What research in maturation suggests for public health. *American Journal of Public Health, 50,* 295–301.

Shedler, J., & Block, J. (1990). Adolescent drug use and psychological health: A longitudinal inquiry. *American Psychologist, 45,* 612–630.

Sklar, S., Annis, H., & Turner, N. (1999). Group comparisons of coping self efficacy between alcohol and cocaine abusers seeking treatment. *Psychology of Addictive Behaviors, 13,* 123–133.

Sorensen, G., Stoddard, A., Hunt, M. K., Hebert, J., Ockene, J., Avrunin, J., et al. (1998). The effects of a health promotion-health protection intervention on behavior change: The WellWorks Study. *American Journal of Public Health, 88*(11), 1685–1690.

Spriggs, M. (2003). Can we help addicts become more autonomous? Inside the mind of an addict. *Bioethics, 17*(5–6), 542–554.

Stein, M., Solomon, D., Herman, D., Anderson, B., & Miller, I. (2003). Depression severity and HIV injection risk behaviors. *American Journal of Psychiatry, 160,* 1659–1662.

Subramaniam, G., Lewis, L., Stitzer, M., & Fishman, M. (2004). Early treatment time course of depressive symptoms in opiate addicts. *Journal of Nervous and Mental Disease, 179*(4), 215–221.

Sylvain, C., Ladouceur, R., & Boisvert, J. (1997). Cognitive and behavioral treatment of pathological gambling: A controlled study. *Journal of Consulting and Clinical Psychology, 65,* 727–732.

U.S. Department of Health and Human Services. (2004a). *Health effects of cigarette smoking.* Retrieved June 25, 2006, from http://www.cec.gov/tobacco/factsheets/HelathEffectsofCigaretteSmoking_Factsheet.htm

U.S. Department of Health and Human Services. (2004b). *Progress review: Substance abuse.* Retrieved June 19, 2006, from http://www.healthypeople.gov/data/2010prog/focus26/

Walton, M., Reischl, T., & Ramanthan, C. (1995). Social settings and addiction relapse. *Journal of Substance Abuse, 7*(2), 223–233.

Washington, O. (2001). Using brief therapeutic interventions to create change in self-efficacy and personal control of chemically dependent women. *Archives of Psychiatric Nursing, XV*(1), 32–40.

Weitzel, M., & Waller, P. (1990). Predictive factors for health-promotive behaviors in white, Hispanic, and black blue-collar workers. *Family and Community Health, 13*, 23–34.

Wilcox, R., & Erikson, C. (2004). Prevention of relapse to addiction: Information for the practitioner. *Texas Medicine, 100*(2), 52–61.

Wilson, M. (2005). Health-promoting behaviors of sheltered homeless women. *Community Health, 28*(1), 51–63.

Witkiewitz, K., & Marlatt, G. A. (2004). Relapse prevention for alcohol and drug problems. *American Psychologist, 59*(4), 224–235.

Young, M., Subere, J., Ahern, J., & Galea, S. (2005). Interpersonal discrimination and the health of illicit drug users. *American Journal of Drug and Alcohol Abuse, 31*, 371–391.

Zeldman, A., Ryan, R., & Fiscella, K. (2004). Motivation, autonomy support, and entity beliefs: Their role in methadone maintenance treatment. *Journal of Social and Clinical Psychology, 23*(5), 675–696.

Chapter 2

Becoming a Problematic Consumer of Narcotics

Ted Goldberg, PhD

This chapter is based on participant observation studies of problematic consumers of narcotics in Stockholm, Sweden, over a period of four and a half
years. When doing fieldwork, a researcher meets many people with different
characteristics, personalities, strengths, and weaknesses. The wealth of data is
so great that it is easy to drown in a sea of details. To formulate the theory
presented here, it has been necessary to look beyond individual differences and
concentrate on what I have come to see as a major underlying pattern common to problematic consumers of narcotics, that is, people who made illicit
substances the central element in their lives. I have developed a dynamic developmental model, or a life-history "career model," to illuminate what brought my
research subjects to "the drug scene" and why they elect to remain on it.

As narcotics consumption is a complex phenomenon regulated by cultural
norms and definitions, place, time, age, gender, and so on, I am unable to determine the extent to which my model can be generalized. It is my hope that readers will be inspired to test its applicability on other populations.

In this chapter the terms *narcotics, illicit substances,* and *illicit drugs* will be
used as synonyms.

ASSUMPTIONS

All knowledge of humans and society, scientific or otherwise, is based on
unproved assumptions. With postulates as a foundation, we build our theoretical understanding (Israel, 1984, p. 16). Differences of opinion in the drug

debate can often be traced to different suppositions. Unfortunately, assumptions in many texts are implicit, leaving it to the reader to unmask them. I shall therefore begin by making explicit the major assumptions upon which my model is based.

Assumptions about Consumers

I assume that the intellectual capacities of those who use narcotics show approximately the same variation as in the population at large, and that those who use illicit drugs understand the consequences of their actions to approximately the same extent that nonconsumers understand their own behavior. Furthermore, I do not agree with those who postulate that it is primarily the chemical effects of the narcotics themselves that determine consumption. Bejerot (1979, p. 90), for instance, writes: "That the individual has become chemically controlled and has serious deficiencies or completely lost self-control vis-à-vis intoxicants is the essential nature of narcotics addiction." Instead, my starting point is that drug consumers should not be seen merely as objects. They are also subjects who actively choose both to use narcotics and to take the consequences thereof.

Assuming that a person is competent to make decisions leads us to ask such questions as: Why does he choose as he does? What alternatives does he believe he has and what alternatives actually are at his disposal? To what extent is he conscious of the motives behind his decisions? The model presented in this chapter will address these kinds of questions.

Nature and Nurture

Certainly, most serious researchers would agree that human behavior is a product of both biochemical and psychosocial processes. However, the relative importance of these two roots in conjunction with drug consumption is the subject of great and ongoing controversy. So even if the term *biopsychosocial* is being used more and more by those who participate in the drug debate, we really aren't in agreement. The question is: How much of human drug behavior should/can be explained by biochemical variables and what is psychosocially determined? This can be illustrated with the help of a continuum. While almost nobody is at either end of the continuum, a person who places himself toward the left side of the continuum is saying something very different from somebody who is near the other end.

Those who assume that human behavior is primarily of biochemical origin see deviance first and foremost as a result of some combination of genetic dispo-

Continuum 1

Behavior .... Behavior
biochemically ....psychosocially
determined .... determined

sition, metabolic disturbance, and/or drug-induced malfunction in vital organs such as the brain or other parts of the central nervous system. For instance, Robinson and Berridge (1993, p. 249) assume that "addictive behavior is due largely to progressive and persistent neuroadaptations caused by repeated drug use." Those who emphasize biochemical determinants are of the opinion that the root of problematic drug consumption lies principally within the individual and/or the narcotics themselves, and that her social experiences are of secondary importance. Solutions are sought by attempting to find substances that will maintain a normal chemical balance within the individual, detoxification, trying to prevent access to illegal psychoactive substances, information, and so on.

By defining the behavior exhibited after drug consumption as a problem lying within the individual and/or the drugs, the biochemical perspective is of major political significance. The implication is that problematic consumption is not an indication of a need for social change.

Researchers emphasizing psychosocial variables analyze either individual characteristics (i.e., personality, life experiences, underlying needs) and/or social structures. On the micro-level, they ask how the individual became such as she is, and look for answers in, for instance, her family and/or other small groups she currently belongs to and/or has belonged to in the past. On the macro-level, they ask what factors in society create problems for parts of the population as a result of their position in the larger social system. Answers are sought in society's social institutions, culture, and history.

The basic assumption among those who place themselves toward the right-hand side of the above continuum is that humans are social beings and their behavior is to a great extent the result of social relationships. Without denying that people differ in their biological make-up, these differences are given subordinate roles. Biology is seen as a framework that sets limits for what we can achieve; social factors are looked upon as determining the extent to which an individual's capabilities will develop. From this point of view, it follows that behavior cannot be analyzed solely in an individual context. We must also look at macro-level processes and political decisions that create possibilities and obstacles both for the individual and the intimate small groups that form her (Mills, 1997).

Complexity and Nonlinear Thinking

Differences of opinion in the drug debate can also be traced to assumptions as to what are causes and what are effects. Some arguments are based on the assumption that biochemical changes induced by illicit drugs produce (undesirable) behavior, such as lack of achievement in school (Nordegren & Tunving, 1984, p. 143), delayed maturation (Dole & Nyswander, 1967, p. 477), and criminality (see Inciardi, 1992, p. 22ff. for some examples of the drastic kinds of statements that have been made and how they have been used politically). Levine (2003, p. 147ff.) uses the term *drug demonization* for the tendency to see illicit drugs as the major cause of just about any behavior we don't approve of in any individual who takes them.

The arguments presented in this chapter will be based on an alternative assumption: neither narcotics nor any other single factor explain human behavior. Instead, we should try to uncover the latticework of multiple factors that increase the probability that some people will choose to take illicit drugs in a problematic way. This implies that rather than principally concentrating on the illicit substances themselves, considerable effort must also be directed toward understanding other factors, such as the consumer's life experiences, her motives, the conditions of her existence, the situations in which illicit drugs are consumed, the society in which her life is being/has been led, and so on.

An assumption upon which the model presented in this chapter is based is that as a result of his social relationships and life experiences, the individual gains knowledge about himself, the society he lives in, and his roles in that society. All of these factors greatly influence the way he will relate to illicit substances, which in turn, has repercussions for his future relationships to others and to society. In other words, there are feedback relationships between the individual, other people, narcotics, and society.

The model presented here is based upon the assumption that narcotics are not the major culprits. While I do not deny that the biochemical effects of psychoactive substances are a part of the equation, human relationships and the societal conditions from which they originate are seen as playing a major role as determinants of both illicit drug consumption and the behavior displayed in conjunction with it.

From this starting point, I ask: What roles do narcotics play in relation to other aspects of the consumer's life? How do illicit substances relate to her past experiences, her present life situation, and her future possibilities? How did she come to contemplate starting to take psychoactive substances? What made her transform these thoughts into action? Once having started taking illicit drugs, why does she choose to continue? One of my fundamental assumptions is that if drug experiences (both chemical and social) are not relevant for a person's life seen as a whole, she will not make them the major focus of her existence.

Therefore, it is an important task for drug research to uncover and describe the relationships between illicit drug consumption and other life experiences.

Simultaneous and Process Models

Characteristic for simultaneous models is the assumption that all of the factors that operate to produce a phenomenon operate concurrently (Becker, 1963/1973, p. 22–23). In such models, we lose sight of the history of both the individual and the society in which he lives. An example of simultaneous thinking is the desperate parent who says: "My son was a wonderful kid until he fell in with the wrong crowd and was enticed into smoking a joint, which lead to his downfall." In this kind of explanation, all of this adolescent's previous life experiences are deemed irrelevant.

To my way of thinking, it is unreasonable to believe that a single event (how traumatic or euphoric it may have been) could eradicate the effects of all of the experiences a person has had in her life. I therefore attempt to develop a sequential model that analyzes processes that start in the past and continue through the present and into the future. To help develop a sequential model, Becker (1963/1973, p. 24) uses the term *career*. Similar to athletes who begin their careers in a sand lot and work their way up through different leagues before becoming professionals, the "deviant" has a career consisting of different stages, where earlier experiences become a fundament upon which later stages rest. In this chapter, I will briefly present the stages in the deviant career model I developed to explain the data I collected during my fieldwork. (The model is expounded upon in Goldberg, 1999, pp. 79–150.)

DIFFERENT KINDS OF CONSUMERS

It is not difficult to understand why we must use different concepts and variables to comprehend why a connoisseur drinks $500 wines with gourmet dinners than we need for an analysis of the drinking patterns of skid-row alcoholics. Both are using the same psychoactive drug but it is obvious that the underlying meanings and motives are very different. A common way to illuminate this distinction is to differentiate between "users" and "misusers."[1] However, I have found that these two concepts are understood in so many different ways in the literature and in everyday speech that they no longer convey meaning in a precise way. We therefore need other terms.

Continuum 2

Abstainers............ Recreational consumers ....Problematic
....consumers
_____
drugs play .... drugs first
no role ....priority

My conceptualization is a continuum with those for whom drugs mean nothing at one end and people who make drugs their first priority at the other. As already noted, *problematic consumers* are people who allow psychoactive substances to play a dominant role in their lives, that is, those who approach the far end of my continuum. *Substantial consumer* will be used as a synonym.

Recreational consumers, on the other hand, consider drugs as one aspect among many in their lives. Borrowing an idea from Norman Zinberg, Stanton Peele (1998, p. 8) writes that nonaddicted drug users "subordinate their desire for a drug to other values, activities, and personal relationships, so that the narcotic or other drug does not dominate their lives. When engaged in other pursuits that they value, these users do not crave the drug or manifest withdrawal on discontinuing their drug use." It is in this sense that I use the term *recreational consumers.*

Although frequency of consumption is a significant aspect in my definitions, it isn't a sufficient criterion. Under certain conditions, it is possible to take drugs regularly without allowing them to govern one's activities. In societies where psychoactive substances are readily accessible, socially accepted, and inexpensive, they can be used in this way. In the Netherlands, for instance, cannabis is more or less socially accepted and can be readily and affordably purchased in any number of coffee shops. It is therefore possible to take this drug on a daily basis with a minimum of social and economic cost. Some people smoke cannabis in a manner comparable to those whose alcohol consumption primarily consists of taking a drink after work or before going to bed. To my way of thinking, people who take illicit substances in this manner shouldn't be considered problematic consumers.

Problematic consumers and recreational consumers may well take the same psychoactive substances, but the meanings behind the act and their motives are very different. A central question in conjunction with all drug consumption is: *What is the individual attempting to accomplish when she takes these substances?*

A number of studies based on different populations have found statistical differences in the psychosocial backgrounds of problematic consumers as compared to recreational consumers. For instance, research on more than 50,000 military conscripts in Sweden (Solarz, 1990) shows that the backgrounds of recreational consumers did not significantly differ from those of nonconsumers. On the other hand, both this and a host of other studies (i.e., Chein, Gerard, Lee, & Rosenfeld, 1964; Puhakka, 2006; Shanks, 2008; Shedler & Block, 1990) clearly indicate that problematic consumers have had unusually negative life experiences predating their initial experience with narcotics. It appears that problematic consumers in postindustrial societies are primarily recruited from those who have many of the following factors in their backgrounds:

- poverty
- at least one parent with a high level of alcohol consumption
- corporal punishment
- serious conflicts in the home
- broken homes
- if the father was physically present, he tended to take little interest in the family
- spoiled or severely frustrated
- subjected to unclear demands
- inconsistent use of punishment
- chronic physical and/or mental illness in the family
- sexual abuse
- overcrowded living conditions
- multiproblem family
- run away from home on multiple occasions
- subjected to discrimination.

These factors play an important role in the development of the individual's self-image, and are major components in the labeling process to be described in this chapter.

The aforementioned studies also indicate that future problematic consumers of illicit substances showed some of the following symptoms prior to their first narcotics consumption:

- depression
- severe headaches
- stomach problems
- low tolerance for stress
- lack of sleep
- anguish
- nervousness
- excessive aggression.

Furthermore, their childhood years were characterized by:

- lack of initiative
- giving up when faced with resistance

+ maladjustment in school (i.e., they have felt themselves mistreated, have received poor grades in both academic subjects and conduct, have been left back and/or placed in a remedial class, have been truant)
+ extensive consumption of tobacco
+ sniffing organic solvents
+ frequent hangovers and/or starting to take pick-me-ups at an early age
+ criminal offenses such as shoplifting, assault and battery, theft, vandalism
+ being registered by the police and/or social authorities
+ not participating in organized leisure time activities
+ having feelings of inferiority
+ a negative self-image.

The prevalence of extremely negative experiences early in the lives of problematic consumers indicates that problematic consumption should not be considered to be primarily an individual predicament. Macro-analysis is necessary for understanding the roots of the problem.

However, people with similar psychosocial backgrounds are not predestined to a given pattern of drug consumption. Individual social experiences and personal characteristics differentiate people from comparable social environments. Therefore, we must also direct our attention to drug consumers as individuals.

Accordingly, explanations for different types of drug consumption should principally be sought:

+ on the macro-level, where people are molded by the society in which they live/have lived
+ on the micro-level, where individuals are shaped through interaction with other people in intimate small groups
+ on the biological level as we differ genetically.

Instead of attempting to cover all of this in one short chapter, I shall concentrate on my fieldwork and the model I developed to explain what I consider to be the most important underlying patterns behind recruitment to the drug scene in Stockholm. Before beginning, I wish to emphasize that the model concerns only problematic consumers and is not relevant for recreational consumers.

THE NEGATIVE SELF-IMAGE AND
SELF-DESTRUCTIVE BEHAVIOR

Early in my fieldwork, I was given the following advice by one of my research subjects: "Don't feel sorry for junkies when they're kicking cold turkey. Addicts are masochists who want to suffer and die." At the time, I found this advice absurd, as the people I had previously associated with wanted to make their lives as satisfactory as possible, and I assumed that everybody had similar aspirations. Furthermore, from the literature I had read about narcotics, I had been given the impression that addicts, if anyone, sought euphoria. At the time, it seemed beyond question that everyone who takes illicit drugs does so because it makes them feel good.

In retrospect, the advice given by this problematic consumer was the key to understanding the essential nature of what I would be observing while in the field. But the idea was so remote from my "preunderstanding" (the ideas I brought with me into the field) that it took a long time before I could accept it.

Few, if any, doubt that problematic consumers of narcotics risk dying young. That they also ruin their health, are disdained by others, can't trust anyone in their surroundings, are obliged to commit crimes or prostitute themselves daily, sometimes "freak out," periodically become "paranoid," and so on is also well known.[2] Why would anybody subject herself to all of this?

A common answer is some variation of the following theme: "Normally both men and animals are steered by the pleasure-pain principle: some degree of effort is required both to obtain pleasure and to avoid discomfort. . . . In drug addiction . . . a 'short circuit' occurs in the biological system and the normal pleasure-pain principle no longer functions" (Bejerot, 1970, pp. 22–23). "When addiction supervenes . . . the drug hunger takes on the strength and character of instinctive drives" (p. 22). "The drug effects take on the strength of libidinal desires and outweigh all mental, physical, social and economic complications arising from the abuse" (p. xvii). In other words, the individual is no longer in control of her actions. All the negative aspects are outweighed by the euphoric effects of drugs that now steer the individual's behavior (see also Bejerot, 1979, p. 28–31, 37–38, 95).

While it is true that some people (but not all) experience moments of euphoria from psychoactive substances, those who start to use drugs on a daily basis quickly discover that there is a flip side to the coin. The proportion between pleasure and pain increasingly tilts toward the latter as the quantity and frequency of narcotics consumption increases.

If one questions them, even those who believe that euphoria is at the root of problematic consumption will usually agree that such is the case. But they argue that the euphoric experiences of the early stages were so powerful that substantial consumers continue in the hope of reexperiencing them, and/or that by the time they discover the negative effects of narcotics it is too late, as they are caught up in a biochemical dependency and can no longer use their own willpower to control their lives.

However, upon closer examination of what the problematic consumers in my study actually did and experienced, I found that "seeking euphoria" does not explain what was taking place. In fact, quite the opposite was true—they were destroying themselves. In saying this, I am not claiming that everything problematic consumers do is directly or even primarily directed at self-destruction. But the long-term effect of their lifestyle points in this direction.

All of the substantial consumers I observed while in the field were self-destructive—but to different degrees. Some took drastic measures such as "cleansing" one's syringe with water from the toilet bowl in a public restroom when there is a sink right next to it, borrowing other people's "works" in spite of the risk of contamination with HIV and/or hepatitis, asking others to smuggle alcohol into the hospital (instead of a drug that is milder on the liver) while being treated for hepatitis, finding a pill on the street and eating it without having the slightest idea what it contains, and so on.

But acts as drastic as these do not constitute the major part of the self-destructiveness on the scene. We get a better understanding of what is going on by observing less dramatic activities that are repeated as a part of everyday life: that is, improper diet, lack of sleep, unsanitary living conditions, physical and/or sexual abuse, prostitution, not brushing one's teeth, not attending to sores, paranoia, poverty, and so forth. All of these are integral parts of the drug scene. In fact, I find it very unlikely that the word *euphoria* would come into anyone's mind while observing the drug scene. Indeed, it would not be an exaggeration to say that little or nothing in the lives of substantial consumers of illicit substances is as much as pleasant.

Another way to try to get around the obvious self-destructiveness of problematic consumers is to presuppose that they do not understand what they are doing. Some assume that substantial consumers must either be intellectually lacking, or are so influenced by drugs that they cannot think straight, or have an exceptional ability to delude themselves. However, my observations do not lend support to these assumptions. Admittedly, it can be difficult to think clearly while under the influence of psychoactive substances, and just about everybody (including problematic consumers of illicit drugs) engages in a certain amount of self-deception. Many substantial consumers put up a front in their contacts with the "straight world," which can easily reinforce the impression that they are fooling themselves, but if one manages to penetrate behind this facade, as I did during my field research, it becomes obvious that while they might not be conscious of all of the consequences of every particular choice they make, sooner or later just about every problematic consumer comes to understand that in the long run the substances they are taking and the life they are leading will destroy them. While narcotics sometimes (but far from always) give a measure of short-term relief, substantial consumers eventually come to an awareness that their lives are rapidly deteriorating.

Since problematic consumers eventually come to understand that both they themselves and everybody else who remains on the scene are on the road to extinction, yet do not change their way of life, there must be a strong self-destructive side in their personalities. People who aren't extremely self-destructive do not remain on the drug scene very long. That is, there are clear differences between problematic and recreational consumers. Recreational consumers experiment with drugs. They seek certain experiences, such as an alternate state of consciousness, sexuality, new sensations and impressions, relaxation, and so on, and are prepared to make some sacrifices to achieve these ends. But they are not willing to destroy their lives. When economic, social, psychological, and/or physiological costs reach an excessive level, recreational consumers either stop taking drugs altogether or greatly reduce consumption. Few people wish to annihilate themselves and this explains why only a small minority of those who experiment with illicit substances maintain a high level of consumption for long periods of time.

But for people with an extremely self-destructive side to their personalities, the negative effects inherent in the lifestyle on the drug scene become an important reason for continuing with narcotics. At least for my research subjects, *problematic consumption of narcotics is a major component in a self-destructive life project.*

However, it is an oversimplification to divide humanity into two categories: those who are self-destructive and those who aren't. Clearly there are degrees of self-destructiveness. The problematic consumers of illicit substances I studied are extremely self-destructive people who lead lives that slope steeply toward extermination. Not quite as self-destructive people might well follow negative paths, but most likely ones that incline at a lesser angle.

A PROCESS MODEL

The model presented here can be seen as a variation of labeling theory and will identify a series of stages that problematic consumers of illicit substances pass through during their careers. However, before I begin, I must define a few concepts.

The *self-image* is an individual's conception of himself in relation to the ideals of his culture. People do not have a self-image at birth and we are not free to choose our self-image at will. Instead the self-image should be seen as developing through social relationships. Those people whose responses contribute to the formulation of an individual's self-image are his *significant others*. Parents (the people who raise the child) are usually his first and the most important significant others. It is through the parents that the child begins to develop his self-image. As he grows older and comes into contact with society outside of the home, some of the people he meets will become significant others and they too will influence his self-image. However, the basis of the self-image has already been established by that time.

A person with a *negative self-image* has learned through interaction with significant others that there is a low degree of correspondence between his personal characteristics and/or behavior and cultural ideals as to how one should be.

Labeling is a process, not a few exceptional events. In the sense that the concept is used here, *labeling* is a course of events consisting of a large number of negative reactions from significant others, which taken as a whole, cause the individual to redefine his self-image in a negative direction.[3] Labeling occurs in many different places, such as in the family, in relationships with contemporaries, in school; and it can be evoked by many different things such as the individual's behavior, appearance, beliefs, sexual preferences, and so on. It is important to keep in mind that labeling is an ongoing process during an extended period of time, and even if one can identify dramatic events in the individual's life, these do not constitute a sufficient explanation. The self-image develops from the sum of large numbers of both prominent and seemingly insignificant experiences and reactions during the entire lifetime of the individual. Therefore, the older we get, the more well established it becomes and the longer it takes to change its essential content, even if adjustments can be achieved in a shorter time frame.

Parental Labeling

With the help of the concept *primary deviance*, I can intimate the course of events that have constituted the beginning of the labeling process for my research subjects. *Primary deviance* consists of acts that do not comply with societal norms but that are not committed with malice aforethought. They are not the product of a well-established negative self-image but rather the result of a lack of understanding of the plausible consequences of one's actions. In the words of a famous anthropologist, the newborn child is "a barbarian invader from another planet"; that is, a baby knows nothing of the culture it is born into. In order to learn societal norms (right from wrong), significant others must respond to the child's spontaneous behavior. *Everybody begins their lives with primary deviance. What distinguishes one person from the other are the ways their significant others react.* Somewhat simplified, one can say that some children learn that they themselves are good, even if what they are doing for the moment is unacceptable. Others learn, after a sufficient number of "unsuitable" reactions, that it is not simply what they are doing for the time being that is unsatisfactory, but rather that there is something basically wrong with them as human beings. This is *parental labeling* and the *first stage* in the deviant careers of my research subjects.

Some parents appear to be unable to help their children develop a positive self-image, and it is reasonable to ask why this is so. Where one seeks answers depends to a large extent upon one's assumptions regarding the relative importance of nature and nurture (see earlier section).

From my point of view, sociological explanations are important as they reveal the societal pressures people in different socioeconomic groups are subjected to, and the increased probability of certain types of behavior. Statistically, such factors as belonging to a minority group, having uneducated parents, living in a slum, and so on, greatly reduce one's choices in life. But societal pressure is only a framework, not an inescapable process that forces people to act (or not act) in a particular way. Indeed, all people in similar social situations do not respond in the same way. Why Smith, but not his neighbor Jones, succumbs to societal pressure and labels his child cannot be explained sociologically. We must therefore also look at psychological and biological variables. However, it is reasonable to assume that if we can reduce societal pressures the number of people who cannot cope should be diminished, thereby decreasing the number of people who label their children.

Societal Labeling

As children grow older, they spend an increasing amount of time out of the home and they come into contact with society, that is, neighbors, day care personnel, elementary school teachers, and so on. During this period, children continue to learn social norms through reactions from others. In their initial contacts with society, the behavior of children is principally characterized by primary deviance, but as they grow older and gain social experience, their actions become increasingly influenced by societal norms. All children exhibit primary deviance in their initial contacts with society. Once again, the most important element is not the behavior but the reactions from significant others. Most children will learn that they are O.K. even if certain things they do are not. But some will learn that the problem lies not in what they are doing, but with them. This is *societal labeling*, the *second stage* in my deviant career model.

However, it is important to keep in mind that not all negative reactions are a part of a labeling process. *Labeling theory does not imply laissez-faire.* People need reactions in order to learn how to function in society. But the reactions must not equate the actions of the moment with the person herself.

Most often, it is not merely a matter of chance if a child is labeled in her contacts with society. Children who have been labeled by their parents run a far greater risk of being subjected to societal labeling. To explain why this is so, I must introduce another concept. *Behavioral incongruity* arises when an individual's behavior isn't in harmony with her self-image. She will react by trying to diminish the incongruity either by changing the behavior or her self-image. Figure 2.1 gives a picture of behavioral incongruity.

However, the picture conveyed by this figure is greatly oversimplified. Firstly, it gives the impression that people are static, when in reality they change. Some of the more important factors influencing changes in my research subjects will be discussed shortly.

Secondly, the self should be regarded as multiple and pluralistic rather than unitary. In, for instance, Robert Ornstein's (1986, 1991) multimind model we have many "small minds." This is because we participate in various social situations and we do not receive the same responses from all of our significant others. This awakens contradictory desires and ambivalent feelings in us. But Ornstein also postulates that there is a "governing self" that decides which of our small minds we are cognizant of at any given time. That is, even if we have

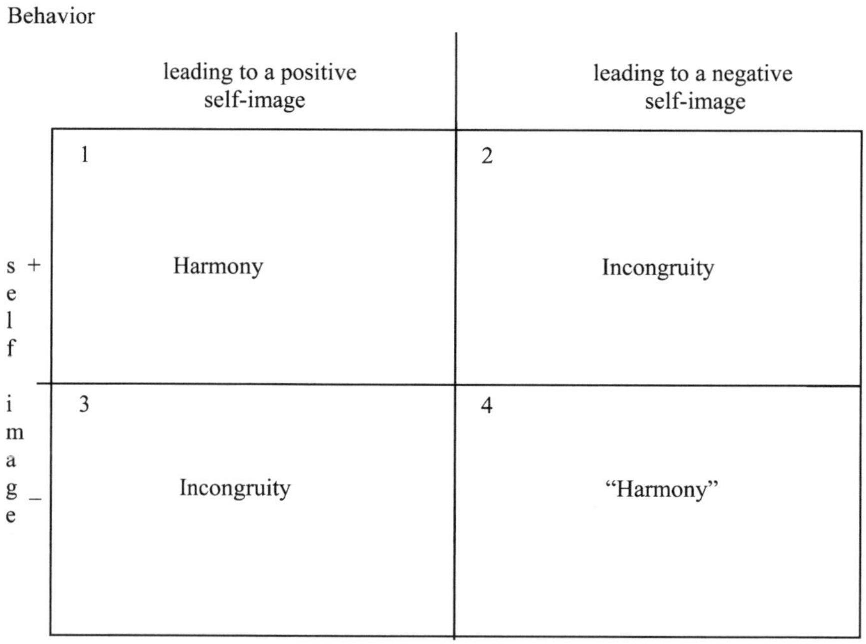

Behavior

	leading to a positive self-image	leading to a negative self-image
s + e l f	1 Harmony	2 Incongruity
i m a g _ e	3 Incongruity	4 "Harmony"

FIGURE 2.1 Behavioral incongruity.

many different "selves" and even if our "identity" changes depending upon the demands of the situation we are in for the moment, all of our identities are not equally important. The *self-image*, as I use the term, can be seen as the *governing self.*

A third complication with the figure is that there are degrees of positive and negative self-images. We can think of the matter as a continuum between those who look upon themselves as a short step under the deity, and those who regard themselves as Satan reincarnated. Depending on where a person stands on this continuum, a certain range of behavior will be acceptable to her; that is, her behavior will not cause incongruity as long as she keeps herself within this domain. However, if she should overstep these boundaries in either direction, that is, either act more positively or more negatively than her self-image will allow for, she will experience incongruity. She must then either discontinue the incongruous activity, place it within the framework of one of her small minds and therefore only be conscious of it in special circumstances, or incorporate it into her governing mind and thereby change her self-image to one that allows for such behavior. Figure 2.2 is a somewhat oversimplified model of these relationships.

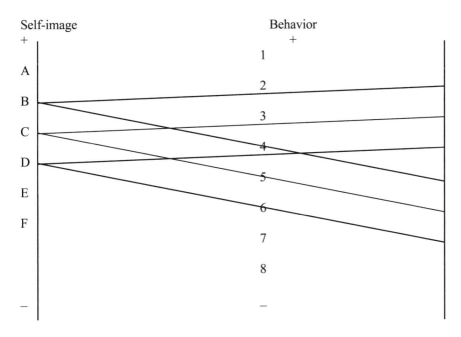

FIGURE 2.2 The relation between self-image and behavior.

An individual with a self-image at position C can behave between points 3 and 6 on the behavior scale without causing incongruity. If he should start acting according to point 2 on the behavior scale, he will either have to change his self-image in a positive direction at least as far as point B, or place the behavior in one of his small minds, or desist from such actions. For instance, upon becoming parents some of my research subjects tried to take care of their children. In doing so, they improved their self-images and this helped to somewhat regulate both their drug consumption and their behavior in general. Indeed, parenthood can be an important factor in getting off the drug scene entirely. But this is certainly not the case for all. Some research subjects who tried to fulfill their roles as parents saw parenthood belonging to a category separate from the rest of their lives. That is, successes in this role were placed in a small mind and not generalized to the self-image. These people tended to limit the amount of time they spent with their children, but when they were with their kids, they exerted themselves. However, it was difficult to see positive effects of this in other situations. And finally, there were those who after a period of time abandoned their children altogether. When I got to know these people well enough for them to confide in me, it became evident that they thought the worse of themselves for having done so. That is, failing to fulfill one's duties as a parent is so important that they didn't merely resume their previous negative self-image, they "devaluated" it further.

Correspondingly, if an individual should start behaving according to point 7 on the behavior scale above, he will either have to change his self-image in a negative direction at least as far as point D, or incorporate the behavior in one of his small minds, or discontinue such activity. Note that the behavior ranges for neighboring points on the self-image scale overlap. This is because people don't change their entire behavioral pattern at once, but rather a little at a time.

An individual with a negative self-image tends to behave so as to provoke others to confirm what he "knows" about himself rather than cause incongruity by acting in a way that would give responses leading to a more positive self-image. For this reason, it is difficult to change an established negative self-image. Negative reactions from significant others tend to modify the behavior of those who basically have a positive self-image, because these reactions are incongruous. For those who already have a negative self-image, admonishments are usually interpreted as a confirmation of what they already believe to be true, and therefore do not lead to behavior more in line with societal norms.

Yet another complication with Figure 2.1 involves the nature of the harmony in cell 1, as compared with the "harmony" in cell 4. In spite of their negative self-images, my research subjects grew up under the influence of mainstream society and have internalized societal norms. Although some authors refer to the drug scene as a *subculture*, I don't find the concept relevant for my observations in Stockholm.[4] For a deviant subculture to arise and remain in existence, its members would have to neutralize the societal norms they have been bombarded with since birth. Although some researchers have gone so far as to itinerate specific methods for achieving this (e.g., see Sykes & Matza, 1957, p. 667ff.), I was unable to distinguish any significant degree of neutralization in my research subjects. When one merely listens to what problematic consumers say in interviews, it is easy to get the impression that they have different norms from the rest of society. But participation observation allows the researcher to establish relationships based on trust, and once this is achieved, one hears entirely different stories. Neither I nor a host of other researchers who have achieved a deeper contact with their informants report any significant degree of neutralization of societal norms (e.g., see Bourgois, 2003; Jonsson, 1973; Yablonsky, 1962). Not only do problematic consumers accept societal norms, but on the whole they tend to have very traditional values. This can be clearly seen, for instance, in what female problematic consumers have to say about sex roles (Lander, 2003, p. 155ff.) and motherhood (Trulsson, 2003, p. 80, 98).

Among the many tragedies in problematic consumers lives is that every day they break rules they themselves feel they should be following. Consequently, their actions cause self-reproach, which is added to all the negative reactions they get from other people. Therefore, the threat of having to devaluate one's self-image is ever present. Deviance bears within itself a certain degree of incongruence. I have indicated this by placing quotes around the word *harmony* in cell 4 in Figure 2.1. As a result of their inability to neutralize societal norms, problematic consumers experience a definite pull toward society; and almost all of those I met during my fieldwork did in fact take tentative steps in this direction on occasion. An example of this is attempting to find a job. If this tentative step is well received, it can initiate a reevaluation of the self-image. If the endeavor fails, it can be more difficult to try again.

In their early contacts with society, children who have been labeled by their parents exhibit the beginning stages of the provocative behavioral patterns easily recognized by everyone who has worked with marginalized people. Although the child's self-image is not firmly established, he can consciously break rules he is aware of, and in doing so provoke negative reactions that serve as a confirmation of what he believes he knows about what kind of person he is. The more frequently a child receives confirmation of his developing negative self-image, the more strongly established it becomes. It is therefore of primary importance that adults who interact with these children have a clear theoretical and/or emotional understanding of what the child is trying to convey with his behavior, so that their reactions do not confirm what the child suspects (that there is something wrong with him) or even worse, become a part of the labeling process (that is, teach the child that he is even worse than he previously believed). Once again, the goal is to teach the child norms without labeling him; to react to what he is doing for the moment, but not against the child himself.

In recent years, politicians in practically all industrialized countries have been making budget cuts. To the extent that they decide to "save money" by withdrawing support from institutions and organizations where children and adolescents establish deeper relationships with adults other than their parents, politicians weaken a possible counterbalance to labeling responses in the home. Examples of such measures are increasing the ratio of children to personnel in community-run day care centers, cramming more pupils into school classes, reducing the number of adults working in schools, withdrawing economic support to youth organizations, cultural organizations, recreation centers, athletic clubs, and so on. With reduced resources, it becomes all the more difficult for the personnel to avoid labeling reactions when responding to children with provocative behavioral patterns, and it is therefore reasonable to expect that more of the children who run the risk of proceeding deeper into a deviant career will in fact do so.

Secondary Deviance

When a child has matured to the point where she has a reasonably clear understanding of societal norms, and has established a self-image based on a substantial number of life experiences, she can enter the *third stage* of the deviant career, *secondary deviance*. The age at which this ensues varies depending upon such factors as the amount and the severity of labeling in the earlier stages. For most of my research subjects, this third stage was established within a few years after becoming a teenager, but in extreme cases it occurred earlier.

Secondary deviance is characterized by acts contrary to societal norms that the individual is cognizant of. Secondary deviance is a product of a relatively well-established negative self-image and is a means of attempting to deal with manifest and/or latent problems arising from labeling. The child has become an adolescent. She has a relatively clear comprehension of right and wrong, and her behavior is increasingly influenced by her negative self-image.

Once a person has accepted that she is not accepted by others, normal social control does not function. People with a positive self-image can be brought to desist from certain behavior by negative reactions because these threaten both their view of themselves and their position as members of a group. But a person with a negative self-image already knows that she is different and an outsider. She doesn't see negative reactions as a guideline to help her gain acceptance because her experiences have taught her that people like her cannot be accepted. So she interprets negative reactions as a further confirmation of how inferior she is. When a person has established a negative self-image, others cannot socially control her by threatening to withdraw love, friendship, or support, since she doesn't feel that she has any of this to begin with. As Bob Dylan succinctly put it: "When you ain't got nothing, you've got nothing to lose."

By defining certain acts as commendable and others as reprehensible, society shows its citizens how to maintain their self-images. For instance, the consumption of certain psychoactive substances is illegal (that is, deplorable). Those who have negative self-images know from their own experiences—the responses they have received from others—that people like them do unacceptable things. They are therefore attracted to illicit drugs. On the other hand, it becomes difficult for people with more positive self-images to consume these substances without experiencing behavioral incongruity. If these people choose to attempt to deal with life's problems by using chemicals, they will go to a doctor to get a prescription for legal drugs. They can do this without causing behavioral incongruity because it is legitimate to take medicine (even if the prescribed drugs should happen to have biochemical effects that are similar to those of narcotics).

If we were to remove current social and legal stigma from illicit substances, the pattern of consumption of these drugs would change. On the one hand, more people would be able to take them as doing so would no longer be experienced as incongruent. On the other hand, those who have a strong negative self-image would either have to take them in an unacceptable manner and/or find new ways to confirm their self-images.

Problematic consumers of narcotics have at least some, and most often all, of the following objectives when they take illegal substances:

1. confirmation of the deeply rooted negative self-image,
2. escape from their own and other people's expectations,
3. self-destruction,
4. revenge.

Due to labeling, problematic consumers of narcotics have drastically negative self-images, initiated prior to their starting to take illicit drugs. Others have deemed them inferior and they have accepted that such is the case. They try to flee, for instance, with the help of psychoactive substances, but they have already internalized the condemnation, and they can't escape from what they bear within. Due to all the negative experiences problematic consumers endure as an integral part of the life they lead on the drug scene, they confirm for themselves that they deserve to be severely punished. After all, they destroy for others and have devastated their own lives. As time passes and the magnitude of negative life experiences escalates, they become all the more convinced that they are reprehensible and that they do not deserve to exist. Increasingly, their life-pattern becomes a process of ensuring that justice is done. Others have condemned them, they have accepted the verdict, and they become their own executioners. But at the same time, by stealing from them, frightening them, giving them a bad conscience, and so on, problematic consumers wreak revenge on those who have passed judgment.

People establish a self-image through others, and they must have help from others to modify it. If we want an individual to change her behavior, we must be willing to take the role of significant other and not only refuse to confirm the negative self-image but also give responses necessary to help her embark upon and endure the long process that leads to a more positive self-image. But this is easier said than done when the labeling process has gone so far that her experiences have taught her to expect negative responses from others. If she is suddenly given positive reactions, the world becomes incomprehensible to her. If, for instance, a social worker or some other significant other does not react as expected, she is looked upon as either being ignorant or simply not having understood what kind of person she is dealing with. This calls for extremely provocative behavior from the problematic consumer to generate the "correct" responses.

If significant others understand that they are being provoked, and are able to find responses that do not label the individual, this can initiate a reevaluation of the negative self-image. But if the provocations are "successful," which sooner or later they usually are, it leads to more labeling and little by little the individual embarks upon the fourth stage in the deviant career.

The Deviance Spiral

The *fourth stage* is called the *deviance spiral* and consists of the following elements, shown in Figure 2.3.

The problematic life experiences that constitute the labeling process create the negative self-image, which in turn leads to secondary deviance, which constitutes failure according to cultural definitions, which induces more labeling, and so on. Each new failure is partially the result of earlier failings but also contributes to future deviance. In this fourth stage, the individual's behavior is usually secondary deviant in several different areas, that is, consuming drugs, selling drugs, theft, prostitution, unemployment, not providing for one's children, homelessness, and so on. As a result, she is subjected to labeling reactions from many different sources.

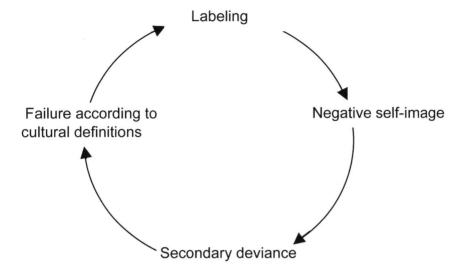

FIGURE 2.3 The deviance spiral.

The deviance spiral is a deterioration of the third stage. As is evident from the name and from Figure 2.3, the problematic consumer of narcotics is now caught in the vortex of a vicious spiral, drawing him downward. This occurs because, when failures and negative reactions accumulate, it becomes all the more difficult to maintain one's self-image at the same (low) level. The individual devalues her self-image still further, which leads to more serious secondary deviance, which other people define as even greater failure and respond to by further labeling, which leads to another devaluation of the self-image, which makes still more serious deviance possible, and so on.

Sooner or later, the deviance spiral leads to everybody who comes into contact with the drug scene getting to the point where they feel that they have had enough. Those who lack self-destructive tendencies usually come to this conclusion quickly and leave the scene shortly after arriving because they don't wish to subject themselves to the rampant negative experiences that surround them. For some people, it takes a little longer before they decide to leave. Only the most self-destructive people stay on the scene so long that they hit rock bottom. That is, they follow the deviance spiral downward to the point where they feel that only two choices remain: either get off drugs, or more directly, commit suicide (e.g., by taking an overdose or by "burning" a pusher who is both willing and able to have them killed). The following example from my fieldwork illustrates the deviance spiral.

When I met R. he was one of the biggest drug dealers in Stockholm. He was unemployed, took narcotics on multiple occasions every day, associated almost exclusively with problematic consumers, and regardless of what the subject of a conversation was initially, it was almost invariably narcotics before the discussion ended. Illicit substances were the hub around which just about everything in his life revolved.

One morning I received a telephone call from him. He was extremely agitated and asked me to come to his apartment. As most problematic consumers do on occasion, he had decided to reappraise his relationship to society. In this particular instance, he was going to try to get a job. When I got to his apartment, he was pacing back and forth nervously, smoking hasch. He told me he had applied for a position as a mailman and that he had an interview at 1:00 P.M. He was certain that nobody would ever employ him, and he was extremely nervous. (In the short run, it was a no-win situation for him. On the one hand, if he was not offered a job, the rejection would have been a blow to his already lacerated self-image. On the other hand, getting a job would have been incongruent to this same self-image.) R. spent several hours smoking one joint after the other and repeating that he wasn't going to get the job. By the time he left for his interview, he was hardly able to communicate. My interpretation of his behavior is that he put himself into a position where if he didn't get the job, he could protect his self-image by claiming that it was because he inadvertently had gotten too stoned.

Amazingly enough, he was given the position, presumably because at the time there was a drastic shortage in the work force in Sweden and the postal authorities were probably desperate.

The most common scenarios when problematic consumers manage to get a job are that they either don't go to it at all, or they show up only sporadically, or they do the job so poorly that they are fired, or they get into conflicts with coworkers and are let go for that reason. Put simply, having a job and doing it well is drastically incongruent to their self-images. With the help of provocation, they get themselves fired and confirm for themselves and others that they are not worthwhile members of society. To illustrate these points I return to R.

On R.'s postal route there were many older four-story walk-ups with only two apartments on each floor (in Sweden the mail is put through a slot in the door of each apartment). One day R. started a conversation with me by saying something to the effect that one of the biggest problems in Sweden is that people are lonely. As he is something of an amateur sociologist, R. presented a long analysis of, among other things, the breakdown of social relationships within the extended family as a result of urbanization. When he finally got to the point, he told me that he had taken it upon himself to do something to help people break their social isolation. In short, he delivered all the mail for each building to just one of the apartments (on the ground floor, of course). That way, he explained, neighbors would have an excuse to ring each other's doorbells and get to know one another.

On several occasions R. told me that some days he couldn't be bothered delivering the mail at all and just threw it into the bushes. As I never actually saw him at this job, I don't really know to what extent he was exaggerating when he spoke of his way of performing his duties. However, I do know that when he had a large shipment of drugs to sell, he didn't go to work at all. He claimed that he usually just didn't show up without calling in sick.

If some of all this is true, R.'s behavior can be seen as an example of the way problematic consumers use provocation to get others to confirm their negative self-images. Normally, an employee who acts the way R. said he did would be asked to leave. However, R. was not fired.

About six months after he started working as a mailman, R. sold an exceptionally large amount of narcotics and had more cash than he'd ever had before. He became concerned about keeping so much money in his apartment while he was waiting for his suppliers to return to Sweden to collect what he owed them. In his own words, he was getting paranoid about the police being on to him, so he made a deal with a problematic consumer he considered a friend that this person would be paid to keep the cash in his apartment. To make a long story short, two of R.'s "friends" who knew about the money stole almost all of it and went off on a spree in southern Europe. R. was left holding the bag and had to pass on the burn. Luckily for him, his suppliers accepted his explanation, because if they hadn't, he would have been killed, as he could not possibly have gotten hold of so much money. However, his problems were far from over. As R. explained it, he now either had to have the two people who burned him murdered or stop dealing; because if word got around that you could get away with cheating him, R. would be ripped off time and again, and he would have to pass on the burns. Sooner or later (presumably sooner), his suppliers would no longer accept any excuses and they would have him eliminated.

In our conversations during this period, R. repeatedly told me that he was many (bad) things but he wasn't a murderer. However, to maintain his position on the drug scene, he now had to become one. To have somebody killed was drastically incongruent with his self-image and he didn't want to do it, but what would/could he do if he were to leave the scene? R. was tormented and frightened but he could not bring himself to sentence two people to death. Instead he fled to the Far East. He had been out there before but this time it wasn't the same. Even this dream was tarnished, and he returned to Stockholm after about a month.

Before leaving Sweden, R. quit his job as a mailman—but resigning is a very different matter than being fired. He had kept a job for more than half a year and could have continued even longer. Becoming a member of society was evidently not as impossible as it once seemed. At the same time, resuming his position on the scene was not really an option as he would literally have to kill to do so. Upon returning to Sweden, R. quickly found a new job and this was one of the major steps in the long process of getting off drugs. Instead of continuing downward in the deviance spiral, R. managed to reverse the process. But if he hadn't already established that he could hold a job, his choices may well have been reduced to killing others or himself. To choose the former would be a major step downward in the deviance spiral. The latter is a choice made by all too many problematic consumers.

When he has hit rock bottom, the individual's small mind that wants to join society but that has been held back, is given higher priority. But if he fails now, all that remains is death. It is therefore not advisable to let the deviance spiral go this far. By not confirming the problematic consumer's negative self-image (e.g., by understanding his provocations and finding nonlabeling responses to them), we can help him break the negative spiral much earlier, preferably before it starts to gain momentum.

As it may be difficult to understand how it is practically feasible to do this, an example may be illuminating. A. S. Neill, former headmaster of Summerhill, a school in England that had among its pupils many "problem children" who had been expelled from other schools, and that used very unusual pedagogical methods, writes: "If I should be painting a door and Robert came along and threw mud on my fresh paint, I would swear at him heartily, because he has been one of us for a long time and what I say to him does not matter. But suppose Robert had just come from a hateful school and his mud slinging was his attempt to fight authority, I would join with him in his mud slinging because his salvation is more important than the door. I know that I must stay on his side while he lives out his hate in order for him to become social" (Neill, 1960, p. 119).

We can summarize my career model by comparing *two extreme kinds of careers*. Both begin with primary deviance, but the reactions received make the careers go in diametrically different directions.

Culturally successful career		Deviant career	
1	Parental acceptance	1	Parental labeling
2	Societal acceptance	2	Societal labeling
3	Normative behavior	3	Secondary deviance
4	Personality enhancement	4	Deviance spiral

The stages in the careers should not be considered completely separate. They can be in progress concurrently and can either reinforce or counteract each other. For instance, parental labeling begins before societal labeling, but can continue for years after the child has made many societal contacts. It is also not necessarily so that an individual will be subjected to the same kinds of reactions from both parents and society, as is the case in the two extreme careers outlined above. Labeling reactions from certain significant others can be counteracted by acceptance from others; in which case, the emerging self-image will neither be extremely positive nor extremely negative (see Figure 2.2). In other words, the number of possible careers far exceeds the two mentioned above. In a welfare state such as Sweden, few people experience the kind of extreme deviant career described here, which makes its prevalence among problematic consumers of narcotics all the more noteworthy.

NOTES

1. Obviously, one can choose to nuance even further. For instance, a report from a governmental commission in the United States distinguished between five different patterns of consumption (see Wurmser, 1995, p. 7).
2. *Paranoid*, as it is used on the drug scene, is slang and should not be equated with its scientific namesake. As in all slang, the concept is not clearly defined. Paranoid denotes vague fears, terrifying experiences, and feelings of persecution. The word is frequently used by problematic consumers because being *paranoid* is a prevalent part of their everyday existence.
3. Logically, one could also think of a positive self-image as being the result of a positive labeling process. However, in this chapter, labeling denotes a negative process.
4. *Subculture* may possibly be a relevant term to describe, for instance, people from eastern Africa who continue to chew *khat* while living in Europe, or Iranians who after emigrating, continue to smoke an opiate on special occasions. While this behavior is not accepted in the majority culture, it is within the bounds of the individual's culture of birth. So in the context of the majority culture the individual is now living in, this might be considered a drug subculture. However, these types of culturally regulated consumption have little to do with the behavior of problematic consumers. If a Somali should chew *khat* or an Iranian should smoke heroin at the expense of his other duties, he would no longer be acting within the framework of his culture and his fellow-countrymen would find his behavior unacceptable.

REFERENCES

Becker, H. S. (1963/1973). *Outsiders*. New York: Free Press.
Bejerot, N. (1970). *Addiction and society*. Springfield, IL: Charles C. Thomas.
Bejerot, N. (1979). *Missbruk av alkohol, narkotika och frihet* [Abuse of alcohol, narcotics and freedom]. Stockholm: Ordfront.
Bourgois, P. (2003). *In search of respect: Selling crack in El Barrio*. Cambridge, UK: Cambridge University Press.

Chein, I., Gerard, D. L., Lee, R. S., & Rosenfeld, E. (1964). *The road to H: Narcotics, delinquency and social policy.* New York: Basic Books.

Dole, V. P., & Nyswander, M. E. (1967). Rehabilitation of the street addict. *Archives of Environmental Health, 14,* 477–480.

Goldberg, T. (1999). *Demystifying drugs: A psychosocial perspective.* New York: St. Martin's Press.

Inciardi, J. A. (1992). *The war on drugs II.* Mountain View, CA: Mayfield.

Israel, J. (1984). *Sociologi: Inledning till det kritiska samhällsstudiet* [Sociology: Introduction to the critical study of society]. Stockholm: BonnierFakta.

Jonsson, G. (1973). *Att bryta det sociala arvet* [Stopping social inheritance]. Stockholm: Folksam.

Lander, I. (2003). *Den flygande maran: En sudie om åtta narkotikabrukande kvinnor i Stockholm* [The floating hag: Ethnography of eight drug using women in Stockholm]. Stockholm: Kriminologiska inst., Stockholms Universitet, Avhandlingsserie nr 11.

Levine, H. G. (2003): Global drug prohibition: Its uses and crises. *International Journal of Drug Policy, 14,* 145–153.

Mills, C. W. (1997). *Den sociologiska visionen* [The sociological imagination]. Lund: Arkiv.

Neill, A. S. (1960). *Summerhill: A radical approach to child rearing.* New York: Hart.

Nordegren, T., & Tunving, K. (1984). *Hasch: Romantik och fakta* [Hasch: Romanticism and facts]. Stockholm: Prisma.

Ornstein, R. (1986). *Multimind.* London: Macmillan.

Ornstein, R. (1991). *The evolution of consciousness: Of Darwin, Freud and cranial fire: The origins of the way we think.* New York: Prentice Hall.

Peele, S. (1998). *The meaning of addiction: An unconventional view.* San Francisco: Jossey-Bass.

Puhakka, O. (2006). *Missbrukare på Sergels Torg 2005* [Misusers in Sergels Torg, 2005]. Stockholm: Stockholms stadsledningskontor, Forsknings- och utvecklingsenheten, FoU-rapport 2006:1.

Robinson, T. E., & Berridge, K. C. (1993). The neural basis of drug craving: An incentive-sensitization theory of addiction. *Brain Research Review, 18,* 247–291.

Shanks, E. (2008). *Utländsk bakgrund och tungt narkotikamissbruk—En kartläggning av levnadsförhållanden* [Foreign background and problematic consumption—An investigation of life experiences]. Stockholm: Rapport i Socialt Arbete nr 125, Institutionen för Socialt Arbete—Socialhögskolan, Stockholms Universitet.

Shedler, J., & Block, J. (1990). Adolescent drug use and psychological health: A longitudinal inquiry. *American Psychologist, 45,* 612–630.

Solarz, A. (1990). *Vem blir drogmissbrukare? Droger, kriminalitet och kontroll* [Who becomes a drug misuser? Drugs, criminality and control]. Stockholm: Brårapport 1990:3, Brottsförebyggande Rådet.

Sykes, G. M., & Matza, D. (1957). Techniques of neutralization: A theory of delinquency. *American Sociological Review, 22,* 664–670.

Trulsson, K. (2003). *Konturer av ett kvinnligt fält: Om missbrukande kvinnors möten i familjeliv och behandling* [Contours of a female domain: On female misuser's experiences of family life and treatment]. Lund: Lund dissertations in Social Work 12, Socialhögskolan, Lunds Universitet.

Wurmser, L. (1995). *The hidden dimension: Psychodynamics in compulsive drug use.* New York: Jason Aronson.

Yablonsky, L. (1962). *The violent gang.* New York: MacMillan.

Chapter 3

Adaptation and Addiction

Ann N. Dapice, PhD

Addiction has been a problem for thousands of years. It involves lasting changes in brain function that may be difficult to reverse. The numbers of "altered brains" include nearly 2 million heroin and cocaine addicts, some 15 million alcoholics, and tens of millions of cigarette smokers in the United States alone (Harvard Mental Health Letter, 2004). Globally, the use of drugs has reached all-time highs (Saah, 2005). As bad as these numbers are, they do not include a far larger array of addictions and numbers of the addicted worldwide.

Research increasingly demonstrates the similarity of, and connections to, a variety of conditions that appear addictive in nature. Some addictions are to external substances (e.g., alcohol, tobacco, cocaine). Some are to external behaviors that stimulate pleasure pathways in the brain (e.g., gambling, online pornography, stalking, and shopping). Some addictions are legal (e.g., food, tobacco, alcohol, prescription drugs, and shopping). Some are not (e.g., cocaine, methamphetamines, stalking). Some substances such as food, alcohol, and prescription painkillers can be used nonaddictively by some people but not by others, and some activities such as gambling, sex, and shopping can be engaged in nonaddictively by some but not others. The consequences of addictions on the addicted and those who are negatively affected by these addictions vary greatly—from chronic disease and slow death, to immediate and sometimes violent death. The social and financial costs of these addictions eventually affect us all. Meanwhile, prevention, intervention, and treatment for addictions, as well as punishment for illegal addictions also vary greatly. Activities such as eating and sexual intercourse are necessary for human survival. In fact, addictions can be seen as originating in behaviors and substances that were once adaptive for the survival of humankind (Dapice, 2006; Fisher, 2004; Popkin, 2007).

Organisms that develop beneficial adaptations increasing the likelihood of their survival are more likely to pass on adaptive genes. The brain's reward system reinforces important behaviors—eating, drinking, sleeping, engaging in sex, but it is easily misled. Computers, the Internet, slot machines, and money can all activate the same regions of the brain as psychoactive drugs (Breiter, Aharon, Kahneman, Dale, & Shizgal, 2001). A recent brain scan study showed that when men were shown erotic pictures, they were more likely to make a larger financial gamble than if they were shown something frightening like a snake, or something neutral like a stapler. The arousing pictures would light up the same area of the brain that lights up when financial risks are taken. This was described as related to the evolutionary need that men have for both money and women. The study was designed to determine cause and effect. The erotic pictures lit up the area in the brain and risk taking followed. When photos of snakes and spiders were shown to the participants, the portion of the brain that is associated with pain, fear, and anger lit up and people were likely to keep their bets low (Knutson, Wimmer, Kuhnen, & Winkelman, 2008). People have different sets of risk factors: neurobiological, psychological, and social. Regardless of the risks to addiction, it is necessary to have exposure to an object of addiction that stimulates a positive experience in the user—relief of discomfort, or creation of pleasure (Walsh, 2007). What causes relief or pleasure varies greatly with the individual and thus the kinds of addictives vary as well.

Food and tobacco are connected to other addictive substances in important evolutionary and physiological ways. Understanding the co-development of mammalian brains and ancient psychotropic plants, as well as the implications of ancient psychotropic substance abuse in altering mammalian brains, helps assess the causes and effects of addiction in today's world. It allows us to come closer to treating the root of the addiction, not the symptoms alone (Saah, 2005). Processes formerly necessary for our safety, well-being, and survival may now serve to make and keep us ill. These include (1) the so-called "thrifty gene" (Popkin, 2007, p. 91), (2) mechanisms for fight and flight (Dapice, 2006; Dapice, Inkanish, Martin, & Brauchi, 2002), and (3) mechanisms for continuation of the species (Fisher, 2004). Our bodies and brains continue to function according to hunting and gathering needs appropriate thousands of years ago.

THRIFTY GENE

Contrary to expectations, skeletons exhumed from 10,000 years ago on the American continent were seen to be healthier than those found since horticulture began (Steckel & Rose, 2002). Early humans stored food substances through the production of insulin in response to the ingestion of carbohydrates. This allowed for fat storage in the body to protect people during winter and times of famine. Similarly, the body and mind sought to limit the amount of energy expanded through physical activity. One ate large amounts when foods were ripe and available, and exercised only as needed for existence (Dapice, 2006, p. 253; Flier & Maratos-Flier, 2007, p. 72; Ozelli, 2007, pp. 84–85).

Food sources became drugs to prevent "decreased fitness" due to starvation and death. Addictive drugs share with "palatable food" the property of increasing extracellular dopamine (Di Chiara & Bassareo, 2007, p. 233). Nicotine, cocaine, and ephedrine sources were first mixed with an alkali substance, most often wood or lime ash, creating a "free base to facilitate diffusion of the drug into the blood stream" (Saah, 2005). Traditionally, American Indians processed corn in a variety of ways using lye or lime ash. Science has since discovered that this process used with corn was required to release complete amino acids and to provide the niacin required to regulate blood sugar. Different tribes had different recipes for treating corn using this method (e.g., Muskogee Creek "softkey," Cherokee "hominy," etc.). Some tribes still have official "corn lyers" (Dapice, Inkanish, Martin, & Montalvo, 2001).

The benefits of civilization have given us mass production and preservation of foods, tobacco, and other substances through agriculture, the industrial revolution, and global transportation. Substances such as tobacco, once rare and localized to a particular geographical area, required first slave labor and then industrialized technologies to produce in amounts sufficient for addiction. Tobacco, once scarce and used for ceremony only, is now plentiful, used in addictive ways, and kills in large numbers worldwide. The World Health Organization estimates that smoking kills more than 4 million people a year. This figure may rise to 10 million per year by 2030 because of rapidly growing tobacco use in developing countries (HealthCentral.com, 2000). As it happens, preservation of tobacco, which includes large amounts of sugar, adds to its addictive qualities by appealing to the brain's natural survival need for carbohydrates (Bennett, Howell, & Doll, 1970).

While tobacco use remains in first place with respect to fatal forms of substance abuse, obesity is rapidly moving ahead as the number-one killer (Tanner, 2004). Research demonstrates that brain circuits involved in drug addiction are also activated by the desire for food. The right orbital-frontal cortex is involved in compulsive behaviors characteristic of addictive states and this same brain region is activated when addicted individuals crave drugs such as cocaine. Food stimulation increases levels of dopamine and when obese individuals were examined, they were found to have fewer dopamine receptors—as has been found in addiction to other substances (Brookhaven National Laboratory, 2004). It is, of course, important that food be satisfying for the survival of the species. Having fewer receptors increases the level of food intake, when possible, and this was once adaptive during winter and famine (Dapice, 2006; Ozelli, 2007). However, in a new understanding of how people become addicted to food, researchers note that taste and palatability are not the only factors since, when the ability to taste is removed, the same dopamine pathways are stimulated by calories (Andrews & Harvath, 2008; De Araujo et al., 2008). Popkin notes that the rapid globalization of obesity has been encouraged by marketing of unhealthy foods worldwide and the food industry has insisted that governments "should not restrict an individual's dietary choices" (2007, p. 93).

The American Cancer Society notes that while a third of the nation's 50 million smokers attempt to quit each year, not unlike statistics on treatment effectiveness in alcohol and drug addiction (Mathews-Larson, 1991; National Institute on Alcohol Abuse and Alcoholism [NIAAA], 1996; Polick, Aarmor, & Bracker, 1980), fewer than 5 percent succeed (Bartosiewicz, 2004). It has been observed and reported (Morgan, 2003) that smokers who try to stop tobacco use through patches and gum become addicted to these as well (Bartosiewicz, 2004). Research has demonstrated that drinking alcohol improves the enjoyment of tobacco. On the average, more than 85 percent of adults with a history of alcohol abuse smoke, and they may be more addicted to nicotine than are smokers without a history of drinking (Abrams, Monti, Niaura, Rohsenow, & Colby, 1996). Carl Anderson, researcher at Harvard University Medical School, reported in a personal communication (September 2004) that the amino acid, L-Glutamine, is missing in the brains of smokers, but not in the brains of those who can take or leave tobacco products. L-Glutamine also helps regulate blood sugar and related cravings for carbohydrates and alcohol (Mathews-Larson, 1991). Again, the cravings can be seen to be adaptive when it is desirable that one take in more of a substance than is needed at the time.

It is known that EEG brain waves are shaped genetically and researchers have demonstrated that reduced amplitude correlates with alcohol dependence. They have identified the chromosomal region that affects the P300 electrical brain wave, previously correlated with alcohol craving and predisposition to relapse. These EEG abnormalities are true both of alcoholics as well as their "alcohol-naïve" (never used) offspring (Begleiter & Porjesz, 1988; Propping, Kruger, & Mark, 1981; Tabakoff & Hoffman, 1988; Volavka, Pollock, Gabrielli, & Mednick, 1985). Studies at the University of Connecticut by Lance Bauer show that relapse to alcohol, cocaine, and opioid dependence can be predicted by brain waves. The high-frequency activity on EEGs was found to far outweigh clinical and demographic variables as a predictor of relapse (Bauer,

2001). Alcoholic P300 brain waves appear as "jagged mountains" compared to the normal appearance of gentle "foothills."

Alcoholism among some groups is partly related to lack of adaptation to certain foods. Alcoholism is highest among peoples who received grains such as wheat, barley, and oats relatively late—Russians and northern Europeans. American Indians have had even less time to adapt to these foods (Mathews-Larson, 1991). Research also shows that hypoglycemia affects up to 95 percent of alcoholics, causing them to become irritable, angry, depressed, hostile, and crave carbohydrates in the form of food or alcohol. Consuming carbohydrates in various forms serves to relieve symptoms temporarily, but with surges of insulin the cycle continues. In the alcoholic community, this phenomenon is known as "dry drunk" and may be observed whether or not individuals have ever used alcohol. Diabetics often experience these same hypoglycemic symptoms and are taught how to respond appropriately with diet (Bell & Martin, 2002; Mathews-Larson, 1991). The cravings are the key to this once-adaptive behavior.

FIGHT/FLIGHT

The fight/flight physiological process protected our ancestors from predators. The mammalian drive to escape danger is driven by the ability to feel negative emotions (Saah, 2005). However, fight/flight responses become destructive when such actions are inappropriate to the situation or when the stress or danger becomes chronic. Cortisol, produced during these times, becomes toxic to cells in the body and the brain, killing brain cells and leaving depression in its wake (Sapolsky, 1996). Especially important is the relationship of stress, cortisol, and predisposition to self-medication. As noted by the National Institute of Drug Abuse (NIDA) in a special issue on stress and drug abuse (2002), studies in the *Journal Psychoneuroendocrinology* indicate (1) stress and cortisol sensitize animals for drug-seeking behaviors and facilitate self-administration, (2) animals that are underaroused and have low levels of cortisol are more prone to develop drug-seeking behaviors, (3) severe stress early in life induces a series of physiological, neurobiological, and hormonal events that result in dysregulation of biological reward pathways in the central nervous system and in stress response systems; these changes seem to prompt self-administration of drugs and alcohol later in life, (4) prenatal exposure to stress and drugs predispose animals to drug-seeking behaviors in adulthood, (5) posttraumatic stress disorder (PTSD) is a risk factor for substance abuse, and (6) the administration of cocaine to humans causes similar physiological reactions such as secretion of adrenalin and cortisol, and psychological reactions similar to arousal caused by stress. Researchers at the Scripps Research Institute in California (Koob, 1999) observed that heavy drinking not only depletes the brain's supplies of neurotransmitters necessary for feelings of well-being and pleasure (dopamine, serotonin, GABA, and opioid peptides), but it also promotes the release of cortisol. This release of cortisol causes tension and depression, which in turn causes the individual to drink more, leading to an ongoing vicious cycle.

Child abuse, neglect, sexual abuse, and verbal abuse cause damage to the cerebellar vermis in the brain, causing electrical irritability that the brain attempts to quell physiologically and the individual attempts to alleviate by abuse of alcohol and drugs. This area of the brain is extremely sensitive to stress hormones (Anderson et al., 1999). Brain imaging technology (Teicher, 2002) demonstrates that there are three major changes observed in the brains of adults who were abused as children: (1) limbic irritability with increased incidence of clinically significant EEG abnormalities, (2) deficient development of the left hemisphere of the brain (throughout the cerebral cortex and hippocampus), and (3) deficient integration of the left and right hemispheres of the brain with diminished development of the middle portions of the corpus callosum that serves as a bridge connecting the left and right brain. These lateralization changes in the brain are similar to those found by many other PTSD researchers. Essentially, the right brain takes control with negative affect and related behaviors (Bremner et al., 2000; Dapice et al., 2002; Sapolsky, 2000). However, the cerebellum has the potential architecturally to continue communication between the left and right brain with the administration of electrical stimulation (C. M. Anderson, personal communication, September 2003). Anderson (2001) has also noted a convergence of data suggesting that abnormalities in the cerebellar vermis may be involved in a wide array of psychiatric disorders, including depression, substance abuse, and ADHD. In *Nearness of Grace*, Arnold Mandell writes that exaggerated pruning of unused neural connections as a result of high levels of stress hormones leads to an extremely reduced range of potential behavior, which results in individuals "who lie without reason, get drunk, binge on promiscuity, steal unneeded things, or withdraw into interpersonal isolation" (2005, p. 30).

The relationship between stress and addiction is not limited to humans. Recent research among primates by Michael Nader of Wake Forest University has demonstrated the impact of unequal power on the one with power—and the ones without. Socially dominant male monkeys showed a brain chemistry change that encouraged resistance to using drugs such as cocaine. This alteration actually increased the number of dopamine receptors. Male monkeys at the bottom of the pecking order displayed *no* boost of the dopamine receptors and readily self-administered large amounts of cocaine (2002, p. 53).

CONTINUATION OF THE SPECIES

An example of yet another normal adaptive response gone awry can be seen in the case of romantic love (Fisher, 2004) and stalking behavior. Unlike addictive substances that are taken into the body, it is an example of external events that stimulate internal responses leading to addiction (Fisher, 2004; Meloy & Fisher, 2006). As an addiction, stalking shows all the symptoms—"tolerance, dependency/craving, withdrawal and relapse" (Meloy & Fisher, 2006, p. 364). Because it serves as a paradigm example of addictions that are not substances taken into the body, because more than 1 million women and nearly 400,000 men are stalked every year in the United States alone, and because stalkers are the most lethal of all criminals (Meloy, 2006, p. 172), space will be taken here to discuss how such an addiction works in the brain.

Stalking seems to originate with once-adaptive mechanisms for mating and reproduction—the sex drive or lust (testosterone), attraction or romantic love (dopamine), and attachment or companion love (vasopressin and oxytocin). The sex drive motivates people to consider a variety of possible partners for survival of the species. Attraction causes people to focus their energies on a specific individual. Attachment motivates people to remain in a relationship long enough to raise their offspring. However, these mechanisms in an individual with personality disorders such as narcissism or borderline personality combine in dangerous and often lethal ways. Stalking perpetrators often have attachment problems from early in life that may be the result of parental loss, neglect, abuse, or abandonment, and may also be related in some cases to genetic defect (Meloy, 2006, p. 278).

Brain imaging studies of stalkers demonstrate elevated activity of dopamine in the reward/motivation system. This activity produces focused attention and unwavering motivation and goal-directed behaviors. These are associated with other feelings, including "exhilaration, increased energy, hyperactivity, and sleeplessness." As noted above, this system can be stimulated by a number of phenomena, including money and cocaine. Activation of these pathways is most likely related to several traits of the "spurned or unrequited" stalker. This response includes heightened energy and intense motivation to "pursue the victim" (Meloy & Fisher, 2006, p. 357). Deactivation of other brain responses may be part of the problem. The right amygdala, involved in fear and other negative emotions, is deactivated and this may cause stalkers to be unable to pay attention to the dangers of their actions.

Another shared characteristic of lovers and stalkers is their obsessive thoughts about the loved one. They report that they cannot get the obtrusive thoughts out of their minds. This is linked to the suppressed activity of central serotonin since research links low serotonin to obsessive thoughts. Low sero-tonin is also linked to another characteristic of lovers and stalkers—impulsivity. There seems to be a negative feedback loop between dopamine and serotonin. Low serotonin elevates dopamine activity and elevated dopamine suppresses serotonin. As the stalker feels energy, attention, and motivation to pursue the victim, rising levels of dopamine suppress serotonin leading to more obsession and dysphoria. As obsession continues, dopamine further lowers serotonin. Other brain systems combine with these processes to produce the symptoms of "energy, impulsivity, dysphoria, fearlessness, and obsession" (Meloy & Fisher, 2006, p. 359). Observers note that these individuals often appear to be on methamphetamines—even when they are not.

Failed in attachment from childhood, caught in the negative feedback loop of increasing dopamine and decreasing serotonin, along with increasing levels of stress cortisol, continued rejection by the victim, all this sets in motion a frustration-attraction response that may increase and sustain the stalker's abil-ity to stalk. They may also experience abandonment rage, which happens when an expected reward is in doubt or unobtainable, stimulating the amygdala in the brain and triggering rage. Both romantic love and rage have a great deal in common. Both produce obsessive thinking, focused attention, motivation, and goal-directed behaviors desiring union or revenge (Meloy & Fisher, 2006, p. 361). When cortisol has been stimulated over time, the levels become abnor-mally low and unlike previously thought, it is low cortisol, not testosterone, that is related to violence in bullies in school and prisoners in jails (MacKeen, 2000).

Fisher and Meloy point out that stalkers are in a state of addiction to their own chemicals. They are seen to relapse in the same way as addicts to cues such as people, events, and songs (Meloy & Fisher, 2006, pp. 364–365). One perpetrator said, "She was like a drug . . . that I needed . . . my high was being with her. . . . I felt like dying when not with her." After the victim obtained a protective order, he murdered her. He said he let his obsession ruin his life. "I lost it all because of my obsession. . . . This obsession was bad. . . . It was like being in heaven and in hell at the same time" (Kienlen, Birmingham, Solberg, O'Regan, & Meloy, 2006, p. 140). It is important to notice the narcissism that focuses only on what happened to him—not the woman he killed. In spite of the fact that stalkers may be one of the worst offenders due to their intelligence and violence, they are rarely arrested for their crimes (Meloy, 1998, p. 3; Meloy, Cowet, Parker, Hofland, & Friedland, 2006, p. 143). Stalking behaviors some-times continue for years, leaving victims in chronic acute traumatic stress where the impact of cortisol damage to victims' brains and other organs is only now beginning to be realized. Stalking behavior needs to be stopped for the sake of both perpetrators and victims.

OTHER BEHAVIORAL ADDICTIONS

Necessary risk taking, mating, and exchange of needed goods are all important to continuation of the species. In "Behavioral Addictions: Do They Exist?," Constance Holden (2001) noted that gamblers get high, show tolerance, have withdrawal symptoms—like drug addicts. Holden gave as example the work of Anna Rose Childress whose brain imaging showed sex addicts to resemble cocaine addicts. Further, Internet abuse is seen as the country's fastest-growing addiction with people addicted online to the same things they are addicted to offline—gambling (including short-term trading), pornography, and shopping, Holden referred to psychiatrist Susan McElroy's statements that the form addictions take has a lot to do with gender. "Men are overwhelmingly represented among sex 'addicts' and outnumber women by about 2 to 1 in gambling and substance abuse." Women are prone to what she calls the "mall disorders"— eating, shopping, and kleptomania—where the ratio of females to males in kleptomania is 2 or 3 to 1 and perhaps 90 percent of compulsive shoppers are women. Bulimia, which is characterized by binging and vomiting, is also seen to be an addiction, unlike anorexia, which involves rigidly controlled behavior and no "high" (Holden, 2001, pp. 980–982). The bulimia-anorexia difference is similar to distinctions between battering and stalking, where stalking is a form of addiction, while brain imaging of batterers demonstrates a misperception of cues causing batterers to mistakenly feel under attack and respond in misplaced attempts to protect themselves (George et al., 2000). Other behaviors such as working and jogging are normally adaptive, but in exaggerated form can take over with the same compulsivity as any other addiction.

A curious example of substance-interaction with addictions thought to be behavioral is the relatively new finding that a prescription drug for "restless leg syndrome" (RLS) can result in a variety of behavioral addictions. Television commercials can be heard regularly listing "side effects" such as pathological gambling, compulsive eating, increased alcohol consumption, and sexual obsession (Mayo Clinic, 2007). What is more interesting is that it is not so widely recognized that over-the-counter diphenhydramine (Benadryl), found in a number of drug combinations for sleep and colds, can elicit RLS (Rye, 2005). The "addictive" behaviors will end with the removal of the RLS medication— and may not begin if diphenhydramine is not taken in the first place.

DISCUSSION

Behaviors once critical to the survival of our species relied on the limits of the environment for regulation. With these limits removed by modern agriculture, transportation, and global trade, we are left with no internal controls

(Saah, 2005) to regulate behaviors where often endless excess is available. In essence, the brain has no brakes. Technology has changed more rapidly than evolutionary adaptations (Walsh, 2007). Drugs of abuse not only stimulate areas of the brain that have evolved to encourage adaptive behaviors, they stimulate these areas more effectively than the survival behaviors themselves (Di Chiara & Bassareo, 2007). In nature, rewards usually come only with effort and after a delay (Harvard Mental Health Letter, 2004). Addictive substances and behaviors provide shortcuts to feeling "fit." Meanwhile, nature and nurture are related in that fight/flight stress makes the brain think famine is coming and so substances are taken in excessively to prepare for the coming "famine." Stress may also exaggerate behaviors that were once adaptive such as sex and risk taking. It is these once-adaptive and interrelated behaviors that now threaten our worldwide health and survival at ever increasing rates.

The understanding of addiction then is complicated and requires both breadth and depth of knowledge from a variety of disciplines if we are to begin to understand its nature. Addiction is no longer about a limited number of substances and people. Many of us, if not most, are addicted to one substance or behavior or another—including the substances and behaviors that are the essence of living itself. The processes that evolved to protect us often do not. It is a new world of addiction—literally and figuratively. Our human "civilization" has made us successful beyond all imagination. First, we learned to gain at least some control of our food supply by planting seeds into the ground so we would not be limited to gathering what Mother Nature provided alone. Instead of hunting untamed animals, we would eventually learn to tend, fence, and breed animals we would depend upon for meat. These actions alone would not prevent hunger from times of famine, but we would also learn to trade with other groups for what we needed but did not have. The movement from hunter-gatherer societies to ones that were pastoral and horticultural required larger families to do the work—as it also provided more food than might once have been available. Larger families would move people from hunter-gatherer egalitarian groups to hierarchical systems where some had more power than others. Eventually, this "civilization," across large societies worldwide, would find slaves helpful in accomplishing even greater amounts of work—allowing others to assume special privilege of class and power. The industrial revolution would come to make slavery no longer necessary, but class and unequal power would generally remain.

Thus the poor may have more abundance than in the past, but it is generally of low quality, full of bad fats and refined carbohydrates that lead to obesity, Type 2 Diabetes, cardiovascular disease, and cancer. Therefore, in what the Food and Agriculture Organization of the United Nations has called the "double burden" of malnutrition, undernutrition exists side by side with rapid rise in overweight people and obesity and related chronic diseases (Spotlight, 2006). Based on a recent study, Dr. Michele Companion of the University of Colorado describes the same phenomenon occurring with American Indians in the United States—as well as in the developing nations of the world (*Native American Times*, 2008).

Human brains seem not to have evolved much from hunter-gatherer times—they continue to depend on a limiting environment for brakes. For most people worldwide, the environment no longer provides these limits. In the modern world, we use cell phones, e-mail, text messaging, wireless computers, and computer games "24/7." Have our electronics, and their messages, made us more attuned to possible dangers from which we must flee or be ready to fight? There seems to be a constant need to be in touch, to know what is happening, a fear of what will happen if we do not stay continuously "tuned in."

CONCLUSION

Not only do we have "old brains," but with new brain imaging, we are able to understand that the brains of people who are addicted are seriously damaged by the drugs of abuse—and may have been damaged by genetic predisposition, or child abuse, or both, long before self-medication began. Science not only can provide us with new information, it can also tell us of past activities such as the use of lye and lime in treating foods and psychotropic plants for nourishment.

The marketing of tobacco and processed foods worldwide, especially to developing countries, has changed the nature of health problems in the world. Tremendous amounts of money are involved in this global trade. New meaning has been given to "international drug traffic." We have tremendous numbers of addicted and a larger array of addictions worldwide. The material cost and human suffering is beyond imagination. Our "old" brains that are capable of developing the technology that can look inside our brains will need to find new ways to stop the damage.

REFERENCES

Abrams, D., Monti, P., Niaura, R., Rohsenow, D., & Colby, S. (1996, March). Intervention for alcoholics who smoke. *Alcohol Health and Research World, 20*(2), 111–117.

Anderson, C. M. (2001). The integrative role of the cerebellar vermis in cognition and emotion. *Consciousness and Emotion, 2*(2), 284–299.

Anderson, C. M., Polcari, A. M., McGreenery, C. E., Maas, L. C., Renshaw, P. F., & Teicher, M. H. (1999). Cerebellar vermis blood flow: Associations with psychiatric symptoms in child abuse and ADHD. *Society for Neuroscience Abstracts, 25* (pt. 2), 1637.

Andrews, Z., & Harvath, T. (2008, March). Tasteless food reward. *Neuron, 57,* 806–808.

Bartosiewicz, P. (2004, May). A quitter's dilemma: Hooked on the cure. *New York Times,* Retrieved March 18, 2008, from http://www.nytimes.com/2004/05/02/business/yourmoney/02smok.html?pagewanted=all&position=

Bauer, L. (2001, September). EEG shown to reliably predict drug and alcohol relapse potential. *Neuropsychopharmacology, 25*(3), 332–340.

Begleiter, H., & Porjesz, B. (1988). Potential biological markers in individuals at high risk for developing alcoholism. *Alcoholism: Clinical and Experimental Research, 12*(4), 488–493.

Bell, L., & Martin K. (2002). A natural prescription for addiction. *Counselor, 3*(4), 40–44.

Bennett, A. E, Howell, R. W., & Doll, R. (1970, May). Sugar consumption and cigarette smoking. *Lancet, 1*(7655), 1011–1014.

Breiter, H. C., Aharon, I., Kahneman, D., Dale, A., & Shizgal, P. (2001). Functional imaging of neural responses to expectancy and experience of monetary gains and losses. *Neuron, 30*(2), 619–639.

Bremner, J., Narayan, M., Anderson, E., Staib, L., Miller, H., & Charney, D. (2000). Hippocampal volume reduction in major depression. *American Journal of Psychiatry, 157,* 115–127.

Brookhaven National Laboratory. (2004). *Exposure to food increases brain metabolism.* Retrieved September 21, 2004, from http://www.bnl.gov/ bnlweb/pubaf/pr/2004/bnlpr041904.htm

Dapice, A. (2006). The medicine wheel. *Journal of Transcultural Nursing, 17*(3), 251–260.

Dapice, A., Inkanish, C., Martin, B., & Brauchi, P. (2002, September). Killing us slowly: When we can't fight and we can't run. *Native American Times.* Retrieved May 25, 2004, from http://www.dlncoalition.org/related_issues/killing_us_slowly.htm

Dapice, A., Inkanish, C., Martin, B., & Montalvo, E. (2001, June). Killing us slowly: The relationship between type II diabetes and alcoholism. *Native American Times.* Retrieved May 25, 2004 from http://vltakaliseji.tripod.com/Vtlakaliseji/id20.html

De Araujo, I., Oliveira-Maia, A., Sotrikova, T., Gainetdinov, R., Caron, M., Nicolelis, M., et al. (2008, March). Food reward in the absence of taste receptor signaling. *Neuron, 57,* 930–941.

Di Chiara, G., & Bassareo, V. (2007). Reward system and addiction: What dopamine does and doesn't do. *Current Opinion in Pharmacology, 9*(2), 233. Retrieved March 10, 2008, from http://www.sciencedaily.com/releases/2004/04/040420214434.htm

Fisher, H. (2004). *Why we love: The nature and chemistry of romantic love.* New York: Henry Holt.

Flier, J., & Maratos-Flier, E. (2007, September). What fuels fat. *Scientific American, 297*(3), 72.

George, D., Hibbeln, J., Ragan, P., Unhau, J., Phillips, M., Doty, L., et al. (2000). Lactate-induced rage and panic in a select group of subjects who perpetrate acts of domestic violence. *Biological Psychiatry, 47,* 804–812.

Harvard Mental Health Letter. (2004). *The addicted brain.* Retrieved March 1, 2008, from http://www.health.harvard.edu/newsweek/The_addicted_brain.htm

HealthCentral.com. (2000). *WHO accuses tobacco companies.* Retrieved March 10, 2008, from http://medicalnewstoday.com/articles/9706.php

Holden, C. (2001, November). Behavioral addictions: Do they exist? *Science, 294,* 980–982.

Kienlen, K., Birmingham, D., Solberg, K., O'Regan, J., & Meloy, J. R. (2006). A comparative study of psychotic and nonpsychotic stalking. In J. R. Meloy (Ed.), *The scientific pursuit of stalking* (pp. 121–142). San Diego: Specialized Training Services.

Knutson, B., Wimmer, G. E., Kuhnen, C., & Winkelman, P. (2008, March). Nucleus accumbens activation mediates the influence of reward cues on financial risk taking. *NeuroReport, 19*(5), 509–513.

Koob, G. (1999). Alcohol stimulates release of stress chemicals. *Scripps Research Institute.* Retrieved March 10, 2008, from http://www.atforum.com/SiteRoot/pages/addiction_resources/webvol_4.pdf

MacKeen, D. (2000). *Hormonal rages: A new study links decreased levels of cortisol with aggressive behavior in boys.* Retrieved September 10, 2002, from http://www.salon.com/health/log/2000/01/14/cortisol

Mandell, A. (2005). *Nearness of grace: A personal science of spiritual transformation.* Retrieved September 15, 2005, from www.cieloinstitute.org/pages/357835/page357835.html?refresh=1111958880143

Mathews-Larson, J. (1991). *Seven weeks to sobriety.* New York: Villard Books.

Mayo Clinic (2007, February 9). Medical therapy for restless legs syndrome may trigger compulsive gambling. *ScienceDaily.* Retrieved March 31, 2008, from http://www.sciencedaily.com/releases/2007/02/070208222800.htm

Meloy, J. R. (1998). *The psychology of stalking: Clinical and forensic perspectives.* San Diego: Academic Press.

Meloy, J. R. (2006). *The scientific pursuit of stalking.* San Diego: Specialized Training Services.

Meloy, J. R., Cowet, P. Y., Parker, S. B., Hofland, B., & Friedland, A. (2006). Domestic protection orders and the prediction of subsequent criminality and violence to protectees. In J. R. Meloy (Ed.), *The scientific pursuit of stalking* (pp. 143–162). San Diego: Specialized Training Services.

Meloy, J. R., & Fisher, H. (2006). Some thoughts on the neurobiology of stalking. In J. R. Meloy (Ed.), *The scientific pursuit of stalking* (pp. 347–372). San Diego: Specialized Training Services.

Morgan, K. (2003, March). More than a kick. *Science News, 163*(12), 184.

Nader, M. (2002, January). Biology of rank: Social status sets up moneys' cocaine use. *Science News, 161*(4), 53.

National Institute of Drug Abuse. (2002, April 8). *NIDA addiction research news.* Retrieved May 25, 2004, from http://www.drugabuse.gov/MedAdv/02/NS-04. html

National Institute on Alcohol Abuse and Alcoholism. (1996). *NIAAA reports Project Match main findings.* Retrieved May 25, 2004, from http://www.niaaa.nih.gov/ NewsEvents/NewsReleases/match.htm

Native American Times. (2008, April). International Relief and Development releases new study of double burden of malnutrition/obesity facing American Indians. Retrieved April 10, 2008, from http://www.nativetimes.com/index.asp?action= displayarticle&article_id=9461

Ozelli, K. L. (2007, September). This is your brain on food. *Scientific American, 297*(3), 84, 85.

Polick, V., Aarmor, D., & Bracker, H. (1980). *The course of alcoholism, four years after treatment* (pp. 169–170). Santa Monica, CA: Rand Corp.

Popkin, B. (2007, September). The world is fat. *Scientific American, 297*(3), 91–93.

Propping, P., Kruger, J., & Mark, N. (1981). Genetic disposition to alcoholism: An EEG study in alcoholics and their relatives. *Human Genetics, 59,* 51–59.

Rye, D. (2005). Restless leg syndrome. Business briefing: *US Neurology Review.* Retrieved March 5, 2008, from http://www.touchbriefings.com/pdf/1239/rye.pdf

Saah, T. (2005). The evolutionary origins and significance of drug addiction. *Harm Reduction Journal, 2*(8). Retrieved March 5, 2008, from http://bmc.ub.uni-potsdam.de/1477–7517-2-8/

Sapolsky, R. (1996). Why stress is bad for your brain. *Science, 273,* 749–750.

Sapolsky, R. (2000). Glucocorticoids and hippocampal atrophy in neuropsychiatric disorders. *Archives of General Psychiatry, 57,* 925–935.

Spotlight. (2006, February). *The double burden of malnutrition: Fighting hunger—and obesity.* Retrieved April 10, 2008, from http://www.fao.org/Ag/Magazine/0602sp1. htm

Steckel, R. H., & Rose, J. C. (2002). *The backbone of history: Health and nutrition in the Western Hemisphere.* New York: Cambridge University Press.

Tabakoff, B., & Hoffman, P. L. (1988). Genetics and biological markers of risk for alcoholism. *Public Health Reports, 103*(6), 690–698.

Tanner, L. (2004). *Study: We're eating ourselves to death.* Associated Press. Retrieved September 21, 2004, from www.cbsnews.com/stories/2004/03/09/health/ main604956.shtml

Teicher, M. H. (2002, March). Scars that won't heal: The neurobiology of child abuse. *Scientific American,* 68–75.

Volavka, J., Pollock, V., Gabrielli, W. F., & Mednick, S. A. (1985). The EEG in persons at risk for alcoholism. *Recent Developments in Alcoholism, 3,* 21–36.

Walsh, E. (2007, May). Addiction and technology—From sex to drugs: Considering evolution and addiction. *Addiction and the Humanities, 3*(4). Retrieved March 5, 2008, from http:www.basisonline.org/2007/05/addiction_the_h.html

Chapter 4

Co-Occurring Trauma and Substance Use Disorders with Criminal Offenders

Scott E. McClure, PhD

It was a moonlit Saturday morning in the slums of London on February 17, 1872, when an event happened that had an indirect yet permanent influence on the English language. Dr. William Chester Minor was a trained physician who served at the Battle of the Wilderness in May 1864 during the American Civil War, a war noted for its gruesomeness and casualties. Dr. Minor's military duties involved the typical medical procedures used to aid the continuous stream of injured soldiers in need of medical treatment. Many of the wounded soldiers needs were far beyond the capabilities of medicine at that time and treatment often resulted in numerous amputations and deaths. In addition to standard medical procedures, Dr. Minor's duties included branding a letter D on the faces of war deserters, many of whom were Irish. These events would later have a profound impact on Dr. Minor's psychological well-being, especially branding Ds on the faces of Irish deserters, a duty he was always reluctant to do. Dr. Minor knew the long-term impact it would have on the Irish, both in the United States and in Ireland where many Irish military veterans planned to return with their newly learned combat skills to fight in the Irish revolts. The branded D would forever label these individuals in the United States as war deserters and would also become an identification mark in Ireland for soldiers of the revolution, thus resulting in rejection by both countries.

Following the Civil War, Dr. Minor's behaviors became impulsive and reckless, often involving alcohol and prostitutes. By 1867 his erratic behavior, accompanied by uncontrolled fits of rage, severe headaches, nightmares, paranoia, and delusions of persecution led to a military discharge and eventually admittance into St. Elizabeth's Lunatic Asylum in Washington, D.C. Upon release from the asylum, Dr. Minor, still haunted by his paranoid delusions that the Irish were after him, moved to London in an attempt to start a new life. Unfortunately, his symptoms of psychological trauma followed him and eventually precipitated the murder of a complete stranger on this winter morning of February 17, 1872. In an ironic turn of events for history, Dr. Minor's assault resulted in his admittance into the English asylum in 1872 where he spent the majority of his remaining life providing thorough and decisive definitions and literary examples for the first comprehensive English dictionary, the *Oxford English Dictionary*.

In today's modern media, a news report titled "Disgruntled Veteran Murders Innocent Family Man" would be a typical headline for the events that happened on February 17, 1872. If the individual was intoxicated at the time of the event, his fate would fare worse, as society generally lacks empathy for violent crime and substance misuse. But, given the entire background and context, provided by Winchester's (1998) book *The Professor and the Madman*, in which Dr. Minor's offense occurred, it is obvious that he was an outstanding citizen and veteran military doctor, who as a result of psychological trauma triggered by the Civil War acted violently in response to his psychiatric symptoms.

In the 1800s we lacked the scientific knowledge and sophistication to provide adequate treatment for trauma symptoms. In modern psychology and psychiatry, we have made major progress in trauma treatment, yet as with Dr. Minor, we still fail to provide this treatment for many individuals who may need it the most, such as criminal offenders.

INMATE POPULATION PROFILE IN THE UNITED STATES

Violence, sexual victimization, racial segregation, substance abuse, and organized crime are prevalent in jails, state, and federal prisons in the United States. This is concerning as more than half of state and federal inmates are nonviolent offenders (Bureau of Justice Statistics, 2001), many of whom are entering prison for the first time. Hence, in order to reduce the odds of victimization and survive prison culture, inmates face the choice to participate in prison politics, which often involves the cost of witnessing and participating in illegal activities and violent behaviors, or to chance not participating in prison politics, which increases the likelihood of victimization.

The number of incarcerated individuals in the United States has nearly quadrupled since 1980. The deinstitutionalization of mental health care and the criminalization of drug policy ("war on drugs") have substantially increased sentencing for nonviolent offenders. Regardless of a decrease in violent and property crimes since the 1990s, our state, federal, and jail inmate populations have steadily risen to 2,245,189 in 2006, which constitutes a 2.8 percent increase since 2005 (William, Todd, & Paige, 2007).

Compared to the general population, prisoners disproportionately come from economically and socially disadvantaged environments. According to the 2002 Bureau of Justice Statistics special report on inmate profile statistics, nearly 70 percent of jail inmates reported regular use of alcohol and drugs, 56 percent of jail inmates grew up in a single-parent home, 1 in 9 lived in a foster home, 31 percent grew up with a parent or guardian who abused alcohol or drugs, and 46 percent reported having a family member who had been incarcerated (Bureau of Justice Statistics, 2004). In addition, more than 50 percent of females and 10 percent of incarcerated males reported being either physically or sexually abused in the past. Abuse rates for male inmates may be underreported. This is particularly true for male offenders victimized while in prison, who are often required to play an ultramasculine role to avoid further victimization and to pertain to the prison cultural values of secrecy and loyalty, which are often needed to survive in this hierarchical society (Goff, Rose, Rose, & Purves, 2007).

Individuals who come from past histories of physical and sexual abuse, who have criminally involved families, and participate in substance misuse, have an increased chance of being incarcerated and experiencing traumatic events. Many incarcerated individuals come from neighborhoods inundated with illicit substances and gang activity. As in prison, to survive in economically disadvantaged neighborhoods, individuals often participate in street politics. As a result, it is nearly impossible to avoid witnessing and at times participating in physical violence and various other illegal activities, which often result in increased vigilance, emotional numbing, increased substance use, and other means of coping with those chaotic environments. Many of these coping skills can become symptoms of posttraumatic stress disorder (PTSD), which will be discussed later in this chapter. Even though many individuals will experience traumatic events in their lifetimes, the development of PTSD is the exception and not the norm.

HISTORICAL DEVELOPMENT OF POSTTRAUMATIC STRESS DISORDER (PTSD)

Prior to the Vietnam War, there were few scientific studies that examined the psychological effects of trauma. Though few studies existed, descriptions of the psychological impact of combat trauma are numerous throughout historical literature. The *Iliad* describes the cold and detached nature of Achilles, who frequently partook in reckless acts of courage fighting hundreds of enemy soldiers without regard for his own life. Ernest Hemingway's short story *Soldier's Home*, which is arguably semiautobiographic, describes in great detail the psychological effects of war trauma on the individual and his surrounding life. This story ends with the main character feeling disconnected and emotionally numb to his current life and lacking motivation and excitement about his future.

During the 1800s military doctors began to diagnose soldiers with "exhaustion" due to a mental shutdown following combat trauma. In the late 1800s Dr. Mendez DaCosta described "Soldier's Heart" as a diagnosis for Civil War combat veterans. Psychological symptoms included hypervigilance and increased startle response, and physiological symptoms included fatigue, heart palpitations, sweating, and tremors. During World War I and World War II, the diagnosis "shell shock" and "combat neurosis" labeled the psychological and physiological symptoms associated with war trauma (Herman, 1992). It was not until the Vietnam War that the scientific examination of the psychological effects of trauma in general and during combat began (Friel, White, & Hull, 2008). The post-Vietnam examination of psychological trauma paved the way for our modern-day classification of PTSD, which first appeared as a diagnosis in the *Diagnostic and Statistical Manual of Mental Disorders Version III (DSM–III)* in 1980 (American Psychiatric Association [APA], 1980).

The *DSM–III* required the following criteria for a PTSD diagnosis: The person experienced or witnessed a distressing event that is outside the range of usual human experience such as a serious threat to one's life or physical integrity. In addition to experiencing this event, the individual must also present with the symptom triad of reexperiencing the event, numbing and/or avoidance, and hyperarousal. These symptoms must persist for more than one month following the event (APA, 1980). The *DSM–III* diagnostic definition of trauma was an important step in the evolution of trauma identification and treatment. The new symptomatic PTSD diagnosis allowed researchers to generalize the traumatic experience beyond victims of war and paved the way for new research regarding the traumatic experiences of incest, rape, domestic violence, child abuse, and other trauma-related topics.

Fourteen years after the publication of the *DSM–III*, the *DSM–IV* was published, to be followed shortly by the evidence-based text revision (*DSM–IV–TR*) in 2000 (APA, 2000). Significant advances in PTSD theory and research enabled the *DSM–IV–TR* PTSD committee to change the primary diagnostic criteria to include a response of intense fear, helplessness, or horror in reaction to the traumatic event as well as to improve upon the original symptom triad.

DSM–IV–TR DIAGNOSTIC CRITERIA FOR PTSD

The *DSM–IV–TR* states that for a diagnosis of PTSD an individual must be confronted with, experience, or witness an event or events that involved actual or threatened death or serious injury, or a threat to the physical integrity of others. The person's response to this event must involve intense fear, helplessness, or horror. In addition to the first two criteria, the individual must experience one or more symptoms of *recurrence* (distressing recollections, distressing dreams, flashbacks, distress or physiological reactivity triggered by internal or external cues associated with the event), three or more symptoms of *avoidance/numbing* (avoid thoughts, feelings, or conversation; avoid activities, places, or people that trigger memories of the event; inability to recall important details associated with the event; diminished interest in activities, feeling detached or estranged from others, restricted affect, foreshortened sense of future), and two or more symptoms of *increased arousal* (sleep difficulties, irritability or anger outbursts, difficulty concentrating, hypervigilance, exaggerated startle response). These symptoms must persist for more than one month following the event and cause clinically significant distress or impairment in social, occupational, or other important areas of functioning (APA, 2000).

TRAUMA AND SUBSTANCE USE DISORDERS IN THE GENERAL POPULATION

Nearly all individuals who participate in substance use treatment programs have experienced psychological trauma. Trauma exposure rates for individuals in both inpatient and outpatient, voluntary and mandated drug treatment programs are near 100 percent (Farley, Golding, Young, Mulligan, & Minkoff, 2004). Approximately 40 percent of clients in drug treatment programs meet the diagnostic criteria for PTSD (Brown, Recupero, & Stout, 1995; Dansky, Roitzsch, Brady, & Saladin, 1997; Farley, et al., 2004; Kessler, Sonnega, Bromet, Hughes, & Nelson, 1995; Triffleman, Marmar, Delucchi, & Ronfeldt, 1995). This is exceptionally high considering that the estimated lifetime prevalence of PTSD among adult Americans is 7.8 percent, with women (10.4%) being twice as likely as men (5%) to have PTSD at some point in their lives (National Center for Posttraumatic Stress Disorders, 2005). It is known that PTSD and other trauma-related problems among substance-abusing populations are associated with many physical, emotional, and interpersonal problems. These problems include an increased risk for chronic health problems, use of "harder" drugs, greater consumption of drugs and alcohol, more frequent relapses, poorer retention in treatment, and more inpatient hospitalizations than having a substance use disorder without trauma exposure (Brown et al., 1995; Jacobson, Southwick, & Kosten, 2001; Cronkite, Henson, Prins, Gima, & Moos, 2004; Ouimette, Finney, & Moos, 1999; Ouimette et. al., 2004). In addition, individuals with PTSD and trauma-related problems are more likely to be unemployed and have less social support than those without (Ouimette et al., 1999).

The physical, emotional, and interpersonal problems associated with individuals who have co-occurring substance use and trauma disorders are alarming. This becomes even more alarming when the overlap between trauma correlates and the criminogenic risk and needs principles used to identify an individual's potential for success in treatment and risk of criminal recidivism are compared.

Marlowe (2007) defines *criminogenic risks* as the characteristics of criminal offenders that increase the likelihood of a relapse to drug misuse and decrease the likelihood for success in treatment, thus increasing the chance of recidivism. The most notable high-risk factors include an earlier onset of substance abuse (especially prior to age 14) or crime (especially prior to age 16), attempting rehabilitation at a younger age (especially before 24 years of age), a recidivist criminal record, previous unsuccessful attempts at rehabilitation, and a co-existing diagnosis of antisocial personality disorder. More strikingly similar are an individual's *psychosocial/criminogenic needs*, which are an individual's areas of dysfunction that, if improved, can considerably reduce the likelihood of continued involvement in substance misuse and criminal behaviors (Marlowe, 2007). Notable high-need factors include compulsive addiction to drugs or alcohol, psychiatric pathology, emotional trauma, brain injury, chronic medical conditions, and illiteracy.

Considering the overlap between criminogenic risk/need factors and those associated with co-occurring trauma and substance use issues, it is fair to assume that many individuals who have not yet participated in the criminal justice system are at substantial risk for incarceration. This is especially true for individuals whose addiction worsens and their need for more and harder substances increase as their tolerance and physiological withdrawal symptoms increase. This progression of addiction usually leads to decreased social functioning and increased criminal behaviors. For example, to achieve the desired level of intoxication needed to numb the emotional pain of past traumas and relieve physical withdrawal symptoms, an individual will likely be in possession of larger amounts of substances and need to participate in other illegal activities such as prostitution, drug sales, theft, and at times violent crimes to financially support his addiction. Hence, for many individuals who go untreated for co-occurring substance misuse and trauma, it is only a matter of time before they enter the revolving doors of the criminal justice system.

CO-OCCURRING TRAUMA AND SUBSTANCE USE DISORDERS WITH CRIMINAL OFFENDER POPULATIONS

Rates of PTSD for both male and females are higher in prison settings than in the general population (Goff et al., 2007; Kubiak, 2004; Trestman, Ford, Zhang, & Wiesbrock, 2007). The PTSD rates are likely to be higher for incarcerated individuals for several reasons. Most incarcerated individuals have participated in substance use, criminal behavior, and come from areas of extreme poverty, all of which increase the risks of trauma exposure (Hochstetler, Murphy, & Simons, 2004). In addition to being at risk prior to incarceration, prison can be the source of new traumas and a trigger for old ones (Kubiak, 2004). As with individuals who experience traumatic events in war or civilian life, individuals who experience traumatic events in prison will have different reactions and varying degrees of adaptation and/or recovery from the event. The effect of a traumatic event while incarcerated will likely vary dependent upon an inmate's genetics, history prior to incarceration, and resources for overcoming and coping with the experience (Hochstetler et al., 2004).

The assessment and treatment of PTSD and other trauma-related symptoms rarely occurs for criminal offender populations. This is disturbing given the disproportionately high incidence of PTSD in this population, the high comorbidity between PTSD and substance use, and the alarmingly high rates of substance use disorders in criminal offender populations.

Inmates are more likely to have histories of substance abuse, mental health problems, and to have witnessed or been victimized by acts of violence than noninmates (Hochstetler et al., 2004). Prevalence rates for PTSD among incarcerated men have been shown to be over four times greater than those of the general population (Ehlers, Maercker, & Boos, 2000) and two times greater for incarcerated women than in the general population (Jordan, Schlenger, Fairbank, & Cadell, 1996). Even these astonishing rates may be an underestimate. Trestman et al. (2007) examined the lifetime prevalence rates of PTSD in a sample of 2,196 incarcerated male and female inmates not identified as acutely mentally ill at intake in Connecticut jails. In this sample, lifetime PTSD prevalence rates for men reached 20 percent and 41.8 percent for women. These findings are alarming as they suggest that many incarcerated individuals who suffer from PTSD often go undetected and untreated.

In addition, Kubiak (2004) explored the differences in treatment adherence, substance relapse, and criminal recidivism in a sample of 199 incarcerated men ($n = 139$) and women ($n = 60$) who volunteered to participate in two residential in-prison substance abuse treatment programs. Fifty-five percent of the treatment population met the criteria for a lifetime prevalence of PTSD with no statistically significant difference in prevalence rates for men (53%) and women (60%). Not surprisingly, due to the aggressive hierarchical nature of men's prisons, men were more likely to report a traumatic experience within the past 12 months while incarcerated than women were. Only one woman reported a traumatic event in the past 12 months compared to 75 percent of men. Most important, statistical analysis identified that both men and women with co-occurring PTSD and a substance use disorder were more likely to recidivate and relapse than those with only a substance use disorder were. This is highly suggestive of the need to address co-occurring substance use and trauma symptoms for incarcerated individuals, as they appear to be highly associated with relapse and criminal recidivism.

Regardless of the high incidence of co-occurring PTSD and substance use with incarcerated individuals, the effects of psychological trauma on substance relapse and criminal recidivism rates are rarely addressed (Kubiak, 2004). This is concerning as several studies have reported high incidence of trauma history among men and women who enter prison (Jordan et al., 1996; Kupers, 1996; Teplin, Abram, & McClelland, 1996), and there is documented evidence of exposure to as well as participation in violence within institutions (Kupers, 1996; Toch, 1998; Websdale & Chesney-Lind, 1998), including sexual victimization for both men and women (Beck & Harrison, 2008; Wolf, Blitz, & Shi, 2007). In fact, an estimated 4.5 percent of state and federal inmates have experienced sexual victimization while incarcerated, with the highest prison rates ranging from 9.3 to 15.7 percent (Beck & Harrison, 2008). This presents a serious problem as 80 percent of federal and state inmate convictions were due to either a drug-related crime, being under the influence during the crime, or having committed a crime to support drug use (Belenko & Peugh, 1998). Approximately 40 percent of clients in drug-treatment programs have PTSD (Brown et al., 1995; Dansky et al., 1997; Farley et al., 2004; Kessler et al., 1995; Triffleman et al., 1995) and up to 50 percent of released inmates who enter community-based treatment programs are thought to have a co-occurring PTSD and substance use disorder and tend to demonstrate poorer long-term treatment outcomes than those without (Ouimette et al., 1999). Hence, in order to reduce recidivism rates with criminal offender populations, the relationship between trauma and substance use disorders needs to be addressed prior to release.

TREATMENT OF CO-OCCURRING SUBSTANCE USE DISORDERS AND TRAUMA

Individuals with PTSD often use substances in an effort to cope with overwhelming emotions, unwanted thoughts and memories, sleep disturbances, anxiety, depression, irritability, and other symptoms associated with trauma. When abstinent from substances, many of these symptoms reoccur with overwhelming intensity and often result in relapse only to further exacerbate PTSD symptoms (Kubiak, 2004). This process makes PTSD different from other mental health issues that co-occur with substance misuse in that trauma symptoms may worsen upon abstinence (Najavits, 2005). Another characteristic that differentiates PTSD from other psychiatric diagnosis is that it is the only mental health diagnosis with a directly identifiable cause that is external from the impacted individual (Najavits, 2005). Fortunately, an identifiable cause makes recovery from PTSD possible. Though recovery is possible, the success of trauma treatment will depend largely on the characteristics of the treated individual (biological vulnerability, genetics, socioeconomic status, single trauma, or chronic exposure), and the selected treatment intervention.

Most addiction treatment programs, whether community- or prison-based, do not assess for trauma history or offer any trauma-related treatment (Dansky et al., 1997). For individuals diagnosed with PTSD, substance use treatment without mental health treatment is less effective than for individuals without PTSD (Kubiak, 2004). For example, studies that have compared individuals in treatment for substance use disorders with and without co-occurring PTSD found higher relapse rates during treatment (Kubiak, 2004), at three-month (Brown, Stout, & Mueller, 1996) and one-year (Ouimette, Ahrens, & Moos, 1997) posttreatment follow-up for individuals with PTSD.

Research has demonstrated better treatment outcomes, for both PTSD symptoms and reduced substance use, when substance use disorders and trauma are addressed simultaneously (Cocozza et al., 2005; Kubiak, 2004; Ouimette et al., 1999). Regardless of this knowledge, most corrections-based addiction treatment programs do not address trauma symptoms. This unfortunate gap between the scientific evidence for effective treatment and its application in frontline treatment delivery may be due to several reasons. For example, trauma assessment rarely occurs in jails or prisons, corrections-based addiction counselors generally lack the knowledge and skills necessary to implement trauma treatment, and most prison-based treatment programs do not utilize clinically licensed supervision to monitor treatment quality.

Currently, there is little empirical research on effective treatment approaches for incarcerated populations. Heckman, Cropsey, and Olds-Davis (2007) conducted an extensive literature review of 156 published empirical articles that addressed trauma treatment in correctional institutions. Only seven articles met the criterion for being empirically oriented and pertaining to PTSD in the criminal justice system. Of those seven, only two studies showed promising results and only one included treatment for co-occurring substance use and trauma disorders (Valentine & Smith, 2001; Zlotnick, Najavits, Rohsenow, & Johnson, 2003). The first study examined an exposure-based approach that utilized repetitive guided imagery of the traumatic event to reduce sensitivity to the event and cognitive restructuring to eliminate irrational beliefs associated with it (Valentine & Smith, 2001). Though the exposure-based treatment had positive results, it did not address substance use and required a trained clinician. This makes it impractical for large substance treatment programs in which the counselors are not clinicians. In addition, exposure-based treatments do not account for the risks associated with doing invasive trauma treatment with substance-abusing individuals whose symptoms may worsen while reliving their traumatic memories.

The second effective treatment intervention utilized *Seeking Safety* (Najavits, 2002), a noninvasive, present-focused, skill-based treatment designed to help individuals cope with both PTSD and substance use disorders (Zlotnick et al., 2003). The strengths of Seeking Safety include a positive current focus, practical coping skills, being manual-based, and noninvasive. Seeking Safety also produced positive outcomes as evidenced by reduced trauma and substance misuse symptoms. Unfortunately, no known empirical studies exist that examine the effectiveness of Seeking Safety treatment with incarcerated men, though it has shown effectiveness with men in the general population (Najavits, 2005).

Presently, there is a substantial need for more research on Seeking Safety's effectiveness with incarcerated individuals, especially for men. Regardless, Seeking Safety appears to be the strongest evidence-based approach to treat co-occurring substance use and trauma disorders with incarcerated individuals. It is present-focused, can be implemented by trained addiction counselors, and is coping skills driven, which makes it a safer intervention for individuals who are at high risk for relapse and may have limited abilities to regulate emotions and impulsivity.

Despite significantly elevated trauma rates and increased exposure to trauma compared to the general population, PTSD treatment for incarcerated individuals is minimal (Heckman et al., 2007). There is limited research on effective treatments for co-occurring PTSD and substance use disorders in the general population (Najavits, 2005) and even fewer for criminal offender populations (Heckman et al., 2007). Hence, there is great need for trauma assessment, treatment, and empirical research for this underserved population (Goff et al., 2007; Heckman et al., 2007; Kubiak, 2004; Trestman et al., 2007).

IMPLEMENTING CO-OCCURRING TRAUMA AND ADDICTION TREATMENT FOR CRIMINAL OFFENDER POPULATIONS

Clients are best served if both trauma and substance use disorders are treated simultaneously, preferably by the same individual or agency (Najavits, 2005). The time has passed where individuals are required to have a sustained period of abstinence prior to treatment. We now better understand the vicious cycle of substance use and PTSD by which substance use reinforces psychological avoidance, a primary symptom of PTSD, which in turn reinforces substance use. The utilization of an integrated treatment approach to address both substance use and trauma symptoms simultaneously may allow for the improvements in one domain to influence improvements in the other (Najavits, 2005). Thus, as the individual develops improved skills to cope with trauma, the individual will be less inclined to utilize substances as a means of coping, and reduced substance use may in turn reduce the potential for subsequent traumas.

In addition to integrated substance use and trauma treatment, individuals with trauma histories may benefit from stage-based treatment interventions (Herman, 1992; Najavits, 2005). Stage-based trauma interventions generally address safety and coping at the first stage, followed by mourning (processing) the traumatic experience, and finally reconnection, the process by which the individual focuses on functioning in work and relationships (Herman, 1992; Najavits, 2005). Safety and coping should be the primary focus for individuals in corrections-based treatment. This is especially true for individuals with severe forms of PTSD and other co-occurring disorders who may decompensate upon addressing trauma symptoms. After clients have successfully developed skills to regulate emotions and cope with trauma symptoms without substance use, they may progress to processing the trauma through exposure therapy, and eventually shift their focus on reconnecting to a functional life. Corrections-based treatment may be the appropriate place to begin the initial phase of trauma treatment, but referral upon release to individual therapy or advanced group therapy by a licensed clinician trained in trauma treatment is recommended for the advanced stages of trauma treatment that utilize processing and exposure techniques.

Successful treatment implementation will depend upon several factors. First and foremost, the positive benefits of treatment must outweigh any negative consequences. If trauma treatment elicits negative thoughts and emotions beyond the treated individual's ability to cope and beyond the addiction counselor's skill level, the client's safety will be violated. Safety is fundamental for successful treatment, if violated individuals may relapse into harmful behaviors such as substance use, physical aggression, and even suicide.

In corrections-based addiction treatment, where safety, security, and trust are of the utmost concern, only the safest and most effective trauma treatments should be applied. Regressive-based treatments such as exposure therapy, Eye Movement Desensitization and Processing (EMDR) therapy, and psychoanalytical treatments, though effective if performed by qualified individuals, are not the best modes of treatment for offenders while incarcerated. One point of concern in regard to treating trauma symptoms in corrections-based addiction treatment programs is the lack of qualified clinicians to address the complex issues that arise when clients discuss and/or relive their trauma histories. Most treatment providers are not equipped with the knowledge, skills, or formal education to work with trauma-related issues and can inadvertently induce harm on the inmate client. Unskilled addiction treatment counselors may mistakenly allow clients to disclose specific trauma details. The disclosure of trauma details without a skilled clinician can be harmful during individual therapy, can elicit trauma symptoms for others during group treatment, and can produce vicarious traumatization for both inmates and treatment staff (Baird & Kracen, 2006). Though disclosure can be effective for regressive- and exposure-based treatments, handling trauma disclosure is beyond the skill level of most addiction treatment counselors.

Even if noninvasive skills-based treatment is applied, adequately trained staff should always deliver it. Trained, licensed clinicians are the optimal choice for treatment delivery, but well-trained addiction counselors supervised by a trained licensed clinician may be as effective and more economically practical for corrections-based treatment. In addition to training frontline treatment staff, all staff, including administrative, corrections, and program management can help improve the treatment atmosphere if trained in *trauma-informed* services (Najavits, 2005).

It is very important that addiction treatment programs understand the difference between *trauma-informed* treatment and *trauma-competent* treatment (Najavits, 2006). Trauma-informed treatment includes giving basic trauma education to all staff at all levels. The Substance Abuse and Mental Health Services Administration (SAMHSA) Women, Co-occurring Disorders and Violence Study (WCDVS) has identified 10 principles that define trauma-informed services (Elliot, Bjelajac, Fallot, Markoff, & Reed, 2005). Though the WCDVS study is specific to women, it seems fair to generalize its principles to men.

The 10 principles include:

1. Trauma-informed services (TIS) recognize the impact of violence and victimization on development and coping strategies.
2. TIS identify recovery from trauma as a primary goal.
3. TIS employ an empowerment model.
4. TIS strive to maximize an individual's choices and control over her recovery.
5. TIS are based in a relational collaboration.
6. TIS create an atmosphere that is respectful of survivors' need for safety, respect, and acceptance.
7. TIS emphasize strengths, highlighting adaptations over symptoms and resilience over pathology.
8. The goal of TIS is to minimize the possibilities of retraumatization.
9. TIS strive to be culturally competent and to understand each individual in the context of her life experiences and cultural background.
10. Trauma-informed agencies solicit consumer input and involve consumers in designing and evaluating services.

While trauma-informed services aim to educate the entire workforce in the basic knowledge, skills, and understanding of the needs of individuals with histories of trauma, trauma-competent treatment seeks to train fewer, carefully selected individuals with the skills necessary for trauma treatment (Najavits, 2006). These individuals need to become educated on manual-based interventions for co-occurring substance and trauma disorders, require clinical supervision, and need formal training on trauma-based interventions. In addition, not all addiction treatment counselors are a good fit for delivering trauma-focused treatment (Najavits, 2006). Individuals who have not learned to cope with their own trauma histories, those who have poor boundaries, and those who are particularly confrontational in their treatment approach may jeopardize the quality of treatment, and at times may cause more harm than good. Fortunately, with proper training, the appropriate staff selection, and clinical supervision, it appears that we can begin to address the ever-evolving problem of co-occurring trauma and substance use disorders with criminal offenders.

CONCLUSION

Clearly, there is a need to improve the assessment, treatment, and research on criminal offender populations with co-occurring trauma and substance use disorders (Goff et al., 2007; Heckman et al., 2007; Kubiak, 2004; Trestman et al., 2007).

Treating both substance use and trauma disorders simultaneously can improve the effectiveness of treatment, as both disorders impact one another. To date, there is limited research on effective trauma treatment interventions for criminal offenders, and even less for criminal offenders with co-occurring PTSD and substance use disorders. Even though there is limited empirical research, it appears that present-focused, noninvasive, standardized, skills-based treatment that emphasizes coping and safety, such as the Seeking Safety treatment design (Najavits, 2002), is the best fit for trauma treatment in correctional institutions.

Until there is increased scientific evidence for effective treatment interventions for criminal offenders with co-occurring trauma and substance use disorders, it seems logical to utilize the most efficient and safest interventions possible. It is this author's opinion that corrections-based treatment is not the place to experiment with treatment modalities that are not evidence-based and scientifically driven. The utilization of nonscientifically driven trauma treatment in correctional institutions, especially by staff that are not trained clinicians, may be borderline unethical behavior as criminal recidivism rates continue to fall between 70 and 80 percent, which indicates that treatment as usual is not highly effective. In addition, there is no room for experimentation in this environment where safety and reduced recidivism is the primary concern. Therefore, the benefits of simultaneously treating trauma and addiction is evident and highly needed, and if done correctly, may substantially reduce criminal recidivism and help formally incarcerated individuals become productive members of society.

REFERENCES

American Psychiatric Association. (1980). *Diagnostic and statistical manual of mental disorders* (3rd ed.). Washington, DC: Author.

American Psychiatric Association. (2000). *Diagnostic and statistical manual of mental disorders* (4th ed. text revision). Washington, DC: Author.

Baird, K., & Kracen, A. C., (2006). Vicarious traumatization and secondary traumatic stress: A research synthesis. *Counseling Psychology Quarterly, 19,* 181–188.

Beck, A. J., & Harrison, P. M. (2008). Sexual victimization in state and federal prisons reported by inmates, 2007. Washington, DC: *Bureau of Justice Statistics Report.*

Belenko, S. & Peugh, C. (1998). *Behind bars: Substance abuse and America's prison population.* New York: Center on Addiction and Substance Abuse at Columbia University.

Brown, P. J., Recupero, P. R., & Stout, R. (1995). PTSD substance abuse comorbidity and treatment utilization. *Addictive Behavior, 20,* 251–254.

Brown, P. J., Stout, R. L., & Mueller, T. (1996). Post-traumatic stress disorder and substance abuse relapse among women. *Psychology of Addictive Behavior, 10,* 124–128.

Bureau of Justice Statistics. (2001). Criminal Offender Statistics. *U.S. Department of Justice: Office of Justice Programs.* Retrieved May 28, 2008, from http://www.ojp. usdoj.gov/bjs/crimoff.htm

Bureau of Justice Statistics. (2004). Profile of jail inmates, 2002. *U.S. Department of Justice: Office of Justice Programs.* Retrieved May 28, 2008, from http://www.ojp. usdoj.gov/bjs/abstract/pji02.htm

Cocozza, J. J., Jackson, E. W., Hennigan, K., Morrissey, J. P., Reed, B. G., & Fallot, R., et al. (2005). Outcomes for women with co-occurring disorders and trauma: Program-level effects. *Journal of Substance Abuse Treatment, 28*(2), 109–120.

Dansky, B. S., Roitzsch, J. C., Brady, K. T., & Saladin, M. E. (1997). Posttraumatic stress disorder and substance abuse: Use of research in a clinical setting. *Journal of Traumatic Stress, 10,* 141–148.

Ehlers, A., Maercker, A., & Boos, A. (2000). Posttraumatic stress disorder following political imprisonment: The role of mental defeat, alienation, and perceived permanent change. *Journal of Abnormal Psychology, 109,* 45–55.

Elliott, D. E., Bjelajac, P., Fallot, R. D., Markoff, L. S., & Reed, B. G. (2005). Trauma-informed or trauma-denied: Principles and implementation of trauma-informed services for women. *Journal of Community Psychology, 33*(4), 461–477.

Farley, M., Golding, J. M., Young, G., Mulligan, M., & Minkoff, J. R. (2004). Trauma history and relapse probability among patients seeking substance abuse treatment. *Journal of Substance Abuse Treatment, 27,* 161–167.

Friel, A., White, T., & Hull, A. (2008). Posttraumatic stress disorder and criminal responsibility. *The Journal of Forensic Psychiatry & Psychology, 19,* 64–85.

Goff, A., Rose, E., Rose, S., & Purves, D. (2007). Does PTSD occur in sentenced prison populations? A systematic literature review. *Criminal Behavior and Mental Health, 17,* 152–162.

Heckman, C. J., Cropsey, K. L., & Olds-Davis, T. (2007). Posttraumatic stress disorder treatment in correctional settings: A brief review of the empirical literature and suggestions for future research. *Psychotherapy: Theory, Research, Practice, Training, 44,* 46–53.

Herman, J. L. (1992). *Trauma and recovery: The aftermath of violence from domestic abuse to political terror.* New York: Basic Books.

Hochstetler, A., Murphy, D. S., & Simons, R. L. (2004). Damaged goods: Exploring predictors of distress in prison inmates. *Crime and Delinquency, 50,* 436–457.

Jacobson, L. K., Southwick, S. M., & Kosten, T. R. (2001). Substance use disorders in patients with posttraumatic stress disorder: A review of the literature. *American Journal of Psychiatry, 158,* 1184–1190.

Jordan, K., Schlenger, W., Fairbank, J., & Cadell, J. (1996). Prevalence of psychiatric disorders among incarcerated women. *Archives of General Psychiatry, 53,* 513–519.

Kessler, R. C., Sonnega, A., Bromet, E., Hughes, M., & Nelson, C. B. (1995). Post-traumatic stress disorder in the National Comorbidity Survey. *Archives of General Psychiatry, 52,* 1048–1060.

Kubiak, S. P. (2004). The effects of PTSD on treatment adherence, drug relapse, and criminal recidivism in a sample of incarcerated men and women. *Research on Social Work Practices, 14*(6), 424–433.

Kupers, T. (1996). Trauma and its sequelae in male prisoners: Effects of confinement, overcrowding, and diminished services. *American Journal of Orthopsychiatry, 66,* 190–196.

Marlowe, D. B., (2007, August 23) *Section on criminal justice research, Treatment Research Institute.* Written testimony to the Commission.

Najavits, L. M. (2002). *Seeking safety: A treatment manual for PTSD and substance abuse.* New York: Guilford Press.

Najavits, L. M. (2005). Theoretical perspective on posttraumatic stress disorder and substance use disorder. *Australian Psychologist, 40,* 118–126.

Najavits, L. M. (2006). Managing trauma reactions in intensive addiction treatment environments. *Journal of Chemical Dependency, 8,* 153–161.

National Center for Posttraumatic Stress Disorders. (2005). *National Comorbidity Survey.* Retrieved June 2, 2008, from http://www.ncptsd.va.gov/ncmain/ncdocs/fact_shts/fs_epidemiological.html

Ouimette, P. C., Ahrens, C., & Moos, R. (1997). Post traumatic stress disorder in substance abuse patients: Relationships to 1-year posttreatment outcomes. *Psychology of Addictive Behaviors, 11,* 34–47.

Ouimette, P. C., Finney, J. W., & Moos, R. H. (1999). Two-year posttreatment functioning and coping of substance abuse patients with posttraumatic stress disorder. *Psychology of Addictive Behaviors, 13,* 105–114.

Ouimette, P. C., Cronkite, R., Henson, B. R., Prins, A., Gima, K., & Moos, R. H. (2004). Posttraumatic stress disorder and health among female and male medical patients. *Journal of Traumatic Stress, 17,* 1–9.

Sabol, W. J., Minton, T. D. & Harrison, P. M. (2007). Prison and jail inmates at mid-year 2006. *U.S. Department of Justice: Office of Justice Programs.* Retrieved November 22, 2008, from http://www.ojp.usdoj.gov/bjs/pub/pdf/pjim06.pdf

Teplin, L., Abram, K., & McClelland, G. (1996). Prevalence of psychiatric disorders among incarcerated women. *Archives of General Psychiatry, 53,* 505–512.

Toch, H. (1998). Hypermasculinity and prison violence. In L. H. Bowker (Ed.), *Masculinities and violence* (pp. 168–178). Thousand Oaks, CA: Sage.

Trestman, R. L., Ford, J., Zhang, W., & Wiesbrock, V. (2007). Current and lifetime psychiatric illness among inmates not identified as acutely mentally ill at intake in Connecticut's jails. *Journal of the American Academy of Psychiatry and Law, 35,* 490–500.

Triffleman, E. G., Marmar, C. R., Delucchi, K. L., & Ronfeldt, H. (1995). Childhood trauma and posttraumatic stress disorder in substance abuse inpatients. *Journal of Nervous and Mental Disease, 183,* 172–176.

Valentine, P. V., & Smith, T. E. (2001). Evaluating incident reduction therapy with female inmates: A randomized controlled clinical trial. *Research on Social Work Practice, 11*, 40–52.

Websdale, N., & Chesney-Lind, M. (1998). Doing violence to women: Research synthesis on the victimization of women. In L. H. Bowker (Ed.), *Masculinities and violence* (pp. 55–81). Thousand Oaks, CA: Sage.

Winchester, S. (1998). *The professor and the madman.* New York: HarperCollins.

Wolf, N., Blitz, C. L., & Shi, J. (2007). Rates of sexual victimization in prison for inmates with and without mental disorders. *Psychiatric Services, 58*, 1087–1094.

Zlotnick, C., Najavits, L. M., Rohsenow, D. J., & Johnson, D. M. (2003). A cognitive-behavioral treatment for incarcerated women with substance abuse disorder and posttraumatic stress disorder: Findings from a pilot study. *Journal of Substance Abuse Treatment, 25*, 99–105.

Chapter 5

The Role of Allergies in Addictions and Mental Illness

Joan Mathews-Larson, PhD, LADC, and

Mark K. Mathews, LADC, BCCR

Understanding allergies as they pertain to addictions and mental health issues requires an analysis of multiple genetic factors. Most agree allergy symptoms are the result of hypersensitive receptors on mast and basophil cells responding to various antigens by triggering the release of inflammatory mediators—particularly histamine. Standard treatment protocols address this underlying flaw with allergy medications, which block the release of histamine, but do nothing to abolish the underlying problem. The consequence of this approach has fueled a rise in addictive patterns with a progressive decline in the health for many allergy-afflicted people. This chapter will examine a genetic basis for allergies more carefully, and present evidence that the pathogenesis of addictions and many mental health problems are actually manifestations of IgG (immunoglobulin G, a serum protein antibody) delayed-onset allergies progressing toward more serious degenerative diseases.

Although the cause of allergies can be explained as an unregulated degranulation of histamine from mast and basophil cells due to gene malfunction, other complex genetic factors contributing to allergy processes need to also be considered (Akdis & Blaser, 2003, p. 15). More than 30 years ago, scientists suspected a genetic connection involving an immune system disorder existed for many diseases, based on structural anomalies in cells. Researcher Chang (1975) states:

> The view that diseases such as cancer, systemic lupus erythemotosus, and agammaglobulinemia can be successfully treated by unilateral manipulation of the

humeral or the cell-mediated immune response per se is probably too simplistic. It has become increasingly clear that many of these disorders of the immune system seem to arise from flaws in cell differentiation, resulting in a hyper- or hypofunction of a particular cell type. (p. 82)

Chang's statement suggests gene-influenced diseases might occur in various ways, and even though unique genetic disorders manifest into different diseases, the process is often accompanied by inflammation (i.e., it incorporates an allergy response).

Geneticist Dr. Chris Reading's insightful reasoning expounds on flaws in cell differentiation, as proposed by researcher Chang. He believes maladapted genes causing allergies must be corrected or prevented from being expressed to prevent the progression of disease. Dr. Ravikovich (2003) aptly states Dr. Reading's concerns:

A slight genetic defect, mostly inherited, occasionally acquired, may remain unnoticed for years. However, time itself and/or cumulative effects of the hazards [allergy provoking substances] may "break the back of the camel." In other words, the initial small defect in the genes may become magnified, and as a result, the operation guided by these genes may cause cells to respond [express] with a pathological reaction to what they would have perceived as harmless before. (p. 7)

Dr. Reading concedes, substances that provoke recurrent allergic responses are especially hazardous for people with underlying genetic defects; but more important, he offers insights into understanding how these structural genetic defects are formed before getting switched on later in life.

Dr. Reading focuses on rogue genes: those present at birth, and distortions that may develop later in life to initiate diseases. Genetic distortions are expressed both structurally and functionally, and with more than 30,000 genes in the nucleus of a single cell, and trillions of cells in the human body, intervening to correct the structural genetic defects causing allergies is impractical, if not impossible (Ravikovich, 2003, p. 8). Instead, Dr. Reading (2002) urges preventative tactics to stop irritating the hypersensitive immune system.

Hypersensitivity reactions result from repeated exposure to a particular substance or to its chemically related substances. . . . The substance, if it is a large polypeptide, acts as an antigen and stimulates the body to form antibodies. Otherwise the substance acts as a hapten and combines with proteins in the body to form antigens. The reaction between an antigen from a later exposure and the corresponding antibodies results in the release of histamine. (Lu & Kacew, 2002, p. 49)

Like Dr. Ravikovich, Dr. Reading recognizes hypersensitive reactions stem from repeated exposures to allergy-provoking foods. But rather than focusing

on correcting the genetic malfunction causing the exaggerated release of histamine, Dr. Reading recommends avoiding allergy foods (Reading, 2002, p. 143).
A delayed allergy response, although clearly tied to the release of histamine,
might not respond to histamine corrective protocols; in fact, the classic exaggerated histamine release, used to define an allergic response, may not even be
the primary problem in an IgG delayed response. After all, cell degranulation
(histamine release) is how healthy tissue should respond when foreign substances (e.g., polypeptides/allergens) come into contact with it (Rocklin, 1982,
pp. 49–70; Sirois & Borgeat, 1982, pp. 205–206).

Recognizing substances that provoke allergy responses may compromise the
health of the host in more ways than just the release of histamine, Dr. Reading
augments previous allergy concepts with a thought-provoking theory that elu-
cidates the pathological progression of diseases, and provides insight into how
such great disparities can exist in people's susceptibility to contract them.

To follow his reasoning, Reading (2002) first offers some clinical facts to be
reviewed:

1. During pregnancy the mother and fetus interact chemically. Dehydroepi-
   androsterone (DHEA) secreted from the adrenal cortex of the fetus stimulates estrogen hormones from the mother's placenta to affect the formation
   (differentiation) of fetal tissues. An adequate supply of vitamins and minerals from the mother is crucial for the process to work.
2. Secondly, the propensity of the most common offending allergy-causing
   foods (grain, milk, egg, beef, and yeast) to trigger allergies is actually caused
   by components of the foods called subfractions: proteins such as gluten,
   a-gliadin, a-casein, and so on.
3. Thirdly, when people consume allergy-provoking foods, they do not properly absorb vitamins and minerals, exacerbating deficiencies in many important nutrients (p. 140).

Dr. Reading reasons when pregnant women consume allergy foods, their
allergy-induced vitamin and mineral deficiency has two deleterious effects on
the forming fetus: it hinders the release of hormones from the mother's placenta, and it lowers levels of vitamins and minerals supplied to the fetus. This
reduces the amount of DHEA being released from the fetus's adrenal cortex,
which further interrupts the supply of estrogens from the placenta, resulting in
an abnormal balance of hormones, vitamins, and minerals. Additionally, damage caused by the toxic subfractions in the foods to which the mother is allergic
may also damage the fetus if the sensitivity to them is passed on genetically. Dr.
Reading (2002) states:

> These subfractions, I believe, cross the placenta and can actually take the place of
> some of the hormones that are [for the reasons outlined above] in short supply.

In other words, the toxic subfractions may actually have a hormone-like action on the fetus. The net result of the faulty hormone-vitamin-mineral balance, plus the presence and hormone-like action of the toxic food fractions, is that some of the fetus's tissues are laid down abnormally. Formed before the immune system has matured, these tissues have a special metabolism that makes them different from normal cells. They are, in fact, premalignant . . . likely to go wild and proliferate in later life, if exposed again to the toxic food fractions and faulty hormone-vitamin-mineral environment that originally helped to form them. (p. 141)

Biochemists recognize cells have receptors for various hormones, proteins, enzymes, and other substances needed to maintain normal growth and division. Each receptor is specially "tuned" to a specific hormone, protein, or enzyme; however, "Cells forming pre-malignant tissue also have receptors for fractions of toxic foods because they took the place of some natural hormones when fetal tissues were forming in the womb" (Reading, 2002, pp. 141–142). Since genes determine the development and activity of all cellular receptors, it is logical to conclude these problems are structural, not functional (Ravikovich, 2003, p. 2). Therefore, to prevent these genes from being switched on, the food fractions originally present when the anomalous genes first formed must be avoided.

Dr. Reading (2002) notes, when allergy-sensitive people ingest allergy-triggering foods, toxic food fractions cross into their bloodstream and stimulate cells with receptors for them. Additionally, these subfractions suppress the immune system by upsetting the balance of hormones, vitamins, and minerals—basically recreating the anomalous environment that was present when the abnormal tissue first formed.

> [Cells of abnormal] tissue take in toxic food fractions just as they did in the womb. And just as they did in the womb, the fractions stimulate the cells to proliferate and reproduce—only this time the uterus is not present to provide growth-regulating hormones to keep the process in check. So cells proliferate wildly and uncontrollably. And when they do so, cancer has begun. (p. 142)

Whenever someone puts forth a theory to explain the disease of cancer, inevitably eyebrows will rise; however, this time we might not want to dismiss Dr. Reading's theory too quickly. His track record for arresting and reversing cancer using allergy elimination diets is impressive.

Reading (2002) believes cancer and many other diseases are actually congenital disorders: "begun by the effect of food allergies on the developing fetus, and exploding out of control when the faulty pre-birth environment reoccurs." He also notes "such cancers are actually mimicking the rapid proliferation of fetal tissues. Or, if you like, they [cancerous cells] are really abnormal fetal tissues starting to proliferate all over again" (p. 142). What makes his argument so compelling is that many cancer cells do in fact release fetal proteins, which are normally seen *only* in unborn babies (Akira et al., 1972, pp. 1–7; Reading, 2002, p. 142).

Addicts and alcoholics, unaware of the biochemical damage stemming from allergic subfractions, are often fooled into thinking they will regain their health and start feeling better by simply being abstinent or avoiding their "primary" addictive substances. However, in abstinence they usually feel worse. So, to counter the misery of withdrawal, alcoholics instinctively and unknowingly indulge their allergies by ingesting copious quantities of foods from which their alcohol was fermented—grains, sugars, yeast, and so forth. Consumption of these allergy-provoking foods sustains an ongoing load of toxins, and biochemical imbalances (Randolph & Moss, 1980, p. 23). Until they break away from their allergy foods, addicts and alcoholics will continue to experience physical and psychological pain. Confused, they'll turn to psychological and spiritual treatment, without understanding the source of the problem is their allergy-riddled diet.

Although restoring proper histamine function, as Dr. Ravikovich directed, may be well suited to address functional problems characterizing IgE immediate onset allergies, countering an IgG delayed allergic reaction is a different, more complex allergy problem. We believe it is most effectively dealt with by avoiding subfraction-containing foods that trigger the formation of immune complexes, and the proliferation of disease-causing cells. In other words, these are structural genetic defects that cannot be corrected, but can be controlled by avoiding the triggers (allergy foods) that switch them on. Unfortunately, foods that switch on allergies are the foods people love to eat again and again, their comfort foods—foods with addictive, drug-like qualities. Why do some foods cause drug-like reactions? A survival mechanism allows the body to override pain by releasing "feel-good" chemicals called endorphins (Braly & Holford, 2006, p. 90). Many analgesic drugs are based on similar chemical structures; all of them, including endorphins, are peptides—small groups of bound amino acids (Terenius, 2000, p. 1). When protein is ingested, it is broken down to peptides, and then, if digestion is working well, those peptides get broken down further to individual amino acids. Unfortunately, allergy foods impair digestion and damage the GI tract, impairing the complete digestion of proteins.

In the laboratory, endorphin-like peptides have been made from wheat, milk, barley, and corn using human digestive enzymes. These peptides have been shown to bind to endorphin receptor sites. Preliminary research shows that certain foods, most commonly wheat and milk, may induce a short-term positive feeling, even if, in the long term, they are causing health problems. (Holford, 2002, p. 73)

Once these peptides reach the bloodstream, they become a problem for the immune system to gather and clear, setting the stage for a classic delayed IgG allergic response.

An IgG delayed-onset food allergy can produce more than 100 allergic symptoms and affect almost every organ or tissue in the body. It is estimated one in three (children and adults), and more than 70 percent of people battling chronic conditions, who are unresponsive to conventional medicine, are also struggling with IgG allergies. In addition, more than 100 medical diseases and conditions have been connected to IgG allergies (Braly & Holford, 2006, p. 16).

> These food allergies occur when your immune system creates an over abundance of IgG antibodies to a particular food allergen. The antibodies, instead of attaching to mast cells like their IgE counterparts, bind directly to the food particles as they enter your bloodstream, creating "immune complexes." The more of these you have floating around the bloodstream, the more on edge your immune system becomes, sending out phagocytes to gobble the complexes up. Basically your immune system gradually goes into red alert. (Braly & Holford, 2006, pp. 15–16)

Unlike the quick response, characteristic of an IgE immediate-onset allergy, IgG symptoms come on slowly—from two hours to several days. Ingesting allergy-provoking foods prompts the gradual formation of immune complexes until finally they overload the immune system's ability to clear them out. That's when symptoms are felt. Unfortunately, the time differential makes symptoms difficult to link to the foods that cause them. And because the initial response to allergy-provoking foods is often a pleasurable, endorphin-like effect, it becomes even more difficult to accept that they are a problem. In the end, a pattern, initiated and sustained by these foods, contributes to an addictive progression of disease.

The starting point of most diseases is in the gut. Allergy foods factor heavily in the etiology of diseases because they damage the GI tract, and impair digestion. In that respect, the deleterious effects from allergies and addictions is the same (Rubin, 2003, pp. 48–55). Furthermore, combining allergy foods with alcohol heaps more stress on the immune system by doing more damage to the gut.

> [For those who drink alcohol], hypersensitivity will continue indefinitely because ethanol greatly increases the permeability of intestinal membranes, making it more likely that macromolecules [polypeptides] will be absorbed into the bloodstream. Alcohol also contributes to immune system hypersensitivity by creating nutritional deficiencies. (Bates, 1987, p. 35)

The problem with alcohol is that it compounds the damage caused by food allergies by increasing permeability in the gut membrane. This destructive effect can be tolerated by the average person, but for the person who already has a food sensitivity problem, just a little bit of alcohol every day will overwhelm the immune system's ability to fight disease and maintain biochemical stability.

> Even a quite moderate use of alcohol will prove to be such an obstacle to healing that the GI tract will never repair itself, and allergies will never cool. Yet these people will turn to alcohol for relief from depression, and it will give a temporary feeling of happiness, giving the impression that it is good medicine. The more you drink, the worse your GI tract will leak allergens into your bloodstream and the more depressed you will become. (Bates, 1987, p. 57)

Bates describes the pathogenesis of alcoholism the same way a food addiction could be described. Whether responding to alcohol, drugs, or allergy foods, allergic/addictive chemistry follows the same course because the body recognizes all these substances as toxins, and turns to the same system—the immune system—to clear them. It's when the toxic load exceeds the immune system's ability to clear it that inflammation begins its destructive process.

Inflammation is a slow progression in some allergic reactions. Unlike quick IgE allergy reactions, where allergens settle directly into tissues to initiate cellular degranulation, many IgG delayed-onset allergies come on slowly. The process begins with antigens clumping to antibodies to form free-floating immune complexes in the blood (Suen & Gordon, 2003, pp. 134–135). Macrophages are then deployed to devour these complexes and take them out of circulation. It's when the immune complexes exceed the immune system's ability to clear them that inflammation occurs—a delayed reaction. Charles Bates (1987) states:

> The body has many ways of dealing with immune complexes. They are large enough to be filtered out of the blood in the liver. Wherever they congregate, they activate the degranulation of mast cells, which release prostaglandins, histamines, leukotrienes, and other inflammatory chemicals called the complement cascade. The result could be heat, pain, or anything from a runny nose to the destruction of healthy tissue. When the immune system destroys healthy tissue in the pancreas, this is called diabetes. Arthritis is the immune system attacking bone and connective tissue. Many diseases of the GI tract follow this pattern. (p. 91)

Recalling the lessons of both Dr. Ravikovich and Dr. Reading, and acknowledging these immune complexes (in delayed-onset food allergies) are clumps of food fractions, the complexity of the biochemical dilemma becomes more obvious. On the one hand, excessive inflammation will lead to tissue destruction and disease—Ravikovich's concern; on the other hand, clumps of food fractions congregating in healthy tissue will recreate an anomalous environment conducive for the proliferation of premalignant cells—Dr Reading's concern. It is not a choice of one or the other. Under stressful conditions of an IgG allergy, the body must deal with these problems simultaneously. In support of Dr. Reading's advice: the best approach to avert this dilemma is to avoid the foods that put the immune system in such a precarious position.

Clearing allergy-provoking foods can be a challenging task. IgG allergies are perpetuated no differently than any other kind of chemical addiction. If the allergic addictive person is deprived of the offending allergen long enough, he or she will go into withdrawal. Philpott and Kalita (2000a) state:

> Adaptive addiction can be described as a state of relative freedom from symptoms, occasioned when the addictive substance is contacted frequently enough and the biological homeostatic state is in good repair. It is, however, a state of chronic stress, precariously balanced, and paves the way for the emergence of an "illness." (p. 28)

Of course, the stress from an ongoing battle with toxic allergens in foods will weaken the immune system. Then, adding seasonal antigens, environmental stresses, physical stresses, or even emotional stress can finally deplete the body's defenses enough so that illness becomes a frequent state.

The similarities of allergies, alcoholism, and addictions are undeniable (i.e., they are the same problem based on similar molecules, following the same etiology). People with IgG allergies and those with other drug/alcohol addictions are engaged in a similar pattern of use—stimulated by the release of endorphin-like substances, and perpetuated by the need to defer the symptoms of withdrawal. Philpott and Kalita (2000a) state:

> The state of partial and temporary relief by contact with allergens is termed "addiction." Understanding addiction as an extension of a maladaptive allergy state is necessary if one is to understand the seriousness of addiction to frequently eaten foods and commonly met chemicals. (p. 28)

Chemically dependent, allergic addictive people may continually submit their bodies to immune-suppressing, disease-initiating chemicals and toxic food fractions for many years before they finally succumb to the fact that it's robbing them of their health, and taking years off their lives.

The truth about allergies is that they are the foundation of addictions. Correcting the genetic malfunction driving IgE immediate-onset allergies (Dr. Ravikovich's work) does not go far enough to break the hold addictive substances have on those unfortunate enough to be genetically predetermined or biochemically altered for IgG delayed-reaction allergies and addictions. As Dr. Reading noted, addictions stem from biochemical anomalies shaped by an endless variety of genetic factors—prenatally and later in life. The scope of allergies can also be expanded to elucidate many mental health disorders. Because they too are rooted in biochemical disruptions tied to allergies, preventative interventions can be incorporated before allergies manifest into more serious diseases.

The brain is a very metabolically active organ. Although it composes only 2 percent of the body's weight, it consumes 20 percent of the body's available oxygen and 25 percent of the body's glucose (Atavistik Pictures, 2006). Transporting all that oxygen and glucose to the brain requires a great deal of blood—the same blood that carries allergy-inciting molecules to other organs in the body. You would think this obvious potential for problems would be of great concern to modern medicine.

> Although allergic mental illness is encountered daily in every doctor's office around the world, it is rarely recognized by physicians because they don't realize allergic reactions often appear as depression, anxiety, irritability, confusion, paranoia, hyperactivity, autism, catatonia, or schizophrenia. Unfortunately, most cases of brain allergies are misdiagnosed as doctors search in vain for emotional causes, while allergic brain malfunctions remain unsuspected. (Mandell & Scanlon, 1979, pp. 90–91)

Compounding the problem of medical ignorance, Dr. Russell Blaylock states:

> Whole foods pass through the intestine, get into the bloodstream and bring forth an immune response. . . . The brain's immune system is also activated, releasing toxic components including glutamate, and that causes neurological dysfunction. You can get all kinds of symptoms triggered from immune reactions: lethargy, stupor, disorientation, paranoia, delusions, hallucinations, agitation, rage, panic attacks, criminal behavior, and even seizures. (Atavistik Pictures, 2006)

In spite of various organic risks to stable brain function, conventional medicine and psychiatry mostly refuses to acknowledge and address the brain's vulnerability to allergens and food subfractions ushered in via the vascular transport system.

Along with food fractions from allergens, many viruses also live and thrive in the blood. The body requires a robust immune system to keep them at bay. A key component in that defense system is endothelial-relaxing factor, or nitric oxide, a natural molecule manufactured in healthy blood vessels that works to destroy invading pathogens. "Nitric oxide is used by the immune system to

stave off infectious bacteria, viruses, and parasites, and it even curtails the proliferation of certain types of cancerous cells" (Ignarro, 2005, p. 48). However,
as vessels harden over time, or if they are poisoned by toxic heavy metals (lead,
mercury, etc.), they lose the ability to manufacture this crucial molecule needed
to protect the brain and body from pathogens in the blood. One way of restoring elasticity to the veins and production of nitric acid is through chelation
therapy. It is believed that by chelating out heavy metals, blood vessels resume
normal production of nitric oxide (Gordon Research Institute, 2000).

But how do viruses contribute to mental illnesses? Philpott and Kalita
(2000b) implicate the origin of *all organic brain disorders* to viral infections from
the herpes family (i.e., Epstein-Barr, cytomegallo, and human herpes virus #6).
If a pregnant mother ingests foods that suppress her immune system (allergy
foods), infections flare up, and may get passed on to her developing fetus. In
addition, infectious viruses might also invade the brain of a young child, particularly because the blood brain barrier is much more vulnerable in the early
years. Then, as that young brain develops, these viruses infect neurons, causing
them to swell. Swelling injures the developing brain, including the temporal
lobe, and particularly the frontal part of the brain, resulting in damage that
impairs perception, judgment, and the ability to concentrate (pp. 148–149).

We believe most mental health disorders can be tied to a symbiotic relationship of allergies (primarily food allergies) and viruses. Unfortunately, viruses do
not fade away or die off. Studies reveal Epstein-Barr, cytomegallo, and human
herpes #6 viral infections remain in the body and the brain for a lifetime,
causing fluctuating symptoms in response to varying levels of stress—and, of
course, allergies are great promoters of stress. When stress flares, these viruses
become more active, which further stresses the immune system. Philpott and
Kalita (2000b) state:

> These are lymphotropic viruses that infect the immune system. B-lymphocytes
> become disordered from the viral infection, producing antibodies and an autoim-
> mune response inappropriately. As a result, the child's immune system becomes
> compromised. The child becomes more reactive to chemicals and inhalants in
> the environment. This additional stress makes the child *much more prone to mal-
> adaptively react to specific foods* [authors' emphasis]. (p. 149)

Interestingly, those specific foods are the ones that help viruses to flourish, and
disrupt mental stability—allergy foods. In addition, they are the ones that get
chosen—even after the infected host has been warned of the gravity of the
situation. It is a hallmark of addictive behavior, but it begs the question: Who's
in charge—the person, or the pathogens? Perhaps addiction is a struggle for
survival between microorganisms that thrive in an acidic, hypoxic environment

and normal cells and tissues that thrive in a more alkaline-hyperoxia environment (Young & Young, 2002, pp. 12–37).

But mental health disorders have been linked to many biochemical abnormalities, not just allergies. Schizophrenia is a branch of mental disorders, in
the extreme. Years ago, Dr. Carl Pfeiffer and colleagues (1970) recognized
schizophrenia as a syndrome, not a single disease. To his credit, he identified
different biochemical deficiencies, which created symptoms interpreted as
schizophrenia. For example, he determined many schizophrenics were pyrolu-
ric, due to metabolic anomalies, which contributed to a zinc and B6 deficiency
(pp. 139–145). Likewise, his contemporary, Dr. Abram Hoffer (2005), saved
many "schizophrenics" from wasting away in mental institutions by elucidating
the true cause of pellagra—a B3 niacin deficiency (p. 70). Dr. Chris Reading
(2002) observed, "While many, or even most, cases of so called schizophrenia
are really allergic conditions or hereditary metabolic disorders, a significant
minority remains that doesn't appear to fit into either category. These can be
called the true schizophrenias" (p. 180). Nevertheless, many symptoms labeled
as schizophrenia can be traced back to biochemical deficiencies or excesses
altering metabolic processes to create distorted expressions of the brain.

So why do these deficiencies or excesses occur in the first place? If it were just
a question of poor nutrition, mental illness would be easy to correct; however,
look deeper and you'll find diet is subordinate to the allergies that drive them.
Indeed, allergies perpetuate cravings for the very foods that sustain the allergic inflammatory conditions that drive degenerative diseases. Again, let's ask,
"Who's in charge, up there in the brain?" Foods that promote inflammation,
hypoxia, and acidity—ideal conditions for viruses to thrive in—are the ones
schizophrenics and allergic/addictive mentally ill patients want to eat, not diets
of nonallergic foods, which cool the inflamed brain, and give support to the
immune system (Young & Young, 2002, pp. 12–37). But why should inflammation of the brain (i.e., chronic encephalitis) result for only some who indulge
their allergic impulses? Are "nonschizophrenics" only spared a miserable fate
of mental anguish because they are not infected with viruses that capitalize on
repeated exposures to allergy foods?

Historically, there have been times when schizophrenics were unable to
obtain foods that would aggravate their allergies, and intensify their viral
infections. During World War II, rations of wheat and rye became scarce in
Scandinavian countries. Based on the unavailability of these gluten-containing
foods, estimates from Finland figured "the mean annual *decrease* in the number
of first admissions [for schizophrenia] from the prewar mean was estimated
to be about 19 percent in 1940–1942 and about 45 percent in 1943–1945"
(Dohan, 1966). This intriguing study shows a strong relationship between

gluten-containing foods and schizophrenia. Unless steady provisions of allergy foods are ingested, the virus cannot maintain its influence over the brain. Famine for the virus equates to sanity for the host.

Allergies are at the foundation of the problem because they distort the terrain of tissues by forming a more acidic environment conducive for viruses to flourish, and microforms to change into more virulent strains (Young & Young, 2002, pp. 21–23). In other words, allergies work hand-in-hand with disease-causing viruses to suppress the immune system, and influence thought processes of the brain. In their clinical experience, Philpott and Kalita (2000b) note:

> Schizophrenia is a state of disordered brain function in areas of perception, mood, thought, and motor function. Acute mental symptoms can be triggered by maladaptive reactions to foods, chemicals, or inhalants to which the subject is allergic, addicted, or otherwise hypersensitive. Several studies have demonstrated that maladaptive reactions to environmental substances, especially foods, are significant factors in evoking mental illnesses. (p. 149)

These "maladaptive reactions to environmental substances" help to promote, sustain, and expand an internal environment (terrain) that fortifies a viral presence in the tissues of the brain. Viral influence affects the way mood, thought, and personality is expressed; finally, even reason is compromised, resulting in irrational behavior and a demeanor perceived as mentally ill.

Fortunately, there is a way to restore stability and give back control to a "mentally ill" brain. The two branches of medicine best equipped to deal with mental health problems brought on by organic-based infections and allergies are ecology medicine and orthomolecular medicine. Both serve to reduce the inflammatory response from allergies, and stabilize the brain. Ecology medicine works by identifying and abstaining from allergy-causing foods, essentially laying siege to viruses and virulent pathogens by keeping out chemicals and foods fractions that help perpetuate the hypoxic, acidic environment they thrive in. The other approach, orthomolecular medicine, works by providing nutrients in optimum amounts needed to restore proper metabolism and health at a cellular level.

Human ecology acknowledges that substances in our environment can have a profound effect on our mental health and behavior. "Evidence suggests that the basic organic forces behind many chronic physical and mental illnesses are addictive reactions to frequently eaten foods and commonly met chemicals" (Philpott & Kalita, 2000a, p. 57). Identifying and avoiding symptom-inducing substances is fundamental to restoring mental stability. Ecology medicine holds the potential for stopping and reversing the pathology of many mental health diseases.

Orthomolecular medicine strives to treat infectious and degenerative diseases by varying the concentration of "right molecules" (i.e., vitamins, minerals, etc.), which are normally present in the human body (Lawson, 2003). Cells inadequately provided with the nutrients needed for proper metabolism and health create a condition for disease. When a cell becomes deficient in even one nutrient, its entire function will be seriously impaired. Multiply that by millions of cells, and tissues and organs may be affected. The brain is an organ composed of million of cells. When its metabolism becomes disordered due to allergic responses, viral attacks, and nutritional deficiencies, it falls into a state of disease. The brain expresses a diseased state with changes in perceptions and cognitive function, resulting in illusions, hallucinations, and delusions (Philpott & Kalita, 2000a, p. 73).

Orthomolecular psychiatry can repair the nutritional imbalances to restore mental health, but that repair is fragile (i.e., it cannot be sustained if *first-cause* ecological factors are not also stopped). The power of ecological and orthomolecular medicine together gives increased therapeutic value beyond either approach alone. Satisfactory clinical results often cannot be achieved unless both systems are combined. Ongoing research into how nutritional factors and ecology medicine support each other in cooling allergies will improve future treatment of mental health problems.

REFERENCES

Akdis, C., & Blaser, K. (2003). Histamine in the immune regulation of allergic inflammation. *Journal of Allergy and Clinical Immunology, 112*, 15–22.

Akira, Y., Kawaharada, M., Ikebe, M., Takahashi, A., Anzai, T., & Wada, T. (1972). Diagnostic significance of two fetal proteins, {alpha}f and rßs, in hepatoma and other neoplastic diseases. *Japanese Journal of Clinical Oncology, 2*, 1–7.

Atavistik Pictures (Producer). (2006). *Nutrition and behavior: A lecture by Russell Blaylock* [DVD]. Ridgeland, MS: Atavistik Pictures.

Bates, C. (1987). *Essential fatty acids and immunity in mental health.* Tacoma, WA: Life Sciences Press.

Braly, J., & Holford, P. (2006). *Hidden food allergies: The essential guide to uncovering hidden food allergies—and achieving permanent relief.* Laguna Beach, CA: Basic Health Publications.

Chang, Y. (1975). Introduction: Prospectives on new immunoregulants. In M. Rosenthale & H. Mansmann (Eds.), *Immunopharmacology* (pp. 79–83). Holliswood, NY: Spectrum Publications.

Dohan, F. C. (January, 1966). Wheat "consumption" and hospital admissions for schizophrenia during World War II: A preliminary report. *American Journal of Clinical Nutrition, 18*, 7–10. Retrieved December 1, 2007, from www.ajcn.org

Gordon Research Institute (Producer). (2000). *Detoxification with the new EDTA program* [Videotape]. New York: Gordon Research Institute.

Hoffer, A. (2005). *Adventures in psychiatry: The scientific memoirs of Dr. Abram Hoffer.* Caledon, ON: KOS Publishing.

Holford, P. (2002). *Improve your digestion.* London: Judy Piakus Publishers.

Ignarro, L. (2005). *No more heart disease: How nitric oxide can prevent—even reverse—heart disease and strokes.* New York: St. Martin's Griffin.

Lawson, S. (2003). *What is orthomolecular medicine?* Retrieved December 10, 2005, from http://lpi.oregonstate.edu/f-w99/orthomolecular.html

Lu, F., & Kacew, S. (2002). *Lu's basic toxicology: Fundamentals, target organs and risk assessment* (4th ed.). New York: Taylor and Francis.

Mandell, M., & Scanlon, L. W. (1979). *Dr. Mandell's 5-day allergy relief system.* New York: Pocket Books.

Pfeiffer, C., Mailloux, R., & Forsythe, L. (1970). *The schizophrenias: Ours to conquer.* Wichita, KS: Bio-Communications Press.

Philpott, W., & Kalita, D. (2000a). *Brain allergies: The psychonutrient and magnetic connections.* Chicago: Keats Publishing.

Philpott, W., & Kalita, D. (2000b). *Magnetic therapy: An alternative medicine definitive guide.* Boulder, CO: Alternative Medicine.com.

Randolph, T., & Moss, R. (1980). *An alternative approach to allergies.* New York: Lippincott & Crowell.

Ravikovich, F. (2003). *The plot against asthma and allergy patients: Asthma, allergies, migraine, chronic fatigue syndrome are curable, but the cure is hidden from patients.* Alton, ON: KOS Publishing.

Reading, C. (2002). *Trace your genes to health.* Ridgeville, CT: Vital Health Publishing.

Rocklin, R. E. (1982). Modulation of inflammatory and immune responses by histamine. In P. Sirois & M. Rola-Pleszczynski (Eds.), *Immunopharmacology: Research monographs in immunology* (pp. 49–74). New York: Elsevier Biomedical Press.

Rubin, J. (2003). *Patient, heal thyself.* Topanga, CA: Freedom Press.

Sirois, P., & Borgeat, P. (1982). Mediators of immediate hypersensitivity. In P. Sirois & M. Rola-Pleszczynski (Eds.), *Immunopharmacology: Research monographs in immunology* (pp. 201–222). New York: Elsevier Biomedical Press.

Suen, R., & Gordon, S. (2003, August–September). A critical review of IgG immunoglobulins and food allergy—implications in systemic health. *Townsend Letter for Doctors and Patients,* 241–242.

Terenius, L. (2000). From opiate pharmacology to opioid peptide physiology. *Upsala Journal of Medical Sciences, 105,* 1.

Young, R. O., & Young, S. R. (2002). *The ph miracle: Balance your diet, reclaim your health.* New York: Warner Wellness.

Part II

BODIES

Chapter 6

Caffeine: Pharmacology and Effects of the World's Most Popular Drug

Kyle M. Clayton, MS, and Paula K. Lundberg-Love, PhD

Caffeine is the most commonly used psychoactive drug in the world (Julien, 2005). A naturally occurring substance derived from more than 60 plants world-wide, caffeine's availability permeates most cultures. In the United States, it is estimated that up to 90 percent of adults consume caffeine on a daily basis, with an average daily intake of 200 to 400 mg per day (Meyer & Quenzer, 2005). The most common sources for daily caffeine intake include coffee, tea, soft drinks, and chocolate. While various factors, including serving size and method of preparation, affect the amount of caffeine found in particular products, the average cup of coffee contains approximately 100 mg of caffeine, while average servings of tea, soft drinks, and chocolate are slightly lower, 50 mg, 40 mg, and 20 mg, respectively. Caffeine tablets of 50–200 mg are available without a prescription (e.g., Vivarin, Nodoz), and various over-the-counter pain relievers, migraine medications, and antihistamines also contain caffeine. Currently, the Food and Drug Administration lists caffeine as safe for consumption, and its use as an additive is not restricted. However, the pervasiveness of caffeine's use, along with the volume of recent research findings on the subject, facilitates the need for exploring the effects of caffeine on the human body.

HISTORY

People have been consuming caffeine in various forms for thousands of years, with early cultures having discovered that the chewing and ingestion of caffeine-containing plants or seeds caused specific positive mood-altering and stimulatory effects. Ancient Chinese legend asserts that Shennong, Emperor of China in approximately 3000 B.C., discovered tea after leaves accidentally fell into boiling water resulting in a fragrant restorative drink (Lu & Yu, 1995). Coffee originated in Africa around A.D. 575, where coffee beans were used for food as well as currency. During the tenth century, coffee was restricted primarily to Ethiopia where its native beans were first cultivated. As Arabic trade expanded, coffee beans moved into other regions including northern Africa, where they were mass-cultivated. Coffee beans eventually entered the European markets where historical sources indicate that coffee initially arrived in Venice as a result of the trade between Europeans and those from North Africa and the Far East.

The appreciation of coffee in Europe was evident in the sixteenth century, and became increasingly popular in the decades to follow. During the seventeenth century, the first "coffee houses" were established, with openings in Britain, Paris, and Venice. Following their inception, coffee houses became popular throughout Western Europe, where they served as a common forum for business and social relations as well as intellectual exchange. Coffee was not widely accepted as the caffeinated drink of choice throughout colonial America until Revolutionary Americans made a nationwide switch from tea to coffee in the eighteenth century. This change occurred as a protest to the Tea Act, in which heavy taxes were levied by the British government on tea imported by Americans. This revolt culminated in the Boston Tea Party, in which large quantities of tea were disposed of in Boston Harbor.

Similar to the coffee bean and tea leaf, the kola nut (cola) also appears to have been rooted in ancient cultural tradition. West African cultures use the kola nut as a euphoric stimulant to restore vitality and ease hunger pangs. Cola was an original additive to many soft drinks, and became the focus of a health scare in 1911 when the U.S. government seized portions of Coca-Cola syrup in Chattanooga, Tennessee, alleging that the product was unsafe due to its caffeine content (Benjamin, Rogers, & Rosenbaum, 1991). Following this seizure, the government initiated litigation (*The United States v. Forty Barrels and Twenty Kegs of Coca-Cola*), in an attempt to force Coca-Cola to remove caffeine from its formula. The public attention brought by the suit led to congressional action, which eventually resulted in the amendment of the Pure Food and Drug Act in 1912, including caffeine on the list of "habit-forming" and "deleterious" substances that must be listed on a product's label.

The earliest evidence of cocoa use comes from residue found inside ancient Mayan pots dated from 600 B.C. to A.D. 250 (Gorman, 2002). Made from the beans of the tropical plant *Theobroma cacao*, cocoa was a favorite drink of ancient Maya and Aztec people in Mesoamerica. Chocolate was consumed in a bitter and spicy beverage called *xocoatl*, often seasoned with vanilla, chile pepper, and achiote. Xocoatl was believed to fight fatigue, a belief possibly attributable to the theobromine and caffeine content. Chocolate was a valuable commodity during this time as cocoa beans were often used as currency in trade. Chocolate was introduced to Europe in the 1500s, and became popular as a beverage by the late seventeenth century. In the latter part of the eighteenth century, chocolate production began in North America, with the establishment of a cocoa bean grinding mill in Massachusetts.

In 1819, pure caffeine was isolated for the first time by German chemist Friedrich Ferdinand Runge (Weinberg & Bealer, 2001). The structure of caffeine was elucidated near the end of the nineteenth century by Hermann Emil Fischer, who was also the first to achieve its total synthesis (Théel, 1902). During this time, cola products began to appear around the world and became one of the most prominent caffeinated beverages. Along with traditional sources of caffeine, including coffee, tea, and chocolate, the twentieth century saw the rise of caffeine intake through energy drinks, additives, and analgesic and appetite suppressant medications. Today the world population consumes more than 100,000 tons of caffeine annually, the equivalent of one caffeinated beverage per person per day.

PHARMACOKINETICS OF CAFFEINE

Taken orally, which is the typical method of drug administration, caffeine is rapidly and completely absorbed. Significant blood levels of caffeine are reached within 30 to 45 minutes of ingestion, with complete absorption occurring within the next 90 minutes (Julien, 2005). Caffeine's absorption occurs within the gastrointestinal tract, beginning in the stomach but occurring primarily within the small intestine. Following absorption, caffeine is distributed freely throughout the body and the brain. Caffeine is highly lipid-soluble, and higher concentrations are found within the brain as compared to plasma (Paton & Beer, 2001). Specifically, animal studies have demonstrated a significant disparity in brain/plasma concentration, with brain levels of caffeine as high as 80 percent (Kaplan, Greenblatt, Leduc, Thompson, & Shader, 1989).

Caffeine is metabolized to paraxanthine, theobromine, and theophylline, each with distinct effects on the body, including the breaking down of stored fat, blood vessel dilation, increased urine volume, and relaxation of bronchi muscles. These metabolites account for virtually all caffeine excretion, with only a small percentage of the original substance being eliminated as nonmetabolized caffeine.

The half-life of caffeine at modest levels of intake is approximately four to six hours in most adults. This period increases with higher levels of intake and for the elderly and those with impaired liver function. Caffeine's half-life is extended significantly in women during the late stages of pregnancy, and in instances of long-term use of oral contraceptive steroids (Chawla & Suleman, 2006). Active cigarette smokers experience a shortened half-life for caffeine, but half-life increases following smoking cessation. Research has suggested that increased levels of caffeine in plasma following smoking cessation may contribute to cigarette withdrawal symptoms in heavy coffee drinkers (Feldman, Meyer, & Quenzer, 1997).

MECHANISM OF ACTION OF CAFFEINE

Caffeine acts through multiple mechanisms to exert a variety of effects on the central nervous system. Caffeine's principal mechanism of action is as an adenosine receptor antagonist (Julien, 2005). Caffeine readily crosses the blood brain barrier, and its similarity in structure to adenosine, a naturally occurring substance in the brain, allows the caffeine molecule to bind to adenosine receptors (particularly adenosine A_1 & A_{2a} receptors) on the surface of cells and block the access of adenosine to its receptors. Recent research suggests that the blockade of adenosine receptors and its ensuing reduction in adenosine activity is responsible for the behavioral stimulation associated with caffeine (Fisone, Borgkvist, & Usiello, 2004). Adenosine plays a key role in the transfer of energy within the body, and its inhibitory function promotes sleep and suppressed arousal, while also producing anti-inflammatory effects as well as acting as a cardiac antiarrhythmic agent. Adenosine also serves as a neuromodulator that produces an overall inhibitory effect by reducing the effects of acetylcholine, dopamine, and glutamate within the central nervous system (CNS). In particular, adenosine inhibits ascending acetylcholine projections to the thalamus and cortex, while inhibiting dopamine activity within the hippocampus, striatum, nucleus accumbens, and prefrontal cortex. In addition, adenosine mediates the effects of glutamate release in the hippocampus during excitotoxicity.

In humans, there are four types of adenosine receptors, including A_1, A_{2a}, A_{2b}, and A_3. Each receptor is encoded by a particular gene and has a specific function. The adenosine A_1 receptor is found throughout the entire body, and generally has an inhibitory function. For example, adenosine A1 receptors found in the brain slow metabolic activity. The adenosine A_1 and A_{2a} receptors both act to regulate myocardial oxygen consumption and coronary blood flow, with the A_1 receptor causing a decrease in heart rate, force of contraction, and responsivity to adrenaline, while the A_{2a} receptor increases blood flow through vasodilatation of coronary arteries. Caffeine antagonism of adenosine receptors prohibits adenosine activity within cells, thus altering their function.

Caffeine's blockade of adenosine receptors increases stimulatory activity, producing changes in mood, increased vigilance, and heightened mental acuity. For example, increased release of acetylcholine associated with adenosine inhibition contributes to caffeine's behavioral arousal effects. The positive stimulatory effects of caffeine are primarily due to the blockade of adenosine receptors that stimulate GABAergic neurons, which in turn typically inhibit the release of dopamine in the reward system of the striatum (Mandel, 2002). This inhibition of GABAergic neurons and the resulting increase in dopaminergic activity within certain areas of the brain may explain many of the behavioral effects associated with caffeine use, including heightened alertness, elevated energy, and increased concentration (Garrett & Griffiths, 1997). In particular, elevated dopamine levels in the prefrontal cortex produced by caffeine appear to contribute to an increase in alertness. In contrast, caffeine does not stimulate the release of dopamine in the nucleus accumbens, which is consistent with the mild behavioral reinforcing properties commonly noted (Acquas, Tanda, & Di Chiara, 2002).

In addition to adenosine antagonistic properties, caffeine is a competitive inhibitor of the enzyme cAMP-phosphodiesterase (cAMP-PDE), which converts cyclic AMP (cAMP) in cells to its noncyclic form, allowing cAMP to build up in cells. Cyclic AMP participates in the messaging sequence produced by cells in response to stimulation by epinephrine. Thus, by blocking the removal of cAMP, caffeine intensifies and prolongs the effects of epinephrine and epinephrine-like drugs such as amphetamine, methamphetamine, and methylphenidate.

The metabolites of caffeine also contribute to caffeine's effects. Theobromine is a caffeine metabolite that serves as a vasodilator, increasing the amount of oxygen and nutrient flow to the brain and muscles. Theophylline, the second of the three primary metabolites, acts as a smooth muscle relaxant that increases heart rate and efficiency. The third metabolic derivative, Paraxanthine, is responsible for an increase in the lipolysis process, which releases glycerol and fatty acids into the blood to be used as a source of fuel by the muscles (Dews, 1987).

BEHAVIORAL AND PHYSIOLOGICAL EFFECTS

The effect of caffeine on humans is largely a function of dosage, frequency of use, and individual sensitivity. Effects are often consistent with those reported by users of other CNS stimulants with very different mechanism of action, including cocaine and amphetamines. At low to moderate daily doses (50–300 mg), commonly reported subjective effects include arousal, increased concentration, elevated mood, increased motivation to work, and decreased sleepiness. The most typical mood-altering effects include increases in energy, alertness, and feelings of well-being (Garrett & Griffiths, 1997). In comparison to the positive effects often reported by respondents consuming low to moderate doses, consumers of higher doses of caffeine increasingly report feelings of anxiety, nervousness, restlessness, and insomnia. The mechanism by which caffeine produces its subjective effects is yet to be determined. Caffeine has not shown to induce dopamine release in the nucleus accumbens of the brain, an action common to drugs with addictive properties, but more likely, exerts effects on mood through indirect stimulation of dopamine in the striatum. Recent research has shown that there is a direct correlation between the experience of positive effects and level of daily use (Attwood, Higgs, & Terry, 2006). Those consuming higher daily doses of caffeine (> 200 mg) were more likely to report positive effects, which may account for their high levels of use. In addition, it was found that while some moderate users did not report significant positive effects, they maintained their schedule of daily consumption, supporting the possibility that low to moderate use may be maintained by other factors, including environmental reinforcement and expectancy. There is controversy regarding the mechanism by which caffeine has shown to elevate mood, as well as performance on tasks utilizing alertness, speed, vigilance, and reaction time. While some have argued that the positive impact of caffeine can be directly attributed to the removal of withdrawal symptoms (James, 2005), more recent research has found improved performance and elevated mood to be a direct result of the stimulatory properties of caffeine, unrelated to effects of withdrawal (Christopher, Sutherland, & Smith, 2005; Hewlett & Smith, 2007; Smith, Sutherland, & Christopher, 2005).

Caffeine-induced anxiety is recognized in the *DSM–IV-TR* as a substance-related disorder characterized by the presentation of prominent anxiety, panic attacks, or obsessions or compulsions directly resulting from the physiological effects of caffeine (American Psychiatric Association [APA], 2000). Moderate daily caffeine consumption (> 200 mg) has been demonstrated to increase anxiety ratings in normal participants (Graham, Schultz, Mayo-Smith, Ries, & Wilford, 2003), while doses of 750 mg have been shown to induce panic attacks (Paton & Beer, 2001). People with a high disposition toward anxiety or those diagnosed with anxiety disorders are often very sensitive to the anxiogenic properties of caffeine, making them particularly vulnerable. Although there is some evidence that those with anxiety disorders tend to limit their exposure to caffeine (Kruger, 1996), it is generally recommended that those with anxiety-related disorders be advised to abstain completely from caffeine use.

Sleep appears to be the physiological process most sensitive to the effects of caffeine. Exposure to caffeine has the ability to produce cerebral stimulatory effects, especially in areas controlling locomotor activity and the sleep-wake cycle, and acute doses exceeding 200 mg are capable of producing significant effects on sleep (Chawla & Suleman, 2006). The *DSM–IV* recognized caffeine-induced sleep disorder as a significant disturbance in sleep brought on by the physiological effects of caffeine (APA, 1994). Caffeine typically disrupts sleep by prolonging sleep latency, shortening total sleep duration, and increasing nocturnal awakenings. Similar to its anxiogenic properties, caffeine's effect on sleep is determined by many factors, including dosage, tolerance, individual sensitivity, and time between ingestion and attempted sleep (Graham et al., 2003). Elevated doses correlate specifically to delays in sleep onset when ingested immediately prior to attempted sleep, and individual differences, such as slower metabolic rate, can increase instances of sleep disruption by extending drug availability. While partial tolerance can decrease caffeine's stimulatory effects, complete tolerance does not occur, leaving even the most habitual users at risk for sleep disturbances. Overall, caffeine's ability to disrupt sleep at high doses is well established, while difficulties at lower to moderate doses appear to be more attributable to individual differences, including sensitivity and schedule of use.

Caffeine also exerts significant effects on cardiovascular function. Research on caffeine's effect on the heart and heart disease is ongoing, and both positive and adverse effects have been demonstrated. Caffeine increases cyclic adenosine monophosphate (cAMP) in heart cells, which simulates the action of epinephrine, causing a slight stimulant effect. This stimulation increases heart rate, cardiac contractility (force of contraction), and cardiac output. Caffeine also has been shown to increase blood pressure, especially in those disposed to hypertension. Repeated blood pressure elevation in habitual users might contribute to an increased risk of heart disease (Lane, Pieper, Phillips-Butte, Bryant, & Kuhn, 2002). In contrast to negative effects, a recent study found that increased caffeine intake provided protection against the risk of heart disease mortality among nonhypertensive elderly participants (Greenberg, Dunbar, Schnoll, Kokolis, & Kassotis, 2007). A conclusive finding regarding the means by which caffeine provides such protection was unavailable; however, Greenberg et al. (2007) suggested that there was evidence to support the hypothesis that caffeine's ability to increase blood pressure counteracts postprandial hypotension. Other possible explanations for caffeine's ability to decrease the risk of heart disease among nonhypertensive elderly patients included commonly demonstrated cardiovascular effects such as increased myocardial contractility (strength of heart contraction), reduced fibrinolysis time (faster clot breakdown), and inhibition of baroreflex activity (increases blood pressure). Also, caffeine's ability to dilate coronary arteries and increase blood flow to the heart has been demonstrated (Rachima-Moaz, Peleg, & Rosenthal, 1998), which might serve to mitigate negative effects in some individuals. With respect to increased risk for the typical adult population, it is possible that caffeine's ability to increase blood pressure is more prominent in coffee consumption than that of tea, as a recent study has indicated that the amino acid theanine (commonly found in tea) may reduce elevated blood pressure (Rogers, Smith, Heatherley, & Pleydell-Pearce, 2008). While there is not a consensus on the effects of caffeine consumption on heart disease, it is generally recommended that individuals with hypertension or heart disease minimize consumption.

As opposed to caffeine's effect on arteries of the heart, where dilation increases oxygen supply, caffeine has the opposite effect on the blood vessels of the brain; cerebral blood vessels are constricted, which decreases blood flow and reduces pressure within the brain (Julien, 2005). This action can prove beneficial for people suffering from headaches, and more specifically, treatment of migraines. Nonprescription medications containing a combination of acetaminophen, aspirin, and caffeine (e.g., Excedrin Migraine) have demonstrated effectiveness in reducing migraine-related symptoms (Chawla & Suleman, 2006).

Additional physiological effects of caffeine include changes in respiratory, urinary, and gastrointestinal function. Caffeine increases both gastric acid secretion and urine output, while producing antiasthmatic effects on lung function. Caffeine causes bronchial relaxation and is commonly used in the treatment of newborn infants who display apneic episodes (periodic suspension of breathing) or bronchopulmonary dysplasia, which is characterized by inflammation and scarring in the lungs. These conditions often occur in low-weight premature babies, and in such cases, caffeine has shown to be an essential aid in normalizing respiration and preventing death.

TOXICITY

Caffeine intoxication is recognized by both the *ICD–10* (World Health Organization [WHO], 1992) and *DSM–IV–TR* (APA, 2000) as a distinct syndrome associated with excessive caffeine use. Caffeine intoxication is defined by a number of clinical features that emerge in response to recent consumption of caffeine. The *DSM–IV* indicates that the diagnosis of caffeine intoxication is dependent on recent daily consumption, generally exceeding 250 mg (more than 2–3 cups of coffee), along with the presentation of intoxicated related symptoms following caffeine use. Common features of caffeine intoxication in adults are similar to the overdose effects of other central nervous system stimulants (e.g., cocaine, amphetamine), and include anxiety, restlessness, excitement, insomnia, rambling flow of thought and speech, irritability, tremor, diuresis, flushed face, gastrointestinal disturbance, psychomotor agitation, and irregular or rapid heartbeat. Caffeine intoxication symptoms in infants include rapid heartbeat, rapid breathing, tremors, shock, muscle tension, nausea, and vomiting. In adult cases of highly elevated doses, symptoms such as fever, hallucinations, delusions, and loss of consciousness have occurred (Medline, 2006). Caffeine intoxication, due to its relatively short half-life (4–6 hours), typically resolves rather quickly with cessation of consumption and supportive care. However, individual reactions differ as related to overall health and caffeine sensitivity. Life-threatening complications, generally related to cardiac dysrhythmias, can occur and immediate medical care may be needed to restore cardiovascular stability. Peritoneal dialysis, hemodialysis, or hemofiltration may also be required in cases of severe caffeine overdose. Extreme dose toxicity can result in death, but such instances are very rare. Lethal dosage is dependent on weight and individual sensitivity to caffeine. However, doses exceeding 5 to 10 grams taken within a limited time frame are generally considered a significant risk. Such a sizeable dose is difficult to achieve under conventional methods (e.g., 50 to 100 average cups of coffee), but can be more readily administered with the ingestion of caffeine tablets. In cases of lethal overdose, the typical cause of death is often described as ventricular fibrillation (Holmgren, Nordén-Pettersson, & Ahlner, 2004).

TOLERANCE, DEPENDENCE, AND WITHDRAWAL

Tolerance refers to a decrease in responsiveness to a drug following repeated exposure in which the dose necessary to achieve the initial reinforcing effect is increased. Tolerance can also refer to the decline of aversive effects typically associated with large doses of the drug. Each of these altered responses to drug exposure can promote the use of increased dosage and repeated administration. Partial tolerance has been shown to develop among chronic caffeine users consuming levels as low as 100 mg per day (Evans & Griffiths, 1999). Caffeine tolerance can develop rather quickly among high-dose consumers. Complete tolerance to the sleep disruption effects of caffeine has been reported after consuming 400 mg of caffeine three times a day for seven days, while complete tolerance to subjective effects such as nervousness, tension, jitters, and elevated energy were observed to develop after consuming 300 mg three times per day for 18 days, and it is possible that such tolerance can occur within a shorter period of time (Griffiths & Mumford, 2000). With respect to chronic users, it should be noted that while tolerance has been shown to develop concerning certain subjective measures (including mood and energy level), tolerance is more prevalent among physiological effects such as respiratory and cardiovascular function, along with sleep disruption.

Substance dependence due to caffeine is recognized as a clinical diagnosis in the *ICD–10* (WHO, 1992). Substance dependence refers to the presentation of cognitive, behavioral, and physiological symptoms related to an individual's continued use of a substance despite significant adverse consequences. Clinical diagnoses of substance dependence can be specified as with or without physiological dependence (evidence of tolerance or withdrawal). While caffeine dependence is not currently recognized as a clinical disorder in the *DSM–IV–TR* (APA, 2000), current research is focusing on whether the diagnosis of caffeine withdrawal or caffeine withdrawal syndrome is warranted for inclusion in future editions of this and other diagnostic texts. Caffeine withdrawal has been documented in numerous empirically validated double-blind experiments (Evans & Griffiths, 1999; Rogers, Martin, Smith, Heatherley, & Smit, 2003; Tinley, Yeomans, & Durlach, 2003). In a recent review of caffeine withdrawal studies, the following symptom categories were indicated as valid: headache, fatigue, decreased energy/activity, decreased alertness, drowsiness, decreased contentment, depressed mood, difficulty concentrating, irritability, and foggy/not clearheaded. It was also noted that additional flu-like symptoms, including nausea/vomiting, tremors, and muscle pain/stiffness are often reported. The most commonly reported symptom in caffeine withdrawal is headache, which occurs in approximately 50 percent of people reporting withdrawal symptoms (Juliano & Griffiths, 2004). Withdrawal symptoms generally begin within 12–24 hours following cessation of caffeine, and reach peak intensity at approximately 20–48 hours with an overall duration of two to seven days. Severity and occurrence of symptoms appear to relate to increases in dosage. However, withdrawal symptoms have been exhibited in those consuming as little as 100 mg/day (approximately one cup of coffee).

REPRODUCTIVE AND PRENATAL CONCERNS

The effect of maternal caffeine consumption on miscarriage and prenatal development remains undetermined, as credible scientific studies have reported a variety of findings. Concerning miscarriage, past studies have shown an increased risk for those consuming high daily doses (> 600 mg) of caffeine, while moderate doses did not increase the risk (Klebanoff, Levine, DerSimonian, Clemens, & Wilkins, 1999). A more recent study found that daily doses exceeding 200 mg were sufficient to increase the risk of miscarriage. In contrast, a recent study by Savitz, Chan, Herring, Howards, and Hartmann

(2008) demonstrated little evidence for risk of miscarriage among women with modest daily caffeine intake. Similar to the issue of miscarriage, caffeine's ability to affect fetal growth is a topic of current debate. A Norwegian study comparing caffeine intake of mothers of small-for-gestational-age (SGA) infants with mothers of non-SGA infants found that high caffeine intake during the third trimester correlated with an increased risk for growth retardation in male fetuses (Vik, Bakketeig, Ulla Trygg, Lund-Larsen, & Jacobsen, 2003). A separate European study reported that caffeine intake was not responsible for increased risk of SGA, and noted that many of the previous studies reporting such an effect had failed to account for other known contributory factors, including smoking and alcohol consumption (Parazzini et al., 2005). In addition to increased risk of SGA, instances of stillbirth also have been studied. In a study by Wisborg, Kesmodel, Hammer Bech, Hedegaard, and Brink Henriksen (2003) containing more than 18,000 pregnant women, those who consumed four to seven cups of coffee a day had an 80 percent increased risk of stillbirth, while women consuming more than eight cups a day had a 300 percent increased risk. While further research is needed to clarify the effects of caffeine on prenatal health and development, current medical recommendations generally advise pregnant women to minimize its consumption.

DRUG INTERACTIONS AND TREATMENT CONSIDERATIONS

Acute administration of high doses of caffeine to individuals diagnosed with panic disorder has been shown to increase cortisol to levels similar to those found in clinically depressed individuals (Paton & Beer, 2001). These elevated levels of cortisol can sometimes mimic the symptoms of depression, leading to false diagnosis. Similarly, caffeine can also interfere with medications prescribed for the treatment of insomnia. Benzodiazepines such as temazepam (Restoril) and triazolam (Halcion) are medications that bind to GABA-A receptors in the brain that enhance the function of GABA and create sedative and hypnotic effects. Caffeine can inhibit the binding of benzodiazepines to their specific receptors on the GABA-A receptor sites, therefore neutralizing the effects of such medications and inhibiting their sedative hypnotic effects (Sawnock, 1995). Such interactions should be considered when evaluating the effectiveness of medications used to treat insomnia. Caffeine screening and monitoring schedules can be an effective tool for proper diagnosis and medication management.

Caffeine also exerts a significant effect on other medications. For example, caffeine additives have demonstrated the ability to increase the effectiveness of pain relievers in the treatment of headaches by as much as 40 percent while helping the body absorb headache medications more quickly, contributing to faster symptom relief. Thus, augmenting such medications with caffeine allows for dose reduction of the analgesic agent, which can reduce the risk for potential side effects and possible drug addiction (WebMD, 2008). With respect to the treatment of smoking cessation, the effect nicotine has on the metabolism of caffeine should be considered. In regular smokers, nicotine increases the metabolism of caffeine, while smoking cessation often decreases the rate of caffeine metabolism. Slower metabolism leads to increased levels of caffeine in blood plasma, and high levels of caffeine following smoking cessation could contribute to nicotine withdrawal symptoms (Julien, 2005).

Caffeine consumption is very common among patients with schizophrenia (Rihs, Muller, & Bauman, 1996). Heavy caffeine users may require higher doses of antipsychotic medication in treatment. The possible explanations for the elevated therapeutic dose requirements include the following: (1) caffeine may increase the severity of psychotic symptoms due to an increase in catecholamine release, which could result in an increase in medication to treat such symptoms; or (2) caffeine may interfere with the effectiveness of antipsychotic medication. Caffeine's blockade of adenosine receptors can result in increased dopamine binding to dopamine D2 receptors, which competes with the action of many antipsychotic agents that target the blockade of dopamine D2 receptors (Paton & Beer, 2001). Paton and Beer (2001) also suggest that caffeine may decrease the effectiveness of iron, lithium, and zinc, and that increases in caffeine could heighten the possibility of clozapine, olanzapine, and tricyclic antidepressant toxicity.

CONCLUSION

Caffeine is readily available around the world and consumed by most adults in the United States. Caffeine is most often ingested in coffee or tea, but can be found in a wide variety of foods, drinks, supplements, and medications. Taken orally, which is the typical method of drug administration, caffeine is rapidly and completely absorbed within the gastrointestinal tract and then metabolized and excreted with a typical half-life of four to six hours. Caffeine functions primarily as a central nervous system stimulant, with its principal mechanism of action as an adenosine A1 and A2a antagonist. Typical stimulatory effects include elevated arousal and concentration, reduced fatigue, and sleep disturbances. Caffeine also produces significant physiological effects on the cardiovascular, respiratory, and gastrointestinal systems, including increased heart rate and blood pressure, antiasthmatic effects, and increased gastric acid secretion and diuresis.

Caffeine intoxication is generally dependent on recent daily consumption exceeding 250 mg, and presents in adults with symptoms such as anxiety, restlessness, insomnia, tremor, gastrointestinal disturbance, and irregular or rapid heartbeat, with rare instances of hallucinations, delusions, and loss of consciousness following highly elevated doses. Caffeine intoxication symptoms in infants include rapid heartbeat, rapid breathing, tremors, shock, muscle tension, nausea, and vomiting. Extremely high doses of caffeine (5–10 g) can be lethal with the cause of death typically attributed to ventricular fibrillation. Tolerance and withdrawal symptoms have been demonstrated in caffeine users with the most prominent symptoms consisting of headache, fatigue, decreased alertness, and irritability. Withdrawal symptoms generally begin within 24 hours following cessation of caffeine, with an overall duration of two to seven days. Severity of symptoms is often a function of elevated doses or individual sensitivity, but caffeine tolerance has been shown to occur in users consuming as little as 100 mg a day, which is equivalent to one average cup of coffee.

Certain clinical uses for caffeine have been demonstrated, including treatment for migraine headaches, treatment of newborn infants who display apneic episodes (periodic suspension of breathing) or bronchopulmonary dysplasia, and as a possible protection against the risk of heart disease mortality among nonhypertensive elderly participants. Caffeine displays significant drug interactions with medications typically prescribed for anxiety, depression, insomnia, pain relief, and schizophrenia. Such interactions should be considered in the treatment of relevant disorders.

There is debate over caffeine's role in heart disease, prenatal and reproductive function, as well as its classification as an addictive substance. Current research is inconclusive, and further exploration regarding the role of caffeine in these and other conditions is warranted. In general, while caffeine appears safe in moderation, certain individuals, including pregnant women, those with anxiety-related disorders, cardiovascular disorders, or insomnia, are advised to limit its consumption.

REFERENCES

Acquas, E., Tanda, G., & Di Chiara, G. (2002). Differential effects of caffeine on dopamine and acetycholine transmission in brain areas of drug-naïve and caffeine-pretreated rats. *Neuropsychopharmacology, 27*(2), 182–193.

American Psychiatric Association. (2000). *Diagnostic and statistical manual of mental disorders* (4th ed., text rev.). Washington, DC: Author.

Attwood, A. S., Higgs, S., & Terry, P. (2006). Differential responsiveness to caffeine and perceived effects of caffeine in moderate and high regular caffeine consumers. *Psychopharmacology, 190*, 469–477.

Benjamin, L.T., Jr., Rogers, A. M., & Rosenbaum, A. (1991). Coca-Cola, caffeine, and mental deficiency: Harry Hollingworth and the Chattanooga trial of 1911. *Journal of the History of the Behavioral Sciences, 27*(1), 42–55.

Chawla, J., & Suleman, A. (2006). Neurologic effects of caffeine. *eMedicine,* Retrieved May 5, 2008, from http://www.emedicine.com/neuro/topic666.htm

Christopher, G., Sutherland, D., & Smith, A. (2005). Effects of caffeine in non-withdrawn volunteers. *Human Psychopharmacology: Clinical and Experimental, 20,* 47–53.

Dews, P. B. (Ed.). (1987). *Caffeine: Perspectives from recent research.* Berlin: Springer.

Evans, S. M., & Griffiths, R. R. (1999). Caffeine withdrawal: A parametric analysis of caffeine dosing conditions. *Journal of Pharmacology and Experimental Therapeutics, 289,* 285–294.

Feldman, R. S., Meyer, J. S., & Quenzer, L. F. (1997). *Principles of neuropsychopharmacology.* Sunderland, MA: Sinauer Associates.

Fisone, G., Borgkvist, A., & Usiello, A. (2004). Caffeine as a psychomotor stimulant: Mechanism of action. *Cellular and Molecular Life Sciences, 61*(7/8), 857–872.

Garrett, B. E., & Griffiths, R. R. (1997). The role of dopamine in the behavioral effects of caffeine in animals and humans. *Pharmacology Biochemistry and Behavior, 57*(3), 533–541.

Gorman, J. (2002, July 20). The original cocoa treat: Chemistry pushes back first use of the drink. *Science News, 162*(3), 38.

Graham, A. W., Schultz, T. K., Mayo-Smith, M. F., Ries, R. K., & Wilford, B. B. (Eds.). (2003). *Principles of addiction medicine* (3rd ed.). Chevy Chase, MD: American Society of Addiction.

Greenberg, J. A., Dunbar, C. C., Schnoll, R., Kokolis, S., & Kassotis, J. (2007). Caffeinated beverage intake and the risk of heart disease mortality in the elderly: A protective analysis. *American Journal of Clinical Nutrition, 85,* 392–398.

Griffiths, R. R., & Mumford, G. K. (2000). *Caffeine: A drug of abuse?* American College of Neuropsychopharmacology. Retrieved April 28, 2008, from http://www.acnp.org/g4/GN401000165/Default.htm

Hewlett, P., & Smith, A. (2007). Effects of repeated doses of caffeine on performance and alertness: New data and secondary analysis. *Human Psychopharmacology: Clinical and Experimental, 22,* 339–350.

Holmgren, P., Nordén-Pettersson, L., & Ahlner, J. (2004). Caffeine fatalities—four case reports. *Forensic Science International, 139,* 71–73.

James, J. E. (2005). Caffeine-induced enhancement of cognitive performance: Confounding due to reversal of withdrawal effects. *Australian Journal of Psychology, 57*(3), 197–200.

Juliano, L. M., & Griffiths, R. R. (2004). A critical review of caffeine withdrawal: Empirical validation of symptoms and signs, incidence, severity, and associated features. *Psychopharmacology, 176,* 1–29.

Julien, R. M. (2005). *A primer of drug action: A comprehensive guide to the actions, uses, and side effects of psychoactive drugs* (10th ed.). New York: Worth Publishers.

Kaplan, G. B., Greenblatt, D. J., LeDuc, B. W., Thompson, M. L., Shader, R. I. (1989). Relationship of plasma and brain caffeine metabolites to benzodiazepine receptor binding and locomotor activity. *Journal of Pharmacology and Experimental Therapeutics 248*, 1078–1083.

Klebanoff, M. A., Levine, R. J., DerSimonian, R., Clemens, J. D., & Wilkins, D. G. (1999). Maternal serum paraxanthine, a caffeine metabolite, and the risk of spontaneous abortion. *New England Journal of Medicine, 341*(22), 1639–1644.

Kruger, A. (1996). Chronic psychiatric patients' use of caffeine: Pharmacological effects and mechanisms. *Psychological Reports, 78*, 915–923.

Lane, J. D., Pieper, C. F., Phillips-Butte, B. G., Bryant, J. E., & Kuhn, C. M. (2002). Caffeine affects cardiovascular and neuroendocrine activation at work and home. *Psychosomatic Medicine, 64*, 595–603.

Lu, Y., & Yu, L. (1995). *Classic of tea: Origins and rituals.* New York: Ecco Press.

Mandel, H. G. (2002). Update on caffeine consumption, disposition and action. *Food and Toxicology, 40*, 1231–1234.

Medline. (2006). *Caffeine overdose.* Retrieved May 1, 2008, from http://www.nlm.nih.gov/medlineplus/ency/article/002579.htm

Meyer, J., & Quenzer, L. (2005). *Psychopharmacology: Drugs, the brain, and behavior.* Sunderland, MA: Sinauer Associates.

Parazzini, F., Chiaffarino, F., Chatenoud, L., Tozzi, L., Cipriani, S., Chiantera, V., et al. (2005). Maternal coffee drinking in pregnancy and risk of small for gestational age birth. *European Journal of Clinical Nutrition, 59*, 299–301.

Paton, C., & Beer, D. (2001). Caffeine: The forgotten variable. *International Journal of Psychiatry in Clinical Practice, 5*, 231–236.

Rachima-Moaz, C., Peleg, E., Rosenthal, T. (1998). The effect of caffeine on ambulatory blood pressure in hypertensive patients. *American Journal of Hypertension 11*, 1426–1432.

Rihs, M., Muller, C., & Bauman, P. (1996). Caffeine consumption in hospitalized psychiatric patients. *European Archives of Psychiatry and Clinical Neuroscience, 246*, 83–92.

Rogers, P. J., Martin, J., Smith, C., Heatherley, S. V., & Smit, H. J. (2003). Absence of reinforcing, mood and psychomotor performance effects of caffeine in habitual non-consumers of caffeine. *Psychopharmacology (Berlin), 167*, 54–62.

Rogers, P. J., Smith, J. E., Heatherley, S. V., & Pleydell-Pearce, C. W. (2008). Time for tea: Mood, blood pressure and cognitive performance effects of caffeine and theanine administered alone and together. *Psychopharmacology, 195*, 569–577.

Savitz, D. A., Chan, R. L., Herring, A. H., Howards, P. P., & Hartmann, K. E. (2008). Caffeine and miscarriage risk. *Epidemiology, 19*(1), 55–62.

Sawnock, J. (1995). Pharmacological rationale for the clinical use of caffeine. *Drugs, 49*, 37–50.

Smith, A., Sutherland, D., & Christopher, G. (2005). Effects of repeated doses of caffeine on mood and performance of alert and fatigued volunteers. *Journal of Psychopharmacology, 19*, 620–626.

Théel, Hj. (1902). *Presentation speech by professor Hj. Théel, president of the Swedish Royal Academy of Sciences on December 10, 1902.* Retrieved May 16, 2008, from http://nobelprize.org/nobel_prizes/chemistry/laureates/1902/press.html

Tinley, E. M., Yeomans, M. R., & Durlach, P. J. (2003). Caffeine reinforces flavour preference in caffeine-dependent, but not long-term withdrawn, caffeine consumers. *Psychopharmacology (Berlin), 166,* 416–423.

Vik, T., Bakketeig, L. S., Ulla Trygg, K., Lund-Larsen, K., & Jacobsen, G. (2003). High caffeine consumption in the third trimester of pregnancy: Gender specific effects on fetal growth. *Paediatric and Perinatal Epidemiology, 17,* 324–331.

WebMD. (2008). *Migraines, headaches, and caffeine.* Retrieved May 1, 2008, from http://www.webmd.com/migraines-headaches/guide/triggers-caffeine?page=2

Weinberg, B. A., & Bealer, B. K. (2001). *World of caffeine: The science and culture of the world's most popular drug.* New York: Routledge.

Wisborg, K., Kesmodel, U., Hammer Bech, B., Hedegaard, M., & Brink Henriksen, T. (2003). Maternal consumption of coffee during pregnancy and stillbirth and infant death in first year of life: Prospective study. *British Medical Journal, 326,* 420–422.

World Health Organization. (1992). *International statistical classification of diseases and related health problems* (10th ed.). *Classification of mental and behavioural disorders: Clinical descriptions and diagnostic guidelines.* Geneva: Author.

Chapter 7

Marijuana Withdrawal: A Survey of Symptoms

Dirk Hanson, MA

More than 14 million Americans smoke marijuana regularly, making it the most commonly used illicit drug in America. In 2006, marijuana was the only drug used by 52.8 percent of illegal drug users (U.S. Department of Health and Human Services, 2006). Over the past 15 years, as addiction researchers have been busily mapping out the chemical alterations in the human nervous system caused by alcohol, cocaine, nicotine, heroin, and tranquilizers, America's most popular illegal drug has remained largely a scientific mystery. Marijuana, the drug millions of Americans have been using regularly for years, is the least studied drug of all.

Why has cannabis research lagged behind that of other drugs of abuse? For decades, the prevailing belief among users and clinical researchers alike was that marijuana did not produce dependency and therefore could not be responsible for major withdrawal symptoms. This thinking is based, quite understandably, on the widespread observation that most marijuana users do not have difficulty going without marijuana, either by choice or by necessity. However, marijuana withdrawal effects are frequently submerged in the welter of polyaddictions common to active addicts. The withdrawal rigors of, say, alcohol or heroin tend to drown out the subtler manifestations of cannabis withdrawal. As Barbara Mason, director of the Laboratory of Clinical Psychopharmacology at Scripps Research Institute, has explained: "People are deciding every day whether to use or not to use marijuana, for medical purposes or otherwise, and there is little scientific information to advise this decision" (2008, 1).

Marijuana withdrawal, which typically affects only heavy smokers, has not been well characterized by the research community. Until recently, there was scant evidence in animal models for marijuana *tolerance* and *withdrawal*, the classic determinants of addiction. Now, however, several researchers have identified the existence of symptoms brought on by the abrupt discontinuation of regular marijuana use in both animal and human studies (de Fonseca et al., 1997). A growing body of evidence supports the existence of a clinically significant marijuana withdrawal syndrome in a subset of marijuana smokers. The syndrome is marked by irritability, restlessness, generalized anxiety, hostility, depression, difficulty sleeping, excessive sweating, loose stools, loss of appetite, a general "blah" feeling, and a mental state that has been described as "inner unrest."

Recent clinical research, combined with anecdotal field reports collected by the author, demonstrate the existence of marijuana withdrawal and the consistency of the most common symptoms of withdrawal and detoxification.

BACKGROUND

In 1992, molecular biologists identified the elusive brain receptor where tetrahydrocannabinol (THC), the primary active ingredient in marijuana, did its work. Shortly after that discovery, researchers at Hebrew University in Jerusalem identified the body's own form of THC, which uses the same CB1 receptors as THC (CB1 is cannabinoid receptor type 1). They christened the internally manufactured substance *anandamide*, after the Sanskrit *ananda*, or "bliss" (Fackelmann, 1993).

Anandamide has a streamlined three-dimensional structure that THC mimics. Both molecules slip easily through the blood brain barrier. Some of the mystery of marijuana's effects was resolved after researchers demonstrated that marijuana definitely increased dopamine activity in the limbic area of the brain. Tanda, Pontieri, and Di Chiara demonstrated that dopamine levels in the nucleus accumbens doubled when rats received an infusion of THC (1997). It appears that marijuana raises dopamine and serotonin levels through the intermediary activation of opiate and Gamma-aminobutyric acid (GABA) receptors (Wilson & Nicoll, 2001). (GABA is the chief inhibitory neurotransmitter in the mammalian central nervous system. The opiate receptor and other brain receptors are proteins located on the surfaces of nerve cells, or neurons.) THC may perform a signaling function in neurons containing GABA and glutamate.

THC and its organic cousin, anandamide, make an impressive triple play in the brain: They effect movement through receptors in the basal ganglia, they alter sensory perception through receptors in the cerebral cortex, and they impact memory by means of receptors in the hippocampus. It is clear that some of the effects of cannabis are produced in much the same way as the effects of other addictive drugs—by means of neurotransmitter alterations along the limbic system's reward pathway.

A great deal of the early research was marred by inconsistent findings and differing definitions of addiction and withdrawal. Most recreational marijuana users find that too much pot in one day makes them lethargic and uncomfortable. Self-proclaimed marijuana addicts, on the other hand, report that pot energizes them, calms them down when they are nervous, or otherwise allows them to function normally. Heavy marijuana users claim that tolerance does build. And when they withdraw from use, many report strong cravings.

Work by Jones, Benowitz, and Herning had helped establish certain baseline symptoms—irritability, insomnia, and lack of appetite—as early as 1981. Studies by Budney, Novy, and Hughes in 1999 further outlined the syndrome in heavy daily marijuana smokers. But the abstinence effects were often inconsistent, and frequently hard to measure. Moreover, their clinical relevance was not always evident.

For marijuana withdrawal to be considered a clinical fact, several criteria had to be met. First, the typically transient pattern of withdrawal effects must be distinguishable from rebound effects. (A rebound effect is defined as the reappearance of a preexisting symptom, and is thus not considered a true withdrawal effect.) In addition, the symptoms must occur reliably, as demonstrated by comprehensive prospective studies (Budney, Hughes, Moore, & Vandrey, 2004). The symptoms under consideration must also be considered clinically significant. Finally, there needs to be a clear and repeatable timeline in evidence for the withdrawal effects.

It has been suggested that the reported symptoms of abrupt marijuana cessation do not rise to the level of withdrawal typically associated with drug detox. It is now possible to lay out the neurochemical basis of marijuana withdrawal, and to demonstrate that marijuana acts on the brain in a fashion similar to other addictive drugs.

There is solid experimental evidence that chronic, heavy cannabis users develop tolerance to its subjective and cardiovascular effects. "In summary," Budney et al. write, "cannabis withdrawal effects clearly occur in the majority of heavy, daily users" (2004, p. 1974). As a rough estimate, approximately 10 percent of marijuana users are at risk for dependence and withdrawal, the classic determinants of drug addiction (Joy, Watson, & Benson, 1999). There is clinical and epidemiological evidence that some heavy cannabis users experience problems in controlling their cannabis use, and continue to use the drug despite experiencing adverse personal consequences of use (Hall, Solowij, & Lemon, 1999). Moreover, there is strong clinical evidence that some users experience a withdrawal syndrome upon the abrupt cessation of cannabis use. The timeline is similar to withdrawal from other addictive drugs.

In 2004, a group at the University of Vermont funded by the US National Institute of Drug Abuse (NIDA), undertook a critical review of all major relevant studies of the validity and clinical significance of marijuana withdrawal (Budney et al., p. 1967). The review of studies demonstrated with certainty that there are people with a propensity for heavy marijuana use who suffer a clearly delineated, verifiable, and frequently vivid set of withdrawal symptoms when they try to quit. One of the most striking pieces of evidence for this is the similarity of symptom sets emerging from the clinical studies to date. The most common "reliable and clinically significant" effects of abrupt withdrawal in heavy pot smokers, according to the University of Vermont research group, included "severity of craving and sleep difficulty, decreased appetite, and increased aggression, anger and irritability" (Budney, et al., p. 1967; Kouri, 2002, p. 30).

As another study author concluded: "Marijuana withdrawal doesn't include dramatic physical symptoms such as the pain, nausea, heavy sweating, and cramps associated with opiate withdrawal. Nevertheless, the symptoms of marijuana withdrawal appear clinically significant" (Zickler, 2002, p. 3). A recent comprehensive outpatient study (Kouri & Pope, 2000, p. 483) with prewithdrawal baselines showed greater levels of anxiety, negative mood, physical discomfort, and decreased appetite during abstinence but not at baseline, compared with two control groups. Moreover, in a "home environment" study, researchers worked with marijuana users who provided self-ratings during marijuana withdrawal; these users smoked an average of 3.6 times daily, did not use other drugs or abuse alcohol, and were free of major psychiatric disorders. The same symptoms predominated, and onset of symptoms occurred reliably within 48 hours of cessation. Moreover, "telephone interviews with collateral observers living with the participants confirmed participants' reports of increased irritability, aggression, and restlessness during abstinence. . . . [T]he validation of symptoms by home-based observers suggested that the effects were of a clinically significant magnitude" (Budney et al., 2004, p. 1971).

Other studies by Budney and colleagues expanded on the list of symptoms that changed significantly from baseline during withdrawal: "anger and aggression, decreased appetite, irritability, nervousness, restlessness, shakiness, sleep difficulty, stomach pain, strange dreams, sweating, and weight loss" (2003, p. 393; 2004, p. 1972). Although most effects were transient, generally lasting no more than two weeks, "strange dreams and sleep difficulties showed significant elevations throughout the study" (2003, p. 394). Budney et al. conclude that, since most symptoms returned to baseline levels in the former users, "these findings were not rebound effects indicative of symptoms that existed before the use of cannabis" (2004, p. 1972). More recent studies by Haney and others "controlled for potential confounders by using placebo conditions and excluding persons who abused other substances, had an active psychiatric disorder, or were taking psychoactive medication" (Haney et al., 2004, p. 158).

Overall, the research cited above confirms that the most common marijuana withdrawal symptom is low-grade anxiety and dysphoria. Anxiety of this sort has a firm biochemical substrate. A peptide known as corticotrophin-releasing factor (CRF) is primarily responsible. Neurologists at the Scripps Research Institute in La Jolla, California, found that CRF levels in the amygdalas of animals in marijuana withdrawal were as much as three times higher than the levels found in animal control groups (Wickelgren, 1997, p. 1967). Long-term marijuana use alters the function of CRF in the limbic system in a manner similar to other addictive drugs (de Fonseca et al., 1997, p. 2051). (CRF receptors in the amygdala also play a direct role in alcohol withdrawal.)

METHOD

Personal observations and selected case histories of frequent marijuana users were gathered from anonymous, unedited comments posted on a blog site maintained by the author. Punctuation, capitalization, and spelling have been normalized in the excerpts included here. Most of the people who have posted comments thus far (more than 100) arrived at the site by means of the search term *marijuana withdrawal*. This may indicate that a large number of posters are heavy smokers seeking information about abstinence symptoms. The popularity of this search phrase on the Google search engine seems to suggest an interest in, and a need for, scientific information about marijuana withdrawal.

What has surprised many observers is that the idea of treatment for marijuana dependence seems to appeal to such a large and diverse group of people. NIDA has been able to find a cohort of withdrawal-prone smokers with relative ease. According to the principal investigator of one NIDA marijuana study, "We had no difficulty recruiting dozens of people between the ages of 30 and 55 who have smoked marijuana at least 5,000 times. A simple ad in the paper generated hundreds of phone calls from such people" (NIDA, 1999, p. 1). This would be roughly equivalent to 14 years of daily pot smoking.

Comments gathered from anonymous users at an open Web forum created for the discussion of marijuana withdrawal symptoms cannot be controlled for confounding variables such as other addictions or psychological disorders. The comment section of the Web site is open to anyone. What such surveys *can* accomplish, however, is the demonstration of parallels, or lack of them, between findings in an experimental setting and anecdotal reports from the field. Survey studies cannot offer indisputable proof. Nonetheless, when combined with the results of formal clinical studies, such surveys offer a window into real-world experience, thus complementing the growing scientific data concerning marijuana withdrawal syndrome.

The comments were generated in large part by heavy, regular smokers who either recognized or have begun to recognize in themselves an addictive propensity toward marijuana. As a group, they have great difficulty—and suffer similar symptoms—whenever, and for whatever reason, they choose to abstain. Perhaps, most important, the present survey adds to the growing documentation of the contention that withdrawal symptoms are a frequent cause of relapse in marijuana smokers attempting to achieve abstinence.

RESULTS

All of the following comments can be found at the Web log *Addiction Inbox* (http://addiction-dirkh.blogspot.com/2007/10/marijuana-withdrawal. html). The unnumbered messages on the Web site are dated, and appear in chronological order.

1. Cave. (2008, February 8):
   "Well I just stopped smoking pot after 4 years of everyday use, 5 days ago. I am feeling the withdrawal symptoms ridiculously hard. No appetite, slight nausea, extreme insomnia."

2. Anonymous. (2008, February 26):
   "My boyfriend (of 6 years) has been a smoker for approximately 16 years. He has tried to give up a few times seriously before but has never quite gotten there yet. His behavior is almost unbearable when he does. It really takes a toll on our relationship. I never realized that it could be so bad and that his actions are so exaggerated by withdrawal."

3. Anonymous. (2008, February 26):
   "I'm a 30-year-old man and have been a heavy cannabis user (3 to 4 joints per day, every day) since I was 19. . . . I've been through intense anxiety, depression, restlessness, lack of appetite. I can't sleep for more than a few hours at a time and when I do, I sweat buckets. I have a terrible appetite, I'm cold all the time, like I can't regulate my temperature."

4. Anonymous. (2008, February 27):
   "I thought I was going crazy because all other sites told me that there were no withdrawal symptoms from pot, I can't think or eat and when I do finally get something down my gullet I get the runs straight after. . . . I feel like I have been hit by a truck and it has only been a week since I gave up."

5. Anonymous. (2008, March 1):
   "I am 31 and a heavy smoker of 10 years. . . . What is really troubling me, however, is the excessive dreaming. . . . The dreams are vivid and strong, enough to wake me up sometimes."

6. Anonymous. (2008, March 3):
   "This idea of 'intense dreaming' is very real and for the first 5 or 6 days after quitting I experienced life-like dreams/nightmares (99% nightmares), which would wake me from my sleep. . . . This idea of breaking out in cold sweat is also very real and quite scary when [it] occurs as [it] got me worried there was something else wrong with me."

7. Scott. (2008, March 3):
   "I was blown away when I saw 'excessive sweating' as I have been experiencing that for a few days. . . . If I could cut back drastically, that would be the ideal situation. But I know from experience that I can't just smoke pot 'a little bit.' If I'm going to reduce, it's going to have to be all the way to zero."

8. Anonymous. (2008, March 7):
   "I'm on day seven of abstinence and boy, do I feel lousy. Night sweats, anxiety, extreme insomnia, and loads of irritability/anger problems. . . . It's a bit like when you have a bad flu. You plain feel rotten. Anything stress-related is magnified ten-fold."

9. Bob. (2008, March 7):
   "I'm 38 years old and have been using weed now daily for almost 21 years. . . . I've been 'clean' now for 4 days and so far it has obviously been difficult, but already I'm showing signs of improvement, the first two days I had no sleep at all. . . . My withdrawal symptoms: Loss of appetite, sweating, irritability, sudden crying fits."

10. Anonymous. (2008, March 8):
    "I am a 25-year-old female and I have been smoking pot since I was 13. I have never stopped even a day that I can remember. Not unless I couldn't get it. I have recently started to realize that it is a drug addiction. I was always on the 'it's not addictive' side. I get very anxious if I think I'm not going to have any. . . . It is out of my control I think, and now I'm starting to not feel high. I really wanna stop, but am so scared of the symptoms. I think I need help."

11. Anonymous. (2008, March 18):
    "Having read all of these comments and questions I no longer feel so abnormal. I have been experiencing most of these symptoms including vivid dreaming. . . . I have been a smoker since I was 15, every day smoking about 2–3 joints."

12. Anonymous. (2008, March 24):
    "I am a 25-year-old female. I started smoking at 18. . . . I quit a few weeks ago. . . . I can't focus on anything. I can't make myself do anything. . . . I snap at everyone, including my boyfriend who has been complaining about my

excessive sweating. I didn't even think of the sweating as a symptom until I
read the other posts here."

13. Anonymous. (2008, April 2):
"I just wanted to say I'm glad I found this site because as many people have
noted the common wisdom is that there are few, if any, symptoms of withdrawal. . . . I've noticed the irritability and mood swings, which I expected,
but didn't make the connection between the vivid and frequent dreams and
waking at night until I read all the other comments."

14. Anonymous. (2008, April 8):
"I finally feel sane again after reading these postings. I am a 48-year-old
male who has been smoking weed since 1975. Anywhere from 2–6 joints
per day of good quality pot for the last four years. Decided to quit about
a week ago and my life has been a living hell since. . . . Haven't eaten a full
meal in a week, very tired and depressed, stomach in knots."

15. Anonymous. (2008, April 25):
"I quit weed 46 days ago. . . . pretty similar symptoms as everyone else
and the most severe anxiety and depression I have ever known. . . . I can't
concentrate or focus, I can't seem to forget about what has happened even
though I want to, it feels as though my brain keeps reminding me about the
'situation' or some general anxious or negative thought just pops into my
consciousness . . . like it's never going to end, like my thoughts are caught
in a vicious circle."

16. Richard. (2008, May 3):
"It's not suicidal ideation but it's the feeling that life will just never 'be
right'. . . . when you suffer from symptoms that you've been told don't exist,
you are left looking for the wrong cause. So, if you're told that marijuana
withdrawal does not increase anxiety, anger, or 'hopelessness,' you want to
look for a cause of those things. . . . I went through withdrawal periods
where I was inappropriately angry at the wrong thing, thinking that specific
people were upsetting me when they were not."

DISCUSSION

The U.S. government's essentially unchanged opposition to marijuana research has meant that, until quite recently, precious few dollars were available
for research. This official recalcitrance is one of the reasons for the belated recognition and characterization of marijuana's distinct withdrawal syndrome.
According to research undertaken as part of the Collaborative Study of the
Genetics of Alcoholism, 16 percent of people with a lifetime history of regular
marijuana use reported a history of cannabis withdrawal symptoms (Schuckit et
al., 1999). In earlier research, Mason discovered that those seeking treatment for

cannabis addiction tended to cluster in two age groups—college age and mid-50s, as reported by Somers (2008).

Budney et al. (2004, p. 1973) write:

> Regarding cross-study reliability, the most consistently reported symptoms are anxiety, decreased appetite/weight loss, irritability, restlessness, sleep problems, and strange dreams. These symptoms were associated with abstinence in at least 70% of the studies in which they were measured. Other clinically important symptoms such as anger/aggression, physical discomfort (usually stomach related), depressed mood, increased craving for marijuana, and increased sweating and shakiness occurred less consistently.

Today, scientists have a much better picture of the tasks performed by anandamide, the body's own form of THC. Among the endogenous tasks performed by anandamide are pain control, memory blocking, appetite enhancement, the suckling reflex, lowering of blood pressure during shock, and the regulation of certain immune responses. This knowledge helps shed light on the wide range of THC withdrawal symptoms, particularly anxiety, chills, sweats, flu-like physical symptoms, and decreased appetite.

Furthermore, we can look to indications for which marijuana is already being prescribed—anxiety relief, appetite enhancement (compounds similar to anandamide have been discovered in dark chocolate), suppression of nausea, relief from the symptoms of glaucoma, and amelioration of certain kinds of pain—for more insight into the common hallmarks of cannabis withdrawal.

What treatment measures can help ameliorate marijuana withdrawal and craving in heavy users who wish to quit? The immediate threat to any decision in favor of abstinence is what might fairly be called the "hair of the dog" effect. Note the findings of a 2004 paper in *Neuropsychopharmacology*: "Oral THC administered during marijuana abstinence decreased ratings of 'anxious,' 'miserable,' 'trouble sleeping,' 'chills,' and marijuana craving, and reversed large decreases in food intake as compared to placebo, while producing no intoxication" (Haney et al., p. 158).

Moreover, "Overall withdrawal severity associated with cannabis alone and tobacco alone was of a similar magnitude. . . . cannabis withdrawal is clinically important and warrants detailed description in the *DSM–V* and *ICD–11*" (Vandrey, Budney, Hughes, & Liguori, 2008, p. 48). It is possible that many more people are trying—and failing—to quit marijuana than researchers have previously suspected. Daily use of marijuana may be driven in part by the desire to avoid or eliminate abstinence symptoms (Haney, Ward, Comer, Foltin, & Fischman, 1999).

To date, there is no effective anticraving medication approved for use against marijuana withdrawal syndrome. More than a decade ago, Ingrid Wickelgren wrote in *Science:* "For instance, chemicals that block the effects of CRF or even relaxation exercises might ameliorate the miserable moods experienced by people in THC withdrawal. In addition, opiate antagonists like naloxone may, by dampening dopamine release, block the reinforcing properties of marijuana in people" (1997, p. 1967). Since stimulation of THC receptors has homologous effects on the endogenous opioid system, various investigators have speculated that naltrexone, the drug used as an adjunct of heroin withdrawal therapy, may find use against symptoms of marijuana withdrawal in people prone to marijuana dependence (Tanda et al., 1997). Further research is needed on the reciprocal relationship between THC and opioid receptor systems.

Serzone (nefazodone), an antidepressant, has been used to decrease some symptoms of marijuana withdrawal in human subjects who regularly smoked six joints per day (Haney et al., 2003). Anxiety and muscular discomfort were reduced, but Serzone had no effect on other symptoms, such as irritability and sleep problems.

Preliminary studies have found that lithium, used to treat bipolar disorder, curbed marijuana withdrawal symptoms in an animal study (Cui, Gu, Hannesson, Yu, & Zhang, 2001). Another drug for mania and epilepsy—Depakote—did not aid significantly in marijuana withdrawal (Haney et al., 2004).

Since difficulty sleeping is one common symptom of withdrawal, common prescription medications might be indicated for short-term use in the case of severe marijuana withdrawal. Some researchers have reported that even brief interventions, in the form of support group sessions, can be useful for dependent pot smokers (Copeland, Swift, & Rees, 2001).

It is also plausible to suggest that the use of marijuana by abstinent substance abusers may heighten the risk of relapse. In a study of 250 patients at a psychiatric/substance abuse hospital in New York, "Postdischarge cannabis use substantially and significantly increased the hazard of first use of any substance and strongly reduced the likelihood of stable remission from use of any substance" (Aharonovich et al., 2005, p. 1507). However, the researchers found that cannabis posed a greater risk to cocaine and alcohol abusers. For heroin, "cannabis use after inpatient treatment did not significantly affect remission and relapse" (Aharonovich, p. 1507).

It is surprising to note the relative paucity of previous clinical data the researchers had to work with in the case of alcohol and marijuana. "The gap in the literature concerning the relationship of cannabis use to the outcome of alcohol dependence was surprising," according to Aharonovich and colleagues. "We were unable to find a single study that examined the effects of cannabis use on post-treatment outcome for alcohol dependence, despite the fact that the majority of patients now in treatment for alcoholism dependence also abuse other drugs. Clearly additional studies of this issue are warranted" (2005, p. 1512).

Addiction researcher Barbara Mason of the Scripps Research Institute of La Jolla, California, is, at the time of this writing, overseeing a four-year study of the neurobiology of marijuana dependence under a grant from NIDA. The comprehensive project will involve both animal and human research, and will make use of state-of-the-art functional brain imaging. The federal grant will also be used as seed money for the new Translational Center on the Clinical Neurobiology of Cannabis Addiction at the Scripps Institute ("Scripps Given," 2008).

Above all, it is time to move beyond the common mistake of assuming that if marijuana causes withdrawal in some people, then it must cause withdrawal in everybody. And if it doesn't, it cannot be very addictive. This thinking has been overtaken by the growing understanding that a minority of people suffer a chemical propensity for marijuana addiction that puts them at high risk, compared to casual, recreational drug users. The fact that most people do not become addicted to marijuana and do not suffer from withdrawal is no more revealing than the fact that a majority of drinkers do not become alcoholics.

The idea of marijuana addiction and withdrawal remains controversial in both private and professional circles. For an unlucky few, a well-identified set of symptoms characterizes abstinence from heavy, daily use of pot. In this, marijuana addiction and withdrawal does not differ greatly from alcoholism—the vast majority of recreational users and drinkers will never experience it.

For those that do, however, the withdrawal symptoms of marijuana abstinence can severely impact their quality of life.

REFERENCES

Aharonovich, E., Liu, X., Samet, S., Nunes, E., Waxman, R., & Hasin, D. (2005). Post-discharge cannabis use and its relationship to cocaine, alcohol, and heroin use: A prospective study. *American Journal of Psychiatry, 162*(8), 1507–1514.

Budney, A. J., Hughes, J. R., Moore, B. A., & Novy, P. L. (2001). Marijuana abstinence effects in marijuana smokers maintained in their home environment. *Archives of General Psychiatry, 58*(10), 917–924. Retrieved February 27, 2008, from http://archpsyc.ama assn.org/cgi/content/full/58/10/917?ck=nck

Budney, A. J., Hughes, J. R., Moore, B. A., & Vandrey, R. (2004, November). Review of the validity and significance of cannabis withdrawal syndrome. *American Jour-*

nal of Psychiatry, 161, 1967–1977. Retrieved April 21, 2008, from http://ajp.psy chiatryonline.org/cgi/content/full/161/11/1967

Budney, A. J., Moore, B. A., Vandrey, R., & Hughes, J. R. (2003). The time course and significance of cannabis withdrawal. *Journal of Abnormal Psychology, 112*, 393–402.

Budney, A. J., Novy, P. L., & Hughes, J. R. (1999, September 1). Marijuana withdrawal among adults seeking treatment for marijuana dependence. *Addiction, 94*, 1311–1322.

Copeland, J., Swift, W., & Rees, V. (2001, January). Clinical profile of participants in a brief intervention program for cannabis use disorder. *Journal of Substance Abuse Treatment, 20*(1), 45–52. Retrieved April 21, 2008, from http://www.ncbi.nlm. nih.gov/pubmed/11239727

Cui, S. S., Gu, G. B., Hannesson, D. K., Yu, P. H., & Zhang, X. (2001, December 15). Prevention of cannabinoid withdrawal syndrome by lithium: Involvement of oxytocinergic neuronal activation. *Journal of Neuroscience, 21*(24), 9867–9876. Retrieved April 27, 2007, from http://www.jneurosci.org/cgi/content/abstract/21/24/9867

de Fonseca, F. R., Rocío, M., Carrera, A., Navarro, M., Koob, G. F., & Weiss, F. (1997, June 27). Activation of corticotropin-releasing factor in the limbic system during cannabinoid withdrawal. *Science, 276*, 2050–2054.

Fackelmann, K. A. (1993, February 6). Marijuana and the brain: Scientists discover the brain's own THC-delta-9-tetrahydrocannabinol. *Science News.* Retrieved March 28, 2008, from http://findarticles.com/p/articles/mi_m1200/is_n6_v143/ai_13434805/pg_1

Hall, W., Solowij, N., & Lemon, J. (1999). *The health and psychological consequences of cannabis use.* (National Task Force on Cannabis Australia, Monograph Series No. 25). Sydney, NSW: University of New South Wales, National Drug and Alcohol Research Centre. Retrieved February 3, 2008, from http://www.drug library.org/schaffer/hemp/medical/home.htm

Haney, M., Hart, C. L., Vosburg, S. K., Nasser, J., Bennetti, A., Zubaran, C., et al. (2004). Marijuana withdrawal in humans: Effects of oral THC or divalproex. *Neuropsychopharmacology, 29*, 158–170.

Haney, M., Hart, C. L., Ward, A. S., & Foltin, R. W. (2003, January). Nefazodone decreases anxiety during marijuana withdrawal in humans. *Psychopharmacology, 165*(2), 157–165.

Haney, M., Ward, A. S., Comer, S. D., Foltin, R. W., & Fischman, M. W. (1999, February). Abstinence symptoms following smoked marijuana in humans. *Psychopharmacology, 141*(4), 395–404.

Hanson, D. (2007, October 17). *Addiction inbox: Marijuana withdrawal.* Retrieved May 3, 2008, from http://addiction-dirkh.blogspot.com/2007/10/marijuana-withdrawal.html

Jones, R. T., Benowitz, N. L., & Herning, R. I. (1981, August–September). Clinical relevance of cannabis tolerance and dependence. *Journal of Clinical Pharmacology,*

8–9(Suppl.), 143–152. Retrieved April 14, 2008, from http://www.ncbi.nlm.nih.gov/sites/entrez

Joy, J. E., Watson, S. J., & Benson, J. A. (1999). *Marijuana and medicine: Assessing the science base.* Institute of Medicine, Division of Neuroscience and Behavioral Health. Washington, DC: National Academy Press. Retrieved March 5, 2008, from http://www.nap.edu/html/marimed/

Kouri, E. M. (2002, February 1). Does marijuana withdrawal syndrome exist? *Psychiatric Times, 19*(2). Retrieved March 17, 2008, from http://www.psychiatrictimes.com/display/article/10168/54701?pageNumber=3

Kouri, E. M., & Pope, H. G., Jr. (2000, November). Abstinence symptoms during withdrawal from chronic marijuana use. *Experimental and Clinical Psychopharmacology, 8*(4), 483–492. Retrieved March 17, 2008, from http://www.ncbi.nlm.nih.gov/pubmed/

Mason, B. (2008, March 15). Scripps given $4M grant to study effects of marijuana. San Diego, *North County Times,* 1.

National Institute on Drug Abuse. (1999, April 20). *Chronic marijuana users become aggressive during withdrawal.* (NIDA News Release). Rockville, MD: Author. Retrieved April 9, 2008, from http://www.nida.nih.gov/MedAdv/99/NR-420.html

Schuckit, M. A., Daeppen, J.-B., Danko, G. P., Tripp, M. L., Li, T.-K., Hesselbrock, V. M., et. al. (1999). Clinical implications for four drugs of the *DSM–IV* distinction between substance dependence with and without a physiological component. *American Journal of Psychiatry, 156,* 41–49.

"Scripps Given $4M Grant to Study Effects of Marijuana." (2008, March 15). *North County Times,* 1. Retrieved March 16, 2008, from http://www.nctimes.com/articles/2008/03/15/news/sandiego/16_02_343_14_08.txt

Somers, T. (2008, March 14). Study aims to clear haze surrounding pot addiction. *San Diego Union,* 1. Retrieved March 16, 2008, from http://www.signonsandiego.com/news/science/20080314–9999–1n14dope.html

Tanda, G., Pontieri, F. E., & Di Chiara, G. (1997, June 27). Cannabinoid and heroin activation of mesolimbic dopamine transmission by a common m1 opioid receptor mechanism. *Science, 276,* 2048–2050.

U.S. Department of Health and Human Services, Substance Abuse and Mental Health Services Administration. (2006). *Results from the 2006 National Survey on Drug Use and Health: National Findings.* Rockville, MD: Office of Applied Studies. Retrieved March 12, 2008, from http://www.oas.samhsa.gov/NSDUH/2k6NSDUH/2k6results.cfm#Ch2

Vandrey, R. G., Budney, A. J., Hughes, J. R., & Liguori, A. (2008, January 1). A within-subject comparison of withdrawal symptoms during abstinence from cannabis, tobacco, and both substances. *Drug and Alcohol Dependence, 92,* 48–54.

Wickelgren, I. (1997, June 27). Marijuana: Harder than thought? *Science, 76,* 1967–1968.

Wilson, R. I., & Nicoll, R. A. (2001, March 29). Endogenous cannabinoids mediate retrograde signalling at hippocampal synapses. *Nature, 410,* 588–592.

Zickler, P. (2002, October 17). Study demonstrates that marijuana smokers experience significant withdrawal. *NIDA Notes, 17(3)*. Bethesda, MD: National Institutes of Health, National Institute on Drug Abuse. Retrieved March 7, 2008,
from http://www.drugabuse.gov/NIDA_notes/NNVol17N3/Demonstrates.
html.

Chapter 8

Marijuana Interaction with Methamphetamine Addiction

Mary F. Holley, MD

The use of marijuana has long been recognized as an antecedent to the use of so-called hard drugs such as methamphetamine. This gateway hypothesis has been roundly debated for many years and attributed to social factors, "peer pressure," and the availability of other drugs in settings in which marijuana is purchased and used. Twin studies have documented the strength of the association between early marijuana use (prior to age 17) and subsequent drug use. In twins discordant for early marijuana use, the marijuana-using twin was more than four times more likely to use and become dependent on stimulants (Lynskey et al., 2003).

The sheer magnitude of marijuana use among adolescents should give us pause to consider the effects of this psychoactive drug on the future of our children. Nearly half of 12th graders have tried marijuana, and 6 percent admit to daily use (Johnston, O'Malley, Bachman, & Schulenberg, 2005), and these are the kids who stayed in school. The rate of marijuana use among high school dropouts is likely to be even higher. The marijuana they are using is also much more potent than the "Iowa Ditch" that grew on the side of the road outside Des Moines in the late 1960s. Marijuana now is grown in high-tech growing labs, with delta-9-tetrahydrocannabinol (TCH) content as high as 15 percent (McLaren, Swift, Dillon, & Allsop, 2008).

This cannabis use is often occurring in adolescence, a time of significant neurologic maturation in areas of executive function, including decision making and impulse control. While multiple predisposing factors predict later drug use, including parental drug use, child abuse, conduct disorder, and novelty seeking as a personality trait, the use of cannabis in adolescence and early adulthood emerged as the strongest risk factor for later involvement in other illicit drugs (Fergusson, Boden, & Horwood, 2008). Even a small increase in risk of addiction becomes socially significant when 50 percent of high school seniors are trying marijuana.

In addition, marijuana has effects on the brain in many of the same areas that methamphetamine changes, including the hippocampus and many areas of the frontal lobes so that injury to these areas caused by initial use of marijuana may be amplified by subsequent and concurrent use of methamphetamine. While scientists prefer to study isolated drug effects for the intellectual satisfaction of knowing precisely how various systems are affected, human behavior rarely cooperates. We are asked to predict the consequences of drug use based on single drug studies, when single drug use is the exception, rather than the norm.

Medication interactions have often been clinically significant in the context of prescription medications. These interactions are likely to be even more significant in the case of two very popular psychoactive drugs of unknown dose and purity used under conditions of concurrent exposure to alcohol, tobacco, and club drugs in people of variable age and underlying health. This chapter will focus on the interaction between marijuana and methamphetamine on brain function and behavior, with an eye to the development and clinical course of dependence on methamphetamine.

BIOCHEMICAL INTERACTIONS

Recent findings have revealed a vast neurotransmission system dubbed the endocannabinoid system due to its sensitivity to cannabinoid stimulation. The endocannabinoid system has been the subject of vigorous research for many years, not just for its interest as related to a drug of abuse, but also for its importance to understanding neurophysiology in general. The endocannabinoid system is in place not just so that people can get high on pot, but also for numerous neurologic processes of neuromodulation. It influences not only the reward system, but also appetite, learning and memory, and executive functions, including impulse control and decision making. We can expect that use of marijuana, particularly at critical developmental stages, prenatal exposure and adolescent drug use, would exert changes in these functions, perhaps long-lasting changes.

The endocannabinoid system has a complex relationship to the reward system of the brain, changing the sensitivity of the neural structures related to the sensation of pleasure. Interactions between cannabinoid receptors and responsiveness to alcohol (López-Moreno et al., 2008), heroin (Solinas, Yasar,

& Goldberg, 2007), and methamphetamine (Landa, Sulcova, & Slais, 2006) have been delineated, with vast implications for the potential addictiveness of these substances. Since marijuana is often used in the context of concurrent use of other drugs, these interactions must be clearly understood in this time of increasing marijuana use.

Marijuana is also a common drug of abuse in the adolescent age range, from age 10–19, and so its impact on adolescent neurodevelopment must be taken into account as well. Functions such as judgment, impulse control, predicting the future consequences of an action, and delayed gratification, are being established. Such executive functions are processed in the frontal and temporal lobes, in areas that are maturing in adolescence. It is likely the psychoactive drugs have an impact on the maturation of these areas, with profound effects on the mature personality.

IMPACT ON THE REWARD CIRCUIT

Marijuana has, first and foremost, effects on the reward circuit of the brain, resulting in a sensation of euphoria and generalized well-being. Rats treated with a cannabinoid CB1 agonist showed significant increases in dopamine release in the nucleus accumbens as an acute effect (Fadda et al., 2006).

Chronic exposure to TCH has been found to increase the length and number of dendritic branches in the shell of nucleus accumbens and also in the medial prefrontal cortex in rats (Kolb, Gorny, Limebeer, & Parker, 2006). Cannabinoid exposure then seems to increase the sensitivity of the reward circuit to dopamine stimulation at a cellular level. This heightened neural capacity for a dopamine response has its basis in changes in the neuroanatomy of the nucleus accumbens.

Specifically, stimulation of the CB1 cannabinoid receptors primes the reward pathway and sensitizes the system to be more responsive to methamphetamine stimulation (Landa et al., 2006) and to a moderate dose of alcohol (López-Moreno et al., 2008) in a persistent manner. The effect is not just a product of acute intoxication, but is rather a change in the neuroanatomy of the nucleus accumbens. This sensitization could result in a situation in which even low doses of lower-purity methamphetamine would be potently rewarding in individuals who have smoked marijuana prior to, or concurrent with, their first experience with methamphetamine.

This finding alone could help explain the widely differing "addiction rate" among methamphetamine users, depending on the social context of their drug use. Lower addiction rates are often seen in those who use methamphetamine occupationally to enhance their work performance (i.e., military personnel) or medically (i.e., for obesity) versus those using it recreationally (Eliyahu, Berlin, Hadad, Heled, & Moran, 2007). While still experiencing the alertness, endurance, or anorectic aspects of methamphetamine, these individuals may be much less sensitive to the euphoric effects of the drug in the absence of previous or concurrent marijuana use.

EXECUTIVE FUNCTION

Marijuana has also been found to have significant effects on the functioning of the frontal lobe as it relates to executive function, including decision making and impulse control. This is of concern as methamphetamine also directly impacts many of the same areas. The use of marijuana may set the anatomic stage for the behavioral and personality changes, including the occupational failure and interpersonal strife, so often seen in methamphetamine addiction. These effects would likely be exaggerated in the case of adolescent users who are still in the process of maturing these brain structures. The combined forces of marijuana use and methamphetamine's effects could amplify the frontal lobe injury that so often complicates substance abuse treatment.

Impairment of the frontal lobe areas involved with executive function has been well documented in heavy marijuana users. Bolla, Brown, Eldreth, Tate, and Cadet in 2002 correlated marijuana use to poor performance in problem solving, learning, inhibition, and reaction time in heavy users who were abstinent for 28 days. To delineate the neurologic basis for this finding, Bolla then compared abstinent marijuana users with controls under positron emission tomography (PET) scanning (Bolla, Eldreth, Matochik, & Cadet, 2005) and found that the marijuana users showed less activation in the right lateral orbitofrontal cortex (OFC) and the right dorsolateral prefrontal cortex (DLPFC) than the control group on the Iowa Gambling Task. Heavy marijuana users did not perform as well as nonusers on this measurement of executive function and decision-making skills.

More recent use of marijuana has far more significant effects on the functioning of these executive functions. Pillay et al. (2008) demonstrated anterior cingulate and prefrontal dysfunction in marijuana users at 24 hours' abstinence that partially normalized after 28 days, though anterior cingulate function was still significantly impaired at 28 days' abstinence. Exposure to marijuana, even remotely—after 28 days of abstinence—compromises inhibitory control and executive function. The degree of cognitive impairment is even greater in the presence of acute intoxication, which is the more common context of an individual's first use of methamphetamine.

In tests of inhibition processing, fMRI testing was done at 28 days' abstinence during a Stroop task involving inhibition of the dominant process of reading words to instead give the colors of words printed in incongruent ink. The cortical activation pattern of the heavy marijuana users reflected reduced activation of the anterior cingulate and more widespread dorsolateral prefrontal lobe compensatory activity (Eldreth, Matochik, Cadet, & Bolla, 2004; Gruber & Yurgelun-Todd, 2005). Marijuana users are thus more dependent on dorsolateral prefrontal lobe activity to be successful in inhibitory processing.

Methamphetamine use significantly compromises these "back-up" areas and further impairs decision making and impulse control. The anatomic basis for this reduced impulse control is demonstrated by several fMRI studies involving human methamphetamine users attempting inhibitory control tasks under fMRI monitoring. Anterior cingulate and dorsolateral prefrontal cortex activity has been shown to be essential in response inhibition and impulse control (Garavan, Ross, Murphy, Roche, & Stein, 2002). Studies have demonstrated reduced task-related activation of the anterior cingulate gyrus in methamphetamine users (Hwuang et al., 2006). Paulus et al. (2002) studied methamphetamine addicts in early recovery by fMRI as they did a two-choice prediction task and a two-choice response task. They demonstrated less activation of dorsolateral prefrontal cortex and failure to activate ventromedial prefrontal cortex during this decision-making task.

These changes appear to be more than just a pharmacologic effect of methamphetamine. There appears to be some cellular destruction of a more permanent nature going on as well. The massive releases of neurotransmitter caused by methamphetamine use result in high levels of nitrogen and oxygen free radical formation (Acikgov et al., 2000). These free radicals are formed by the metabolism of methamphetamine, and also by the breakdown of the huge amounts of monoamine neurotransmitters that have been released both intra and extra cellularly. These monoamine neurotransmitters must also be broken down, and MAO, the usual enzyme to do that, is inhibited by methamphetamine. Alternative metabolic routes are used, resulting in the generation of large amounts of hydroxyl free radicals nitric oxide and peroxynitrite, which are extremely toxic to brain cells (Jeng, Ramkissoon, Parman, & Wells, 2006).

Free radical compounds denature proteins, damage DNA, and generally wreak havoc in the areas of the brain in which they are concentrated (Cubells, Rayport, Rajendran, & Sulzer, 1994). Because most of the neurotransmitters are released in the midbrain, nucleus accumbens, and striatum, and in the prefrontal cortex, those areas are disproportionately affected by methamphetamine abuse with progressively worsening cognitive and executive function (Li,

Wang, Qiu, & Luo, 2008). Nordahl et al. (2005) did magnetic resonance spectroscopy (MRS) measures of N-acetylaspartate-creatine and phosphocreatine (NAA/Cr), choline-creatine and phosphocreatine (Cho/Cr), and choline-N-acetylaspartate (Cho/NAA) ratios in the anterior cingulate cortex of abstinent meth users and found evidence of cellular compromise that only partially corrected after prolonged periods (years) of abstinence.

These changes have implications for addiction recovery and relapse as function in crucial frontal lobe areas is compromised. Methamphetamine users had significantly impaired inhibitory control on a Stop Signal Test measuring latency to inhibit a motor response (Monterosso, Aron, Cordova, Xu, & London, 2005). Impulsivity is also related to impaired perception of time intervals, with methamphetamine abusers consistently overestimating time intervals and accelerating fingertaps (Wittmann, Leland, Churan, & Paulus, 2007). This "trigger fingered" impaired capacity for inhibitory processing would reduce the ability to resist impulses, delay gratification, and thus, increase the likelihood of relapse. In a landmark study, Paulus, Tapert, and Schuckit (2005) showed that those addicts who eventually relapsed had markedly reduced activation of the dorsolateral prefrontal cortex and anterior cingulate gyrus compared to addicts who did not subsequently relapse. Subjects were followed for up to three years to observe for relapse, and the predictive power of this functional measure of brain activity in these areas was impressive.

MEMORY AND LEARNING

In addition to its direct effects on the reward circuit and executive function, marijuana has significant effects on the hippocampus and various areas of the frontal lobe that could also affect memory and learning, in a way that could increase the likelihood that a person would use and become dependent on methamphetamine, and increase the neurologic impact of his methamphetamine use. A hippocampus, for instance, that is already compromised by marijuana use might be more vulnerable to the neurotoxic effects of methamphetamine.

Long- and short-term heavy cannabis use leads to impaired verbal memory and fluency, attention, and psychomotor speed at 24 hours after last use (in the absence of intoxication), which has implications for occupational performance and driving safety (Messinis, Kyprianidou, Malefaki, & Papathanasopoulos, 2006). Short-term abstinent cannabis users had deficits in verbal fluency, visual recognition, delayed visual recall, and short- and long-interval prospective memory. There were no differences for immediate visual recall (McHale & Hunt, 2008). Recent users also demonstrated abnormal brain activation patterns during a working memory task, with recruitment of additional regions not typically used for this type of working memory (Kanayama, Rogowska, Pope, Gruber, & Yurgelun-Todd, 2004).

Even after 28 days of abstinence, performance was significantly worse in both long- and short-term memory for heavy users. Nestor, Roberts, Garavan, and Hester (2008) demonstrated that cannabis-using adults had significantly lower activity in the superior temporal gyrus, and several areas of the frontal lobe, compared to controls during learning in a name-face task. Results also showed that cannabis-using adults had significantly lower activity in the frontal and temporal lobes, and higher activity in the right parahippocampal gyrus, during learning. These changes indicate functional deficits and compensatory processes in cannabis users.

Heavy use is defined as daily smoking of at least one joint per day, a condition met by about 6 percent of all high school seniors (Johnston et al., 2005). While moderate recreational users of marijuana had normal performance on tests of working memory and selective attention, cannabis users displayed a significant alteration in brain activity in the left superior parietal cortex after 10 days of abstinence (Jager, Kahn, Van Den Brink, Van Ree, & Ramsey, 2006), indicating that even moderate use has an effect on brain function. But again, those same frontal lobe structures compromised by marijuana use may be more susceptible to the more serious neurotoxic effects of methamphetamine when it is used after or concurrent with marijuana.

The toxicity of methamphetamine is profound, and the cognitive changes seen in methamphetamine addicts are far more pronounced than those associated with marijuana. Methamphetamine abusers have cognitive deficits, abnormal metabolic activity, and structural deficits in frontal, temporal, and para hippocampal cortices, and reduced hippocampal volume. The magnitude of disruption in these areas is correlated with cognitive deficits in attention, memory, and executive function in many domains (London et al., 2005; Thompson et al., 2004). Scott et al. (2007) did a meta-analysis of available data on the neuropsychological effects of methamphetamine abuse/dependence. They revealed deficits in episodic memory, executive functions, information-processing speed, motor skills, language, and visuoconstructional abilities in methamphetamine users that were far more prominent and easily measurable than those found in marijuana users. Primate studies of methamphetamine-exposed animals have demonstrated profound impairment in cognitive function, particularly spatial working memory and long-term associative memory that were related to dopamine deficiencies in the prefrontal cortex, cingulate cortex, and striatum (Castner, Volser, & Goldman-Rakic, 2005). These cognitive deficits greatly impair ability to participate in cognitive behavioral therapy as a component of rehabilitation. Memory, attention span, and information processing slowly improve over the course of 12–18 months, requiring prolonged treatment at great cost.

DEVELOPMENTAL CONSIDERATIONS

A large number of the people who are initiating methamphetamine use are in the adolescent age group, with an average age of 19 (Brecht, Greenwell, & Anglin, 2006), and nearly all of them use alcohol, tobacco, and/or marijuana prior to first use of methamphetamine. Adolescents are more likely to smoke or snort meth than to inject it at their first use (Wood et al., 2008) and to do so in the context of marijuana use. Youth and young adults are in a developmental phase in which the rate of maturation and development of the brain is exceeded only by that of infancy and early childhood. In this extremely important developmental window, our teenagers are exposing themselves to neurotoxic drugs that will affect their lives and opportunities significantly.

The vulnerability of the adolescent brain is just beginning to be understood. The endocannabinoid inhibition of synaptic function in the hippocampus was more pronounced in adolescent rats than adults, which may account for the increased sensitivity of adolescent animals to TCH-induced memory impairment (Kang-Park, Wilson, Kuhn, Moore, & Swartzwelder, 2007). Adolescent THC exposure resulted in CB1/G protein uncoupling in the hippocampus that persisted into adulthood (Rubino et al., 2008), suggesting that a cannabinoid-related disconnection can be expressed in adulthood as a developmental deficit. These animal studies support the conclusion that the neurologic changes seen with human marijuana use do not likely precede drug use (as predisposing factors), but are in fact consequences of adolescent marijuana use in normal teens.

Normal adolescent neurodevelopment includes extensive remodeling of the frontal lobes, occurring between the ages of 12 and 21 (Gogtay et al., 2004; Shaw et al., 2008). This process involves myelination of white matter tracts and synaptic pruning in areas of the frontal lobes involved in executive function, including judgment, prediction of future consequences, inhibitory processes, and impulse control. All of these functions are important when resisting peer pressure and controlling alcohol and drug intake.

Tapert et al. (2007) measured brain function by an fMRI technique during a go/no-go task, indicating inhibitory control in adolescent marijuana users compared to controls (controlled for alcohol intake). Marijuana users performed as well as nonusers, but recruited additional cortical areas in the frontal and parietal lobes, in order to perform the task. These changes were noted after 28 days of abstinence and thus reflect a persistent finding. These findings suggest that a key capability of executive function, inhibition of impulses, is impaired not just when an individual is intoxicated, as classical gateway theories have posited, but for weeks afterward, during a developmental period in which forebrain maturation is taking place.

The effects of marijuana on other cognitive functions have also been found to be more significant in adolescents than in adults. Memory and learning are critical functions for academic and occupational success and have been found to be distorted in adolescent marijuana users. Schweinsburg et al. (2008) showed that marijuana-using adolescents, after one month of abstinence, performed normally on a spatial working memory assessment, but had markedly different cortical activation patterns, reflecting different attention mental strategies used to achieve the same end result. In another fMRI study of marijuana-using adolescents studied in a spatial working memory task, users showed changes in recruitment of the anterior cingulate gyrus, temporal cortex, and hippocampal gyrus, again at 28 days' abstinence (Padula, Schweinsburg, & Tapert, 2007).

Not all of the studies have shown equivalent performance for marijuana-using adolescents. Medina and Tapert's group has done extensive research into the state of the hippocampus in adolescents who use marijuana, alcohol, and both, and found significant differences in hippocampal volumes. They also demonstrated, after a month of monitored abstinence, marijuana users had slower psychomotor speed, poorer complex attention, poorer story memory, and reduced planning and sequencing ability, all correlated with lifetime marijuana exposure and controlling for alcohol use (Medina et al., 2007). Smaller hippocampal volumes in the marijuana-using youth were also associated with more depressive symptoms on the Beck Depression Inventory (Medina, Nagel, Park, McQueeny, & Tapert, 2007).

These studies suggest long-lasting changes in the neuroanatomy of important areas in the frontal lobes related to the acquisition of executive functions. If these areas do not mature properly during adolescence, a developmental window of opportunity is missed. We often find in the course of working with addicted young adults that their emotional maturity matches the chronologic age at which they first began abusing substances. One of the challenges of addiction treatment is encouraging our clients to "grow up." Subsequent maturation can and does occur, but with a great deal more effort on the part of both client and therapist than would be the case with normal adolescence. We must seriously consider such neuroanatomic findings before we blithely accept the fact that 50 percent of our young people are using pot.

PRENATAL EXPOSURE TO POT

Our final concern will be with the issue of prenatal exposure to marijuana and its effects on the unborn child. The young adults and adolescents we have been describing are predominantly of childbearing age. In Barcelona, Spain, 5.3 percent of newborns had a meconium screen positive for marijuana exposure, while only 1.7 percent of mothers admitted to using it during pregnancy (Lozano et al., 2007). In the United States, 6 percent of newborns in four major cities were positive for marijuana in 2003, an increase from 3 percent in 1993 (Derauf et al., 2007).

Parental substance abuse is a well-known risk factor for the development of substance abuse in children. Children witnessing the substance abuse of a parent are much more likely to view substance abuse as normal and acceptable behavior. They are also likely to have experienced numerous adverse childhood events, including abuse and neglect, which also predispose to addiction as they grow older (Dube et al., 2003).

But there is a little more to it than that. Prenatal exposure to marijuana predicted early use of marijuana by offspring by the age of 14, even after controlling for the child's current alcohol and tobacco use, pubertal stage, sexual activity, delinquency, peer drug use, family history of drug abuse, and characteristics of the home environment, including parental depression, current drug use, and strictness/supervision (Day, Goldschmidt, & Thomas, 2006). Prenatal exposure to marijuana produces changes in the neurologic make-up of the child that independently predispose to later substance abuse.

The endocannabinoid system is key to the early development of the central nervous system, serving as a traffic cop, directing the proliferation, migration, differentiation, and synapse formation of functional neural circuits throughout the developing brain (Harkany et al., 2007). Rats exposed to THC prenatally had increased anxiety scores measure by peeps when removed from the nest, inhibited juvenile social interaction, and play among adolescents, extending into adulthood with impaired elevated maze performance (Trezza et al., 2008). Emotional development has been found to be impaired in humans also. Prenatal marijuana exposure in the first and third trimesters predicted significantly increased levels of depressive symptoms in 10-year-old children (Gray, Day, Leech, & Richardson, 2005).

Prenatal marijuana exposure is also associated with cognitive deficits in children as measured by the Stanford-Binet verbal reasoning and short-term memory scales at ages three, four, and six (Day, Richardson, Goldschmidt, Robles, & Taylor, 1994; Fried & Watkinson, 1990; Goldschmidt, Richardson, Willford, & Day, 2008). Childhood cognitive deficits and learning disabilities represent a nonenvironmental risk factor for subsequent substance abuse. More significantly, prenatal marijuana exposure is associated with impaired executive function and impulse control at age 9–12 (Fried, Watkinson, & Gray, 1998), with poorer Wide Range Achievement Test-Revised (WRAT-R) reading comprehension and spelling scores at age 10 (Goldschmidt, Richardson, Cornelius, & Day, 2004), and with impaired higher-order mental function, analysis, and integration at age 13–16 (Fried, Watkinson, & Gray, 2003). These deficits are strong predisposing factors placing children at risk for substance abuse in those vulnerable adolescent years, even if their role models are drug free (Karacostas & Fisher, 1993).

CONCLUSION

Marijuana use is a common antecedent to methamphetamine use, and both drugs affect similar structures in the brain. While methamphetamine is by far the more toxic of the two, causing significant functional disability that may take months or even years of therapy to reverse, marijuana may contribute more to this injury than has been previously acknowledged. Marijuana sensitizes the reward circuit to respond to methamphetamine more robustly, and predisposes to addiction to methamphetamine. Marijuana also appears to aggravate the injury to cognitive structures by impairing the function of the key areas involved in memory and higher-order thinking capacity. These effects are magnified even further when drug use occurs in adolescence, as the brain is going through a major remodeling in preparation for adulthood. When key maturation events fail to occur, there may not be an opportunity for a redo.

Clearly, the scientific findings related to marijuana need to be evaluated whenever the legalization of this drug is considered. The long-term implications of the widespread use of any psychoactive drug should be carefully thought out. If alcohol were up for evaluation by the FDA as a potential addition—and danger—to our society, the data would probably argue for its exclusion. Alcohol causes untold social harm and personal tragedy. Do we really need another intoxicant in our already overly intoxicated society?

REFERENCES

Acikgov, O., Gapnenas, S., Kayatekin, B. M., Pekasetin, C., Uysal, N., Dayi, A., et al. (2000). The effects of a single dose of methamphetamine on lipid peroxidation levels in the rat striatum and prefrontal cortex. *European Neuropsychopharmacology*, *10*(5), 415–418.

Bolla, K. I., Brown, K., Eldreth, D., Tate, K., & Cadet, J. L. (2002). Dose-related neurocognitive effects of marijuana use. *Neurology*, *59*(9), 1337–1343.

Bolla, K. I., Eldreth, D. A., Matochik, J. A., & Cadet, J. L. (2005). Neural substrates of faulty decision making in abstinent marijuana users. *Neuroimage*, *26*(2), 480–492.

Brecht, M. L., Greenwell, L., & Anglin, M. D. (2006). Substance use pathways to methamphetamine use among treated users. *Addictive Behaviors, 32*(1), 24–38.

Castner, S. A., Volser, P. S., & Goldman-Rakic, P. S. (2005). Amphetamine sensitization impairs cognition and reduces dopamine turnover in primate prefrontal cortex. *Biologic Psychiatry, 57,* 743–751.

Cubells, J. F., Rayport, S., Rajendran, G., & Sulzer, D. (1994). Methamphetamine neurotoxicity involves vacuolization of endocytic organelles and dopamine dependent intracellular oxidative stress. *Journal of Neuroscience, 14*(4), 2260–2271.

Day, N. L., Goldschmidt, L., & Thomas, C. A. (2006). Prenatal marijuana exposure contributes to the prediction of marijuana use at age 14. *Addiction, 101*(9), 1313–1322.

Day, N. L., Richardson, G. A., Goldschmidt, L., Robles, N., & Taylor, P. M. (1994). Effect of prenatal marijuana exposure on the cognitive development of offspring at age three. *Neurotoxicologic Teratology, 16*(2), 169–175.

Derauf, C., LaGasse, L. L., Smith, L. M., Grant, P., Shah, R., Arria, A., et al. (2007). Demographic and psychosocial characteristics of mothers using methamphetamine during pregnancy: Preliminary results of the infant development, environment, and lifestyle study (IDEAL). *American Journal of Drug and Alcohol Abuse, 33,* 281–289.

Dube, S. R., Felitti, V. J., Dong, M., Chapman, D. P., Giles, W. H., & Anda, R. F. (2003). Childhood abuse, neglect, and household dysfunction and the risk of illicit drug use: The adverse childhood experiences study. *Pediatrics, 111*(3), 564–572.

Eldrith, D. A., Matochik, J. A., Cadet, J. L., & Bolla K. L. (2004). Abnormal brain activity in prefrontal brain regions in abstinent marijuana users. *Neuroimage, 23,* 914–920.

Eliyahu, U., Berlin, S., Hadad, E., Heled, Y., & Moran, D. S. (2007). Psychostimulants and military operations. *Military Medicine, 172*(4), 383–387.

Fadda, P., Scherma, M., Spano, M. S., Salis, P., Melis, V., & Fattore, L. (2006). Cannabinoid self-administration increases dopamine release in the nucleus accumbens. *Neuroreporter, 17*(15), 1629–1632.

Fergusson, D. M., Boden, J. M., & Horwood, L. J. (2008). The developmental antecedents of illicit drug use: Evidence from a 25-year longitudinal study. *Drug and Alcohol Dependence, 96*(1–2), 165–177.

Fried, P. A., & Watkinson, B. (1990). 36- and 48-month neurobehavioral follow-up of children prenatally exposed to marijuana, cigarettes, and alcohol. *Journal of Developmental and Behavioral Pediatrics, 11*(2), 49–58.

Fried, P. A., Watkinson, B., & Gray, R. (1998). Differential effects on cognitive functioning in 9- to 12-year-olds prenatally exposed to cigarettes and marihuana. *Neurotoxicoogicl Teratology, 20*(3), 293–306.

Fried, P. A., Watkinson, B., & Gray, R. (2003). Differential effects on cognitive functioning in 13- to 16-year-olds prenatally exposed to cigarettes and marihuana. *Neurotoxicologic Teratology, 25*(4), 427–436.

Garavan, H., Ross, T. J., Murphy, K., Roche, R. A., & Stein, E. A. (2002). Dissociable executive function in the dynamic control of behavior: Inhibition, error detection, and correction. *Neuroimage, 27,* 1820–1829.

Gogtay, N., Giedd, J. N., Lusk, L., Hayashi, K. M., Greenstein, D., Vaituzis, A. C., et al. (2004). Dynamic mapping of human cortical development during childhood through early adulthood. *Proceedings of the National Academy of Science U S A, 101*(21), 8174–8179.

Goldschmidt, L., Richardson, G. A., Cornelius, M. D., & Day, N. L. (2004). Prenatal marijuana and alcohol exposure and academic achievement at age 10. *Neurotoxicologic Teratology, 26*(4), 521–532.

Goldschmidt, L., Richardson, G. A., Willford, J., & Day, N. L. (2008). Prenatal marijuana exposure and intelligence test performance at age 6. *Journal American Academy of Child and Adolescent Psychiatry, 47*(3), 254–263.

Gray, K. A., Day, N. L., Leech, S., & Richardson, G. A. (2005). Prenatal marijuana exposure: Effect on child depressive symptoms at ten years of age. *Neurotoxicologic Teratology, 27*(3), 439–448.

Gruber, S. A., & Yurgelun-Todd, D. A. (2005). Neuroimaging of marijuana smokers during inhibitory processing: A pilot investigation. *Brain Research: Cognitive Brain Research, 23*(1), 107–118.

Harkany, T., Guzmán, M., Galve-Roperh, I., Berghuis, P., Devi, L. A., & Mackie, K. (2007). The emerging functions of endocannabinoid signaling during CNS development. *Trends in Pharmacologic Science, 28*(2), 83–92.

Hwang, J., Lyoo, I. K., Kim, S. J., Sung, Y. H., Bae, S., Cho, S. N., et al. (2006). Decreased cerebral blood flow of the right anterior cingulate cortex in long term and short term abstinent methamphetamine users. *Drug and Alcohol Dependence, 28,* 177–181.

Jager, G., Kahn, R. S., Van Den Brink, W., Van Ree, J. M., & Ramsey, N. F. (2006). Long-term effects of frequent cannabis use on working memory and attention: An fMRI study. *Psychopharmacology (Berlin), 185*(3), 358–368.

Jeng, W., Ramkissoon, A., Parman, T., & Wells, P. G. (2006). Prostaglandin H synthase catalysed bioactivation of amphetamine to free radical intermediates that cause CNS regional DNA oxidation and nerve terminal degeneration. *Federation of American Societies for Experimental Biology Journal, 20,* 638–650.

Johnston, L. D., O'Malley, P. M., Bachman, J. G., & Schulenberg, J. E. (2005). *Monitoring the future national results on adolescent drug use 1975–2004: Vol 1. Secondary school students* (NIH Publication No. 05–5727). Bethesda, MD: National Institute on Drug Abuse.

Kanayama, G., Rogowska, J., Pope, H. G., Gruber, S. A., & Yurgelun-Todd, D. A. (2004). Spatial working memory in heavy cannabis users: A functional magnetic resonance imaging study. *Psychopharmacology (Berlin), 176*(3–4), 239–247.

Kang-Park, M. H., Wilson, W. A., Kuhn, C. M., Moore, S. D., & Swartzwelder, H. S. (2007). Differential sensitivity of GABA A receptor-mediated IPSCs to cannabinoids in hippocampal slices from adolescent and adult rats. *Journal of Neurophysiology, 98*(3), 1223–1230.

Karacostas, D. D., & Fisher, G. L. (1993). Chemical dependency in students with and without learning disabilities. *Journal of Learning Disabilities, 26*(7), 491–495.

Kolb, B., Gorny, G., Limebeer, C. L., & Parker, L. A. (2006). Chronic treatment with Delta 9 tetrahydrocannabinol alters the structure of neurons in the nucleus accumbens shell and medial prefrontal cortex of rats. *Synapse, 60*(6), 429–436.

Landa, L., Sulcova, A., & Slais, K. (2006). Involvement of cannabinoid CB1 and CB2 receptor activity in the development of behavioral sensitization to methamphetamine effects in rats. *Neuro Endocrinology Letters, 27*(1–2), 63–69.

Li, X., Wang, H., Qiu, P., & Luo, H. (2008). Proteomic profiling of proteins associated with methamphetamine-induced neurotoxicity in different regions of rat brain. *Neurochemistry International, 52,* 256–264.

London, E. D., Berman, S. M., Voytek, B., Simon, S. L., Mandelkern, M. A., Monterosso, J., et al. (2005). Cerebral metabolic dysfunction and impaired vigilance in recently abstinent methamphetamine abusers. *Biological Psychiatry, 58*(10), 770–778.

López-Moreno, J. A., Scherma, M., Rodríguez de Fonseca, F., González-Cuevas, G., Fratta, W., & Navarro, M. (2008). Changed accumbal responsiveness to alcohol in rats pre-treated with nicotine or the cannabinoid receptor agonist WIN 55,212–2. *Neuroscience Letters, 433*(1), 1–5.

Lozano, J., García-Algar, O., Marchei, E., Vall, O., Monleon, T., Giovannandrea, R. D., et al. (2007). Prevalence of gestational exposure to cannabis in a Mediterranean city by meconium analysis. *Acta Paediatrica, 96*(12), 1734–1737.

Lynskey, M. T., Heath, A. C., Bucholz, K. K., Slutske, W. S., Madden, P. A., Nelson, E. C., et al. (2003). Escalation of drug use in early onset cannabis users vs co-twin controls. *Journal of the American Medical Association, 289,* 427–433.

McHale, S., & Hunt, N. (2008). Executive function deficits in short-term abstinent cannabis users. *Human Psychopharmacology, 23*(5), 409–415.

McLaren, J., Swift, W., Dillon, P., & Allsop, S. (2008). Cannabis potency and contamination: A review of the literature. *Addiction, 103*(7), 1100–1109.

Medina, K. L., Hanson, K. L., Schweinsburg, A. D., Cohen-Zion, M., Nagel, B. J., & Tapert, S. F. (2007). Neuropsychological functioning in adolescent marijuana users: Subtle deficits detectable after a month of abstinence. *Journal of the International Neuropsychological Society, 13*(5), 807–820.

Medina, K. L., Nagel, B. J., Park, A., McQueeny, T., & Tapert, S. F. (2007). Depressive symptoms in adolescents: Associations with white matter volume and marijuana use. *Journal of Child Psychology and Psychiatry, 48*(6), 592–600.

Messinis, L., Kyprianidou, A., Malefaki, S., & Papathanasopoulos, P. (2006). Neuropsychological deficits in long-term frequent cannabis users. *Neurology, 66*(5), 737–739.

Monterosso, J. R., Aron, A. R., Cordova, X., Xu, J., & London, E. D. (2005). Deficits in response inhibition associated with chronic methamphetamine abuse. *Drug and Alcohol Dependence, 79*(2), 273–277.

Nestor, L., Roberts, G., Garavan, H., & Hester, R. (2008). Deficits in learning and memory: Parahippocampal hyperactivity and frontocortical hypoactivity in cannabis users. *Neuroimage, 40*(3), 1328–1339.

Nordahl, T. E., Salo, R., Natsuaki, Y., Galloway, G. P., Waters, C., Moore, C. D., et al. (2005). Methamphetamine users in sustained abstinence: A proton magnetic resonance spectroscopy study. *Archives of General Psychiatry, 62*(4), 444–452.

Padula, C. B., Schweinsburg, A. D., & Tapert, S. F. (2007). Spatial working memory performance and fMRI activation interaction in abstinent adolescent marijuana users. *Psychology of Addictive Behaviors, 21*(4), 478–487.

Paulus, M. P., Hozack, N. E., Zauscher, B. E., Frank, L., Brown, G. G., Braff, D. L., et al. (2002). Behavioral and functional neuroimaging evidence for prefrontal dysfunction in methamphetamine dependent subjects. *Neuropsychopharmacology, 26*, 53–63.

Paulus, M. P., Tapert, S., & Schuckit, M. A. (2005) Neural activation patterns of methamphetamine dependent subjects during decision making predict relapse. *Archives of General Psychiatry, 62*, 761–768.

Pillay, S. S., Rogowska, J., Kanayama, G., Gruber, S., Simpson, N., Pope, H.G., Yurgelun-Todd, D. A. (2008). Cannabis and motor function: fMRI changes following 28 days of discontinuation. *Experimental and Clinical Psychopharmacology, 16*, 22–32.

Rubino, T., Vigano, D., Realini, N., Guidali, C., Braida, D., Capurro, V., et al. (2008). Chronic delta(9)-tetrahydrocannabinol during adolescence provokes sex-dependent changes in the emotional profile in adult rats: Behavioral and biochemical correlates. *Neuropsychopharmacology, 33*(11), 2760–2771.

Schweinsburg, A. D., Nagel, B. J., Schweinsburg, B. C., Park, A., Theilmann, R. J., & Tapert, S. F. (2008). Abstinent adolescent marijuana users show altered fMRI response during spatial working memory. *Psychiatry Research, 163*(1), 40–51.

Scott, J. C., Woods, S. P., Matt, G. E., Meyer, R. A., Heaton, R. K., et al. (2007). Neurocognitive effects of methamphetamine: A critical review and meta-analysis. *Neuropsychological Review, 17*(3), 275–297.

Shaw, P., Kabani, N. J., Lerch, J. P., Eckstrand, K., Lenroot, R., Gogtay, N., et al. (2008). Neurodevelopmental trajectories of the human cerebral cortex. *Journal of Neuroscience, 28*(14), 3586–3594.

Solinas, M., Yasar, S., & Goldberg, S. R. (2007). Endocannabinoid system involvement in brain reward processes related to drug abuse. *Pharmacologic Research, 56*(5), 393–405.

Tapert, S. F., Schweinsburg, A. D., Drummond, S. A., Martin, P., Paulus, M. P., Brown, S. A., et al. (2007). Functional MRI of inhibitory processing in abstinent adolescent marijuana users. *Psychopharmacology, 194*(2), 173–183.

Thompson, P. M., Hayashi, K. M., Simon, S. L., Geaga, J. A., Hong, M. S., Sui, Y., et al. (2004). Structural abnormalities in the brains of human subjects who use methamphetamine. *Journal of Neuroscience, 24*, 6028–6036.

Trezza, V., Campolongo, P., Cassano, T., Macheda, T., Dipasquale, P., Carrata, M. R., et al. (2008). Effects of perinatal exposure to delta-9-tetrahydrocannabinol on the emotional reactivity of the offspring: A longitudinal behavioral study in Wistar rats. *Psychopharmacology (Berlin), 198*(4), 529–537.

Wittmann, M., Leland, D. S., Churan, J., & Paulus, M. P. (2007). Impaired time perception and motor timing in stimulant-dependent subjects. *Drug and Alcohol
Dependence, 90*(2–3), 183–192.

Wood, E., Stoltz, J. A., Zhang, R., Strathdee, S. A., Montaner, J. S., & Kerr, T. (2008).
Circumstances of first crystal methamphetamine use and initiation of injection
drug use among high-risk youth. *Drug and Alcohol Review, 27*(3), 270–276.

Chapter 9

What Is Methamphetamine and How and Why Is It Used?¹

Herbert C. Covey, PhD

WHAT IS METHAMPHETAMINE?

Methamphetamine, also known as *speed, crystal, ice, crank*, or *chalk*, is a power-fully addictive stimulant that chemically affects the central nervous system by producing intoxication through the increased stimulation of the dopamine and norepinephrine receptors in the brain. Dopamine is associated with pain sup-pression, appetite control, and the brain's self-reward center. Norepinephrine activates the body's fight-or-flight response in emergencies. Meth acts on the brain reward pathway by increasing the release of the neurotransmitters nora-drenaline, dopamine, and serotonin and reducing the reuptake of dopamine. These neurotransmitters carry messages from one nerve to another and are critical to the individual's sense of pleasure. Meth provides the user, at least initially, with a tremendous sense of pleasure.

Meth is a synthetic stimulant commonly used as a recreational drug. Physicians legally prescribe the drug as a treatment for attention deficit dis-order (ADD) under the brand name Desoxyn, for both children and adults. The illegal form of the drug is made easily in clandestine labs with over-the-counter ingredients. For addicts, it is relatively inexpensive to purchase and has desired effects that last for hours. Some users find it appealing because it causes decreased appetite (resulting in weight loss), heightens energy levels, enhances attention, enables people to be physically (sexually) active for long periods, and provides a general sense of well-being and euphoria similar to that of cocaine. The desired effects of meth use can last between six and eight hours, which are then followed by a coming-down period when the user becomes agitated and potentially violent. It is particularly addictive for females because of the "benefit" of its corresponding weight loss.

Meth is a Schedule II stimulant in the United States, meaning that it is illegal to buy, sell, or possess without a prescription. Outside of the United States, it is legally controlled in most countries and is only available by prescription. The federal government classifies methamphetamine as a controlled substance. The 1970 Controlled Substances Act placed strict limitations on the importing, manufacture, and retail availability of amphetamine-related drugs. The 2000 Methamphetamine Anti-Proliferation Act applied further limits on the sale of precursor ingredients used in other products.

Criminal sentencing for crystal meth is determined by U.S. sentencing guidelines, which are based on the statutory sentences, including quantity-based mandatory minimum sentences, in the Controlled Substances Act. For meth, the statute and guidelines both set forth alternative formulations for determining quantity-based sentences, because "actual" or "pure" meth is distinguished from "a mixture or substance containing" meth. Under federal law, meth trafficking carries a minimum of five years in prison and fines of $2 million for individuals or $4 million for more than one individual for first offenses involving 50 grams or less. Life imprisonment is the maximum penalty for trafficking with two or more prior offenses. U.S. sentencing guidelines should be consulted for specific penalties for trafficking, purity, quantity, forms, and other legal considerations. Unprescribed meth is illegal in every state.

HISTORY OF METHAMPHETAMINE AND ITS USE

Closely related to meth is the drug amphetamine. Amphetamine was first synthesized in 1887 in Germany by a scientist named L. Edeleano, who named it phenylisopropylamine. Initially, amphetamine had no known medical application. During the 1920s, researchers investigated it as a treatment for depression, as a decongestant, and for other medical purposes. By the 1930s, retailers marketed amphetamine as Benzedrine, which was an over-the-counter inhaler used to treat nasal congestion. By the late 1930s, physicians prescribed amphetamine for narcolepsy, attention-deficit/hyperactivity disorder, and depression. During WWII, military organizations used amphetamines (and methamphetamine) to keep soldiers ready and available for duty. As use of amphetamines spread, so did their abuse. To some, amphetamines became a cure-all for such things as weight control and treating mild depression.

In 1919, a Japanese chemist named A. Ogata produced the first meth. In contrast to amphetamine, meth is more powerful and easier to manufacture. Meth's progenitor is ephedrine, which is naturally found in Mahuang, a Chinese plant whose stimulant properties have been documented for over 5,100 years (Holthouse & Rubin, 1997a, 1997b). During WWII, the Japanese military used meth to improve military performance. It was also sold over the counter in Japan to increase work performance and endurance during the war (Anglin, Burke, Perrochet, Stamper, & Dawud-Noursi, 2000). Following the war, its use, including intravenously, became epidemic in Japan, as supplies were readily available (Wermuth, 2000). It has been suggested that Adolf Hitler may have been a heavy user.

Following the war, Dexedrine (dextroamphetamine) and Methedrine became readily available in the United States. College students, truck drivers, motorcycle gangs, and athletes used the drug to stay awake and to improve concentration and performance.

In the mid-1960s, people were using meth in San Francisco and parts of the West Coast. In 1967, the first meth lab bust occurred in Santa Cruz, California (Holthouse & Rubin, 1997b). By 1970, use of the drug declined following the 1970 Controlled Substances Act, which restricted the production of injectable meth (Wermuth, 2000). However, meth made inroads in the gay community by the late 1970s (Bonné, 2004) and spread in popularity in California during the late 1980s (Leinwand, 2003). Hawaii, California, and Arizona were some of the earliest and hardest impacted states. California was hit particularly hard because of the smuggling of ephedrine, a critical ingredient in the production of meth, across the Mexican border. With tighter federal controls over ephedrine, pseudoephedrine became a replacement ingredient. In 1996, Congress passed the Methamphetamine Control Act of 1996. This Act doubled the maximum penalties for possession of the drug and increased the penalty for the possession of equipment used to manufacture meth from 4 to 10 years. The Act cracked down on large purchases of the ingredients, such as red phosphorous and iodine, and increased civil penalties for companies that sell precursor chemicals to people that manufacture meth. It did not, however, stop the flow of ephedrine into the United States.

By the 1990s, some young adults found methamphetamine to be a popular alternative to cocaine and heroin. White motorcycle gangs controlled production and distribution of meth before the 1990s (Gibson, Leamon, & Flynn, 2002). Small home labs and Mexican-based criminal organizations eventually took over production and distribution of meth. Mexican-based criminal organizations established "superlabs" in California and Mexico that were capable of producing large amounts of highly pure meth. In congressional testimony to the Senate Judiciary Committee, authority Donnie R. Marshall reported that about 85 percent of all methamphetamine used in the United States in 2000 was produced by these superlabs (Marshall, 2000). During the 1990s and up to the present day, another shift occurred as cooks started to produce meth in small, home-based clandestine labs.

The meth on the streets today is often more powerful than that available in earlier years. Today, meth cooks have refined recipes to the point that some batches have as much as six times the potency of meth cooked in the 1960s (Mills, 1999). This meth is not always sold on the street, but rather cooks circulate (give or sell) it among friends and acquaintances.

Today, meth is a Schedule II drug that is available only through a highly restricted prescription procedure. Physicians have used meth to treat overeating disorders, depression, Parkinson's disease, obesity, attention deficit disorder, and narcolepsy.

STREET AND SLANG TERMS FOR METHAMPHETAMINE

Users and others have developed a set of terms for meth and its related behaviors similar to those used with other street drugs. These terms can be divided into street terms for the drug itself, the behaviors associated with its use, and the types of users. The terms in Table 9.1 are an extensive compilation of words used to refer to meth (Mills, 1999; Office of National Drug Control Policy, 2003), with the most commonly used terms boldfaced.

STREET AND SLANG TERMS FOR METHAMPHETAMINE ADDICTS

Just as there are different terms for meth, there are terms for its addicts. Many street terms have evolved to describe or refer to meth addicts: Basehead, Battery Bender, Cluckers, Chicken-Headed Clucks, Crack Heads, Crackies, Crankster, Cranker, Doorknobbers, Fienda, Fiends, Fiendz, Gacked, Geek(ers), Geekin, Geeter, Go Go Loser, Jibby, Jibby Bear, Jibbhead, Krista, Loker or Lokers, Neck Creature, Shadow People (due to an aversion of users to light), Sketchpad or Schetchers, Skitzers, Sketch Cookie, Sketch Monster, Speed Freak, Spin Doctor, Spinsters, Tweakers, Tweekin/the Go, or Wiggers.

STREET AND SLANG TERMS FOR BEHAVIORS/FEELINGS

Meth addicts have developed a number of terms they use to describe their state of mind when using meth: Ampin, Amped, Awake, Bache Knock 2 Rock, Bachin, "Bob" (as in discombobulated), Buzzed, Cranked Up, Crank

Table 9.1
Slang Terms for Methamphetamine

Albino Poo, Alffy, All Weekend Long, All Tweakend Long, **Amp**, Anny, Anything Going On, Bache Knock, Bache Rock, Bag Chasers, Baggers, Barney Dope, Batak (Philippine), Bato (Philippine), Batu Kilat (Philippine), Batu or Batunas (Hawaii), Batuwhore, Beegokes, Bianca, Bikerdope, Bikers Coffee, Billy (Great Britain) Bitch, Biznack, Blanco, Blizzard, Blue Acid, Blue Belly, Blue Funk, Blue Meth, Bomb, Booger, Boorit-Cebuano (Filipino), Boo-Yah, Brian Ed, Buff Stick, Buggar Sugar, Buggs, Bumps, Buzzard Dust, Caca, Candy, Cankinstien, CC, Chach, Cha Cha Cha, Chalk, Chalk Dust, Chank, Cheebah, Cheese, Chicken Feed, Chicken Flippin, Chikin or Chicken, Chicken Feed, Chingadera, Chittle, Chizel, Chiznad, Choad, Cinnamon, Clavo, Coco, Coffee, Cookies, Crack Whore, **Crank**, Cri Cri (Mexican border), Criddler, Cringe, Crink, Critty, Cristy, Crizzy, Croch Dope, CR (California), Crow, Crunk, Crypto, **Crystal**, **Crystal Meth**, Crystalight, Cube, Debbie, Tina, and Crissy, Desocsins, Devil Dust, Devil's Dandruff, Devil's Drug, Dingles, Dirt, Dirty, Dizzy D, D-monic or D, Do Da, Doody, Doo-My-Lau, Dope, Drano, Dummy Dust, Dyno, Epimethrine, Epod, Ersar Dust, Ethyl-M, Evil Yellow, Fatch, Fedrin, Fil-Layed, Fizz Whizz, Gackle-a Fackle-a, Gak, Gas, Geep, Gemni, Glass, Go Speed, Glass, Go Fast, Go-ey, Go-Go, Go-Go Juice, Gonzales, Goop, Got Anything, Granulated Orange, Grit, Gumption, Gyp, Hawaiian Salt, Hank, Hanyak, High Speed Chicken Feed, Highten, Hillbilly Crack, Hippy Crack, Homework, Hoo, Horse Mumpy, Hot Ice, Hydro, Hypes, **Ice**, Ice Cream, Icee, Ish, Izice, Jab, Jasmine, Jenny Crank Program, Jet Fuel, Jib, Jib Nugget, Jinga, Juddha, Juice, Junk, Kaksonjac, Kibble, Killer, KooLAID, Kryptonite, L.A., L.A. Glass, Lamer, Laundry Detergent, Lemon Drop, Life, Lily, Linda, Lost Weekend, Love, Low, Lucille, M Man, Magic, **Meth**, Meth Monsters, Methaine, Methandfriend, Methandfriendsofmine, Methanfelony, Methatrim, methmood, Method, Motivation (Colorado), Nazi Dope, Ned, Newday, No Doze, Nose Candy, On a Good One, OZs, Patsie, Peaking, Peanut Butter, Peel Dope, Pepsi (means meth), Pepsi One (Crystal meth), Phazers, Phets, Philopon (East Asia), Pieta, Pink, Poison, Poop, Poo'd Out, Poor Man's Cocaine, Pootanany, Powder, Power Monkeys, Powder Point, Project Propellant, Puddle, Pump, Q'd , Quartz, Quick (Canada), Quill, Racket jaw, Rails, Rank, Redneck Heroin, Richie Rich, Rip, Rock, Rocket Fuel, Rocky Mountain High, Rosebud, Rudy's Rumdumb, Running Pizo, Sack, Sam's Sniff, Sarahs, Satan Dust, Scante, Scap, Schlep Rock, Scooby Snax, Scud, Scwadge, Shab, Shabu, Sha-bang, Shabs, Shabu, **Shards**, Shit, Shiznack, Shiznac, Sciznac, Shiznastica, Shiznit, Shiznitty, Shizzo, Shnizzie Snort, Agua, Shwack, Skeech, Sketch, Ski, Skitz, Sky Rocks, Sliggers, Smiley Smile, Smurf Dope, Smzl, Snaps, Sniff, Snow (Colorado), space Food, Spaceman, Spagack, Sparacked, Sparked, Sparkle, Speed, Speed Racer, Spin Spin Spin, Spinack, Spindarella, Spinney Boo, Spinning Spishak Spook, Spoosh, Sprack, Sprizzlefracked, Sprung (Mississippi), Spun Ducky Woo, Squawk, Stallar, Sto-pid, Stove Top, Styels, Sugar, Super Ice, Sweetness, Swerve, Syabu (Asia), Talkie, Tasmanian Devil, Tenna, Tenner, The New Prozac, The White House, Tick Tick, Tical, Tina, Tish, Tobats, Toots, Torqued, Trash, Trippin Trip, Tubbytoast, Tutu (Hawaii), Twack, Twacked Out, Tweak, Tweedle Doo, Tweek, Tweezwasabi, Twiz, Twizacked, 222 (Chicago Area) Ugly Dust, Vanilla Pheromones, Wake, Way, Wash, WE WE We, Whacked, White Bitch, White Cross (after pill form), White Crunk, White Ink, White Junk, White Lady, White Pony, White, Who-Ha, Wigg, **Working Man's Cocaine**, Xaing, Yaba, Yama, Yammer Bammer, Yank, Yankee, Yay, Yead Out, Yellow Barn, Yellow Powder, Zingin, Zip, Zoiks, and Zoom.

It should be noted that some of these terms are used interchangeably with amphetamine, such as "speed."

Whore Jamie, Feelin Shitty, Foiled, Fried, Gakked, Gassing, Gear or Gear-up, Geeked, Geekin, Gurped, Heated, High, Jacked, Lit, Peaking, Pissed, Pumped, Psychosis, Ring Dang Doo, Riped, Rollin or Rollin Hard, Scattered, Schlep Heads, Sketching, Spin-Jo, Speeding, Sparked, Spracked, Spun, Spun Monkey or Spun Turkey, Stoked, Talkie, Trippin, Twacked, Tweaking, Tweeked, Twisted, Wide Open, Wired, Worked, Woop Chicken, Zipper, and Zoomin. When the user is experiencing the initial rush from using meth, he is "amping." Amping refers to the "amplified" euphoria users feel during the rush.

MISCELLANEOUS METH-RELATED TERMS

The meth drug trade has its own set of terms, including those used by meth addicts and distributors for the sales and distribution of the drug. An *eightball* refers to one-eighth of an ounce of meth. A *teenager*, *Tina*, or *Teena* refers to one-sixteenth of an ounce, and a *paper* is a term for a quarter gram of meth.

Paraphernalia is a general term for medical supplies or equipment used to make or use meth. Addicts refer to needles as *points*, *rigs*, or *slammers*. They sometimes call a straw or device used to snort meth a *tooter*. Those involved in making it need to shop or otherwise acquire the precursors (materials) needed to make the drug in a manner and in quantities that do not arouse suspicion. This acquisition of supplies is called *smurfing*.

The meth subculture has developed other terms related to use. For example, *crank*, *craters*, *crank bugs*, and *spider bites* refer to sores on the face and body resulting from prolonged meth use. *Meth mouth* refers to the terrible dental conditions addicts have from long-term use.

HOW IS METH USED?

Users can inject, smoke, orally ingest, anally insert, or snort meth. The method the user selects influences how the drug is experienced. Meth is a bitter-tasting powder that easily dissolves in beverages. The powder form of the drug is often snorted, which produces a less intense but much longer-lasting high. In 1993, 42 percent of meth and amphetamine treatment admissions reported they used the drug in this manner, according to the Substance Abuse and Mental Health Services Administration (SAMHSA, 2006). By 2003, only 15 percent of the treatment admissions reported they snorted or inhaled the drug. Recent Treatment Episode Data Set (TEDS) data found that in 2003, 56 percent of primary meth and amphetamine admissions reported smoking the drug, which was up from the 15 percent reported in 1993 (SAMHSA, 2006). In 1993, 29 percent indicated that they injected the drug, which compares to 22 percent in

2003. Smoking or injecting the drug produces a short but more intense and pleasurable "rush." In 1993, oral ingestion represented 13 percent and "other" accounted for 1 percent of the routes of administration. By 2003, oral administration declined to 6 percent and other routes of administration remained unchanged at 1 percent (SAMHSA, 2006).

Powdered meth is a hydrochloride salt form that quickly absorbs water from the air. This form of meth is smokable, as is *crystal meth* or *ice*, which refers to meth grown into crystals. Although some people believe that crystal meth is a freebase form of meth, this is not true. Meth that is grown into crystals is simply easier to smoke. Meth in crystal form, rather than powder, also is more likely to be relatively pure because of the difficulty of growing crystals from impure chemicals. According to SAMHSA (2004), in 1992, 12 percent of meth and amphetamine treatment admissions reported they smoked meth. By 2002, 50 percent of the treatment admissions reported they smoked meth in its crystal form. This represents a major shift from inhaling to smoking over this 10-year span.

Another relatively new way of consuming meth is called "booty bumping." This process involves the user heating meth into liquid form and mixing it with water. The user then draws the fluid into a syringe that lacks a needle. The syringe is then inserted in the anus and meth shot into the user's body. Users rely on this technique because the drug is readily absorbed into the bloodstream.

The crystal form of meth is referred to as *crystal, ice,* or *glass.* If heat is introduced, the user can smoke or inject crystal meth. Smoking it is a much faster and intense way to get high than swallowing the drug. The user places a small amount of crystal in a glass pipe (often called a *tooter*), heats it, and inhales the resulting vapors. Crystal meth or ice melts into a liquid when heated and returns to its crystal form when cooled. Boiling crystal turns it into a semiliquid referred to as *snot,* which can be smoked or placed up the nose. Users view smoking meth as ideal because it can be used almost anywhere, since the vapors are odorless and undetectable.

The rush or high felt by the user is the direct result of the release of dopamine into the section of the brain that controls feelings of pleasure. The rush or high associated with its use is relatively long-lasting compared to other drugs. The effects of meth use can last as long as 12 hours. If it is snorted, the user usually experiences effects within about 5 minutes. If it is orally ingested, the user will feel a rush in around 20 minutes. Oral meth use tends to lack rushing, has less euphoric effects, and tends to cause far less of a feeling of wanting to do it again than the other methods.

The fastest rushes occur when the user smokes or injects meth. The user usually experiences an immediate and powerful response. Smoking and injecting are associated with stronger, faster, and more euphoric effects. While injecting results in a faster reward, it also results in a faster crash. Users learn to manage the rapid crashes by trying to attain another rush by taking more of the drug. These effects are more associated with compulsive or addictive user patterns. The general use trend is more toward smoking meth because of this immediacy and the strength of the initial rush. It should be noted that many addicts have an aversion to using needles and never inject the drug.

Standard-shaped light bulbs are easily converted into meth pipes. Meth pipes lack a screen found with pipes used to smoke cocaine or marijuana. The user places the meth inside the bowl of the glass pipe and then heats it until it turns into a liquid and then emits a gas (vapor). Once it turns to a gas, the user inhales it through the stem of the pipe. Over time, a white milky residue builds up on the sides of the bowl. Because the glass bowl gets very hot, users will sometimes have burn marks on their fingertips from holding the hot bowls or closing off the hole at the top of the pipe to keep the gas from escaping (see Figure 9.1).

After being heated, unused crystal meth returns to its crystal state when cooled by ice or a cool wet rag. Users will cool down unused liquid meth to its crystal form because it is easier to transport and use at another time.

Regardless of the method of use, meth addicts will frequently use it with other drugs such as cocaine, marijuana, and alcohol. Because of their poly-drug use, it is sometimes difficult to sort out the effects of the meth from other drugs. Users rely on other drugs or alcohol to either enhance or supplement the meth high or cushion their withdrawal and depression when coming down.

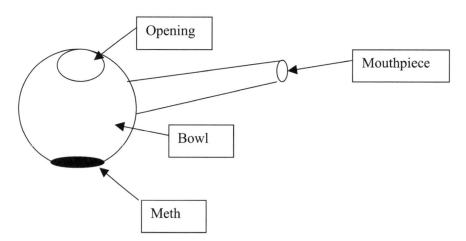

FIGURE 9.1 Typical design of pipe used to smoke methamphetamine.

WHAT DOES METH LOOK LIKE?

Meth is usually found on the street as powder or crystal. Street meth, like many other street drugs, is often diluted or cut with other substances. Powdered meth is cut with a filler or is crushed up with amphetamine or methylphenidate (Ritalin) tablets. Sometimes street meth is not really the drug at all but some other compound. Street meth that is clear and crystal is referred to as *glass* or *crystal*. Meth comes in many colors, including white, yellow, brown, orange, pink, red, or darker colors; it can also be almost transparent. The method of manufacture and chemicals used affects the color meth assumes, but most meth is white. Meth can take such forms as powder, granulated crystals (crystal meth or ice), tablets (pills sometimes called Yaba), or capsules. Crystal meth is made by adding a small molecule group (hydrochloric acid). The Yaba form is a tablet that is often comprised of meth and caffeine and is produced in Asia and Southeast Asia. The tablets are small (they can generally fit through a straw) and most often are reddish orange or green. Yaba tablets sometimes have corporate logos, such as Toyota, MTV, or Calvin Klein, that are popular in the rave scene. Examples of crystal meth can be found in the following photo.

Methamphetamine in crystal ("ice") form. Photo courtesy of the Drug Enforcement Administration.

METH DOSES

When meth is taken in a pill or tablet form, between 0.05 and 0.1 of a gram represents a dose. When it is smoked, the amount needed is smaller—as little as 0.01 of a gram may be all that is needed. The dosage amounts differ based on the purity of the drug, tolerance of the user, frequency of use, and individual reactions that are based on body physiology, metabolism, and method of use. The Erowid (2006) Web site provides some general guidelines for dosage amounts for an infrequent user of pure meth. Caution should be taken with any dosage amount because of the varying individual reactions to the drug. Thus, Table 9.2 lists what some are indicating are dosage estimates and should not be considered a guide for anyone.

The important things to remember about the doses are that a number of factors influence the amount needed to get high—the doses can be very small, and with prolonged use, more of the drug is needed to get the desired results. Erowid (2006) identified vomiting, headaches, dizziness, cold sweats, shaking, and, ultimately, death as possible results from overdosing on meth.

Table 9.2
Approximate Doses by Method of Abuse

	Oral Dosages	Insufflated (Snorted)	Smoked	Injected (IV)
Threshold	5 mg	5 mg	5–10 mg	5 mg
Light Stimulation	5–15 mg	5–15 mg	10–20 mg	5–10 mg
Common	10–30 mg	10–40 mg	10–40 mg	10–40 mg
Strong (some rushing)	20–50 mg	30–60 mg	30–60 mg	30–60 mg
Very Strong (rushing)		501 mg	501 mg	50–100 mg (strong rushing; intense euphoria)
Onset	20–70 minutes (depending on form and stomach contents)	5–10 minutes	0–2 minutes	0–2 minutes
Duration	3–5 hours	2–4 hours	1–3 hours	1–3 hours
Coming Down	2–6 hours	2–6 hours	2–4 hours	2–4 hours
Normal Aftereffects	up to 24 hours	up to 24 hours	up to 24 hours	up to 24 hours

METH USE AND DRUG TESTS

Meth is detectable using standard drug tests of urine from three to five days following use. It is detectable in hair tests for approximately 90 days and in blood samples for one to three days. A number of substances can result in false positives, including ephedrine, pseudoephedrine, and other substances found in such over-the-counter medications as Sudafed, Allerest, Contact, Nyquil, Robitussin, and others. Diet aids, nasal sprays, asthma medications, and several prescription medications may suggest meth use when it has not been used.

WHY DO PEOPLE USE METH?

People use the drug for a number of reasons (Morgan & Beck, 1995). The short-term effects of meth use are desired: the sense of euphoria and pleasure; a high that lasts 8 to 12 hours or more; energy enhancement and alertness; weight loss because of decreased appetite; decreased fatigue; relief from chronic depression; a sense of social bonding with other users; and improved sexual pleasure and drive. Rawson (2005) found that more than 35 percent of the women who used the drug said they did so to lose weight, compared to 10 percent of meth-using men. Rawson also found that about 35 percent of the women used it to relieve depression, compared to about 25 percent of the men. Meth users have reported on what it feels like to use the drug. One indicated, "It made me feel confident, self-assured," then added, "Then it took on a whole new meaning to me. I became a partier" (Bonné, 2004). Another said she felt "this very intense surge of energy through the body." She added, "I felt like I was superhuman because I would think more, I could accomplish more."

Meth users also experience negative short-term effects that are not desired, including increased respiration, higher pulse rate (irregular heartbeat or cardiac arrhythmia), higher blood pressure, increased body temperature (hyperthermia), convulsions, irritability, hyperexcitability, grinding of teeth, nervousness, dilated pupils resulting in an aversion to light, and death, according to the National Institute on Drug Abuse (2002), Anglin et al. (2000), Anglin, Kalechstein, Maglione, Annon, and Fiorentine (1997), and Leshner (2000).

LONG-TERM UNDESIRED EFFECTS OF METH USE

Several agencies, including the Drug Enforcement Administration (DEA) and other authorities (Greenwell & Brecht, 2003; Leshner, 2000; London et al., 2004; National Institutes of Health, 2001, 2004; Volkow et al., 2001a,

2001b) have identified long-term effects of meth use that include severe psychological and physical dependence (addiction); violent behavior that eventually gets coupled with paranoia, making the users even more dangerous; chronic fatigue; talkativeness; overall lifestyle disruption; sleep problems such as insomnia (inability to sleep); cognitive impairments and reduced functioning; confusion; fight-or-flight responses to stimuli; visual and auditory hallucinations; uninhibited sexual functioning with prolonged use; severe depression; picking at the skin and scratching imaginary bugs, which causes open sores and infections. Morals and values are abandoned. The inability to think and act sequentially is impaired and, with heavy, prolonged use, disappears. For example, meth users find it difficult to follow directions or listen to instructions. Heavy use may also lead to homicidal or suicidal thoughts.

Physically, long-term use may result in seizures, chest pain, dry mouth, cardiac valve thickening, death, dramatic weight loss because users lose interest in food and eventually suffer from malnutrition, and brain damage (methamphetamine is neurotoxic). Prolonged use can lead to what is called "amphetamine psychosis," resulting in paranoia, auditory and visual hallucinations, self-absorption, irritability, and aggressive and erratic behavior. Amphetamine psychosis is a disorder similar to paranoid schizophrenia. Individuals with amphetamine psychosis may exhibit bizarre behavior that is sometimes violent.

PATTERNS OF METH USE—LOW INTENSITY, BINGE, AND HIGH INTENSITY

There are three basic patterns of meth use: low intensity, binge, and high intensity. Low intensity is a pattern of use where the user is not psychologically addicted to meth but relies on it for specific perceived benefits, such as a work enhancer or diet-aid drug. Typically, low-intensity users snort or swallow the drug.

Low-Intensity Users

According to Narconon (2002), low-intensity use is characterized by the snorting of powdered meth or ingestion of pills. Users at this level use meth to keep themselves awake and alert for special tasks, or to lose weight. Users at this level are able to hold down jobs, attend school, and otherwise appear to act normal and operate normal lives. Some over-the-road truckers, overtime workers, night-shift workers, stay-at-home parents needing to get several tasks done, and students use it for these purposes. Low-intensity users are unlikely to come into contact with law enforcement, social service, health, or child welfare caseworkers because of problems resulting from this pattern of use.

Professionals may encounter or be working with low-intensity users and not be aware of their use of meth. It is important to note that chronic low-intensity users often view it as a "functional drug." That is, they see it as helping them get things done, such as lose weight, focus on tasks, or get work done. They believe that they "can stop anytime" or "have it under control." Over the long run, this functionality turns out to be a myth.

Narconon (2002) notes that, while use of meth in this fashion seems to be managed, low-intensity users are a short step away from becoming binge users. Low-intensity users have experienced the rush associated with heavier use and generally only need to smoke or inject to cross over the line into binge-use patterns. When they do so, the problems with their use escalate.

Binge Users

Binge users smoke or inject to experience the euphoria that comes from a more intense use of meth. During a binge, the user will periodically use the drug to maintain the high. It is these strong euphoric experiences that move the user from a low-intensity to a psychologically addicted user. A common and unhealthy use pattern for meth is to re-dose repeatedly for several days in a row. Depending on whether the intention is to stay awake, remain high, or attempt to continue to get "rushing" effects, doses are repeated every 3 to 8 hours to stay awake, or every 30 minutes to 4 hours to remain "high." A user re-dosing often takes the same amount of meth as the first dose. As re-dosing continues beyond 48 hours, the user's dosages tend to increase.

HIGH-INTENSITY USERS

High-intensity users have a goal of never crashing or coming down but maintaining a state of euphoria and the perfect rush. Given the nature of meth and its effects on the body, this becomes an impossible goal. For the chronic user, following the first injection or smoke, each successive rush or high becomes more difficult to obtain, and more of the drug is needed. The user remembers the initial high but can never reach that point again no matter how much of the drug is used.

High-intensity users may start out with a pattern of needing from $20 to $40 a day to support their addiction. This increases several-fold as more and more of the drug is needed to maintain the high they are seeking. The high cost of heavy use drives many to criminal behavior to support their addiction. For some, crime is the only alternative.

Phases of High-Intensity Use

High-intensity users experience meth use as a series of phases. Depending on how often they use, their history of use, method of use, and dosage amounts, the length and nature of each phase differ but follow a general pattern. In order of occurrence, the general phases follow.

The Rush

The rush is the initial sense of intense euphoria that the user experiences immediately after smoking or injecting meth. Low-intensity users do not experience a rush when snorting or swallowing the drug. During the rush, the user experiences an intense feeling of pleasure and a burning sensation. The initial rush can last between 5 and 30 minutes, which is longer than the rush associated with the stimulant cocaine. Some users, especially injectors, report an initial burning sensation as the meth is introduced into the body. During the rush, the user's metabolic rate increases, blood pressure elevates, and pulse soars. Users compare the experience of the rush as being the equivalent to having multiple sexual orgasms.

The reason for the rush is that meth triggers the adrenal gland to release a hormone called epinephrine (adrenaline), which puts the body in a battle mode—fight or flight. In addition, the physical sensation the rush provides results from the explosive release of dopamine in the pleasure center of the user's brain. Dopamine is released in the brain's pleasure center. Long-term users find that much of their life is devoted to maintaining a constant rush.

The High

The rush is followed by a high that can last between 4 and 16 hours. This is a longer period than that experienced by cocaine users. Some circles refer to being high as the "shoulder." While being high on meth, the user has a sense of being smarter, more focused, argumentative, and aggressive. High users frequently interrupt those around them.

The Binge

When the user continues to use while high, this is known as binging. Binging is an effort by the user to maintain a prolonged high by taking more meth. During the binge the user becomes hyperactive. Because of severe depression and other negative effects that begin when the drug starts to wear off, users try to avoid crashing or coming down. They may binge to stay high and awake for many days at a time. The law of diminishing returns operates for the user, as the desired effects of meth diminish with each dose. This may cause the user to consume even more to reach the initial rush or stay high. Eventually, there is no rush or high resulting from further consumption, and the user stops.

Tweaking

When the binge ends, a stage of the cycle known as tweaking occurs. The user has a sense of emptiness and dysphoria. Taking more meth will not alleviate the negative feelings experienced by the tweaking user. This stage is not comfortable for the user and some turn to other drugs to self-medicate their feelings. For some, alcohol or other illegal substances are used for self-medications. Tweaking is assumed by many to be the most dangerous stage to professionals, such as law enforcement officers and social workers. Tweakers have not slept for days and as a result are irritable. Think about how moody you get when you don't have enough sleep and then multiply this feeling several times over. Tweakers are unpredictable and short-tempered. Tweakers sometimes are frustrated because they can't find enough of a dose to experience that initial high, and this frustration translates into a sense of unease and aggression. When coupled with the paranoia that results from long-term use, they are loose cannons on the deck able to go off at any time.

Tweakers appear to have rapid and brisk movements. They are overstimulated. Their eyes will rapidly dart around, speech will be rapid, eyes will be clear, and speech concise. A tweaker's eyes may roll back into the head. Tweakers are obsessive about things. For example, they will clean the same thing over and over but ignore other things that need cleaning. The kitchen may be spotless but the house or yard may be full of unfinished projects and filth. In addition, tweakers can become obsessed with dismantling things, such as appliances, with no idea of why they are doing it. They might dismantle a television, washing machine, or any number of objects without a clue about how to put things back together.

Because tweakers hear and see things differently, it can be difficult for law enforcement or caseworkers to predict what, if anything, will set them off. Tweakers have such an altered sense of reality that virtually anybody or anything could set them off into a rage or confrontation. Because many become paranoid, a caseworker, law enforcement officer, family member, or other person could become an unsuspecting target. Because some users fear authorities, they have many weapons around the house. This requires that caseworkers and other professionals be cautious around tweaking individuals.

There is considerable folklore on how long a user can tweak. Reports of 15 to almost 40 days without sleep have been reported to the author. While it is true that addicts do stay awake for very long periods of time, what is likely is they actually take short naps and float in and out of consciousness. They never fall into a deep and replenishing sleep until later in the cycle. While meth is not a hallucinogen or a psychedelic, it is easy to understand how prolonged sleep deprivation would result in bizarre behaviors and thoughts. Sleep deprivation can result in profoundly disturbing hallucinations. For example, many addicts will describe the "shadow people" that seem to appear and be very real to them (Holthouse & Rubin, 1997a).

The Crash

Eventually, because of a lack of sleep and loss of epinephrine, the body becomes exhausted and falls into a deep sleep. This is known as the crash. When high-intensity users stop taking meth they experience depression, anxiety, fatigue, paranoia, aggression, and an intense craving for the drug (London et al., 2004; National Institute on Drug Abuse, 2002). Tweakers sleep like they are dead when the time comes to crash, and they sleep for days afterwards. The crash can last for days, as the body replenishes its supply of epinephrine. Users may try to cushion the crash by using tranquilizers or downer drugs, such as marijuana, heroin, or alcohol (Gibson et al., 2002). Users that are crashing usually pose no real threat to caseworkers, law enforcement officers, or other professionals. However, crashing parents or guardians cannot provide basic care to children and often are neglectful of them and may place them at risk. Protecting, feeding, and overseeing children are not possible for the crashing user, and sometimes their children go without food, sleep, care, and supervision. Some children learn to survive on their own when parents or guardians are crashing. They eat and drink whatever they can find. Crashes may last between one and three days.

Normalcy

Meth addicts eventually return to a state of normalcy for a few days. This stage can last between 2 and 14 days, depending on frequency of use. The high-intensity user never really gets back to complete normalcy because of the physiological damage done to the body, specifically the brain. This is not to say the high-intensity user cannot recover and lead a normal life.

Withdrawal

Users who withdraw from meth experience symptoms of physical distress. Withdrawal from the drug is a prolonged process, and users in withdrawal experience depression and are initially unable to experience pleasure. They also may experience fatigue, paranoia, and aggression, and have psychotic symptoms that may persist for months or years following use (Office of National Drug Control Policy, 2005). They become lethargic and have no energy. Users, because of poor eating habits, also may experience extreme hunger. If the cravings for meth are strong, some may become suicidal. If more meth is used, their sense of pleasure increases and their depression will temporarily be alleviated. Some suggest that this is a major reason why meth addicts are some of the most difficult to treat and why recidivism rates are high.

Experts agree that meth is a highly addictive stimulant drug (National Institutes of Health, 2001). According to the U.S. Drug Enforcement Administration (2005), "Methamphetamine has a phenomenal rate of addiction, with some experts saying users can get hooked after just one use." Anecdotal accounts and clinical experience suggest that addiction can occur in less than a year. The Center for Substance Abuse Treatment (1999) Tip 33: Treatment for Stimulant Use Disorders notes in chapter 2 that addiction typically occurs after using the drug for two to five years. Prolonged or binge use of meth causes significant tolerance and psychological dependence. Some report addiction after the first use, but this is not typical for most.

THE PHYSICAL APPEARANCE OF METH USERS

It would be inaccurate to stereotype high-intensity meth users as looking a certain way. There is no set appearance for all meth users and addicts. They can assume a variety of appearances depending on a number of factors, including the amount and frequency they are using. Low-intensity meth users can look reasonably normal in appearance. However, if the individual is using meth on a regular basis, obvious physical indications develop over time. It should be noted that as dramatic as the outside appearance may be, there is also physiological damage occurring on the inside of the body. Three excellent Web sites that have examples of the progression of deterioration from meth use are: 2stopmeth. org; www.co.multnomah.or.us/sheriff/faces_of_meth.htm; and www.mappsd. org. The reader can view some examples of the physical deterioration resulting from prolonged meth use on these sites.

Crank Bugs and Meth Mites

Open sores on the skin are the result of the individual scratching imaginary "crank bugs" or "meth mites." Long-term meth users develop the sensation that insects are crawling on their skin, causing them to scratch themselves. The scratching associated with these imaginary insects (known as formication) eventually leads to lesions in the skin, topical infections, sore areas, and scabs. These open sores are aggravated by the addict continuing to scratch and thus spreading the infection. The user's lack of proper hygiene contributes to the spread of infection. Those who inject frequently develop abscesses, ulcerations, and scars around the injection sites. These injection sites may become infected and also a target of scratching.

"Meth Mouth"

The long-term or heavy use of meth also leads to severe dental problems, which professionals and addicts refer to as "meth mouth." The American Dental Association (ADA, 2005) concluded that "the oral effects of methamphetamine can be devastating." Long-term drug addicts, especially those using meth, do not take good care of their teeth and do not visit their dentists on a regular basis. Meth addicts do not brush their teeth often, have poor diets, and avoid medical and dental professionals to hide their addiction. Meth acts on the gums and teeth as a corrosive. It softens the teeth, and they basically melt away. When a user smokes meth, the chemicals used to make it, such as sulfuric or muriatic acid, are heated and vaporize and spread around the mouth. The user's mouth is irritated and burned by the chemicals, and sores eventually develop that become infected. This infection spreads throughout the mouth and gums. When coupled with the corrosive action of chemicals on tooth enamel, eventually the teeth rot away to well below the gum line. The gums are also affected because meth use causes blood flow to decrease and thus gums to break down and become diseased. For these and other reasons, it is common for the roots to show and the loss of teeth to occur.

The decay occurring can also be attributed to the effect of meth use on saliva production, or what is medically referred to as "dry mouth" (ADA, 2005). Meth dries out the salivary glands and thus the production of saliva. Normally, the body uses saliva to clean the teeth and neutralize acids, and to control harmful bacteria. With less saliva, the user's mouth cannot perform these functions. Consequently, the acids in anything consumed are free to decay the teeth and gums. The sense of a "dry mouth" or "cottonmouth" (xerostomic) causes some users to drink lots of sugary sodas, which also add to tooth decay (ADA, 2005). Damage to the mouth is not limited to those who smoke the drug; it can also be caused by snorting meth, as caustic chemicals flow through the nasal passage to the back of the mouth.

Another fundamental process that destroys the user's teeth is the grinding that occurs during use. Meth use causes the user to feel anxious or nervous, and the unintentional teeth grinding that consequently occurs leads to cracks and breaks. Meth users often grind their teeth down hard, causing teeth to break and nerve endings to become exposed. The user may also lose fillings because the teeth grinding causes them to fall out. Just breathing through the mouth and having air pass over the teeth and gums can cause some users to feel pain. Whether from smoking or snorting, the user will eventually develop meth mouth, and many users simply use more meth to alleviate the pain.

The best way to visualize and understand meth mouth is to view some of the images of the mouths of long-term users. The color insert section contains examples of meth mouth and the corresponding tooth and gum decay resulting from prolonged meth use. The consequences of meth mouth go beyond pain and disfiguration. Some long-term recovering users with damaged teeth may be reluctant or unable to find dental help. If they do find it, they may lack the money for dental repairs. With poor teeth, they find it difficult to obtain work because potential employers are turned off by unsightly teeth (mouths), and users face social rejection.

THE COMPARATIVE LOW COST OF METH

In addition to the desired effects of meth on the user, one of the reasons for the drug's popularity is its relative low cost. It is relatively inexpensive to produce, but more important, lasts longer than alternative stimulants, such as cocaine. Prices for the drug vary across the United States:

It costs $20 to $60 for a quarter gram, which is slightly lower than cocaine but lasts significantly longer (Bonné, 2001).

The National Council of State Governments estimated a $100 batch of methamphetamine would sell on the street for about $1,000 (Kraman, 2004).

Meth prices range between $5 and $15 a dose (Leinwand, 2003).

The Drug Enforcement Administration in 2001 provided a price range from $3,500 to $23,000 per pound, $350 to $2,700 per ounce, and $20 to $300 per gram (Drug Policy Information Clearinghouse, 2003).

The price of crystal meth runs higher because of its purity and additional manufacturing steps. The National Drug Intelligence Center (2005), using Drug Enforcement Administration data, reported the prices for powdered and crystal meth shown in Table 9.3.

Although prices seem high to the nonuser, they represent a good value to the addict. The long-term high of the drug is a good value compared to cocaine or other substances. Likewise, meth quickly becomes expensive as addicts must use increasing amounts of the drug and do so more frequently over time in pursuit of that lasting high and avoidance of the crash. The consequence is that

Table 9.3
National Price Ranges of Methamphetamine, 2003

Quantity	Powder	Crystal
Pound	$1,600–$45,000	$6,000–$70,000
Ounce	$270–$5,000	$500–$3,100
Gram	$20–$300	$60–$700

Source: National Drug Intelligence Center 2005.

the price of meth becomes very high for children as their needs compete with the meth for family resources.

HOW DOES METH COMPARE TO COCAINE?

Because both are powerful psycho stimulants, meth is often compared with cocaine (National Drug Intelligence Center, 2002). Users who have used both drugs report similar experiences, such as a sense of euphoria. Users of both drugs report experiencing an initial rush, and a longer high and sense of euphoria with meth. If the cocaine is in crack form, the rush and high are much shorter. Users can smoke, inject, snort, or swallow either illicit drug. Both drugs may produce anxiety, increased blood pressure, increased temperature, higher pulse rates, and possible death. Short-term effects of both include increased activity, decreased appetite, and respiration. Prolonged use of either drug can lead to psychotic behaviors, hallucinations, mood disturbances, and/or violence. When users of either drug withdraw, they report craving, paranoia, and depression (London et al., 2004).

Differences between the two drugs exist. Cocaine is derived from the refined leaves of the South American coca plant; consequently, almost all cocaine in the United States is imported. The meth found in the United States is also imported from Mexico, Southeast Asia, and other countries. However, unlike cocaine, it can be domestically manufactured in large or small operations. Large spaces, while often desirable, are not required for production. Meth can be produced in small rooms or spaces. The production of meth is relatively easy compared to importing cocaine. All of the necessary chemicals to produce meth are relatively available, thus making law enforcement control of the illicit drug difficult.

Cocaine and meth abusers have different use patterns. For example, meth users report that they use the drug on a more regular basis than that reported by cocaine users. Meth's effects require less-frequent administration than cocaine, because meth leaves the system more slowly and thus has a longer half-life than cocaine. Meth has a half-life of between 10 and 12 hours, compared with only about one hour for cocaine (Wermuth, 2000). While cocaine is quickly and almost completely metabolized in the body, meth has a longer duration, and a larger percent of the drug remains unchanged in the body (Center for Substance Abuse Prevention/National Prevention Network, 2006; National Institute on Drug Abuse, 2002). Thus, the brain is affected for more prolonged spans of time. Cocaine is not neurotoxic to dopamine and serotonin neurons, but meth is neurotoxic. "Meth has more long-term, serious effects on the brain than cocaine" (National Institute on Drug Abuse, 2002).

Another difference is cost. Meth is cheaper on the street than cocaine. Meth has a longer duration for the initial rush and high. Crack cocaine offers a high of about 15–20 minutes and meth a high of 8–24 hours. The perceived cost-benefit ratio to the user is much greater for the meth addict. Rawson, Anglin, and Ling (2002, p. 7) wrote, "Methamphetamine effects are long lasting and methamphetamine users typically spend about 25 percent as much money for methamphetamine as that spent by cocaine users for cocaine."

According to research by Dr. Sara Simon sponsored by the National Institute on Drug Abuse (NIDA), abuse patterns differ between meth and cocaine abusers (Zickler, 2005). Meth abusers typically take the drug early in the morning and in two- to four-hour intervals, similar to being on a medication. In contrast, cocaine abusers typically take the drug in the evening and take it over a period of several hours that resembles a recreational-use pattern. They typically continue using until all of the cocaine is gone. In addition, another pattern showed that continuous use was more common among meth abusers than among those abusing cocaine. According to other NIDA-sponsored research by Dr. Simon, the effects of meth and cocaine abuse resulted in similar cognitive deficits, but meth abusers had more problems than cocaine abusers at tasks requiring attention and the ability to organize information (Zickler, 2005).

In the 1980s, cocaine use became epidemic, but in recent years, use has declined among the middle class. Crack cocaine remains a serious blight in some inner cities. Cocaine's use, similar to other drugs, is cyclic, with periodic increases and decreases (Rawson et al., 2002). In contrast, meth has the potential of enduring, similar to marijuana and alcohol.

Cocaine addicts typically experience profound life changes in a relatively short time frame because of higher costs of use and use patterns, which involve binging. Cocaine users typically hit bottom sooner than many meth users. Meth addicts experience the same losses and also hit bottom, but in many cases, do so over a longer period. Some meth addicts use at levels that allow them to maintain jobs, homes, some money, and at least, the appearance of being in control.

NOTE

1. From: *The Methamphetamine Crisis,* Herbert C. Covey; Chapter 1, pp. 3–22, "What Is Methamphetamine and How and Why Is It Used?," by Herbert C. Covey. Copyright © 2006 by Herbert C. Covey. Reproduced with permission of Greenwood Publishing Group, Inc., Westport, CT.

REFERENCES

American Dental Association. (2005, August 9). *Dental topics A to Z: Methamphetamine use.* Retrieved from www.ada.org/prof/resources/topics/methmouth.asp

Anglin, M. D., Burke, C., Perrochet, B., Stamper, E., & Dawud-Noursi, S. (2000). History of the methamphetamine problem. *Journal of Psychoactive Drugs, 32,* 137–141.

Anglin, M. D., Kalechstein, A., Maglione, M., Annon, J., & Fiorentine, R. (1997). *Epidemiology and treatment of methamphetamine abuse in California: A regional report.* Unpublished manuscript, Los Angeles: UCLA, Drug Abuse Research Center.

Bonné, J. (2001). Meth's deadly buzz. *Msnbc.com special report.* Retrieved from msnbc.msncom/id/3071772

Bonné, J. (2004). Hooked in the Haight: Life, death or prison. *Msnbc interactive.* Retrieved from msnbc.com/id/3071769

Center for Substance Abuse Prevention/National Prevention Network. (2006). *Methamphetamine: A resource kit.* Rockville, MD: Substance Abuse and Mental Health Services Administration.

Center for Substance Abuse Treatment. (1999). *Tip 33: Treatment for stimulant use disorders: Treatment improvement protocol* (TIP Series No. 33). Rockville, MD: Substance Abuse and Mental Health Services Administration.

Drug Policy Information Clearinghouse. (2003). *Methamphetamine: Fact sheet.* Rockville, MD: Office of National Drug Control Policy.

Erowid. (2006, March 31). *Meth.* Retrieved from www.erowid.org.

Gibson, D. R., Leamon, M. H., & Flynn, N. (2002). Epidemiology and public health consequences of methamphetamine use in California's central valley. *Journal of Psychoactive Drugs, 34,* 313–319.

Holthouse, D., & Rubin, P. (1997a, December 18). *Methodology—Part I: New Times.* Retrieved from www.phoenixnewtimes.com/issues/1997–12–18/feature2

Holthouse, D., & Rubin, P. (1997b, December 18). *Methodology—Part II: New Times.* Retrieved from www.phoenixnewtimes.com/issues/1997–12–18/feature4

Kraman, P. (2004). *Drug abuse in America—Rural meth.* Lexington, KY: Council of State Governments.

Leinwand, D. (2003). "Meth" moves east. *USA Today,* July 29.

Leshner, A. I. (2000). Addressing the medical consequences of drug abuse. *NIDA Notes, 15,* 3–4.

London, E. D, Simon, S. L., Berman, S. M., Mandelkern, M. A., Lichtman, A. M., Bramen, J., et al. (2004). Mood disturbances and regional cerebral metabolic abnormalities in recently abstinent methamphetamine abusers. *Archives of General Psychiatry, 61,* 73–84.

Marshall, D. R. (2000, July 6). *Congressional testimony to the Senate Judiciary Committee.*

Martin, K. R. (2002). Prenatal exposure to methamphetamine increases vulnerability to the drug's neurotoxic effects in adult male mice. *NIDA Notes, 17,* 1–3.

Mills, K. (1999, December 13). Meth of old has morphed into epidemic proportions. *Seattle Post-Intelligencer.*

Morgan, P., & Beck, J. (1995). The legacy of the paradox: Hidden contexts of methamphetamine use in the United States. In H. Klee (Ed.), *Amphetamine misuse: International perspectives on current trends.* Amsterdam: Harwood Academic Publishers.

Narconon. (2002). *Methamphetamine information: Abuse patterns.* Retrieved from www.narconon.org/druginfo/methamphetamine addiction

National Drug Intelligence Center. (2002, August). Crystal methamphetamine. *Information Bulletin.* (Product Number 2002-L0424–005). Johnstown, PA: U.S. Department of Justice.

National Drug Intelligence Center. (2005). *Methamphetamine drug threat assessment.* Johnstown, PA: U.S. Department of Justice.

National Institute on Drug Abuse. (2002). *Research report: Methamphetamine abuse and addiction.* Bethesda, MD: Author.

National Institutes of Health. (2001, March 1). Methamphetamine abuse leads to long-lasting changes in the human brain that are linked to impaired coordination and memory. *NIH News.* Washington, DC: U.S. Department of Health and Human Services. Retrieved from www.nih.gov/news/pr/mar2001/nida

National Institutes of Health. (2004, January 5). New study suggests methamphetamine withdrawal is associated with brain changes similar to those seen in depression and anxiety. *NIH News.* Washington, DC: U.S. Department of Health and Human Services.

Office of National Drug Control Policy. (2003). *Methamphetamine: Fact sheet.* Rockville, MD: Drug Policy Information Clearinghouse. Retrieved from www.whitehousedrugpolicy.gov/drugfact/methamphetamine

Office of National Drug Control Policy. (2005, November 30). *Fact sheet: Methamphetamine.* Retrieved from www.whitehousedrugpolicy.gov/publications/factsht/methamph/

Rawson, R. A., Anglin, M. D., & Ling, W. (2002). Will the methamphetamine problem go away? *Journal of Addictive Diseases, 21,* 5–19.

Substance Abuse and Mental Health Services Administration. (2004). *Drug abuse warning network, 2003: Interim national estimates of drug-related emergency department visits.* Rockville, MD: Author.

Substance Abuse and Mental Health Services Administration. (2006, March 15). Trends in methamphetamine/amphetamine admissions to treatment: 1993–2003. *The DASIS Report.*

U.S. Drug Enforcement Administration. (2005). *Factsheet: Fast facts about meth.* Washington, DC: Author. Retrieved from www.usdoj.gov/dea/pubs/pressrel/meth fact03.html

Volkow, N. D., Chang, L., Wang, G.-J., Fowler, J. S., Franceschi, D., Sedler, M. J., et al. (2001a). Higher cortical and lower subcortical metabolism in detoxified methamphetamine abusers. *American Journal of Psychiatry, 158*(3), 383–389.

Volkow, N. D., Chang, L., Wang, G.-J., Fowler, J. S., Leonido-Yee, M., Franceschi, D., et al. (2001b). Association of dopamine transporter reduction with psychomotor impairment in methamphetamine abusers. *American Journal of Psychiatry, 158*(3), 377–382.

Wermuth, L. (2000). Methamphetamine use: Hazards and social influences. *Journal of Drug Education, 30*, 423–433.

Zickler, P. (2005). Methamphetamine, cocaine abusers have different patterns of drug use, suffer cognitive impairments. *NIDA Notes, 16*, 1–2.

Chapter 10

The Short- and Long-Term Medical Effects of Methamphetamine on Children and Adults[1]

Kathryn M. Wells, MD

HISTORY OF MEDICAL USE

Methamphetamine is a drug that has been around and known to the medical community for many years. Chemically, it is a synthetic drug that belongs to the amphetamine class of drugs. Medically, its stimulant effects act on both the central and peripheral nervous systems. Throughout history it has had various medical uses, but it has increasingly been used illicitly.

Meth was first synthesized in 1887 by a German chemist. It was not used therapeutically until the 1930s when it began to be promoted by American pharmaceutical companies for various ailments and was thought to be without risk of addiction. At about the same time, Japan began to produce large quantities of meth in the pill form for domestic consumption. After the war, Japanese pharmaceutical companies launched a large campaign to increase the use of over-the-counter meth pills that were in abundance in former military warehouses. This consequently led to the first large-scale epidemic of meth use and abuse (Kato, 1990). In the United States, a prescription was still needed to legally obtain amphetamines, but by the 1950s, the nonmedical use of amphetamines had spread to the civilian population, most commonly being used by individuals who needed to stay awake for long periods of time or to perform well at monotonous tasks. Additionally, meth was being prescribed for the treatment of hyperactivity, obesity, narcolepsy (a disorder causing spontaneous sleep), and depression (Beebe & Walley, 1995).

The "second wave" of the meth epidemic in the United States occurred in the 1960s when intravenous use of the drug became more popular. These users were the first individuals to take the drug solely for its euphoric effects (Wolkoff, 1997). During this period, users had created a way to manufacture meth on the street called the P2P (phenyl-2-propanone) method. This wave was controlled by law enforcement and public efforts to educate potential abusers and treat users. This method of manufacturing meth used lead acetate as a chemical reagent and, because there were often large quantities of lead in the final product, placing the user at risk for lead poisoning, there was the risk of hepatitis, nephritis, and encephalopathy (Allcott, Barnhart & Mooney, 1987).

The "third wave" of meth use in the United States occurred in the 1980s as a result of the advent of another, faster, and easier method for meth manufacturing called the pseudoephedrine reduction method. This method, further discussed elsewhere in this text, contributed to the rapidly rising accessibility and popularity of the drug on the street in the 1990s and 2000s. It produced a more potent and psychoactive form of the drug with a higher percentage of the dextro-isomer of the drug compared to the P2P method, which produced equal proportions of the dextro- and levo-isomers (Burton, 1991; Center for Substance Abuse Treatment, 1997; Cho, 1990). This is important because dextro-methamphetamine is three to four times more potent to the central nervous system (CNS) than levo-methamphetamine (Sowder & Beschner, 1993). The extent of the potential consequences of the impurities of this manufactured form of meth is unclear (unintended by-products and reagent residuals as well as processing errors), but this is of great concern, as many of these laboratories are operated by uneducated "chemists" who get their recipes from unpublished sources or through the Internet and who are frequently using the drug while processing it.

Additionally, on the street a potent, smokable form of meth, known as *crystal*, *glass*, or *ice*, began to gain popularity, and its use grew rapidly because of the more potent and longer "high." For these reasons, many cocaine users began to be attracted to the use of meth (Wolkoff, 1997). By the 1990s, the use of prescription meth was almost completely discontinued due to the understanding of its potential for addiction. Meth is currently classified as a Schedule II stimulant, meaning that it is known to have a high potential for abuse and is available only by prescription. The only accepted medical indications for use of meth are for the treatment of narcolepsy and attention-deficit/hyperactivity disorder, and the dosages prescribed are much smaller than what is used by the abusers.

HOW IS METH USED?

Meth may be snorted, smoked, orally ingested, injected, or absorbed through any mucous membranes such as sublingually, rectally, or vaginally. It is readily absorbed from the gut, nasopharynx (back of the nose and throat), muscle (when injected), mucosa, and placenta. It alters the mood differently depending on the route of ingestion. When the drug is snorted or taken orally, the user describes a feeling of euphoria or a feeling of extreme well-being called a "high." Smoking or injecting the drug results additionally in a more immediate, brief, intense sensation called a "flash" or a "rush." Users describe this as extremely pleasurable, and it has been characterized by some individuals as being equivalent to multiple orgasms. This is then followed by the euphoria. The "high" and the "rush" are both a result of the release of very high levels of the neurotransmitter dopamine into areas of the brain that regulate feelings of pleasure. Further description of the effect of this drug on the brain will be discussed in a later section.

Different methods of use produce different response within the user's body. The length of time until onset of symptoms is dependent upon the method of use. If the drug is snorted, effects occur within 3–5 minutes due to the rapid uptake of the drug through highly vascular nasal passages. If, however, the drug is ingested orally, it must be taken up through the lining of the digestive system, with effects not occurring for 15–20 minutes. Smoking meth usually allows the drug to reach the brain even more rapidly than injecting it (MacKenzie & Heischober, 1997). This is felt to be related to the small particle size of the drug, allowing it to penetrate deep into the lung tissue, where it rapidly crosses into the pulmonary circulation. In fact, meth is available to the body and brain very rapidly after use as it, unlike cocaine, does not have to be converted to a "free base" in order to be smoked effectively (MacKenzie & Heischober, 1997). The stimulant effects of meth have been reported to last up to 24 hours, most commonly 8–12 hours, compared to cocaine's high of only 20–30 minutes (National Institute on Drug Abuse, 1998). Additionally, the route of administration plays a role in the potential for dangerous and unintended consequences or side effects. Intravenous use is frequently associated with additional illnesses related to the administration of the drug (i.e., sharing of needles) such as hepatitis, HIV infection, tuberculosis, pneumonia, cellulitis (tissue infection), bacterial or viral endocarditis (infection of the lining of the heart), wound abscesses, sepsis (blood infection), thrombosis (blood clot in the blood vessels), thrombophlebitis (infection of lining of the blood vessel), and kidney injury (Šlamberová, Charousová, & Pometlová, 2005; Sowder &

Beschner, 1993). Snorting the drug may be associated with sinusitis (infection of the sinuses), loss of the sense of smell, congestion, atrophy (thinning) of the nasal mucosa, nosebleeds, perforation or damage to the nasal septum, hoarseness, and difficulty with swallowing (Sowder & Beschner, 1993; Gold, 1997).

Meth is commonly used in a "binge and crash" pattern—this means that the user will continue to use the drug ("binge") until they completely "crash." Many users go on a "run," during which time they may forgo food and sleep while binging. This period of use can last for several days. After the heavy binge cycle and before the "crash," the user may experience extreme paranoia, hallucinations, aggression, and agitation. This period of use is called "tweaking" and is felt to be the most physiologically dangerous time for the user as he or she may have a tremendous amount of drug in their body. It is also the time period when the user is potentially the most dangerous, due at least in part to their propensity for violence and feelings of paranoia. The "crash" is believed to occur because the chemical messenger (neurotransmitter) dopamine is depleted from the nerve terminals. It will slowly reaccumulate (at least to some level) while the user is crashing, but during this time the user may sleep for days, not even awakening to take care of regular bodily needs such as eating. Unfortunately, this often leads to increased use of the drug following the crash and eventually to difficulty in feeling any pleasure at all as the nerve terminals become injured. This is further discussed below in the section on central nervous system effects.

Tolerance to meth occurs within minutes, and the pleasurable effects disappear even before the blood concentrations fall. This partially explains the lack of direct correlation between blood level and clinical effects seen with meth. Tolerance means that users often need to take repeatedly higher doses and dose more frequently to get the desired effect. In addition, users often change their method of intake to a method that provides the additional "rush" or "flash" but is also more addictive (injection or smoking). However, there is no tolerance for the negative effects on the user's judgment, impulsivity, aggression, and susceptibility to paranoia, delusions, and hallucinations. In fact, it frequently takes an increasingly smaller amount of the drug to produce these symptoms.

When users discontinue their meth use, they will experience at least some symptoms of withdrawal. The more problematic and prominent withdrawal is the psychological withdrawal, which consists of depression, anxiety and agitation, fatigue, paranoia, aggression, and an intense craving for the drug. Physical withdrawal may also occur and is characterized by excessive hunger (polyphagia) and excessive sleepiness (hypersomnolence). Seizures may occur when the user is withdrawing from this drug. Studies have shown that there are brain abnormalities similar to those seen in people with mood disorders such as anxiety and depression (London et al., 2004) in individuals who have recently discontinued their meth use. This poses additional challenges for individuals in treatment for this addiction.

CLINICAL EFFECTS OF METH USE

There are many factors that may contribute to how a person's body responds to meth use and abuse. The clinical effects from the use of meth are related to the form of the drug used, the dose, the frequency of use, the route of administration, and the length and amount of use. Additionally, the user may have underlying mental health problems for which he or she is trying to self-medicate with the use of the meth. The user may also be using other drugs in conjunction with meth, which may compound and complicate the effects of the drug. Finally, the methods of manufacturing this drug vary greatly, as does the purity of the final product. Therefore, the chemicals used in the manufacturing process as well as unwanted by-products may remain in the final product. This makes it very difficult to differentiate the effects of the drug alone from the effects of the other chemicals and by-products present. These variables also make it very difficult to predict, with any great certainty, the effects of the drug on each individual user.

Short-Term Effects

Pharmacologically, meth is a strong stimulant and is therefore in a class of drugs that includes cocaine, caffeine, and amphetamines. It is structurally similar to amphetamine as well as some of the body's natural neurotransmitters (chemical messengers) such as dopamine, serotonin, epinephrine (adrenaline), and norepinephrine. Meth has a much greater effect on the central nervous system than other amphetamines. Additionally, it seems to exert fewer peripheral nervous system effects (Beebe & Walley, 1995).

Many users report that they began taking meth to try to increase their alertness and to stay awake for longer periods of time, while others begin taking the drug use to lose weight. Still other users begin using to increase their sexual appetite, using it socially to go dancing or "clubbing."

A large portion of the acute physiological symptoms displayed after the use of meth are related to its peripheral effects on the autonomic nervous system and include dilated pupils, dry mouth, suppressed appetite (and consequent weight loss), elevated blood pressure (hypertension), tachycardia (high heart rate), rapid respiratory rate (tachyon), bruxism (involuntary teeth grinding), insomnia (inability to sleep or decreased need for sleep), tremors, and blurry vision. Additionally, meth is a vasoconstrictor of peripheral blood vessels, which causes decreased oxygen delivery to the extremities, resulting in poor circulation. This may contribute to the multiple skin lesions that users often have, which are further worsened by the frequent picking behavior that the user demonstrates while perseverating on the lesions. Users also often perseverate on other tasks such as taking electronic items apart but then are unable to focus adequately in order to reassemble them (Center for Substance Abuse Treatment, 1999).

The central nervous system effects of meth ingestion are the result of the structural similarity of meth and the neurotransmitters active in the brain (dopamine, serotonin, epinephrine or adrenaline, and norepinephrine). Meth use can initially create feelings of euphoria (well-being), elevated energy, increased sensory perception, improved attention, excitation, intensification of emotions, perception of elevated self-esteem, increased alertness, agitation, aggression, restlessness, irritability, repetitive stereotyped behaviors, and increased physical activity (Jaffe, 1995). Conversely, it can decrease physical appetite with subsequent often marked and rapid weight loss. Users may have pressured speech and flight of ideas with rapid shifts in thinking, poor concentration, exaggerated self-esteem, hypervigilance, enhanced sensory awareness, fearlessness, suspiciousness, impaired judgment, poor impulse control, aggression, and emotional liability (Center for Substance Abuse Treatment, 1999).

Users have described markedly increased feelings of sexual desire, but despite this increased libido (sex drive), they usually begin to have difficulty in sexual performance. It is believed that the result of meth-stimulated serotonin release in the brain gives an initial antidepressant effect and elevates feelings of empathy. However, it is also responsible for bizarre mood changes, psychotic behavior, aggressiveness, and bruxism (involuntary grinding of the teeth). Some users may also experience feelings of nausea and dizziness.

The central nervous system effects of acute ingestion may include psychotic behaviors such as hallucinations and paranoia, which can lead to bizarre, irrational, and even violent, behavior. These effects may persist for days or weeks after the drug was discontinued (Beebe & Walley, 1995). These individuals may therefore have a great potential for violence, are at risk for homicidal and suicidal behavior (Szuster, 1990), and can be very dangerous to approach in any setting. A condition called methamphetamine psychosis has been described in the literature (Murray, 1998). This illness consists of several features, including extreme paranoia, well-formed delusions, hypersensitivity to environmental stimuli including light and sound, stereotyped "tweaking" behavior, panic, extreme fearfulness, and a high potential for violence. In fact, there is a described "hyperviolence syndrome" where the victim is frequently a part of the perpetrator's delusional belief system. A weapon such as a knife or gun is commonly used in committing a crime and frequently there are multiple wounds inflicted, sometimes even days after the victim's death (MacKenzie & Heischober, 1997). Additionally, agitated delirium has been described in cases of meth-psychotic states and has also been linked to sudden cardiac death in meth users.

Overdose of the drug may be lethal and can even occur in a first-time user who ingests a single large dose (Jaffe, 1990). Acute symptoms of toxic ingestion may include dizziness, tremor, irritability, confusion, hostility, hallucinations, panic, headache, skin flushing, chest pain, palpitations, increased core body temperature (hyperthermia), irregular heart rhythms (arrhythmias), vomiting, cramps, excessive sweating, and severe high blood pressure (hypertension). This can result in brain hemorrhage or stroke, heart attack (myocardial infarction), and acute pulmonary edema (abnormal accumulation of fluid in the lungs) (Furst, Fallon, Reznik, & Shah, 1990; Nestor, Tamamoto, Kam, & Schultz, 1989a, 1989b). Additionally, the hyperthermia may be exacerbated by increased muscular activity due to agitation and can result in massive muscle breakdown (rhabdomyolysis) and potentially, kidney failure (Beebe & Walley, 1995). The development of a very high fever, rapid heart rate, severe hypertension, convulsions, toxic delirium, and cardiovascular collapse may signal a life-threatening situation (Ellinwood, Sudilovsky, & Nelson, 1973; Rowbotham, 1993; Wetli, 1993).

Medical treatment for overdose of meth consists primarily of supportive care. Other potential causes of presentation must be excluded. There are no specific medications or antidotes for the treatment of meth intoxication.

Sedation and rapid cooling may be used to manage the hyperthermia and agitated movements (Ellinwood et al., 1973; Gold, 1997). Ventilation and oxygenation may need to be provided and medications may need to be used to manage hypertension and seizures. Evaluation for cardiac arrhythmias and injury may need to be undertaken as well.

Long-Term Effects

The long-term effects of meth use can be particularly challenging when dealing with a chronic meth abuser. The use and abuse of this drug commonly leads to progressive social and occupational deterioration. Many who work with meth addicts report that the changes caused by the drug lead to a complete rearrangement of the user's priorities. For this reason, meth causes the heavy user to withdraw from anything and everything that is important to them. The reality is that studies now show that these effects are related to brain changes, many of which may be permanent. Individuals who have used meth for long periods of time demonstrate many features of dependence. It is clear that meth is highly addictive and may lead to a chronic, relapsing disease. Addiction to meth is characterized by compulsive drug-seeking behavior, which is the result of functional and molecular changes in the brain. There is a stronger potential for addiction when utilizing the more rapid-acting routes of administration such as injection or smoking the drug, since there is stronger positive reinforcement for the use with the extremely pleasurable feelings that immediately follow (National Institute on Drug Abuse, 1998).

Chronic users often exhibit concerning behavioral changes, which consist of paranoia, auditory and visual hallucinations, mood disturbances, and delusions. This may result in homicidal or suicidal thoughts. Chronic users may also demonstrate excessive anxiety, confusion, insomnia, weight loss, and extremely violent behavior. It is important to be aware of this when dealing with someone addicted to the drug as they may exhibit very dangerous, unprovoked rages. Additionally, long-term users may display unusual motor movements that appear very similar to a Parkinsonian tremor. When the drug is discontinued, the user may experience depression, anxiety, fatigue, paranoia, aggression, and an intense craving for the drug. Studies have shown that the behavioral changes may persist for months or years after use of the drug is discontinued (National Institute on Drug Abuse, 1998). Chronic meth abuse may lead to the "kindling" phenomenon or "reverse tolerance" where the user can be pushed into frank psychosis by even very small amounts of any stimulant (methamphetamine, amphetamine, caffeine, or nicotine). This is felt to involve alterations that occur in the brain (Jaffe, 1990). Recent studies have suggested that meth psychosis may also spontaneously be brought on by mild stressors (Yui, Goto, Ikemoto, Ishiguro, & Kamata, 2000). Finally, there is another condition called chronic psychosis or "withdrawal" or "abstinence" psychosis, but it is unclear if this may be related to latent schizophrenia that was uncovered by the meth use (Streltzer & Leigh, 1977; Tomiyama, 1990).

Another feature of long-term meth use and abuse relates to the heightened sexuality linked to the use of this drug. After meth use for any length of time, users frequently describe changes in their sexual behaviors. They report that frequently activities that would previously give them sexual gratification no longer do, which leads many users to turn to increasingly bizarre sexual behaviors to meet their sexual needs. This can lead to predatory sexual behavior, increased promiscuity, and the extensive use of pornography. Frequent, often unprotected, sexual activity results in many unplanned pregnancies as well as the transmission of sexually transmitted and blood-borne infections, including HIV/AIDS and multiple forms of viral hepatitis (particularly hepatitis B and C). These risks are increased further when the users are injecting the drug and sharing the injection equipment. In fact, the use of methamphetamine is so closely linked to sexual behavior that some studies have shown that sexual photos presented to meth users can trigger desire to use, even after long-term abstinence.

Dental decay has become a hallmark of chronic meth use and abuse. This complication has been termed by many as "meth mouth" and is likely multi-factorial. First, meth use markedly reduces the production of saliva, causing a very dry mouth (xerostomia). Since saliva normally serves to bathe the teeth and reduce decay-causing bacteria, its reduction may lead to dental decay. Additionally, users often have a high intake of sugary soft drinks, which, coupled with a lack of oral hygiene as well as poor nutrition, may contribute to dental decay (Shaner, 2002). Finally, the significant vasoconstriction caused by meth use may also decrease blood flow to the teeth through the dental pulp, causing further damage. Another hallmark of chronic meth abuse is skin lesions. This is discussed in detail below in the section on the dermatologic system.

MEDICAL COMPLICATIONS OF METH USE

Meth use can affect any major organ system in the body. It has the most profound effect on the brain and central nervous system, but can also affect other organs.

Central Nervous System

The greatest systemic medical concern about meth use is the serious effect that the drug has on the brain of the user. The effects of meth on the central nervous system are numerous. First, this drug affects the brain at the very cel-lular level, causing nerve damage and loss.

In order to understand the complex effect that meth has on brain cells, it is important to understand the way that brain cells normally work. Nerve cells pass messages from one cell to another through the assistance of chemicals called neurotransmitters. These chemicals are necessary, because the nerve cells do not actually touch and therefore must pass their messages by the release and uptake of a neurotransmitter. These chemical messengers, such as dopamine, epinephrine, norepinephrine, and serotonin, are stored in structures called ves-icles that float around in a fluid called cytoplasm within the presynaptic (send-ing) nerve cell. They remain there until the cell is given the signal to release the chemical. At that time the vesicle moves to the edge of the presynaptic cell, binds to the cell wall, and releases the neurotransmitter into the synapse (the space between the two nerve cells). The message is then picked up by the postsynaptic (receiving) cell when the neurotransmitter attaches to a receptor on the cell wall. If there is more neurotransmitter in the synapse than is needed, it will either be destroyed or taken back up into the presynaptic cell for storage until it is needed again. This is done through a mechanism in the cell wall of the presynaptic cell called a transporter.

Dopamine is the neurotransmitter most affected by meth, because the two chemicals are very similar in structure. Dopamine is normally released when something pleasurable occurs, since it acts in the regions of the brain that regulate feelings of pleasure. It also elicits effects in the areas of the brain that regulate movement, emotion, judgment, and motivation. Once meth enters the body, regardless of the manner, it makes its way to the brain cells, among other places, where it causes the cells to release dopamine into the nerve synapse. This is what creates the stimulant effects of the drug that the user desires. Early studies showed that meth decreased the transporter function in dopamine neurons (Brown, Hanson, & Fleckenstein, 2000). However, newer studies have shown that the meth actually enters the presynaptic cell and causes massive release of dopamine from the storage vesicles into the cell cytoplasm as well as an additional massive release of dopamine from the presynaptic cell. This causes flooding of the synapse with the dopamine. There are only a limited number of receptors on the postsynaptic cell, and once they are full of the dopamine, they can no longer take up more of the chemical. Therefore, there is an excess of dopamine left in the synapse. Researchers believe that the excess dopamine is broken down by chemicals in the synapse and is ultimately turned into breakdown products that are toxic to the nerve cells. Additionally, the excess dopamine released into the presynaptic cell's cytoplasm is believed to be damaging to the cell.

Studies using a noninvasive brain imaging technique called magnetic resonance spectroscopy (MRS) have shown that the damage done to nerve cells is long-term and is similar to that caused by strokes or Alzheimer's disease (Ernst, Chang, Leonido-Yee, & Speck, 2000). Another study by Dr. Volkow used positron emission tomography (PET) scans to show that dopamine transporter levels in the striatum of the brain were 24 percent lower in meth users than in control subjects. Additionally, the meth users performed more poorly than nonusers on tests that evaluated brain function associated with the striatum, including fine motor skills, gross motor skills, and memory. The reduction in performance was proportional to the deficits in dopamine transporters. She concluded that compared with the normal 6–7 percent reduction in dopamine transporters found in aging, users saw losses roughly equivalent to 40 years of aging (Volkow et al., 2001).

Damage caused by meth to the dopamine system has been compared to that seen in patients with Parkinson's disease, a brain disease characterized by the progressive loss of dopamine neurons in the regions of the brain involved in movement. Although damage to the brains of Parkinson's patients is more severe than that in meth users, researchers now believe that long-term meth use may lead to symptoms very similar to Parkinson's disease (Volkow et al., 2001). It is unknown if sustained abstinence from meth use will result in recovery of brain changes. Early studies suggested that abstinence was accompanied by dopamine transporter recovery, but a parallel recovery in cognitive function has been more difficult to identify. It is clear that recovery is related to the individual's baseline prior to use, the length of use, and the length of the abstinence (Volkow et al., 2001). A recent study using proton magnetic resonance spectroscopy suggested that following cessation of meth use, adaptive changes occur in the brain, which was felt to potentially contribute to some improvement in function (Nordahl et al., 2005). However, another recent publication suggests that meth use causes persistent hypometabolism in the frontal white matter of the brain with impairment in frontal executive function (Kim et al., 2005). Many studies are ongoing in this important area.

The release of serotonin is also stimulated by meth ingestion. This neurotransmitter has been implicated in states of consciousness, mood, depression, and anxiety. It is believed that meth has a little bit less serotonin effect than dopamine effect. However, damage to cells responsive to this chemical may explain the problems with depression that recovering addicts face.

As the nerve terminals are injured, the user eventually is unable to feel the pleasure that he began to use the drug for. This can contribute to the cycle of addiction and many of the chronic effects that are seen in long-term users.

Meth use can cause seizure activity, strokes, and spontaneous brain bleeds. It can also lead to chronic psychosis as well as movement disorders.

Cardiovascular System

Because meth is a stimulant, it has multiple effects on the cardiovascular system. These effects appear to be manifest at all dose levels and routes of administration even in otherwise healthy young adults. Virtually any kind of heart disease has been linked to meth use and abuse. First, use of this drug causes an increase in heart rate (tachycardia) as well as elevation of blood pressure (hypertension), both of which can be marked and very dangerous. Additionally, meth use can cause sudden cardiac death as well as the sudden rupture of an aneurysm. Meth is a blood vessel constrictor (vasoconstrictor), and that abnormal constriction of blood vessels of the heart can cause heart damage or a heart attack. This may be worsened or exacerbated by the fact that meth use causes increased platelet aggregation, which may clog cardiac vessels. Primarily because of the catecholamine (epinephrine and other neurotransmitted) excess, meth abuse may result in cardiotoxicity. This may be manifest as inflammation of the heart muscle (myocarditis) or the heart lining (endocarditis) and abnormalities in the heart muscle itself (cardiomyopathy) (Hong, Matsuyama, & Nur, 1991; Gold, 1997). Finally, chronic meth abuse can cause damage to any vessels throughout the body, further damaging the tissues those vessels supply.

Respiratory System

Respiratory system complications from meth abuse include shortness of breath (dyspnea) and severe chest pain. Coughing spasms following inhalation of the drug may result in pulmonary barotrauma and consequent leakiness of air into the pleural cavity, chest cavity (mediastinum), and soft (subcutaneous) tissues of the chest. Pulmonary edema (excess fluid in the lungs) has been noted in meth fatalities and is felt to be the result of deep inhalation of the drug and subsequent aggravation of preexisting conditions (Nestor et al., 1989a, 1989b). Granulomas may form as a result of chronic irritation from adulterants added to the drugs, and constriction of the blood vessels in the lungs may ultimately affect oxygen exchange, potentially leading to chronic lung disease (Center for Substance Abuse Treatment, 1997).

Dermatologic System

The skin of the chronic user is often in poor condition and may be covered in sores. Poor circulation to the skin, poor nutrition, and tactile hallucinations all contribute to this quickly identifiable problem. Users often report that they believe that there are bugs crawling on their skin (a phenomenon called "formication") and will perseverate on trying to pick at the bugs, often with instruments such as knives. These lesions frequently have difficulty healing well and become readily apparent in chronic users. Some parents will even believe that their children have bugs on their skin and cover the children in insect spray or pick at the child's skin. These lesions may be confused with another skin disorder if the drug use is not identified.

There may be evidence of healed burns if the user participated in manufacturing and was burned—often these individuals do not get medical care for the burns when they occur and attempt to treat the injury themselves. Recent data in the literature suggests that if such a burn patient seeks medical care, he needs to be managed differently from routine burn patients, requiring two to three times the usual amount of fluid resuscitation (Warner, Connolly, Gibran, Heimback, & Engrav, 2003).

Immunologic System

Drug abuse has been linked to increased risk of HIV and Hepatitis B, C, and D infection due to high-risk behaviors of users such as unprotected sexual activity and the sharing of injection paraphernalia. Preliminary animal studies have suggested that meth may also affect HIV disease progression by a more rapid and increased brain HIV viral load. Another study suggested that HIV-positive meth users may be at a greater risk of developing acquired immune deficiency syndrome (AIDS) than non–meth-using HIV-positive patients. Finally, additional studies have suggested that interactions between meth and the HIV virus itself may lead to greater neuronal damage and neuropsychological impairment (Volkow, 2005).

Other Organs

Other organs can be affected by meth use as well. Muscle damage can occur as a result of severely elevated body temperature (rhabdomyolysis). This can lead to major organ system damage, including the kidney, liver, and brain. Giant gastrointestinal ulcers can occur as a result of vasoconstriction decreasing blood supply to the intestines. There have also been reports of acute liver failure following intravenous meth use (Kamijo, Soma, Nishida, Namera, & Ohwada, 2002). One recent study showed significantly decreased calcification in the bone of chronic meth users, suggesting possible chronic effects on bone metabolism (Katsuragawa, 1999).

EFFECTS OF METH USE IN PREGNANCY

Meth use during pregnancy is believed to place the unborn fetus at risk, as does the use of other illicit drugs and alcohol. However, the full extent of maternal use of meth on the fetus and newborn infant is not completely known, and the fact that a mother uses a drug while pregnant does not, in and of itself, ensure that the unborn fetus will be affected. In fact, it is very difficult to differentiate the effects of meth exposure from a multitude of other factors such as maternal nutritional status and health, genetics, socioeconomic status, lack of prenatal care, and concomitant exposure to other drugs, including nicotine and alcohol. Additionally, the effect of any prenatal exposure on the fetus is also related to the gestational period during which the drug was used as well as the amount and form of use (Plessinger, 1998). Exposures in the first and second trimester of pregnancy are more likely to result in systemic abnormalities, while exposures later in pregnancy are linked with growth abnormalities.

There is currently a multicenter study underway to further describe this issue but, preliminarily, the investigators report that the effects appear to be similar to those of cocaine-exposed infants. However, although meth and cocaine are both sympathomimetic agents, it is known that meth has a much longer duration of action, potentially complicating its effects further.

There are several components of the potential risk to the fetus in a pregnancy complicated by maternal meth use. First, the effects of the use of the drug on the mother and father, including fertility, must be considered. Studies have shown that chronic, high-dose stimulant use affects reproductive and sexual functioning in both males and females. Male users report loss of sexual interest, impotence, and difficulty in maintaining an ejaculation, while female users may have abnormalities in their menstrual cycles leading to amenorrhea and infertility, as well as difficulty in achieving an orgasm (Gold, 1997). In the pregnant woman, meth may cause hypertension (high blood pressure), tachycardia, and vasoconstriction. Additionally, the mother's poor nutritional habits, high-risk behaviors, and commonly poor prenatal care may contribute to potential risk to the fetus.

Next, the risks to the placenta and the fetus must be considered. Based on its sympathomimetic function, meth is thought to have direct cardiovascular effects on both the fetus and the placenta, potentially causing fetal hypertension (high blood pressure), tachycardia (high heart rate), and vasoconstriction. These effects may result in premature delivery, intrauterine growth retardation, placental hemorrhage, fetal distress, or spontaneous abortion. Additionally, because the placenta provides the source of nutrition for the fetus, constriction of these blood vessels, as caused by meth, may result in reduced blood flow to the fetus and ultimately reduced oxygen and nutrient supply. These findings are consistent with the pharmacologic properties of meth, as it is known that elevated levels of norepinephrine can cause placental vasoconstriction and increased uterine contractility (Lederman, Lederman, Work, & McCann, 1978; Sherman & Gautieri, 1972). One sheep study released in 1993 showed that methamphetamine readily crosses the placenta and produces significant and long-lasting maternal and fetal cardiovascular effects (Stek et al., 1993). It is also known that meth passes through the placenta to the fetus and can cause elevated fetal blood pressure, potentially leading to prenatal strokes and heart or other major organ damage. The drug can cause an increased or extremely variable heart rate in the fetus and slowing or alteration of fetal growth. Additionally, simultaneous with an increase in maternal blood pressure following meth abuse, there is a decreased blood supply as well as oxygen supply to the placenta and fetus. This impaired oxygen supply can retard fetal development (Stewart & Meeker, 1997). Another study in sheep, released in

1994, showed that maternal administration of meth was found to be associated with a short-term increase in circulating fetal catecholamines, which was followed by hyperglycemia, lacticacidemia, and hyperinsulinism. This began to suggest an alteration of fetal sympathoadrenal activity, which may contribute to the perinatal complications seen with meth use (Dickinson, Andres, & Parisi, 1994). Additionally, it has been shown that the norepinephrine transporter and, to a lesser extent, the serotonin transporter are cellular targets in the human placenta for both amphetamine and meth (Ramamoorthy, Ramamoorthy, Leibach, & Ganapathy, 1995).

Another aspect of prenatal meth exposure that must be considered is any possible direct effect on the fetus. Fetal development abnormalities have been described sporadically in the medical literature, but no true syndrome specifically linked with maternal use of meth in the prenatal period has been described. There are limited numbers of studies in this area, particularly studies focusing on human infants. Additionally, most of the research in this area combines all amphetamines (often including cocaine), and only few studies isolate meth exposures. It is known that because of its low molecular weight and lipid solubility, there is considerable transfer of meth from maternal to fetal blood. This, in addition to the immaturity of fetal metabolic activities, may account for the reason that the drug remains in fetal circulation much longer than it does in maternal blood (Inaba & Cohen, 1993; Stek et al., 1993). Multiple studies looking at human exposures to amphetamines have indicated an association between meth or amphetamine use during pregnancy and cleft lip (Little, Snell, & Gilstrap, 1988; Nelson & Forfar, 1971; Saxen, 1975; Thomas, 1995), cardiac defects (Little et al., 1988; Nelson & Forfar, 1971; Nora, McNamara, & Clarke-Fraser, 1967; Nora, Vargo, Nora, Love, & McNamara, 1970), low birth weight (Little et al., 1988; Oro & Dixon, 1987), growth reduction and reduced head circumference (Eriksson, Larsson, & Zetterström, 1981; Little et al., 1988; Oro & Dixon, 1987), biliary atresia (Golbus, 1980; Levin, 1971), prematurity and stillbirth (Ericksson, Larsson, Windbladh, & Zetterström, 1978), hyperbilirubinemia requiring transfusion (Ericksson et al., 1978), cerebral hemorrhage (Dixon & Bejar, 1989), low body fat, and undescended testes (Little et al., 1988). Although these things have been noted to be associated with meth or amphetamine use prenatally, there is little data to suggest any kind of causative relationship, and the direct link between fetal abnormalities and maternal methamphetamine use is not clearly discernable. One study by Oro and Dixon showed that in utero exposure to cocaine or methamphetamine was adversely, negatively associated with gestational age, birth weight, length, and occipitofrontal circumference. They also showed that "the increased rate of prematurity, intrauterine growth retardation, and perinatal complications associated with prenatal exposure to cocaine or methamphetamine was greater than that predicted by coexisting risk factors and was consistent with the pharmacologic properties of these drugs" (Oro & Dixon, 1987). Another study by Smith et al. showed an association between decreased growth in infants exposed to meth throughout pregnancy relative to those infants only exposed in the first and second trimesters (Smith et al., 2003). Therefore, it is felt that birth outcomes may improve if the mother stops using the drug in the last one to three months of pregnancy. In addition, this study revealed significantly more small-for-gestational-age infants in the methamphetamine-exposed group than those in the nonexposed group (Smith et al., 2003). There also appeared to be a significant decrease in growth in the meth-exposed infants who were born to mothers who additionally smoked cigarettes compared to those who did not smoke (Smith et al., 2003). Finally, these infants may be at increased risk of blood-borne diseases such as HIV, Hepatitis B, and hepatitis C because of the frequent high-risk behaviors of the mother.

Early studies of amphetamine-exposed infants indicated that many of these infants had difficulties with poor feeding and extreme drowsiness throughout the first several weeks to as long as a year of life (Ericksson et al., 1978, 1981; Ramer, 1974). Some of these infants (like infants with exposures to narcotics) may display an array of behavioral disturbances after birth characterized by tremors, irritability, abnormal sleep patterns, and poor feeding, which may represent direct drug effects rather than withdrawal, as the metabolites were found in the infants' urine for up to seven days after birth (Oro & Dixon, 1987). One study that analyzed 294 mother-infant pairs (134 exposed and 160 unexposed) found that 49 percent of exposed infants displayed evidence of withdrawal symptoms and documented the need for pharmacologic intervention for the treatment of withdrawal symptoms in 4 percent of these infants (Smith et al., 2003). Following this initial hyperirritable phase (usually only displayed in the first several days of life), some meth-exposed infants were so extremely drowsy that they required tube feedings, approximating the prolonged sleep, lethargy, and depression ("crash") seen in adult users (Oro & Dixon, 1987). This period of time through the first four weeks of life is felt to be related to the dopamine depletion syndrome and may be characterized by lethargy in the infant with excessive periods of sleep, poor suck and swallow coordination, sleep apnea, and poor habituation (Shah, 2006). Exposed infants may have irregular sleep patterns, poor feeding, tremors, and increased muscle tone. Their poor ability to habituate or self-regulate, especially under stressful situations, will be further intensified if their environment is noisy and chaotic. They will not tolerate this well, which will likely lead to increased irritability and potential for abuse. In the next four months of life, the infant may display symptoms of CNS immaturity, including effects on motor development; sensory integration problems including tactile, defensive, and texture issues; and neurobehavioral symptoms affecting their interaction and social development. This period is frequently followed by a symptom-free period or the honeymoon phase from 6 to 18 months. However, from 18 months to 5 years, the children may again begin to exhibit difficulties with sensory integration, poorly focused attention, easy distractibility, poor anger management, and aggressive outbursts (Shah, 2006).

Because of the multitude of confounding variables such as other potential drug exposures, genetic predisposition, and environmental factors, it is difficult to identify postnatal features that are directly related to in utero meth exposure. However, scientists have begun to study infants exposed to meth in utero to attempt to identify potential outcomes. One study by Hansen, Struthers, & Gospe (1993) of infants exposed to meth in utero has identified visual cognitive effects (poorer visual recognition memory—a measure correlated with subsequent IQ) and changes in behavior that appear to be permanent in these infants. Several additional studies in rats have demonstrated similar concerns for spatial learning in adult animals exposed to meth in utero (Crawford, Williams, Newman, McDougall, & Vorhees, 2003; Williams, Vorhees, Boon, Saber, & Cain, 2002; Williams et al., 2003).

Several studies have shown that prenatally meth-exposed infants may go on to exhibit further difficulties in childhood. Children exposed to meth in utero may face difficulties with what is called executive-level functioning. This functioning is related to the brain's ability to absorb information, interpret the information, and make decisions based on it. Difficulties in this level of functioning may help explain the problems that many of these children face with impulsivity, judgment, and connecting behavior with consequence. Although there are mounting studies on the effects of meth on adult brains, studies on the brains of infants exposed to meth in utero are limited but beginning to emerge. One study by Smith et al. attempted to study the possible neurotoxic effects of prenatal meth exposure on the developing brain using brain proton magnetic resonance spectroscopy (Smith et al., 2003). In this study, the researchers found the suggestion of an abnormality in the energy metabolism in the brains of children exposed to meth in utero, but acknowledged the need for more studies and the interpretation of this study with caution due to their small sample size and limited behavioral assessments (Smith et al., 2003). The study, however, may have important clinical implications, since the area found to be affected is the frontal-striatal pathway, which is involved in executive-level functioning.

Studies done in Sweden following the short-term legalization of drugs of abuse in the 1960s looked at populations of children exposed to amphetamines prenatally who were then monitored for their progress and performance (Plessinger, 1998). Several reports indicated difficulties with altered growth and behavior in the exposed children (Plessinger, 1998). Looking at matched groups of exposed and unexposed children at 8 years and then 14 years of age, a larger number of amphetamine-exposed children did more poorly than unexposed controls in mathematics, language, and physical training (Cernerud, Eriksson, Jonsson, Steneroth, & Zetterström, 1996; Ericksson et al., 1978, 1981). These studies also showed that once these exposed children were past puberty, the boys were taller and heavier and the girls were shorter and lighter than the Swedish standards used for comparison (Cernerud et al., 1996). These findings may suggest an effect of in utero exposure of methamphetamines on normal neural development and maturation of the adenohypophysis, which raises concern that the use of amphetamines during pregnancy may cause a wide variety of effects (Plessinger, 1998).

Additional work is being done in an effort to better define any association there may be between prenatal drug exposures and later drug use and medical complications in young adults and adults. One recent study at the University of Chicago indicated that males who were exposed to meth in utero and then went on to take the drug themselves as teens or adults may have hastened onset of brain disorders such as Parkinson's Disease (Heller, Bubula, Lew, Heller, & Won, 2001).

Finally, there have been reports of deaths in fetuses and infants felt to be related to maternal meth use. Although the actual number of these cases reported in the literature is low, there is concern about the risk of death in infant's exposure to this drug either prenatally or in the postnatal period. One study reviewed the deaths of eight fetuses/infants aged from 20 weeks estimated gestational age to a 1-month-old infant (Stewart & Meeker, 1997). In these cases, it was believed that the maternal use of meth played a role in the deaths of the fetuses/infants, and the authors cited the increased vulnerability of the developing nervous system and potential compromise due to fetal acidosis, hypoxernia, decreased uterine blood flow, changes in fetal blood gases, and an increase in fetal glucose levels (Stewart & Meeker, 1997). There have also been some studies suggesting a possible link between cocaine exposure in utero and sudden infant death syndrome (SIDS), but the nature of this connection is unclear. However, because of this potential link as well as the possibility that the infant may have ingested the drug, California law now requires that all SIDS deaths be tested for certain drugs, including meth.

PARENTING ISSUES IN METH USE

A very important factor that must be considered regarding children that are exposed to meth is the environment in which the child is raised. There are additional and potentially very dangerous consequences that may occur if a child grows up in an environment where there is active use of methamphetamine. These risks include the actual environment, which may include many hazards including the exposure to the drug itself, as well as the actual quality of parenting that the child receives.

The environment of a meth abuser is one that may contain many risks for growing children. These risks include exposure to the actual drug itself (see the next section), weapons, an unkempt and dirty home, inadequate food, inappropriate sleeping conditions, multiple unsavory visitors, and exposure to violence and sexual content and activity. The child may be neglected while the parents sleep for long periods of time during a "crash." They frequently do not receive adequate medical, dental, emotional, and educational care. Additionally, children living in these homes are at an increased risk of sexual abuse, either from witnessing sexually explicit activity or material or from becoming the actual targets of bizarre sexual activity in the home. They may also be physically abused or even killed when the parent becomes easily frustrated or the child becomes the target of the parent's homicidal ideations.

There are few studies in this area, but one study in which meth was administered to premating, gestational, and lactational rat pups demonstrated that the drug had a negative effect on maternal behavior toward the pups (Šlamberová et al., 2005).

EFFECTS ON CHILDREN

When meth is used in a home where children reside, there are several routes of potential exposure and subsequent danger to the children. First, when there is active use in the home, the drug itself is frequently readily accessible to children, often lying on surfaces within easy reach of a curious child. Children display frequent hand-to-mouth behavior, placing them at risk for picking up the drug itself and ingesting it, resulting in a continuum of possible effects ranging from minor physiologic response to significant intoxication, seizures, and death. Although this is not an uncommon event, there are only a few such cases reported in the literature. In 1998 Kolecki reported 18 cases in which children less than 13 years of age were confirmed to be victims of oral methamphetamine poisoning. In these cases, the drugs had been left out with easy access for the children. The children displayed agitation (9), inconsolability (6), increased heart rate (18), abdominal pain, vomiting (6), seizures, muscle breakdown, fever (1), and ataxia (1). Prior to identification of the cause for the children's illness, multiple tests and treatments were undertaken such as head CTs (5), spinal taps (3), and administration of spider (Centruroides sculpturatus) antivenom (3), since the presentation closely resembled spider envenomation. In fact, one child developed an anaphylactic reaction to the antivenom (Kolecki, 1998). Another case reported in 1995 by Gospe profiled the case of an 11-month-old boy who presented to medical care with irritability and transient cortical blindness and involuntary turning of the head and tested positive for meth. Symptoms resolved after 12 hours of supportive care. Mother reported that she had found the infant chewing on a small plastic bag (Gospe, 1995). An additional case was reported by Narogka, who described a 13-month-old girl whose symptoms of restlessness and roving eye movements were initially felt to be from scorpion envenomation, but when she did not respond to antivenom, a urine drug screen was obtained and found to be positive for meth (Nagorka & Bergeson, 1998).

Effects of exposures to meth through breastfeeding must also be considered. Meth, like most drugs, is transferred to the breast milk when a lactating mother uses the drug. Therefore, the American Academy of Pediatrics does not recommend breastfeeding when the mother is using meth, as it is believed that the infant will receive the drug through breast milk, and this has been reported to cause irritability and poor sleeping patterns (American Academy of Pediatrics, Committee on Drugs, 2001).

At this time, there is not enough scientific data in the literature to fully understand the amount of exposure that a child may receive when living in an environment where meth is actively being smoked or used. There is no information on the potential for intake of the drug through transdermal absorption or passive inhalation. Research in this area is clearly needed.

CONCLUSION

Meth use and abuse in this country has far-reaching ramifications for not only the user but for society. While we currently understand a great deal about the medical effects of this drug on both adults and children, there is far more that needs to be studied. Additionally, the nature and extent of the effects on the user of the by-products and other chemicals that may remain in the meth following the manufacturing process are unknown at this time. The studies that are currently available have only addressed the effect of the actual drug. The National Institute of Drug Abuse (NIDA) is aggressively supporting a comprehensive research program to better understand meth's mechanism of action, physical and behavioral effects, risk and protective factors, treatments, and potential predictors of treatment success (Volkow, 2005). Continued collaborative efforts are critical to advancements in understanding the medical effects of meth on the users and children who are exposed.

NOTE

1. From: *The Methamphetamine Crisis*, Herbert C. Covey; Chapter 4, pp. 57–74, "The Short- and Long-Term Medical Effects of Methamphetamine on Children and Adults," by Kathryn Wells. Copyright © 2006 by Herbert C. Covey. Reproduced with permission of Greenwood Publishing Group, Inc., Westport, CT.

REFERENCES

Allcott, J. V., III, Barnhart, R. A., & Mooney, L. A. (1987). Acute lead poisoning in two users of illicit methamphetamine. *Journal of the American Medical Association, 258,* 510–511.

American Academy of Pediatrics, Committee on Drugs. (2001). The transfer of drugs and other chemicals into human milk. *Pediatrics, 108*(3), 776–789.

Beebe, D. K, & Walley, E. (1995). Smokable methamphetamine ("ice"): An old drug in a different form. *American Family Physician, 51*(2), 449–453.

Brown, J. M., Hanson, G. R., & Fleckenstein, A. E. (2000). Methamphetamine rapidly decreases vesicular dopamine uptake. *Journal of Neurochemistry, 74*(5), 2221–2223.

Burton, B. T. (1991). Heavy metal and organic contaminants associated with illicit methamphetamine production. In M. A. Miller & N. J. Kozel (Eds.), *Methamphetamine abuse: Epidemiologic issues and implications* (pp. 47–59). (NIDA Research Monograph Series, No. 115. DHHS Publication No. [ADM] 91–1836). Rockville, MD: National Institute on Drug Abuse.

Center for Substance Abuse Treatment. (1997). Proceedings of the national consensus meeting on the use, abuse, and sequelae of abuse of methamphetamine with implications for prevention, treatment, and research (DHHS Publication No. [SMA] 96–8013). Rockville, MD: Substance Abuse and Mental Health Services Administration.

Center for Substance Abuse Treatment. (1999). *Tip 33: Treatment for stimulant use disorders: Treatment improvement protocol* (TIP Series No. 33). Rockville, MD: Substance Abuse and Mental Health Services Administration.

Cernerud, L., Eriksson, M., Jonsson, B., Steneroth, G., & Zetterström, R. (1996). Amphetamine addiction during pregnancy: 14-year follow-up of growth and school performance. *Acta Pediatrica, 85,* 204–208.

Cho, A. K. (1990). Ice: A new dosage form of an old drug. *Science, 249,* 631–634.

Crawford, C. A., Williams, M. T., Newman, E. R., McDougall, S. A., & Vorhees, C. V. (2003). Methamphetamine exposure during the preweaning period causes prolonged changes in dorsal striatal protein kinase A activity, dopamine Ds-like binding sites, and dopamine content. *Synapse, 48,* 131–137.

Dickinson, J. E., Andres, R. L., & Parisi, V. M. (1994). The ovine fetal sympathoadrenal response to the maternal administration of methamphetamine. *American Journal of Obstetrics and Gynecology, 170,* 1452–1457.

Dixon, S. D., & Bejar, R. (1989). Echoencephalographic findings in neonates associated with cocaine and methamphetamine use: Incidence and clinical correlates. *Journal of Pediatrics, 115*, 770–778.

Ellinwood, E. H., Jr., Sudilovsky, A., & Nelson, L. M. (1973). Evolving behavior in the clinical and experimental amphetamine (model) psychosis. *American Journal of Psychiatry, 130*, 1088–1092.

Ericksson, M., Larsson, C., Windbladh, B., & Zetterström, R. (1978). The influence of amphetamine addiction on pregnancy and the newborn infant. *Acta Paediatrica Scandinavica, 67*(1), 95–99.

Eriksson, M., Larsson, G., & Zetterström, R. (1981). Amphetamine addiction and pregnancy. II: Pregnancy, delivery and the neonatal period: Socio-medical aspects. *Acta Obstetricia et Gynecologica Scandinavica, 60*, 253–259.

Ernst, T., Chang, L., Leonido-Yee, M., & Speck, O. (2000). Evidence for long-term neurotoxicity associated with methamphetamine abuse: A 1H MRS study. *Neurology, 54*, 1344–1349.

Furst, S. R., Fallon, S. P., Reznik, G. N., & Shah, P. K. (1990). Myocardial infarction after inhalation of methamphetamine [Letter to the editor]. *New England Journal of Medicine, 49*, 389–391.

Golbus, M. S. (1980). Teratology for the obstetrician: Current status. *Obstetrics and Gynecology, 55*, 269–277.

Gold, M. S. (1997). Cocaine (and crack): Clinical aspects. In J. H. Lowenson, P. Ruiz, R. B. Millman, & J. G. Langrod (Eds.), *Substance abuse: A comprehensive textbook* (3rd ed.). Baltimore: Williams and Wilkins.

Gospe, S. (1995). Transient cortical blindness in an infant exposed to methamphetamine. *Annals of Emergency Medicine, 26*, 380–382.

Hansen, R. L., Struthers, J. M., & Gospe, S. M., Jr. (1993). Visual evoked potentials and visual processing in stimulant drug-exposed infants. *Developmental Medicine and Child Neurology, 35*, 798–805.

Heller, A., Bubula, N., Lew, R., Heller, B., & Won, L. (2001). Gender-dependent enhanced adult neurotoxic response to methamphetamine following fetal exposure to the drug. *Journal of Pharmacology and Experimental Therapeutics, 298*(2), 769–779.

Hong, R., Matsuyama, E., & Nur, K. (1991). Cardiomyopathy associated with the smoking of crystal methamphetamine. *Journal of the American Medical Association, 265*(9), 1152–1154.

Inaba, D., & Cohen, W. (1993). *Uppers, downers, all arounders* (2nd ed.). Ashland, OR: CNS Productions.

Jaffe, J. H. (1990). Drug addiction and drug abuse. In A. G. Gilman, T. W. Rall, A. S. Nies, & P. Taylor (Eds.), *Goodman and Gilman's the pharmacological basis of therapeutics* (8th ed., pp. 539–545). New York: Pergamon.

Jaffe, J. H. (1995). Amphetamine (or amphetamine-like)-related disorders. In H. I. Kaplan, & B. J. Sadock (Eds.), *Comprehensive textbook of psychiatry* (6th ed., pp. 791–798). Baltimore: Williams and Wilkins.

Kamijo, Y., Soma, K., Nishida, M., Namera, A., & Ohwada, T. (2002). Acute liver failure following intravenous methamphetamine. *Veterinarian and Human Toxicology*, *44*(4), 216–217.

Kato, M. (1990). Brief history of control, prevention, and treatment of drug dependence in Japan. *Drug Alcohol Dependency*, *25*(2), 213–214.

Katsuragawa, Y. (1999). Effect of methamphetamine abuse on the bone quality of the calcaneus. *Forensic Science International*, *101*, 43–48.

Kim, S. J., Lyoo, I. K., Hwang, J., Sung, Y. H., Lee, H. Y., Lee, D. S., et al. (2005). Frontal glucose metabolism in abstinent methamphetamine users. *Neuropsychopharmacology*, *30*(7), 1383–1391.

Lederman, R. P., Lederman, E., Work, B. A., Jr., & McCann, D. S. (1978). The relationship of maternal anxiety, plasma catecholamines and plasma cortisol to progress in labor. *American Journal of Obstetrics and Gynecology*, *132*, 495–500.

Levin, J. N. (1971). Amphetamine ingestion with biliary atresia. *Pediatrics*, *79*, 130–131.

Lewis, D. C., & Millar, D. G. (2005, July 27). Open letter: To whom it may concern.

Little, B. B., Snell, L. M., & Gilstrap, L. C., III. (1988). Methamphetamine use during pregnancy: Outcome and fetal effects. *Obstetrics and Gynecology*, *72*, 541–544.

London, E. D, Simon, S. L., Berman, S. M., Mandelkern, M. A., Lichtman, A. M., Bramen, J., et al. (2004). Mood disturbances and regional cerebral metabolic abnormalities in recently abstinent methamphetamine abusers. *Archives of General Psychiatry*, *61*, 73–84.

MacKenzie, R. G., & Heischober, B. (1997). Methamphetamine. *Pediatrics in Review*, *18*(9), 305–309.

Murray, J. B. (1998). Psychophysiological aspects of amphetamine-methamphetamine abuse. *Journal of Psychology*, *132*(2), 227–237.

Nagorka, A. R., & Bergeson, P. S. (1998). Infant methamphetamine toxicity posing as scorpion envenomation. *Pediatric Emergency Care*, *14*, 350–351.

National Institute on Drug Abuse. (1998, April). *Methamphetamine abuse and addiction*. (National Institute on Drug Abuse Research Report Series. NIH Publication No. 98–4210). Bethesda, MD: Author.

National Institutes of Health. (2004, January 5). New study suggests methamphetamine withdrawal is associated with brain changes similar to those seen in depression and anxiety. *NIH News*, Washington, DC: U.S. Department of Health and Human Services.

National Jewish Medical and Research Center. (2004). *Toxic brew of chemicals cooked up in methamphetamine labs*. Denver, CO: Author. Retrieved from www.national jewish.org/news/meth

Nelson, M. M., & Forfar, O. (1971). Associations between drugs administered during pregnancy and congenital abnormalities of the fetus. *British Medical Journal*, *1*, 523–527.

Nestor, T. A., Tamamoto, W. I., Kam, T. H., & Schultz, T. (1989a). Crystal methamphetamine-induced acute pulmonary edema: A case report. *Hawaii Medical Journal, 48*, 457–460.

Nestor, T. A., Tamamoto, W. I., Kam, T. H., & Schultz, T. (1989b). Acute pulmonary edema caused by crystalline methamphetamine. *Lancet, 2*(8674), 1277–1278.

Nora, J. J., McNamara, D. G., & Clarke-Fraser, F. (1967). Dexamphetamine sulphate and human malformations. *Lancet, 2*, 1021–1022.

Nora, J. J., Vargo, T. A., Nora, A. H., Love, K. E., & McNamara, D. G. (1970). Dexamphetamine: A possible environmental trigger in cardiovascular malformations. *Lancet, 1*(7659), 1290–1291.

Nordahl, T. E., Salo, R., Natsuaki, Y., Galloway, G. P., Waters, C., Moore, C. D., et al. (2005). Methamphetamine users in sustained abstinence: A proton magnetic resonance spectroscopy study. *Archives of General Psychiatry, 62*, 444–452.

Oro, A. S., & Dixon, S. D. (1987). Perinatal cocaine and methamphetamine exposure: Maternal and neonatal correlates. *Journal of Pediatrics, 111*, 571–578.

Plessinger, M. A. (1998). Prenatal exposure to amphetamines: Risks and adverse outcomes in pregnancy. *Obstetrics and Gynecology Clinics of North America, 25*, 119–139.

Ramamoorthy, J. D., Ramamoorthy, S., Leibach, F. H., & Ganapathy, V. (1995). Human placental monoamine transporters as targets for amphetamines. *American Journal of Obstetrics and Gynecology, 173*, 1782–1787.

Ramer, C. M. (1974). The case history of an infant born to an amphetamine-addicted mother. *Clinical Pediatrics, 13*, 596–597.

Rowbotham, M. C. (1993). Cocaine levels and elimination in inpatients and outpatients: Implications for emergency treatment of cocaine complications. In H. Sorer (Ed.), *Acute cocaine intoxication: Current methods of treatment* (pp. 147–155). (NIDA Research Monograph Series, No. 123. DHHS Publication No. [ADM] 93–3498). Rockville, MD: National Institute on Drug Abuse.

Saxen, I., (1975). Associations between oral clefts and drugs taken during pregnancy. *International Journal of Epidemiology, 4*, 37–44.

Shah, R. (2006, February 21). *Infants exposed prenatally to methamphetamines: Developmental effects and effective interventions.* Teleconference Series, National Abandoned Infants Assistance Resource Center.

Shaner, J. W. (2002, September). Caries associated with methamphetamine abuse. *Journal of the Michigan Dental Association, 84*(9), 42–47.

Sherman, W. T., & Gautieri, R. F. (1972). Effect of certain drugs on perfused human placenta. X. Norepinephrine release by bradynin. *Journal of Pharmacological Science, 61*, 870–873.

Šlamberová, R., Charousová, P., & Pometlová, M. (2005). Methamphetamine administration during gestation impairs maternal behavior. *Developmental Psychobiology, 46*, 57–65.

Smith, L., Yonekura, M. L., Wallace, T., Berman, N., Kuo, J., & Berkowitz, C. (2003). Effects of prenatal methamphetamine exposure on fetal growth and drug withdrawal symptoms in infants born at term. *Journal of Developmental Behavior and Pediatrics, 24*(1), 17–23.

Sowder, B., & Beschner, G. (Eds.). (1993). *Methamphetamine: An illicit drug with high abuse potential.* Unpublished report from NIDA Contract No. 271–90–0002. Rockville, MD: T. Head and Company.

Stek, A. M., Fisher, B. K., Baker, R. S., Lang, U., Tseng, C. U., & Clark, K. E. (1993). Maternal and fetal cardiovascular responses to methamphetamine in the pregnant sheep. *American Journal of Obstetrics and Gynecology, 169*(4), 888–897.

Stewart, J. L., & Meeker, J. E. 1997. Fetal and infant deaths associated with maternal methamphetamine abuse. *Journal of Analytical Toxicology, 21,* 515–517.

Streltzer, J., & Leigh, H. (1977, January–February). Amphetamine abstinence psychosis—Does it exist? *Psychiatric Opinion,* 47–50.

Szuster, R. R. (1990). Methamphetamine in psychiatric emergencies. *Hawaii Medical Journal, 49,* 389–391.

Tandy, K. P. (2004, March 24). Statement before the U.S. House of Representatives, Committee on Appropriations, Subcommittee for the Departments of Commerce, Justice, State, the Judiciary and Related Agencies. Washington, DC.

Thomas, D. B. (1995). Cleft palate, mortality and morbidity in infants of substance abusing mothers. *Journal of Paediatric Child Health, 31,* 457–460.

Tomiyama, G. (1990). Chronic schizophrenia-like states in methamphetamine psychosis. *Japanese Journal of Psychiatry and Neurology, 44*(3), 531–539.

Volkow, N. D. (2005, April 21). Methamphetamine abuse—Testimony before the Senate Subcommittee on Labor, Health and Human Services, Education, and Related Agencies—Committee on Appropriations. Washington, DC.

Volkow, N. D., Chang, L., Wang, G.-J., Fowler, J. S., Leonido-Yee, M., Franceschi, D., et al. (2001). Association of dopamine transporter reduction with psychomotor impairment in methamphetamine abusers. *American Journal of Psychiatry, 158*(3), 377–382.

Warner, P., Connolly, J. P., Gibran, N. S., Heimback, D. M., & Engrav, L. H. (2003). The methamphetamine burn patient. *Journal of Burn Care and Rehabilitation, 24*(5), 275–278.

Wetli, C. V. (1993). The pathology of cocaine: Perspectives from the autopsy table. In H. Sorer (Ed.), *Acute cocaine intoxication: Current methods of treatment* (pp. 172–183). (NIDA Research Monograph Series, No. 123. DHHS Publication No. [ADM] 93–3498). Rockville, MD: National Institute on Drug Abuse.

Williams, M. T., Morford, L. L., Wood, S. L., Wallace, T. L., Fukumura, M., Broening, H. W., et al. (2003). Developmental D-methamphetamine treatment selectively induces spatial navigation impairments in reference memory in the Morris water maze while sparing working memory. *Synapse, 48,* 138–148.

Williams, M. T., Vorhees, C. V., Boon, F., Saber, A. J., & Cain, D. P. (2002). Methamphetamine exposure from postnatal day 11 to 20 causes impairments in both behavioral strategies and spatial learning in adult rats. *Brain Research, 958,* 312–321.

Wolkoff, D. (1997). Methamphetamine abuse: An overview for health care professionals. *Hawaii Medical Journal, 56,* 34–36, 44.

Yui, K., Goto, K., Ikemoto, S., Ishiguro, T., & Kamata, Y. (2000). Increased sensitivity to stress in spontaneous recurrence of methamphetamine psychosis: Noradrenergic hyperactivity with contribution from dopaminergic hyperactivity. *Journal of Clinical Psychopharmacology, 20*(2), 165–174.

Chapter 11

Vapors May Be Dangerous If Inhaled: An Overview of Inhalants and Their Abuse

Jace Waguspack, BS, and Paula K. Lundberg-Love, PhD

The word *inhalant* is a broad term used to describe a heterogeneous group of chemicals that share a common route of administration. In addition to the drugs identified as "inhalants," there are other drugs that are inhaled, but they are excluded from this group as they fall under other drug classifications (i.e., cigarettes, marijuana, or crack cocaine). Inhalants can be effectively subdivided into three separate groups known as volatile substances, nitrous oxide, and nitrites (Balster, 1998).

The first group, volatile substances, is the most commonly abused of the inhalants, and it includes a wide variety of substances that give off vapors at room temperature (Brouette & Anton, 2001). This group typically includes solvents, adhesives, aerosols, cleaning agents, and gasoline (Sharp & Rosenberg, 1997). There are many different types of chemicals that constitute this group, but some of the more common chemicals include toluene, acetone, butane, trichloroethylene, hexane, propane, fluorocarbons, and others (Sharp & Rosenberg, 1997). These chemicals can be found in a variety of easily acquired products, including some glues, spray paint, dry cleaning agents, paint thinner, nail polish remover, and typewriter correction fluid (Sharp & Rosenberg, 1997). The relative ease with which one can acquire these products is one of the proposed explanations for their widespread abuse, especially among young people (McHugh, 1987).

The chemical that constitutes the second group of inhalants is nitrous oxide. Nitrous oxide is commonly known as laughing gas, and can be acquired by those who have access to medical supplies because it is used in dentistry as a type of anesthetic. It also is often used as a propellant in whipped cream, which makes it available in grocery stores (Brouette & Anton, 2001).

The final group of inhalants comprises chemicals referred to as nitrites. Nitrites include the chemicals butyl nitrite, amyl nitrite, and isobutyl nitrite, and are commonly found in room odorizers (Brouette & Anton, 2001). Due to the fact that they enhance sexual experiences, they are also often sold in sex shops (Brouette & Anton, 2001).

There are several methods by which these chemicals are inhaled, including "sniffing," "huffing," "spraying," and "bagging." "Sniffing" involves inhaling vapors from an open container (Dinwiddie, 1994). "Huffing" is a practice whereby an individual soaks a rag in the chemical of choice and then holds the rag to his or her face to be inhaled (Brouette & Anton, 2001). Inhalant users sometimes directly spray the desired inhalant into the mouth or nose (Brouette & Anton, 2001). "Bagging," on the other hand, involves filling a bag with the chemical and then breathing from the bag (Brouette & Anton, 2001). The practice of bagging can be quite dangerous, as the drowsiness that inhalants induce coupled with the lack of fresh oxygen received when breathing from the bag may cause the individual to lose consciousness. When adhesives are being used in this manner, the bag may seal to the person's face, causing death by asphyxiation if the individual loses consciousness (Brouette & Anton, 2001).

HISTORY AND EPIDEMIOLOGY

The abuse of inhalant drugs is a relatively recent phenomenon. Inhalant use first began to receive public attention in the 1960s, when sniffing glue became popular (Fredlund, Spence, & Maxwell, 1989). During this time, abuse of nitrites began to emerge as well (Haverkos, Kopstein, Wilson, & Drotman, 1994). Nitrites became particularly popular among homosexual men due to the enhancement of sexual experience from vasodilation (widening of blood vessels) resulting in penile engorgement, combined with relaxation of smooth muscle tissue (Goode & Troiden, 1979), as well as prolonged orgasm (Newell, Spitz, & Wilson, 1988). Chronic use of nitrites has several negative hematological effects, including effects on lymphocyte number and function, reduction of monocyte adherence, and the suppression of natural killer cells. Nitrite abuse also compromises T-dependent antibody induction, cytotoxic T cell induction, and the tumoricidal activity of macrophages (Brouette & Anton, 2001; Dax, Lange, & Jaffe, 1989; Soderberg, Chang, & Barnett, 1996). Due to nitrites' negative hematological effects, as well as a high correlation of nitrite use in AIDS patients, it was once postulated that nitrites were in fact the cause of AIDS (Brouette & Anton, 2001). Because of the discovery of the HIV virus, this theory was disproved. A positive side effect of the association of nitrites and possible susceptibility to AIDS was that the use of nitrites sharply decreased and has never regained its former popularity (Brouette & Anton, 2001).

However, the use of other inhalant substances remains high, particularly among young people. Some sources even report that inhalants have surpassed marijuana in popularity among 12-year-olds (Meyer & Quenzer, 2005). A recent study found that 17 percent of eighth graders in the United States have used inhalants (Johnston, O'Malley, Bachman, & Schulenberg, 2006). It has been proposed that the magnitude of this number is due to the ease of access to inhalants through a variety of common household substances (Ridenour, Bray, & Cottler, 2007). In fact, because they are so readily available, research indicates that inhalants are the gateway drugs for many children (McHugh, 1987).

While inhalant abuse is most common in young people, prevalence rates vary among different ethnic groups. Use among Hispanic Americans was found to be high, but these data are thought to be confounded by the low socioeconomic status and social dysfunction of the particular group of Hispanics studied (Padilla, Padilla, Morales, Olmedo, & Ramirez, 1979). Prevalence of inhalant use by Native American youths on reservations has been reported to be as high as 34 percent of 8th graders and 20 percent of 12th graders (Beauvais, 1992). Conversely, use of inhalants has been found to be particularly low in African Americans as opposed to other ethnic groups (Compton, Cottler, Dinwiddie, Mager, & Asmus, 1994).

Geographically, while inhalant abuse is seen across the United States, it is most pronounced in Alaska, where as many as 22 percent of high school students report having used inhalants (Meyer & Quenzer, 2005). Appropriately, one of the few inhalant abuse treatment centers in the United States, the Tundra Swan Inhalant Treatment Center, is located in Bethel, Alaska (Meyer & Quenzer, 2005).

COMORBIDITY OF PSYCHIATRIC DISORDERS AND INHALANT USE

Inhalant use has a very high rate of comorbidity with psychological disorders. Research indicates that 70 percent of inhalant users met criteria for a mental disorder at some point during their lifetime and 38 percent met criteria for a mental disorder within a year of the survey (Wu & Howard, 2007). Furthermore, female inhalant users exhibit mental disorders more often than do male inhalant users, and female users exhibit multiple mental disorders more often than do their male counterparts (Wu & Howard, 2007). Major depression was the most common mental disorder found comorbid with inhalant use (41%), and antisocial personality disorder was the second most common mental disorder (32%) (Wu & Howard, 2007). Of the 70 percent of inhalant users that met the criteria for one lifetime mental disorder, 49 percent met the criteria for three or more disorders. The high rate of comorbidity between inhalant use and psychological disorders has important implications for the treatment of inhalant abuse, which will be discussed later in this chapter. Although, at this time, a causal relationship cannot be inferred between inhalant use and psychiatric disorders, it is interesting to note that in the majority of cases, inhalant use precedes the onset of most mood and anxiety disorders identified in inhalant users, and that the onset of these psychiatric disorders tends to occur earlier in inhalant users versus nonusers (Wu & Howard, 2007).

MECHANISMS OF ACTION

Volatile Substances

The physiological mechanisms of action of the volatile substances are the least understood of all of the inhalants. However, recent research has made some progress in identifying and understanding how these agents affect neurons and brain neurochemistry. Many of the mechanisms of action of these substances are similar to those of ethanol. Moreover, these substances exert specific and nonspecific effects on the brain. With respect to their nonspecific mechanisms, volatile substances interact directly with the cell membranes of neurons, thereby fluidizing them (Brouette & Anton, 2001). Such a process reduces the efficiency of neural processing and results in overall central nervous system (CNS) depression. They also interact with and enhance the activity of gamma-aminobutyric acid (GABA)-A receptors and stimulate glycine receptors. Both GABA and glycine are two different neurotransmitter systems whose activation leads to inhibition of the CNS (Beckstead, Weiner, Eger, Gong, & Mihic, 2000). Chemicals in the volatile substance class of inhalants also appear to inhibit the activity of the N-methyl-D-aspartate (NMDA) glutamate receptors, a neurotransmitter system often responsible for central nervous system excitation (Cruz, Balster, & Woodwar, 2000) and the potentiation of learning and memory. This action further induces inhibition of CNS activity. Some volatile substances (specifically toluene) activate dopamine neurons in the ventral tegmental area, a part of the brain involved in the reinforcing effects of many drugs of abuse (Riegel, Zapata, Shippenberg, & French, 2007). Finally, recent research has shown that volatile solvents enhance the activity of serotonin 3A receptors (5-HT 3A), which are also believed to be involved in the reinforcement of drug-seeking behavior (Lopreato, Phelan, Borghese, Beckstead, & Mihic, 2003). The mechanisms behind this involvement are not well understood. However, some researchers have demonstrated that activation of 5-HT 3A receptors can stimulate dopamine release in the nucleus accumbens, a structure involved in the reinforcing effects of many drugs of abuse (Chen, van Praag, & Gardner, 1991).

Nitrous Oxide

The mechanisms by which nitrous oxide exerts its effects on human behavior are in dispute. Some argue that nitrous oxide works primarily through the opiate receptor system, and that it modulates the release of beta-endorphins and binds to the three types of opiate receptors: mu, kappa, and delta (Brouette & Anton, 2001; Gillman & Lichtigfeld, 1998). This theory would explain the analgesic effects of nitrous oxide, as activation of opiate receptors is known to produce analgesia (Gillman & Lichtigfeld, 1998). Activation of certain opiate receptors is also known to induce euphoria, which is also observed in nitrous oxide intoxication (Beckman, Zacny, & Walker, 2006). However, other research contradicts the opiate receptor theory of nitrous oxide analgesia and intoxication effects. In one such study, naloxone, a known opiate receptor antagonist, was administered following administration of nitrous oxide (Zacny et al., 1999). If the analgesia and euphoria caused by nitrous oxide were the result of opiate receptor activation, administration of naloxone should have reduced both of these effects. Instead, this study found that there was no significant reduction in analgesia or euphoria following naloxone administration, suggesting a separate mechanism of action for both of these effects (Zacny et al., 1999). Further research is necessary to determine the role of the opiate receptors in the analgesic and intoxicating effects of nitrous oxide, though it would appear that there is more current research that supports some degree of opiate receptor involvement. Less disputed is the theory that nitrous oxide blocks NMDA glutamate receptors (Brouette & Anton, 2001; Yamakura & Harris, 2000). This action is likely to underlie the short-term memory deficits often experienced by those under the influence of nitrous oxide (Brouette & Anton, 2001).

Nitrites

The mechanism of action of the third group of inhalants, nitrites, is quite different from the previous two groups. Instead of binding to specific neurotransmitter receptors, nitrites induce vasodilation, which results in the relaxation of blood vessels, and increased blood flow (Brouette & Anton, 2001).

Vasodilation of cerebral arteries is thought to underlie the psychological effects of nitrite intoxication (Brouette & Anton, 2001), while vasodilation of peripheral blood vessels results in lower blood pressure, flushing, syncope (fainting), throbbing sensations, and feelings of warmth (Balster, 1998). Nitrites also cause relaxation of smooth muscle tissue (Brouette & Anton, 2001).

ACUTE EFFECTS

Intoxication

The symptoms observed in inhalant intoxication vary depending upon the class of the inhalant used. Volatile substances cause drowsiness, diplopia (double vision), dysarthria (slurred speech), ataxia (an inability to walk and balance), and general disorientation (Brouette & Anton, 2001). When inhaled in higher concentrations, visual hallucinations can occur (Brouette & Anton, 2001). Because volatile substances have a similar mechanism of action to that of ethanol, it is not surprising that inhalant intoxication closely resembles that of ethanol. Disinhibition is accompanied by perceptual distortions and incoordination (Dinwiddie, 1994). Furthermore, users often experience nausea and vomiting, headaches, coughing, and excessive salivation (Dinwiddie, 1994). Occasionally, one may develop a rash around the nose and mouth (Dinwiddie, 1994). Some abusers even develop delusions, such as the belief that they can fly, which results in injury if these individuals subsequently jump out of windows or trees (Evans & Raistrick, 1987). There is evidence that tolerance develops with prolonged use of volatile substances (Ron, 1986).

In contrast, the symptoms of nitrous oxide intoxication often mimic those of psychedelic drugs as opposed to alcohol (Atkinson & Green, 1983). Nitrous oxide intoxication is often described as a dissociative experience (Brouette & Anton, 2001). While it does not produce the same reaction in all users, those that abuse it report that it induces euphoria, tingling, numbness, dizziness, hallucinations, and sensations of warmth (Brouette & Anton, 2001). Short-term memory loss has also been observed to occur as a result of nitrous oxide intoxication (Brouette & Anton, 2001).

The final group of inhalant drugs, nitrites, induces euphoria, floating sensations, increased tactile sensitivity, disinhibition, heightened sexual arousal, relaxation of the anus, and prolonged orgasm (Newell et al., 1988).

Sudden Sniffing Death Syndrome

Sudden sniffing death syndrome refers to a phenomenon whereby inhalation of chemicals from the volatile substance class of inhalants sensitizes the heart to the neurotransmitter epinephrine, which is involved in startle and stress responses (Bass, 1970). When the user is then frightened or stressed, as can happen from being caught inhaling by an adult or a startling visual hallucination, the hypersensitivity of the heart to epinephrine can trigger a fatal cardiac arrhythmia (Committee on Substance Abuse, 1996). Such a fatality can occur at any time, even upon an individual's first use of the substance (Committee on Substance Abuse, 1996). There also may be a higher risk of sudden death associated with fuel gases and aerosols than with adhesives (King, Smialek, & Troutman, 1985).

CHRONIC ORGAN EFFECTS

Chronic abuse of the volatile substance class of inhalants can have deleterious effects on multiple organ systems throughout the body. Hepatotoxicity, or toxicity of the liver, is associated with several of the volatile substances (Brouette & Anton, 2001). However, liver toxicity usually decreases shortly after cessation of inhalant use (Fornazzari, 1988). Pulmonary disease, emphysema, and chemical pneumonitis have also been found in individuals chronically exposed to volatile substances (Dinwiddie, 1994). Furthermore, heart complications, such as those found in sudden sniffing death syndrome, are a serious risk (Brouette & Anton, 2001). Some volatile substances, toluene in particular, can cause renal dysfunction (Brouette & Anton, 2001). Other research has even linked volatile substance abuse to bone marrow suppression (Flanagan, Ruprah, Meredith, & Ramsey, 1990). There are no known long-term complications of nitrous oxide abuse, as the side effects of nitrous oxide subside following abstinence (Brouette & Anton, 2001). Meanwhile, the most common complication resulting from chronic abuse of nitrites is a reduction in the functioning and efficacy of the immune system through various mechanisms, as discussed previously (Brouette & Anton, 2001).

CENTRAL NERVOUS SYSTEM EFFECTS

There are multiple brain structures affected by chronic inhalant abuse. Cell death in the cerebellum, a structure vital for balance and gait, often occurs (Fornazzari, Wilkinson, Kapur, & Carlen, 1983). With prolonged use, this damage may become permanent (Lazar, Ho, Melen, & Daghestani, 1983). Furthermore, destruction of white matter via neuronal demyelination is also observed in many chronic volatile substance abusers (Brouette & Anton, 2001). Myelin is a substance that insulates neurons such that the neural transmission of myelinated neurons is much more rapid than that of nonmyelinated neurons.

Therefore, the destruction of myelin in the central nervous system can produce a wide array of neurobehavioral deficits. In severe cases, this may even produce dementia (Meadows & Verghese, 1996). A recent MRI study confirmed neurological abnormalities in subcortical brain structures and white matter in 44 percent of the solvent abusers studied, as opposed to only 25.5 percent of other drug users studied (Rosenberg, Grigsby, Dreisbach, Busenbark, & Grigsby, 2002). These results imply that volatile solvents are neurotoxic, and that they produce neurological abnormalities more often than do other drugs, such as cocaine, marijuana, alcohol, amphetamines, and opiates.

Neuropsychological Deficits and Organic Solvent Neurotoxicity

Neuropsychological testing of chronic inhalant abusers has revealed a variety of neurobehavioral consequences. These include deficits in auditory discrimination, psychomotor speed, visuo-motor functioning, and memory impairment (Tsushima & Towne, 1977). Furthermore, some research suggests that the length of inhalant use correlates with lower neuropsychological test scores in these areas (Tsushima & Towne, 1977). Impairments in executive function (i.e., impulse control, planning, strategy formation, self-monitoring, and problem solving) have also been observed in chronic volatile substance abusers. These types of impairments may interfere with the effective treatment of these individuals due to the individual's lack of insight into his problems or an inability to follow steps to resolve such problems (Rosenberg et al., 2002).

Some individuals exposed to volatile solvents over a prolonged period of time develop a disorder called organic solvent neurotoxicity (OSN). This disorder is characterized by three levels of severity (Ogden, 1993). Symptoms of Type 1 OSN include fatigue, irritability, depression, and anxiety. This is the mildest form of OSN, and no significant types of neuropsychological impairment have been demonstrated in individuals with this type of OSN (Ogden, 1993). With continued abstinence from solvent ingestion, the symptoms diminish and ultimately disappear (Ogden, 1993). Symptoms of Type 2 OSN include personality and mood disturbances, deficiencies in motivation and impulse control, and deficits in memory, learning, concentration, and psychomotor speed (Ogden, 1993). Symptoms of Type 2 OSN generally improve somewhat, although not completely, after abstinence from exposure to solvents (Ogden, 1993). Type 3 OSN is the most severe form of the disorder, characterized by severe dementia accompanied by progressive deterioration of memory, cognitive abilities, and emotional functioning (Ogden, 1993). This condition is irreversible (Ogden, 1993).

FETAL EFFECTS

Administration of inhalants has been shown to affect the fetus in both animals and humans. Due to their high lipid solubility, most volatile substances rapidly and easily cross the placenta (Brouette & Anton, 2001). In animal studies, prenatal exposure to the solvent toluene resulted in lower birth weight and minor malformations (Bowen, Mohammadi, Batis, & Hannigan, 2007). A condition closely mimicking fetal alcohol syndrome has been identified in human infants born to volatile substance abusers (Toutant & Lippmann, 1979). Symptoms include facial deformities, limb abnormalities, growth retardation, and developmental delays. There is also evidence that the infant can be born with a withdrawal syndrome if the mother had used inhalants a few days before the child's birth (Tenenbein, Casiro, & Seshia, 1996).

INHALANT WITHDRAWAL SYNDROME

Despite the fact that a withdrawal syndrome for inhalants is not classified in the *DSM–IV–TR* (American Psychiatric Association, 2000), research indicates that some individuals do have withdrawal symptoms upon abstinence from inhalants. Symptoms include anhedonia, irritability, sleep disturbances, psychomotor slowing, dry mouth, lacrimation (watery eyes), drug craving, headaches, and heart palpitations (Muralidharan, Rajkumar, Mulla, Kayak, & Benegal, 2008; Shah, Vankar, & Upadhyaya, 1999). Pharmacological treatment of inhalant withdrawal symptoms has not been well established, but some research suggests that the administration of benzodiazepines may be effective (Brouette & Anton, 2001). Some new research indicates that baclofen, a GABA-B agonist may be an effective treatment option (Muralidharan et al., 2008).

TREATMENT OF INHALANT ABUSE

The current approach to the treatment of inhalant abuse in the United States is inadequate (Beauvais, Jumper-Thurman, Plested, & Helm, 2002). There are several factors that limit the effectiveness of the treatment of inhalant abuse, including a need for extended detoxification (Reidel, Hebert, & Bird, 1995), common comorbid psychological disorders (Wu & Howard, 2007), the presence of neurological damage (Beauvais et al., 2002), a lack of treatment centers dedicated to inhalant abuse (Beauvais et al., 2002), and an incomplete understanding of the mechanisms of action of many inhalant drugs (Shen, 2007). Furthermore, as a result of these limitations, treatment centers that do accept inhalant abusers are often pessimistic about the successful rehabilitation of these individuals (Beauvais et al., 2002).

Despite barriers to effective treatment, some recent progress has been made with respect to the primary prevention of inhalant abuse. Primary prevention focuses on stopping potential users from trying the drug. A recent study examined the response of junior high students to anti-inhalant messages (Crano, Siegel, Alvaro, & Patel, 2007). This study exposed inhalant users, vulnerable nonusers, and resolute nonusers to a variety of different anti-inhalant advertisements. The researchers discovered that indirect messages (i.e., messages not overtly targeting the viewer) were more effective in influencing users and vulnerable nonusers. Furthermore, users responded more negatively to messages that threatened physical harm (as opposed to negative social consequences) as a result of inhalant abuse. Finally, vulnerable nonusers were affected more by messages from someone their age, while users were affected more by messages from an adult doctor. The findings of this study can be used to construct more influential and persuasive anti-inhalant messages based upon the target audience. Anti-inhalant messages that are more effective in overcoming users' resistance have greater potential to influence users to quit before they develop patterns of abuse, dependence, and brain impairment.

Despite the incomplete understanding of the mechanisms of action through which inhalants exert their effects, some preliminary pharmacological treatments for inhalant abuse are under investigation. Some research suggests that inhalants act as 5-HT3-A receptor agonists, similar to one of the known mechanisms of action of alcohol (Lopreato et al., 2003). Based on the success of some 5-HT3 receptor antagonists in decreasing alcohol consumption in rodent models and human test subjects, these researchers suggest that antagonism of 5-HT3 receptors may also decrease inhalant abuse (Lopreato et al., 2003). A single subject case study involving administration of lamotrigine (Lamictal) may support this hypothesis. Lamotrigine blocks voltage gated sodium channels, modulates the release of glutamate and aspartate, inhibits dopamine uptake, blocks 5-HT3-A receptors, and may have some effect on calcium channels (Shen, 2007). In this study, administration of lamotrigine to a chronic inhalant abuser decreased craving symptoms and helped the subject remain abstinent throughout the six-month experimental period (Shen, 2007). While these studies show promise for the future of the pharmacological treatment of inhalant abuse, more research must be conducted to investigate the reliability and efficacy of lamotrigine.

There are other research studies that have examined the pharmacological treatment of withdrawal symptoms of inhalant dependence. In a brief three-subject case series study, Muralidharan et al. (2008) administered baclofen, a GABA-B agonist, in order to reduce or eliminate the withdrawal symptoms of inhalant dependence. Baclofen's agonism of GABA-B receptors appears to modulate the activity of alcohol (and possibly inhalants) on GABA-A receptors. The three subjects in this study all reported a significant decrease in withdrawal symptoms as well as in inhalant cravings within 48 hours of initiation of baclofen treatment. Furthermore, the symptoms and cravings remained low throughout the course of treatment. The researchers also suggest that baclofen may be useful in relapse prevention.

A large number of drug treatment center directors believe that the treatment of inhalant abusers takes longer than recovery from other types of substance abuse, that it is more difficult, and thus is overall less successful (Beauvais et al., 2002). Furthermore, due to the extended length of detoxification, the high comorbidity of mental disorders with inhalant abuse, and the wide range of social dysfunction seen in many inhalant abusers, many treatment center professionals believe that standard treatment programs, which are highly structured with a brief progress schedule, will not be effective for the treatment of inhalant abusers (Beauvais et al., 2002). Many directors of treatment centers also noted that by the time detoxification of chronic users was complete and effective treatment could begin, the patient had to be discharged, often due to third-party payer restrictions on length of treatment (Beauvais et al., 2002). Moreover, many treatment providers believed that chronic inhalant abusers suffered significant neurological damage, which negatively affected their optimism for a positive outcome for these patients (Beauvais et al., 2002). Therefore, the inclusion of professionals trained in neuropsychological assessment and rehabilitation is important in the treatment of chronic inhalant users. These professionals are essential for detecting whether neurological damage has occurred, how extensive the damage may be, and the development of successful techniques for the neuropsychological rehabilitation of these individuals to help them overcome or compensate for their deficits. Furthermore, with as many as 70 percent of inhalant users meeting the criteria for one or more psychological disorders, therapy and/or pharmacological treatment may be necessary to effectively treat the inhalant abuse. The wide range of social dysfunction present in inhalant users must be addressed as well, and young users typically require significant case management (Beauvais et al., 2002). Education is also an important factor in treatment, as more than 27 percent of drug treatment center directors surveyed indicated that a lack of knowledge by the general public and treatment professionals significantly compromised effective treatment (Beauvais et al., 2002).

CONCLUSION

Inhalants are a diverse group of chemicals that share a common route of administration and are not included in other categories of drugs of abuse that are inhaled (i.e., nicotine, marijuana, or crack cocaine). Inhalants can be divided into three groups of chemicals: volatile substances, nitrous oxide, and nitrites. Common methods of administration include "sniffing," "huffing," "spraying," and "bagging." Inhalant use began to receive public attention in the 1960s, and has since become a significant problem, particularly among young people. Use varies among different ethnic groups. While Hispanics and Native Americans show higher-than-average prevalence rates, African Americans show exceptionally low prevalence rates. Inhalant abuse is also particularly high in Alaska. Furthermore, a high percentage of inhalant users have one or more comorbid mental disorders, with major depression and antisocial personality disorder being the most common.

The mechanisms of action of the volatile substances are not completely understood. However, current research indicates that they fluidize cell membranes, enhance the activity of GABA-A and glycine receptors, inhibit the activity of NMDA glutamate receptors, activate dopamine neurons in the ventral tegmental area, and enhance the action of 5-HT-3A receptors. Nitrous oxide is thought by some to be mediated via the actions on a variety of opiate receptors, although others dispute this hypothesis. It also inhibits the action of NMDA glutamate receptors. Nitrites induce central and peripheral vasodilation and the relaxation of smooth muscle tissue.

The acute effects of inhalant use include intoxication and sudden sniffing death syndrome. In volatile substances, intoxication includes drowsiness, diplopia, dysarthria, ataxia, disorientation, and in higher doses, visual hallucinations and delusions. Nitrous oxide intoxication can induce euphoria, tingling, numbness, dizziness, hallucinations, warmth, and short-term memory loss. Nitrite intoxication results in euphoria, floating sensations, increased tactile sensitivity, disinhibition, heightened sexual arousal, relaxation of the anus, and prolonged orgasm. Sudden sniffing death syndrome occurs when a volatile substance sensitizes the heart to the action of epinephrine and the user is then startled. The subsequent release of epinephrine into the sensitized heart can produce a fatal cardiac arrhythmia. This can potentially happen at any time, even during an individual's first use.

The chronic use of inhalants can have potentially damaging effects on multiple organ systems. In the volatile substance group, these can include hepatotoxicity, pulmonary disease, heart complications, renal dysfunction, and bone marrow suppression. Chronic abuse of nitrites can have negative effects on the immune system. The effects of prolonged use of inhalants upon the central nervous system include cerebellar atrophy, diffuse destruction of white matter, and the possibility of dementia. Chronic inhalant abuse may also result in deficits in auditory discrimination, psychomotor speed, visuo-motor functioning, and memory. Furthermore, a condition called organic solvent neurotoxicity, which is characterized by a variety of cognitive and mood disturbances may develop. Inhalant use by a mother can also affect an unborn child. There are documented impairments in both animal and human models of the disorder, and in human infants, a condition similar to fetal alcohol syndrome can occur. Moreover, the child can also show withdrawal symptoms upon birth if the mother has recently used inhalants.

Withdrawal of inhalants is not included as a diagnostic entity in the *DSM-IV–TR*, but withdrawal effects have been documented. They include anhedonia, irritability, sleep disturbances, psychomotor slowing, dry mouth, lacrimation, craving, headaches, and heart palpitations. This withdrawal syndrome may be treated with some success by using benzodiazepines or baclofen.

Treatment of inhalant abuse is complicated and may be confounded by many factors. However, important areas to address include primary prevention, pharmacological treatment, neuropsychological evaluation and rehabilitation, treatment of comorbid mental disorders, and education about the disorder. Pharmacological intervention is currently rather limited, but there has been preliminary success in treating an inhalant abuser with lamotrigine.

Inhalant abuse continues to be a serious problem, particularly among young people. The incomplete knowledge of the mechanisms of action for some of these substances, combined with insufficient resources for the treatment of the abusers and the complexity of the issues surrounding inhalant abuse, make it difficult for these individuals to receive the help that they need. Further research into these topics is warranted and necessary, and more resources must be devoted to the study and treatment of inhalant abuse to effectively combat this growing problem.

REFERENCES

American Psychiatric Association. (2000). *Diagnostic and statistical manual of mental disorders* (4th ed., text rev.). Washington, DC: Author.

Atkinson, R. M., & Green, J. D. (1983). Personality, prior drug use, and introspective experience during nitrous oxide intoxication. *International Journal of Addiction*, 18(5), 717–738.

Balster, R. L. (1998). Neural basis of inhalant abuse. *Drug and Alcohol Dependence*, 51, 207–214.

Bass, M. (1970). Sudden sniffing death. *Journal of the American Medical Association*, 212(12), 2075–2079.

Beauvais, F. (1992). Comparison of drug use rates for reservation Indian, non-reservation Indian, and Anglo youth. *American Indian and Alaska Native Mental Health Research*, 5(1), 13–31.

Beauvais, F., Jumper-Thurman, P., Plested, B., & Helm, H. (2002). A survey of attitudes among drug user treatment providers toward the treatment of inhalant users. *Substance Use and Misuse*, 37(11), 1391–1410.

Beckman, N. J., Zacny, J. P., & Walker, D. J. (2006). Within-subject comparison of the subjective and psychomotor effects of a gaseous anesthetic and two volatile anesthetics in healthy volunteers. *Drug and Alcohol Dependence*, 81, 89–95.

Beckstead, M. J., Weiner, J. L., Eger, E. I., II, Gong, D. H., & Mihic, S. J. (2000). Glycine and gamma-aminobutyric acid-A receptor function is enhanced by inhaled drugs of abuse. *Molecular Pharmacology*, 57, 1199–1205.

Bowen, S. E., Mohammadi, M. H., Batis, J. C., & Hannigan, J. H. (2007). Gestational toluene exposure effects on spontaneous and amphetamine-induced locomotor behavior in rats. *Neurotoxicology and Teratology*, 29, 236–246.

Brouette, T., & Anton, R. (2001). Clinical review of inhalants. *American Journal on Addictions*, 10, 79–94.

Chen, J. P., van Praag, H. M., & Gardner, E. L. (1991). Activation of 5-HT3 receptor by 1-phenylbiguanide increases dopamine release in the rat nucleus accumbens. *Brain Research*, 543, 354–357.

Committee on Substance Abuse and Committee on Native American Child Health. (1996). Inhalant abuse. *Pediatrics*, 97(3), 420–423.

Compton, W. M., Cottler, L. B., Dinwiddie, S. H., Mager, D. E., & Asmus, G. (1994). Inhalant use: Characteristics and predictors. *American Journal on Addiction*, 3(3), 263–272.

Crano, W. D., Siegel, J. T., Alvaro, E. M., & Patel, N. M. (2007). Overcoming adolescents' resistance to anti-inhalant appeals. *Psychology of Addictive Behaviors*, 21(4), 516–524.

Cruz, S. L., Balster, R. L., & Woodwar, J. J. (2000). Effects of volatile solvents on recombinant N-methyl-D-aspartate receptors expressed in xenopus oocytes. *British Journal of Pharmacology*, 131, 1303–1308.

Dax, E. M., Lange, W. R., & Jaffe, J. H. (1989). Allergic reactions to amyl nitrite inhalation. *American Journal of Medicine*, 86, 732.

Dinwiddie, S. H. (1994). Abuse of inhalants: A review. *Addiction*, 89, 925–939.

Evans, A. C., & Raistrick, D. (1987). Phenomenology of intoxication with toluene-based adhesives and butane gas. *British Journal of Psychiatry*, 150, 769–773.

Flanagan, R. J., Ruprah, M., Meredith, T. J., & Ramsey, J. D. (1990). An introduction to the clinical toxicology of volatile substances. *Drug Safety*, 5, 359–383.

Fornazzari, L. (1988). Clinical recognition and management of solvent abusers. *Internal Medicine for the Specialist*, 9(6), 2–7.

Fornazzari, L., Wilkinson, D. A., Kapur, B. M., & Carlen, P. L. (1983). Cerebellar cortical and functional impairment in toluene abusers. *Acta Neurologica Scandinavica, 67*, 319–329.

Fredlund, E. V., Spence, R. T., & Maxwell, J. C. (1989). *Substance use among students in Texas secondary schools, 1988.* Austin: Texas Commission on Alcohol and Drug Abuse.

Gillman, M. A., & Lichtigfeld, F. J. (1998). Clinical role and mechanisms of action of analgesic nitrous oxide. *International Journal of Neuroscience, 93*(1–2), 55–62.

Goode, E., & Troiden, R. R. (1979). Amyl nitrite use among homosexual men. *American Journal of Psychiatry, 136*, 1067–1069.

Haverkos, H. W., Kopstein, A. N., Wilson, H., & Drotman, P. (1994). Nitrite inhalants: History, epidemiology, and possible links to AIDS. *Environmental Health Perspective, 102*, 858–861.

Johnston, L. D., O'Malley, P. M., Bachman, J. G., & Schulenberg, J. E. (2006). *Monitoring the future national results on adolescent drug use: Overview of key findings.* Bethesda, MD: National Institute on Drug Abuse.

King, G. S., Smialek, J. E., & Troutman, W. G. (1985). Sudden death in adolescents resulting from the inhalation of typewriter correction fluid. *Journal of the American Medical Association, 253*, 1604–1606.

Lazar, R. B., Ho, S. U., Melen, O., & Daghestani, A. N. (1983). Multifocal central nervous system damage caused by toluene abuse. *Neurology, 33*, 1337–1340.

Lopreato, G. F., Phelan, R., Borghese, C. M., Beckstead, M. J., & Mihic, S. J. (2003). Inhaled drugs of abuse enhance serotonin-3 receptor function. *Drug and Alcohol Dependence, 70*, 11–15.

McHugh, M. J. (1987). The abuse of volatile substances. *Pediatric Clinics of North America, 34*, 333–340.

Meadows, R., & Verghese, A. (1996). Medical complications of glue sniffing. *Southern Medical Journal, 89*(5), 455–462.

Meyer, J. S., & Quenzer, L. F. (2005). *Psychopharmacology: Drugs, the brain and behavior.* Sunderland, MA: Sinauer Associates.

Muralidharan, K., Rajkumar, R. P., Mulla, U., Kayak, R. B., & Benegal, V. (2008). Baclofen in the management of inhalant withdrawal: A case series. *Primary Care Companion Journal of Clinical Psychiatry, 10*(1), 48–51.

Newell, G. R., Spitz, M. R., & Wilson, M. B. (1988). Nitrite inhalants: Historical perspective. *National Institute on Drug Abuse Research Monogram Series, 83*, 1–14.

Ogden, J. A. (1993). The psychological and neuropsychological assessment of chronic organic solvent neurotoxicity: A case series. *New Zealand Journal of Psychology, 22*(2), 82–93.

Padilla, E. R., Padilla, A. M., Morales, A., Olmedo, E. L., & Ramirez, R. (1979). Inhalant, marijuana, and alcohol abuse among barrio children and adolescents. *International Journal of the Addictions, 14*(7), 945–964.

Reidel, S., Hebert, T., & Bird, P. (1995). *Inhalant abuse: Confronting the growing challenge. Treating Alcohol and Other Drug Abusers in Rural and Frontier Areas* (Technical Assistance Publication Series No. 17). Rockville, MD: Center for Substance Abuse Treatment.

Ridenour, T. A., Bray, B. C., & Cottler, L. B. (2007). Reliability of use, abuse, and dependence of four types of inhalants in adolescents and young adults. *Drug and Alcohol Dependence, 91,* 40–49.

Riegel, A. C., Zapata, A., Shippenberg, T. S., & French, E. D. (2007). The abused inhalant toluene increases dopamine release in the nucleus accumbens by directly stimulating ventral tegmental area neurons. *Neuropsychopharmacology, 32,* 1558–1569.

Ron, M. A. (1986). Volatile substance abuse: A review of possible long-term neurological, intellectual, and psychiatric sequelae. *British Journal of Psychiatry, 148,* 235–246.

Rosenberg, N. L., Grigsby, J., Dreisbach, J., Busenbark, D., & Grigsby, P. (2002). Neuropsychologic impairment and MRI abnormalities associated with chronic solvent abuse. *Clinical Toxicology, 40*(1), 21–34.

Shah, R., Vankar, G. K., & Upadhyaya, H. P. (1999). Phenomenology of gasoline intoxication and withdrawal symptoms among adolescents in India: A case series. *American Journal on Addictions, 8,* 254–257.

Sharp, C. W., & Rosenberg, N. L. (1997). *Substance abuse: A comprehensive textbook.* Baltimore, MD: Williams and Wilkins.

Shen, Y. (2007). Treatment of inhalant dependence with lamotrigine. *Progress in Neuro-Psychopharmacology and Biological Psychiatry, 31,* 769–771.

Soderberg, L. S., Chang, L. W., & Barnett, J. B. (1996). Elevated TNF-alpha and inducible nitric oxide production by alveolar macrophages after exposure to a nitrite inhalant. *Journal of Leukocyte Biology, 60*(4), 459–464.

Tenenbein, M., Casiro, O. G., & Seshia, M. M. (1996). Neonatal withdrawal from maternal volatile substance abuse. *Archives of Disease in Childhood—Fetal and Neonatal Edition, 74*(3), F204–F207.

Toutant, C., & Lippmann, S. (1979). Fetal solvents syndrome [Letter to the editor]. *Lancet, 1*(8130), 1356.

Tsushima, W. T., & Towne, W. S. (1977). Effects of paint sniffing on neuropsychological test performance. *Journal of Abnormal Psychology, 86,* 402–407.

Wu, L., & Howard, M. O. (2007). Psychiatric disorders in inhalant users: Results from the National Epidemiologic Survey on Alcohol and Related Conditions. *Drug and Alcohol Dependence, 88,* 146–155.

Yamakura, T., & Harris, R. A. (2000). Effects of gaseous anesthetics nitrous oxide and xenon on ligand-gated ion channels. *Anesthesiology, 93,* 1095–1101.

Zacny, J. P., Conran, A., Pardo, H., Coalson, D. W., Black, M., Klock, P. A., et al. (1999). Effects of naloxone on nitrous oxide actions in healthy volunteers. *Pain, 83,* 411–418.

Chapter 12

The Effects and Abuse Potential of GHB: A Pervasive "Club Drug"

Bethany L. Waits, BA, and Paula K. Lundberg-Love, PhD

Gamma-hydroxybutyrate, or GHB, is a widely used drug whose popularity has increased dramatically since its discovery in the late 1960s (Miotto et al., 2001). Once ingested, GHB acts by depressing or downregulating the activity of the central nervous system (CNS), including the brain and the spinal cord, and its effects are similar to other CNS depressants such as alcohol and benzodiazepines (BZD). Although GHB was initially synthesized for use as an intravenous anesthetic for surgical procedures, it has since been marketed therapeutically as a dietary supplement, an anabolic agent, and a drug for the treatment of narcolepsy. Moreover, it has been implicated in preclinical trials for the relief of withdrawal symptoms for several addictive substances, particularly alcohol (Julien, 2005; Levinthal, 2006). In its purest form, GHB is a white powdery substance that is soluble in water (Gonzalez & Nutt, 2005). Although GHB can be obtained as a tablet or a capsule, it is usually distributed, both legally and illegally, as a colorless, odorless, and tasteless solution, and it is typically packaged in small bottles, similar in size to those used for shampoo in hotel rooms (Meyer & Quenzer, 2005). Thus, while oral administration is the most common form of ingestion associated with GHB, the drug is sometimes injected directly into the bloodstream (Jones, 2001).

While GHB was initially developed for medicinal purposes, in recent years it primarily has become a drug of abuse, and is frequently referred to as a "club drug" (Britt & McCance-Katz, 2005). According to Levinthal (2006), a *club drug* is a term that describes a group of drugs utilized primarily by young adults at dance parities, or "raves," which occur at night clubs. Other common "club drugs" include MDMA (ecstasy), ketamine, Rohypnol, methamphetamine, and LSD (Britt & McCance-Katz, 2005, Levinthal, 2006). The club drugs, including GHB, are readily accessible to purchase at raves and are often combined with other substances to heighten their effects. For instance, one study of GHB users found that 53 percent combined GHB with ecstasy, 50 percent with marijuana, 43 percent with cocaine, 40 percent with amphetamines, and 37 percent with alcohol. The same study reported that 40 percent of the participants used GHB intentionally to increase, or extend, the "high" from other drugs. Overall, 71 percent mentioned using GHB with other substances (Miotto et al., 2001).

In addition to raves and night clubs, GHB can be obtained illegally on the street and on the Internet (Britt & McCance-Katz, 2005; Nicholson & Balster, 2001). Common street names include liquid X, liquid E, grievous bodily harm, G, Georgia home boy, G-rrifick, salty water, scoop, somatomac, gamma 10, gamma g, goop, easy lay, cherry meth, blue nitro, nature's quaalude, GH revitalize, revivarant, renew/trient, and fantasy (Britt & McCance-Katz, 2005; Julien, 2005; Levinthal, 2006). At times, it has also been referred to as "liquid ecstasy" due to its ability to produce a state of euphoria similar to MDMA (Jones, 2001). Recently, GHB has become indirectly available on the Internet in the form of "chemistry kits." These kits contain the biological precursors of GHB, gamma-butyrolactone (GBL) and 1, 4,-butanediol (BD), and instructions that describe how to convert GBL or 1, 4,–BD into GHB (Nicholson & Balster, 2001). Furthermore, according to Jones (2001), several Web sites have GHB "recipes" that illustrate ways to produce GHB in a household kitchen.

The increase in the sale and distribution of GHB has been documented in several studies conducted by the U.S. government. The Drug Abuse Warning Network (DAWN) is a national surveillance agency controlled by the U.S. Substance Abuse Mental Health Service Administration that collects data concerning drug-related visits to hospital emergency rooms throughout the United States. DAWN also documents information concerning drug-related fatalities reported by medical examiners and coroners. According to DAWN, in 1994, 683 emergency departments at various hospitals recorded GHB-related visits. By 2000, this number rose to 4,969 documentations of GHB-related incidents, which is approximately seven times the number reported in 1994 (Meyer & Quenzer, 2005; Rosenthal & Solhkhah, 2005). Due to the increase in information concerning GHB misuse, it is important to discuss the hazardous effects and abuse potential associated with this drug. A review of the current research concerning GHB's history, therapeutic indications, and mechanisms of action in the brain will be discussed. Additionally, the behavioral and physiological effects of GHB as well as its toxicity, withdrawal effects, and approaches to treatment considerations will be addressed in the following sections.

HISTORY

The pharmacological properties of GHB were first reported in 1960 by Dr. Henri Laborit, a French scientist well known for his discovery of Thorazine, the first antipsychotic drug (Meyer & Quenzer, 2005). As a surgeon, Laborit was interested in identifying a compound similar to gamma-aminobutyric acid (GABA), a newly discovered inhibitory neurotransmitter that depressed the activity of the CNS. If such a substance could be identified, Laborit speculated, it would produce sedation and might be utilized as an anesthetic in surgical procedures (Gonzalez & Nutt, 2005; Meyer & Quenzer, 2005). After its synthesis was achieved, it was apparent that GHB was a GABA analog that easily crossed the blood brain barrier (a semipermeable membrane that prevents nonlipid soluble substances from entering the brain). Thus, GHB was capable of directly affecting the brain's biochemistry (Carlson, 2007). Early studies on laboratory animals confirmed Laborit's suspicion that GHB produced sedation and anesthesia. Based on this information, GHB was widely used as an anesthetic in Europe, and is still used for this purpose in some European countries (Meyer & Quenzer, 2005). Recently, however, its use has declined as new studies have revealed that its anesthetic effects are not as therapeutic as other drugs that are currently available, due in part to its lack of analgesic (pain-reducing) properties (Gonzalez & Nutt, 2005).

In the United States, GHB received little attention until the 1980s, when health food stores across the nation began to market the drug as a nutritional supplement and as a sleep aid. Due to manufacturers' claims that GHB had the potential to reduce body fat and increase muscle mass, it became a highly sought after drug (Meyer & Quenzer, 2005). Advertisements stated that GHB had a low risk of toxicity and little danger of dependence, and because of these endorsements, GHB soon became popular among many different groups (Miotto et al., 2001). For instance, its use was particularly prevalent among bodybuilders who used GHB as an allegedly safe alternative to anabolic steroids (Jones, 2001). According to researchers, the most frequent users of GHB, other than bodybuilders, included athletes, gym members, models, and habitual travelers across time zones (Gonzalez & Nutt, 2005). Unfortunately, the distribution and sale of GHB was virtually ignored by the medical community and by public health officials for approximately a decade after it was first released in the United States (Nicholson & Balster, 2001). However, by the 1990s, the Food and Drug Administration (FDA) began to receive numerous reports concerning GHB-related illnesses (Meyer & Quenzer, 2005). For instance, seizures and comas were frequently reported by those using supplements containing GHB (Levinthal, 2006). Additionally, the FDA became concerned about the dramatic increase in GHB use for sedation and growth enhancement. Many agreed that GHB should be prescribed by a medical doctor to minimize the dangers of over-the-counter misuse (Meyer & Quenzer, 2005).

At the same time, GHB began to be used as a date rape drug, often in combination with alcohol, and such reports began to increase public awareness about its dangerous effects (Julien, 2005; Meyer & Quenzer, 2005; Nicholson & Balster, 2001). Because GHB is a colorless, odorless, and virtually tasteless liquid, it can easily be slipped into alcoholic beverages without it being detected by the drinker (Levinthal, 2006). Like other date-rape drugs (i.e., Rohypnol), GHB's ability to produce unconsciousness, especially in combination with alcohol, has been the primary reason for its use in sexual assault. Moreover, because GHB is rapidly absorbed in the body, unconsciousness persists for several hours after ingestion, making it impossible for a victim to resist the attack (Britt & McCance-Katz, 2005). Although little evidence suggests that GHB enhances sexuality, many believe that it disinhibits sexual inhibitions, making sexual assault easier to accomplish. Furthermore, because GHB is excreted from the body in approximately 12 hours, detection of the drug in blood or urine samples is very difficult.

Thus, the victim's attempts to prosecute are often unsuccessful due to lack of medical evidence (Jones, 2001).

Few published cases exist concerning GHB's alleged role in date rape (Gable, 2004). In one study that investigated cases of drug-related sexual assault, GHB was implicated in only 4.1 percent of the total number evaluated (Nicholson & Balster, 2001). According to Gable (2004), this is not necessarily an indication that GHB is rarely used in date rape. Because few laboratories have the capacity to determine the presence of GHB in the body, it is difficult to establish the true prevalence of GHB involved in cases of sexual assault (Gable, 2004).

These types of events led the FDA to designate the drug as a Schedule I controlled substance in March 2000 (Gable, 2004). As a result, GHB could no longer be obtained over the counter, and it became illegal under FDA regulations to possess or manufacture the drug. However, in 2002, the FDA approved GHB for the treatment of narcolepsy under the trade name Xyrem, and it became a Schedule III controlled substance when utilized for this purpose (Meyer & Quenzer, 2005). According to Nicholson and Balster (2001), GHB's current FDA regulation is similar to tetrahydrocanabinol (THC), or marijuana. For example, THC is classified as a Schedule I controlled substance, but the FDA-approved formulation Marinol, which is used to treat nausea associated with chemotherapy, is designated as a Schedule III drug.

THERAPEUTIC INDICATIONS FOR GHB

As previously mentioned, GHB has been utilized as an anesthetic, a growth promoter, a dietary supplement, a treatment for narcolepsy, and a medication to reduce the adverse effects associated with certain types of drug withdrawal (Hernandez, McDaniel, Costanza, & Hernandez, 1998). Even so, the importance of understanding the biological basis concerning GHB's therapeutic indications cannot be disregarded. For instance, GHB's use as a growth promoter and weight loss supplement was largely supported by research demonstrating its ability to enhance the release of human growth hormone. This effect is a result of GHB's ability to increase stages 3 and 4 sleep, also known as slow-wave sleep (SWS), which is a deeper, more restorative sleep state (Carlson, 2007). Since human growth hormone is primarily released during SWS, GHB indirectly increases its release by amplifying the amount of slow-wave sleep an individual experiences through the night (Gonzalez & Nutt, 2005). Thus, by enhancing the level of growth hormone in the body, it was assumed that GHB ingestion would increase overall muscle mass, similar to anabolic steroids (Rosenthal & Solhkhah, 2005). Although manufacturers of GHB-containing products relied on this research to assert its efficacy (Nicholson & Balster, 2001), there is no scientific evidence supporting GHB's capacity to increase muscle development significantly.

While GHB's efficacy as a growth promoter remains equivocal, it appears to be a useful medication for the treatment of narcolepsy. Narcolepsy is a genetic disorder whose symptoms typically appear during adolescence. It is characterized by excessive daytime sleepiness and a disordered sleep stage architecture with rapid eye movement (REM) sleep occurring at sleep onset (Julien, 2005). One of the most frequent daytime symptoms associated with narcolepsy is cataplexy, a complete loss of muscle tone resulting in paralysis. When a cataplexy attack occurs, a fully awake individual will suddenly fall to the ground unable to move (Carlson, 2007). According to Julien (2005), approximately 60–75 percent of patients with narcolepsy experience cataplexy, and it is usually precipitated by strong emotional reactions such as laughter, anger, surprise, or excitement.

When searching for possible substances to treat narcolepsy, researchers speculated that GHB's ability to promote sleep might eliminate certain symptoms of the disorder, namely, cataplexy attacks. For instance, oral doses of approximately 30–50 mg of GHB produce a state of somnolence, which is readily reversible by external events and is virtually indistinguishable from normal sleep (Nicholson & Balster, 2001). Furthermore, the results of sleep studies evaluating participants' behavior and electroencephalogram (EEG) patterns suggest that GHB-induced sleep mimics physiological sleep by increasing both SWS and REM sleep (Galloway et al., 1997; Rosenthal & Solhkhah, 2005). GHB's ability to produce a normal sleep state underlies its effectiveness in alleviating the symptoms of narcolepsy. Indeed, when GHB is taken at night, it consolidates sleep, restores sleep patterns to normal levels, and reduces hypnagoic hallucinations (i.e., vivid dreams that occur at sleep onset). Also, GHB improves daytime symptoms by reducing cataplexy attacks and daytime sleepiness (Nicholson & Balster, 2001). To date, the only FDA-approved therapeutic indication of GHB is for the treatment of cataplexy attacks associated with narcolepsy. As mentioned earlier, it is distributed under the trade name, Xyrem, and is manufactured by Jazz Pharmaceuticals (Rosenthal & Solhkhah, 2005).

Currently, researchers are investigating GHB's effectiveness in treating the withdrawal symptoms of several addictive substances, specifically alcohol, opiates, and cocaine (Gonzalez & Nutt, 2005). Support for this hypothesis has been provided by Gallimberti, Schifano, Forza, and Miconi (1994), who found GHB reduced alcohol withdrawal symptoms, including tremors and seizures, in laboratory rats. In clinical studies, GHB has been shown to diminish depression, nausea, and anxiety among alcoholics in detoxification programs (Jones, 2001). Furthermore, the long-term usefulness of GHB among alcoholics in detoxification suggests that the drug significantly increases the number of abstinent days experienced by these individuals (Galloway et al., 1997). GHB also has been found to ease the abstinence syndrome produced by opiate withdrawal. Researchers suspect that GHB may stimulate the release of endogenous opiates, thereby relieving the symptoms associated with opiate abstinence (Nicholson & Balster, 2001). Additionally, one preclinical study conducted by Fattore, Martellotta, Cossu, and Fratta (2000) found data to support the use of GHB for the treatment of cocaine addiction. However, no other studies have replicated these findings. While the use of GHB for the treatment of various withdrawal symptoms is promising, it has not yet been approved by the FDA for the treatment of either alcohol or opiate withdrawal. Therefore, more research must be conducted to determine whether the treatment of certain types of drug withdrawal is, indeed, a therapeutic indication of GHB (Addolorato, Caputo, Capristo, Stefanini, & Gasbarrini, 2000).

MECHANISMS OF ACTION

According to Meyer and Quenzer (2005), two competing hypotheses exist concerning GHB's mechanism of action, or sites of action, in the brain. The first theory states that GHB is an agonist at the GABA-B receptor. An agonist is any drug that binds to a specific receptor and either facilitates or enhances the naturally occurring effects of that particular receptor. As mentioned previously, GABA, or gamma-aminobutyric acid, is an inhibitory neurotransmitter that depresses, or downregulates, the activity of the central nervous system (Meyer & Quenzer, 2005). Thus, a GABA agonist is any substance that activates GABA receptors causing a CNS-depressant effect. There are two types of GABA receptors in the human brain: GABA-A and GABA-B receptors. Many CNS-depressants (i.e., alcohol, benzodiazepines, and barbiturates) stimulate certain subunits on the GABA-A receptor, and cause behavioral effects such as sedation and relief from anxiety. The GABA-B receptor, when activated, leads to similar behavioral effects, and it is hypothesized that GHB acts on this receptor. Evidence supporting this assumption is based on research showing that the behavioral and physiological effects of GHB in animals can be inhibited by GABA-B receptor antagonists. GHB's anesthetic properties and ability to produce sedation may be the result of its GABA-B receptor agonist properties (Miotto et al., 2001; Meyer & Quenzer, 2005).

The second theory concerning GHB's mechanism of action states that its effects are mediated by specific GHB receptors found in the human brain (Kemmel et al., 1998; Meyer & Quenzer, 2005). This hypothesis was first introduced by Roth and Giarman, who demonstrated that GHB was an endogenous substance and, therefore, might act as a neurotransmitter or neuromodulator in various brain regions (Galloway et al., 1997). Current research indicates that GHB fulfills many of the characteristics associated with neurotransmitters or neuromodulators. For instance, it is released in a calcium-dependent manner. It possesses a distinct reuptake system that transports it into synaptic vesicles. It has specific enzymes that remove it from the synaptic cleft after it is released, and, as previously discussed, it has its own particular receptor sites throughout the brain (Meyer & Quenzer, 2005; Nicholson & Balster, 2001). Furthermore, in rats, monkeys, and humans, GHB-binding receptor sites have been identified in the hippocampus, caudate nucleus, cerebral cortex, and cerebellum. In addition, certain substances have been synthesized in laboratories that specifically bind to GHB receptors. One such substance, NCS-382, is a selective antagonist at GHB receptors, blocking GHB's effects in the brain (Meyer & Quenzer, 2005). This research, along with studies supporting GHB's role as a GABA-B receptor agonist, provide a strong scientific foundation in the understanding of GHB's mechanisms of action.

BEHAVIORAL AND PHYSIOLOGICAL EFFECTS

The behavioral and physiological effects associated with GHB are largely dependent on the amount of the drug an individual ingests. When administered for therapeutic purposes, typical doses of GHB range from 15 to 30 mg. Unfortunately, GHB is frequently misused as a recreational drug, and regular users have been known to ingest as much as 57 to 71 mg (Nicholson & Balster, 2001). According to Jones (2001), addiction to GHB is highly probable if an individual consumes between 30 and 50 mg on a daily basis. Therefore, like many other substances, GHB's therapeutic effectiveness and potential for abuse is influenced by the dosage of the drug that a person takes.

Although GHB results in many behavioral and physiological effects, it is typically abused for its ability to induce euphoria, or an "out-of-body" high (Levinthal, 2006). Many researchers believe that this "euphoric" effect underlies its potential for abuse (Julien, 2005). Experiments with laboratory animals, using conditioned place preference, have supported the hypothesis that GHB has reinforcing effects. Conditioned place preference, or CPP, is an experimental procedure in which an animal is given a drug, in this case GHB, and is then placed in a specific compartment to create an association between that environment and the effects of the drug. The animal is also given a placebo and placed in a different compartment. After this place-conditioning is established, researchers allow the animal to have access to both compartments at the same time, and measure the amount of time the animal spends in each environment. Thus, if the animal finds the drug rewarding, it spends the majority of its time in the compartment associated with the drug (Meyer & Quenzer, 2005). In a study by Martellotta, Fattore, Cossu, and Fratta (1997), GHB was shown to induce a CPP, meaning that the laboratory animal preferred the compartment paired with GHB administration to the compartment paired with the placebo. However, it took approximately six drug exposures for a CPP to occur, which is significantly more than other addictive drugs, such as cocaine and the opiates, which produce a CPP after two exposures. This finding suggests that while GHB can be classified as a reinforcer, its effects are much weaker than other highly rewarding drugs. Moreover, those that abuse GHB typically believe that it acts as an aphrodisiac, and that it has the ability to increase or enhance sexual experiences (Julien, 2005; Rosenthal & Solhkhah, 2005). While other substances, like alcohol, have been reported to heighten sexuality, there is no evidence that GHB, or other depressants, aid in sexual performance (Julien, 2005).

When a person consumes GHB, it takes approximately 5 to 15 minutes for it to cross the blood brain barrier, and affect behavior. Theses effects can last between four and seven hours. However, in some cases, users report dizziness for up to two weeks after GHB ingestion (Galloway et al., 1997). Small doses of GHB, 10 to 20 mg or less, typically produce muscle relaxation and relief from anxiety. Additionally, disinhibition, sociability, and light inebriation have been reported. Those using GHB at low doses often describe an alcohol-like experience, with behavioral effects similar to those experienced after drinking two alcoholic beverages (Gable, 2004). Several clinical studies suggest that GHB at low doses has no effect on attention, vigilance, alertness, short-term memory, or psychomotor skills. The only adverse symptoms mentioned by participants included slight dizziness (Nicholson & Balster, 2001). At moderate doses, between 20 and 40 mg, GHB's behavioral and physiological effects are accentuated. For instance, moderate doses of GHB generally induce sleep and produce euphoria (Rosenthal & Solhkhah, 2005). In addition, other common symptoms include physical disequilibrium, grogginess, tactile sensitivity, increased gag reflex, nausea, and vomiting (Gable, 2004; Gonzalez & Nutt, 2005). According to Nicholson and Balster (2001), at 30 to 40 mg, users may experience mild hypothermia, loss of peripheral vision, confusion, agitation, enuresis, myoclonic jerks, tremors, ataxia, aggression, and hallucinations. Furthermore, as doses increase above 40 or 50 mg, users often become unconscious and may experience severe respiratory depression (Levinthal, 2006). Although high doses of GHB are not generally associated with seizures, some users have reported the occurrence of tonic-clonic (i.e., grand mal) seizures after ingestion of 60 to 70 mg of GHB. Furthermore, as doses increase above 70 mg, individuals often experience a state of unarousable sleep or coma, which can last from approximately one to five hours. Researchers speculate that a lethal dose of GHB is approximately 5–15 times higher than a dose producing unconsciousness (Nicholson & Balster, 2001). Finally, in several rare cases, high doses of GHB, over a period of time, have led to Wernicke-Korsakoff syndrome, which is characterized by a deficiency in thiamine and is often observed in alcoholics (Friedman, Westlake, & Furman, 1996; Gonzalez & Nutt, 2005).

In a noteworthy study conducted by Miotto and colleagues (2001), GHB users were interviewed about the subjective effects of the drug. Of the 42 participants in the study, 75–100 percent reported euphoria, feelings of happiness, increased sexuality, increased well-being, heightened sense of touch, relaxation, talkativeness, tranquility, disinhibition, pleasant drowsiness, and optimism after using GHB. Furthermore, 50–74 percent experienced increased intensity of orgasms, increased energy, giddiness, sensitivity to sound, sweatiness, and loss of consciousness. A smaller percentage, 25–49 percent mentioned symptoms of nausea, auditory and visual hallucinations, headaches, frequent urination, and vomiting. Finally, 1–24 percent of those who participated experienced amnesia or seizures. This research suggests that GHB has the potential to cause serious health effects in individuals who consume large quantities of the substance. More information regarding GHB's toxic effects will be discussed in the following section.

TOXICITY

The term *toxicity* refers to a chemical substance's ability to induce functional or anatomical damage to a living organism. While the toxic effects of many drugs have been documented in the medical literature, GHB's toxicity has been more difficult to determine. This is largely due to the fact that certain amounts of GHB naturally occur in the human brain. Also, GHB is rapidly metabolized after ingestion, giving researchers less time to determine its biological effects (Gable, 2004). Because many physicians have little experience with GHB toxicity, the incidence rates of GHB use are difficult to obtain. Only a few laboratories have the capability to detect the presence of GHB in the body, and clinicians can rarely determine actual blood or tissue levels of the drug (Hernandez et al., 1998; Nicholson & Balster, 2001). Moreover, if a laboratory does have the ability to test for GHB, only a specific type of urinalysis, which tests for the presence of one drug, can determine if GHB was ingested by the individual (Gable, 2004). According to Nicholson and Balster (2001), this makes the evaluation of GHB's toxicity very difficult, because the majority of cases involving hospitalization involve the co-ingestion of other substances, such as alcohol.

While only a limited amount of information in the medical literature exists concerning GHB toxicity, evidence obtained from users, clubs, health food stores, gyms, and the street suggest that the prevalence of GHB overdose is much higher than previously suspected (Hernandez et al., 1998). For example, among one sample of first-time GHB users, approximately 53 percent overdosed on the substance (Degenhardt, Darke, & Dillon, 2003). This percentage increased to 75 percent among users who had ingested GHB on more than 15 occasions (Gonzalez & Nutt, 2005). Typically, an overdose from GHB occurs if an individual takes multiple doses over a short period of time, if there is a higher concentration of GHB in the bottle than expected, or if the drug is taken in combination with alcohol or other sedative drugs (Meyer & Quenzer, 2005).

GHB toxicity, or overdose, can lead to a wide variety of medical conditions, which in some cases, may be life-threatening (Hernandez et al., 1998). Since GHB is a depressant, it is not surprising that the most common manifestations of toxicity involve cardiac, respiratory, and central nervous system depression (Gonzalez & Nutt, 2005). Indeed, a nonfatal overdose of GHB is often characterized by respiratory depression and an unarousable coma. According to Gonzalez and Nutt (2005), unconsciousness may be so unexpected that the patient may be injured as a result of the sudden loss of muscle tone. Although individuals typically regain consciousness after five hours, if other sedatives, such as alcohol, have been taken in combination with GHB, an individual may remain in a comatose state for up to eight days (Nicholson & Balster, 2001).

However, it is not uncommon for patients spontaneously to regain conscious-ness after several hours. As they become more alert, many report feelings of extreme agitation and combativeness (Rosenthal & Solhkhah, 2005). Clearly, respiratory depression and coma are the most common consequences of GHB overdose; other symptoms have been reported by patients. These include stu-por, delirium, nausea, vomiting, vertical nystagmus, hypotension, tachycardia, tremor, anxiety, ataxia, jerking movements, bradycardia, disorientation, and muscle stiffening (Gonzalez & Nutt, 2005; Julien, 2005; Miotto et al., 2001). Additionally, seizures have been reported in rare cases (Meyer & Quenzer, 2005).

As mentioned, the toxic effects of GHB are greatly potentiated when com-bined with other substances, such as alcohol, opiates, barbiturates, and benzo-diazepines (Miotto et al., 2001). Unfortunately, many individuals that abuse GHB do so in order to heighten the effects of other abusive drugs. For instance, the euphoric effects produced by alcohol and some stimulants are enhanced when combined with GHB (Nicholson & Balster, 2001). Additionally, when taken with other club drugs such as ketamine and ecstasy, GHB can reduce several of the adverse effects, such as teeth grinding and jaw-clenching, while simultaneously increasing euphoria and disinhibition (Rosenthal & Solhkhah, 2005). Thus, it is not surprising that many users who overdose on GHB are also under the influence of other substances, often exacerbating GHB's toxic-ity. Indeed, an increase in the adverse reactions to GHB, when combined with other drugs, has been documented in several case reports of overdose victims. One group of researchers evaluated 88 cases of GHB overdose reported by the emergency room of San Francisco General Hospital. Of these cases, approxi-mately 50 percent involved co-ingestion of one or more additional substances other than GHB. Furthermore, the most common substances taken with GHB included alcohol, amphetamine, and MDMA (Chin, Sporer, Cullison, Dyer, & Wu, 1998). While it is rare that an overdose of GHB will lead to death, the majority of GHB-related fatalities have been associated with other drugs of abuse. One death, reported by Ferrara, Tedeschi, Frison, and Rossi (1995), involved ingestion of GHB in combination with heroin. However, according to Gable (2004), GHB toxicity is the most life-threatening when mixed with alcohol.

WITHDRAWAL EFFECTS

Clinical evidence suggests that chronic use of GHB can produce severe withdrawal symptoms among habitual users (McDonough, Kennedy, Glasper, & Bearn, 2004). Those that consume regular doses of GHB at two- to four-hour intervals throughout the day are thought to be the most susceptible to experiencing a withdrawal syndrome after discontinuation. Furthermore, many of the symptoms associated with GHB withdrawal are similar to the withdrawal symptoms of other CNS depressants (i.e., alcohol, barbiturates, and benzodiazepine). If an individual is also dependent on a substance other than GHB, the withdrawal syndrome associated with GHB may be more complicated (Rosenthal & Solhkhah, 2005). In general, an individual experiences withdrawal symptoms several hours after the last dose of GHB. However, these symptoms tend to worsen and typically last from 3 to 15 days (Julien, 2005). According to McDonough et al. (2004), the mean duration for GHB withdrawal is approximately 9 days, which is very similar to that of alcohol and other sedative-hypnotics. Several reports have characterized the withdrawal syndrome associated with GHB to occur in two phases. In the first phase (2–12 hours after the last dose), milder symptoms such as insomnia, tremor, anxiety, increased heart rate, confusion, and vomiting have been documented (Britt & McCance-Katz, 2005). According to Meyer and Quenzer (2005), the most common withdrawal symptoms initially seen in patients are insomnia, anxiety, and tremors. Additional withdrawal symptoms commonly seen during the first 12 hours include feelings of doom, sweating, craving for the drug, mood lability, abdominal cramping, heart palpitations, diaphoresis, tachycardia, and miosis (Gonzalez & Nutt, 2005; Jones, 2001; Rosenthal & Solhkhah, 2005). The second phase begins 2 to 3 days after the last dose of GHB, when symptoms become more severe (Britt & McCance-Katz, 2005). Disorientation, fever, horizontal nystagmus, severe agitation, confusion, seizures, paranoia, delusional thinking, and auditory or visual hallucinations have been reported among patients (Rosenthal & Solhkhah, 2005). In some severe cases, full-blown psychosis may develop, and it is not uncommon for many patients to experience delirium during withdrawal (Britt & McCance-Katz, 2005; Meyer & Quenzer, 2005). Indeed, patients who were heavy users prior to cessation are more likely to have withdrawal delirium than those who used the drug less frequently (McDonough et al., 2004). In a meta-analysis conducted by McDonough and colleagues (2004), 38 cases of GHB withdrawal were reviewed, and over half of the patients reported sustained delirium after discontinuation of GHB. In another study, withdrawal delirium and agitation were the most long-lasting symptoms and continued for approximately two weeks after the last dose of GHB (Miotto et al., 2001).

TREATMENT CONSIDERATIONS

In cases of GHB overdose, the most common form of treatment involves supportive medical care, often in the form of cardiovascular and respiratory assistance (Julien, 2005). However, according to Gonzalez and Nutt (2005), for a patient to receive the best possible care, it is important to discover the amount of the drug that was ingested, as well as any other substances currently in the body. As mentioned, GHB toxicity often leads to unconsciousness and sometimes to unarousable coma. Respiratory support is often mandatory, but the majority of patients typically regain consciousness several hours after GHB overdose, and many are well enough to be discharged after waking. In a study conduced by Chin et al. (1998), similar findings were reported with approximately 13 percent of overdose patients requiring intubation. However, the majority of patients recovered within five hours and were discharged from the emergency department.

Although no specific antidote has been identified for the treatment of GHB overdose, several substances have been used in combination with cardiovascular and respiratory support (Julien, 2005). For instance, naloxone, or Narcan, a drug typically used to counter the effects of opiate overdose, has been utilized to reverse the comatose state associated with GHB toxicity (Jones, 2001). Other drugs such as physostigmine or neostigmine, acetylcholinesterase inhibitors, also have been effective in reviving patients. However, evidence suggests that using these drugs may induce more serious side effects (i.e., seizures). The benzodiazepine antagonist, Romazicon, used for the treatment of benzodiazepine toxicity, also has been administered to patients. Unfortunately, this drug has not proven effective in reversing GHB-related coma (Gonzalez & Nutt, 2005). Clearly, more research is required in order to establish an effective treatment for GHB overdose.

As with overdose, the withdrawal syndrome associated with GHB can be difficult to treat (Gonzalez & Nutt, 2005). According to McDonough et al. (2004), GHB detoxification is usually unplanned, and medical assistance is given only after patients are admitted to emergency departments in a state of crisis. Additionally, users who consume large doses of GHB, at short intervals, are often refractory to treatment during withdrawal, making it difficult for medical professionals to stabilize their symptoms. Even after the first two weeks of detoxification, life-threatening withdrawal symptoms may occur. Therefore, it is crucial for individuals to remain in the hospital for several weeks. If patients are allowed to return home too quickly, there is a high risk that they will relapse and recommence GHB use (Gonzalez & Nutt, 2005).

Several drugs have been implicated in the treatment of GHB withdrawal. These typically include benzodiazepines, mood stabilizers, antipsychotics, and at times, GHB substitutes. Usually, a benzodiazepine is the first drug of choice to suppress withdrawal symptoms (Gonzalez & Nutt, 2005). The most common BZDs prescribed to patients include Valium and Ativan (Glasper, McDonough, & Bearn, 2005). During the first few hours after admission, medical professionals monitor the individual and determine the amount of

BZD required to ease her symptoms. Once this dose has been established, it is given to the patient several times a day for approximately one to two weeks. After the second week, daily doses of BZD are reduced and eventually discontinued (Gonzalez & Nutt, 2005). Although BZDs are typically effective in treating symptoms, in extreme cases, an intravenous anesthetic, such as Propofol, may be administered to those that are unresponsive to high doses of benzodiazepines (Gonzalez & Nutt, 2005). Moreover, if a patient experiences withdrawal delirium, a mood stabilizer, such as Neurontin, is often combined with the BZD to decrease agitation (Miotto et al., 2001).

In addition to mood stabilizers, antipsychotics can be used in conjunction with BZDs to reduce the psychotic symptoms associated with GHB withdrawal (i.e., hallucinations, delusions, and paranoia) (Glasper et al., 2005). For instance, low doses of Haldol, an older antipsychotic, have been successful in alleviating several of these symptoms (Jones, 2001). Additional antipsychotics, such as Zyprexa and Clozaril, are effective in treating the hallucinations and paranoia often seen in patients undergoing withdrawal (Rosenthal & Solhkhah, 2005). Finally, a new alternative in the treatment of GHB withdrawal involves the use of Xyrem, a form of GHB used for the treatment of narcolepsy. During inpatient detoxification, the appropriate dose of Xyrem is given instead of benzodiazepines and then is slowly reduced based on the patient's needs. While this new treatment method is rarely used, it is suspected that its popularity may increase in the coming years (Gonzalez & Nutt, 2005).

CONCLUSIONS

GHB is a white powdery substance that is soluble in water, and is usually distributed, both legally and illegally, as a colorless, odorless, and tasteless solution. Although GHB has been used therapeutically as an anesthetic, a growth promoter, a dietary supplement, a treatment for narcolepsy, and a medication to reduce the adverse effects associated with withdrawal, in recent years it has primarily become a drug of abuse and is commonly referred to as a "club drug." Other common club drugs include MDMA (ecstasy), ketamine, Rohypnol, methamphetamine, and LSD. These drugs, along with GHB, are readily accessible for purchase at "raves" (i.e., dance parties) and are often combined with other substances to heighten their effects. Moreover, GHB can be obtained illegally on the street under the following names: liquid X, liquid E, grievous bodily harm, G, Georgia home boy, G-rrifick, salty water, scoop, gamma 10, gamma g, easy lay, and cherry meth. Recently, GHB has become indirectly available on the Internet in the form of "chemistry kits," which contain the biological precursors of GHB with instructions that describe how to convert the precursors into the drug. These preceding events, along with GHB's alleged use in sexual assault, led the FDA to designate GHB as a Schedule I controlled substance in March 2000.

According to Meyer and Quenzer (2005), two competing hypotheses exist concerning GHB's mechanism of action in the brain. The first theory states that GHB is a GABA-B agonist, meaning that the drug activates GABA receptors causing a CNS-depressant effect. The second theory states that GHB's effects are mediated by specific GHB receptors found in the human brain. Current research indicates that GHB fulfills many of the characteristics associated with neurotransmitters or neuromodulators. These include its release in a calcium-dependent manner, its distinct reuptake system, and its own endogenous receptor system in the brain.

Furthermore, when an individual consumes GHB, it takes approximately 5 to 15 minutes for it to cross the blood brain barrier and affect behavior. Small doses of GHB typically produce muscle relaxation and relief from anxiety. Moderate doses of GHB induce sleep and euphoria, as well as physical disequilibrium, grogginess, tactile sensitivity, increased gag reflex, nausea, and vomiting. When doses increase above 40 or 50 mg, users often become unconscious and may experience severe respiratory depression. At toxic levels, GHB can produce unarousable coma and seizures. Other symptoms involved in GHB overdose include stupor, delirium, nausea, vomiting, vertical nystagmus, hypotension, tachycardia, tremor, anxiety, ataxia, jerking movements, bradycardia, disorientation, and muscle stiffening. Furthermore, when a patient is admitted to the hospital for GHB overdose, the most common form of treatment involves supportive medical care (i.e., cardiovascular and respiratory assistance). Drugs such as naloxone, physostigmine, neostigmine, and Romazicon have been given to patients in combination with supportive medical care to relieve the toxic effects of GHB.

Individuals that consume regular doses of GHB at two- to four-hour intervals throughout the day are thought to be the most susceptible to experiencing withdrawal after discontinuation. The most common withdrawal symptoms initially seen in patients include insomnia, anxiety, and tremors. As the withdrawal syndrome progresses, feelings of doom, sweating, craving for the drug, mood lability, abdominal cramping, heart palpitations, diaphoresis, tachycardia, and miosis occur. The most severe withdrawal symptoms that patients are likely to experience can involve fever, horizontal nystagmus, severe agitation, confusion, seizures, paranoia, delusional thinking, and auditory or visual hallucinations. Several drugs have been implicated in the treatment of GHB withdrawal. These typically consist of benzodiazepines, mood stabilizers, antipsychotics, and GHB substitutes. For instance, Valium and Ativan are the most common

BZDs prescribed to those in withdrawal. If a patient experiences withdrawal delirium, a mood stabilizer, such as Neurontin, is often combined with the BZD to decrease agitation. Additionally, antipsychotics can be used to reduce the psychotic symptoms associated with GHB withdrawal, and GHB substitutes (i.e., Xyrem) may be given instead of BZDs to reduce symptoms.

REFERENCES

Addolorato, G., Caputo, F., Capristo, E., Stefanini, G., & Gasbarrini. (2000). Gamma-hydroxybutyric acid efficacy, potential abuse, and dependence in the treatment of alcohol addiction. *Alcohol, 20*, 217–222.

Britt, G. C., & McCance-Katz, E. F. (2005). A brief overview of the clinical pharmacology of "club drugs." *Substance Use and Misuse, 40*, 1189–1201.

Carlson, N. R. (2007). *Physiology of behavior*. Boston: Allyn and Bacon.

Chin, R. L., Sporer, K. A., Cullison, B., Dyer, J. E., & Wu, T. D. (1998). Clinical course of gamma-hydroxybutyrate overdose. *Annals of Emergency Medicine, 31*, 716–722.

Degenhardt, L., Darke, S., & Dillon, P. (2003). The prevalence and correlates of gamma-hydroxybutyrate (GHB) overdose among Australian users. *Addiction, 98*, 199–204.

Fattore, L., Martellotta, M. C., Cossu, G., & Fratta, W. (2000). Gamma-hydroxybutyric acid: An evaluation of its rewarding properties in rats and mice. *Alcohol, 20*, 247–256.

Ferrara, S. D., Tedeschi, L., Frison, G., & Rossi, A. (1995). Fatality due to gamma-hydroxybutyric acid (GHB) and heroin intoxication. *Journal of Forensic Science, 40*, 501–504.

Friedman, J., Westlake, R., & Furman, M. (1996). "Grievous bodily harm": Gamma hydroxybutyrate abuse leading to the Wernicke-Korsakoff syndrome. *Neurology, 46*, 469–471.

Gable, R. S. (2004). Acute toxic effects of club drugs. *Journal of Psychoactive Drugs, 36*, 303–313.

Gallimberti, L., Schifano, F., Forza, G., & Miconi, L. (1994). Clinical efficacy of gamma-hydroxybutyric acid in treatment of opiate withdrawal. *European Archives of Psychiatry and Clinical Neuroscience, 244*, 113–114.

Galloway, G. P., Frederick, S. L., Staggers, F. E., Gonzales, M., Stalcup, S. A., & Smith, D. E. (1997). Gamma-hydroxybutyrate: An emerging drug of abuse that causes physical dependence. *Addiction, 92*, 89–96.

Glasper, A., McDonough, M., & Bearn, J. (2005). Within-patient variability in clinical presentation of gamma-hydroxybutyrate withdrawal: A case report. *European Addiction Research, 11*, 152–154.

Gonzalez, A., & Nutt, D. J. (2005). Gamma hydroxyl butyrate abuse and dependency. *Journal of Psychopharmacology, 19*, 195–204.

Hernandez, M., McDaniel, C. H., Costanza, C. D., & Hernandez, O. J. (1998). GHB-induced delirium: A case report and review of the literature on gamma hydroxy-butyric acid. *American Journal of Alcohol Abuse, 24,* 179–183.

Jones, C. (2001). Suspicious death related to gamma-hydroxybutyrate (GHB) toxicity. *Journal of Clinical Forensic Medicine, 8,* 74–76.

Julien, R. M. (2005). *A primer of drug action.* New York: Worth Publishing.

Kemmel, V., Taleb, O., Perard, A., Andriamampandry, C., Siffert, J. C., Mark, J., et al. (1998). Neurochemical and electrophysiological evidence for the existence of a functional gamma-hydroxybutyrate system in NCB-20 neurons. *Neuroscience, 86,* 989–1000.

Levinthal, C. F. (2006). *Drugs, behavior, and modern society.* Boston: Allyn and Bacon.

Martellotta, M. C., Fattore, L., Cossu, G., & Fratta, W. (1997). Rewarding properties of gamma-hydroxybutyric acid: An evaluation through place preference paradigm. *Psychopharmacology, 132,* 1–5.

McDonough, M., Kennedy, N., Glasper, A., & Bearn, J. (2004). Clinical features and management of gamma-hydroxybutyrate (GHB) withdrawal: A review. *Drug and Alcohol Dependence, 75,* 3–9.

Meyer, J. S., & Quenzer, L. F. (2005). *Psychopharmacology: Drugs, the brain and behavior.* Sunderland, MA: Sinauer Associates.

Miotto, K., Darakjian, J., Basch, J., Murray, S., Zogg, J., & Rawson, R. (2001). Gamma-hydroxybutyric acid: Patterns of use, effects and withdrawal. *American Journal on Addictions, 10,* 232–241.

Nicholson, K. L., & Balster, R. L. (2001). GHB: A new and novel drug of abuse. *Drug and Alcohol Dependence, 63,* 1–22.

Rosenthal, R. N., & Solhkhah, R. (2005). Club drugs. In D. A. Ciraulo & H. R. Kranzler (Eds.), *Clinical manual of addiction psychopharmacology* (pp. 243–267). Washington, DC: American Psychological Publishing.

Chapter 13

HIV and Addiction from an African Perspective: Making the Link

Mary Theresa Webb, PhD with Donald Omonge, BA

Since U.S. president George W. Bush announced the first AIDS awareness day in 2005, billions of U.S. dollars (President's Emergency Plan for AIDS Relief [PEPFAR]) and euro funds have gone into relieving the suffering of millions of Africans infected by the HIV virus and AIDS. African researchers and leaders came together in a conference in Dar Es Salaam, Tanzania, hosted by USG agencies through PEPFAR on August 29–31, 2005, to discuss alcohol/HIV risk behaviors and transmission in Africa. In a media presentation, Senior Technical Advisor and Prevention Technical Team Leader, Office of U.S. Global AIDS Coordinator Caroline A. Ryan, MD, MPH, stated that only 3 percent of all PEPFAR funding in African countries, notably Botswana and Rwanda, has supported programs that dealt with these alcohol-abusive behaviors that effect the transmission of the HIV virus through sexual contact.

All of the funded programs at that time were engaged in community forums and trainings to raise awareness. In Botswana, the community action forums had three components: the formation of a Citizen's Action Committee on Alcohol, the Botswana Alcohol AIDS Project, and the Botswana Movement against Destructive Decision (BMADD). BMADD held trainings for the health care sector on the issues of family dysfunction, co-dependency, alcohol use and abuse, depression, boundaries, grief, loss and bereavement, and self-worth/self-identity. In Namibia, Health Communication, in partner with Johns Hopkins University, held a series of community action forums in 38 sites across the country. Community leaders in all of the six areas surveyed for feedback noted that alcohol abuse combined with unemployment and poverty were the main problems contributing to the spread of the HIV virus. Rwanda also held community discussions around the same time period.

In 2006, a year after this conference, the Global Outreach in Addiction Leadership and Learning (GOAL) Project, located in Pittsburgh, Pennsylvania, received the first in three rounds of a New Partner's Initiative in PEPFAR funding for supporting the Kenya-based Substance Abuse Rehabilitation and HIV/AIDS (SARAH) Network of grassroots projects to help in the prevention of the spread of the HIV virus by educating communities, teachers, clergy, probation officers, and others in the disease of addiction and its role in the spread of the virus. The Kenya SARAH Network is highlighted here.

MAKING THE LINK

In the World Health report of 2002, cited in the Resolution of the Fifty-eighth World Health Assembly (2006), the resolution pointed out that 4 percent of disease and 3.2 percent of all deaths are attributed to alcohol, and alcohol is the biggest risk factor in developing countries. The resolution called on member states to recognize the threats to public health and to implement programs to reduce the harmful use of alcohol. Presentations a year earlier at the African Regional Conference (sponsored by USG agencies, 2005), had pointed out the consequences of alcohol consumption for HIV transmission and progression: (1) alcohol consumption is a risk factor; (2) misuse of alcohol affects adherence to HIV medication regimens; and (3) there is increased risk because of the interaction between alcohol, noninjection and injection drug use. In Eastern and Southern Africa, estimated alcohol consumption per person aged 15 years or older is 16.6 liters with 43 percent of the entire population within this age bracket being drinkers (WHO, 2004).

Prior to the resolution from the World Health Report of 2002, injecting heroin was widely known to be a major risk factor in the spread of the HIV virus. Since the rise of independent autonomous African countries and the development of these countries in the twentieth century, alcohol consumption had became a greater risk than injecting heroin because alcohol use and misuse had been on the rise among both young and old (Odejide, 2006). Dr. Flisher at the University in Cape Town in South Africa, clearly defined the causes of harmful use: (1) personal factors, such as low self-esteem, depression, sensation seeking and genetics; (2) interpersonal factors, such as peer pressure, relationship problems, negative responses of health care providers, and other environmental influences; and (3) cultural factors and structural factors, such as poverty (Flisher, 2006). Dr. Kasirye, representing the Uganda Youth Development League, Kampala, Uganda, in the same journal (CRISA, 2006, p. 27) stressed that drinking alcohol increases the risk of being infected with the HIV virus and that those who are under the influence of alcohol are less likely to be concerned about the use of condoms. Even domestic violence is on the increase in areas with high alcohol consumption.

Africa is second only to Eastern Europe in the level of absolute alcohol consumed, and eastern and southern African countries have the highest consumption per drinker in the world. Burundi, Nigeria, South Africa, Swaziland, and Uganda have the highest recorded per capita consumption (Ashley, Levine, & Needle, 2006, p. 193; Obot, 2006, p. 19). These researchers arrived at the consensus that interventions to lessen the spread of the AIDS virus must also target reducing alcohol consumption. They point out that many studies link alcohol use and sexual arousal, acting on that arousal, as well as condom nonuse increases the risk of HIV infection. Alcohol consumption also reduces adherence to antiviral medications and Tuberculosis medications as well as compliance to treatment (Ashley et al., 2006, p. 193). The same authors raised the issue of gender-based violence (GBV) or violence against women in this journal article (p. 195). The UN Population Fund (UNFPA) Gender Theme Group defines GBV as "violence involving men and women, in which the female is usually the victim; and which is derived from unequal power relationships between men and women. It includes, but is not limited to, physical, sexual and psychological harm" (UNFPA, [defined by United Nations Population Fund Gender Theme Group] 1998; Ashley et al., p. 195). In most African countries, GBV is about 40–60 percent. This explains the alarming rates of the rise of the HIV virus among women and children in Sub-Saharan African countries. This inequality of power was made vivid in a skit put on by a Kenyan team training area clergy in Kakamaga, Kenya, one of the towns in western Kenya. In the skit, a husband and wife were discussing what to do about a son's drinking and drug abuse. The husband sat in a chair while the wife sat on the floor at his feet, as it is the custom for the female to sit lower than the male. A peer-based support group, formed for women whose husbands drink too much in the Kisumu District of Kenya, meets in a mud hut. When this author visited with them, she asked the 15 young mothers and wives present how many had been tested for HIV/AIDS. Three women raised their hands. She asked the others what was keeping them from being tested. "We would be beaten," one member said. The rest nodded their heads in agreement. If any of these women do manage to sneak away to be tested and their tests prove positive, they will probably be shunned by their families and fellow villagers.

RECOMMENDATIONS

According to Ashley et al. (2006), the key step to addressing reducing the spread of HIV/AIDS is to reduce alcohol abuse. They recommend: (1) coalition building, (2) community empowerment, (3) professional capacity building and evidence-based treatment accessibility, (4) national policies and interventions, and (5) changing alcohol-imbibing cultures and behaviors (p. 196). They advocate for changing socially acceptable African male drinking patterns, training public health officials, and school-based interventions. They recommend cross-training in HIV and addiction and voluntary counseling and testing (VCT) (Ashley et al., 2006).

In addition to Botswana, Nambia, and Rwanda, in Uganda churches partnering with the government and NGOS are encouraging alcohol abstinence as a way forward in reducing the spread of the HIV virus. This chapter will highlight a Kenya prevention model, the SARAH Network, funded by the GOAL Project under President Bush's New Partner's Initiative under PEPFAR, and a treatment model in Egypt that is having an impact in that African country.

THE SARAH NETWORK MODEL (KENYA)

In 2005, the Anglican Bishop for Western Maseno Province in Kenya invited a G.O.A.L. Project team to train Kenyans in addictive disease and its relationship to HIV/AIDS. Margaret Namirembe Oketch, a Kenyan leader, and her colleague, invited 52 potential local leaders, community workers, clergy, teachers, and probation officers to the Brackenhurst Conference Center near Limuru for a two-week training. An American all-volunteer professional team worked with Ms. Oketch to put together an addiction/HIV/AIDS training package that included dramatic skits, PowerPoint presentations, and modeling 12 Step recovery and HIV/AIDS support groups (AA and Al-Anon) during the first week of the training. During the second week, the participants grouped themselves by various interests and worked together to prepare their action plans (mini proposals) that they presented to the whole group and made a commitment to follow through with their plans. Meanwhile, the combined GOAL/Kenya team formed a model structure for supervision and follow-up (Figure 13.1) that gave birth to the SARAH Network.

The SARAH Network can be a model for other African countries faced with the escalating rate of HIV/AIDS due to substance abuse addiction because it meets most of the guidelines recommended by Ashley et al. (2006) for successfully reducing the impact of risky behaviors due to the abuse of alcohol. Two recommendations, coalition building and community empowerment, are listed with examples.

A coalition of grassroots projects make up the SARAH Network. The Aniga Women's Initiative is located in western Kenya, in the Kisumu dis-

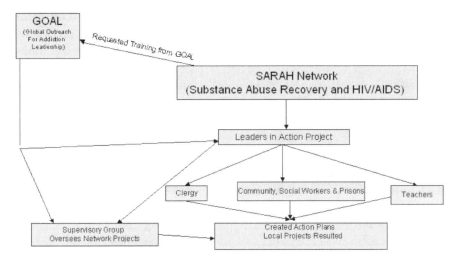

FIGURE 13.1 GOAL/SARAH Network Organizational Chart.

trict, where the statistics for both legal and illegal alcohol abuse and HIV/AIDS among women and children are higher than anywhere else in Kenya. The Kisumu region is also a rural area where village widowed women brew 80 percent proof alcohol called *Chang'aa* and/or are subject to GBV by drunken husbands if they risk going for VCT testing. The women in the Aniga project have been encouraged by their leader to form support groups and to reach out to other village women.

Five new support groups have mushroomed in a two-year period of time. Both men and women in these villages are now planting crops, bee keeping, rearing dairy goats, and raising chickens to bring in sustainable income as alternatives to chang'aa brewing. A mobile unit (van) brings VCT services directly to them.

The Aniga Women Initiative holds community mobilization daylong events in their district. In August, 2007, 2,000 people attended and more than 100 took advantage of VCT located in a tent nearby where the villagers were entertained by skits, poems, and songs that told the HIV and substance abuse prevention message. One reason for the success of this particular project has been the involvement of the local tribal chiefs and community leaders in all of the trainings and that, rather than attempting to change the local customs, such as spousal inheritance, skits are planned around cultural customs to encourage VCT testing by all parties.

Caring Mothers, a group of commercial sex workers in the coastal region of Mombasa, is another rural project. Although commercial sex workers are difficult to work with, the group has grown from 15 to 36 and, with the persistence of their leader; the women are now in peer-based support groups and are learning to protect themselves from acquiring the virus and to stop using alcohol and other drugs. As economic necessity drives many of these women into prostitution, they have begun alternative income-generating activities, such as soap making, growing crops, and hair dressing.

Wholeness Among People Project (WAPIS) is an peri-urban project located in the Banana region, Kiambu District. This project, directed by a member of the Church Army (similar to the Salvation Army), is geared to helping young male drivers of commuting passenger service vehicles called *Matatus* stop using and dealing in drugs. Drunk-driving traffic accidents have been the major causes of death on Kenyan roads. With the encouragement of their pastor leader and with training in substance abuse prevention and the formation of recovery support groups, about 50 young male drivers now are reaching out to local schools, training peer educators, and doing drug prevention with primary and high school students.

Also, in the Kawangware slums of Nairobi, another pastor has been training peer educators and has started an Alcoholics Anonymous recovery support group at his Upako Center. Under a tin-roofed shack, the young volunteer high school peer educators educate AIDS orphans.

PROFESSIONAL CAPACITY BUILDING

SARAH Network staff conducts weeklong addiction HIV/AIDS training events for clergy, probation officers, and teachers. In a study done in the Kisumu district of Kenya in 1994, the findings indicated that community and church members look up to clergy as trusted community leaders and those impaired seek help (Oketch, 2005). GOAL/SARAH facilitators have trained more than 48 clergy and lay leaders with proven behavior change communication methods and modeling mutual help 12 Step recovery support groups, based on SARAH's motto *Each One Reach One*. These clergy have informed and educated 4,800 persons. SARAH staff collected data and qualitative results using a simple monitoring and evaluation form and followed up with telephone calls, e-mails, and personal visits.

At each workshop, clergy are given a supply of addiction recovery educational books and pamphlets and a list of rehabilitation centers for possible referrals. SARAH also helps affected and infected clergy seek treatment by sponsoring and referring them to a nearby treatment center.

EVIDENCE-BASED TREATMENT ACCESSIBILITY

Although SARAH-trained clergy and teachers refer those persons who request help to existing treatment centers, the majority of Kenyan treatment centers charge a fee and most Kenyans cannot afford to pay those fees. Also, the counselors in these facilities are recovering addicts themselves and have had very little addiction counselor training. Through the SARAH Network, the International Association of Therapeutic Communities, the U.S. Academic Education Development (AED), the Kenya National Campaign Against Drug Abuse Authority (NACADAA), the Support for Addiction Prevention and Treatment in Africa Trust (SAPTA) and the Centre for Addiction Studies and Services in Africa (CASSA), efforts are underway to develop evidence-based interventions, to train addiction counselors, to set up new treatment programs in existing hospitals, and to start a countrywide school and community drug-prevention program.

SARAH Network's motto, *Each One Reach One*, has been successful in spreading the message of hope in healing for both alcohol and other drug abusers and addicts and those infected with HIV/AIDS. Although there are a handful of mutual help 12 Step–based recovery support groups, it will take another 10 years for these to multiply. In Kenya, especially in western Kenya, many more of these peer-based anonymous groups are needed. These recovery support groups have proven successful worldwide for helping addicts stay clean and sober.

CHANGING ALCOHOL-IMBIBING CULTURES AND BEHAVIORS

Alcohol and other drugs have been used and consumed in Kenya as part of the cultural traditions for centuries, but there were certain rules and values of use up until the period just after colonialism and the subsequent breakup of family and tribal cultures. It had been permissible for adults to use alcohol and tobacco, but youth and women were discouraged from using either until after childbearing years. Traditionally, alcohol, including illegal *Bhang'aa* has been used and abused during weddings, birthdays, harvest festivals, funeral ceremonies, and other social events (SINAM/Levi Trust, 1999). However, drunkenness has never been acceptable. In fact, those who exhibit drunkenness as well as those who test positive for the HIV virus become social outcasts. In all their trainings, SARAH staff and project leaders teach the brain disease concept of addiction and the realities of alcohol dependency and the resultant laxity in regard to sexual behaviors.

Khat production and exportation is a booming business among in Kenya. Due to the excessive availability, the abuse of khat is an common activity among long distance truck drivers and others. Among other dangers, excessive use of khat has been blamed for rendering men impotent and hence wives seeking other sexual partners and thus increasing the spread of HIV/AIDS. SARAH staff educates vulnerable individuals on the dangers of the abuse of khat in their HIV prevention activities.

The SARAH staff trainers and project leaders employ dramatic skits, role plays, and dialogues to dispel folklore and myths surrounding alcohol and other drug use. In clergy trainings, clergy also practice methods learned to dispel myths, teach facts, and reduce stigma.

CROSS-TRAINING IN HIV AND ADDICTION AND VCT

Although HIV/AIDS training is now readily available in African countries, thanks to generous funding from the United States, the United Nations, and the European Union, very few programs provide the cross-training in HIV and addiction, as well as modeling both peer-based recovery and HIV+ support groups. SARAH emphasizes a similar mutual help group step for both groups. The basic weeklong training consists of two days of knowledge in drug prevention and treatment, two days in HIV/AIDS prevention and treatment, and one day in implementation planning. SARAH facilitators train people with proven behavior change communication methods. Trainers present topics geared to the specific group to be trained. Participants fill out an action planning sheet provided by the SARAH staff indicating what actions they will undertake and how many persons they anticipate reaching.

The Freedom Center in Egypt, on the continent of Africa and considered a country in the Arab Middle East, an emerging new treatment model that combines the Minnesota Model (i.e., based in peer–based mutual help recovery support group) with a six-week therapeutic community model has been found to be effective. This, combined with a treatment model that includes one-on-one and group counseling as well as attendance at outside recovery support groups, has been accompanied by extensive prevention awareness through television and radio and has taught that treatment for alcohol and other drug addiction is possible.

Three thousand heroin addicts and alcoholics in this Arab African country now wait to get a bed in one of two dozen treatment centers. The Freedom Center, founded by Ehab Elkharrat, MD, former president of the International Substance Abuse and Addiction Coalition (ISAAC) and who now is United Nations Development Programme (UNDP) representative for all Arab countries, has started other treatment centers in and around Cairo where both heroin and alcohol addiction are huge challenges. Narcotics Anonymous (12 Step) support groups have mushroomed in the past six years. Working on the principle of one addict reaching out to help another and sponsorship, the Egyptian Narcotics Anonymous (NA) support groups have become the lifeline for addicts and are spreading the message of hope in recovery.

CONCLUSIONS

Implementing model programs specifically suited to African cultures and customs to combat the spread of HIV/AIDS must include training components that cross both disciplines, (HIV/AIDS and alcohol and other drugs) that have proven effective for prevention and treatment. They must be geared to those within the culture who are most effective as change agents. The SARAH Network has targeted community opinion-shapers who include clergy, teachers, probation officers, and grassroots community organizers as the most effective as prevention agents.

Difficulties still lie ahead in African countries in meeting the challenges that alcohol and other substance abuse and addiction cause in the spread of HIV/AIDS. Much still needs to be done to assist in the formation of and support for evidence-based treatment facilities, especially for those populations less able to pay. Treatment should embody the establishment and sustaining of mutual help—addiction recovery and HIV+ support groups. Also, unless GBV and rape of vulnerable women and children is curtailed through establishing shelters and a legal protection system, very little hope exists for curbing the spread of the HIV virus in Kenya as well as in other African countries. Limited research has been done to investigate the correlations between HIV and substance abuse issues in Kenya. Despite this fact the SARAH Network's interventions have proven to be effective based on what has worked in other countries. Research-guided interventions would facilitate localized interventions and possibly yield better outcomes. For the existing treatment centers, both public and private, addiction counselor training and certification should be strengthened. More counselor training is needed for family member issues, relapse prevention, therapeutic strategies such as motivational interviewing, and stages of change, as well as a country-wide certification process. These should be put in place in each of the infected African countries.

The Kenya SARAH Network Prevention model and the Egyptian Freedom Center treatment model signal a great new beginning for the African continent in its fight against the spread of the HIV virus.

REFERENCES

African Centre for Research and Information on Substance Abuse (CRISA); R. Kasirye. (2006). Commentary. *African Journal of Drug and Alcohol Studies*. CRISA Publications 5(1), 27–38.

Africa Regional Conference. (2005, August 29–31). (USG agencies: Health and Human Services (HHS), Center for Disease Control (CDC), County Assistance Plans (cAP), National Institute of Alcohol Abuse and Alcoholism (NIAAA), Department of Defense (DoD), and United States Agency for International Development (USAID) President's Emergency Plan for AIDS Relief (PEPFAR) *Alcohol, HIV risk behaviors and transmission in Africa: Developing programs for the United States Emergency Plan for AIDS relief.* Dar Es Salaam, Tanzania 13-32.

Ashley, J. W., Levine, B., & Needle, R. (2006). Summary of the proceedings on alcohol, HIV risk behaviors and transmission in Africa: Developing programmes for the United States President's Emergency Plan for AIDS relief (PEPFAR). *African Journal of Drug and Alcohol Studies*, 5(2), 192–200.

Fifty-eighth World Health Assembly Resolution on Public Health Problems Caused by Harmful Use of Alcohol. (2005, May). In *African Journal of Drug and Alcohol Studies* (2006), CRISA Publications 5(1), 71–72.

Flisher, A. (2006). Public health problems caused by harmful use of alcohol. *African Journal of Drug and Alcohol Studies*, 5(1), CRISA Publications, 73–74.

Obot, I. S. (2006). Alcohol use and related problems in Sub-Saharan Africa. *African Journal of Drug and Alcohol Studies* CRISA Publications 5(1), 17–26.

Odejide, O. A. (2006). Public health problems caused by harmful use of alcohol. *African Journal of Drug and Alcohol Studies*. CRISA Publications 5(1), 17–26.

Oketch, M. (2005). *Substance use and abuse—Kenya*. Presentation at First National Addiction Conference in Kisumu, Kenya.

SINAM/Levi Trust. (1999). Some observations on the misuse of drugs in Mombasa. Unpublished paper.

UNFPA (defined by United Nations Population Fund Gender Theme Group). (1998). Violence against girls and women. From http://www.unfpa.org/intercenter/violence/ntro.htm. Cited also on p. 21, g. Woelk. Alcohol and Gender-Based Violence. Africa Regional Meeting Report, Dar es Salaam, Tanzania. August 29–31, 2005.

World Health Organization (WHO). (2004). Global Status Report on Alcohol, 2004. World Health Organization, Department of Mental Health and Substance Abuse, from http://www.who.int/substance_abuse/publications/alcohol/en/index.html.

Chapter 14

Drug Abuse–Related HIV/AIDS Epidemic in India: Situation and Responses

Atul Ambekar, MD, and Meera Vaswani, PhD

HIV EPIDEMIC IN INDIA: CONTRIBUTION OF INJECTING DRUG USE

The first case of HIV was detected in India in 1986. In the past two decades since then, the HIV epidemic continues to grow unabated in India. As per the latest estimates, there are about 2.5 million people living with HIV in the country. The prevalence of HIV among the general population is estimated to be about 0.36 percent, with a much higher prevalence among men as compared to women (0.43% vs. 0.29%). Prevalence is also high in the young, productive age group with 88.7 percent of all infections occurring in the age group of 15–49 years (National AIDS Control Organization [NACO], 2007a). In other words, there is still no generalized epidemic (defined as more than 1% HIV prevalence in the general population; Joint United Nations Programme on HIV/AIDS and World Health Organization [UNAIDS/WHO], 2004) of HIV in India at the national level.

The national level data, however, should be interpreted with caution. India, being a vast and heterogeneous country, has a heterogeneous HIV situation. It has often been commented that there is not one, but many, simultaneous HIV epidemics currently spreading in India (Monitoring the AIDS Pandemic [MAP], 2004). In three states of the country, the epidemic is generalized, that is, these states have HIV prevalence of more than 1 percent in the general population. These three states are Andhra Pradesh, Manipur, and Nagaland. It must also be remembered that though these states have a higher *proportion* of

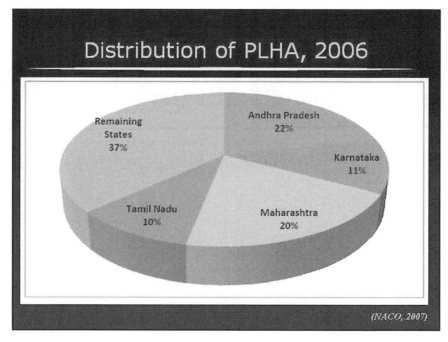

FIGURE 14.1   Distribution of proportion of people living with HIV/AIDS (PLHA) in India, 2006. From *HIV Sentinel Surveillance and HIV Estimation, 2006*, by National AIDS Control Organization, 2007, New Delhi: Ministry of Health and Family Welfare, Government of India.

people living with HIV/AIDS (PLHA), there are other states with far higher *absolute numbers* of people living with HIV (see Figure 14.1).

Besides these three states in the country, there are many other states that are in the "concentrated" stage of the epidemic (UNAIDS/WHO, 2004), in that the prevalence of HIV, though less than 1 percent in the general population, is more than 5 percent in the high-risk groups (HRGs). Certain groups of individuals, based on their enhanced vulnerability to HIV infection, are seen as HRGs. These include female sex workers (FSW), men having sex with men (MSM), and injecting drug users (IDUs). Among these, it is noteworthy that the highest prevalence of HIV at the national level has been found among IDUs (as shown in Figure 14.2).

Since the beginning of the HIV epidemic in India, the major route of transmission has always been heterosexual intercourse, though the proportion of HIV infections attributed to heterosexual intercourse (Correa & Gisselquist,

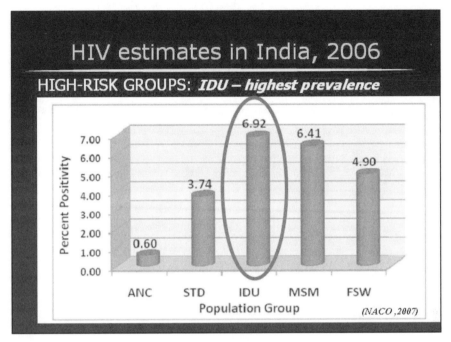

FIGURE 14.2 HIV prevalence among various groups in India, 2006. From *HIV Sentinel Surveillance and HIV Estimation, 2006,* by National AIDS Control Organization, 2007, New Delhi: Ministry of Health and Family Welfare, Government of India.

2006), particularly heterosexual commercial sex (Gisselquist & Correa, 2006), has been debated in the literature. The contribution of injecting drug use (IDU) and consequent sharing of contaminated injection equipment has usually been estimated to be around 2–3 percent of the total HIV infections (Correa & Gisselquist, 2006). Until recently, it has been largely believed that HIV infection among IDUs is concentrated only in the northeastern states (Manipur and Nagaland) and certain large cities of the country (Chennai, Delhi, and Mumbai). Findings from the recent round on sentinel surveillance (conducted annually, at a national level), however, reveal that the HIV infection among IDUs has spread in many states of the country (NACO, 2007a). As seen in Figure 14.3, as many as seven areas of the country have crossed the threshold for a concentrated epidemic among IDUs.

Additionally, many smaller, clinic-based studies have reported high prevalence of HIV infection among injecting drug users in India (Jindal, Arora, &

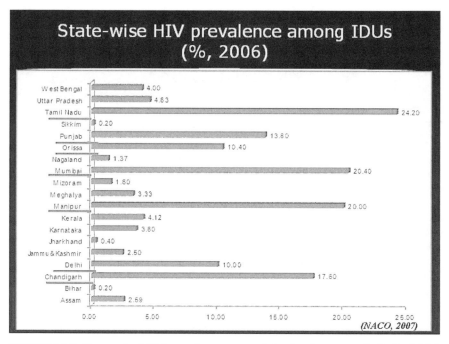

FIGURE 14.3 State-wise HIV prevalence among injecting drug users in India, 2006. From *HIV Sentinel Surveillance and HIV Estimation, 2006*, by National AIDS Control Organization, 2007, New Delhi: Ministry of Health and Family Welfare, Government of India.

Singh, 2008; Saraswathi & Dutta, 2007; Vaswani & Desai, 2004; Vaswani & Rao, 2006). Thus, injecting drug use is a major risk factor for transmission of HIV in India. While, in two of the states (Manipur and Nagaland), it is the primary factor behind a generalized HIV epidemic, the phenomenon may be significantly contributing to the spread of the HIV epidemic elsewhere in the country as well.

INJECTING DRUG USE IN INDIA

Historically, the use of certain intoxicating substances has been prevalent in India for many centuries now. Traditionally, various cannabis derivatives and locally brewed alcohol were the substances of use. There was also a certain degree of social sanction to use of these substances (Dhawan, 1998). Until the early twentieth century, many of the substances of abuse, which are currently illicit, were available through licit channels. Nonmedical or nonprescription use of psychotropic medications was also observed. Besides opium, cannabis, and alcohol, use of cocaine and even khat was reported in India until 1940. However, many reports up to the late 1960s suggested that most users of these substances used in moderation and only a few did become habitual users or used in excess (Reid & Costigan, 2002).

In the 1980s, however, with the introduction of heroin in India, the situation changed to a great degree. Earlier, opium was available through licensed vendors and a sizable number of registered opium addicts existed in the 1950s (Ray, 1998). Over the years, this practice has been discontinued and new registration of opium addicts has been stopped. In the early 1990s, only a few of the registered opium users were alive and drawing their quota of opium. Consequently, many users of a traditional, plant-based (and relatively less potent) drug like opium were forced to shift to a modern, synthetic (and more potent) drug, that is, heroin (Ambekar, Lewis, Rao, & Sethi, 2005).

Over next few years, many heroin users switched to injecting modes of taking opioid drugs. The phenomenon was first noted in the northeastern states of Manipur and Nagaland, which share their border with Myanmar—the world's second-largest illicit opium-producing country (United Nations Office on Drugs and Crime, Regional Office for South Asia, and Ministry of Social Justice and Empowerment [UNODC/MSJE], 2005). Since taking opioids through an injection route provides a better and quicker high, the injecting route is perceived by the drug users as more cost-effective (UNODC/MSJE, 2004a, 2004b, 2005). The phenomenon was first noted in the northeastern states of Manipur and Nagaland (Sarkar et al., 1991, 1995), which share their border with Myanmar—the world's second-largest illicit opium-producing country (United Nations Office on Drugs and Crime, Regional Office for South Asia, and Ministry of Social Justice and Empowerment [UNODC/ MSJE], 2005).

Currently, India figures among the developing and transitional countries with the "largest populations of IDUs," along with Brazil, China, and Russia (Aceijas et al., 2006). However, there are no reliable estimates regarding the number or prevalence of IDUs in the country. The largest of the epidemiological studies in the country—the National Household Survey—found a prevalence of 0.1 percent of IDUs among the adult male population of the country (UNODC/MSJE, 2004a). However, it is widely accepted that household samples are not appropriate to pick up hidden and potentially stigmatizing phenomena such as injecting drug use (Joint United Nations Programme on HIV/AIDS and Family Health International [UNAIDS/FHI], 2003). The same multimodality study (UNODC/MSJE, 2004a) also collected information from patients seeking treatment for substance use problems from more than 200 treatment centers throughout the country through a survey—the

Drug Abuse Monitoring System (DAMS). In this survey, prevalence of injecting drug use ("ever" in lifetime) among treatment seekers was reported to be 14 percent (UNODC/MSJE, 2002a). Yet another component of the same study was the Rapid Assessment Survey (RAS), in which data were collected from drug users contacted at streets in 14 urban locations across the country. Here, the prevalence of injecting drug use was 43 percent (UNODC/MSJE, 2002b). International experts (Aceijas et al., 2004) in a global overview of HIV among IDUs have quoted a rather wide range—from 563,000 to 2,025,000—for the estimated number of IDUs in India.

   Like the HIV situation, however, the spread of IDU is also heterogeneous in the country. For a long time now it has been believed that the phenomenon of IDU is a matter of concern only in the northeastern states (Manipur and Nagaland) and the metro cities of the country (Chennai, Mumbai, and Delhi). There have been multiple studies, however, that have produced evidence that IDU is not limited to the aforementioned areas. The 14-city Rapid Assessment Survey (UNODC/MSJE, 2002b) documented the presence of injecting drug use in many other cities of the country other than the northeastern states and metropolitan cities (see Figure 14.4).

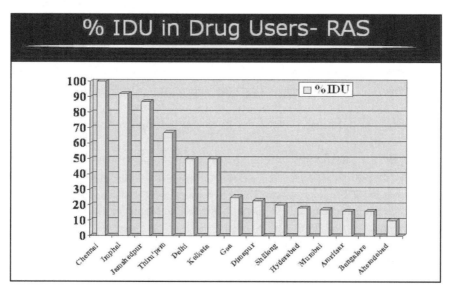

FIGURE 14.4   Proportion of injecting drug users in the total sample of drug users in the Rapid Assessment Survey of Drug Use in India. From *The Extent, Pattern and Trends of Drug Abuse in India: National Survey*, by United Nations Office on Drugs and Crime, Regional Office for South Asia, and Ministry of Social Justice and Empowerment, 2004, New Delhi: UNODC and MSJE.

SHARAN, an NGO working in the area of drugs and HIV, has recently documented the presence of IDU in many parts of the country, including Uttar Pradesh, Maharashtra, Goa, Kerala, and Tamil Nadu (SHARAN, 2007). Similarly, in two of the recent, large-scale studies, presence of IDUs has been documented in many north Indian states, including Punjab, Haryana, Uttar Pradesh, Bihar, Jharkhand, and Orissa (Ambekar & Tripathi, 2006, 2007, 2008).

Thus, there is considerable evidence that IDU is well established in many parts of India. The worrying aspect of this is the presence of IDU in smaller towns and rural areas of the country.

PROFILE OF IDUS IN INDIA

Most of the studies in India have found IDUs to be in their late 20s or early 30s. Notably, most injecting drug users in India are those, who, in the initial phase of their drug-use career, use opioids through a noninjecting route (most commonly, heroin, through smoking or "chasing" routes) and later switch to the injection mode of using opioids. There is usually a time lag—ranging from 2 to 10 years—when people switch from noninjecting to injecting mode of taking drugs (UNODC/MSJE, 2004b). The factors behind initiation of injecting in India have also been studied and are summarized in the accompanying box.

BOX 1

Factors behind Initiation of Injecting Drug Use by Drug Users in India

+ Nonavailability of heroin (for smoking or "chasing")
+ High cost of heroin (for smoking or "chasing")
+ Easy availability of pharmaceutical opiates and other sedatives (inject-able) in pharmacies (without prescription)
+ Perception that taking drugs through the injecting route produces better and quicker highs and immediate relief from withdrawal symptoms
+ Iatrogenic, that is, administration of opioid injections by a health professional
+ Curiosity
+ Peer pressure

Source: Injecting Drug Use and HIV in India: An Emerging Concern, by United Nations Office on Drugs and Crime, Regional Office for South Asia, and Ministry of Social Justice and Empowerment, 2004, New Delhi: UNODC and MSJE; "My First Time: Initiation into Injecting Drug Use in Manipur and Nagaland, North-East India," by M. Kermode, V. Longleng, B. C. Singh, J. Hocking, B. Langkham, and N. Crofts, 2007, *Harm Reduction Journal, 4,* p. 19.

Most injecting drug users in India prefer to inject either heroin or pharma-ceutical preparations. The pharmaceutical preparations include injectable opi-oids like buprenorphine and pentazocine, which are usually mixed with other sedatives like diazepam, promethazine, and chlorpheniramine. A distinct pat-tern of using dextropropxyphene capsules for injection has also been observed, particularly from the northeastern states of Manipur, Nagaland, and Mizoram (UNODC/MSJE, 2004b, 2005; Kermode et al., 2007; Ambekar & Tripathi, 2006, 2008).

RISK BEHAVIORS AMONG IDUS: INJECTING RISKS

The risk of transmission of HIV and other blood-borne virus infections due to sharing of contaminated injection equipment is well documented. Injecting serves as an efficient vehicle for transmission of HIV. The injecting route is about three to five times more efficient than the sexual route (0.67% risk for HIV transmission per episode of intravenous needle or syringe exposure as compared to 0.1%–3% risk for HIV transmission per episode of receptive penile-anal sexual exposure and 0.1%–0.2% risk per episode of receptive vagi-nal exposure; Centers for Disease Control and Prevention [CDC], 1998).

There is ample evidence from the community-based as well as clinic-based studies that a sizable proportion of IDUs in India share their injection equip-ment and thus are vulnerable to transmission of HIV and other blood-borne virus infections. In the Rapid Assessment Survey of Drug Abuse in India (UNODC/MSJE, 2002b, 2004), injecting drug use was reported to be a group activity. Needle sharing was reported to be "common" among injecting drug users and varied between 52 and 81 percent. Indirect sharing (e.g., shar-ing of cotton swab, filter, and spoons, etc.) was also common. About half of the IDUs who shared reported that they had shared syringes and needles the last time they injected. Most did not clean the needles and syringes. In the first round of the Behavioral Surveillance Survey (BSS) conducted in India by the National AIDS Control Organization (NACO, 2002a) among 1,355 IDUs, about 44 percent shared injection equipment in the preceding month, while 4 percent reported that they "always" shared injection equipment. In the latest round of BSS also (NACO, 2007b), a large majority of IDUs in Manipur, Delhi, Chennai, and Mumbai reported sharing of injection material. Many of them reported sharing on more than 50 percent of the occasions. In yet another recent study (Ambekar & Tripathi, 2006) conducted at multiple sites nation-wide among 5,603 IDUs, 59 percent reported sharing of injections "ever." A large majority of them (77%) shared at the last occasion of injecting. In clinic-based studies, high prevalence of risk behaviors as well as HIV infection has been reported among IDUs, particularly when compared to non-IDUs (i.e., drug users who take drugs through a noninjecting route). Vaswani and Desai (2004) found a high prevalence of risky injection behavior among IDUs in their sample of 154 consecutive drug users attending a treatment center. Notably, the prevalence of HIV was significantly higher among IDUs (8.2%) as compared to non-IDUs (1.8% in heroin smokers and 0% in alcohol-dependent individuals).

Thus, in this backdrop of widespread injecting drug use and associated practice of sharing contaminated injection equipment, rapid escalation of the prevalence of HIV remains a very likely possibility in India. Some parts of the country have witnessed explosive HIV epidemics among IDUs in the past. For instance, in Manipur in northeast India, the first case of HIV among IDUs was detected in 1989. Six months later, prevalence among IDUs had increased to 50 percent (Sarkar et al., 1993).

RISK BEHAVIORS AMONG DRUG USERS: SEXUAL RISKS

While injecting-related risk for transmission of HIV is well recognized, the contribution of substance use (alcohol as well as illicit drugs like cannabis and opioids) to enhanced transmission of HIV is not recognized so well. There is evidence that substance use (injecting or otherwise) is associated with an enhanced vulnerability to high-risk sexual behavior.

Men who have been drinking alcohol report more contact and noncontact sexual problems as compared to those who do not use alcohol (Verma, Sharma, Singh, Rangaiyan, & Pelto, 2001). In a study on assessment of the risk factors in sexually transmitted diseases (STD), alcohol was one of the risk factors found to be significantly associated with the acquisition of STD (Sharma & Chaubey, 1996). Among studies looking at sexual behavior and its relationship with substance use, in a study from northeast India, among 200 students, sexual behavior was found to be strongly associated with alcohol use (Longkumer, Shrivastava, & Murugesan, 2000). Similarly, in yet another study among adolescents in slums of Mumbai, alcohol use was associated with risky sexual behavior along with the perception that consumption of alcohol before sex heightens sexual pleasure and makes it long-lasting (Singh, Schensul, & Gupta, 2004). Such an association between alcohol and substance use and high-risk sexual behaviors is more evident among groups regarded to be at high risk of HIV such as sex workers and truckers. The number of clients visiting the sex workers decreases during the "dry" (i.e., alcohol-free) periods (Ambwani & Gilada, 1998).

Tripathi, Malhotra, and Sharma (2004) have reported findings of their study carried out in the city of Delhi as a part of a multinational study sponsored by the World Health Organization (WHO). Primary data on alcohol use and sexual risk behavior were obtained from interviews of key informants (KIs), sex workers, truck drivers, and restaurant workers. Among the significant findings, alcohol was found to be a common substance of use among various population subgroups, including sex workers. A clear relationship between use of alcohol and sexual behavior was evident. Though from the general population about 25 percent of respondents reported sexual arousal and enhanced sexual pleasure following consumption of alcohol, among high-risk population groups (sex workers, transport workers, etc.), between 60 and 100 percent reported such feelings. Of more concern was the finding that condom use was uniformly low among all the population subgroups except for sex workers. Consistent condom use was even lower (Tripathi et al., 2004).

Apart from alcohol, other substance use has also been linked to high-risk sexual behaviors. High prevalence of substance use has been found among sex workers and their clients in India. In a nationwide Behavioral Surveillance Survey, among a total of 5,572 female sex workers (FSWs), 22 percent reported that they consumed alcohol every day in the last month (NACO, 2001). Overall, around 15 percent of FSWs reported that they drink regularly before sex. Some (about 6%) had tried other (nonalcohol) addictive drugs, including injections, in the past 12 months. In the same study, among a total of 5,684 clients of FSWs, the proportion of respondents drinking at least once a week was 45 percent and the proportion of those drinking daily was nearly 23 percent. Nearly 13 percent of the respondents regularly consumed alcoholic drinks before having sex with their commercial partners. Around 22 percent reported use of other compounds like cannabis and opium. Some of these respondents (10%) had injected drugs in the last 12 months (NACO, 2001).

In a study from India, comparing the sexual behavior of drug users (excluding alcohol and tobacco) with nondrug users randomly selected from the same community, the average number of sexual partners was found to be significantly higher among drug users (7.4 vs. 4) as compared to nondrug users (Sharma, Aggarwal, & Dubey, 2002). In a recent nationwide study among 12,580 drug users, about 37 percent reported sex with multiple partners. More than a third (35%) reported *never* having used a condom (Ambekar & Tripathi, 2006).

The sexual behaviors of injecting drug users have also been studied. There is evidence that many injecting drug users are sexually active and do visit sex workers (UNODC/MSJE, 2004a, 2004b). In a clinic-based study (Vaswani & Rao, 2006), among 154 consecutive treatment seekers, a significantly higher proportion of IDUs (83.6%) was found to have multiple sex partners as compared to non-IDUs (57.4%). Women IDUs have been found to be engaging in sex work to sustain their livelihoods (Panda et al., 2001). There is also evidence that HIV infection is being transmitted from injecting drug users to their non-injecting wives and sexual partners (Panda et al., 2000, 2005, 2007).

Thus, in India, a definite association is clearly seen between drug use and high-risk sexual behavior. This association is visible in the general population as well as the known "high-risk" population groups.

RESPONSE TO IDU-RELATED HIV: HARM REDUCTION

While it is well known that drug dependence is a complex, chronic, relapsing condition that is often accompanied by severe health, psychological, economic, legal, and social consequences—or "harms" (McLellan, Lewis, O'Brien, & Kleber, 2000)—with the advent of the HIV epidemic, substance use, in particular, injecting drug use (IDU), is now seen as a major public health issue rather than just a social/legal issue. Injecting drug users are particularly vulnerable to HIV and other blood-borne infections (such as hepatitis C) as a result of sharing contaminated injecting equipment. There is ample evidence from the recent literature that IDUs in India have a high sero-positivity not only for HIV but hepatitis B and C as well (Das, Borkakoty, Mahanta, Medhi, & Chelleng, 2007; Datta et al., 2006; Jindal et al., 2008; Saraswathi & Dutta, 2007; Sarkar et al., 2006). Some of the harms associated with drug use may be attributable to the effects of the drug itself on the body and the mind. More often, drug-related harm is the result of the many social, economic, legal, cultural, and political factors that influence the availability of illicit (illegal) drugs and the conditions under which they are used. Poverty, migration, and social discrimination affect people's vulnerability to the drug-related harm. Stringent laws, unpragmatic policies, and the social stigmatization and discrimination of illicit drug users serve to drive them further toward isolation and away from their social support like family, as well as from various health and social services (Ambekar, Agrawal, & Tripathi, 2008).

Additionally, it should be remembered that "zero tolerance"–based strategies such as legal prohibition of substances and emphasis only on the abstinence-oriented treatment have not been able to eliminate substance use from the society. Despite being illicit and controlled substances, the use of certain drugs like heroin, cocaine, and others is still prevalent in the society and the worldwide illegal trade of these substances is burgeoning (UNODC, 2007). Moreover, making a drug illegal may even increase the harms associated with its use by contributing to the marginalization of a drug user and criminalization of his drug use behavior. There is a growing understanding that the utopian rhetoric, like "a drug-free society" or "a world without drugs," is unrealistic and unachievable. The global community is now realizing that some drug abuse would occur in any society, despite the best efforts at curbing it. Consequently, a pragmatic response would be to employ strategies that could reduce the harms associated with this drug use. One of the approaches to bring about desirable changes in the behavior of substance-using individuals—and thus reducing the risks of harms—is harm reduction.

While the concept of harm reduction has been used in the context of a variety of risky behaviors, primarily it has been seen as an intervention and management strategy for the individuals using psychoactive substances. Various definitions for the term *harm reduction* (also termed sometimes as *harm minimization*) have been put forward (Lenton & Single, 1998). The International Harm Reduction Association (IHRA) defines harm reduction as "policies and programs, which aim to reduce the health, social and economic harms associated with the use of psychoactive substances" (IHRA, 2006). A defining feature of such policies and programs is their focus on the prevention of drug-related harm rather than the prevention of drug use per se (Hunt, 2003). Instead of viewing drug problems as phenomena caused by individual psychological (or moral) deficiencies, harm reduction views any society's patterns of drug use collectively—holding that many of the most destructive consequences and refractory problems of illicit drug use are not solely attributable to the drugs per se. Rather, many of these problems are more closely linked to the failure of the policies employed to control them (Ambekar & Balhara, 2007; Ambekar et al., 2008).

The adjoining box summarizes some of the key principles of harm reduction (Ritter & Cameron, 2005).

BOX 2

Some Key Features and Principles of Harm Reduction

+ The primary goal is reducing harm rather than drug use per se
+ Built on evidence-based analysis
+ Acceptance that drugs are a part of society and may never be eliminated
+ Provides a comprehensive public health framework
+ Priority is placed on immediate (and achievable) goals
+ Pragmatic—does not seek to pursue policies or strategies that are unachievable or likely to create more harm than good
+ Recognizes individual human right—rooted in an acceptance of individual integrity and responsibility

Source: Adapted from *A Systematic Review of Harm Reduction,* by A. Ritter and J. Cameron, 2005, DPMP, Monograph Series No. 06, Fitzroy, Australia: Turning Point Alcohol and Drug Centre.

Though there are many strategies that have been proposed to reduce the harms associated with injecting drug use, in the following section, we limit our discussion to only a few of them. These include (1) needle-syringe exchange programs, (2) agonist maintenance treatment, (3) outreach activities, and (4) legal and policy reforms.

Needle-Syringe Exchange Programs

The programs for needle and syringe exchange are more readily associated with the harm reduction approach than any other type of intervention. At its most basic level, this strategy involves supplying new, clean needles and syringes to IDUs, in exchange for old, used, and potentially contaminated needles and syringes.

As discussed earlier, a sizable number of IDUs in India share their used and potentially contaminated injections with each other, putting themselves and their partners at the risk of acquiring HIV and other blood-borne virus infections. Availability of new, clean injecting equipment, free of cost, would provide these IDUs with an opportunity to protect themselves and their injecting partners from transmission of HIV. Additionally, these programs also provide a point of continuous contact with the drug users that enable these practices and a wide range of other health matters to be discussed. Indeed, most such programs do not limit themselves only to providing sterile injecting equipment but also incorporate a variety of other services such as risk reduction education, condom distribution, bleach distribution, education on needle disinfection, and referrals to substance abuse treatment and other health and social services (Wodak, 2004).

The effectiveness of these programs in preventing the spread of HIV has been a matter of controversy, mainly due to a number of methodological shortcomings in the studies conducted to evaluate their effectiveness. In a review, Gibson, Flynn, & Perales (2001) reported findings from 42 studies, of which 28 found positive effects (reduction in drug-related HIV risk behavior, including self-reported sharing of needles and syringes, unsafe injection and disposal practices, and frequency of injection) and 14 found either no association or a combination of positive and negative effects. Overall, this provides reasonable evidence of the positive impact of needle-syringe exchange programs on HIV risk behavior and HIV infection. Wodak (2004), after his extensive review of 48 studies for the World Health Organization (WHO), has also concluded that not only was there compelling evidence of the effectiveness of needle-syringe exchange programs in reducing HIV infection substantially, there was compelling evidence for their cost-effectiveness as well. Moreover, there was no convincing evidence of any major, unintended negative consequences. However, and more important, he concluded that these programs on their own are not enough to control HIV infection among IDUs.

Agonist Maintenance Treatment

These programs, known by a variety of names such as "opioid replacement therapy" or "oral substitution treatment" rely on the principle of substituting an illicit, unsafe, short-acting, and more addictive drug with a legal medication of known purity and potency. The origins of opioid replacement therapies can be traced back to the landmark study on the role of methadone maintenance in opioid-dependent subjects (Dole & Nyswander, 1965). Since then, a number of drugs have been used for this purpose such as methadone, LAAM, buprenorphine, slow release oral morphine, and others. However, the search for an ideal agent continues to remain elusive. All of the replacement medications have been shown to be effective in reducing use of illicit drugs, reducing the risk of injecting, reducing the risk of overdose, reducing involvement in illegal activities, and improving socio-occupational functioning (Gowing, Farrell, Bornemann, & Ali, 2004; Mattick, Breen, Kimber, & Davoli, 2003; Mattick, Kimber, Breen, & Davoli, 2003).

For India, these programs are especially relevant because the most favored drugs by the IDUs in India are opioids (Ambekar et al., 2005; Ray & Ambekar, 2005). Though methadone is not available in India as of now, another agent—buprenorphine—is available, and the country has gathered enough experience and expertise in the area of buprenorphine maintenance programs (Dhawan & Sunder, 2008).

Outreach Activities

Several of the drug-using populations may not be accessible through the conventional center-based services. Such populations may remain "hidden" due to a number of factors such as inaccessibility of services, unattractiveness of facilities, distance, stigma, and so forth. Outreach was conceived to overcome these barriers and to reach out to people within their own communities or local milieu, outside of the usual service settings. Community-based outreach involves a number of activities such as establishing contact and rapport with the target populations in their natural environments, providing information about unsafe as well as risk behaviors, and promoting and supporting safe behaviors.

Outreach services have been proved to be effective for reaching hard-to-reach, hidden populations of drug users and provide the means for enabling IDUs to reduce their risk behaviors. According to a WHO review, a significant proportion of IDUs receiving outreach-based interventions reduces their risk behaviors in drug using, needle, and sexual practices and increases their protective behaviors (Needle et al., 2005).

Outreach services are especially relevant in India, since help seeking among drug users has been found to be low and delayed (UNODC/MSJE, 2004a; Ambekar et al., 2005). Outreach-based activities aimed at identifying and reaching out to hidden IDUs have been employed at many centers in India (Hangzo, Chatterjee, & Sarkar, 1997; Kumar, Mudaliar, & Daniels, 1998). The preliminary evidence from the country suggests that outreach services for IDUs produce significant changes in risk behaviors, especially the injecting-related risk behaviors (Kumar et al., 1998; Kumar, 2008).

Legal and Policy Reforms

The general approach toward drug use in most countries has been "criminalization." This approach may be beneficial in handling drug trafficking but has been shown to be detrimental for an individual drug user, as it promotes marginalization and enhances harm due to increased prices of the prohibited drugs. Such an approach is now under scrutiny and debate. It is now increasingly recognized that by reducing the association of drug use with criminal prosecution, the reform of punitive legal policies can produce clear benefits in the realm of public health and social order.

Since all the harm reduction measures deal basically with illegal drugs and individuals who use these illegal drugs, they are affected by the prevailing legal and policy environment. For instance, there is a possibility that under the existing Indian laws, an agency (or its staff) engaged in providing needle-syringe exchange services in India can be booked under the relevant laws on the grounds of abetment to the crime, that is, facilitating or encouraging drug use by the injecting drug users by providing needle-syringe services to them (Lawyers Collective, 2007).

IDU-RELATED HIV EPIDEMIC IN INDIA: THE INDIAN RESPONSE

The following section will focus upon a critical overview of the response to the IDU-related HIV epidemic in India at the legal, policy, and programmatic level and will attempt to highlight certain existing gaps.

Legal and Policy Issues

In the area of "supply reduction" of drug abuse, India is signatory to all three major international conventions related to drug use, namely, Single Convention on Narcotic Drugs, 1961, Convention on Psychotropic Substances 1971, and Convention against the Illicit Traffic in Narcotic Drugs and Psychotropic Substances, 1988 (Ambekar et al., 2005). In India, the broad legislative framework on narcotic drugs and psychotropic substances is contained in the three Central Acts: Drugs and Cosmetics Act, 1940, The Narcotics Drugs and Psychotropic Substances Act, 1985 (NDPS Act 1985), and the Prevention of Illicit Traffic in Narcotic Drugs and Psychotropic Substances Act, 1988. The NDPS Act lays down the focus and direction of drug control strategy in the country. Importantly, this Act does attempt to differentiate between a drug user and drug peddler (on the basis of the quantity of the illicit drug found in possession) and also provides for the treatment of drug users (Lawyers Collective, 2007).

India's policy on narcotic drugs and psychotropic substances is based on Article 47 of the Directive Principles of State Policy, Constitution of India, where the "Duty of the State [is] to raise the level of nutrition and the standard of living and to improve public health." However, India does not have a national drug control policy or an apex organization in respect of drug control. The National Health Policy 2002 of India (Ministry of Health and Family Welfare [MOHFW], 2002) does not specifically mention drug use as a component or concern. On HIV/AIDS issues, however, there are explicitly stated and documented policies in the country. The policy document of the National AIDS Control Organization (NACO, 2002b)—National AIDS Prevention and Control Policy (NAPCP)—recognizes various harm reduction measures, as the appropriate strategies to prevent HIV among injecting drug users, although the policy further admits that in India the harm reduction approach is yet to find wider acceptability because of ethical and moral considerations.

As far as the "drug demand reduction" activities are concerned, the nodal agency for drug demand reduction in India is the Ministry of Social Justice and Empowerment (MSJE), and not the Ministry of Health, implying indirectly that drug demand reduction is seen as more of a social justice and welfare issue rather than a health-related issue. The Ministry of Social Justice and Empowerment has developed a three-pronged strategy for drug demand reduction in India. The three components are: (1) building awareness and educating people about ill effects of drug abuse; (2) dealing with addicts through a program of motivation, counseling, treatment, follow-up, and social reintegration; and (3) imparting drug abuse prevention rehabilitation training to service providers. The ministry (MSJE) implements its programs mainly by supporting NGOs all over the country. Currently, the ministry is supporting around 450 drug dependence treatment centers throughout the country, which are being run by NGOs (Ambekar et al., 2005). In addition, the Union Ministry of Health and Family Welfare and the Health Departments of the States and Union Territories also provide treatment and hospitalization services related to substance use. There are about 122 de-addiction centers, supported at least in part, by the Ministry of Health and Family Welfare (Panda, 2007).

Thus, to summarize, at the policy level, drug use and related issues do not receive a priority status in the health agenda of the government of India. The legal environment in the country, though, is conducive to providing adequate treatment and harm reduction services to injecting drug users.

Programmatic and Service-Delivery Issues

As discussed earlier, treatment services to drug users are delivered through the NGOs (supported by the government, the social welfare sector) as well as the government-run de-addiction centers as part of the health sector. However, it has been repeatedly commented that many of these services remain inadequately utilized (Ambekar et al., 2005; UNODC/MSJE, 2004a). Additionally, the National AIDS Control Organization is also engaged in providing harm reduction services ("Targeted Interventions") to the injecting drug users through NGOs, under the National AIDS Control Programme (NACP), which has just entered its third phase (NACO, 2006).

As of now, there are about 120 targeted interventions in various parts of the country (but concentrated mainly in the northeastern states and the bigger cities), delivering harm reduction (outreach and needle-syringe exchange but *not* agonist maintenance) services to about 90,000 IDUs (Rao & Khumukcham, 2008). This amounts to about 53 percent coverage. As of 2007, there were about 48 intervention sites for buprenorphine substitution also (largely implemented through NGOs, without any direct support from the government), providing services to only a few thousand IDUs (Dhawan & Sunder, 2008). The NACP–III plans, ambitiously, to scale up the existing IDU intervention with various harm reduction services so as to cover about 80 percent of the total number of IDUs in the country (Rao & Khumukcham, 2008). Among the newer initiatives, the NACO proposes to implement oral substitution therapy, in addition to needle-syringe exchange to the IDUs. Clearly, extensive scaling-up of the existing services is required in order to provide adequate coverage to injecting drug users in India to be able to achieve the stated goal of the National AIDS Control Programme—halt and reverse the HIV epidemic (NACO, 2006).

While the effectiveness of the needle-syringe exchange programs in India has not been studied systematically, there is some evidence that these programs may have been successful in bringing IDUs closer to various services, reduction of risky injection practices, and reducing the prevalence of HIV (Ngully, 2008; Sharma et al., 2003). Similarly, the preliminary evidence regarding the Indian experience with opioid substitution therapy is also encouraging. Dhawan and Sunder (2008), in a brief overview of buprenorphine substitution in India, have concluded that buprenorphine substitution programs have been success-ful in decreasing the harm associated with drug use, as well as decreasing the drug use per se and improving the quality of life.

To summarize, though various harm-reduction services in India are in place, they remain too few and far in between. There is a visible and obvious gap in terms of the number of services available and the requirements of these ser-vices. Without a rapid scale-up in the number and the quality of the services, it would be difficult to provide adequate coverage to the IDU population. This would make it very challenging to realize the goal of halting and reversing the HIV epidemic.

CONCLUSION AND RECOMMENDATIONS

The available evidence indicates that substance use and related HIV is fairly prevalent in almost all parts of India; although, in terms of the HIV prevalence among drug users, different areas within the country are at different stages of the epidemic. However, the presence of risky behaviors—both injecting-related as well as sexual—among drug users would mean continued vulner-ability in the country for rapid escalation of the HIV epidemic among drug users and eventually to the general population. Fortunately, among the general population, HIV prevalence is still low in India. The current stage of the HIV epidemic thus should be seen as a window of opportunity for implementing large-scale, evidence-based programs for HIV prevention. Presented below are a few specific measures, which should be urgently adopted by India.

BOX 3

Recommendations for Drug-Related HIV Prevention Programs in India

+ Better assessment of epidemiological situation and monitoring/surveil-lance
+ Convergence of abstinence-oriented drug abuse treatment and HIV prevention ("harm reduction") services
+ Interventions to address both injecting-related and sexual risk behaviors

---

Expanding the Knowledge Base

There is an urgent need to expand the knowledge base about drug abuse and vulnerabilities to HIV/AIDS in India. Thus, extensive epidemiological data of adequate quality are urgently required. Additionally, the monitoring and surveillance systems need to be periodically reviewed and, if required, be strengthened and expanded. Behavioral data, wherever possible, should be linked with the biological data. Data collected from clinics by way of "sentinel surveillance" should be supplemented by data collected from the community, that is, the general population. Such an approach has recently been adopted in India for the general population, resulting in a major revision of the HIV estimates in the country (NACO, 2007; UNAIDS, 2007). Finally, a very important research agenda for the country is that of the effectiveness and appropriateness of HIV prevention interventions.

Convergence of "Abstinence" and "Harm-Reduction" Approaches

Services for the treatment for substance use disorders, while available almost everywhere in India, have largely tended to focus upon complete abstinence from drugs. Approaches regarded as "harm reduction" should be urgently scaled up in India. Indeed, both of these—abstinence and harm reduction— should not be seen as two opposite approaches. Rather, emphasis should be on provision of a whole continuum of care, whereby all the services that drug users may require—those aimed at achieving a drug-free life, those aimed at reducing the drug use itself, and those aimed at reducing the consequences of drug use—should be made available to them. Such a comprehensive approach has been recently endorsed by the United Nations as well (UNODC, 2008). Specifically, the country urgently requires oral substitution programs for opioid injectors using agonist agents like methadone and buprenorphine.

Broadening the Scope of the Interventions

Most drug users including IDUs are sexually active and engage in risky sexual behavior. Moreover, a sizable number are married and can potentially transmit the HIV infection to their spouses and regular sexual partners. There is evidence that HIV infection can be transmitted from IDUs to their noninjecting wives leading, ultimately to a generalized epidemic. Thus, it is of utmost importance that interventions aimed at prevention of HIV among IDUs should reach out to their sexual partners as well. Along with the injecting-related risk behaviors, sexual risk behaviors should also be the targets of various behavior change interventions.

REFERENCES

Aceijas, C., Friedman, S. R., Cooper, H.L.F., Wiessing, L., Stimson, G. V., Hickman, M., on behalf of the Reference Group on HIV/AIDS Prevention and Care among IDU in Developing and Transitional Countries. (2006). Estimates of injecting drug users at the national and local level in developing and transitional countries, and gender and age distribution. *Sexually Transmitted Infections, 82*(Suppl. 3), iii10-iii17.

Aceijas, C., Stimson, G. V., Hickman, M., Rhodes, T., on behalf of the Reference Group on HIV/AIDS Prevention and Care among IDU in Developing and Transitional Countries. (2004, November 19). Global overview of injecting drug use and HIV infection among injecting drug users. *AIDS, 18*(17), 2295–2303.

Ambekar, A., Agrawal, A., & Tripathi, B. M. (2008, March). Harm reduction: An overview. In A. Ambekar & B. M. Tripathi (Eds.), *Drug abuse: News-n-views* (Harm reduction: Prevention of HIV among drug users) (pp. 5–7). New Delhi: National Drug Dependence Treatment Centre, All India Institute of Medical Sciences.

Ambekar, A., & Balhara, Y. P. S. (2007). Harm reduction. In R. Lal & S. Gupta (Eds.), *Substance use disorders: A manual for nursing personnel* (pp. 102–111). New Delhi: National Drug Dependence Treatment Centre, All India Institute of Medical Sciences.

Ambekar, A., Lewis, G., Rao, S., & Sethi, H. S. (2005). *South Asia regional profile: Drugs and crime, 2005.* New Delhi: United Nations Office on Drugs and Crime, Regional Office for South Asia.

Ambekar, A., & Tripathi, B. M. (2006). *Knowledge, attitude, behaviour and practices of drug users in India.* Report submitted to Society for Promotion of Youth and Masses under the peer-led intervention—supported by the Department for International Development (DFID), New Delhi.

Ambekar, A., & Tripathi, B. M. (2007). *Size estimation of IDU at 300 sites in India.* Report submitted to Society for Promotion of Youth and Masses under the peer-led intervention—supported by DFID, New Delhi.

Ambekar, A., & Tripathi, B. M. (2008). *Size estimation of injecting drug use in Punjab and Haryana.* New Delhi: Joint United Nations Programme on HIV/AIDS and Society for Promotion of Youth and Masses.

Ambwani, P. N., & Gilada, I. S. (1998). *Dry alcohol days during festivals to prevent HIV/AIDS.* XII International Conference on AIDS, Geneva. AIDSLINE ICA 12/98410386.

Centers for Disease Control and Prevention. (1998). Management of possible sexual, injecting-drug-use, or other nonoccupational exposure to HIV, including considerations related to antiretroviral therapy. *Morbidity and Mortality Weekly Report* (MMWR), *50*(No. RR-17), 1–14.

Correa, M., & Gisselquist, D. (2006, November). Routes of HIV transmission in India: Assessing the reliability of information from AIDS case surveillance. *International Journal of STD and AIDS, 17*(11), 731–735.

Das, H. K., Borkakoty, B. J., Mahanta, J., Medhi, G. K., & Chelleng, P. K. (2007, September–October). Hepatitis C virus infection and risk behaviors among injection drug users of Nagaland. *Indian Journal of Gastroenterology, 26*(5), 253–254.

Datta, S., Banerjee, A., Chandra, P. K., Mahapatra, P. K., Chakrabarti, S., & Chakravarty, R. (2006, December). Drug trafficking routes and hepatitis B in injection drug users, Manipur, India. *Emerging Infectious Diseases, 12*(12), 1954–1957.

Dhawan, A. (1998). Traditional use. In R. Ray (Ed.), *South Asia drug demand reduction report 1998*(pp. 44–45). New Delhi: United Nations Office on Drugs and Crime, Regional Office for South Asia.

Dhawan, A., & Sunder, S. (2008, March). Opioid substitution therapy: The Indian experience. In A. Ambekar & B. M. Tripathi (Eds.), *Drug abuse: News-n-views* (Harm reduction: Prevention of HIV among drug users) (pp. 8–10). New Delhi: National Drug Dependence Treatment Centre, All India Institute of Medical Sciences.

Dole, V. P., & Nyswander, M. (1965, August). A medical treatment for diacetylmorphine (heroin) addiction: A clinical trial with methadone hydrochloride. *Journal of the American Medical Association, 23*(193), 646–650.

Gibson, D. R., Flynn, N. M., & Perales, D. (2001). Effectiveness of syringe exchange programmes in reducing HIV risk behaviour and HIV seroconversion among injecting drug users. *AIDS, 15*(11), 1329–1341.

Gisselquist, D., & Correa, M. (2006, November). How much does heterosexual commercial sex contribute to India's HIV epidemic? *International Journal of STD and AIDS, 17*(11), 736–742.

Gowing, L., Farrell, M., Bornemann, R., & Ali, R. (2004, October 18). Substitution treatment of injecting opioid users for prevention of HIV infection. *Cochrane Database of Systematic Reviews* (4), CD004145.

Hangzo, C., Chatterjee, A., & Sarkar, S. (1997). Reaching beyond the hills: HIV prevention among injecting drug users in Manipur, India. *Addiction, 92*(7), 813–820.

Hunt, N. (2003). *A review of the evidence-base for harm reduction approaches to drug use.* Forward thinking on drugs: A release initiative. Retrieved December 2, 2008, from http://www.forward-thinking-on-drugs.org/review2-print.html

International Harm Reduction Association. (2006). *What is harm reduction?* Retrieved December 2, 2008, from http://www.ihra.net/Whatisharmreduction

Jindal, N., Arora, U., & Singh, K. (2008). Prevalence of human immunodeficiency virus (HIV), hepatitis B virus, and hepatitis C virus in three groups of populations at high risk of HIV infection in Amritsar (Punjab), Northern India. *Japanese Journal of Infectious Diseases, 61*(1), 79–81.

Joint United Nations Programme on HIV/AIDS. (2007). *Fact-sheet: The process behind India's revised AIDS estimates.* Geneva: Author.

Joint United Nations Programme on HIV/AIDS and Family Health International. (2003). *Estimating the size of populations at risk for HIV: Issues and methods.* Geneva and Washington, DC.

Joint United Nations Programme on HIV/AIDS and World Health Organization. (2004). *Making HIV prevalence and AIDS estimates.* UNAIDS/WHO Working Group on Global HIV/AIDS and STI Surveillance. Retrieved December 2, 2008, from www.who.int/entity/hiv/strategic/en/neff_walker_estimations methods.ppt

Kermode, M., Longleng, V., Singh, B. C., Hocking, J., Langkham, B., & Crofts, N. (2007). My first time: Initiation into injecting drug use in Manipur and Nagaland, north-east India. *Harm Reduction Journal, 4*: 19.

Kumar, M. S. (2008, March). Outreach services: The Indian experience. In A. Ambekar & B. M. Tripathi (Eds.), *Drug abuse: News-n-views* (Harm reduction: Prevention of HIV among drug users) (pp. 11–12). New Delhi: National Drug Dependence Treatment Centre, All India Institute of Medical Sciences.

Kumar, M. S., Mudaliar, S., & Daniels, D. (1998). Community based outreach HIV intervention for street-recruited drug users in Madras, India. *Public Health Reports, 113*(Suppl. 1), 58–66.

Lawyers Collective. (2007). *Legal and policy concerns related to IDU harm reduction in SAARC countries: A review commissioned by UNODC.* New Delhi: Lawyers Collective HIV/AIDS Unit and United Nations Office on Drugs and Crime.

Lenton, S., & Single, E. (1998). The definition of harm reduction. *Drug and Alcohol Review, 17,* 213–220.

Longkumer, M., Shrivastava, H. C., & Murugesan, P. (2000). *Alcohol abuse and risky sexual behavior among the indigenous college students in Shillong, India.* Mumbai: International Institute for Population Sciences.

Mattick, R. P., Breen, C., Kimber, J., & Davoli, M. (2003). Methadone maintenance therapy versus no opioid replacement therapy for opioid dependence. *Cochrane Database of Systematic Reviews* (2), CD002209.

Mattick, R. P., Kimber, J., Breen, C., & Davoli, M. (2003). Buprenorphine maintenance versus placebo or methadone maintenance for opioid dependence. *Cochrane Database of Systematic Reviews* (2), CD002207.

McLellan, T., Lewis, D., O'Brien, C., & Kleber, H. (2000). Drug dependence, a chronic mental illness: Implications for treatment, insurance, and outcomes evaluation. *Journal of the American Medical Association, 284*(13), 1689–1695.

Ministry of Health and Family Welfare, Government of India. (2002). *National health policy 2002.* Retrieved from http://mohfw.nic.in/np2002.htm

Monitoring the AIDS Pandemic. (2004). *AIDS in Asia: Face the facts.* Monitoring the AIDS Pandemic (MAP) Network. Retrieved from http://www.mapnetwork. org/docs/MAP_AIDSinAsia2004.pdf

National AIDS Control Organization. (2001). *National Baseline High Risk and Bridge Population Behavioural Surveillance Survey 2001. PART 1: Female sex workers and their clients.* Ministry of Health and Family Welfare, Government of India. Retrieved December 2, 2008, from www.nacoonline.org

National AIDS Control Organization. (2002a). *National Baseline High Risk and Bridge Population Behavioural Surveillance Survey 2002. PART 2: Men who have sex with men and injecting drug users.* Ministry of Health and Family Welfare, Government of India. Retrieved December 2, 2008, from www.nacoon line.org

National AIDS Control Organization. (2002b). *National AIDS prevention and control policy.* Ministry of Health and Family Welfare, Government of India. Retrieved December 2, 2008, from http://www.nacoonline.org/program.htm

National AIDS Control Organization. (2006). *National AIDS Control Programme Phase III (2007–2012): Strategy and implementation plan.* Ministry of Health and Family Welfare, Government of India. Retrieved December 2, 2008, from http://www.nacoonline.org/program.htm

National AIDS Control Organization. (2007a). *HIV sentinel surveillance and HIV estimation, 2006.* Ministry of Health and Family Welfare, Government of India. Retrieved December 2, 2008, from www.nacoonline.org

National AIDS Control Organization. (2007b). *Endline Behavioural Surveillance Survey 2006.* Ministry of Health and Family Welfare, Government of India. Retrieved December 2, 2008, from www.nacoonline.org

Needle, R. H., Burrows, D., Friedman, S. R., Dorabjee, J., Touzã, G., Badrieva, L., et al. (2005). Effectiveness of community-based outreach in preventing HIV/AIDS among injecting drug users. *International Journal of Drug Policy, 16*(1), 45–57.

Ngully, P. (2008, March). Needle syringe exchange program (NSEP): Experience from Nagaland. In A. Ambekar & B. M. Tripathi (Eds.), *Drug abuse: News-n-views* (Harm reduction: Prevention of HIV among drug users) (p. 15). New Delhi: National Drug Dependence Treatment Centre, All India Institute of Medical Sciences.

Panda, D. (2007). Drug de-addiction programmes in India. In R. Lal & S. Gupta (Eds.), *Substance use disorders: A manual for nursing personnel* (pp. 10–14). New Delhi: National Drug Dependence Treatment Centre, All India Institute of Medical Sciences.

Panda, S., Bijaya, L., Sadhana, N., Devi, S. N., Foley, E., Chatterjee, A., et al. (2001, July–August). Interface between drug use and sex work in Manipur. *National Medical Journal of India, 14*(4), 209–211.

Panda, S., Chatterjee, A., Bhattacharya, S. K., Manna, B., Singh, P. N., Sarkar, S., et al. (2000, July). Transmission of HIV from injecting drug users to their wives in India. *International Journal of STD and AIDS, 11*(7), 468–473.

Panda, S., Kumar, M. S., Lokabiraman, S., Jayashree, K., Satagopan, M. C., Solomon, S., et al. (2005). Risk factors for HIV infection in injection drug users and evidence for onward transmission of HIV to their sexual partners in Chennai, India. *Journal of Acquired Immune Deficiency Syndrome, 39,* 9–15.

Panda, S., Kumar, M. S., Saravanamurthy, P. S., Mahalingam, P., Vijaylakshmi, A., Balakrishnan, P., et al. (2007). Sexually transmitted infections and sexual practices in injection drug users and their regular sex partners in Chennai, India. *Sexually Transmitted Diseases, 34*(4), 250–253.

Rao, R., & Khumukcham, S. (2008, March). Prevention of drug related HIV: Role of NACO. In A. Ambekar & B. M. Tripathi (Eds.), *Drug abuse: News-n-views* (Harm reduction: Prevention of HIV among drug users) (pp. 17–18). New Delhi: National Drug Dependence Treatment Centre, All India Institute of Medical Sciences.

Ray, R. (1998). *South Asia drug demand reduction report 1998.* New Delhi: United Nations Drug Control Programme (UNDCP) Regional Office for South Asia.

Ray, R., & Ambekar, A. (2005). *Drug abuse and HIV/AIDS situation in South Asia: Vulnerabilities and responses.* New Delhi: Report submitted to the United Nations Office on Drugs and Crime, Regional Office for South Asia.

Reid, G., & Costigan, G. (2002, January). *Revisiting the hidden epidemic: A situation assessment of drug use in Asia in the context of HIV/AIDS.* Australia: The Centre for Harm Reduction, The Burnet Institute.

Ritter, A., & Cameron, J. (2005). A systematic review of harm reduction. DPMP [Drug Policy Modeling Project], Monograph Series No. 06. Fitzroy, Australia: Turning Point Alcohol and Drug Centre.

Saraswathi, K., & Dutta, A. (2007, April). Study of human immunodeficiency virus and HCV infections in intravenous drug users in Mumbai. *Indian Journal of Microbiology, 25*(2), 174–175.

Sarkar, K., Bal, B., Mukherjee, R., Chakraborty, S., Niyogi, S. K., Saha, M. K., et al. (2006). Epidemic of HIV coupled with hepatitis C virus among injecting drug users of Himalayan West Bengal, Eastern India, Bordering Nepal, Bhutan, and Bangladesh. *Substance Use and Misuse, 41*(3), 341–352.

Sarkar, S., Das, N., Panda, S., Naik, T. N., Sarkar, K., Singh, B. C., et al. (1993). Rapid spread of HIV among injecting drug users in north-eastern states of India. *Bulletin of Narcotics, 45*(1), 91–105.

Sarkar, S., Mookerjee, P., Roy, A., Naik, T. N., Singh, J. K., Sharma, A. R., et al. (1991, September). Descriptive epidemiology of intravenous heroin users—a new risk group for transmission of HIV in India. *Journal of Infections, 23*(2), 201–207.

Sarkar, S., Panda, S., Sarkar, K., Hangzo, C. Z., Bijaya, L., Singh, N. Y., et al. (1995, July–September). A cross-sectional study on factors including HIV testing and counselling determining unsafe injecting practices among injecting drug users of Manipur. *Indian Journal of Public Health, 39*(3), 86–92.

SHARAN. (2007). *A national scale up of IDU interventions across nine states in India: Rapid Assessment.* New Delhi: Author.

Sharma, A. K., Aggarwal, O. P., & Dubey, K. K. (2002, May). Sexual behavior of drug-users: Is it different? *Preventive Medicine, 34*(5), 512–515.

Sharma, A. K., & Chaubey, D. (1996). Risk factors in sexually transmitted diseases. *Indian Journal of Sexually Transmitted Diseases, 17*, 8–10.

Sharma, M., Panda, S., Sharma, U., Singh, H. N., Sharma, C., & Singh, R. R. (2003). Five years of needle syringe exchange in Manipur, India: Programme and contextual issues. *International Journal of Drug Policy, 14*, 407–415.

Singh, S. K., Schensul, J. J., & Gupta, K. (2004, July 11–16). *Alcohol use and risky sexual behavior among adolescents in low income slum communities in Mumbai, India.* Abstract No. C11731. Bangkok, Thailand: International Conference on AIDS.

Tripathi, B. M., Malhotra, S., & Sharma, H. K. (2004). *Alcohol and high-risk sexual behaviour.* New Delhi: National Drug Dependence Treatment Centre, All India Institute of Medical Sciences and World Health Organization.

United Nations Office on Drugs and Crime. (2007). *World drug report 2007.* Vienna, Austria: Author.

United Nations Office on Drugs and Crime. (2008). *Reducing adverse health and social consequences of drug abuse: A comprehensive approach—Discussion Paper.* Vienna, Austria: Author.

United Nations Office on Drugs and Crime, Regional Office for South Asia, and Ministry of Social Justice and Empowerment. (2002a). *Drug Abuse Monitoring System.* New Delhi: Authors.

United Nations Office on Drugs and Crime, Regional Office for South Asia, and Ministry of Social Justice and Empowerment. (2002b). *A Rapid Assessment Survey of Drug Abuse in India.* New Delhi: Authors.

United Nations Office on Drugs and Crime, Regional Office for South Asia, and Ministry of Social Justice and Empowerment. (2004a). *The extent, pattern and trends of drug abuse in India: National Survey.* New Delhi: Authors.

United Nations Office on Drugs and Crime, Regional Office for South Asia, and Ministry of Social Justice and Empowerment. (2004b). *Injecting drug use and HIV in India: An emerging concern.* New Delhi: Authors.

United Nations Office on Drugs and Crime, Regional Office for South Asia, and Ministry of Social Justice and Empowerment. (2005). *Drug use in the north eastern states of India.* New Delhi: Authors.

Vaswani, M., & Desai, N. G. (2004). HIV infection and high-risk behaviors in opioid dependent patients: The Indian context. *Addictive Behaviors, 29*(8), 1699–1705.

Vaswani, M., & Rao, R. (2006). Risk behaviors and HIV infection in alcohol/drug abuse: Indian scenario. *Addictive Disorders and Their Treatment, 5*(1), 35–40.

Verma, R., Sharma, S., Singh, R., Rangaiyan, G., & Pelto, J. (2003, May–June). Beliefs concerning sexual health problems and treatment seeking among men in an Indian slum community. *Culture Health and Sexuality, 5*(3), 265–276.

Wodak, A. (2004). *Effectiveness of sterile needle and syringe programming in reducing HIV/AIDS among injecting drug users.* Evidence for Action Technical Papers. Geneva: World Health Organization.

Part III

PSYCHOBIOLOGIES

Chapter 15

Alcohol Abuse: Impact on Vital Brain Functions and Societal Implications

Mary Theresa Webb, PhD

Recent neuroscientific research provides an important scientific and societal basis for raising an international alarm about the risk of binge or heavy alcohol drinking. Heavy alcohol use damages sections of the brain that modulate emotions, controls intellectual functioning, and thus may contribute to an increase in societal violence, family disruption, and diseases, such as HIV/AIDS.

Heavy drinking before the brain is fully matured arrests the development of the frontal lobe, especially the area of executive function, according to neuroscientific research. For adults, heavy drinking over a long period of time risks the loss of cognitive abilities and increases the risk of having cardiovascular incidents and alcoholic dementias, taxing health care systems.

Statistics from a 2006 European Union Study show that countries who have lowered their legal drinking age to 18 or 16 years old show an increase in binge drinking in these age groups at the same time that 100 American college presidents have suggested lowering the drinking age from 21 to 18 years old (Amethyst Initiative, 2008).

ALCOHOL AND BRAIN RESEARCH

The Centers for Disease Control (CDC) has classified alcohol (ethanol), the addictive drug in all alcoholic beverages, as a central nervous system depressant. Alcohol abuse has plagued humankind since people learned to turn barley and corn into mead. Even today, in many rural regions of Africa, villagers brew maise and turn it into 80-proof alcoholic drinks. In America, until the turn of the twentieth century, a bottle of alcohol was kept in the family medicine cabinet and used as an anesthetic in surgical procedures. Today, in twenty-first-century America, about 7.7 percent of the population are dependent on or abuse alcohol (Lemonick & Park, 2007, p. 44), one-third of all teenagers binge drink (Kann, et.al, 2000), nearly half of all college students binge drink (Leinwand, 2007), and an uncounted number of young, middle-aged, and older adults abuse alcohol. A *binge* is a pattern of drinking alcohol that brings blood alcohol concentration (BAC) to 0.08 gram-percent or above. For a typical adult, this pattern corresponds to consuming five or more drinks (male), or four or more drinks (female), in about two hours. According to estimates by the U.S. Substance Abuse and Mental Health Services Administration (SAMSHA), 3 to 25 percent of older adults are classified as heavy alcohol users and 2.2 to 9.6 percent abuse alcohol (SAMSHA & National Council on Aging, 1998, p. 4).

Alcohol intake in small and infrequent doses can be flushed out of the body through the action of a catalytic enzyme, alcohol dehydrogenese, that metabolizes alcohol into its constituent chemical components to be eliminated from the body, thus reducing the risk of any toxic residual effects. However, when alcohol rushes into the body through excessive drinking, it is like torrential rain causing a river to rise over its banks, saturating the ground and destroying whatever is in its path. In the case of rapid or excessive intake of alcohol, instead of the alcohol being metabolized and flushed out of the body, the excessive alcohol floods the bloodstream and goes into the brain. Although most mature adults can tolerate consuming 58 liters annually or no more than two drinks a day with little or no effect on cognitive abilities (with the exception of women who have a lower amount of the enzyme alcohol dehydrogenese), alcohol is still toxic to neurons if the drug reaches the brain (Lezak, 1995, pp. 250–251). The more alcohol consumed, depending on age and sex, the greater the risk of permanent brain damage. Areas most affected are the frontal lobe or prefrontal cortex and the cerebellum, as shown in Figure 15.1 (Oscar-Berman and Marinkovic, 2004, p. 4).

The frontal area of the brain contains the neurons that regulate emotions as well as executive functioning, or attention, abstract reasoning, organization, mental flexibility, planning, self-monitoring, and the capacity to use external clues to govern behavior. The prefrontal cortex in a human's brain is 120 percent larger than that of other mammals, giving humans higher intellectual functions than any other mammal. However, alcohol abuse impairs and often destroys those intellectual abilities (Phil, 2003).

Synapses and Neurotransmitter Conductivity

Although it has been known for several decades that drugs such as alcohol replace the neurotransmitter, dopamine, that permits the flow of neurons in

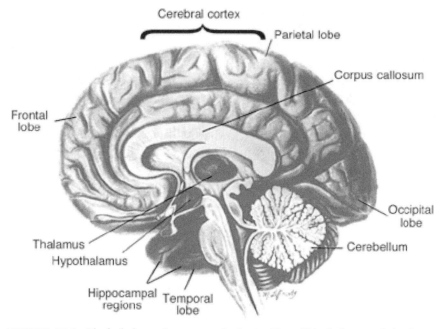

FIGURE 15.1 Alcohol abuse: Impact on the brain. From "Alcoholism and the Brain: An Overview," in *The Neurobiology of Addiction: Introduction to the Brain and the Reward Pathway and Addiction*, by M. Oscar-Berman and K. Marinkovic, 1997, Washington, DC: National Institute on Alcohol Abuse and Alcoholism (NIAAA), p. 4.

the synapse from one nerve ending to another, it has only been in the last 10 years that magnetic resonance imaging (MRI) research studies can show colored pictures of the brain. See Figure 15.2 for how neurotransmitters flow from one synapse to another.

Patterns of brain development and the impact of early onset alcohol use or long-time alcohol abuse and the resultant brain damage have been thus recorded. Through time lapse imaging, researchers at the U.S. National Institute of Mental Health (NIMH) and the University of California showed that the prefrontal cortex doesn't fully develop until young adulthood, for males that is about the age of 25; for females, about the age of 22 (Gogtay, Rapoport, Thompson, Toga, Lusk, and colleagues, 2004). If heavy alcohol use arrests this development, then important executive functions in the prefrontal cortex cannot fully mature.

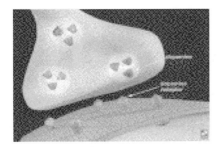

FIGURE 15.2 Synapses and neurotransmitter conductivity. From *Teaching Packets: The Neurobiology of Drug Addiction. Section 1: Introduction to the Brain,* National Institute on Drug Abuse, http://www.nida.nih.gov/pubs/teaching/Teaching2/Teaching2.html

CONCERNS FOR YOUTH

The 2006 European Union study (Anderson & Baumberg, 2006, p. 76) concludes that almost all 15- to 16-year-old students have drunk alcohol, beginning at 12.5 years of age, and start getting drunk at 14 years. Most countries studied show a rise in binge drinking with the prevalence of heavy drinking greatest among young boys (Grube, 2005, p. 3). The highest prevalence of drunkenness and binging among youth being recorded is in Denmark, the Netherlands, Germany, the Isle of Man, Ireland, and the United Kingdom. In countries that have a more positive view of alcohol and have lower legal drinking ages, youth binge drinking increases (p. 108). In this comprehensive report by the Prevention Research Center of the Pacific Insititute for Research and Evaluation prepared for the U.S. Department of Justice (update on ESPAD and MTF surveys, 2003), drinking rates and alcohol-related problems among teenagers (10th graders) in all EU countries and the United States were compared (see Figure 15.3). With the exception of Turkey, the rate of binge drinking was lowest in the United States. Although this comparative study did not prove that the higher legal drinking age in the United States was a deterrent, the fact that binge drinking among youth was lower than in the EU indicates that the U.S. higher legal drinking age (21) should be considered as one of the factors for this finding. In fact, the author concludes, based on his analysis (Grube , 2005), that the perception that American youth drink more and have more problems than their European counterparts is not true. According to this study there is then no support for changing the minimum drinking age in the United States.

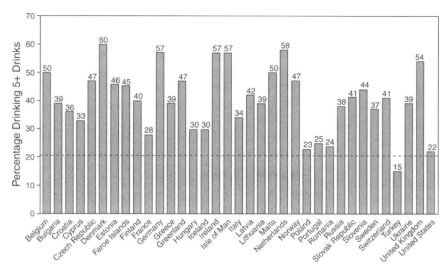

FIGURE 15.3 Prevalence of heavy drinking in the past 30 days: United States and Europe. From Joel Grube of the Prevention Research Center, Pacific Institute for Research and Evaluation, May, 2005 in *Youth Drinking Rates and Problems: A Comparison of European Countries and the United States,* for the U.S. Department of Justice, Office of Juvenile Justice and Delinquency Prevention, Update of 2003 ESPAD and 2003 MTF surveys, Calverton, MD.

The signers of the Amethyst Initiative recognize that binge drinking is a serious problem, with nearly half of America's 5.4 million full-time college students binge drinking once a month, (Leinwand, 2007) many of whom (30% of high school youth) started binge drinking in their high school years (Kann et al., 2000), 2007, p. 1). However, changing the legal age to 18 will not solve this problem. Aggressive measures need to be taken to change the drinking culture on college campuses.

If early alcohol abuse (before the age of 25) damages the brain's intellectual functioning, the ability to think, reason, and make wise decisions, then educating youth to be responsible and intelligent citizens is compromised. Not only might alcohol abuse by adolescents and youth under the age of 25 cause arrested brain development and potential permanent damage, but the resultant brain damage in turn will probably lead to early alcohol and other drug dependency (addiction) and chronic relapse. Improper executive functioning of the prefrontal cortex makes recovery difficult because recovery involves learning to control triggers and cravings. An alcohol-impacted brain also shrinks in size and has less white matter, leading to cognitive impairment in later life (EU [European Union] Commission, 2006 p. 150).

Occasional or weekend binge drinking, five or six drinks in a row whose purpose is to become intoxicated, popular among teenagers and college students, has long-lasting implications not only for education but for the future of developed and developing countries. As noted in the 2007 U.S. Surgeon General's Report (SAMHSA, 2007), the long-term dangers to America's youth have rung enough alarm bells that the U.S. government has proposed remedial and preventative actions, as has the European Institute of Alcohol Studies in its report to the European Union for implementing public health policies.

CONCERNS FOR OLDER ADULTS

Underdeveloped brains of youth and young adults under the age of 25 are not the only brains affected by chronic heavy alcohol consumption. In a study of male veterans receiving treatment at the Durham Veterans Affairs Medical Center (in the US), researchers Swartzwelder, Zinn, and Stein (2004) administered memory and executive function tests to both alcohol-dependent and age-appropriate primary care outpatients. The alcohol-dependent group scored lower on abstract reasoning, memory, and effectiveness of timed tasks. Although some U.S. National Institute on Alcohol Abuse and Alcoholism (NIAAA) researchers indicate that moderate alcohol use (one drink a day for individuals over 65) reduces the risk of cardiovascular disease and dementia among older adults (Gunzerath, Faden, Zakhari, & Warren, 2004), other researchers (Oscar-Berman & Marinkovic, 2004, p. 5) demonstrated that older adults who had been alcohol users or alcohol abusers as youth had significant brain shrinkage and right hemisphere weakening and were thus more prone to hemorrhagic strokes. Note the shrinkage in cortical grey matter in Figure 15.4.

This condition, known as *alcoholic dementia*, shows cognitive deterioration typically associated with the prefrontal cortex or frontal lobe (Lezak, 1995, p. 255). When years of chronic drinking causes such a stroke in the weakened part of the brain, the frontal lobe in the right brain hemisphere is most often impaired. The affected person can no longer make judgments, use abstract reasoning, or plan and carry out activities without supervision. An estimated 2.3 million older Americans who have or have had problems with alcohol also have this kind of dementia, making it difficult for physicians and caregivers to distinguish between the alcohol-induced dementia and Alzheimer's disease. Two kinds of these dementias, vascular dementia and Wernick-Korsakoff syndrome, are often misdiagnosed as Alzheimer's disease. Korsakoff psychosis (WKS) is a more severe form of alcohol-induced dementia that includes amnesia and

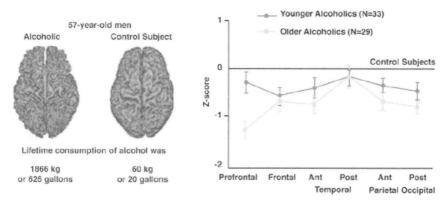

FIGURE 15.4 Cortical gray matter volumes. From "Alcoholism and the Brain: An Overview," in *The Neurobiology of Addiction: Introduction to the Brain and the Reward Pathway and Addiction*, by M. Oscar-Berman and K. Marinkovic, 1997, Washington, DC: National Institute on Alcohol Abuse and Alcoholism (NIAAA). Source: Pfefferbaum et al, 1997.

has an accompanying thiamine deficiency with even more pronounced brain shrinkage and damage. Those older adults so affected have very little ability to change self-destructive behaviors.

CONCERN FOR AN INCREASE IN VIOLENCE

According to the most recent studies in the report from the European Union Commission (Anderson & Baumberg, 2006) concerning alcohol and its societal impact, the authors have some evidence that alcohol abuse is linked with crime, especially violent crime. Heavy alcohol use has been associated with about one-quarter of all assaults and harm done through domestic violence and with about 16 percent of child abuse and neglect. Four out of 10 homicides are attributed to alcohol use (p. 211). These statistics do not take into account unintentional drunk-driving accidents, one of the leading causes of traffic fatalities in all countries.

Because alcohol damages the prefrontal lobe area of the brain where emotions are modulated, it naturally follows that this accounts for the lack of anger control, road rage, rage against women and children, that is, spousal and child abuse. Alcohol is also a central nervous system depressant so that heavy alcohol use is a significant factor in intentional deaths, that is, suicides or rage against oneself.

RECOMMENDATIONS FOR ACTION

The 2007 U.S. Surgeon General's Call for Action recognizes the many developmental and environmental influences on youth drinking and recommends that school officials, parents, and community members come together to determine preventative actions to stop early youth use of alcohol, undertake brief interventions to begin treatment early, and change the way the treatment community treats youth who are already impaired. Some of these are already in place in the United States and may be the reason that the United States has a lower rate of heavy drinking among youth than countries in the European Union. However, as evidenced in the July 2008 Amethyst Initiative, college administrations are still struggling to curb the alarming increase in heavy drinking among college students. Both parents and youth should weigh what potential damage alcohol abuse will do to education and career plans and make choices to avoid those institutions of higher learning whose administrations and alumni continue to permit heavy undergraduate drinking behavior and don't undertake aggressive measures to curb such behavior and treat those so affected. Unfortunately, alcoholic beverage companies contribute to the problem as they target underage youth by sponsoring college sporting events.

Health care professionals, clinicians, and social workers need more training in how to utilize alcohol screening instruments with patients and clients, incorporating them into routine health examinations and patient histories. They also need more training in brief interventions to arrest the alcohol abuse prior to further brain shrinkage and alcohol-induced dementias. Newer treatment options that are based on results of neuropsychological testing to determine the extent of executive function impairment are also needed for both older adults and youth who have abused or are addicted to alcohol and may be in recovery to determine appropriate treatment planning.

There is an absence of robust comparable and comprehensive data on the relation between alcohol and crime. More research is needed in this area (Anderson & Baumberg, 2006, p. 200). Although it has long been estimated that 70–90 percent of those incarcerated have committed a crime while under the influence of alcohol or other drugs, these are only estimates. Interviewing prisoners and asking them whether they would have committed the crime if they had not been drunk was one methodology recommended and used in the EU Commission study. Twenty-four percent of those interviewed in a Canadian study acknowledged they had committed crimes when they were drunk at the time of the crime. However, this low figure is probably due to prisoners still in denial, prisoners high on other drugs, and cultural attitudes toward drinking.

Providing facts and dispelling myths is one of the best ways to change public attitudes and cultural practices surrounding alcohol abuse and addiction. Countries around the world can no longer afford to ignore the public health crisis caused by heavy alcohol use. Smoking cigarettes has become unpopular and now has a negative cultural image in many Western countries due to the efforts of alarmed government public health officials. These enlightened officials have acted upon the knowledge of the dangers of passive smoke and have undertaken aggressive intervention and treatment strategies to help people quit. The same aggressive public health campaign can also change the positive image of heavy alcohol use to a negative one and help those who are abusing or addicted to alcohol to abstain. The long-term biological and societal consequences are too great to ignore. Slogans such as this one, *My brain matters, does yours?*, could change the way the public views alcohol use.

REFERENCES

Amethyst Initiative. http://www.amethystinitiative.org

Anderson, P., & Baumberg, B. (2006). *Alcohol in Europe: A public health perspective.* London: Institute of Alcohol Studies.

Centers for Disease Control (CDC). http://www.cdc.gov/alcohol/faqs.htm#1
Gogtay, N., Rapoport, J., Thompson, P., Toga, A., Lusk, L. Vaituzis, C., et al. (2004, May 17). Imaging study shows brain maturing. *Science News.* Retrieved February 22, 2008, from www.nimh.nih.gov/science-news/2004/pressrelease

EU (European Union) Commission. (2006). Anderson, P., and Blaumberg, B. Alcohol in Europe, a public health perspective. Institute of Alcohol Studies, UK.

Grube, J. (2005). *Youth drinking rates and problems: A comparison of European countries and the United States.* Calverton, MD: Prevention Research Center, Pacific Institute for Research and Evaluation in support of Office of Juvenile Justice and Delinquency Prevention. www.udetc.org

Gunzerath, L., Faden, V., Zakhari, S., & Warren, K. (2004). Alcoholism: Clinical and experimental research. National Institute on Alcohol Abuse and Alcoholism Report on Moderate Drinking. *Alcoholism Clinical and Experimental Research, 28*(6), 829–847.

Kann, L. S., Kinchen, B., Williams, J., Ross, R., Lowry, J., Grunbaum, J., et al. , (2000, June 9). *Youth risk behavior surveillance—United States, 1999.* Retrieved February 22, 2008, from www.marininstitute.org/youth/alcoho0l_youth.htm

Leinwand, D. (2007). College drug use, binge drinking rise. *USA Today.* Retrieved February 22, 2008, from. www.usatoday.com/news/nation/2007-03-15-college-drug-use_N.htm

Lemonick, M. D., & Park, A. (July 16,2007). The science of addiction. *Time,* 42–48.

Lezak, M. D. (1995). Alcohol related disorders. *Neuropsychological Assessment* (3rd ed.), *Theory and practice of neuropsychological assessment* (pp. 246–258). New York: Oxford University Press.

Oscar-Berman, M., & Marinkovic, K. (1997). Alcoholism and the brain: An overview. The neurobiology of addiction: Introduction to the brain and the reward pathway and addiction. *NIAAA. Office of Science Education.* Slides retrieved February 27, 2008.

Oscar-Berman, M., & Marinkovic, K. (2004). Alcoholism and the brain: An overview. *NIAAA.* Retrieved February 22, 2008, from http://pubs.niaaa.nih.gov/publica tions/arh27-2/125-133.htm

Phil, R. O., & Peterson, J. B. (2003, May 14). Alcohol impairs executive cognitive functioning much longer than expected. *Alcoholism: Clinical and Experimental Research.* Retrieved February 22, 2008, from www.eurkalert.org/pub_releases/2003-05. ace-aie050703

Substance Abuse and Mental Health Services Administration. (2007). *The Surgeon General's call to action to prevent and reduce underage drinking.* Retrieved February 27, 2008, from www.surgeongeneral.gov

Substance Abuse and Mental Health Services Administration & National Council on Aging. (1998). *Substance abuse among older adults.*

Sullivan, E. V. (2003). Alcohol may compound its damaging effects through frontocerebellar circuitry. *Alcoholism: Clinical and Experimental Research.* Retrieved February 22, 2008, from www.eurkalert.org/pub_releases/2003-09/ace-amc090803. php

Swartzwelder, H. S., Zinn, S., & Stein, R. (2004). *Certain components of the brain's executive functions are compromised early in abstinence.* Retrieved December 30, 2007, from medicalnewstoday.com

Chapter 16

Addiction and Cognitive Control

Vicki W. Chanon, PhD, and Charlotte A. Boettiger, PhD

Substance use disorder, or addiction, is a neurobehavioral disorder characterized by a compulsion to ingest psychoactive substances (such as alcohol, prescription narcotics, nicotine, opiates, stimulants, and marijuana) despite repeated serious negative consequences. Addiction is a widespread problem, occurring among all ethnic groups and socioeconomic classes. Under normal conditions, our base motivations of hunger, thirst, and healthy fear of death or bodily harm are so powerful that they ensure that our basic needs for food, water, and physical safety are met. The need for emotional companionship, financial security, and sexual gratification also normally motivate our actions. However, for those with substance use disorders, some or all of these drives become secondary to obtaining and consuming their abused substance. This misdirection of motivation can lead to bodily harm, loss of vital relationships, loss of employment, loss of shelter, and even death. Observing addiction from the outside can be extremely frightening and puzzling. Why do addicts risk such harm? Evidence suggests that brain circuits that normally guide goal-directed behavior are malfunctioning in addicts. Recent evidence also suggests that perturbations of cognitive control are hallmarks of addiction. These cognitive aspects of addiction and their neural bases are relatively unexplored, but the advent of cognitive neuroscience tools, which allow exploration of brain activity in humans, may allow us to make quantum leaps in our understanding of the brain mechanisms of substance use disorders in the near future.

HOW DOES ADDICTION RELATE TO
COGNITIVE CONTROL?

Cognitive control is a broad term describing processes essential to our survival and well-being, encompassing one's ability to act and react in a situation-specific manner (Miller & Cohen, 2001). Appropriate reactions to a specific stimulus can vary greatly from one time or situation to another. For example, a large cobra behind the glass at the zoo may evoke intrigue and cause you to stop at the exhibit to look closer, while the same snake encountered on a wooded hiking trail may evoke fear and cause you to run away. This flexibility in our cognitive control not only allows us to make key decisions through complex and changing contexts, but also allows us to direct our attention to what we find significant and to create important memories of and associations with those things. Disruptions in this cognitive control, or "dysexecutive" behaviors, are an important and defining characteristic in addictive disorder, as people with this disease are often unable to make situation-appropriate responses to stimuli or events.

Moreover, recent evidence suggests that at least two specific cognitive control faculties are functioning abnormally in addicts: attentional control and decision making. Specifically, addicts disproportionately direct their attentional resources toward stimuli associated with their abused substance. For example, the attention of an alcoholic is biased toward items, images, and words that he or she associates with drinking alcohol. This bias, which is directly related to the likelihood of relapse in abstinent individuals, may be the product of profound associative learning in addicts, whereby drug-related cues and the actions of drug seeking and drug taking are tightly linked within the brain (Robinson & Berridge, 2003). These associations are likely to underlie the intense cravings that present a major barrier to maintaining abstinence from drug use. In addition to attentional abnormalities, clinical evidence suggests that decision-making abnormalities exist among people with substance use disorders as well. For example, a number of laboratory studies consistently find that, across a broad spectrum of addictive disorders, addicts show an immediate reward bias; that is, they are more likely than nonaddict participants to choose a smaller immediate reward over a larger reward for which they would need to wait (Reynolds, 2006). This tendency holds true for various types of rewards, including the addict's drug of choice and monetary rewards. Laboratory-controlled gambling tasks have also linked abnormal decision making with addictive disorders (Bechara, 2005; Clark & Robbins, 2002). These cognitive processes (decision making, attentional control, and reinforcement-based associative learning) are all processes that fall under the general umbrella of executive function and are associated with frontal circuits within the brain. It is still unclear, though, whether these abnormalities always co-occur, or whether they are separate dysfunctions, each of which occurs in some addicts but not others. Some data suggest that the attentional biases may precede addictive disorders, but comparable data are not available in the decision-making domain. Therefore, it is not yet clear whether decision-making abnormalities contribute to the development of addictive disorders, or are instead a byproduct of addiction or prolonged drug abuse.

ADDICTION AND ATTENTIONAL BIAS

Numerous behavioral studies point to an abnormality in attentional allocation to drug cues in addicts. Attention is quickly captured by and/or held on items associated with an addict's substance of choice (Robbins & Ehrman, 2004). A variety of cognitive tasks have been used to explore and measure this bias, one of the most prevalent being the spatial cuing task. In this task, participants are presented with two visual stimuli (or "cues"), one on each side of the screen. Generally one of the cues, which could be words or images, is a drug-related stimulus while the other is neutral. After the cues disappear, a target item requiring some response by the participant appears in the same location that was occupied by one of the two cues. Addicts respond more quickly to targets when they appear in the location where the drug-related cue had appeared than when they appeared in the location of the neutral cue. This finding suggests that, in addicts, attention is preferentially captured or held by drug-related cues. Another task that has been used to measure drug-related bias is a modified Stroop task (MacLeod, 1991; Stroop, 1935). The original Stroop task presents words (including color names) displayed in different ink (or screen) colors, and tests participants on their speed of naming the font color. For example, if the word *red* was printed in blue ink, the correct response would be *blue*. Participants are generally slower at naming the ink color for color words that do not match the ink than they are at naming neutral, noncolor words, and color words written in a congruent font color. This "Stroop Effect" is thought to occur because attention devoted to reading the word interferes with naming the font color. The task has been modified to study drug-related attentional bias, by presenting drug-related words in varying ink colors, rather than color-related words. Such studies find that, in addicts, drug-related words demand more attentional resources than do neutral words.

While the majority of evidence for drug-related attentional bias comes from spatial cuing and modified Stroop studies, such bias has also been detected using other types of cognitive tasks. For example, change blindness tasks, in which participants detect slight changes between two rapidly alternating visual scenes, demonstrate that addicts more readily detect drug-related changes in the scene. Another task, the attentional blink paradigm, has also recently been used to measure addiction-related attentional abnormalities. In this task, a stream of visual stimuli is rapidly presented, and participants are instructed to detect two specified target stimuli within the stream. When the first target (T1) and the second target (T2) are separated by about 200–400 milleseconds, participants are more likely to miss the second target because attentional resources are already allocated to processing T1. This phenomenon is referred to as the "attentional blink." If T1 is an addiction-related stimulus, addicts demonstrate a larger and more extended attentional blink. In contrast, when T2 is an addiction-related stimulus, an addict's attentional blink is reduced (Liu, Li, Sun, & Ma, 2008). Together, these studies indicate that, in addicts, words and images associated with their drug use have a heightened capacity to capture and hold attention, and that such stimuli interfere with attention to other things in their environment.

This heightened attention toward drug-related stimuli occurs in a wide variety of addictions, including cannabis, cocaine, opiates, tobacco, alcohol, caffeine, and even gambling. Attention abnormalities have been most thoroughly studied for the most commonly abused substances: tobacco and alcohol. Thus, studies exploring attention in alcohol and nicotine addictions have provided a greater understanding of some complex properties of addiction-related attentional bias. For example, data suggest that attentional bias toward tobacco cues requires the stimuli to be consciously perceived; when the smoking cues are presented too quickly or are masked by another stimulus, they do not affect attentional allocation. Data also show that demographic factors, like age and race, and mood factors, like depression, do not impact attentional bias toward alcohol cues in alcoholics. Studies of alcohol attentional bias have found that heavy social drinkers (but not light drinkers) show attentional bias toward alcohol cues, suggesting that such bias may serve as an early warning sign of alcohol addiction; these findings also bring up another possible explanation for the bias: stimulus familiarity. Previous cognitive psychology studies suggest that familiar or overlearned stimuli can affect attentional allocation (Chanon & Hopfinger, 2007). A contribution of familiarity effects to addiction-related attentional bias is suggested by an alcohol-related bias evident among staff members at a treatment center; however, the magnitude of the attentional bias toward alcohol stimuli was predicted by measures of alcohol dependence among the staff members, suggesting that the root cause of the attention bias goes beyond mere stimulus familiarity.

There is abundant evidence that attention is directed disproportionately to drug-related stimuli in addictive disorders, but do such attention abnormalities really matter? Studies that correlate addiction-related attentional bias with treatment outcomes say "Yes!" Mounting evidence suggests that the magnitude of this attention bias is directly proportional to relapse risk (Munafò & Albery, 2006). Moreover, many studies suggest that the size of the attentional bias is also directly proportional to the level of craving during drug abstinence. This clinical relevance underscores the importance of understanding the neural mechanisms of addiction-related attention bias. As noted above, repeated use of an addictive substance may produce changes in the brain that cause the brain to attribute excessive significance or "salience" to people, places, and things associated with drug use; the development of such hypersensitivity is referred to as "incentive salience" learning (Robinson & Berridge, 2003). Understanding which neural processes are affected and contribute to this increased salience of drug cues could lead to new ideas for better treatments for substance use disorders. Thus far, there has been almost no exploration into these neural correlates; however, studies looking at other aspects of attention and addiction provide some hypotheses about the parts of the brain that are involved.

NEURAL CORRELATES OF ATTENTIONAL CONTROL

While empirical studies of the neural mechanisms of attentional bias toward addictive substances remain incomplete, general studies of attentional allocation provide some clues. For example, neuropsychological studies suggest that patients with damage to the parietal lobes have difficulty disengaging and reorienting their attentional focus (Posner, Walker, Friedrich, & Rafal, 1984). The importance of the posterior parietal cortex (PPC) in attentional orienting also comes from neuroimaging studies, which particularly emphasize the intraparietal sulcus (IPS) (Corbetta & Shulman, 2002). Data from single-cell recording in nonhuman primates and fMRI studies in humans also provide evidence that attention leads to increased perceptual processing. For example, enhanced visual attention leads to increased neural activity in the nonprimary visual cortical areas. Study of the childhood development of attention networks has further enhanced our understanding of the neural mechanisms of attentional control. Explorations into the behavior, brain structure, and brain function related to reorienting and executive control of attention in children versus adults implicate a fronto-parietal network in attentional control. As expected, children showed poorer attentional control behaviorally, and they showed reduced brain activity in right temporo-parietal junction (TPJ) and dorsolateral prefrontal cortex (DLPFC). These behavioral and functional brain differences between children and adults were associated with structural brain differences; poorer performance and reduced brain activity were associated with less gray matter in the TPJ and DLPFC (Konrad et al., 2005). These studies of typically functioning brains give us a place to begin exploring possible sites of brain dysfunction in addiction, but studies specifically exploring these neural mechanisms in addict populations are in great demand.

While addiction-related attentional bias has not been studied at the neural level, other studies of the addicted brain shed some light on possible mechanisms. Attentional bias toward drug-related cues relies greatly on the fact that these cues have become strongly associated with the use of the drug itself. Based on this deep association, the cues that become associated with drug use can produce an intense craving and relapse both in animals and humans (Robinson & Berridge, 2003). Animal studies that have directly examined the effects of cocaine administration on learned associations suggest that drug administration disrupts orbitofrontal pathways to the striatum, causing impairment in the ability to inhibit previously conditioned responses (Everitt et al., 2007). While it is likely that this cognitive inflexibility plays a role in the attentional bias toward drug-related stimuli, the neural underpinnings of the bias remain a mystery for now. Ongoing studies using emerging neuroimaging and pharmacology techniques to explore the underlying neural mechanisms of addiction-related attentional bias aim to fill this gap in our understanding and to suggest new ways in which to treat addictive disorders.

ADDICTION, DECISION MAKING, AND ACTION SELECTION

Two symptoms used as diagnostic criteria for substance dependence according to the *Diagnostic and Statistical Manual of Mental Disorders* (American Psychiatric Association, 1994) are (1) a persistent desire or unsuccessful efforts to cut down or control substance use, and (2) continued substance use despite knowledge of having a persistent or recurrent physical or psychological problem that is likely to have been caused or exacerbated by the substance. Research suggests that addiction is related not only to deficits in decision making related to substance use, but also to deficits in more general decision-making processes, and even to deficits in the selection of simple responses to stimuli.

One of the most frequently used tasks to study simple responses selection and inhibition is the "go/no-go" paradigm. This task generally involves presentation of different types of cues that indicate to the participant whether to respond or to refrain from responding on a given trial. Substance-dependent individuals have difficulty inhibiting planned responses to no-go targets (Lubman, Yucel, & Pantelis, 2004; Verdejo-Garcia, Bechara, Recknor, & Perez-Garcia, 2006). While addicts may demonstrate some generalized inhibitory impairment, one can observe that such impairments appear most evident in the presence of drugs or drug-associated cues. Consistent with this observation, in laboratory go/no-go studies, addicts demonstrate greater inhibitory impairment when drug-related cues are present.

In addition to investigations of simple response selection and inhibition, several neurocognitive studies of addicts have probed higher-level forms of decision making, focusing on two primary forms. The first that we will discuss are known as "gambling tasks," and include the Iowa Gambling Task (IGT) and the Cambridge Gambling Task (CBT) (Bechara, 2005; Clark & Robbins, 2002; Rogers et al., 1999). The IGT requires participants to pick virtual playing cards, one at a time, from one of four decks of cards displayed on a computer screen. Each choice results in either a gain or loss of money. The four decks vary in terms of their riskiness and in their ultimate payoff. Two of the decks have relatively low gains, but even lower losses, while the other two have high gains, and even higher losses; the latter decks also have more frequent losses. Performance on these gambling tasks is assessed by participants' abilities to pick the statistically best decks (i.e., the low-risk decks). One concern with the IGT is that in addition to measuring decision-making behavior, the task is also implicitly measuring learning, as participants learn which decks are best on the basis of their choices. Thus slow learners could be misinterpreted as being poor decision makers. Indeed, some studies have found that performance on the IGT depends on IQ, suggesting an important role for learning in this task. Developed later, the CBT requires participants to guess whether a reward token will randomly appear in a blue box or red box and subsequently place a bet on their decision. There are 10 boxes across the top of the screen and the ratio of red boxes to blue boxes varies from trial to trial (Rogers et al., 1999). Findings with addicts in gambling task studies have been inconsistent; some have found substance abusers to have impairments on the tasks, while others have not. These discrepancies raise the possibility that the type of addiction and/or the duration of abstinence may be important factors affecting performance on the gambling tasks, but greater exploration of these issues is needed before definitive conclusions can be drawn.

The other type of decision-making task most commonly used to study addicts is the so-called delay discounting task. Performance on these tasks has been shown to be IQ independent, and robustly distinguishes between addicts and control subjects. Generally, this type of task requires participants to decide between a reward (e.g., a sum of money) available sooner and a larger reward available at a later time. The exact implementation of such task varies from lab to lab, but in general, in comparison to control participants, addicts tend to choose the smaller, immediate rewards more often. As with addiction-related attentional bias, delay discounting has been reported for a variety of addictive disorders, including cigarette smokers, alcoholics, amphetamine users, cocaine users, opiate users, and gamblers (Bickel & Marsch, 2001; Reynolds, 2006). While this tendency for addicts to more steeply or more frequently discount delayed monetary rewards is quite consistent, it appears that rewards consisting of the drug of choice are temporally discounted even more severely by addicts (Bickel & Marsch, 2001; Reynolds, 2006). Of clinical and public health significance, heroin-dependent individuals who are willing to participate in risky needle-sharing behavior show greater delay discounting of both heroin and monetary rewards. Together, these findings suggest a generalized mechanism for overvaluing immediate consequences over delayed consequences that may help perpetuate continued drug use in the face of adverse consequences.

NEURAL CORRELATES OF ACTION SELECTION

Numerous studies using various techniques implicate frontal circuits in action selection processes (Duncan & Owen, 2000; Ostlund & Balleine, 2007; Rushworth, Walton, Kennerley, & Bannerman, 2004). For example, studies exploring response selection in nonhuman primates find neuronal activity in prefrontal cortex neurons related to go-no/go responses. Neuropsychological studies of patients with frontal lobe damage have also provided evidence for a role of frontal areas in action selection and response inhibition. In particular, deficits in these functions are frequently observed in frontotemporal dementia (FTD) patients. The term *FTD* is used to describe non-Alzheimer dementias associated with atrophy in the frontal and temporal lobes. Numerous studies indicate that such atrophy, particularly when it involves the orbitofrontal cortex, impairs response selection and the ability to inhibit inappropriate responses (Viskontas, Possin, & Miller, 2007). Similarly, patients with lesions in the right frontal lobe have slower reactions to signals directing them to inhibit their responses than do patients with intact frontal lobes (Aron, Fletcher, Bullmore, Sahakian, & Robbins, 2003). Finally, a large amount of evidence implicating frontal areas in action selection and complex decision making comes from recent neuroimaging data. The frontal lobes, specifically in the right hemisphere, have been implicated in response inhibition tasks when inhibiting responses to external stimuli (Brass, Derrfuss, Forstmann, & von Cramon, 2005; de Wit, Enggasser, & Richards, 2002; McClure, Ericson, Laibson, Loewenstein, & Cohen, 2007; McClure, Laibson, Loewenstein, & Cohen, 2004). Similarly, an area of the fronto-median cortex plays a role in voluntary response inhibition when the decision to withhold a response is internally rather than externally cued (Brass & Haggard, 2007). Based on accumulated evidence, Michael Frank and colleagues have recently developed models of natural action selection that posit a central role of the basal ganglia (BG) frontal circuits (Frank, Scheres, & Sherman, 2007). These models point to two separate pathways, with each pathway's contribution regulated by dopamine (DA) levels. These pathways, one of which initiates responses and the other of which inhibits them, derive from two separate populations of cells within the striatum, which in turn target divergent pathways through the BG nuclei, thalamus, and cortex.

While many neuroimaging studies have probed the neural correlates of simple response selection, including several studies in addicted populations, investigations into the neural bases of decision making are less numerous. Fewer studies still have assessed the neural signature of behavioral differences between substance-abusing and non–substance-abusing populations (Bickel et al., 2007). Some fMRI evidence suggests that a dysfunction in the orbito-frontal cortex (OFC) is responsible for response selection differences seen in behavioral studies (Goldstein & Volkow, 2002). For example, cocaine addicts and alcoholics both show greater activation in the OFC correlated with poorer performance on a Stroop task, while controls show the opposite pattern, that is, greater OFC activation is related to better performance in controls. These findings suggest the brains of substance abusers are generally working harder to recruit the usual brain areas needed to perform the task, but that some neural inefficiency is impeding effective response inhibition. In terms of more complex decision making, Bechara (2005) describes a neural framework that would account for our ability to make decisions based on future outcomes. Bechara's theory suggests that two interacting brain systems, an impulsive amygdala-driven system and a more reflective prefrontal-driven system, become unbalanced with drug use, resulting in an overactive amygdala driven system. This imbalance between systems is then proposed to impair a drug user's ability to consider distant future outcomes when choosing whether to continue drug use despite probable negative consequences. Neuroimaging data have also explored complex decision making using delay discounting tasks, with results suggesting that activity differences in frontal and amygdala areas are related to differences in choosing smaller, sooner versus larger, later rewards (Boettiger et al., 2007; McClure et al., 2004, 2007).

While neuroimaging studies are one common means for investigating the neural underpinnings of differences in cognitive functions among addict populations, another valuable method is the use of behavioral pharmacology. This tool has been employed most extensively in studies assessing delay discounting behavior. These studies have determined that acutely elevating dopamine levels with amphetamine *decreases* discounting of delayed rewards (de Wit et al., 2002) and that acutely depressing serotonin levels *increases* discounting of delayed rewards (Schweighofer et al., 2008). Two further studies point to the importance of dopamine in regulating discounting behavior. First, blockade of endogenous opioids with naltrexone (NTX; one of the few FDA-approved treatments for some forms of addiction) changed delay discounting behavior in a personality-dependent fashion (Mitchell, Tavares, Fields, D'Esposito, & Boettiger, 2007). The personality measure, the "Locus of Control" score, measures one's tendency to perceive outcomes as under his or her own control or as controlled by external forces (Rotter, 1966), and is theoretically linked to brain dopamine levels (Declerck, Boone, & De Brabander, 2006). This finding that this cognitive effect of NTX is personality-dependent suggests that its therapeutic effects could be as well. The second finding linked a genetic polymorphism that regulates cortical dopamine levels with delay discounting performance (Boettiger et al., 2007). Further investigation is needed, but these data highlight the importance of the modulatory systems targeted by drugs of abuse (Everitt & Robbins, 2005) in influencing decision-making behavior.

CONCLUSION

Animal studies have been undeniably instrumental in furthering our understanding of the neurobiology of addiction. Such studies have determined which circuits in the brain play a role in addictive behavior, how these areas are connected, and how these circuits are regulated by neuromodulators. Important components of these circuits include a brainstem site called the ventral tegmental area (VTA), the prefrontal cortex, and two areas located deep in the brain, the amygdala and the nucleus accumbens. The VTA neurons produce dopamine, which they release into the other three brain areas listed above. Such dopamine release normally occurs in response to natural rewards like food, water, and sex, but it also occurs in response to all drugs of abuse. These circuits are affected by learning, with the result being that cues associated with rewards also come to trigger dopamine release. Chronic intake of drugs of abuse results in an intensified version of such learning, producing extreme hypersensitivity to drug-related cues. This knowledge gathered in animal studies has enabled scientists to take a more educated approach to empirical studies of addiction in humans.

Despite the importance of these animal studies, it is important to recognize that addiction is a human disorder that does not generally occur in animals outside of a laboratory context. With the advent of cognitive neuroscience tools, we are beginning to understand the neurobiology of addiction in a new way. These tools now allow the investigation of cognitive aspects of addiction, and thus to ask scientific questions that are only addressable by testing human populations. A growing body of research has begun to specifically focus on addiction as a dysfunction of cognitive control. While it is evident that dysfunctions in cognitive control may be central to the disease of addiction, a vast amount remains to be learned about the underlying neural mechanisms of these dysfunctions. A better understanding of the neural mechanisms underlying cognitive control dysfunctions in addiction will lead to a more complete understanding of how cognitive control systems function normally. In addition, this knowledge will stimulate new avenues for treatment development (both behavioral and pharmacological), ultimately increasing the variety and effectiveness of options for treating substance use disorders.

REFERENCES

American Psychiatric Association. (1994). *Diagnostic and statistical manual of mental disorders* (4th ed.). Washington, DC: Author.

Aron, A. R., Fletcher, P. C., Bullmore, E. T., Sahakian, B. J., & Robbins, T. W. (2003). Stop-signal inhibition disrupted by damage to right inferior frontal gyrus in humans. *Nature Neuroscience, 6*(2), 115–116.

Bechara, A. (2005). Decision making, impulse control and loss of willpower to resist drugs: A neurocognitive perspective. *Nature Neuroscience, 8*(11), 1458–1463.

Bickel, W. K., & Marsch, L. A. (2001). Toward a behavioral economic understanding of drug dependence: Delay discounting processes. *Addiction, 96*(1), 73–86.

Bickel, W. K., Miller, M. L., Yi, R., Kowal, B. P., Lindquist, D. M., & Pitcock, J. A. (2007). Behavioral and neuroeconomics of drug addiction: Competing neural systems and temporal discounting processes. *Drug and Alcohol Dependence, 90*(Suppl. 1), S85–S91.

Boettiger, C. A., Mitchell, J. M., Tavares, V. C., Robertson, M., Joslyn, G., D'Esposito, M., et al. (2007). Immediate reward bias in humans: Fronto-parietal networks and a role for the catechol-O-methyltransferase 158(Val/Val) genotype. *Journal of Neuroscience, 27*(52), 14383–14391.

Brass, M., Derrfuss, J., Forstmann, B., & von Cramon, D. Y. (2005). The role of the inferior frontal junction area in cognitive control. *Trends in Cognitive Sciences, 9*(7), 314–316.

Brass, M., & Haggard, P. (2007). To do or not to do: The neural signature of self-control. *Journal of Neuroscience, 27*(34), 9141–9145.

Chanon, V., & Hopfinger, J. (2007). Memory's grip on attention: The influence of item memory on the allocation of attention. *Visual Cognition, 16*(2 & 3), 325–340.

Clark, L., & Robbins, T. (2002). Decision-making deficits in drug addiction. *Trends in Cognitive Sciences, 6*(9), 361–363.

Corbetta, M., & Shulman, G. L. (2002). Control of goal-directed and stimulus-driven attention in the brain. *Nature Reviews Neuroscience, 3*(3), 201–215.

de Wit, H., Enggasser, J. L., & Richards, J. B. (2002). Acute administration of d-amphetamine decreases impulsivity in healthy volunteers. *Neuropsychopharmacology, 27*(5), 813–825.

Declerck, C. H., Boone, C., & De Brabander, B. (2006). On feeling in control: A biological theory for individual differences in control perception. *Brain and Cognition, 62*(2), 143–176.

Duncan, J., & Owen, A. M. (2000). Common regions of the human frontal lobe recruited by diverse cognitive demands. *Trends in Neurosciences, 23*(10), 475–483.

Everitt, B. J., Hutcheson, D. M., Ersche, K. D., Pelloux, Y., Dalley, J. W., & Robbins, T. W. (2007). The orbital prefrontal cortex and drug addiction in laboratory animals and humans. *Annals of the New York Academy of Sciences, 1121,* 576–597.

Everitt, B. J., & Robbins, T. W. (2005). Neural systems of reinforcement for drug addiction: From actions to habits to compulsion. *Nature Neuroscience, 8*(11), 1481–1489.

Frank, M. J., Scheres, A., & Sherman, S. J. (2007). Understanding decision-making deficits in neurological conditions: Insights from models of natural action selection. *Philosophical Transactions of the Royal Society of London B: Biological Sciences, 362*(1485), 1641–1654.

Goldstein, R. Z., & Volkow, N. D. (2002). Drug addiction and its underlying neurobiological basis: Neuroimaging evidence for the involvement of the frontal cortex. *American Journal of Psychiatry, 159*(10), 1642–1652.

Konrad, K., Neufang, S., Thiel, C. M., Specht, K., Hanisch, C., Fan, J., et al. (2005). Development of attentional networks: An fMRI study with children and adults. *Neuroimage, 28*(2), 429–439.

Liu, N., Li, B., Sun, N., & Ma, Y. (2008). Effects of addiction-associated and affective stimuli on the attentional blink in a sample of abstinent opiate dependent patients. *Journal of Psychopharmacology, 22*(1), 64–70.

Lubman, D. I., Yucel, M., & Pantelis, C. (2004). Addiction, a condition of compulsive behaviour? Neuroimaging and neuropsychological evidence of inhibitory dysregulation. *Addiction, 99*(12), 1491–1502.

MacLeod, C. M. (1991). Half a century of research on the Stroop effect: An integrative review. *Psychological Bulletin, 109*(2), 163–203.

McClure, S. M., Ericson, K. M., Laibson, D. I., Loewenstein, G., & Cohen, J. D. (2007). Time discounting for primary rewards. *Journal of Neuroscience, 27*(21), 5796–5804.

McClure, S. M., Laibson, D. I., Loewenstein, G., & Cohen, J. D. (2004). Separate neural systems value immediate and delayed monetary rewards. *Science, 306*(5695), 503–507.

Miller, E. K., & Cohen, J. D. (2001). An integrative theory of prefrontal cortex function. *Annual Review of Neuroscience, 24,* 167–202.

Mitchell, J. M., Tavares, V. C., Fields, H. L., D'Esposito, M., & Boettiger, C. A. (2007). Endogenous opioid blockade and impulsive responding in alcoholics and healthy controls. *Neuropsychopharmacology, 32*(2), 439–449.

Munafò, M., & Albery, I. P. (Eds.). (2006). *Cognition + Addiction.* Oxford: Oxford University Press.

Ostlund, S. B., & Balleine, B. W. (2007). The contribution of orbitofrontal cortex to action selection. *Annals of the New York Academy of Sciences, 1121,* 174–192.

Posner, M. I., Walker, J. A., Friedrich, F. J., & Rafal, R. D. (1984). Effects of parietal injury on covert orienting of attention. *Journal of Neuroscience, 4*(7), 1863–1874.

Reynolds, B. (2006). A review of delay-discounting research with humans: Relations to drug use and gambling. *Behavioral Pharmacology, 17*(8), 651–667.

Robbins, S. J., & Ehrman, R. N. (2004). The role of attentional bias in substance abuse. *Behavioral and Cognitive Neuroscience Reviews, 3*(4), 243–260.

Robinson, T. E., & Berridge, K. C. (2003). Addiction. *Annual Review of Psychology, 54,* 25–53.

Rogers, R. D., Everitt, B. J., Baldacchino, A., Blackshaw, A. J., Swainson, R., Wynne, K., et al. (1999). Dissociable deficits in the decision-making cognition of chronic amphetamine abusers, opiate abusers, patients with focal damage to prefrontal cortex, and tryptophan-depleted normal volunteers: Evidence for monoaminergic mechanisms. *Neuropsychopharmacology, 20*(4), 322–339.

Rotter, J. B. (1966). Generalized expectancies for internal versus external control of reinforcement. *Psychological Monographs, 80*(1), 1–28.

Rushworth, M. F., Walton, M. E., Kennerley, S. W., & Bannerman, D. M. (2004). Action sets and decisions in the medial frontal cortex. *Trends in Cognitive Sciences, 8*(9), 410–417.

Schweighofer, N., Bertin, M., Shishida, K., Okamoto, Y., Tanaka, S. C., Yamawaki, S., et al. (2008). Low-serotonin levels increase delayed reward discounting in humans. *Journal of Neuroscience, 28*(17), 4528–4532.

Stroop, J. (1935). Studies of interference in serial verbal reactions. *Journal of Experimental Psychology, 18*(6), 643–662.

Verdejo-Garcia, A., Bechara, A., Recknor, E. C., & Perez-Garcia, M. (2006). Executive dysfunction in substance dependent individuals during drug use and abstinence: An examination of the behavioral, cognitive and emotional correlates of addiction. *Journal of the International Neuropsychological Society, 12*(3), 405–415.

Viskontas, I. V., Possin, K. L., & Miller, B. L. (2007). Symptoms of frontotemporal dementia provide insights into orbitofrontal cortex function and social behavior. *Annals of the New York Academy of Sciences, 1121,* 528–545.

Chapter 17

Schizophrenia and Substance Misuse

Giuseppe Carrà, MD, MSc, PhD, and
Sonia Johnson, MSc, MRCPsych, DM

Comorbid drug and alcohol problems ("dual diagnosis") are growing concerns among people with schizophrenia and other severe psychoses because of large increases in prevalence and their association with poorer clinical (Margolese, Negrete, Tempier, & Gill, 2006) and psychosocial (Hunt, Bergen, & Bashir, 2002) outcomes. Dual diagnosis clients present more difficulties also from a diagnostic and clinical management perspective than do single diagnosis clients. Substance use has been found to exacerbate positive symptoms (Drake, Osher, & Wallach, 1989; Margolese, Malchy, Negrete, Tempier, & Gill, 2004; Negrete, Knapp, Douglas, & Smith, 1986; Pulver, Wolyniec, Wagner, Moorman, & McGrath, 1989) and to increase aggression and violence (Angermeyer, 2000; Soyka, 2000), as well as medication noncompliance (Bhanji, Chouinard, & Margolese, 2004; Coldham, Addington, & Addington, 2002; Kamali et al., 2001; Margolese et al., 2004; Olfson et al., 2000; Swartz et al., 1998) in people with schizophrenia. Furthermore, time to readmission or community survival is significantly reduced among "dually diagnosed" compared to nonabusing subjects, even when controlling for noncompliance (Hunt et al., 2002).

Improved clinical management of dual diagnosis has been among main concerns of several European National Health Services (Banerjee, Clancy, & Crome, 2002; Carrà & Clerici, 2006; Dervaux et al., 2001; Gouzoulis-Mayfrank, 2004). Options for service development have been widely discussed (Johnson, 1997; Weaver et al., 1999), as models from the United States might perform differently within the context of well-established community mental health services. A variety of treatments exist, but the drive from the United States has been to provide programs integrating treatment of both substance misuse and severe mental illness. Such programs require additional resources and may require radical redesign of service delivery systems. Actual prevalence rates in European countries and impact on clinical and psychosocial outcomes can inform evidence-based allocation of resources in terms of services and training needed (Johnson, 1997).

THE PREVALENCE OF SUBSTANCE USE IN PEOPLE WITH SCHIZOPHRENIA: STILL AN OPEN QUESTION?

Since the late 1980s, a number of studies have reported that substance use disorders occur at high rates in schizophrenia. U.S. data indicate that approximately 30–50 percent of people with schizophrenia have a lifetime substance use disorder. Nonetheless, whether these rates are generalizable to different countries remains controversial. A number of methodological issues must be considered, which may affect evidence about dual diagnosis prevalence. The first concern is about ascertainment. Most investigations of comorbidity in schizophrenia have been conducted with clinical samples of convenience and this can bias comorbidity rates in an upward direction (Berkson, 1946), and limit generalizability to the general population of individuals with schizophrenia. Studies such as the Epidemiologic Catchment Area (ECA; Regier, Farmer, & Rae, 1990), the National Comorbidity Survey (NCS; Kendler, Gallagher, Abelson, & Kessler, 1996) and the National Psychiatric Morbidity Survey (Jenkins et al., 1997) avoid such sampling problems in that assessments were conducted on both community and institutional populations. Nevertheless, data from these studies are also somewhat limited as the lay interview assessments of psychotic disorders used have been shown to have poor agreement with interviews conducted by clinicians (Kendler et al., 1996). Such poor agreement is indeed common in large-scale surveys and gives rise to expressions of concern among psychiatric epidemiologists (Taub et al., 2005) about validity of evidence. Similarly, the assessment of substance use can also be problematic. Designs often failed to utilize available diagnostic standards of abuse or dependence but instead identify samples based on use, problem use, or combine all levels of severity into one category. Consequently, direct comparisons of rates are limited by the variety of methods of substance use assessment. Reliable multimodal assessment is recommended for dually diagnosed patients (Goldfinger et al., 1996).

The following are the main methods that should be used to assess substance use (Drake, Alterman, & Rosenberg, 1993), with decreasing validity: consensus method (i.e., at least structured diagnosis plus other sources); self-report using formal diagnostic interviews; staff ratings; self-report using screening instrument. A related problem lies in the high prevalence of multiple substance use. This makes it critical to carry out a broad assessment of substance use and interpretations are limited by the use of more than one substance. Thus, given the frequent occurrence of multiple substance use diagnoses (particularly between alcohol and other drugs), any attempt to attribute observed findings associated with comorbid substance use to a single substance or class of substances is often difficult if not impossible. Finally, a further concern in this research is in relation to the failure to specify time criteria in samples, that is, whether substance diagnoses are based on current, past, or lifetime. Collapsing across current and past use may either obscure or mix up enduring use rates and transient states of intoxication or withdrawal.

WHY AND HOW DO SUBSTANCE-RELATED DISORDERS DEVELOP AMONG PEOPLE WITH SCHIZOPHRENIA?

As mentioned above, comorbidity rates have important implications for nosological issues. The study of comorbidity may enhance the generalizability of research findings. A better understanding both of causal processes underlying comorbidity and of the interplay of individual disorders involved is also needed. Despite the prevalence of substance use disorders in schizophrenia and the worrying effects of dual diagnosis, little is known about its causes. However, attempting to overcome the "chicken and egg" paradox (Meyer, 1986), a number of explanatory models of substance use in schizophrenia have been proposed in the last two decades.

Genetics

There has been accumulating evidence that genetics play a role in schizophrenia (e.g., Sullivan, Kendler, & Neale, 2003), and twin studies have indicated a genetic component to alcohol dependence (Heath et al., 2001; Prescott & Kendler, 1999) and to dependence on other drugs (Kendler, Jacobson, Prescott, & Neale, 2003; Tsuang et al., 1996). Rather more complex is the contribution of genetics to the comorbidity of the two illnesses. Indeed, the available evidence currently suggests little or no genetic relationship between schizophrenia and alcoholism (Kendler & Gardner, 1997), and it may well be that the comorbidity of schizophrenia and substance use disorders reflects the effects of two separate genetic risks in the same individual (Kendler, 1985).

Substance Abuse Leads to Increased Risks of Psychosis

This widely debated association is essentially based on the stress-vulnerability model (Zubin & Spring, 1977), implicating substance use as a stressor precipitating the onset of schizophrenia in vulnerable individuals. Thus, comorbid substance use and schizophrenia may have reciprocal interactions in terms of onset, course, severity, and clinical characteristics (Mueser, Drake, & Wallach, 1998), assuming that the use of substances actually increases the risk of schizophrenia. Indeed, the available evidence supports the hypothesis that cannabis is actually an independent risk factor, both for psychosis and for the development of psychotic symptoms (see Semple, McIntosh, & Lawrie, 2005 for a recent systematic review), with public health concerns (e.g., Fergusson, Poulton, Smith, & Boden, 2006).

Self-Medication Model

An intriguing hypothesis proposes that self-medication by substance abuse is a coping attempt by people with schizophrenia, matching the pharmacological properties of substances with the particular psychiatric symptoms and states experienced (Khantzian, 1985, 1997). However, this should imply diagnostic and symptomatological differences in substance selection (e.g., choice of stimulants and negative symptoms should be associated). Neither prediction is supported by research evidence. Among people suffering from schizophrenia, no replicable patterns of substances chosen and symptoms experienced have been identified (Brunette, Mueser, Xie, & Drake, 1997; Cuffel & Chase, 1994; Hamera, Schneider, & Deviney, 1995), despite preliminary findings supporting the self-medication hypothesis (Schneier & Siris, 1987). As a matter of fact, given the frequent occurrence of multiple substance misuse as discussed above, it is not possible to attribute any observed symptomatological and clinical difference to a single drug class. The only strong evidence is that regarding the association between fewer negative symptoms and dual diagnosis, though it is not still clear whether this may involve lifespan or just current misuse (see Potvin, Sepehry, & Stip, 2006 for a review). Furthermore, the pattern of substance use in schizophrenia is similar to that found in other diagnostic groups (e.g., El-Guebaly & Hodgins, 1992), and reflects a substance use pattern in the general population (Mueser, Yarnold, & Bellack, 1992; Regier et al., 1990) where the sampling took place. However, a less definitive form of the self-medication hypothesis that does have some supporting evidence suggests that substances are used to relieve dysphoria and anxiety and to alleviate tension (Addington & Duchak, 1997; Baigent, Holme, & Hafner, 1995) rather than medicating core psychotic symptoms.

Social and Cross-Cultural Differences

A final framework that may contribute to the model of how substance use and schizophrenia are linked is to assess epidemiological data to determine if demographic or sociocultural differences in substance use are related to the relative risk for use by people with schizophrenia (Phillips & Johnson, 2001). Availability of substances but also the social context in terms of individual and local or national cultural factors is likely to contribute to the prevalence of dual diagnosis. Internationally, and within a consistent simultaneous sampling framework, the World Mental Health Surveys (WHO World Mental Health Survey Consortium, 2004) reported general population 12-month prevalence for substance disorders ranging between 0.1 and 6.4 percent (IQR, 0.8%–2.6%). This might support the hypothesis about the influence of socioeconomic and cultural factors on dual diagnosis prevalence rates, probably mediated by availability (RachBeisel, Scott, & Dixon, 1999).

THE FIRST WAVE OF EVIDENCE: THE UNITED STATES

Most evidence about the prevalence of this comorbid condition comes from the United States. The largest of these investigations, the Epidemiologic Catchment Area (ECA) study, has shown that the odds of meeting criteria for a substance use disorder are 4.6 times higher for individuals with schizophrenia compared with the rest of the population (Regier et al., 1990). In the National Comorbidity Survey (NCS), roughly half of respondents who met criteria for a substance use disorder at some time in their life also met criteria for one or more lifetime mental disorders (Kessler et al., 1996). Similarly, half of those who met criteria for a mental disorder also met those for a lifetime substance use one. Regarding the general population, the ECA study found that 47 percent of patients with schizophrenia had a comorbid substance abuse disorder, 34 percent related to alcohol, and 28 percent to other drugs (Regier et al., 1990). Further data from the NCS (Kendler et al., 1996) showed that 44.8 percent of individuals with nonaffective psychosis were classified as having a dual diagnosis.

Is Dual Diagnosis Simply Inherent to Psychotic Illness?

Also in the United States, studies in mental health settings suggest variations in dual diagnosis rates, ranging between 20 and 65 percent of persons who have a diagnosis of a severe mental illness (Cuffel, Shumway, Chouljian, & MacDonald, 1994; Drake et al., 1989). For instance, 38 percent of clients of mental health services in a California county reported one or more alcohol dependence symptoms in the previous year, and 21 percent the use of three or more types of illicit drugs (Weisner & Schmidt, 1993), but the prevalence of current substance use in an emergency room among clients with schizophrenia has been reported at 47 percent (Barbee, Clark, Crapanzano, Heintz, & Kehoe,

1989) and among inpatients, it ranges from 12 to 60 percent (Brady, Casto, Lydiard, Malcom, & Arana, 1991; Brady et al., 1990; Dixon, Haas, Weiden, Sweeney, & Frances, 1991; Drake et al., 1989; Havassy & Arns, 1998). On the whole, rates seem higher among patients with psychosis receiving emergency or inpatient treatment (Mueser et al., 1992). The recent Clinical Antipsychotic Trials of Intervention Effectiveness (CATIE) study, recruiting at 57 mixed U.S. clinical sites, found 37 percent with current evidence of substance use disorders (Swartz et al., 2006).

However, some U.S. literature also suggests that dual diagnosis rates might vary between rural or urban areas (Mueser, Essock, Drake, Wolfe, & Frisman, 2001), and different backgrounds (Lambert, Griffith, & Hendrickse, 1996; Mowbray, Ribisl, Solomon, Luke, & Kewson, 1997). These variations may reflect factors such as acute versus nonacute illnesses and differences according to mental health care settings sampled (Drake et al., 1989; Havassy & Arns, 1998) and the availability of illicit drugs in the study location (RachBeisel et al., 1999).

Variations in rates reported from the United States prompt questions about the extent to which comorbidity is a product of local social circumstances rather than vulnerability to substance misuse being an inherent clinical feature of psychosis. A number of such social factors could be studied also in order to implement effective preventive and treatment programs (Jeffery, Ley, McLaren, & Siegfried, 2000) as currently research is focused on assessing whether extra resources, required to deliver substance misuse treatment integrated with mental health care for people with severe mental health problems, will lead to benefit. A number of environmental factors may mediate higher incidence of psychotic illnesses in urban areas (e.g., Allardyce et al., 2001), in its turn potentially mediated by social deprivation or migration into urban areas (Freeman, 1994; Van Os, 2004). Analogous social factors—both at individual level and at local/national level—might mediate incidence of substance abuse in people with schizophrenia, explaining part of the variation in dual diagnosis prevalence rates.

SUGGESTIONS FROM ALCOHOL AND DRUG ABUSE PREVALENCE IN THE GENERAL POPULATION

Evidence about the epidemiology of "pure" drug and alcohol abuse in the general population is particularly useful to explore prevalence variations in different cultural and social contexts. First, in reestimating prevalence values by calibration of case definitions (i.e., imposing methodological constraints to unify case definitions), differences were found between the United States and the UK in prevalence of active drug dependence, which was estimated as 1.4

percent in the United States and 0.5 percent in the UK, just somewhat attenuated when the effect of living in an urban setting was controlled (Furr-Holden
& Anthony, 2003). The difference was found despite symptom profiles among
active cases being very similar. In both countries, being male, unmarried, of a
low socioeconomic status (SES), and living in an urban setting were associated with an increased occurrence of drug dependence. Furthermore within
the European Union, differences in lifetime and current prevalence of alcohol
and drug abuse have long been assessed by the European Monitoring Centre
for Drugs and Drug Addiction (EMCDDA) in its annual reports, and despite
the general trend toward increasing rates, variations between countries in
prevalence rates of both alcohol and drugs abuse remain wide (EMCDDA,
2005). However, accurate comparisons between countries are still problematic
because both strengths and weaknesses of different general population surveys on drug use prevalence vary in conjunction with the survey methodology
(EMCDDA, 1997). The EMCDDA 2005 annual report attempted to update
figures from recently published national surveys, estimating lifetime dependence prevalence rates in the EU countries ranging from 1.1 to 11.9 percent
for alcohol, and between 1.0 and 6.9 percent for any other drug (EMCDDA,
2005). Two recent systematic reviews have provided an overview of prevalence
of current alcohol (Rehm, Room, van den Brink, & Jacobi, 2005a) and drug
(Rehm, Room, van den Brink, & Jacobi, 2005b) use disorders in EU countries and Norway. Including only studies using the *DSM–III–R* or *DSM–IV,*
or *ICD–10*, plus validated instruments to assess alcohol use disorders, prevalence rates for dependence ranged from 0.4 to 7.5 percent for males and 0.1 to
2.1 percent for females. Regarding drug dependence, including cannabis, the
12-month prevalence rates varied between 0.3 and 2.9 percent. Overall, these
figures suggest wide variations in the extent of alcohol and drug dependence
between different Western countries and support the need to explore whether
there are similar variations in the dual diagnosed population.

EUROPEAN EVIDENCE ABOUT PREVALENCE
OF DUAL DIAGNOSIS

Until fairly recently, little evidence has been available about the epidemiology of dual diagnosis in other countries and whether prevalence and patterns
resemble those found in the United States. The literature on dual diagnosis
remains very limited in many European countries (EMCDDA, 2004), but a
body of evidence of moderate size has been accumulating in the UK since the
beginning of the 1990s (Carrà & Johnson, in press) and, though at a different
pace, also in other European countries.

Apart from its importance to service planning and policy making in the European Union, this literature is of general interest in two respects. First, it allows assessment of whether American findings regarding the epidemiology of dual diagnosis generalize to other Western countries or whether, as with general population figures, there are substantial differences between the United States and European countries. Second, unlike the United States, EU mental health services are generally catchment area based, serving the whole population of a specific geographical area. This means that findings from EU studies regarding variations between countries are considerably more likely to be representative of the underlying population than those from the United States, where a variety of factors other than place of residence are likely to influence who uses which service (Mueser, Bond, Drake, & Resnick, 1998; Wang et al., 2005). It also allows exploration of the relationship between comorbidity and the characteristics of the local area and its population.

Most recent UK studies report rates between 20 and 37 percent in mental health settings (Menezes et al., 1996; Weaver et al., 2003), but appear to be especially high in inpatient (Phillips & Johnson, 2003) and crisis team (Johnson et al., 2005a, 2005b) and forensic (Wheatley, 1998) settings. In terms of geography, rates appear highest in inner-city areas (McCreadie et al., 2002). Evidence from France is less homogeneous with reported lifetime use rates from a cross-sectional survey (Launay, Petitjean, Perdereau, & Antoine, 1998) of 50 percent for alcohol and 27 percent for cannabis, and current rates for inpatients of 8 percent (Verdoux, Mury, Besancon, & Bourgeois, 1996). However, inner-city inpatients (Dervaux et al., 2003) reported rates of 43 percent for lifetime and 30 percent for current comorbid disorders. In Germany, schizophrenic inpatients consecutively admitted in the Munich (Soyka et al., 1993) area showed a lifetime prevalence for substance use disorders of 43 percent, while a representative first-episode sample reported a lifetime history of abuse due to alcohol (24%) or other drugs (14%) (Hambrecht & Hafner, 1996). In Italy, recent data based on multistage household probability samples yield a 12-month prevalence of World Mental Health Composite International Diagnostic Interview for alcohol abuse and dependence of 0.1 (0.0–0.2), and for a serious mental disorder of 1.0 (0.4–1.7) (WHO, 2004), although cross-national comparisons are hampered by inconsistencies in diagnostic methods. Nevertheless, some Italian data are available from specific clinical populations, namely, on opiate users in residential treatment (Clerici, Carta, & Cazzullo, 1989), with 30 percent having *DSM–III* Axis I and 59 percent Axis II disorders, and on patients on a methadone maintenance treatment program (Pani, Trogu, Contu, Agus, & Gessa, 1997), with 54 percent having *DSM–III–R* Axis I and 43 percent Axis II disorders. Sampling from community addictions services, it was found that dually diagnosed clients represented 36 percent of the entire caseload (Carrà, Scioli, Monti, & Marinoni, 2006). Furthermore, one multicenter survey in the Lombardy region (Clerici & Carta, 1996), using standardized diagnostic instruments on 606 opiate users in six outpatient or residential treatment programs, showed that, according to *DSM–III*, 108 (17.8%) suffered only from a substance use disorder, 160 (26.4%) had a further comorbid psychiatric diagnosis (except personality disorders), and 338 (55.8%) had a further Axis II diagnosis. A more nationally representative survey (although it was biased by a large rate of refusals for the CIDI's diagnostic assessment) (Pozzi, Bacigalupi, & Tempesta, 1997) on 11 addicts' outpatient clinics located all over Italy showed an overall lifetime psychiatric comorbidity of 32.3 percent, including psychotic (10%), mood (63%), anxiety (19%), and other mental disorders (8%).

THE CLINICAL IMPACT OF ALCOHOL AND DRUG USE ON THE COURSE OF PSYCHOSIS

Numerous studies report that dual diagnosis is strongly associated with youth and male sex (e.g., DeQuardo, Carpenter, & Tandon, 1994; Mueser et al., 1990; Zammit, Allebeck, Andreasson, Lundberg, & Lewis, 2002). More important, comparing with their nonabusing counterparts, those with a comorbid substance abuse present more difficulties from a clinical management perspective. As a matter of fact, higher rates of mental health services use are reported (Bartels et al., 1993). People with this comorbidity spend significantly more days as inpatients (Menezes et al., 1996; Schofield, Quinn, Haddock, & Barrowclough, 2001; Wright, Gournay, Glorney, & Thornicroft, 2000) and in psychiatric intensive care units (Isaac, Isaac, & Holloway, 2005); and use more Accident and Emergency Departments (A&E) out-of-hours (Todd et al., 2005), assertive outreach (Graham et al., 2001), and community (McCrone et al., 2000) psychiatric services. Such evidence about mental health services use suggests the need to explore clinical and psychosocial characteristics dual diagnosis is associated with. These issues should be the main targets of treatment in terms of clinical management. The topic of the effect of substance abuse on the course and outcome of the psychosis has been extensively studied in the last decade. Several reviews have dealt with the topic, providing useful overviews (Crawford, Crome, & Clancy, 2003; Murray, Grech, Phillips, & Johnson, 2003; Ridgely & Johnson, 2001).

Positive Psychotic Symptoms

Substance use has been found to exacerbate psychiatric symptoms in people with schizophrenia, and it has been especially associated with more prominent positive psychotic symptoms on various measures (e.g., D'Souza et al., 2005; Green, Zimmet, Strous, & Schildkraut, 1999; Lieberman, Kane, & Alvir, 1987; Lysaker, Bell, Beam-Goulet, & Milstein, 1994; Margolese et al., 2004). A recent meta-analysis (Talamo et al., 2006) reviewed eight studies providing Positive and Negative Syndrome Scale (PANSS) (Kay, Fiszbein & Opler, 1987) ratings in both comorbid and noncomorbid clients suffering from schizophrenia. Studies using different definitions of substance abuse and measuring PANSS ratings and substance misuse simultaneously (Addington & Addington, 1998; Bersani, Orlandi, Kotzalidis, & Pancheri, 2002; Lysaker et al., 1994; Margolese et al., 2004; Scheller-Gilkey, Moynes, Cooper, Kant, & Miller, 2004) or at different times (Compton, Furman, & Kaslow, 2004; Gut-Fayand et al., 2001; Sevy, Kay, Opler, & van Praag, 1990) were pooled. Moreover, scores for individual PANSS items, subscale scores for individual subjects, and many other clinical details were not analyzed, nor were other psychopathological and sociodemographic features, that might covary with dual diagnosis, controlled for. On pooling means among 725 subjects, comorbid patients had very significantly higher PANSS-positive, and lower PANSS-negative, scores (Talamo et al., 2006). Also, the recent U.S. CATIE study (Swartz et al., 2006) that recruited 1,460 subjects (37% comorbid) showed higher positive symptoms as well as lower negative symptoms scores on PANSS in comorbid subjects. The clinical relevance of these findings also derives from evidence that the main aspect of mental state associated with violence is the presence of persecutory delusions (Junginger, 1996). Positive symptoms associated with dual diagnosis may thus lead to the increased aggression and violence rates shown by comorbid clients and probably to their use of acute services and inpatient wards. Dual diagnosis patients are as a matter of fact more likely to commit violent offenses (Angermeyer, 2000), and they seem more likely to be convicted of criminal activity (Soyka, 2000) compared to those who do not abuse substances (40.1% vs. 13.7%).

Negative Psychotic Symptoms

Evidence that dual diagnosis patients experience fewer negative symptoms is relevant to the debate on the self-medication hypothesis. People with schizophrenia might attempt to cope with negative symptoms by stimulant pharmacological properties. In fact, studies testing the self-medication hypothesis in dual diagnosis schizophrenia have not been conclusive, with some studies showing that they experience fewer negative symptoms (e.g., Compton et al., 2004; Goswami, Mattoo, Basu, & Singh, 2004; Serper, Chou, Allen, Czobor, & Cancro, 1999), and others not (e.g., Addington & Addington, 1997; Gut-Fayand et al., 2001).

This topic is probably more complex than that in relation to positive symptoms for several reasons. First, negative symptoms need clear conceptualization and description (Andreasen, 1985). This concept—already implicit in Bleuler's distinction between fundamental and accessory symptoms—was developed particularly by Strauss, Carpenter, and Bartko (1974), explicitly classifying the positive and negative symptoms and differentiating the latter from social dysfunction. Indeed, Bleuler's early descriptions are closely aligned with the current nosological description of negative symptoms as restrictions in the range and intensity of emotional expression (affective flattening), in the fluency and productivity of thought and speech (alogia), and in the initiation of goal-directed behavior (avolition). The loss of the ability to feel pleasure (anhedonia) has also been identified as an associated feature, but controversy remains (American Psychiatric Association, 1994). Andreasen described the first operationalized criteria for positive and negative schizophrenia (Andreasen & Olsen, 1982).

Accordingly, the concept of positive versus negative symptoms in schizophrenia led to the development of several rating scales. Clinical investigations in dual diagnosis have used the Brief Psychiatric Rating Scale (BPRS; Overall & Gorham, 1962), the PANSS (Kay, Fiszbein & Opler, 1987), and the Scale for the Assessment of Negative Symptoms (SANS; Andreasen, 1983), along with numerous other scales. The psychometric properties of some of these scales lead to somewhat heterogeneous results in terms of factor-analytic characteristics of positive and negative symptoms. In SANS three dimensions (i.e., psychosis, disorganization, negative) best represent the scale's factor structure. The PANSS shows five factors—positive, negative, depressive, disorganization, and excitement (Lindenmayer, Bernstein-Hyman, & Grochowsky, 1994). In addition: (1) the SANS is explicitly chosen to measure negative symptoms, whereas other scales assess schizophrenia symptoms in broader terms; (2) it covers cognitive symptoms in a less confusing way than the PANSS; and (3) four out of five SANS fall within the negative factor (Buchanan & Carpenter, 1994). However, the most important difference lies in the lack of an anhedonia item in all scales but SANS because of the controversies over including it among negative features. In practice, the self-medication hypothesis assumes that anhedonia is the main target of substance abuse (Khantzian, 1997). In a recent meta-analysis of studies that used just the SANS (Potvin et al., 2006), people with schizophrenia plus a substance use disorder experienced fewer negative symptoms than abstinent ones, and the largest effect size was observed for the anhedonia subscale. Other important findings from this meta-analysis were that the reduction in negative symptoms was associated with the abuse of cocaine and cannabis, but not alcohol.

A number of other studies using the PANSS were recently pooled in a meta-analysis that showed that comorbid patients had significantly lower PANSS-negative scores (Talamo et al., 2006). Nevertheless, even these findings must be considered in the light of several reservations. The results in relation to substance of choice certainly seem consistent with the self-medication hypothesis. However, in terms of neurobiology, the negative symptoms of schizophrenia have been associated with a dopaminergic deficit in the prefrontal cortex (Finlay, 2001), but it remains unclear why people with schizophrenia should select substances that share the common property of acutely increasing dopamine release in the prefrontal cortex (Devous, Trivedi, & Rush, 2001; Volkow et al., 1996). By taking alcohol and other drugs, people with schizophrenia would be self-medicating their neurotransmitter deficits within the prefrontal system, and eventually, their negative symptoms. In addition, the fact that a difference in negative symptoms was observed only for lifetime dependent people with schizophrenia suggests that this does not depend on the *acute* effects of drugs. However, drugs seem unlikely to have long-term effects on negative symptoms. Moreover, further potential hypotheses remain to be tested. Depression, compliance with medication, or factors not yet identified are candidate variables that could explain this relationship. In terms of reverse explanation, patients with fewer negative symptoms might be simply more prone to substance abuse (Kirkpatrick et al., 1996; Kirkpatrick, Messias, & Tek, 2003). Longitudinal studies are required to resolve this issue as well as to explore whether the exposure to current or lifetime substance abuse is related to negative symptoms. More important, several different patient profiles exist among the dual diagnosis population in terms of social skills (e.g., Salyers & Mueser, 2001). Planning and organization skills are required to obtain substances of abuse and maintain substance use. Therefore, these patients would be able to continue their addiction because they have better cognitive function and fewer negative symptoms (Joyal, Hallé, Lapierre, & Hodgins, 2003).

Quality of Life and Social Functioning

In relation to quality of life (QoL) in severely mentally ill substance abusers, the evidence is still somewhat contradictory. In "pure" alcohol dependent subjects, abstinence, controlled, or minimal drinking are associated with improved QoL and psychiatric comorbidity is an important factor in determining a poor QoL (Foster, Powell, Marshall, & Peters, 1999). A few studies examining the effect of substance abuse on outpatients with established severe mental illness (Brunette, Noordsy, Xie, & Drake, 2003; Lam & Rosenheck, 2000) and with first-episode psychosis (Addington & Addington, 1997, 1998) found significantly lower quality-of-life scores in those with dual diagnosis compared with patients with schizophrenia with no past history of substance abuse, but these findings were not replicated in a similar later study (Van Mastrigt, Addington, & Addington, 2004). Furthermore, Herman (2004) found that dually diagnosed inpatients express higher levels of satisfaction with their quality of life compared to the non–substance-abusing patients with schizophrenia. However, hypotheses emerge from the literature that might explain differences in findings and which deserve further testing. In dually diagnosed people, quality of life also seems related to medication adherence, with findings from a first-episode psychosis cohort showing poorer quality of life in nonadherent patients (Coldham et al., 2002). Also, social skills and cognition and likewise psychotic negative symptoms are features that might explain part of the variance in quality of life, and they should be controlled for when the influence of dual diagnosis is assessed (Joyal et al., 2003; Salyers & Mueser, 2001). Finally, QoL has been the outcome measure in several trials for the dually diagnosed population, often (Bellack, Bennett, Gearon, Brown, & Yang, 2006; Drake et al., 1998; Schaar & Ojehagen, 2003; Shaner, Eckman, Roberts, & Fuller, 2003), but not always (Lehman, Herron, Schwartz, & Myers, 1993), showing improvements.

Medication Compliance

Approximately 40 percent of patients with schizophrenia stop prescribed medication within one year and 75 percent by two years (Owen, Fischer, Booth, & Cuffel, 1996; Perkins, 1999). As mentioned above, it seems possible that increased symptoms expressed by people with comorbid substance abuse and schizophrenia can be accounted for by medication noncompliance as well as by the direct effect of substances on psychiatric symptoms. Findings from numerous studies (Buchanan, 1992; Drake et al., 1989; Kashner et al., 1991; Kovasznay et al., 1997; Owen et al., 1996; Razali & Yahya, 1995; Swartz et al., 1998) reported lower medication compliance in comorbid patients. Furthermore, a recent history of substance abuse or dependence may more accurately predict future medication compliance than a more remote history of a substance use disorder (Olfson et al., 2000). Poor compliance with neuroleptic regimens in comorbid people seem to be associated with more negative subjective or dysphoric responses, but when comorbid substance misuse and other confounding variables are controlled for, level of insight is a significant factor in determining whether a patient is regularly compliant (Kamali et al., 2001). Thus, a better understanding of reasons for noncompliance might be helpful also in quantifying the amount of noncompliance mediated by increasing positive symptoms and that attributable just to comorbid substance abuse (Kamali et al., 2001). Indeed, when comorbid patients are adequately treated for their psychiatric illness, there is considerable amelioration in their positive psychotic symptoms (Margolese et al., 2006), even when their substance use remains unchanged.

CONCLUSIONS

Dual diagnosis rates among people with schizophrenia in mental health settings are high. Social factors may be very important in explaining dual diagnosis rates in people with schizophrenia.

People with schizophrenia and dual diagnosis—compared with those without a comorbid disorder—have greater positive and fewer negative symptoms, and report poorer adherence to medication compliance and worse global subjective satisfaction with life. However, the self-medication hypothesis needs further research. Conceptualization and measuring of negative features in dual diagnosis are further candidate areas for research.

The negative impact in dual diagnosis on the symptomatological features and on psychosocial functioning is cause of concern. The high rates of dependence (not simply abuse) on alcohol or other drugs, and their impact on different outcomes deserves attention and cautious consideration also in terms of health service research. Standard treatments provided in community mental health centers might not be appropriate in dealing with dual diagnosis. Results on dual diagnosis prevalence cannot assume to be generalizable from one country to another. Furthermore, for social and cultural reasons, people might not want to admit substance misuse, which could also be more stigmatized in some countries than others.

However, social factors such as area of residence are very important in explaining dual diagnosis rates in people with schizophrenia. Periodic, local, surveys are needed to explore the extent of the comorbidity. Mental health and addiction services should take into account results on local prevalence when planning their treatment programs. Staffing, training, and configuration of health services are all areas to be designed and implemented according to relevant evidence. Better identification and treatment of comorbid dependence in adequate settings should be among treatment priorities. Treatment needs of the comorbid population need to be met in order to guarantee a subjective quality of life at least as high as that of their nondependent counterparts. Further research is also needed to explore whether variations in dual diagnosis rates between centers are the result of different distributions of individual social characteristics (e.g., poverty, unemployment, single marital status, etc.) or of area-level social characteristics (e.g., drug availability, stigma experienced by the mentally ill, benefits regime, etc.).

REFERENCES

Addington, J., & Addington, D. (1997). Substance abuse and cognitive functioning in schizophrenia. *Journal of Psychiatry and Neuroscience, 22,* 99–104.

Addington, J., & Addington, D. (1998). Effects of substance misuse in early psychosis. *British Journal of Psychiatry Supplement, 172*(33), 134–136.

Addington, J., & Duchak, V. (1997). Reasons for substance use in schizophrenia. *Acta Psychiatrica Scandinavica, 96,* 329–333.

Allardyce, J., Boydell, J., Van Os, J., Morrison, G., Castle, D., Murray, R. M., et al. (2001). Comparison of the incidence of schizophrenia in rural Dumfries and Galloway and urban Camberwell. *British Journal of Psychiatry, 179,* 335–339.

American Psychiatric Association. (1994). *Diagnostic and statistical manual of mental disorders* (4th ed.). Washington, DC: Author.

Andreasen, N. C. (1983). *The Scale for the Assessment of Negative Symptoms.* Iowa City: University of Iowa.

Andreasen, N. C. (1985). Positive vs. negative schizophrenia: A critical evaluation. *Schizophrenia Bulletin, 11,* 380–389.

Andreasen, N. C., & Olsen, S. (1982). Negative vs. positive schizophrenia: Definition and validation. *Archives of General Psychiatry, 39,* 789–794.

Angermeyer, M. C. (2000). Schizophrenia and violence. *Acta Psychiatrica Scandinavica, Supplement, 407*(102), 63–67.

Baigent, M., Holme, G., & Hafner, R. J. (1995). Self reports of the interaction between substance abuse and schizophrenia. *Australian and New Zealand Journal of Psychiatry, 29,* 69–74.

Banerjee, S., Clancy, C., & Crome, I. (2002). *Coexisting problems of mental disorder and substance misuse (dual diagnosis): An information manual.* London: Royal College of Psychiatrists Research Unit.

Barbee, J. G., Clark, P. D., Crapanzano, M. S., Heintz, G. C., & Kehoe, C. E. (1989). Alcohol and substance abuse among schizophrenic patients presenting to an emergency psychiatric service. *Journal of Nervous and Mental Disease, 177,* 400–407.

Bartels, S. J., Teague, G. B., Drake, R. E., Clark, R. E., Bush, P. W., & Noordsy, D. L. (1993). Substance abuse in schizophrenia: Service utilisation and costs. *Journal of Nervous and Mental Disease, 181,* 227–232.

Bellack, A. S., Bennett, M. E., Gearon, J. S., Brown, C. H., & Yang, Y. (2006). A randomized clinical trial of a new behavioral treatment for drug abuse in people with severe and persistent mental illness. *Archives of General Psychiatry, 63,* 426–432.

Berkson, J. (1946). Limitations of the application of the fourfold table analysis to hospital data. *Biometrics, 2,* 47–53.

Bersani, G., Orlandi, V., Kotzalidis, G. D., & Pancheri, P. (2002). Cannabis and schizophrenia: Impact on onset, course, psychopathology and outcomes. *European Archives of Psychiatry and Clinical Neuroscience, 252,* 86–92.

Bhanji, N. H., Chouinard, G., & Margolese, H. C. (2004). A review of compliance, depot intramuscular antipsychotics and the new long-acting injectable atypical antipsychotic risperidone in schizophrenia. *European Neuropsychopharmacology, 14,* 87–92.

Brady, K., Anton, R., Ballenger, J. C., Lydiard, R. B., Adinoff, B., & Selander, J. (1990). Cocaine abuse among schizophrenic patients. *American Journal of Psychiatry, 147,* 1164–1167.

Brady, K., Casto, S., Lydiard, R. B., Malcom, R., & Arana, G. (1991). Substance abuse in an inpatient psychiatric sample. *American Journal of Drug and Alcohol Abuse, 17,* 389–397.

Brunette, M. F., Mueser, K. T., Xie, H., & Drake, R. E. (1997). Relationships between symptoms of schizophrenia and substance abuse. *Journal of Nervous and Mental Disease, 185,* 13–20.

Brunette, M. F., Noordsy, D. L., Xie, H., & Drake, R. E. (2003). Benzodiazepine use and abuse among patients with severe mental illness and co-occurring substance use disorders. *Psychiatric Services, 54,* 1395–1401.

Buchanan, A. (1992). A two-year prospective study of treatment compliance inpatients with schizophrenia. *Psychological Medicine, 22,* 787–797.

Buchanan, R. W., & Carpenter, Jr., W. T. (1994). Domains of psychopathology and approach to the reduction of heterogeneity in schizophrenia. *Journal of Nervous and Mental Disease, 182,* 193–204.

Carrà, G., & Clerici, M. (2006). Dual diagnosis-policy and practice in Italy. *American Journal on Addictions, 15,* 125–130.

Carrà, G., & Johnson, S. (in press). Variations in rates of comorbid substance use in psychosis between mental health settings and geographical areas in the UK. A systematic review. *Social Psychiatry and Psychiatric Epidemiology,* DOI 10.1007/s00127-008-0458-2.

Carrà, G., Scioli, R., Monti, M. C., & Marinoni, A. (2006). Severity profiles of substance-abusing patients in Italian community addiction facilities: Influence of psychiatric concurrent disorders. *European Addiction Research, 12,* 96–101.

Clerici, M., & Carta, I. (1996). Personality disorders among psychoactive substance users: Diagnostic and psychodynamic issues. *European Addiction Research, 2,* 147–155.

Clerici, M., Carta, I., & Cazzullo, C. L. (1989). Substance abuse and psychopathology: A diagnostic screening of Italian narcotic addicts. *Social Psychiatry and Psychiatric Epidemiology, 24,* 219–226.

Coldham, E. L., Addington, J., & Addington D. (2002), Medication adherence of individuals with a first episode of psychosis. *Acta Psychiatrica Scandinavica, 106,* 286–290.

Compton, M. T., Furman, A. C., & Kaslow, N. J. (2004). Lower negative symptom scores among cannabis-dependent patients with schizophrenia-spectrum disorders: Preliminary evidence from an African American first-episode sample. *Schizophrenia Research, 71,* 61–64.

Crawford, V., Crome, I. B., & Clancy, C. (2003). Co-existing problems of mental health and substance misuse (dual diagnosis): A literature review. *Drugs: Education, Prevention and Policy, 10,* 1–74.

Cuffel, B. J., & Chase, P. (1994). Remission and relapse of substance use disorders in schizophrenia: Results from a one-year prospective study. *Journal of Nervous and Mental Disease, 182,* 342–348.

Cuffel, B. J., Shumway, M., Chouljian, T. L., & MacDonald, T. (1994). A longitudinal study of substance use and community violence in schizophrenia. *Journal of Nervous and Mental Disease, 182,* 704–708.

DeQuardo, J. R., Carpenter, C. F., & Tandon, R. (1994). Patterns of substance abuse in schizophrenia: Nature and significance. *Journal of Psychiatric Research, 28,* 267–275.

Dervaux, A., Bayle, F. J., Laqueille, X., Bourdel, M. C., Le Borgne, M. H., Olié, J. P., et al. (2001). Is substance abuse in schizophrenia related to impulsivity, sensation seeking or anhedonia? *American Journal of Psychiatry, 158,* 492–494.

Dervaux, A., Laqueille, X., Bourdel, M. C., Leborgne, M. H., Olié, J. P., Lôo, H., et al. (2003). Cannabis and schizophrenia: Demographic and clinical correlates. *Encephale, 29,* 11–17.

Devous, M. D., Trivedi, M. H., & Rush, A. J. (2001). Regional cerebral blood flow response to oral amphetamine challenge in healthy volunteers. *Journal of Nuclear Medicine, 156,* 19–26.

Dixon, L., Haas, G., Weiden, P. J., Sweeney, J., & Frances, A. J. (1991). Drug abuse in schizophrenic patients: Clinical correlates and reasons for use. *American Journal of Psychiatry, 148,* 224–230.

Drake, R. E., Alterman, A. I., & Rosenberg, S. R. (1993). Detection of substance use disorders in severely mentally ill patients. *Community Mental Health Journal, 29,* 175–192.

Drake, R. E., McHugo, G. J., Clark, R. E., Teague, G. B., Xie, H., Miles, K., et al. (1998). Assertive community treatment for patients with co-occurring severe mental illness and substance use disorder: A clinical trial. *American Journal of Orthopsychiatry, 68,* 201–215.

Drake, R. E., Osher, F. C., & Wallach, M. A. (1989). Alcohol use and abuse in schizophrenia: A prospective community study. *Journal of Nervous and Mental Disease, 177,* 408–414.

D'Souza, D. C., Abi-Saab, W. M., Madonick, S., Forselius-Bielen, K., Doersch, A., Braley, G., et al. (2005). Delta-9-tetrahydrocannabinol effects in schizophrenia: Implications for cognition, psychosis and addiction. *Biological Psychiatry, 57,* 594–608.

El-Guebaly, N., & Hodgins, D. C. (1992). Schizophrenia and substance abuse: Prevalence issues. *Canadian Journal of Psychiatry, 37,* 704–710.

European Monitoring Centre for Drugs and Drug Addiction. (1997). *Improving the comparability of general population surveys on drug use in the European Union.* Luxembourg: Office for Official Publications of the European Communities.

European Monitoring Centre for Drugs and Drug Addiction. (2004). Comorbidity: Drug use and mental disorders. *Drugs in Focus, 14,* 1–4.

European Monitoring Centre for Drugs and Drug Addiction. (2005). *The state of the drugs problem in the European Union and Norway.* Luxembourg: Office for Official Publications of the European Communities.

Fergusson, D. M., Poulton, R., Smith, P. F., & Boden, J. M. (2006). Cannabis and psychosis. *British Medical Journal, 332,* 172–175.

Finlay, J. M. (2001). Mesoprefontal dopamine neurons and schizophrenia: The role of development abnormalities. *Schizophrenia Bulletin, 27,* 431–442.

Foster, J. H., Powell, J. E., Marshall, E. J., & Peters, T. J. (1999). Quality of life in alcohol-dependent subjects—a review. *Quality of Life Research, 8,* 255–261.

Freeman, H. (1994). Schizophrenia and city residence. *British Journal of Psychiatry Supplement, 164*(23), 39–50.

Furr-Holden, C. D., & Anthony, J. C. (2003). Epidemiologic differences in drug dependence: A US-UK cross-national comparison. *Social Psychiatry and Psychiatric Epidemiology, 38,* 165–172.

Goldfinger, S. M., Schutt, R. K., Seidmanm, L. J., Turnerm, W. M., Penk, W. E., & Tolomiczenko, G. S. (1996). Self-report and observer measures of substance abuse among homeless mentally ill persons in the cross-section and over time. *Journal of Nervous and Mental Disease, 184,* 667–672.

Goswami, S., Mattoo, S. K., Basu, D., & Singh, G. (2004). Substance abusing schizophrenics: Do they self-medicate? *American Journal on Addictions, 13,* 139–150.

Gouzoulis-Mayfrank, E. (2004). Doppeldiagnose Psychose und Sucht. Von den Grundlagen zur Praxis. *Nervenarzt, 75,* 642–650.

Graham, H. L., Maslin, J., Copello, A., Birchwood, M., Mueser, K., McGovern, D., et al. (2001). Drug and alcohol problems amongst individuals with severe mental health problems in an inner city area of the UK. *Social Psychiatry and Psychiatric Epidemiology, 36,* 448–455.

Green, A. I., Zimmet, S. V., Strous, R. D., & Schildkraut, J. J. (1999). Clozapine for comorbid substance use disorder and schizophrenia: Do patients with schizophrenia have a reward-deficiency syndrome that can be ameliorated by clozapine? *Harvard Review of Psychiatry, 6,* 287–296.

Gut-Fayand, A., Dervaux, A., Olié, J. P., Lôo, H., Poirier, M. F., & Krebs, M. O. (2001). Substance abuse and suicidality in schizophrenia: A common risk factor linked to impulsivity. *Psychiatry Research, 102,* 65–72.

Hambrecht, M., & Hafner, H. (1996). Substance abuse and the onset of schizophrenia. *Biological Psychiatry, 40,* 1155–1163.

Hamera, E., Schneider, J. K., & Deviney, S. (1995). Alcohol, cannabis, nicotine, and caffeine use and symptom distress in schizophrenia. *Journal of Nervous and Mental Disease, 183,* 559–565.

Havassy, B. E., & Arns, P. G. (1998). Relationship of cocaine and other substance dependence to well-being of high-risk psychiatric patients. *Psychiatric Services, 49,* 935–940.

Heath, A. C., Whitfield, J. B., Madden, P. A., Bucholz, K. K., Dinwiddie, S. H., Slutske, W. S., et al. (2001). Towards a molecular epidemiology of alcohol dependence: Analysing the interplay of genetic and environmental risk factors. *British Journal of Psychiatry Supplement, 40*, 33–40.

Herman, M. (2004). Neurocognitive functioning and quality of life among dually diagnosed and non-substance abusing schizophrenia inpatients. *International Journal of Mental Health Nursing, 13*, 282–291.

Hunt, G. E., Bergen, J., & Bashir, M. (2002). Medication compliance and comorbid substance abuse in schizophrenia: Impact on community survival 4 years after a relapse. *Schizophrenia Research, 54*, 253–264.

Isaac, M., Isaac, M., & Holloway, F. (2005). Is cannabis an anti-antipsychotic? The experience in psychiatric intensive care. *Human Psychopharmacology, 20*, 207–210.

Jeffery, D. P., Ley, A., McLaren, S., & Siegfried, N. (2000). Psychosocial treatment programmes for people with both severe mental illness and substance misuse. *The Cochrane Database of Systematic Reviews, 2*. Art. No.: CD001088. DOI: 10.1002/14651858.CD001088.

Jenkins, R., Bebbington, P., Brugha, T., Farrell, M., Gill, B., Lewis, G., et al. (1997). The National Psychiatric Morbidity Surveys of Great Britain—Strategy and methods. *Psychological Medicine, 27*, 765–774.

Johnson, S. (1997). Dual diagnosis of severe mental illness and substance misuse: A case for specialist services? *British Journal of Psychiatry, 171*, 205–208.

Johnson, S., Nolan, F., Hoult, J., White, I. R., Bebbington, P., Sandor, A., et al. (2005a). Outcomes of crises before and after introduction of a crisis resolution team. *British Journal of Psychiatry, 187*, 68–75.

Johnson, S., Nolan, F., Pilling, S., Sandor, A., Hoult, J., McKenzie, N., et al. (2005b). Randomised controlled trial of acute mental health care by a crisis resolution team: The North Islington crisis study. *BMJ, 331*, 599–602.

Joyal, C. C., Hallé, P., Lapierre, D., & Hodgins, S. (2003). Drug abuse and/or dependence and better neuropsychological performance in patients with schizophrenia. *Schizophrenia Research, 63*, 297–299.

Junginger, J. (1996). Psychosis and violence: The case for a content analysis of psychotic experience. *Schizophrenia Bulletin, 22*, 91–103.

Kamali, M., Kelly, L., Gervin, M., Browne, S., Larkin, C., & O'Callaghan, E. (2001). Insight and comorbid substance misuse and medication compliance among patients with schizophrenia. *Psychiatric Services, 52*, 161–163.

Kashner, T. M., Rader, L. E., Rodell, D. E., Beck, C. M., Rodell, L. R., & Muller, K. (1991). Family characteristics, substance abuse, and hospitalization patterns of patients with schizophrenia. *Hospital and Community Psychiatry, 42*, 195–197.

Kay, S. R., Fiszbein, A., & Opler, L. A. (1987). The Positive and Negative Syndromes Scale (PANSS) for schizophrenia. *Schizophrenia Bulletin, 13*, 261–276.

Kendler, K. S. (1985). A twin study of individuals with both schizophrenia and alcoholism. *British Journal of Psychiatry, 147*, 48–53.

Kendler, K. S., Gallagher, T. J., Abelson, J. M., & Kessler, R. C. (1996). Lifetime prevalence, demographic risk factors, and diagnostic validity of nonaffective psychosis as assessed in a US community sample. *Archives of General Psychiatry, 53,* 1022–1031.

Kendler, K. S., & Gardner, C. O. (1997). The risk for psychiatric disorders in relatives of schizophrenic and control probands: A comparison of three independent studies. *Psychological Medicine, 27,* 411–419.

Kendler, K. S., Jacobson, K. C., Prescott, C. A., & Neale, M. C. (2003). Specificity of genetic and environmental risk factors for use and abuse/dependence of cannabis, cocaine, hallucinogens, sedatives, stimulants, and opiates in male twins. *American Journal of Psychiatry, 160,* 687–695.

Kessler, R. C., Nelson, C. B., McGonagle, K. A., Edlund, M. J., Frank, R. G., & Leaf, P. J. (1996). The epidemiology of co-occurring addictive and mental disorders: Implications for prevention and service utilization. *American Journal of Orthopsychiatry, 66,* 17–31.

Khantzian, E. J. (1985). The self-medication hypothesis of addictive disorders: Focus on heroin and cocaine dependence. *American Journal of Psychiatry, 142,* 1259–1264.

Khantzian, E. J. (1997). The self-medication hypothesis of substance use disorders: A reconsideration and recent applications. *Harvard Review of Psychiatry, 4,* 231–244.

Kirkpatrick, B., Amador, X. F., Flaum, M., Yale, S. A., Gorman, J. M., Carpenter, W. T. Jr., et al. (1996). The deficit syndrome in the *DSM–IV* Field Trial: I. Alcohol and other drug abuse. *Schizophrenia Research, 20,* 69–77.

Kirkpatrick, B., Messias, E. M., & Tek, C. (2003). Substance abuse and the heterogeneity of schizophrenia: A population-based study. *Schizophrenia Research, 62,* 293–294.

Kovasznay, B., Fleischer, J., Tanenberg-Karant, M., Jandorf, L., Miller, A. D., & Bromet, E. (1997). Substance use disorder and the early course of illness in schizophrenia and affective psychosis. *Schizophrenia Bulletin, 23,* 195–201.

Lam, J. A., & Rosenheck, R. A. (2000). Correlates of improvements in quality of life among homeless persons with serious mental illness. *Psychiatric Services, 51,* 116–118.

Lambert, M. T., Griffith, J. M., & Hendrickse, W. (1996). Characteristics of patients with substance abuse diagnoses on a general psychiatry unit in a VA Medical Center. *Psychiatric Services, 47,* 1104–1107.

Launay, C., Petitjean, F., Perdereau, F., & Antoine, D. (1998). Conduites toxicomaniaques chez les malades mentaux: Une enquête en Ile-de-France. *Annales Médico-psychologiques, 156,* 482–485.

Lehman, A. F., Herron, J. D., Schwartz, R. P., & Myers, C. P. (1993). Rehabilitation for adults with severe mental illness and substance use disorders. *Journal of Nervous and Mental Disease, 181,* 86–90.

Lieberman, J. A., Kane, J. M., & Alvir, J. (1987). Provocative tests with psychostimulant drugs in schizophrenia. *Psychopharmacology, 91,* 415–433.

Lindenmayer, J. P., Bernstein-Hyman, R., & Grochowsky, S. (1994). Five factor model of schizophrenia. *Journal of Nervous and Mental Diseases, 182*, 631–638.

Lysaker, P., Bell, M., Beam-Goulet, J., & Milstein, R. (1994). Relationship of positive and negative symptoms to cocaine abuse in schizophrenia. *Journal of Nervous and Mental Disease, 182*, 109–112.

Margolese, H. C., Malchy, L., Negrete, J. C., Tempier, R., & Gill, K. (2004). Drug and alcohol use among patients with schizophrenia and related psychoses: Levels and consequences. *Schizophrenia Research, 67*, 157–166.

Margolese, H. C., Negrete, J., Tempier, R., & Gill, K. (2006). A 12-month prospective follow-up study of patients with schizophrenia-spectrum disorders and substance abuse: Changes in psychiatric symptoms and substance use. *Schizophrenia Research, 83*, 65–75.

McCreadie, R. G., & Scottish Comorbidity Study Group. (2002). Use of drugs, alcohol and tobacco by people with schizophrenia: Case-control study. *British Journal of Psychiatry, 181*, 321–325.

McCrone, P., Menezes, P. R., Johnson, S., Scott, H., Thornicroft, G., Marshall, J., et al. (2000). Service use and costs of people with dual diagnosis in south London. *Acta Psychiatrica Scandinavica, 101*, 464–472.

Menezes, P. R., Johnson, S., Thornicroft, G., Marshall, J., Prosser, D., Bebbington, P., et al. (1996). Drug and alcohol problems among individuals with severe mental illness in south London. *British Journal of Psychiatry, 168*, 612–619.

Meyer, R. E. (1986). How to understand the relationship between psychopathology and addictive disorders: Another example of the chicken and the egg. In R. E. Meyer (Ed.), *Psychopathology and addictive disorders* (pp. 3–16). New York: Guilford Press.

Mowbray, C. T., Ribisl, K. M., Solomon, M., Luke, D. A., & Kewson, T. P. (1997). Characteristics of dual diagnosis patients admitted to an urban, public psychiatric hospital: An examination of individual, social, and community domains. *American Journal of Drug and Alcohol Abuse, 23*, 309–326.

Mueser, K. T., Bond, G. R., Drake, R. E., & Resnick, S. G. (1998). Models of community care for severe mental illness: A review of research on case management. *Schizophrenia Bulletin, 24*, 37–74.

Mueser, K. T., Drake, R. E., & Wallach, M. A. (1998). Dual diagnosis: A review of etiological theories. *Addictive Behaviors, 23*, 717–734.

Mueser, K. T., Essock, S. M., Drake, R. E., Wolfe, R. S., & Frisman, L. (2001). Rural and urban differences in patients with a dual diagnosis. *Schizophrenia Research, 48*, 93–107.

Mueser, K. T., Yarnold, P. R., & Bellack, A. S. (1992). Diagnostic and demographic correlates of substance abuse in schizophrenia and major affective disorder. *Acta Psychiatrica Scandinavica, 85*, 48–55.

Mueser, K. T., Yarnold, P. R., Levinson, D. F., Singh, H., Bellack, A. S., Kee, K., et al. (1990). Prevalence of substance abuse in schizophrenia: Demographic and clinical correlates. *Schizophrenia Bulletin, 16*, 31–35.

Murray, R. M., Grech, A., Phillips, P., & Johnson, S. (2003). What is the relationship between substance abuse and schizophrenia? In R. M. Murray, M. Cannon, P. Jones, et al. (Eds.), *The epidemiology of schizophrenia* (pp. 317–342). Cambridge: Cambridge University Press.

Negrete, J. C., Knapp, W. P., Douglas, D. E., & Smith, W. B. (1986). Cannabis affects the severity of schizophrenic symptoms: Results of a clinical survey. *Psychological Medicine, 16,* 515–520.

Olfson, M., Mechanic, D., Hansell, S., Boyer, C. A., Walkup, J., & Weiden, P. J. (2000). Predicting medication noncompliance after hospital discharge among patients with schizophrenia. *Psychiatric Services, 51,* 216–222.

Overall, J. E., & Gorham, D. R. (1962). Brief Psychiatric Rating Scale. *Psychology Reports, 10,* 799–812.

Owen, R. R., Fischer, E. P., Booth, B. M., & Cuffel, B. J. (1996). Medication non-compliance and substance abuse among persons with schizophrenia. *Psychiatric Services, 47,* 853–858.

Pani, P. P., Trogu, E., Contu, P., Agus, A., & Gessa, G. L. (1997). Psychiatric severity and treatment response in a comprehensive methadone maintenance treatment program. *Drug and Alcohol Dependence, 48,* 119–126.

Perkins, D. O. (1999). Adherence to antipsychotic medications. *Journal of Clinical Psychiatry Supplement, 60,* 25–30.

Phillips, P., & Johnson, S. (2001). How does drug and alcohol misuse develop among people with psychotic illness? A literature review. *Social Psychiatry and Psychiatric Epidemiology, 36,* 269–276.

Phillips, P., & Johnson, S. (2003). Drug and alcohol misuse among inpatients with psychotic illnesses in three inner-London psychiatric units. *Psychiatric Bulletin, 27,* 217–220.

Potvin, S., Sepehry, A. A., & Stip, E. (2006). A meta-analysis of negative symptoms in dual diagnosis schizophrenia. *Psychological Medicine, 36,* 431–440.

Pozzi, G., Bacigalupi, M., & Tempesta, E. (1997). Comorbidity of drug dependence and other mental disorders: A two-phase study of prevalence at outpatient treatment centres in Italy. *Drug and Alcohol Dependence, 46,* 69–77.

Prescott, C. A., & Kendler, K. S. (1999). Genetic and environmental contributions to alcohol abuse and dependence in a population-based sample of male twins. *American Journal of Psychiatry, 156,* 34–40.

Pulver, A. E., Wolyniec, P. S., Wagner, M. G., Moorman, C. C., & McGrath, J. A. (1989). An epidemiologic investigation of alcohol-dependent schizophrenics. *Acta Psychiatrica Scandinavica, 79,* 603–612.

RachBeisel, J., Scott, J., & Dixon, L. (1999). Co-occurring severe mental illness and substance use disorders: A review of recent research. *Psychiatric Services, 50,* 1427–1434.

Razali, M. S., & Yahya, H. (1995). Compliance with treatment in schizophrenia: A drug intervention program in a developing country. *Acta Psychiatrica Scandinavica, 91,* 331–335.

Regier, D. A., Farmer, M. E., & Rae, D. S. (1990). Co-morbidity of mental disorders with alcohol and other drug abuse: Results from the Epidemiological Catchment Area (ECA) study. *Journal of the American Medical Association, 264*, 2511–2518.

Rehm, J., Room, R., van den Brink, W., & Jacobi, F. (2005a). Alcohol use disorders in EU countries and Norway: An overview of the epidemiology. *European Neuropsychopharmacology, 15*, 377–388.

Rehm, J., Room, R., van den Brink, W., & Jacobi, F. (2005b). Problematic drug use and drug use disorders in EU countries and Norway: An overview of the epidemiology. *European Neuropsychopharmacology, 15*, 389–397.

Ridgely, M. S., & Johnson, S. (2001). Drug and alcohol services. In G. Szmukler & G. Thornicroft (Eds.), *Textbook of community psychiatry* (pp. 347–367). Oxford: Oxford University Press.

Salyers, M. P., & Mueser, K. T. (2001). Social functioning, psychopathology, and medication side effects in relation to substance use and abuse in schizophrenia. *Schizophrenia Research, 48*, 109–123.

Schaar, I., & Ojehagen, A. (2003). Predictors of improvement in quality of life of severely mentally ill substance abusers during 18 months of co-operation between psychiatric and social services. *Social Psychiatry and Psychiatric Epidemiology, 38*, 83–87.

Scheller-Gilkey, G., Moynes, K., Cooper, I., Kant, C., & Miller, A. H. (2004). Early life stress and PTSD symptoms in patients with comorbid schizophrenia and substance abuse. *Schizophrenia Research, 69*, 167–174.

Schneier, F. R., & Siris, S. G. (1987). A review of psychoactive substance use and abuse in schizophrenia: Patterns of drug choice. *Journal of Nervous and Mental Disease, 175*, 641–652.

Schofield, N., Quinn, J., Haddock, G., & Barrowclough, C. (2001). Schizophrenia and substance misuse problems: A comparison between patients with and without significant carer contact. *Social Psychiatry and Psychiatric Epidemiology, 36*, 523–528.

Semple, D. M., McIntosh, A. M., & Lawrie, S. M. (2005). Cannabis as a risk factor for psychosis: Systematic review. *Journal of Psychopharmacology, 19*, 187–194.

Serper, M. R., Chou, J. C., Allen, M. H., Czobor, P., & Cancro, R. (1999). Symptomatic overlap of cocaine intoxication and acute schizophrenia at emergency presentation. *Schizophrenia Bulletin, 25*, 387–394.

Sevy, S., Kay, S. R., Opler, L. A., & van Praag, H. M. (1990). Significance of cocaine history in schizophrenia. *Journal of Nervous and Mental Disease, 178*, 642–648.

Shaner, A., Eckman, T., Roberts, L. J., & Fuller, T. (2003). Feasibility of a skills training approach to reduce substance dependence among individuals with schizophrenia. *Psychiatric Services, 54*, 1287–1289.

Soyka, M. (2000). Substance misuse, psychiatric disorder and violent and disturbed behaviour. *British Journal of Psychiatry, 176*, 345–350.

Soyka, M., Albus, M., Kathmann, N., Finelli A., Hofstetter S., Holzbach, R., et al. (1993). Prevalence of alcohol and drug abuse in schizophrenic inpatients. *European Archives of Psychiatry and Clinical Neuroscience, 242*, 362–372.

Strauss, J. S., Carpenter, W. T., & Bartko, J. (1974). The diagnosis and understanding of schizophrenia. III: Speculations on the processes that underlie schizophrenic symptoms and signs. *Schizophrenia Bulletin, 1*, 61–69.

Sullivan, P. F., Kendler, K. S., & Neale, M. C. (2003). Schizophrenia as a complex trait: Evidence from a meta-analysis of twin studies. *Archives of General Psychiatry, 60*, 1187–1192.

Swartz, M. S., Swanson, J. W., Hiday, V. A., Borum, R., Wagner, H. R., & Burns, B. J. (1998). Violence and severe mental illness: The effects of substance abuse and non-adherence to medication. *American Journal of Psychiatry, 155*, 226–231.

Swartz, M. S., Wagner, H. R., Swanson, J. W., Stroup, T. S., McEvoy, J. P., Canive, J. M., et al. (2006). Substance use in persons with schizophrenia: Baseline prevalence and correlates from the NIMH CATIE study. *Journal of Nervous and Mental Disease, 194*, 164–172.

Talamo, A., Centorrino, F., Tondo, L., Dimitri, A., Hennen, J., & Baldessarini, R. J. (2006). Comorbid substance-use in schizophrenia: Relation to positive and negative symptoms. *Schizophrenia Research, 86*, 251–255.

Taub, N. A., Morgan, Z., Brugha, T. S., Lambert, P. C., Bebbington, P. E., Jenkins, R., et al. (2005). Recalibration methods to enhance information on prevalence rates from large mental health surveys. *International Journal of Methods in Psychiatric Research, 14*, 3–13.

Todd, J., Green, G., Pevalin, D. J, Harrison, M., Ikuesan, B. A., Self, C., et al. (2005). Service uptake in a sample of substance misuse and community mental health service clients: A case control study. *Journal of Mental Health, 14*, 95–107.

Tsuang, M. T., Lyons, M. J., Eisen, S. A., Goldberg, J., True, W., Lin, N., et al. (1996). Genetic influences on *DSM–III–R* drug abuse and dependence: A study of 3,372 twin pairs. *American Journal of Medical Genetics, 67*, 473–477.

Van Mastrigt, S., Addington, J., & Addington, D. (2004). Substance misuse at presentation to an early psychosis program. *Social Psychiatry and Psychiatric Epidemiology, 39*, 69–72.

Van Os, J. (2004). Does the urban environment cause psychosis? *British Journal of Psychiatry, 184*, 287–288.

Verdoux, H., Mury, M., Besancon, G., & Bourgeois, M. (1996). Comparative study of substance dependence comorbidity in bipolar, schizophrenic and schizoaffective disorders. *Encephale, 22*, 95–101.

Volkow, N. D., Gillespie, H., Mullani, N., Tancredi, L., Grant, C., Valentine, A., et al. (1996). Brain glucose metabolism in chronic marijuana users at baseline and during marijuana intoxication. *Psychiatry Research, 67*, 29–38.

Wang, P. S., Lane, M., Olfson, M., Pincus, H. A., Wells, K. B., & Kessler, R. C. (2005). Twelve-month use of mental health services in the United States: Results from the National Comorbidity Survey Replication. *Archives of General Psychiatry, 62*, 629–640.

Weaver, T., Madden, P., Charles, V., Stimson, G., Renton, A., Tyrer, P., et al. (1999). Severe mental illness and substance misuse comorbidity: Research is needed to inform policy and service development. *BMJ, 318*, 37–38.

Weaver, T., Madden, P., Charles, V., Stimson, G., Renton, A., Tyrer, P., et al. (2003). Comorbidity of substance misuse and mental illness in community mental health and substance misuse services. *British Journal of Psychiatry, 183*, 304–313.

Weisner, C., & Schmidt, L. (1993). Alcohol and drug problems among diverse health and social service populations. *American Journal of Public Health, 83*, 824–829.

Wheatley, M. (1998). The prevalence and relevance of substance misuse in detained schizophrenic patients. *Journal of Forensic Psychiatry, 9*, 114–129.

WHO World Mental Health Survey Consortium. (2004). Prevalence, severity, and unmet need for treatment of mental disorders in the World Health Organization World Mental Health Surveys. *Journal of the American Medical Association, 291*, 2581–2590.

Wright, S., Gournay, K., Glorney, E., & Thornicroft, G. (2000). Dual diagnosis in the suburbs: Prevalence, need, and in-patient service use. *Social Psychiatry and Psychiatric Epidemiology, 35*, 297–304.

Zammit, S., Allebeck, P., Andreasson, S., Lundberg, I., & Lewis, G. (2002). Self reported cannabis use as a risk factor for schizophrenia in Swedish conscripts of 1969: Historical cohort study. *BMJ, 325*, 1199–1204.

Zubin, J., & Spring, B. (1977). Vulnerability—a new view of schizophrenia. *Journal of Abnormal Psychology, 86*, 103–126.

Chapter 18

Neural Basis for Methamphetamine Addiction—Rethinking the Definition of Dependence

Mary F. Holley, MD

Addiction to methamphetamine is a serious disabling condition that affects individuals, families, and communities as end-stage addicts destroy their lives, abuse their children, and lose their jobs. The availability of effective treatment is limited by the economic resources available to treat what many consider an incurable moral failure. Taxpayers and donors are often unwilling to devote large amounts of money to rehabilitate people who voluntarily ingest drugs of abuse. The need for prolonged periods of rehabilitation and extended supervision is even greater for methamphetamine addiction than for addiction to other drugs of abuse. A better understanding of the biologic nature of addiction is needed on all fronts, by addicts, their families, health care policy makers and payers, the legal and judicial fields, and the community at large.

Because of the lack of available treatment, an overwhelming burden is being placed on our corrections system by the sheer volume of inmates sentenced primarily for drug offenses. Corrections facilities are designed to punish and deter antisocial behavior in rational persons. They are now being asked to intervene in the disease of addiction although they are neither funded nor staffed to treat addiction. Addicts do not usually make rational choices but rather are driven by a brain disease that must be treated to prevent the recidivism that plagues our current system.

Even in the field of psychiatry, there is tremendous reluctance to admit that methamphetamine is a neurotoxin and that brain tissue is damaged by it. This in spite of the persuasive animal and human data confirming the serious neurotoxicity, particularly to the frontal lobes, related to methamphetamine use. And this reluctance is seen in card-carrying Darwinists. Can methamphetamine be a neurotoxin in all known animal models and yet fall harmless to the ground when confronted with the mystical, magical human brain? There is nothing special about human neurons that render them impervious to the oxygen free radical compounds released by methamphetamine.

If we wish to convince the general public and health care policy makers that addiction is a brain disease and not merely a moral failure, we must define it in objective terms, not just in behavioral terms. Our current definition of dependence has as much to do with the tolerance of the patient's employer for poor performance as it does the patient's behavior. We should instead define it in terms of neurochemical, behavioral, and personality changes, which appear early in the clinical course, long before "dependence" is diagnosed under the current paradigm.

NEUROTRANSMISSION

Changes in the neurotransmitter levels of the brain underlie many of the personality changes and mental illnesses associated with methamphetamine. The principal chemicals affected by the use of meth are the monoamines dopamine, serotonin, norepinephrine, and cortisol, a stress hormone.

Methamphetamine stimulates a massive release of monoamines, especially norepinephrine, a 2,000 percent increase (Rothman, Bauman, Dersch, Romero, & Rice, 2001), dopamine, a 500–1,000 percent increase (Gough, Imam, Blough, Slikker, & Ali, 2002; Izawa, Yamanashi, Asakura, Misu, & Goshima, 2006), and serotonin, a 300–500 percent increase (Ago, Nakamura, Baba, & Matsuda, 2008) by both presynaptic and postsynaptic mechanisms. Meth causes the accelerated release of vesicles containing these neurotransmitters, and reverses the presynaptic transporter molecule that normally reabsorbs neurotransmitter once released (Zaczek, Culp, & De Souza, 1991). Methamphetamine changes the conformation of the transporter molecule causing the "vacuum cleaner" to go into reverse and spew neurotransmitter out instead of reabsorbing it (Yudko, Hall, & McPherson, 2003, p. 39). This is in contrast to cocaine, which only blocks the reabsorption of neurotransmitter.

Postsynaptically, meth inhibits the enzyme monoamine oxidase (MAO), which is responsible for metabolizing these neurotransmitters once they are released. This increases the length of time the transmitter is active at the receptor site and thus its effects in the brain (Ramsay & Hunter, 2003). When MAO is inhibited, alternate routes of metabolism are used, resulting in delayed metabolism and hydroxy free radical formation. Methamphetamine stimulation also triggers an increase in gluatamine receptor density in nucleus accumbens, acutely increasing its responsiveness to repetitive stimulation (Chao, Ariano, Peterson, & Wolf, 2002).

Methamphetamine also disrupts the hypothalamic pituitary axis, causing a release of cortisol, a stress hormone. Higher cortisol levels are associated with greater dopamine release in the striatum and more positive subjective drug effects (Oswald et al., 2005). Glucocorticoid receptors in the midbrain are affected in the striatum and hippocampus, which is thought to underlie stress-related relapse (Wang et al., 2005).

SENSITIZATION STAGE OF ADDICTION

Methamphetamine addiction progresses through two distinct biochemical stages. Only the later stage is characteristically recognized as *addiction* or *dependence* in the terminology of *DSM–IV.* Those patients still in the initial sensitization stage are considered users, but have not yet had negative sequellae from their drug use and so have not tried to quit or cut down. In sensitization, each dose feels even better than before, lasts longer, and is more intense. Having heard about tolerance, the user understands that only when his drug use accelerates would he be considered an addict, so during this early stage, he assures himself he must be ok. He does not believe his methamphetamine use is having any effect on his brain.

During the sensitization period, neural tracts that are hyperstimulated on an occasional basis by low intensity use become more responsive to methamphetamine. These neural tracts have been shown to increase their sensitivity to repeated doses of methamphetamine, both by increasing numbers of receptors for monoamine neurotransmitters, and also by increasing numbers of glutamate receptors in the brain (Xui, Koeltzow, Cooper, Robertson, & White, 2002). We add more lanes to accommodate increased traffic.

And in the sensitization period, the neurons still have a reserve of intracellular neurotransmitter that can be mobilized by axonal transport, to replenish the terminals with fresh supplies of neurotransmitter, thus enabling the cells to function in the face of massive losses in their neurotransmitter supplies (Yudko et al., 2003). This is why, in the early stage of addiction, function is maintained between "highs" and the "crash" after using is just a mild depression, not even as bad as the hangover after an evening of heavy alcohol intake.

This phase may last for years in the case of oral use of small doses of methamphetamine, and there are medical uses for methamphetamine for treatment of Attention Deficit Hyperactivity Disorder (ADHD), narcolepsy, and weight loss in small closely monitored doses. The military has used methamphetamine in small closely regulated doses for many years with a long record of safety.

Unmonitored use, however, readily lends itself to compulsive and repetitive use with resultant personality changes—what any unbiased observer would call *addiction*.

At this early stage the addict is almost never willing to admit she has a problem. She uses frequently, but perhaps not daily. She feels focused and energetic while on methamphetamine. Her family members notice her personality changes, her short temper and impatience, but she thinks everything is fine. She cannot quit using for any prolonged length of time—what the average person would consider addiction—but she has never really tried to quit, nor does she consider herself impaired in any way, and so a psychiatrist would not diagnose her *dependent*. Psychiatry has rejected the word *addiction* as a diagnostic term. It is used here purely as a functional term referring to the habitual and compulsive use of a substance.

Dependence is diagnosed only when strict criteria are met, including three of the following conditions:

Tolerance
Withdrawal symptoms
Escalation of use
Effort to control use
Occupies time, effort
Replaces other activities
Use despite impairment

Only in the later stage of addiction, when drug use impairs functioning and replaces normal healthy activities, resulting in the loss of relationships or employment, does a psychiatrist consider the individual an addict (dependent). This functional definition has more to do with the reaction of his wife and the demands of his employer than it does with the biochemical effects the drug is having in his brain. He won't make an effort to control his use until threatened with an employee drug test. The level of denial in such a person guarantees that the subjective measures used to define dependence will not apply to him until a set of handcuffs has been applied at least once. The changes in his brain are at an advanced stage by now. By the time dependence is diagnosed, serious mental health problems are often evident, and recovery of normal cognition and personality features will require months, if not years, of intense therapy.

Early diagnosis and intervention are impossible with the current definition of dependence (or addiction) used by psychiatry. In fact, people requesting treatment for their addiction are sometimes turned away by mental health providers because they are "not addicted enough," particularly in the public sector.

LATE-STAGE ADDICTION

In later-stage addiction, neurotransmitter reserves have been depleted as continued massive releases of monoamines have exhausted the cell's capacity to manufacture these complex chemicals de-novo (Vacca, Ahn, & Phillips, 2006). Presynaptic function is also impaired by chronic methamphetamine exposure, with corresponding behavioral changes, an effect that persists at least four months into recovery in an animal model (Melega et al., 2008). Striatal dopamine concentration (reserve) is reduced by 20 percent and presynaptic dopamine transporter density is reduced by 35 percent. Chronic presynaptic depression of function is "renormalized" in cortico-striatal pathways by read-ministration of methamphetamine, restoring the system to apparent normalcy (Bamford et al., 2008).

At the same time, the postsynaptic side has responded to the massive hyper-stimulation by phospohorylating, sequestering, and degrading its receptors (Volkow et al., 2001). While D1 receptors in the striatum are preserved, they are delinked from the adenylyl cyclase that serves as its second messenger in the postsynaptic cell (Tong et al., 2003). The dopamine response is suppressed in response to both psycho stimulants and natural rewards in withdrawal from methamphetamine (Vacca et al., 2006). More and more stimulation is required to trigger a postsynaptic response. The crash becomes more symptomatic and longer lasting as neurotransmitters and receptors are depleted. The addict accelerates his drug dose and interval in an effort to reclaim the high and/or avoid the crash.

As dopamine transmission is impaired in the reward circuit, higher doses of methamphetamine are required to maintain function. The recreational user can't wait until Friday to use again, and the functional user needs higher doses to maintain his current level of productivity. As higher doses are used, side effects, including jitteriness and disorganization, are seen, which impair his occupational adjustment. He is generally oblivious to this change and to the personality changes that are also occurring. His boss and his wife, however, usually are not oblivious to these changes.

His irritability has by now progressed to domestic violence—either verbal or physical. His children are afraid of him. His work performance has become erratic and customers and coworkers are complaining. Personality changes are the hallmark sign of the methamphetamine user. They are much more promi-nent than those seen in heroin or even cocaine users, and they affect every aspect of life. Some of these personality changes are quite reversible since they are mediated by biochemical changes in brain function, not by structural changes.

But they improve very slowly, over the course of many months of abstinence as neurotransmission is reestablished (Wang et al., 2004).

Other changes seen in later-stage methamphetamine addiction are not as readily reversible. The loss of memory, cognitive ability, motivation, and reality testing are related to structural damage to brain tissue caused by cellular damage to the brain (Thompson et al., 2004). These changes also result in the deepening of the addiction as key structures related to self-control are compromised.

CYTOTOXICITY

The massive release of neurotransmitters caused by high dose and chronic methamphetamine use results in high levels of nitrogen and oxygen free radical formation (Acikgov et al., 2000). These free radicals are formed by the metabolism of methamphetamine, and also by the breakdown of the huge amounts of monoamine neurotransmitters that have been released both intra- and extracellularly. These monoamine neurotransmitters must also be broken down, and MAO, the usual enzyme to do that, is inhibited by methamphetamine. Alternative metabolic routes are used, resulting in the generation of large amounts of hydroxyl free radicals nitric oxide and peroxynitrite, which are extremely toxic to brain cells (Jeng, Ramkissoon, Parman, & Wells, 2006).

Free radical compounds denature proteins, damage DNA, and generally wreak havoc in the areas of the brain in which they are concentrated (Cubbells, Rayport, Rajendran, & Sulzer, 1994). Because most of the neurotransmitters are released in the midbrain, nucleus accumbens, and striatum, and in the prefrontal cortex, those areas are disproportionately affected by methamphetamine abuse with progressively worsening cognitive and executive function (Li, Wang, Qiu, & Luo, 2008).

The power of these free radicals to damage the human brain was demonstrated most vividly by Thompson in 2004 when he and his colleagues demonstrated up to 15 percent loss of brain tissue in large areas of the brain, including both cortical and subcortical tissue in methamphetamine users. These findings were correlated with cognitive and memory defects in the subjects studied. Thompson described it as a "forest fire of brain damage" with real-world consequences in occupational failure, disintegration of relationships, and challenges in treatment.

Methamphetamine use causes persistent hypometabolism in the frontal white matter and impairment in frontal executive function on positron emission tomography (PET) scanning (Kim, Lyoo, Hwang, Sung, & Lee, 2005). Abstinent meth users showed impaired performance on the Wisconsin card-sorting test associated with reduced metabolism in the right superior frontal lobe. Hypo-frontality in methamphetamine addicts has been thought to contribute to the significant cognitive deficits, memory loss, and poor impulse control that cause significant social failure and complicate treatment participation and success (Homer et al., 2008). A realistic assessment of the nature and extent of these deficits is essential to developing effective treatment programs.

THE PLEASURE CIRCUIT

The pleasure circuit has been well described, and consists of the nucleus accumbens, anterior bed nuclei, anterior lateral hypothalamus, stria terminalis, lateral preoptic area, median forebrain bundle, ventral tegmental area, ventral pallidum, and prefrontal cortex. These areas are profoundly affected by methamphetamine administration, with altered sensitivity and receptor changes in animal models (Brady, Glick, & O'Donnell, 2005; Broom & Yamamoto, 2005; Yong & Kauer, 2003).

Direct stimulation of the nucleus accumbens by dopamine results in euphoria. The ventral tegmental area sends numerous dopaminergic neurons to the nucleus accumbens, contributing to reward and motivation in response to natural pleasures. Methamphetamine increases dopamine in the nucleus accumbens by up to 1,000–1,200 percent, provoking a powerful pleasurable sensation and triggering a powerful motivator. As these dopamine receptors are damaged by overstimulation, natural rewards are not appreciated, and motivation is impaired.

The prefrontal cortex is an integral part of the reward circuit. Pleasures are experienced in all their richness in the prefrontal cortex, and cravings originate in these areas as marked by intense neural activity on exposure to triggers (Kalivas, Volkow, & Seamans, 2005). Prefrontal cortex is hyperresponsive to drug cues, driving the nucleus accumbens, while at the same time, executive function is reduced, diminishing cognitive control. Wilson's analysis of these studies showed the orbitofrontal and dorsolateral orbitofrontal cortex more active in addicts anticipating drug usage, while anterior cingulate cortex was more activated in those trying to resist the urge to drug usage—treatment-seeking individuals (Wilson, Sayette, & Fiez, 2004).

Appeals to the pleasure circuit to explain all aspects of addictive behavior are found wanting in that as addiction proceeds, pleasurable sensations decline, and addicts are often motivated to use substances that no longer give them very much pleasure. Motivation shifts from obtaining pleasure and avoiding the pain and anxiety of withdrawal to compulsive use in the face of serious adverse consequences. The ability of the conscious mind to control behavior is seriously compromised in addiction, particularly methamphetamine addiction, even when competent cognitive behavioral therapy is received and mastered. This suggests a parallel and separate anatomic basis for behavior control apart from hedonic perception.

THE CONTROL CIRCUIT

The control circuit is less understood, and is not included in most textbooks on the neurophysiology of addiction. The original literature, however, supports the existence of a dedicated set of structures that serve to facilitate control of behavior in the face of desire or craving. This control circuit consists of the prefrontal cortex, anterior cingulate gyrus, the lateral habenula, and fasciculus retroflexus, which exerts inhibitory GABA-A control over the midbrain craving centers in the ventral tegmental area (Ji & Shepard, 2007). There are also direct inhibitory connections between prefrontal cortex and VTA that are also GABA-mediated (Carr & Sesack, 2000).

The influence of this circuit in the modulation of addiction has been delineated in several human studies. Volkow and colleagues in 2001 demonstrated a loss of dopamine receptors in the entire orbitofrontal cortex in abstinent methamphetamine users. More specifically, methamphetamine users showed significantly reduced cerebral blood flow in the anterior cingulate gyrus, with a significant persistent reduction even after six months' abstinence. This suggests a structural change, not just a functional neurotransmitter mediated effect, in the anterior cingulate gyrus, an important area for control of impulses and behavior (Hwang et al., 2006).

Multiple studies have demonstrated reduced task-related activation of the anterior cingulated gyrus in methamphetamine users. Paulus, Tapert, and Schuckit in 2005 showed that those addicts who eventually relapsed had markedly reduced activation of the dorsolateral prefrontal cortex and anterior cingulate gyrus compared to addicts who did not subsequently relapse. Subjects were followed for up to three years to observe for relapse, and the predictive power of this functional measure of brain activity in these areas was impressive.

The cingulum bundle conducts impulses from anterior cingulate gyrus and other prefrontal areas posteriorly, primarily to the hippocampus, but also to multiple other midbrain structures, including the lateral habenula. The cells in this transmission line are exquisitely sensitive to methamphetamine, with destruction of more than 90 percent of the cingulum bundle demonstrated after just a single intoxicating dose of methamphetamine in animal models (Zhou & Bledsoe, 1996). This is not just a change in the sensitivity of the neurons, but the destruction of a key pathway between the cingulate gyrus and midbrain structures, including hippocampus and lateral habenula.

The lateral habenula itself is sensitive to the effects of methamphetamine with specific degeneration of large areas of lateral habenula with continuous exposure to meth as would be seen in a binge pattern of self-administration (Ellison, 1992). In 2000, Carlson and colleagues reported that many drugs of abuse impair function in the habenula and fasciculus retroflexus, dubbing it "the weak link in addiction." This line of research was then almost completely neglected for many years until recent studies have further delineated the significance of Ellison's and Carlson's findings.

The lateral habenula is a significant processing center conveying information from cognitive cortical areas to subcortical areas. Habenular lesions result in learning deficits, and reductions in memory and attention consistent with its central role in cognition (Lecourtier & Kelly, 2007). In humans, the lateral habenula is especially responsive to feedback about errors, exerting inhibitory impulses when errors are detected and response patterns need to be changed (Ullsperger & Cramon, 2003).

Lateral habenula neurons in the primate are activated in a no-reward condition, exerting inhibitory control over dopamine release from the ventral tegmental area (Matsumoto & Hikosaka, 2007). In this study even weak stimulation of lateral habenula elicited strong inhibition of dopamine release. Dopamine levels are thus decreased when predicted rewards do not occur, a biological basis for disappointment (Pagnoni, Zink, Montague, & Berns, 2002).

Specifically, lateral habenula in turn exerts a powerful inhibitory effect on dopamine transmission by the ventral tegmental area via the fasciculus retroflexus, a GABAergic pathway. Ji and Shepard (2007) did the definitive study of this tract, demonstrating that single-pulse stimulation of the lateral habenula effectively shut down the activity of 97 percent of the dopaminergic neurons in the substantia nigra and ventral tegmental area. Stimulation of the lateral habenula resulted in a complete cessation of spontaneous firing in nearly all dopamine neurons in the substantia nigra and ventral tegmental areas. Lesions of the fasciculus retroflexus completely blocked this strongly inhibitory effect on dopamine neurons.

These ventral tegmental dopaminergic signals are responsible for recurrent drug-taking behaviors even in the absence of an external trigger for the hedonic reward pathway (Nakajima et al., 2004). Uncontrolled ventral tegmental stimulation of the nucleus accumbens produces dopamine signals that are experienced in the frontal cortex as cravings and the desire to get high. If sufficient inhibitory control in the frontal cortex is not present to suppress these signals, behavior is likewise uncontrolled.

PROPOSED TREATMENTS

Since a number of interrelated adaptations to drug use occur in multiple areas of the brain, it would be expected that intervention would also have to occur at multiple levels for successful rehabilitation. There are adaptations in the reward areas, motivation and drive, memory and conditioning, and inhibitory control areas that result in long-lasting changes in a person's responsiveness to natural rewards, cognitive ability, and inhibitory control. While acute drug intake increases dopamine release, chronic use impairs it not only in the reward centers but also in the frontal lobes (cognitive ability) and cingulate gyrus (inhibitory control) (Volkow, Fowler, & Wang, 2004).

GABA-mediated inhibitory control is a target for many of the newly proposed treatments for addiction, including baclofen, gabapentin, and vigabatrin. These drugs are GABA A agonists (baclofen), or GABA transaminase inhibitors (gabapentin and vigabatrin), essentially amplifying the inhibitory signals and thus improving impulse control and reducing craving. Animal studies were very promising (Barrett, Negus, Mello, & Caine, 2005; Di Ciano & Everitt, 2004; Filip et al., 2007), as were open-label studies using baclofen and gabapentin (Urschell, Hanselka, Gromov, White, & Baron, 2007) and vigabatrin (Brodie, Fiqueroa, Laska, & Dewey, 2005; Fechtner, Khouri, Figueroa, Ramirez, & Federico, 2006). However, double-blind studies of baclofen and gabapentin showed no effect (Heinzerling et al., 2006; Shoptaw et al., 2003). A randomized controlled trial of vigabatrin is needed. Though vigabatrin has been linked to visual field defects with long-term use, its safety in short-term use is suggested by the open-label studies completed (Brodie et al., 2005).

Reducing the reward value of methamphetamine is another biochemical target area that is open to intervention. As in the case of heroin addiction and its partial agonist buprenorphine, there is a partial agonist for stimulant drugs in the form of modafinil. In animal studies, modafinil substituted partially for both cocaine and amphetamine in rats trained to discriminate these stimulants from saline, but was much less potent (Dopheide, Morgan, Rodvelt, Schachtman, & Miller, 2007). While it is not a dopamine receptor agonist, it has a similar clinical profile to stimulants with alertness and cognitive improvement and does increase dopamine release in the nucleus accumbens (Murillo-Rodríguez, Haro, Palomero-Rivero, Millán-Aldaco, & Drucker-Colín, 2007). A double-blind controlled trial of modafinil showed it is effective in reducing cocaine dependence with few adverse effects (Dackis, Kampman, Lynch, Pettinati, & O'Brien, 2005). It is especially beneficial in improving cognitive performance and thus participation with cognitive behavioral therapy (Makris,

2007; Minzenberg & Carter, 2008). Buproprion, a dopamine and norepineph-rine reuptake blocker, has also been shown effective in a subset of men using low doses of methamphetamine, but was not effective for the population at large (Elkashef et al., 2008; Shoptaw et al., 2008).

Alternatively, dopamine blockade has been evaluated for effectiveness in reducing stimulant relapse. Selective D3 receptor antagonists reduced cocaine seeking behavior in rats (Xi et al., 2006; Cervo, Cocco, Petrella, & Heidbreder, 2006). Available D2 blockers including arapiprozole (Beresford et al., 2005) and olanzapine (Smelson et al., 2006) relieve cravings in comorbid schizo-phrenic stimulant addicts, but with the usual anhedonic side effects character-istic of these medications.

NONPHARMACOLOGIC APPROACHES

But there are nonpharmacologic ways of influencing the self-control tract of the brain and enhancing its function, some of which the rehabilitation industry has used for years without really understanding the neurobiology behind them. One of them is the "boot camp" approach. All rehabilitation programs include at least a component of this approach, and some are almost exclusively a boot-camp experience. Chores and schedules and responsibilities are expected and are recognized as important to recovery from addiction.

The value of these interventions consists of the conditioning, and in some cases, regeneration, of damaged tissue, restoring function in the areas of the brain mediating self-control. Classical rehabilitation techniques are used from the physical therapy paradigms and applied to behavioral rehabilitation with good success. When a neural tract is impaired, for instance, after a stroke, reha-bilitation consists of forcing the relevant area of the brain to work, thus facili-tating the recruitment of surrounding surviving cells to take over the function of the diseased tissue, a process called activity-dependent plastic change, or neuroplasticity (Ward, 2005).

In the same way, when the self-control pathway is compromised, rehabilita-tion consists of imposing conditions that force the patient to exert inhibitory control over her behavior, facilitating recruitment of surviving cells to take over the function of the diseased tissue. This is particularly effective at the corti-cal level in retraining the anterior cingulate cortex to control behavior. Addicts are "forced" to get up at a given time, do chores, and keep a schedule, so that impulse inhibiting areas are stimulated to function on a regular basis. The prin-ciples of neuroplasticity ensure that such "exercise" will stimulate recovery of function by increases in brain-derived neurotrophic factor (BDNF), dendritic arborization, and synaptic plasticity.

Contingency management capitalizes on these same principles, as an external motivator is used to improve compliance and modify behavior. Coupled with cognitive behavioral therapy and the social support found in the group therapy setting, success in treatment of methamphetamine addiction is comparable to treatment of other addictions. Cognitive and attentional problems limit the application of cognitive behavioral techniques in early abstinence, but as the brain heals and remodels, retention and insight improve and treatment outcomes are comparable to those obtained with treatment of cocaine and other drug addictions (Rawson et al., 2000).

FUTURE DIRECTIONS

Until now, most neuropharmacology research has been devoted to understanding the reward system of brain physiology with an eye toward blocking the rewards associated with drug abuse with dopamine blockers of various types. Atypical antipsychotic medications have been used and found effective, but anhedonia is a frequent side effect. Clinical usefulness is limited to those patients who are willing to forgo all rewards for an indefinite period of time. Compliance with such therapy is usually confined to the court-ordered population. Substitution therapy with modafinil is more likely to be effective and acceptable to patients, but carries its own risks of exacerbating mental illnesses such as bipolar disorder and psychosis, and also cardiovascular complications (Kampman, 2008).

More attention should be directed toward the self-control system to develop new treatments based on enhancing the addict's control over her own behavior. GABAergic medications offer the potential to amplify normal inhibitory neural tracts to improve impulse control at the midbrain level, while behavioral modification and cognitive behavioral therapy addresses the cortical components of the self-control circuit. This could lead to improvements in the effectiveness of our current contingency management and motivational enhancement techniques, both of which are components of effective cognitive behavioral treatment. A greater understanding of the neurologic components and functional biochemistry of the self-control factor would extend pharmacologic and non-pharmacologic support to empower addicts to control their own lives instead of being controlled by drugs of abuse.

Our enhanced biological understanding of addiction would also permit a more objective definition of drug dependence itself, thus avoiding the denial and deception that complicates the accurate diagnosis of addiction. We are in dire need of an accessible biochemical or radiological marker for drug dependence that does not rely on subjective discomfort, third-party report, or personal desire for change, all of which can be missing in a person who is shooting up daily and sustaining serious neurologic damage. The level of denial and deception among drug users is legendary. A scan documenting the loss of dopamine activity in the midbrain might be fairly motivating to a patient considering rehabilitation for her drug problem. Earlier intervention would be possible if addiction could be diagnosed at an earlier stage before significant frontal lobe damage has occurred.

Much work needs to be done to identify dopamine, serotonin, or norepinephrine metabolites in peripheral blood, develop scanning techniques to identify brain cell dysfunction, or cognitive testing, or scales of personality parameters that could inform users of the effect drug use is having on their brains before their condition worsens to the point of serious disability. We are close to having the capability of doing just that. Morris, Normandin, and Schiffer (2008) have validated a PET-based technique that accurately measures microdialysis confirmed dopamine levels noninvasively. Our reliance on the recognition of late behavioral changes diagnostic of addiction under *DSM IV* is keeping us behind the curve when assessing the impact methamphetamine is having on individual lives and on society as a whole.

Addiction must be defined and diagnosed in neurologic terms if it is to be recognized as a "brain disease" deserving of comprehensive and compassionate treatment and not a "moral failure" subject to incarceration. A better public understanding of addiction as a brain disease would move it out of the court system and into the therapist's office, with corresponding improvements in public perception, patient self-image, relegation of public resources, and insurance coverage.

REFERENCES

Acikgov, O., Gapnenas, S., Kayatekin, B. M., Pekasetin, C., Uusal, N., Dayi, A., et al. (2000). The effects of a single dose of methamphetamine on lipid peroxidation levels in the rat striatum and prefrontal cortex. *European Neuropsychopharmacology, 10*(5), 415–418.

Ago, Y., Nakamura, S., Baba, A., & Matsuda, T. (2008). Neuropsychotoxicity of abused drugs: Effects of serotonin receptor ligands on methamphetamine and cocaine induced behavioral sensitization in mice. *Journal of Psycopharmacologic Sciences, 106*(1), 15–21.

Bamford, N. S., Zhang, H., Joyce, J. A., Scarlis, C. A., Hanan, W., Wu, N. P., et al. (2008). Repeated exposure to methamphetamine causes long lasting presynaptic cortiostriatal depression that is normalized with drug readministration. *Neuron, 58*(1), 89–103.

Barrett, A. C., Negus, S. S., Mello, N. K., & Caine, S. B. (2005). Effect of GABA agonist and GABA A receptor modulators on cocaine and food maintained responding and cocaine discrimination in rats. *Journal of Pharmacology and Experimental Therapeutics, 315*, 858–871.

Beresford, T. P., Clapp, L., Martin, B., Wiberg, J. L., Alfers, J., Beresford, H. F. (2005). Aripiprazole in schizophrenia with cocaine dependence: A pilot study. *Journal of Clinical Psychopharmacology, 25*, 363–366.

Brady, A. M., Glick, S. D., & O'Donnell, P. (2005). Selective disruption of nucleus accumbens gating mechanisms in rats behaviorally sensitized to methamphetamine. *Journal of Neuroscience, 25*, 6687–6695.

Brodie, J. D., Fiqueroa, E., Laska, E. M., & Dewey, S. L. (2005). Safety and efficacy of GVG for the treatment of methamphetamine and/or cocaine addiction. *Synapse, 55*(2), 122–125.

Broom, S. L., & Yamamoto, B. K. (2005). Effects of subchronic methamphetamine exposure on basal dopamine and stress induced dopamine release in the nucleus accumbens shell of rats. *Psychopharmacology, 181*, 467–476.

Carlson, J., Armstrong, B., Switzer, R. C., & Ellison, G. (2000). Selective neurotoxic effects of nicotine on axons in fasciculus retroflexus further support evidence that this is a weak link in brain across multiple drugs of abuse. *Neuropharmacology, 39*(13), 2792–2798.

Carr, D. B., & Sesack, S. (2000). Projections from the rat prefrontal cortex to the ventral tegmental area: Target specificity in the synaptic associations with meso accumbens and mesocortical neurons. *Journal of Neuroscience, 20*(10), 3864–3873.

Cervo, L., Cocco, A., Petrella, C., & Heidbreder C. A. (2006). Selective antaqgonism at dopamine D3 receptors attenuates cocaine-seeking behavior in the rat. *International Journal of Neuropsychopharmacology, 23*, 1–15.

Chao, S. Z., Ariano, M. A., Peterson, D. A., & Wolf, M. E. (2002). D1 dopamine receptor stimulation increases GluR1 surface expression in nucleus accumbens neurons. *Journal of Neurochemistry, 83*(3), 704–712.

Cubells, J. F., Rayport, S., Rajendran, G., & Sulzer, D. (1994). Methamphetamine neurotoxicity involves vacuolization of endocytic organelles and dopamine dependent intracellular oxidative stress. *Journal of Neuroscience, 14*(4), 2260–2271.

Dackis, C. A., Kampman, K. M., Lynch, K. G., Pettinati, H. M., & O'Brien, C. P. (2005). A double blind, placebo controlled trial of modafinil for cocaine dependence. *Neuropsychopharmacology, 30*(1), 205–211.

Di Ciano, P., & Everitt, B. J. (2004). Contribution of the ventral tegmental area to cocaine seeking maintained by a paired drug conditioned stimulus in rats. *European Journal of Neuroscience, 19*, 1991–1997.

Dopheide, M. M., Morgan, R. E., Rodvelt, K. R., Schachtman, T. R., & Miller, D. K. (2007). Modafinil evokes striatal [(3)H]dopamine release and alters the subjective properties of stimulants. *European Journal of Pharmacology, 568*(1–3), 112–123.

Elkashef, A. M., Rawson, R. A., Anderson, A. L., Li, S. H., Holmes, T., Smith, E. V., et al. (2008). Buproprion for the treatment of methamphetamine dependence. *Neuropsychopharmacology, 33*(5), 1162–1170.

Ellison, G. (1992). Continuous amphetamine and cocaine have similar neurotoxic effects in lateral habenular nucleus and fasciculus retroflexus. *Brain Research, 598,* 352–356.

Fechtner, R. D., Khouri, A. S., Figueroa, E., Ramirez, M., & Federico, M. (2006). Short term treatment of cocaine and or methamphetamine abuse with vigabatrin: Ocular safety pilot results. *Archives of Ophthalmology, 124,* 1257–1262.

Filip, M., Frankowska, M., Zaniewska, M., Goada, A., Przegaliaski, E., & Vetulani, J. (2007). Diverse effects of GABA mimetic drugs on cocaine evoked self administration and discriminative stimulus effects in rats. *Psychopharmacology, 192,* 17–26.

Gough, B., Imam, S. Z., Blough, B., Slikker, W., Jr., & Ali, S. F. (2002). Comparative effects of substituted amphetamines (PMA, MDMA, and METH) on monoamines in rat coudate: A microdialysis study. *Annals NY Academy of Science, 965,* 410–420.

Heinzerling, K. G., Shoptaw, S., Peck, J. A., Yang, X., Liu, J., Roll, J., et al. (2006). Randomized placebo controlled trial of baclofen and gabapentin for the treatment of methamphetamine dependence. *Drug and Alcohol Dependence, 85,* 177–184.

Homer, B. D., Solomon, T. M., Moeller, R. W., Mascia, A., DeRaleau, L., & Halkitis, P. N. (2008). Methamphetamine abuse and impairment of social functioning: A review of the underlying neurophysiological causes and behavioral implications. *Psychological Bulletin, 134*(2), 301–310.

Hwang, J., Lyoo, I. K., Kim, S. J., Sung, Y. H., Bae, S., Cho, S.N., et al. (2006). Decreased cerebral blood flow of the right anterior cingulate cortex in long term and short term abstinent methamphetamine users. *Drug and Alcohol Dependence, 28,* 177–181.

Izawa, J., Yamanashi, K., Asakura, T., Misu, Y., & Goshima, Y. (2006). Differential effects of methamphetamine and cocaine on behavior and extracellular levels of dopamine and 3,4 dihydroxyphenylalanine in the nucleus accumbens of conscious rats. *European Journal of Pharmacology, 549,* 84–90.

Jeng, W., Ramkissoon, A., Parman, T., & Wells, P. G. (2006). Prostaglandin H synthase catalysed bioactivation of amphetamine to free radical intermediates that cause CNS regional DNA oxidation and nerve terminal degeneration. *The FASEB journal : Official publication of the Federation of American Societies for Experimental Biology, 20,* 638–650.

Ji, H., & Shepard, P. (2007). Lateral habenula stimulation inhibits rat midbrain dopamine neurons through a GABA A receptor mediated mechanism. *Journal of Neuroscience, 27,* 6923–6930.

Kalivas, P. W., Volkow, N., & Seamans, J. (2005). Unmanageable motivation in addiction: A pathology in prefrontal–accumbens glutamate transmission. *Neuron, 45,* 647–650.

Kampman, K. M. (2008). The search of medication to treat stimulant dependence. *Addiction Science and Clinical Practice, 4,* 28–35.

Kim, S. J., Lyoo, I. K., Hwang, J., Sung, Y. H., Lee, H. Y., Lee, D. S., et al. (2005). Frontal glucose hypometabolism in abstinent methamphetamine users. *Neuropsychopharmacology, 30*(7), 1383–1391.

Lecourtier, L., & Kelly, P. H. (2007). A conductor hidden in the orchestra? Role of the habenular complex in monoamine transmission and cognition. *Neuroscience and Behavioral Reviews, 31,* 658–672.

Li, X., Wang, H., Qiu, P., & Luo, H. (2008). Proteomic profiling of proteins associated with methamphetamine-induced neurotoxicity in different regions of rat brain. *Neurochemistry International, 52,* 256–264.

Makris, A. P., Rush, C. R., Frederich, R. C., Taylor, A. C., Kelly, T. H. (2007). Behavioral and subjective effects of d-amphetamine and modafinil in healthy adults. *Experimental and Clinical Psychopharmacology, 15,* 123–133.

Matsumoto, M., & Hikosaka, O. (2007). Lateral habenula as a source of negative reward signals in dopamine neurons. *Nature, 447,* 1111–1115.

Melega, W. P., Jorgensen, M. J., Laatan, G., Way, B. M., Pham, J., Morton, G., et al. (2008). Long term methamphetamine administration in the vervet monkey models aspects of a human exposure: Brain neurotoxicity and behavioral profiles. *Neuropsychopharmacology, 33*(6), 1441–1452.

Minzenberg, M. J. & Carter, C. S. (2008). Modafinil: A review of neurochemical actions and effects on cognition. *Neuropsychopharmacology, 33,* 1477–1502.

Morris, E. D., Normandin, M. D., & Schiffer, W. K. (2008). Initial comparison of ntPET with microdialysis measurements of methamphetamine induced dopamine release in rats: Support for estimation of dopamine curves from PET data. *Molecular Imaging and Biology, 10*(2), 67–73.

Murillo-Rodríguez, E., Haro, R., Palomero-Rivero, M., Millán-Aldaco, D., & Drucker-Colín, R. (2007). Modafinil enhances extracellular levels of dopamine in the nucleus accumbens and increases wakefulness in rats. *Behavioural Brain Research, 176*(2), 353–357.

Nakajima, A., Yamada, K., He, J., Zeng, N., Nitta, A., & Nabeshima, T. (2004). Anatomical substrates for the discriminative stimulus effects of methamphetamine in rats. *Journal of Neurochemistry, 91*(2), 308–317.

Oswald, L. M., Wong, D. F., McCaul, M., Zhou, Y., Kuwabara, H., Choi, L., et al. (2005). Relationships among ventral striatal dopamine release, cortisol secretion, and subjective responses to amphetamine. *Neuropsychopharmacology, 30*(4), 821–832.

Pagnoni, G., Zink, C. F., Montague, P. R., & Berns, G. S. (2002). Activity in human ventral striatum locked to errors of reward prediction. *Nature and Neuroscience, 5,* 97–98.

Paulus, M. P., Tapert, S., & Schuckit, M. A. (2005). Neural activation patterns of methamphetamine dependent subjects during decision making predict relapse. *Archives of General Psychiatry, 62,* 761–768.

Ramsay, R. R., & Hunter, D. J. (2003). Interactions of D-amphetamine with the active site of monoamine oxidase-A. *Inflammopharmacology, 11*(2), 127–133.

Rawson, R., Huber, A., Brethen, P., Obert, J., Gulati, V., Shoptaw, S., et al. (2000). Methamphetamine and cocaine users: Differences in characteristics and treatment retention. *Journal of Psychoactive Drugs, 32*(2), 233–238.

Rothman, R. B., Bauman, M. H., Dersch, C. M., Romero, D. V., & Rice, K. C. (2001). Amphetamine type central nervous system stimulants release norepinephrine more potently than they release dopamine and serotonin. *Synapse, 39*, 32–41.

Shoptaw, S., Heinzerling, K. G., Rotheram-Fuller, E., Steward, T., Wang, J., Swanson, A. N., et al. (2008). Randomized, placebo-controlled trial of bupropion for the treatment of methamphetamine dependence. *Drug and Alcohol Dependence, 96*(3), 222–232.

Shoptaw, S., Yang, X., Rotheram-Fuller, E. J., Hsieh, Y. C., Kintaudi, P. C., Charuvastra, V. C., et al. (2003). Randomized placebo controlled trial of baclofen for cocaine dependence: Preliminary effects for individuals with chronic patterns of cocaine use. *Journal of Clinical Psychiatry, 64*, 1440–1448.

Smelson, D. A., Ziedonis, D., Williams, J., Losonczy, M. F., Williams, J., & Steinberg, M. L. (2006). The efficacy of olanzapine for decreasing cue-elicited craving in individuals with schizophrenia and cocaine dependence: A preliminary report. *Journal of Clinical Psychopharmacology, 26*, 9–12.

Thompson, P. M., Hayashi, K. M., Simon, S. L., Geaga, J. A., Hong, M. S., Sui, Y., et al. (2004). Structural abnormalities in the brains of human subjects who use methamphetamine. *Journal of Neuroscience, 24*, 6028–6036.

Tong, J., Ross, B. M., Schmunk, G. A., Peretti, F. J., Kalsinsky, K. S., Yoshiaki, F., et al. (2003). Decreased striatal dopamine D1 receptor stimulated adenylyl cyclase activity in human methamphetamine users. *American Journal of Psychiatry, 160*, 896–903.

Ullsperger, M., & Cramon, Y. V. (2003). Error monitoring using external feedback: Specific roles of the habenular complex, the reward system, and the cingulate motor area revealed by functional magnetic resonance imaging. *Journal of Neuroscience, 23*, 4308–4314.

Urschel, H. C., Hanselka, L., Gromov, I., White, L., & Baron, M. (2007). Open label study of a proprietary treatment program targeting Type A GABA receptor dysregulation in methamphetamine dependence. *Mayo Clinic Proceedings, 82*, 1170–1178.

Vacca, G., Ahn, S., & Phillips, A. G. (2006). Effects of short term abstinence from escalating doses of D-amphetamine in drug and sucrose evoked dopamine efflux in the rat nucleus accumbens. *Neuropsychopharmacology, 32*, 932–939.

Volkow, N. D., Chang, L., Wang, G. J., Fowler, J. S., Ding, Y. S., Sedler, M., et al. (2001). Low level of brain dopamine D2 receptors in methamphetamine abusers: Association with metabolism in the orbitofrontal cortex. *American Journal of Psychiatry, 158*, 2015–2021.

Volkow, N. D., Fowler, J. S., & Wang, G. J. (2004). The addicted human brain viewed in the light of imaging studies: Brain circuits and treatment strategies. *Neuropharmacology, 47*(Suppl. 1), 3–13.

Wang, B., Shaham, Y., Zitzman, D., Azari, S., Wise, R. A., & You, Z. B. (2005). Cocaine experience establishes control of midbrain glutamate and dopamine by cotricotropin releasing factor: A role in stress induced relapse to drug seeking. *Journal of Neuroscience, 25,* 5289–5296.

Wang, G. J., Volkow, N., Chang, L., Miller, E., Sedler, M., Hitzemann, R., et al. (2004). Partial recovery of brain metabolism in methamphetamine abusers after protracted abstinence. *American Journal of Psychiatry, 161,* 242–248.

Ward, N. (2005). Neural plasticity and recovery of function. *Progress in Brain Research, 150,* 527–535.

Wilson, S. J., Sayette, M. A., & Fiez, J. A. (2004). Prefrontal responses to drug cues: A neurocognitive analysis. *Nature Neuroscience, 7,* 211–214.

Xi, Z. X., Newman, A. H., Gilbert, J. G., Pak, A. C., Peng, X. Q., Ashby, C. R. Jr, et al. (2006). The novel dopamine D3 receptor antagonist NGB 2904 inhibits cocaine's rewarding effects and cocaine-induced reinstatement of drug seeking behavior in rats. *Neuropsychopharmacology, 31,* 1393–1405.

Xui, T. H., Koeltzow, T. E., Cooper, T. E., Robertson, G. S., & White, F. J. (2002). Repeated ventral tegmental area amphetamine administration alters dopamine D1 receptor signaling in the nucleus accumbens. *Synapse, 45,* 159–170.

Yong, L., & Kauer, J. (2003). Repeated exposure to amphetamine disrupts dopaminergic modulation of excitatory synaptic plasticity and neurotransmission in nucleus accumbens. *Synapse, 51,* 1–10.

Yudko, E., Hall, H. V., & McPherson, S. B. (2003). *Methamphetamine use: Clinical and forensic aspects.* Boca Raton, FL: CRC Press.

Zaczek, R., Culp, S., & De Souza, E. B. (1991). Interactions of [3H]amphetamine with rat brain synaptosomes. II: Active transport. *Journal of Pharmacologic and Experimental Therapeutics, 257*(2), 830–835.

Zhou, F. C., & Bledsoe, S. (1996). *Methamphetamine causes rapid varicosis, perforation and definitive degeneration of serotonin fibers: An immunocytochemical study of serotonin transporter.* Retrieved November 15, 2004, from http://www.neuroscience.com/chi0796/htm/main.html

Chapter 19

Neurobiological Mechanisms and Cognitive Components of Addiction

Jorge Juárez, PhD, and Olga Inozemtseva, PhD

Addictive behavior can be seen as either a public health concern or as a problem of inadequate social adaptation. The boundaries between these two concepts become rather unclear once we consider that such disturbances may be determined by an altered genetic condition or by acquisition in any stage of development due to external agents, including the aforementioned social adaptation factor. Several studies support the position that addictive behavior has a genetic substratum, a condition that may lead individuals to seek contact with drugs and to become dependent on them even after only one or a few exposures. Other hypotheses argue that any healthy subject can become addicted if he or she is exposed to a drug with some frequency. A third point of view holds that repeated exposure to a drug by a subject with a certain genetic charge that confers specific biological or personality characteristics may be more prone to acquiring an addiction than another individual with distinct characteristics. The problem is that we have not yet identified with precision just what those characteristics are that may predispose a person to more easily acquire an addiction. What is more, if such traits do exist, they would not necessarily be the same for all potentially addictive substances. Beyond looking at causes, other studies are focusing on analyses of the mechanisms of action of the different substances that can produce addictive behavior in the organism, in an effort to provide information that may lead to possible forms of treatment. The integrated analysis of causes, mechanisms of action, and treatment is an ideal condition for studying addictions, but analyzing each one of these components apart from the others also constitutes an important task for scientists, one that requires a great deal of research that will contribute data and information to each objective of study on a daily basis. This chapter focuses primarily on describing the mechanisms of action in the brain of several substances of abuse and analyzing some of the cognitive components that have been associated with addictive behavior by cause and effect.

Generally speaking, addictive behavior is associated with the consumption of one or more of a variety of illicit substances, though it can also be related to the compulsive consumption of completely licit substances, such as certain foods, or to practicing a broad range of social and physical activities that can go from obsessive physical exercise to the behavior of the compulsive gambler. It is clear that addictions can be exemplified by a wide variety of behaviors, but for the purposes of this chapter, discussion is limited to those substances better known as drugs of abuse, the consumption of which is widespread in the population, generally in a form called *recreational* use. The chemical characteristics of such drugs vary greatly and are responsible for each one's particular properties of diffusion and distribution in the body, as well as for the specific mechanisms of action that affect different tissues in the organism. Despite the heterogeneity in the characteristics of the different drugs of abuse, it is clear that they may act on the same sites in the brain and that their activity may produce similar neurophysiologic responses.

THE MESOLIMBIC-CORTICAL SYSTEM

This system is also known as the pleasure circuit. It is intimately associated with reinforcing mechanisms and is of particular importance here because several potentially addictive substances act upon it in one way or another. For this reason, it is necessary to describe in broad terms its composition, both anatomical and neurochemical. From the anatomical perspective, the mesolimbic-cortical system is made up of the ventral tegmental area (VTA), the accumbens nucleus (Acc), the prefrontal cortex (pfC), and the amygdala (Am). Most of these structures have reciprocal connections in which diverse neurotransmitters intervene; the most important of which in terms of its reinforcing action linked to addictive conduct is dopamine (DA). The main dopaminergic projections of this circuit are those that project from VTA to Acc, pfC, and Am (Ford, Mark, & Williams, 2006). The pfC, in turn, sends glutamatergic projections to the VTA and to the Acc, while the basolateral Am sends this same type of projections to pfC. The opioid system also plays an important role in this system's functioning, as the beta-endorphins liberated in the hypothalamus are able to facilitate the liberation of dopamine indirectly. Moreover, the activation of kappa receptors has an inhibiting effect on the dopaminergic neurons of the VTA (Margolis, Hjelmstad, Bonci, & Fields, 2005). Other neurotransmitters and modulators of neuronal activity are involved in the function of the mesolimbic-cortical system, but as it is not the purpose of this chapter to present an exhaustive description of them, they will be mentioned only to the degree in which they are pertinent to the description of the mechanisms of action of the drugs examined.

NICOTINE (C10H14N2)

Nicotine is a natural alkaloid, a nitrogenated compound that acts as a base in relation to acids. It was first isolated from tobacco leaves by Posselt and Reiman in 1828, and is found in concentrations as high as 5 percent. The nicotine content of a cigarette is normally from 1 to 2 percent. Nicotine is a tertiary amine that penetrates membranes easily and is absorbed through the mucosa, skin, and lungs. From there, it spreads through the bloodstream in just a few seconds. Like many other molecules, nicotine requires receptors to produce its biological action. Receptors are proteins that can be found in the membrane, the cytosol, or the cell nucleus. The nicotine receptors, called nicotinic, are found in the cell membrane joined to ionic channels and may be activated by acetylcholine or nicotine. Once the ligand, in this case nicotine, binds to the receptor, it generally produces excitability in the cell. At the peripheral level, it stimulates the autonomous ganglions and the suprarenal medulla, thus increasing blood pressure and cardiac frequency. Its action on the neuromuscular union increases muscle tone. In the central nervous system, it acts on several regions where there are nicotinic receptors, while in terms of its effects related to the acquisition of addiction, it acts upon nicotinic receptors in the mesolimbic-cortical system that, as mentioned above, is related to reinforcing mechanisms.

The neurons in the ventral tegmental area synthesize DA, which is released by specific stimuli. It is precisely in those neurons that we find nicotinic receptors that upon being stimulated by nicotine produce the release of DA by these neurons (Keath, Iacoviello, Barrett, Mansvelder, & McGehee, 2007). This action is associated with the euphoric effects, the increased state of alertness and, probably, nicotine's addictive potential. The activation of other neurotransmission systems also seems to play an important role in the effects of nicotine, as this drug has the ability to inhibit monoaminoxidase (MAO), an enzyme that in addition to degrading DA also degrades norepinephrine (NE) and serotonin (5-HT). In this way, the inhibiting of this enzyme by nicotine provides a greater availability of these three neurotransmitters and thus increases their activity in neuronal communication. Nicotine's action has a specific characteristic in that during chronic exposure it produces a desensitization of the receptors and their inactivation (Corringer et al., 1998), an effect that may be associated with satiating the desire to smoke; however, in the short term, this inactivation produces an increase in the number of receptors as a compensating phenomenon, a mechanism known as receptor up-regulation that, it has been suggested, may be associated with the abstinence syndrome and the compulsive urge to smoke. Hence, this alternation between the deactivation of the receptors and their up-regulation may generate dependence and, therefore, the cyclical desire to smoke.

ALCOHOL (ETHANOL)

Alcohol is another substance the consumption of which is legal, though we know that it is by no means exempt from abuse and can cause a behavioral state of dependence. Ethanol is an alcohol produced through fermentation, whose molecular formula is CH_3CH_2OH. Its high degree of solubility in water allows it to penetrate practically all of the organism's tissues, including the brain. Additionally, it has a certain degree of liposolubility that allows it to interact with the lipid bilayer of the cell membrane in such a way that it modifies some of its properties. Alcohol is classified as a substance that depresses the central nervous system, a property intimately related to its affinity for the type-A receptors of gamma aminobutyric acid (GABA), which are widely distributed in the central nervous system. These receptors are inserted in the cell membrane and have different subunits that surround an ionic canal that permits the flow of chlorine (Cl^-). The activation of these GABA receptors makes the chlorine—a negatively charged ion—flow toward the interior of the cell, producing an even higher negative potential there, a phenomenon known as *hyperpolarization* that raises the threshold of cell activation that, in turn, produces an inhibiting action upon it. The activity of these GABA receptors is potentialized by alcohol, thus increasing its inhibiting action. The ansiolitic properties of alcohol, amply described in the literature, seem also to be associated with alcohol's action on the GABA receptors.

In addition, alcohol produces an increase in the liberation of beta-endorphin (an endogenous opioid) by the hypothalamus that, as already described, may be associated with the gratifying and analgesic properties of alcohol. Moreover, some authors have postulated that one of the causes of alcoholism may be associated with a compensatory action on the part of the opioid system that acts through the consumption of alcohol; this, because it has been found that alcoholic subjects present a deficiency of beta-endorphins (Genazzani et al., 1982). Hence, the release of beta-endorphins by alcohol would generate a more pleasant effect in subjects who have this endogenous opioid deficiency than in normal subjects. Though the direct effect of the release of beta-endorphins by alcohol may be reinforcing per se, there is another mechanism that affects the mesolimbic-cortical system and that seems to potentialize or complement the gratifying properties of alcohol. This mechanism operates as follows: the activity of certain GABAergic type neurons in the VTA exercises an inhibiting effect on the dopaminergic neurons of the VTA and their role is to modulate the dopaminergic discharge toward the accumbens nucleus (Olson & Nestler, 2007). These GABA neurons contain opioid receptors whose activity has an inhibiting effect on the secretion of these same neurons; that is, on the secretion of GABA (Steffensen et al., 2006), such that when beta-endorphins are liberated through alcohol consumption, they bind to the opioid receptors at the GABA terminals and inhibit them (Xiao & Ye, 2008). Given that these receptors then exercise an inhibiting action on the dopaminergic cells of the VTA, the final result is an inhibiting of the inhibition that produces the release of dopamine toward the Acc and the pfC. As mentioned above, this produces a gratifying effect. It is well known that alcohol interacts with other neurotransmission systems; however, as far as its addictive properties are concerned, the action on the opioid and dopaminergic system plays a preponderant role. Alcohol consumption also depends on the functional state of the organism, and that is where the endocrine system seems to play an important role, as studies have described that estrogens can affect alcohol consumption in two ways (Juárez, Vázquez-Cortés & Barrios De Tomasi, 2005); that is, there is evidence that estrogen treatment initially decreases alcohol consumption, but if the subjects are exposed to alcohol after several days of estrogen treatment, consumption increases significantly, a result that seems to depend on the action of the estrogens on the greater or lesser availability of opioid receptors. These data are relevant from the clinical perspective, as estrogens play a very important role in the development of both men and women, and are especially significant in the case of the latter due to their dynamic presence during the reproductive life of women and their subsequent declination during the postmenopausal period.

DRUGS THAT ACT ON THE OPIOID SYSTEM

As is well known, the organism produces its own opioids, molecules derived from amino acids called peptides. These substances are derived from different precursor molecules, and in some cases, are joined to common receptors, though this union presents different degrees of affinity. The principal endogenous opioid peptides are beta-endorphins—enkephalins and dinorphins— that are found widely distributed at both the peripheral and central levels.

Their mu (μ), delta (δ), and kappa (κ) receptors are also widely distributed in the organism, and their activation has been related to multiple functions, some of the most important of which are analgesia, the hedonistic aspects of behavior, and the modulation of nervous activity in the brain (Barrios De Tomasi & Juárez, 2007). It may seem paradoxical that the same type of opioid peptide is secreted in conditions characterized by pain and by pleasure, but it is not really so once we consider that reducing or eliminating pain can be just as pleasant as the presence of an agreeable stimulus. The most common drugs of abuse that act on the opioid system are morphine and heroin, the first of which is often used in clinical medicine because of its powerful analgesic properties, while the second is preponderant in recreational use. Both have a significant addictive potential and produce an intense abstinence syndrome that can be described in two phases: the early phase is generally marked by sweating, rhinorrhea, irritability, dysphoria, trembling, agitation, anorexia, tearing, gooseflesh, and drug craving; the later phase may be characterized by an increase in the signs and symptoms of the early phase, plus nausea, vomiting, diarrhea, increased blood pressure and heart rate, depression, generalized muscle spasms, dehydration, and a low threshold for convulsive crises (Carvey, 1998, chap. 4).

One point of discussion has been whether the dependence on these substances results from the individual seeking the drug intensely in order to eliminate the signs and symptoms of the abstinence syndrome, or if the euphoric effects and reinforcement of such drugs suffice to maintain dependence on them. These hypotheses may, in fact, be complementary rather than mutually exclusive because, as mentioned above, eliminating a harmful stimulus can be just as pleasing as positive reinforcement. Either way, the results would sustain the substance-seeking behavior of the addict. We know that blocking the m opioid receptors in the caudal region of the accumbens nucleus decreases the self-administration of heroin in rats (Martin, Kim, Lyupina, & Smith, 2002), which suggests that in this structure opioid activity on its own produces reinforcing effects that lead the addict to continue consuming the drug. However, the opioids have other mechanisms of action, produced indirectly through the activation or inhibition of other neurotransmission systems that may play an even more important part in the acquisition and continuance of addictions to these drugs. One of the most important of these is precisely the effect on the dopaminergic mesolimbic-cortical system. In this action, the agonistic opioid, which could be morphine or heroin, would act in a way similar to that described for the beta-endorphins liberated by alcohol. In this scenario, these drugs would bind preferentially to the m receptors of the GABA neurons in the ventral tegmental area, and thus inhibit them. This inhibition would, in turn, facilitate the liberation of dopamine. The different opioid receptors may seem to have different functions in the release of dopamine toward the VTA, as it has been reported that the activation of the kappa receptors inhibits the release of dopamine toward the prefrontal cortex, but not toward the accumbens (Margolis et al., 2006). This finding supports the notion of the different functionality of the DA in the Acc and pfC, and suggests that the release of DA from the VTA toward these structures may take place independently.

PSYCHOSTIMULANTS

Drugs that stimulate the central nervous system (CNS) include substances with diverse structural characteristics that share the common effect of raising a person's state of alertness and level of motor activity. They are also known as sympathomimetic substances, as they increase or imitate the activity of the autonomous sympathetic nervous system. The best-known stimulant drugs are amphetamines, methamphetamines, and cocaine in all of its forms.

Amphetamine and Methamphetamine

Amphetamines are aromatic amines (C9H13N) that exercise a powerful stimulant action on the CNS. Their most common effects are raising the state of alertness, improving concentration, increasing motor activity, producing a sensation of well-being or euphoria, inhibiting sleep, anorexia, and stimulating respiration, among others. In clinical medicine, they have been prescribed to treat obesity, narcolepsy, attention-deficit hyperactivity disorder, and depression, as well as for problems of asthma, as they also have a bronchodilator effect. Because of their euphoric effects and the increased state of alertness they produce, plus their induction of an emotional state of well-being, they are used and abused recreationally. Methamphetamines (C10H15N) are the methylated form of amphetamines; that is, they are differentiated from the latter by the presence of a methyl group in the amine group, a small structural change that reduces their peripheral effects and results, it would appear, in lessening the undesirable effects associated with the activation of the sympathetic nervous system. At the central level, however, the effects of methamphetamines are quite similar to those described for amphetamines, though they tend to be preferred for recreational use because of their lesser undesirable effects. Moreover, methamphetamines are pyrolized more easily and commonly inhaled, which favors their distribution through the lungs, quickly generates higher levels in the brain and, therefore, generates a more intense "high."

Chemical-structural variations between amphetamines and methamphetamines may give them a greater or lesser degree of activity on each neurotransmitter involved; however, given that their mechanisms of action at the cerebral level are practically the same, this activity will be described indistinctly for both substances. Consuming amphetamines or methamphetamines generates a greater availability of dopamine and noradrenaline in the synaptic space and, at least in the olfactory bulb, amphetamines are more efficient in liberating DA than NE (Mesfioui et al., 1998). The action on serotonin seems to be less when compared to that on the other two neurotransmitters, though it has been reported that some amphetamine analogues may present a greater effect on serotonin traffic.

There are basically three mechanisms of action at the cellular level that produce a greater availability of the neurotransmitter: (1) these drugs facilitate the non–calcium-dependent release of the neurotransmitter; there is evidence that amphetamines act on the recently synthesized neurotransmitter and on the contents of the vesicles, given that the previous administration of reserpine, a substance that depletes the neurotransmitter from the vesicles that contain it, attenuates the effect of amphetamines on the release of dopamine (Sabol & Seiden, 1998); (2) they act on the mechanisms that recapture the neurotransmitter and compete with it in its transportation toward the interior of the cell, a competition that makes the neurotransmitter remain available to be utilized by the postsynaptic receptors and thus exercise its effects for a longer period of time (Jayanthi & Ramamoorthy, 2005); and (3) they inhibit the degradation of the DA, NE, or 5-HT by acting competitively on the mononaminoxidase enzyme (MAO), which is in charge, precisely, of deactivating these neurotransmitters. As can be seen, the common result of these mechanisms is a greater availability of the neurotransmitter and, therefore, an increase in its activity. The fact that amphetamines compete with the neurotransmitter in its transportation toward the interior of the cell at the same time as it competes with it to be externalized by that same transporter prevents a dopaminergic overstimulation from occurring with increased doses of amphetamines, because of the greater quantity of amphetamines inside the cell, competition for the transporter favors the amphetamine, while the externalization of dopamine is attenuated. This permits a wider safety margin from harm due to overdoses, compared to that of other drugs whose blocking of the transporter is noncompetitive.

Cocaine (C17H21NO4)

This is an alkaloid obtained from the leaf of the coca plant, which contains approximately 0.5 to 0.7 percent of the active substance. Its most common version is cocaine hydrochloride in powder form that is administered intranasally (snorted) or intravenously (Schuckit, 2000, chap. 5). Another often used form is called *crack*, which is obtained by adding a base—usually ammonia or sodium bicarbonate—to cocaine hydrochloride previously dissolved in water and then filtered. This form of cocaine has a lower point of fusion than cocaine hydrochloride, which allows it to be inhaled (smoked by itself or in combination) at the moment it is pyrolized, and thus take effect more quickly than when it is aspirated. The name *crack* is onomatopoeic of the sound "crack" makes when pyrolized (Carvey, 1998, chap. 12; Schuckit, 2000, chap. 5). Many of cocaine's effects on behavior and the individual's state of mind are similar to those obtained through the consumption of amphetamines or methamphetamines, though there are important differences in the intensity and duration of its effects. Cocaine produces an intense state of euphoria that may be related to the size of the dose taken. It also increases the state of alertness and mental sharpness, creates a sensation of energy, self-confidence, and egocentricity, and apparently augments sensorial sensitivity, while decreasing appetite, the need to sleep, and the signs and symptoms of the activation of the sympathetic nervous system (Gold & Jacobs, 2005, chap. 13). Its mechanism of cellular action consists in blocking the recapture proteins in the presynaptic terminal, where dopamine is primarily released, but it also acts in a similar way in the recapture of noradrenaline and serotonin. However, unlike amphetamines, cocaine does not establish a competitive action with the neurotransmitter through its entry into the cell's cytosol, but simply blocks its entry by producing a greater availability of it in the synaptic cleft, which in turn produces an increase in the dopaminergic, noradrenergic, or serotonergic activity, according to the type of neurotransmitter that is compromised.

As can be appreciated, the common denominator in the action of the drugs described above is their effect on dopaminergic transmission in the mesolimbic-cortical system, which has been related, as discussed above, to the motivational and reinforcing mechanisms in different species of mammals, including humans. Although there can be no question, given the evidence described in the literature, that all of these drugs exercise a common action on the brain, we know that they also affect other systems of neurotransmission that, acting in concert, produce the effects characteristic of each different, potentially addictive substance. The effects of these drugs have varying degrees of severity on the functional state of the organism in general and of the brain in particular. During the acute phase of a drug's action, a series of neuroadaptive changes takes place. In some cases, these changes are reversible, such that once the effect of the drug passes, the organism returns to homeostasis. In other cases, however, the brain may suffer irreversible damage due to the acute or chronic consumption of the substance. In some cases, the magnitude of the damage is so great that it can be perceived both anatomically and behaviorally, while in others, the harm may be functional and thus more difficult to detect. Nonetheless, it may manifest itself and be detected through testing of the individual's cognitive capacities, and this is precisely the objective of the analysis described in the following section of this chapter.

NEUROPSYCHOLOGICAL COMPONENTS IN ADDICTED SUBJECTS

The main objective of the neuropsychological analysis of addictions is to search for the relationship between the use of substances and the neuropsychological impairments that may become manifest at the behavioral, cognitive, emotional, and personality levels. These neuropsychological impairments have been studied primarily in patients with different degrees of dependency or addiction to one particular substance or among polyabusers. Koob et al. (2004) conceptualize the addictive state as a disorder that progresses from impulsivity to compulsivity through a cycle; that is, in order for the patients to reach the addictive state they must follow a path that leads from the occasional, controlled use of a drug to a point at which they lose behavioral control over the search for, and consumption of, that substance; a situation defined as chronic addiction. The *Diagnostic and Statistical Manual of Mental Disorders* (*DSM–IV–TR*; American Psychiatric Association, 2002) defines substance dependency as "a cluster of cognitive, behavioural, and physiologic symptoms that indicate that the person has impaired control of psychoactive substance use and continues use of the substance despite adverse consequences (p. 218)." Substance abuse and its chronic use may result in the individual presenting the adverse neuropsychological deficits examined below, based on studies carried out with patients addicted to two of the most widely used and easily accessible kinds of psychostimulants: cocaine and methamphetamines.

As mentioned previously, cocaine is a potent psychostimulant that acts upon the monoaminergic neurotransmission systems, especially the dopaminergic system. The most frequently reported cognitive deficits in cocaine-addicted patients in abstinence indicate problems related to memory, attention, abstract reasoning, and the executive functions. Several researchers have reported deterioration of verbal and visual memory, in the phase of immediate and delayed recall, as well as in verbal learning (Beatty, Katzung, Moreland, & Nixon, 1995; Gillen et al., 1998; Horner, 1997; Rosselli & Ardila, 1996; Serper et al., 2000). The deficit in attention and concentration processes has been evidenced in both visuoperceptual and verbal tasks (Rosselli & Ardila, 1996; Strickland et al., 1993; Toomey et al., 2003). Finally, the decrease in the capacity for abstract reasoning has been observed in problem-solving tasks (Beatty et al., 1995; Rosselli & Ardila, 1996). In addition to a deficit in specific cognitive abilities (memory, attention, abstract reasoning), studies have reported a more general decrease in intellectual levels (Rosselli & Ardila, 1996), and in global neuropsychological functioning (Robinson, Heaton, & O'Malley, 1999). Given that cocaine acts primarily on the dopaminergic system, several studies have also revealed some deterioration in motor functions (Robinson et al., 1999; Toomey et al., 2003).

Addiction to cocaine is often associated with addictions to other substances, most often alcohol. Findings in the literature on the comorbid effect of chronic cocaine and alcohol abuse are contradictory, as some studies report no effect of the comorbidity of cocaine and alcohol on cognitive functions, while in others the consumption of "pure" cocaine is associated with more marked deficiencies in certain functions. Thus, Beatty et al. (1995) compared a group of "pure" cocaine addicts and a group of "pure" alcohol addicts to a third group made up of healthy participants. They reported that both groups of addicts presented a significantly poorer execution than the control group in most of the measurements of learning, memory, problem solving, executive functions, and perceptual motor-speed. Furthermore, they considered that the general pattern of neuropsychological impairment was similar in the two addict groups. In contrast, Robinson et al. (1999) compared cocaine addicts, cocaine-alcohol addicts, and healthy persons using the Halstead-Reitan neuropsychological test battery. There, the cocaine addicts presented a significantly lower execution than the cocaine-alcohol co-abusers in both complex and simple motor functioning, as well as on a measure of global neuropsychological functioning. However, the results attained by the cocaine-alcohol co-abusers did not differ significantly from those of the control group in most of the applied tasks. Brown, Seraganian, and Tremblay (1994) found no differences in the execution of a variety of neuropsychological tests between a group of cocaine- and alcohol-dependent patients and individuals addicted only to alcohol.

The complex nature of cocaine addiction includes changes at different levels of the functioning of the organism (including modifications at the level of genetic expression) that may be long-lasting or even permanent (Nestler, 2005). In this vein, Juárez (2004) has suggested that the repeated and prolonged exposure to a variety of drugs, such as cocaine, is capable of producing homeorretic modifications in the organism, which are understood as adaptive changes in different systems within the organism that may be permanent or transitory. Therefore, it is logical to ask: Is the neuropsychological deterioration in addicted patients transitory or permanent? The most natural way of responding to this question would be through studies of patients in long-term abstinence, or through longitudinal studies. In this area, Strickland et al. (1993) reported the presence of attention and concentration deficit, learning difficulties, and a deterioration of visual and verbal memory in patients addicted to crack cocaine after six months of abstinence. These researchers came to the conclusion that prolonged exposure to cocaine produces a persistent neuropsychological deficit. Di Sclafani, Tolou-Shams, Price, and Fein (2002) examined cognitive functions in abstinent crack-dependent and crack- and alcohol-dependent individuals after six weeks and six months of abstinence. Both groups of addicted patients presented deficits in attention, executive functions, spatial processing, memory (immediate and delayed), and in the global clinical impairment store after six weeks of abstinence. The substance-dependent groups were still significantly impaired at six months of abstinence. Bolla, Funderbuk, and Cadet (2000) detected an association between the dose of both cocaine and alcohol and performance on neuropsychological tasks among patients addicted to cocaine with and without alcohol use at 1–3 days of abstinence. The same effect observed in the first evaluation persisted in the second procedure, carried out with the same patients after four weeks of abstinence.

Cocaine addiction produces a deterioration of the CNS and then proceeds to exercise a negative effect on general neuropsychological functioning and specific cognitive functions, which appears to persist even after the person ceases to consume the drug for a prolonged period of time.

Methamphetamines are another, relatively recent, powerful psychostimulant that have become very popular among the addict population in the past couple of decades. Similar to cocaine, methamphetamines or deoxyephedrine, commonly known as *ice* or *crystal*, act primarily on the dopaminergic system, though their mechanism of action is somewhat different from that of cocaine, as described above. The difference in the mechanism of action at the cellular level between these two psychostimulants may be determinant for the profile of the neuropsychological deficits in persons addicted to one or another of these two substances. We have not found any studies in the literature that report a comparative analysis of the cognitive characteristics of addicts to these two drugs, though numerous works have focused on one or the other of the two. The most frequently reported deficits in methamphetamine addicts are related to learning processes and immediate and delayed verbal memory (Kalechstein, Newton, & Green, 2003; Rippeth et al., 2004; Simon et al., 2000), working memory (Rippeth et al., 2004), attention (Kalechstein et al., 2003; Nordahl, Salo, & Leamon, 2003; Rippeth et al., 2004), psycho-motor speed (Kalechstein et al., 2003), executive functions (Kalechstein et al., 2003; Salo et al., 2005; Simon et al., 2000), motor abilities (Rippeth et al., 2004; Volkow et al., 2001), and abstract reasoning (Simon et al., 2000). No reduction in the premorbid intellectual level, as measured by the Shipley-Hartford Vocabulary test (Simon et al., 2000), has been reported for methamphetamine addicts. The studies reviewed here in regard to this group of patients point to a profile of neuro-psychological impairments similar to that of cocaine addicts. However, additional work is necessary to answer the question whether the neurotoxic effects of cocaine and methamphetamine produce conspicuous differences in the neuropsychological profile of these patients.

The neuropsychological impairments in the area of addictions frequently accompany findings on the functioning of the CNS. The most commonly used techniques in this field are positron emission tomography (PET), functional magnetic resonance imaging (fMRI), and single photon emission computed tomography (SPECT), among others, all of which make it possible to detect changes in patterns of brain blood fluid (CBF) and the metabolism of brain glucose. In relation to cocaine addicts, studies with neuroimaging techniques report a reduction in CBF, both globally and regionally, because, as it turns out, cocaine is a powerful vasoconstrictor. Regional hypoperfusion appears to be more prominent in zones rich in dopamine. Many studies conducted with patients addicted to cocaine report a marked reduction in CBF in the regions of the prefrontal cortex, particularly in the anterior cingulate (Bolla et al., 2004; Volkow et al., 1993) and the orbitofrontal cortex (Adinoff et al., 2003; Volkow et al., 2005). In addition, the activity of the SNC in these patients has been negatively correlated with the consumption dose of the drug (Bolla et al., 2004; Johnson et al., 2005). Moreover, studies of these patients have revealed changes in the pattern of the activation of the limbic system, which is traditionally associated with motivation and the compulsive drug intake (Lu et al., 2005). In contrast, Childress et al. (1999) demonstrated an increased blood flow in the amygdala and anterior cingulate in addicts as compared to healthy individuals when all were shown a video on the consumption of cocaine.

In methamphetamine addicts, neuroimaging studies have been widely used to detect the availability of dopamine transporters (DAT) in the neuronal terminals. It has been shown that methamphetamine addicts present DAT loss in the orbitofrontal and dorsolateral regions of the prefrontal cortex, the amygdala, and other subcortical regions (Ernst, Chang, Leonido-Yee, & Speck, 2000; Sekine et al., 2003; Volkow et al., 2001). Furthermore, in several studies, the density of the DAT correlated negatively with the years of use of the substance (Sekine et al., 2003; Volkow et al., 2001). Sekine et al. related the low density of DAT in the orbitofrontal and dorsolateral cortex to the severity of patients' psychiatric symptoms. Volkow et al. observed DAT loss in the striatum (caudate 27.8% and putamen 21.1%) in methamphetamine addicts, compared to control subjects, associated with a persistent motor deficit. Other alterations of the SNC have also been reported for this type of addict. For example, Ernst et al., using the proton magnetic resonance spectroscopy (MRS) technique, found a significant reduction in the frontal white matter and basal ganglia. Nordahl et al. (2005) reported a reduction in the metabolism of the anterior cingulate and in the insular cortex (London et al., 2005). Furthermore, Thompson et al. (2004) demonstrated a cortical and hyppocampal structural deficit in patients addicted to methamphetamines.

The prefrontal cortex has been associated with cognitive executive functions (Luria, 1982, p. 185), which Lezak (1995, p. 650) referred to as dimensions of human behavior that are related to the way in which behavior is expressed. They are abilities related to forming objectives, planning, carrying out goal-directed behavior, and the effectiveness of production. Lezak added that these abilities are necessary for appropriate, socially responsible, self-sufficient behavior.

In a review study, Verdejo-García, López-Torrecillas, Giménez, & Pérez-García (2004) referred to the executive functions as those that permit anticipation and the establishment of objectives; the designing of plans and programs; self-regulation and task-monitoring; an appropriate selection, organization, and sequencing of behavior in space and time; monitoring of behavior with respect to affective and motivational states; adaptive decision making; efficiency of execution; and feedback.

In those addicted to several types of substances, including psychostimulants, studies have described impairments in the executive functions that find expression in a lack of cognitive flexibility, verbal fluency (Kalechstein et al., 2003; Simon et al., 2000; Verdejo-García & Pérez-García, 2007), inhibition (Ardila, Rosselli, & Strumwasser, 1991; Kalechstein et al., 2003; Nordahl et al., 2003; Rosselli, Ardila, Lubomski, Murray, & King, 2001), abstract reasoning (Ardila et al., 1991; Rosselli et al., 2001; Simon et al., 2000), and planning and organization (Bechara, 2005). Bechara et al. (2001) and Damasio (1994) consider that substance addicts present a deterioration of the executive functions related mainly to motivational aspects and decision making linked to the orbitofrontal cortex.

At the clinical level, detecting the deficit in executive functions and developing possible treatments have important implications. The problems that addicted patients experience in the area of executive functions are often cited to explain their failure to remain in rehabilitation programs, and their frequent relapse and desertion from treatment. On the other hand, various authors mention that deficiencies in the executive functions prior to addiction may create a predisposition to addiction among these patients through such mechanisms as excessive sensibility to reinforcers, or their inability to control their impulsivity (Rogers & Robbins, 2001; Verheul, 2001). However, to date we have no answer to the question: Is the executive deficit in addicted patients premorbid, or is it the consequence of the use of substances? It is still difficult to find a response to this question given the methodological complications involved, but advances in scientific knowledge in the area of neuroscience will allow us to posit new research strategies designed to search for answers to questions such as these that may have repercussions for the rehabilitation and treatment of addicts.

REFERENCES

Adinoff, B., Devous, M. D., Cooper, D. B., Best, S. E., Chandler, P., Harris, T., et al. (2003). Resting regional cerebral blood flow and gambling task performance in cocaine-dependent subjects and healthy comparison subjects. *American Journal of Psychiatry, 160,* 1892–1894.

American Psychiatric Association. (2002). *Diagnostic and statistical manual of mental disorders* (4th ed., text rev.). Washington, DC: Author.

Ardila, A., Rosselli, M., & Strumwasser, S. (1991). Neuropsychological deficits in chronic cocaine abusers. *International Journal of Neuroscience, 57,* 73–79.

Barrios De Tomasi, E., & Juárez, J. (2007). Antagonistas opioides y consumo de alcohol. *Revista de Neurología, 45,* 155–162.

Beatty, W. W., Katzung, V. J., Moreland, V. J., & Nixon, S. J. (1995). Neuropsychological performance of recently abstinent alcoholics and cocaine abusers. *Drug and Alcohol Dependence, 37,* 247–253.

Bechara, A. (2005). Decision making, impulse control and loss of willpower to resist drugs: A neurocognitive perspective. *Nature Neuroscience, 8,* 1458–1463.

Bechara, A., Dolan, S., Denburg, N., Hindes, A., Anderson, S. W., & Nathan, P. E. (2001). Decision-making deficits, linked to a dysfunctional ventromedial prefrontal cortex, revealed in alcohol and stimulant abusers. *Neuropsychologia, 39,* 376–389.

Bolla, K., Ernst, M., Kiehl, K., Mouratidis, M., Eldreth, D., Contoreggi, C., et al. (2004). Prefrontal cortical dysfunction in abstinent cocaine abusers. *Journal of Neuropsychiatry and Clinical Neurosciences, 16,* 456–459.

Bolla, K. I., Funderbuk, F. R., & Cadet, J. L. (2000). Differential effects of cocaine and cocaine + alcohol on neurocognitive performance. *Neurology, 54,* 2285–2292.

Brown , T. G., Seraganian, P., & Tremblay, J. (1994). Alcoholics also dependent on cocaine in treatment: Do they differ from "pure" alcoholics? *Addictive Behaviors, 19,* 105–112.

Carvey, P. M. (1998). *Drug action in the central nervous system.* New York: Oxford University Press.

Childress, A. R., Mosley, D., McElgin, W., Fitzgerald, J., Reivich, M., & O'Brien, C. P. (1999). Limbic activation during cue-induced cocaine craving. *American Journal of Psychiatry, 156,* 11–15.

Corringer, P. J., Bertrand, S., Bohler, S., Edelstein, S. J., Changeux, J. P., & Bertrand, D. (1998). Critical elements determining diversity in agonist binding and desensitization of neuronal nicotinic acetylcholine receptors. *Journal of Neurosciences,* *18,* 648–657.

Damasio, A. R. (1994). *Descartes' error: Emotion, reason and the human brain.* New York: Grosset/Putnam.

Di Sclafani, V., Tolou-Shams, M., Price, L. J., & Fein, G. (2002). Neuropsychological performance of individuals dependent on crack-cocaine, or crack-cocaine and alcohol, at 6 weeks and 6 months of abstinence. *Drug and Alcohol Dependence,* *66,* 161–171.

Ernst, T., Chang, L., Leonido-Yee, M., & Speck, O. (2000). Evidence for long-term neurotoxicity associated with methamphetamine abuse: A 1H MRS study. *Neurology,* *54,* 1344–1349.

Ford, C. P., Mark, G. P., & Williams, J. T. (2006).Properties and opioid inhibition of mesolimbic dopamine neurons vary according to target location. *Journal of Neurosciences,* *26,* 2788–2797.

Genazzani, A. R., Nappi, G., Facchinetti, F., Mazzella, G. L., Parrini, D., Sinforiani, E., et al. (1982). Central deficiency of ∃-endophin in alcohol addicts. *Journal of Clinical Endocrinology and Metabolism,* *55,* 583–586.

Gillen, R. W., Kranzler, H. R., Bauer, L. B., Burleson, J. A., Samarel, D., & Morrison, D. J. (1998). Neuropsychological findings in cocaine-dependent outpatients. *Progress in Neuro-Psychopharmacology and Biological Psychiatry,* *22,* 1061–1076.

Gold, M. S., & Jacobs, W. S. (2005). Cocaine and crack: Clinical aspects. In J. H. Lowinson, P. Ruiz, R. B. Millman, & J. G. Langrod (Eds.), *Substance abuse: A comprehensive textbook* (pp. 218–251). Philadelphia: Lippincott, Williams & Wilkins.

Horner, M. D. (1997). Cognitive functioning in alcoholic patients with and without cocaine dependence. *Archives of Clinical Neuropsychology,* *12,* 667–676.

Jayanthi, L. D., & Ramamoorthy, S. (2005). Regulation of monoamine transporters: Influence of psychostimulants and therapeutic antidepressants. *The American Association of Pharmaceutical Scientists Journal,* *27,* 728–738.

Johnson, B. A., Dawes, M. A., Roache, J. D., Wells, L. T., Ait-Daoud, N., Mauldin, J. B., et al. (2005). Acute intravenous low- and high-dose cocaine reduce quantitative global and regional cerebral blood flow in recently abstinent subjects with cocaine use disorder. *Journal of Cerebral Blood Flow and Metabolism,* *25,* 928–936.

Juárez, J. (2004). Neurobiología de las adicciones. In J. Velásquez-Moctezuma (Ed.), *Temas selectos de neurociencias III* (pp. 225–235). Distrito Federal, Mexico: Universidad Autónoma Metropolitana (UAM).

Juárez, J., Vázquez-Cortés, C., & Barrios De Tomasi, E. (2005). Different stages in the temporal course of estrogen treatment produce opposite effects on voluntary alcohol consumption in male rats. *Alcohol,* *36,* 55–61.

Kalechstein, A. D., Newton, T. F., & Green, M. (2003). Methamphetamine dependence is associated with neurocognitive impairment in the initial phases of abstinence. *Journal of Neuropsychiatry and Clinical Neurosciences,* *15,* 215–220.

Keath, J. R., Iacoviello, M. P., Barrett, L. E., Mansvelder, H. D., & McGehee, D. S. (2007). Differential modulation by nicotine of substantia nigra versus ventral tegmental area dopamine neurons. *Journal of Neurophysiology,* *98,* 3388–3396.

Koob, G. H., Ahmed, S. H., Boutrel, B., Chen, S. A., Kenny, P. J, Markou, A., et al. (2004). Neurobiological mechanisms in the transition from drug use to drug dependence. *Neuroscience and Biobehavioral Reviews, 27,* 739–749.

Lezak, M. D. (1995). *Neuropsychological assessment.* New York: Oxford University Press.

London, E. D., Berman, S. M., Voytek, B., Simon, S. L., Mandelkern, M. A., Monterosso, P., et al. (2005). Cerebral metabolic dysfunction and impaired vigilance in recently abstinent methamphetamine abusers. *Biological Psychiatry, 58,* 770–778.

Lu, L., Hope, B. T., Dempsey, J., Liu, S. Y., Bossert, J. M., & Shaham, Y. (2005). Central amygdala ERK signaling pathway is critical to incubation of cocaine craving. *Nature Neuroscience, 8,* 212–219.

Luria, A. R. (1982). *El cerebro en acción.* Habana, Cuba: Edición Revolucionaria.

Margolis, E. B., Hjelmstad, G. O., Bonci, A., & Fields, H. L. (2005). Both kappa and mu opioid agonists inhibit glutamatergic input to ventral tegmental area neurons. *Journal of Neurophysiology, 93,* 3086–3093.

Margolis, E. B., Lock, H., Chefer, V. I., Shippenberg, T. S., Hjelmstad, G. O., & Fields, H. L. (2006). Kappa opioids selectively control dopaminergic neurons projecting to the prefrontal cortex. *Proceedings of the National Academy of Sciences of the United States of America, 103,* 2938–2942.

Martin, T. J., Kim, S. A., Lyupina, Y., & Smith, J. E. (2002). Differential involvement of mu-opioid receptors in the rostral versus caudal nucleus accumbens in the reinforcing effects of heroin in rats: Evidence from focal injections of beta-funaltrexamine. *Psychopharmacology, 161,* 152–159.

Mesfioui, A., Math, F., Jmari, K., El Hessni, A., Choulli, M. K., & Davrainville, J. L. (1998). Effects of amphetamine and phenylethylamine on catecholamine release in the glomerular layer of the rat olfactory bulb. *Biological Signals and Receptors, 7,* 235–243.

Nestler, E. J. (2005, December). The neurobiology of cocaine addiction. *Science and Practice Perspectives,* 4–11.

Nordahl, T. E., Salo, R., & Leamon, M. (2003). Neuropsychological effects of chronic methamphetamine use on neurotransmitters and cognition: A review. *Journal of Neuropsychiatry and Clinical Neurosciences, 15,* 317–325.

Nordahl, T. E., Salo, R., Natsuaki, Y., Galloway, G. P., Watres, C., & Moore, C. D. (2005). Methamphetamine users in sustained abstinence: A proton magnetic resonance spectroscopy study. *Archives of General Psychiatry, 62,* 444–452.

Olson, V. G., & Nestler, E. J. (2007). Topographical organization of GABAergic neurons within the ventral tegmental area of the rat. *Synapse, 61,* 87–95.

Rippeth, D. J., Heaton, K. R., Carey, L. C., Marcotte, D. T., Moore, J. D., González, R., et al. (2004). Methamphetamine dependence increases risk of neuropsychological impairment in HIV infected persons. *Journal of the International Neuropsychological Society, 10,* 1–14.

Robinson, J. E., Heaton, R. K., & O'Malley, S. S. (1999). Neuropsychological functioning in cocaine abusers with and without alcohol dependence. *Journal of the International Neuropsychological Society, 5,* 10–19.

Rogers, R. D., & Robbins, T. W. (2001). Investigating the neurocognitive deficits associated with chronic drug misuse. *Current Opinion in Neurobiology, 11*, 250–257.

Rosselli, M., Ardila, A., Lubomski, M., Murray, S., & King, K. (2001). Personality profile and neuropsychological test performance in chronic cocaine-abusers. *International Journal of Neuroscience, 110*, 55–72.

Rosselli, M., & Ardila, A. (1996). Cognitive effects of cocaine and polydrug abuse. *Journal of Clinical and Experimental Neuropsychology, 18*, 122–135.

Sabol, K. E., & Seiden, L. S. (1998). Reserpine attenuates D-amphetamine and MDMA-induced transmitter release in vivo: A consideration of dose, core temperature and dopamine synthesis. *Brain Research, 806*, 69–78.

Salo, R., Nordahl, T. E., Moore, C., Waters, C., Natsuaki, Y., Galloway, G. P., et al. (2005). A dissociation in attentional control: Evidence from methamphetamine dependence. *Biological Psychiatry, 57*, 310–313.

Schuckit, M. A. (2000). Drug alcohol abuse: A clinical guide to diagnosis and treatment. New York: Kluwer Academic/Plenum.

Sekine, Y., Minabe, Y., Ouchi, Y., Takei, N., Iyo, M., Nakamura, K., et al. (2003). Association of dopamine transporter loss in the orbitofrontal and dorsolateral prefrontal cortices with methamphetamine-related psychiatric symptoms. *American Journal of Psychiatry, 160*, 1699–1701.

Serper, M. R., Bergman, A., Copersino, M. L., Chou, J.C.Y., Richarme, D., & Cancro, R. (2000). Learning and memory impairment in cocaine-dependent and comorbid schizophrenic patients. *Psychiatric Research, 93*, 21–32.

Simon, S. L., Domier, C., Carnell, J., Brethen, P., Rawson, R., & Ling, W. (2000). Cognitive impairment in individuals currently using methamphetamine. *American Journal on Addictions, 9*, 222–231.

Steffensen, S. C., Stobbs, S. H., Colago, E. E., Lee, R. S., Koob, G. F., Gallegos, R. A., et al. (2006). Contingent and non-contingent effects of heroin on mu-opioid receptor-containing ventral tegmental area GABA neurons. *Experimental Neurology, 202*, 139–151.

Strickland, T. L., Mena, I., Villanueva-Meyer, J., Miller, B. L., Cummings, J., Mehringer, C. M., et al. (1993). Cerebral perfusion and neuropsychological consequences of chronic cocaine use. *Journal of Neuropsychiatry and Clinical Neurosciences, 5*, 419–427.

Thompson, P. M., Hayashi, K. M., Simon, S. L., Geaga, J. A., Hong, M. S., Sui, Y., et al. (2004). Structural abnormalities in the brains of human subjects who use methamphetamine. *Journal of Neurosciences, 24*, 6028–6036.

Toomey, R., Lyons, M. J., Eisen, S. A., Xian, H., Chantarujipakong, S., Seidman, L. J., et al. (2003). A twin study of the neuropsychological consequences of stimulant abuse. *Archives of General Psychiatry, 3*, 303–310.

Verdejo-García, A., López-Torrecillas, F., Giménez, C. O., & Pérez-García, M. (2004). Clinical implications and methodological challenges in the study of the neuropsychological correlates of cannabis, stimulant, and opioid abuse. *Neuropsychology Review, 14*, 1–41.

Verdejo-García, A., & Pérez-García, M. (2007). Profile of executive deficits in cocaine and heroin polysubstance users: Common and differential effects on separate executive components. *Psychopharmacology, 190,* 517–530.

Verheul, R. (2001). Comorbidity of personality disorders in individuals with substance use disorders. *European Psychiatry, 16,* 274–282.

Volkow, N. D., Chang, L., Wang, G., Fowler, J. S., Franceschi, D., Sedler, M. J., et al. (2001). Higher cortical and lower subcortical metabolism in detoxified methamphetamine abusers. *American Journal of Psychiatry, 158,* 383–389.

Volkow, N. D., Fowler, J. S., Wang, G.-J., Hitzemann, R., Logan, J., Shlyer, D. J., et al. (1993). Decreased dopamine D2 receptor availability is associated with reduced frontal metabolism in cocaine abusers. *Synapse, 14,* 169–177.

Volkow, N. D., Wang, G.-J., Ma, Y., Fowler, J. S., Wong, C., Ding, Y.-S., et al. (2005). Activation of orbitofrontal and medial prefrontal cortex by methylphenidate in cocaine-addicted subjects but not in controls: Relevance to addiction. *Journal of Neurosciences, 25,* 3932–3939.

Xiao, C., & Ye, J. H. (2008). Ethanol dually modulates GABAergic synaptic transmission onto dopaminergic neurons in ventral tegmental area: Role of mu-opioid receptors. *Neuroscience, 153,* 240–248.

Chapter 20

Fetal, Neonatal, and Early Childhood Effects of Prenatal Methamphetamine Exposure

Mary F. Holley, MD

Drugs of abuse have a long legacy of causing significant impairment in the development of the human brain. Alcohol abuse during pregnancy results in significant changes that include facial dysmorphisms, neurobehavioral problems such as Attention Deficit Hyperactivity Disorder (ADHD), and mental retardation. The full complex of alcohol-related dysfunction is known as fetal alcohol syndrome. Methamphetamine exposure has not been identified with a syndrome or an identifiable pattern of malformation or dysfunction, but clusters of symptoms have been associated with neurologic deficits identified on sophisticated brain scanning of children exposed to methamphetamine (Chang et al., 2004). These findings require our attention and reasonable changes in our patterns of practice in the prenatal clinic and the nursery.

There are a number of developmental risk factors that are common to all drugs of abuse and that may overlap with the effects of lower socioeconomic status. These include genetic influences, nutrition status of the mother, poverty and associated stressors, mental illness either as a predisposing factor to addiction or as a consequence of drug use, infectious diseases, and lack of prenatal care. Each of these factors contributes to the environmental stressors impacting the development of the child born into a family affected by drug abuse. We will also consider the risk factors specific to methamphetamine use, including placental insufficiency, preterm labor, congenital malformations, and the neurotoxic effects of methamphetamine on the developing brain.

Early identification of drug-exposed infants and children is crucial to our efforts to intervene in the lives of these children. Early childhood development is strongly affected by the drug use of parents, particularly mothers. Proactive intervention, however, demands that we know at the infancy or preschool stage that a child is at risk for drug- or alcohol-related developmental challenges. In order to effectively intervene in these children's lives, we have to know who they are, and be willing to take action to protect them. The consequences of our failure to do so will be made manifest in the juvenile detention centers of the next decade.

INTRODUCTION

In the United States, methamphetamine use among pregnant women doubled over the six-year span from 1998 to 2004 (Cox, Posner, Kourtis, & Jamieson, 2008), as methamphetamine has gradually replaced cocaine as the drug of choice in many areas of the nation among Americans in general and women of childbearing age in particular. Unlike cocaine, methamphetamine is used by women at rates equal to men (Cohen, Greenberg, Uri, Halpin, & Zweben, 2007), primarily for weight loss and increased energy. Methamphetamine is a much more toxic drug than cocaine, causing more rapid and intense addiction (Gonzalez, Castro, Barrington, Walton, & Rawson, 2000), more symptoms of mental illness (McKetin, McLaren, Lubman, & Hides, 2006), and more rapid personal and family disintegration. For all these reasons, methamphetamine has exacted a higher toll on the family, higher even than cocaine, which has already destroyed countless families across this nation.

Both cocaine and methamphetamine produce sexual arousal and promote promiscuous sexual behavior, but methamphetamine produces this effect for far longer than cocaine, and is commonly used by addicts to enhance their sexual experience. As the people using methamphetamine are predominantly of childbearing age, this drug poses greater risks to their unborn children than other comparable drugs of abuse. Increased risk of disease transmission, including sexually transmitted diseases (STD), hepatitis C, and HIV, higher risk of obstetric complications, prematurity and growth restriction, are of particular concern as methamphetamine use increases in the mothers of our children (Smith, LaGasse, Derauf, Grant, & Shah, 2006).

Of major concern are the numerous anecdotal reports of significant neurologic dysfunction in children exposed to methamphetamine in utero. Caretakers of these children have reported cases of severe ADHD, conduct disorders, learning disabilities, and developmental delays in the children of methamphetamine users. These reports have been of great concern to the family members, adoptive and foster parents who are taking responsibility for these children. Scientifically valid information regarding their prognosis and effective interventions is greatly needed.

Education professionals are concerned about the impact of methamphetamine abuse on the special education demands placed on their schools as large numbers of children with learning disabilities and attention deficits are enrolled in the nation's public school system. And since children with learning disabilities and academic failure have higher rates of delinquency (Aseltine, Gore, & Gordon, 2000), methamphetamine-exposed children are more likely to grow up to be wards of the juvenile justice system, further straining our criminal justice system. Early identification of the drug-affected child would permit intervention and training opportunities before entry into the school system, at a time when such interventions are most likely to be effective. But early identification requires drug testing of neonates at or shortly after birth.

True primary prevention would require identification of the drug-using mother in the first trimester of pregnancy, a time when many mothers are amenable to interventions to help their children. Drug testing in the prenatal clinic, however, is generally not done because of fears such testing would deter women from seeking prenatal care. Lacking reliable prenatal information, we are left with secondary prevention, limiting the effects of a disease by controlling its complications—damage control. This we seek to do by neonatal drug testing to detect exposure early and offer remedial assistance to the child and rehabilitation to the mother after prenatal exposure has already occurred.

There is a great deal of controversy over the utility and validity of drug testing of neonates. There are concerns over the accuracy of the tests, false positive results, interactions with prescribed medications, and possible lawsuits by mothers alleging breaches of their privacy rights. There are also concerns over possible legal prosecution against the mothers of these children, actions taken by child protective services workers, including termination of parental rights, custody battles, and the lack of rehabilitation facilities accepting mothers with their young children.

An accurate understanding of and response to the epidemic of drug use in this nation (and around the world) is essential to prevent a public health disaster of epic proportions as today's children become tomorrow's parents. In view of the significant neurotoxicty of methamphetamine, the anecdotal reports of neurologic dysfunction and learning disability in methamphetamine-affected children cannot be dismissed altogether as unreliable. These reports instead must be investigated and fully understood in order to institute preventative measures and offer meaningful intervention to affected children and their families.

NONSPECIFIC RISK FACTORS

Nutrition is a strong variable associated with poor outcomes in drug-using pregnancies (Knight et al., 1994). Some drugs of abuse, such as alcohol, replace normal food intake and compete with nutrients for entry into the mother. Other drugs are potent anorectics, among them cocaine and methamphetamine. These drugs can cause profound nutritional deficiencies in chronic users, to the point of starvation. Vitamin deficiencies, anemia, and protein calorie malnutrition are significant risks to a pregnancy already complicated by substance abuse.

Poverty is also strongly associated with drug abuse, as addicts are unable to hold down a job or manage their finances appropriately. Some methamphetamine addicts are employed and hold middle-income jobs, but all of their resources go to procure drugs and alcohol, and adequate housing and nutrition are not priorities for these people. Uninsured mothers living in poverty are less likely to attend prenatal clinics and more likely to have untreated infections and poor nutrition regardless of their drug abuse status.

Chronic stress is often a characteristic of the lifestyle of drug-abusing mothers (Derauf et al., 2007). Homelessness is common, and many addicts move from place to place with no permanent address. Addicts sometimes live in cars or abandoned buildings without utilities or a stable food supply, conditions not conducive to a healthy pregnancy. Legal problems are common with multiple arrests, bonds, and fines. Criminal activity and domestic violence are especially common in methamphetamine-affected households. Methamphetamine addicts are irritable and impatient, and with the onset of psychotic symptoms, sometimes become violent. This violence is often directed at family members.

Mental illness is very common in substance abusers, especially methamphetamine abusers. Addicts sometimes have preexisting major illnesses such as bipolar disorder or schizophrenia, but more often, they develop methamphetamine-induced symptoms of mental illness, which may or may not clear after a period of detoxification (Mahoney, Kalechstein, De La Garza, & Newton, 2008). Addicts may become paranoid, suspicious, and hypervigilant. Real and apparent threats are ubiquitous. Addicts feel threatened by other addicts, aggressive dealers, "snitches," and the authorities and often develop delusions surrounding these and other threats. Their mental problems lead directly to severe distress, and indirectly to occupational failure, economic distress, noncompliance with prenatal care, and poor parental adjustment. Long-term methamphetamine use can cause a form of dementia with memory loss and frontal lobe dysfunction, leading to severe impairment in some users (McCann et al., 2007).

Infectious disease is common in drug-abusing populations regardless of the substance used. Sexually transmitted diseases flourish in the climate of promiscuity, the sex-for-dope economy, and reduced precautions characteristic of methamphetamine abuse. Methamphetamine increases sexual desire and drive much more than other drugs of abuse, and so is associated with extremely high rates of infection with STDs. Methamphetamine users experience drying of mucous membranes due to the vasoconstrictive effects of the drug. Methamphetamine addicts engage in higher rates of unprotected sex and larger numbers of anonymous partners. They are less likely to present for medical care and less compliant with treatment for STDs.

Increased risks of hepatitis B and C and HIV are well known, particularly in IV drug users and sexually promiscuous users. Methamphetamine appears to act as an adjuvant, increasing the risk of infection when exposed to either hepatitis C (Ye et al., 2008) or HIV (Mahajan et al., 2006; Nair et al., 2006; Talloczy et al., 2008). These infections are transmitted vertically to the neonate at birth. While measures can be taken to protect the developing fetus from HIV, there are currently no prophylactic treatments available to prevent hepatitis C from transmitting to the newborn.

Substance abusers are also less likely to present for prenatal care and so are less likely to have been tested and treated for their infectious diseases. Methamphetamine abusers often first present to the hospital in advanced labor having no prior relationship with any health care provider. Fearing involvement with the legal system, they frequently deny illegal drug exposure. Their drug use can only be detected by drug testing in the presence of high-risk behavioral indicators.

METHAMPHETAMINE SPECIFIC RISK FACTORS

Aside from the general risk factors associated with abuse of any drug, there are also a host of risk factors specific to methamphetamine abuse. These include obstetric complications, poor neonatal growth, increased risk of congenital malformations, and neurologic injury to the neonatal brain related to exposure to a potent neurotoxin. The human fetus and placenta lack enzymes that could metabolize methamphetamine as it crosses the placental barrier (Dixon, 1989). Since methamphetamine crosses the placenta very efficiently, blood and tissue levels in the fetus are comparable to maternal blood and tissue levels (Stek et al., 1993; Won, Bubula, & Heller, 2001). Methamphetamine has a much longer half-life than cocaine, particularly in the human fetus. These factors can result in the accumulation of active drug in the fetus, and higher blood levels of the drug have been seen in the developing fetus than seen in the mother under conditions of chronic administration (Stewart & Meeker, 1997).

The immature organ systems of the fetus are therefore exposed to "big people" doses of a potent stimulant drug with all of its vasoconstrictor and cellular toxic properties. The picture is further complicated by the fact that more than 80 percent of methamphetamine-using mothers also use one or more additional drugs of abuse, most commonly alcohol (Brecht, Greenwell, & Anglin, 2007). The impact on the developing fetus is thus increased exponentially in its clinical presentation.

Obstetric complications are significantly increased in methamphetamine-abusing pregnant mothers. Because of its prolonged half-life in humans—12 to 20 hours—chronic vascular disruption is seen, leading to long-term complications. Placental insufficiency is often seen, leading to intrauterine growth restriction in the fetus (Smith et al., 2006). Some congenital malformations may also be associated with the intense vasoconstriction associated with methamphetamine use (Hoyme et al., 1990). Maternal hypertension associated with methamphetamine is of much longer duration than similar findings in cocaine abusers and can lead to obstetric catastrophe with abruption and fetal distress or fetal demise (Stewart & Meeker, 1997).

Maternal hypertension is often mistaken for preeclampsia or co-occurs with preeclampsia (Elliott & Rees, 1990). Accurate diagnosis is essential since the treatment differs for methamphetamine abusers. Treatment with beta blockers such as Labetolol can have untoward results in methamphetamine abusers as these drugs do not block the alpha adrenergic effect of methamphetamine and can lead to rapidly progressive heart failure in methamphetamine-abusing gravidas (Samuels, Maze, & Albright, 1979 and author's personal experience). Older antihypertensives are preferred, such as appressoline or nipride, which block alpha receptors and control the hypertension seen in methamphetamine abuse. These drugs must be dosed carefully and slowly to prevent overshoot hypotension and resulting fetal distress.

Preterm labor, premature rupture of membranes, and chorioamnionitis are all increased in methamphetamine-affected pregnancies (Eriksson, Larsson, & Zetterström, 1981). The result is often a low birth weight newborn with signs of drug withdrawal, including tremors, lethargy, poor feeding, excess irritability, and other neurobehavioral abnormalities (Smith et al., 2003). Physical signs of withdrawal in the neonate include tachycardia, hypertension, hyper-reflexia, often mixed with symptoms related to the concurrent use of narcotics such as heroin. The Neonatal Abstinence Scoring system is validated for neonates exposed to all drugs of abuse, although the findings can be widely different for infants withdrawing from heroin versus those exposed to stimulants (Oro & Dixon, 1987). Many of these children are exposed to multiple drugs with conflicting effects, leading to confusing findings and missed detection of exposed children.

The incidence of congenital malformations has been studied in chart review studies (Forrester & Merz, 2006, 2007), or retrospective studies of affected children (Torfs, Velie, Oechsli, Bateson, & Curry, 1994), but these studies did not include a routine neonatal drug-testing protocol and instead relied on patient report and sporadic drug testing in response to risk factors over the course of normal obstetric care. Both methods of detection are fraught with difficulty as only 25 percent of drug-abusing mothers admit to drug use when questioned (Ostrea, Brady, Gause, Raymundo, & Stevens, 1992), and drug testing is often done based on stereotype, missing many drug-using mothers who do not fit the profile of the "drug addict." As a result, we do not know the true incidence of congenital malformations in the infants of methamphetamine-abusing mothers. Anecdotal reports have linked methamphetamine abuse with gastroschisis, eye and ear malformations, cardiac defects, renal anomalies, and limb reduction defects, all of which are exceedingly rare (Bays, 1991).

Effects of methamphetamine exposure on the developing brain have been extensively studied, particularly in light of the overwhelming evidence that methamphetamine is a neurotoxin in the adult brain (for a review, see Yamamoto & Bankson, 2005). Most of these studies have been done on rodent species. Very few human studies have been done to assess human brain development in methamphetamine-exposed children, but those that have been done suggest a significant effect, and a long-lasting effect, with behavioral changes and increased social problems extending into adolescence.

METHAMPHETAMINE'S EFFECT ON BRAIN DEVELOPMENT

Theoretically, methamphetamine should have a significant impact on brain development. It is a potent vasoconstrictor, reducing blood supply to the placenta and thus delivery of oxygen and nutrients to the developing fetus. It is also a potent neurotoxin, releasing free radical compounds that cause neural cell death (Yamamoto & Bankson, 2005). And indeed stimulants do impact embryogenesis of the developing central nervous system. Cell proliferation and migration are impacted and synaptogenesis is impaired (Weissman & Caldecott-Hazard, 1995). There is reduction in neural growth factor and a marked increase in reactive oxygen species and free radicals (Jeng, Wong, Ting-A-Kee, & Wells, 2005; Wells et al., 2005). These toxic chemicals are known neurotoxins and have been implicated in the progression of cellular damage to the brain in adult methamphetamine users (Acikgoz et al., 2000).

Animal models, rats, mice, and gerbils, have been used to study the fetal effects of many drugs, including methamphetamine. Rodents metabolize methamphetamine differently from humans; the half-life of methamphetamine in rodents is only around 1 hour, compared with 12 hours in humans (Cho, Melega, Kuczenski, & Segal, 2001). Rodents also mature their central nervous system in the first month postnatally while humans do so in the third trimester of pregnancy (Gomez-DeSilva, Silva, & Tavares, 1998). Rodents are born at an earlier gestational maturity than humans, and so are usually dosed 10 to 20 days after birth to simulate third-trimester human exposure. Neonatal rodents have been found to be relatively resistant to the effects of methamphetamine compared to adults. These factors explain the significant differences in dosing of animals compared to typical human use patterns. These differences often cloud interpretation of animal data by clinicians who accuse animal researchers of vastly overdosing the animals. Because of the markedly reduced half-life of methamphetamine in rodents, these studies more likely underestimate the impact of fetal methamphetamine exposure, rather than overestimating it. Overall, methamphetamine appears to be a much more neurotoxic drug than cocaine, as might be expected based on its metabolic profile.

A summary of the most recent research in the field of methamphetamine effect on brain development reveals some disturbing trends. Acevedo, de Esch, and Raber (2006) studying mice found significant disruption of hippocampus dependent cognitive function in adult animals exposed to methamphetamine in the neonatal stage. Cognitive functions affected included spatial learning, memory, and object recognition. Vorhees, Skelton, and Williams (2007) looked at rats and also found spatial learning and memory deficits that persisted into adulthood, suggesting a permanent structural change in brain development. In an older but well-done study, Hildebrandt, Teuchert-Noodt, and Dawirs (1999) localized the site of methamphetamine-induced injury to the dentate gyrus of the hippocampus, specifically to impaired granule cell proliferation (a 34 percent deficit). Even low-dose methamphetamine exposure caused significant spatial learning deficits in rats, suggesting that there is no safe level of exposure during pregnancy (Williams, Moran, & Vorhees, 2004).

Gomez-DeSilva and colleagues (2004) demonstrated increased catecholamines in neonatal rat brains exposed to methamphetamine, particularly in the substantia nigra, caudate putamen, and nucleus accumbens. Williams, Brown, and Vorhees (2004) demonstrated injury to the hippocampus, nucleus accumbens, and parietal lobes in rats exposed to methamphetamine. These findings have been replicated repeatedly by numerous researchers, demonstrating a significant neurotoxic effect of methamphetamine in brain development with functional loss of memory and coordination.

The mechanism of this damage was elucidated by Jeng et al. (2005), who investigated the metabolic pathways by which methamphetamine damages developing neural tissue. They found that methamphetamine causes oxidative cell injury in the brains of mice exposed to neonatal methamphetamine. Oxygen free radicals are produced by the metabolism of both methamphetamine and the monoamine neurotransmitters released in response to methamphetamine. These free radicals are potent neurotoxins. The fetal brain lacks key alternate enzymes needed to metabolize monoamines and methamphetamine, leading to the build-up of high levels of oxygen free radicals and consequent long-term impairment of brain development (Wells et al., 2005).

These neurotoxic changes persist into adulthood and sensitize the adult brain to the effects of adult exposure to methamphetamine, particularly in males. Neurotoxicity to the dopaminergic projections in response to methamphetamine challenge in adulthood was significantly increased in animals that had been exposed to methamphetamine prenatally, suggesting a persistent sensitivity (Heller, Bubula, Lew, Heller, & Won, 2001). This finding has significant implications for meth-exposed children growing up in meth-abusing homes who learn early in life how to solve their problems with a pipe.

HUMAN STUDIES OF METHAMPHETAMINE IMPACT

Clearly, methamphetamine should not be given to neonatal rats, mice, or gerbils. It damages their little brains. But what about humans? Do the animal studies apply to the human infant? Most human methamphetamine users are polydrug users and have multiple other risk factors in addition to their drug use, including poverty, stress, nutritional deficiencies, and infections, to name a few. For these reasons, the rodent studies more likely *underestimate* the impact of the total prenatal environment on the human fetus and its development.

The earliest studies on human response to fetal methamphetamine exposure were grim indeed. Tests of visual recognition in human infants exposed to methamphetamine showed significant decreases (Hansen, Struthers, & Gospe, 1993) and corresponding differences in attention, distractibility, and activity level (Struthers & Hansen, 1992). Changes in visual recognition in the infant are strongly associated with cognitive function later in life, and lack of eye contact can also impair maternal–infant bonding in the first days of life. Dixon and Bejar at UCSD (1989) found that 35 percent of neonates exposed to cocaine and/or methamphetamine in utero had abnormalities in brain structure at birth, including intraventricular hemorrhage, necrotic echodensities, and cavitary lesions. These lesions were thought to be due to the severe vasoconstrictive effects of stimulant drugs of abuse. A significant number of stimulant-exposed infants (10%) had ventricular dilation, reflecting diffuse atrophy of cortical tissue.

But the human brain is not the same as a rodent brain. Cortical areas are much more richly developed in humans, and the human cortex continues postnatal development over the first 21 years of life, especially in the first 3 years of life. The developmental window that extends from birth to age three is a time of explosive growth in cognitive, emotional, verbal, and social development. Given adequate interaction, stimulation, and nutrition, the human cortex increases in size significantly. If the meth-exposed child is sent home with responsible parents, much (though perhaps not all) of the brain injury sustained before birth could be compensated for and its impact diminished. Early intervention in methamphetamine-exposed children could be extremely important to the long-term prognosis for human cognitive and social development.

And indeed that is what the studies demonstrate. When methamphetamine-exposed children are studied at age 8 to 10 years, the cavitary lesions and ventricular dilation are no longer seen (Smith et al., 2001). All of the children in this study had been exposed to methamphetamine with very low levels of exposure to other drugs of abuse, including alcohol. Children with diagnosed developmental delay, impaired growth, seizure disorders, or ADHD were excluded. Only those children who looked perfectly normal were studied. Although these children did have signs of metabolic changes in the basal ganglia, no cavitary lesions were found.

In a follow-up study by the same group, Chang et al. in 2004 investigated further the changes seen in the basal ganglia of methamphetamine-exposed children. Using some of the same subjects, again excluding children with obvious developmental delays or ADHD, significant subcortical changes were seen. Methamphetamine-exposed children had significantly smaller hippocampus, globus palidus, putamen, and caudate (17%–26% smaller), the same areas that are impaired in the animal studies.

A corresponding decrement in neuropsychological testing was also observed in these methamphetamine-exposed children. They scored lower on measures of visual-motor integration, attention, verbal memory, and long-term spatial memory, all essential functions in efficient learning. Again, these were children who had not been identified as having a developmental delay or ADHD by teachers or caregivers. These children looked perfectly normal and were performing normally in school, but they were challenged by the effects of their prenatal methamphetamine exposure.

Long-term follow-up of methamphetamine-exposed children over a period of up to 15 years shows the impact of these challenges. Billings, Eriksson, Jonsson, Steneroth, and Zetterström (1994) demonstrated increased aggressive behavior and poor adjustment in children 8 to 10 years old exposed to methamphetamine prenatally. The same children followed up to 15 years of age (Cernarud, Eriksson, Jonsson, Steneroth, & Zetterström, 1996; Eriksson, Jonsson, Steneroth, & Zetterström, 2000) showed higher rates of academic failure and poor social adjustment. These methamphetamine-exposed children were three times more likely to be behind in school (15% were one year or more behind) and had lower grades than nonexposed peers.

These long-term studies did not attempt to control for alcohol exposure. Indeed, 81 percent of these children were also exposed to alcohol prenatally. Fetal alcohol syndrome has clearly been linked to significant neurobehavioral abnormalities, including ADHD, learning disability, verbal memory deficits, and mental retardation (Pie, Rinaldi, Rasmussen, Massey, & Massey, 2008). Most of these children (80%) were also exposed to nicotine, which has been linked to abnormalities of the auditory association area (Dwyer, Broide, & Leslie, 2008) and dysregulation of emotion and attention (Shea & Steiner, 2008). The majority (78%) of these children did not live with their birth mothers throughout childhood. Many were wards of the state and had moved from foster home to foster home, a condition that is strongly linked to academic failure and delinquency (National Center on Addiction and Substance Abuse at Columbia University, 2004).

We do not know the true incidence or severity of psychomotor or neurocognitive disability in children exposed to methamphetamine because routine drug testing is not being done, and so the majority of affected children are not identified at birth or assessed as they mature. Human studies will always be complicated by concurrent alcohol and other drug abuse, since most meth addicts use other drugs as well. We do not yet have the necessary data to assess the true incidence and risk of methamphetamine exposure to the development of the human brain.

EARLY DETECTION AND INTERVENTION

Primary prevention of drug-related disability in the infant requires that the drug-abusing mother be identified and counseled early in the prenatal course so that disease and impairment is prevented. Screening of obstetric patients for drug and alcohol abuse is required by the laws of most states, yet is inconsistently done by most providers and even more seldom reported or acted upon during the pregnancy. This is in spite of the fact that a poor obstetric outcome is likely in the event of drug abuse during pregnancy, and that the poor outcome is likely to be attributed to substandard obstetric care if the existence of drug abuse has not been documented.

Prenatal screening is fraught with difficulty because of the fear that the drug-abusing gravida will simply avoid prenatal care if serious attention is directed to her drug or alcohol abuse, especially in the form of drug testing. Screening is thus limited to verbal questioning with its attendant underestimation of the extent of the problem at hand.

For verbal screening to be effective, questioning should be incorporated into the routine intake interview so that a rapport is established with the health care provider and suspicion as to the intentions of the provider is minimized.

Questioning should begin with an inquiry into family history of substance abuse, ideally in the context of a general family history review. This line of questioning is less threatening to the patient and less likely to raise resistance than a direct assault on her fitness to be a mother. If the family history of addiction is then recorded as an illness, not a moral failure, the patient may be more likely to admit to her own "addictive illness" than she would be to admit to her "illegal drug use" with its criminal intonations.

Early prenatal identification of a drug or alcohol problem permits primary prevention of the neonatal complications—the ideal situation—rather than just the damage containment obtainable with neonatal drug testing. Prenatal identification requires an informed, concerned, and honest patient, who has been apprised of the risks drug abuse poses to her and her baby's health, a nonjudgmental attitude on the part of the medical provider, and the availability of appropriate inpatient or outpatient treatment facilities.

Since primary prevention is often not accomplished, we are left with damage containment measures that focus on identification of the affected newborns and rehabilitation of their mothers after delivery. But even postdelivery "damage control" interventions are often not carried out because of poor detection of drug and alcohol abuse in the neonatal stage. The period of hospitalization presents our best opportunity to detect and intervene in the addiction process because of the prolonged period of intense observation by skilled professionals in the labor and delivery suite. Professionals trained in recognition of the signs of addiction can identify mothers and infants with risk factors for addiction, and in most states, can order a neonatal drug test at the slightest hint of a problem. The most seriously affected children are likely to be identified in this way; however, not all drug addicts look, act, and smell like drug addicts. Not all labor and delivery professionals are alert to the signs and symptoms of addiction, and not all doctors and hospitals permit drug testing on their favored (insured) patients. Some doctors and hospitals, wishing to avoid all the hassle associated with drug testing, do testing on only the most egregious cases, missing many affected children. The extremely short hospitalizations for delivery that are now common also limit the ability of trained professionals to observe mothers over an extended time and recognize abnormal patterns of behavior and failures in bonding.

Most children exposed to drugs of abuse are not identified at birth, and most of them go home with their drug-abusing parents without any intervention. These children, who have already been exposed to a potent neurotoxin, are then exposed to poor nutrition, domestic violence and child abuse, infectious diseases, and a host of environmental problems associated with poverty and addiction. They are at significant risk for academic and social failure if their problems are not addressed in a proactive manner. Proactive intervention, how-ever, demands that we know at the infancy or preschool stage that a child is at risk for drug- or alcohol-related developmental challenges. Early identification offers us the opportunity to intervene in the development of a child and reduce the likelihood of a poor outcome.

Despite a long history of neonatal testing for medical problems and inborn errors of metabolism in our newborns (e.g., PKU [phenylketonuria] and hypo-thyroid), the United States has no systematic program for testing all neonates for exposure to neurotoxic drugs of abuse. This is in spite of the large numbers of children thought to suffer from these exposures and the ease of testing by meconium or hair analysis (Garcia-Bournissen, Rokach, Karaskov, & Koren, 2007). Testing is instead based on stereotypes and behavioral indications that may unfairly stigmatize some segments of the population, and at the same time, fail to detect the majority of cases. Basic public health science tells us that this is a totally inadequate system of detection of a major public health risk.

In a large study of meconium drug testing, 44 percent of all neonates in an inner-city hospital tested positive for illicit drug exposure. The majority of children with prenatal exposure to illegal drugs appeared normal at birth, and so would not have been tested under most protocols. Only one in four drug-abusing mothers admitted to her drug use on questioning in the perinatal setting (Ostrea et al., 1992). Of those who admitted to drug use at any time during pregnancy, around 90 percent of their infants had a positive meconium drug screen at birth.

Current neonatal indications for drug testing include obvious withdrawal symptoms, low birth weight, neurobehavioral abnormalities, seizures, stroke, cardiac problems, and necrotizing enterocolitis in a term baby. Only severely affected infants will display symptoms this severe—around 4 percent of meth-amphetamine-positive neonates (Smith et al., 2003). Most methamphetamine-affected children (> 50%) do not have any significant withdrawal symptoms, yet are still at risk for developmental delay or learning disability. Identification of these children is essential for effective intervention to prevent social and aca-demic failure.

Current maternal indications for neonatal drug testing include a known his-tory of drug abuse, lack of prenatal care, home delivery or precipitous delivery, preterm labor, poor weight gain in pregnancy, hypertension without proteinuria, abruption, fetal distress, sexually transmitted disease, and obvious intoxication. Poor, single, or homeless mothers are much more likely to be tested for drug abuse than mothers who are employed and have stable family relationships.

The currently practiced methods for drug testing of neonates rely heavily on stereotypes of how drug-abusing mothers typically behave. This approach is dangerous and misleading for two reasons. First, women from disadvantaged backgrounds may fit the "profile" of the drug-abusing mother and may be selected for testing at a higher rate. This risk factor–based testing leads to a stigmatized feeling of reproach, being held under suspicion merely for being poor or unmarried or homeless.

Second, stereotype-based drug testing misses many infants whose mothers do not fit the profile but who are abusing illegal drugs, especially methamphetamine. Methamphetamine differs from other major drugs of abuse in that many low-dose users do not consider themselves "drug users." Methamphetamine abusers are often well educated, highly functioning individuals, working two jobs, highly driven and successful. They use methamphetamine to work harder and longer, get more focus and enhance attention, or to lose weight and/or prevent weight gain. They consider methamphetamine a "medication," not a "drug," and so will deny "drug use." Methamphetamine users frequently do not fit the stereotype of the "addict." Drug testing based on stereotypes misses this sizable population of mothers, and so their methamphetamine-exposed newborns are not detected.

Universal drug testing offers a major improvement to our current protocols based on perceived risk factors. The currently high cost of meconium drug testing would be greatly reduced if all newborns were tested with resulting economies of scale, just as the cost of the PKU test was reduced when it became part of standard care. State laws to provide for testing of all newborns for exposure to drugs of abuse, just as we currently test all neonates for PKU and thyroid dysfunction, would permit detection of the vast majority of drug-affected newborns. The basis for testing for PKU and thyroid dysfunction is that early intervention is life saving and prevents severe disability in affected children. This rationale also applies to the drug-exposed newborn. Identified mothers could be offered treatment and counseling, and a major cause of child abuse would be prevented. Children could be screened for learning disabilities and receive the special attention they need to develop normally.

We currently screen children for learning disabilities in early elementary school, long after the best window of opportunity for intervention—birth to age three—has passed. Universal neonatal testing for drug exposure would permit earlier intervention in the child's cognitive and social development, and would also permit earlier intervention for the mothers of drug-exposed children, allowing more of them to obtain the treatment they need to preserve the family. None of these interventions can happen if we do not know a newborn has been exposed to substance abuse.

If all newborns were tested, no mother would feel singled out or stigmatized, and no drug-affected children would be missed. Counseling and follow-up could be offered to mothers and their children, and early detection of learning difficulties could be facilitated. Early detection could lead to better outcomes for children and their families as addictions are identified in earlier stages when treatment outcomes are more favorable. Earlier detection of the subtle learning disabilities associated with methamphetamine exposure permits educational intervention to mitigate the long-term impact of these challenges.

The major limitation of universal neonatal meconium drug testing is that it would only detect late second- and third-trimester use, and would miss those children whose mothers didn't like the hyperemesis treatment offered by their obstetrician, and elected to use their college friend's hangover treatment instead. These women are extremely unlikely to admit to drug use, and if their children exhibit learning difficulties or neurologic injury, they will find someone else to blame.

Another limitation is the incidence of false positive results even with the use of gas chromatography or mass spectrometry confirmation testing. Meconium screens are not reliable for PCP (Phencyclidine) exposure—the use of dextromethorphine (Robitussin) cough medicine is enough to make the PCP screen positive. The meconium screen would also be positive for amphetamines in the case of prescription use of stimulants such as Adderall and Desoxyn. These drugs are not recommended for use in pregnancy (Category C) as alternative treatments are readily available for their indications.

But the most common reason for failure to obtain a drug test is denial, usually based on stereotyping of the mother and fear of offending the favored (insured) patient. Patients are in denial, their families are in denial, and often health care workers join them in the assurance that everything must be just fine. A good girl like her couldn't possibly be using illegal drugs. Denial is generally discouraged in the medical field, since lives are at risk if a serious diagnosis is missed.

DENIAL DOESN'T WORK

Denial on a societal scale is just as dangerous as denial on an individual level. Our reluctance to "label" drug-affected children results in a complete inability to assist them since we do not know who they are. Universal drug testing of neonates would break down barriers to treatment and intervention for children and their families. Family drug courts could assure compliance with treatment on the part of parents and assemble the wide range of services and programs that could prevent the disintegration of these fragile families.

When affected children are missed, opportunities for intervention are missed.

We lose opportunities to impact the child and family with drug-treatment options, prevent child abuse and neglect, improve cognitive performance, and prevent academic failure. We miss the opportunity to prevent second-generation drug abuse in these children as they grow up with poor self-esteem and fall into delinquency. Universal drug testing offers us an inroad to identify and assist families and children at risk. We would be remiss if we fail to take action.

REFERENCES

Acikgoz, O., Gonenc, S., Kayatekin, B. M., Pekcetin, C., Uysal, N., Daye, A., et al. (2000). The effects of a single dose of methamphetamine on lipid peroxidation levels in the rat striatum and prefrontal cortex. *European Journal of Neuropsychopharmacology. 10*(5), 415–418.

Acevedo, S. F., de Esch, I. J., & Raber, J. (2007). Sex and histamine dependent long term cognitive effects of methamphetamine exposure. *Neuropsychopharmacology, 32*(3), 665–672.

Aseltine, R. H., Gore, S., & Gordon, J. (2000). Life stress, anger, and anxiety, and delinquency: An empirical test of general strain theory. *Journal of Health and Social Behavior, 41,* 256–275.

Bays, J. (1991). Fetal vascular disruption with prenatal exposure to cocaine or methamphetamine. [Letter to the Editor]. *Pediatrics, 87,* 416–417.

Billings, L., Eriksson, M., Jonsson, B., Steneroth, G., & Zetterström, R. (1994). The influence of environmental factors on behavioral problems in eight year old children exposed to amphetamine during fetal life. *Child Abuse and Neglect, 15,* 3–9.

Brecht, M. L., Greenwell, L., & Anglin, M. D. (2007). Substance use pathways to methamphetamine use among treated users. *Addictive Behaviors, 32*(1), 24–38.

Cernarud, L., Eriksson, M., Jonsson, B., Steneroth, G., & Zetterström, R. (1996). Amphetamine addiction during pregnancy: 14 year follow-up of growth and school performance. *Acta Pediatrics, 85,* 204–208.

Chang, L., Smith, L. M., LoPresti, C., Yonekura, L. M., Kuo, J., Walot, I., et al. (2004). Smaller subcortical volumes and cognitive deficits in children with prenatal methamphetamine exposure. *Psychiatry Research and Neuroimaging, 132,* 95–106.

Cho, A. K., Melega, W. P., Kuczenski, R., & Segal, D. S. (2001). Relevance of pharmacokinetic parameters in animal models of methamphetamine abuse. *Synapse, 39,* 161–166.

Cohen, J. B., Greenberg, R., Uri, J., Halpin, M., & Zweben, J. E. (2007). Women with methamphetamine dependence: Research on etiology and treatment. *Psychoactive Drugs, 4,* 347–351.

Cox, S., Posner, S. F., Kourtis, A. P., & Jamieson, D. J. (2008). Hospitalizations with amphetamine abuse among pregnant women. *Obstetrics and Gynecology, 111,* 341–347.

Derauf, C., LaGasse, L. L., Smith, L. M., Grant, P., Shah R., Arria, A., et al. (2007). Demographic and psychosocial characteristics of mothers using methamphetamine during pregnancy: Preliminary results of the infant development, environment, and lifestyle study (IDEAL). *American Journal of Drug and Alcohol Abuse,* 33, 281–289.

Dixon, S. D. (1989). Effects of transplacental exposure to cocaine and methamphetamine on the neonate. *Western Journal of Medicine, 150*(4), 436–442.

Dixon, S. D., & Bejar, R. (1989). Echoencephalographic findings in neonates associated with maternal cocaine and methamphetamine use: Incidence and clinical correlates. *Journal of Pediatrics, 115,* 770–778.

Dwyer, J. B., Broide, R. S., & Leslie, F. M. (2008). Nicotine and brain development. *Birth Defects Research Part C: Embryo Today, 84*(1), 30–44.

Elliott, R. H., & Rees, G. B. (1990). Amphetamine ingestion presenting as eclampsia. *Canadian Journal of Anaesthesiology, 37,* 130–133.

Eriksson, M., Jonsson, B., Steneroth, G., & Zetterström, R. (2000). Amphetamine abuse during pregnancy: Environmental factors and outcome after 14–15 years. *Scandinavian Journal of Public Health, 28*(2), 154–157.

Eriksson, M., Larsson, G., & Zetterström, R. (1981). Amphetamine addiction and pregnancy. II: Pregnancy, delivery and the neonatal period: Socio-medical aspects. *Acta Obstetrics and Gynecology Scandinavia, 60*(3), 253–259.

Forrester, M. B., & Merz, R. D. (2006). Comparison of trends in gastroschisis and prenatal illicit drug use rates. *Journal of Toxicology and Environmental Health,* A 69, 1253–1259.

Forrester, M. B., & Merz, R. D. (2007). Risk of selected birth defects with prenatal drug use, Hawaii 1986–2002. *Journal of Toxicology and Environmental Health,* A 70, 7–18.

Garcia-Bournissen, F., Rokach, B., Karaskov, T., & Koren, G. (2007). Methamphetamine detection in maternal and neonatal hair: Implications for fetal safety. *Archives of Disease in Childhood: Fetal Neonatal Ed., 92,* F332–F333.

Gomez-DeSilva, J., de Miguel, R., Fernandez-Ruiz, J., Summavielle, T., & Tavares, M. A. (2004). Effects of neonatal exposure to methamphetamine: Catecholamine levels in brain areas of the developing rat. *Annals of New York Academy of Science, 1025,* 602–611.

Gomez-DeSilva, J., Silva, M. C., & Tavares, T. (1998). Developmental exposure to methamphetamine: A neonatal model in the rat. *Annals of New York Academy of Science, 844,* 310–313.

Gonzalez Castro, F., Barrington, E. H., Walton, M. A., & Rawson, R. A. (2000). Cocaine and methamphetamine: Differential addiction rates. *Psychology of Addictive Behaviors, 14,* 390–396.

Hansen, R. L., Struthers, J. M., & Gospe, S. M., Jr. (1993). Visual evoked potentials and visual processing in stimulant drug exposed infants. *Developmental and Medical Child Neurology, 35,* 798–805.

Heller, A., Bubula, N., Lew, R., Heller, B., & Won, L. (2001). Gender dependent enhanced adult neurotoxic response to methamphetamine following fetal exposure to the drug. *The Journal of Pharmacology and Experimental Therapeutics, 298,* 769–779.

Hildebrandt, K., Teuchert-Noodt, G., & Dawirs, R. R. (1999). A single neonatal dose of methamphetamine suppresses dentate granule cell proliferation in adult gerbils which is restored to control values by acute doses of haloperidol. *Journal of Neural Transmission, 106,* 549–558.

Hoyme, H. E., Jones, K. L., Dixon, S. D., Jewett, T., Hanson, J. W., Robinson, L. K., et al. (1990). Prenatal cocaine exposure and fetal vascular disruption. *Pediatrics, 85*(5), 743–747.

Jeng, W., Wong, A. W., Ting-A-Kee, R., & Wells, P. G. (2005). Methamphetamine enhanced embryonic oxidative DNA damage and neurodevelopmental deficits. *Free Radical Biology and Medicine, 39,* 317–326.

Knight, E. M., James, H., Edwards, C. H., Spurlock, B. G., Oyemade, U. J., Johnson, A. A., et al. (1994). Relationships of serum illicit drug concentrations during pregnancy to maternal nutritional status. *Journal of Nutrition, 124,* 973S–980S.

Mahajan, S. D., Hu, Z., Reynolds, J. L., Aalinkeel, R., Schwartz, S. A., & Nair, M. P. (2006). Methamphetamine modulates gene expression patterns in monocyte derived mature dendritic cells: Implications for HIV-1 pathogenesis. *Molecular Diagnostics and Therapeutics, 10,* 257–269.

Mahoney, J. J., III, Kalechstein, A. D., De La Garza, R., II, & Newton, T. F. (2008). Presence and persistence of psychotic symptoms in cocaine- versus methamphetamine- dependent participants. *American Journal of Addiction, 17*(2), 83–98.

McCann, U. D., Kuwabara, H., Kumar, A., Palermo, M., Abbey, R. Brasic, J., et al. (2007). Persistent cognitive and dopamine transporter deficits in abstinent methamphetamine users. *Synapse, 62*(2), 91–100.

McKetin, R., McLaren, J., Lubman, D. I., & Hides, L. (2006). The prevalence of psychotic symptoms among methamphetamine users. *Addiction, 101*(10), 1473–1478.

Nair, M. P., Mahajan, S., Sykes, D., Bapardekar, M. V., & Reynolds, J., (2006). Methamphetamine modulates DC SIGN expression by mature dendritic cells. *Journal of Neuroimmune Pharmacology,* (3), 296–304.

National Center on Addiction and Substance Abuse at Columbia University. (2004). *Criminal neglect: Substance abuse, juvenile justice, and the children left behind.* New York: Author.

Oro, A. S., & Dixon, S. D. (1987). Perinatal cocaine and methamphetamine exposure: Maternal and neonatal correlates. *Pediatrics, 111*(4), 571–578.

Ostrea, E. M., Brady, M., Gause, S., Raymundo, A. L., & Stevens, M. (1992). Drug screening of newborns by meconium analysis: A large scale, prospective, epidemiologic study. *Pediatrics, 89,* 107–113.

Pei, J. R., Rinaldi, C. M., Rasmussen, C., Massey, V., & Massey, D. (2008). Memory patterns of acquisition and retention of verbal and nonverbal information in children with fetal alcohol spectrum disorders. *Canadian Journal of Clinical Pharmacology, 15*(1), e44–56.

Samuels, S. I., Maze, A., & Albright, G. (1979). Cardiac arrest during cesarean section in a chronic amphetamine abuser. *Anesthesia and Analgesia, 58,* 528–530.

Shea, A. K., & Steiner, M. (2008). Cigarette smoking during pregnancy. *Nicotine and Tobacco Research, 10*(2), 267–278.

Smith, L. M., Chang, L., Yonekura, M. L., Grob, C., Osborne, D., & Ernst, T. (2001). Brain proton magnetic resonance spectroscopy in children exposed to methamphetamine in utero. *Neurology, 57*, 255–260.

Smith, L. M., LaGasse, L. L., Derauf, C., Grant, P., & Shah, R. (2006). The infant development, environmental, and lifestyle study: Effects of prenatal methamphetamine exposure, polydrug exposure, and poverty on intrauterine growth. *Pediatrics, 118*, 1149–1156.

Smith, L., Yonekura, M. L., Wallace, T., Berman, N., Kuo, J., & Berkowitz, C. (2003). Effects of prenatal methamphetamine exposure on fetal growth and drug withdrawal symptoms in infants born at term. *Journal of Developmental and Behavioral Pediatrics, 24*, 17–23.

Stek, A. M., Fisher, B. K., Baker, R. S., Lang, U., Tseng, C. Y & Clark, K. E. (1993). Maternal and fetal cardiovascular responses to methamphetamine in the pregnant sheep. *American Journal of Obstetrics and Gynecology, 169*(4), 888–897.

Stewart, J. L., & Meeker, J. E. (1997). Fetal and infant deaths associated with maternal methamphetamine abuse. *Journal of Analytic Toxicology, 21*, 515–517.

Struthers, J. M., & Hansen, R. L. (1992). Visual recognition memory in drug-exposed infants. *Behavioral Pediatrics, 13*, 108–111.

Talloczy, Z., Martinez, J., Joset, D., Ray, Y., Gacser, A., Toussi, S., et al. (2008). Methamphetamine inhibits antigen processing, presentation, and phagocytosis. *Plos Pathogens, 4*, e28.

Torfs, C. P., Velie, E. M., Oechsli, F. W., Bateson, T. F., & Curry, C. J. (1994). A population based study of gastroschisis: Demographic, pregnancy, and lifestyle risk factors. *Teratology, 50*(1), 44–53.

Vorhees, C. V., Skelton, M. R., & Williams, M. T. (2007). Age dependent effects of neonatal methamphetamine exposure on spatial learning. *Behavioral Pharmacology, 18*, 549–552.

Weissman, A. D., & Caldecott-Hazard, S. (1995). Developmental neurotoxicity to methamphetamines. *Clinical and Experimental Pharmacology and Physiology, 22*, 372–374.

Wells, P. G., Bhuller, Y., Chen, C. S., Jeng, W., Kasapinovic, S., Kennedy, J. C., et al. (2005). Molecular and biochemical mechanisms in teratogenesis involving reactive oxygen species. *Toxicology and Applied Pharmacology, 207*(2 Suppl.), 354–366.

Williams, M. T., Brown, R. W., & Vorhees, C. V. (2004). Neonatal methamphetamine administration induces region specific long term neuronal morphologic changes in the rat hippocampus, nucleus accumbens, and parietal cortex. *European Journal of Neuroscience 19*, 3165–3170.

Williams, M. T., Moran, M. S., & Vorhees, C. V. (2004). Behavioral and growth effects induced by low dose methamphetamine administration during the neonatal period in rats. *International Journal of Developmental Neuroscience, 22*, 273–283.

Won, L., Bubula, N., & Heller, A. (2001). Methamphetamine concentrations in fetal and maternal brain following prenatal exposure. *Neurotoxicology and Teratology, 23*(4), 349–354.

Yamamoto, B. K., & Bankson, M. G. (2005). Amphetamine neurotoxicity: Cause and consequence of oxidative stress. *Critical Reviews of Neurobiology, 17,* 87–117.

Ye, L., Peng, J. S., Wang, X., Wang, Y. J., Luo, G. X., & Ho, W. Z. (2008). Methamphetamine enhances hepatitis C virus replication in human hepatocytes. *Journal of Viral Hepatitis, 15,* 261–270.

Chapter 21

Endocannabinoid Hypothesis of Drug Addiction

Emmanuel S. Onaivi, MSc, PhD

In reviewing the history of human drug addictions, one finds previous mis-conceptions that people addicted to drugs lacked willpower and were morally weak. But we now know that drug addiction is a chronic relapsing brain disease characterized by the compulsive use of addictive substances despite adverse consequences to the individual and society. For more than 50 years, it has been assumed that all drugs of abuse release dopamine in the brain's reward sys-tem to produce pleasure and euphoria and, consequently, lead to addiction in vulnerable individuals (Salamone, Correa, Mingote, & Weber, 2005; Spanagel & Weiss, 1999). However, many agents, such as inhalants, barbiturates, or benzodiazepines, do not activate midbrain dopamine-mediated transmission consistently, despite the fact that these drugs have rewarding properties and are heavily abused (Spanagel & Weiss, 1999). Therefore, dopamine is not a simple marker of reward or hedonia, and it might no longer be tenable to sug-gest that drugs of abuse are simply activating the brain's "natural reward system" (Salamone et al., 2005). In this chapter, I propose that the dopamine hypothesis of drug abuse and reward is another misconception. The dopamine projections in the brain do not convey a specific "reward" signal because dopamine release occurs not only to all drugs of abuse but also to stress, foot shock, aversive and salient stimuli (Horvitz, 2000; Roll, 2005). Mice that cannot make dopamine (DD mice) have been used to test the hypothesis that dopamine is neces-sary for reward. The results show that dopamine is not required for natural reward (Cannon & Palmiter, 2003) and morphine-induced reward (Hnasko, Sotak, & Palmiter, 2005). Thus, there are numerous problems associated with

Table 21.1
Problems Associated with Dopamine Hypothesis of Reward

Beyond the nucleus accumbens and dopamine hypothesis of reward
• Not all studies point to a unitary role for dopamine in one brain circuitry as the most relevant system in drug abuse.
• Dopamine may not be involved in brain reward mechanisms as previously thought.
• Reward centers in the brain consist of multiple systems and neuroanatomical sites other than the mesoaccumbens dopamine circuitry.
• Dopamine-independent mechanisms involving other neurotransmitters like glutamate, GABA, serotonin, endocannabinoids, stress hormones, and dynorphin are potential substrates for the rewarding effects of abused substances.
• In schizophrenics, dopamine excess in mesoaccumbens causes heightened state of arousal and not pleasure.
• Smokers and cocaine addicts continue to take hits long after the cigarettes become distasteful or after the effects of cocaine have worn off.
• Addictions arise from a complex pattern of pathogenetic and environmental situations.
• Differential effects of abused substances on the complex network of genes, hormones, neurotransmitters, and modulators do not support the concept of a single reward transmitter.
• Manipulation of dopamine circuitry as a pharmacology target should provide medication for substance abuse.
• There is no causal relationship for dopamine as a pleasure or reward transmitter triggered by abused substances.
• Activation of dopamine pathways is not involved in brain-stimulation reward of all brain sites relevant to addiction.
• Electrolytic lesions and 6-OH dopamine lesion studies of dopamine cell bodies in the ventral tegmental area and other brain sites did not attenuate brain-stimulation reward.

dopamine hypothesis of reward (Table 21.1). For example, self-administration of opiates and alcohol occurs even when the mesolimbic dopamine system is lesioned (Koob & Le Moal, 1997) and interference with accumbens dopamine transmission does not substantially blunt the primary motivation for natural rewards (Salamone et al., 2005). Although we cannot underestimate the role of dopamine in the central nervous system, recent studies in schizophrenia, where dopamine hypothesis had dominated the treatment approaches, now show that glutamate receptor offers promise for a new class of antipsychotic agents (Patil et al., 2007).

It appears that the strong and long-held belief of dopamine hypothesis as a basis for drug reward and addiction will not change overnight. However, the recent evidence indicating that the endocannabinoid system plays a pivotal role in reward processes (Solinas, Goldberg, & Piomelli, 2008) suggests that the endocannabinoid system may be a target for the treatment of addictive behaviors. So the activation of the "natural reward system," supposedly mediated by the accumbens dopamine, cannot reasonably be used as a general explanation for drug abuse and addiction (Salamone et al., 2005). Furthermore, the discovery that dopamine neurons fail to respond when animals receive anticipated reward contradicts the neurobiological model of acute drug reward and reinforcement associated with the mesolimbic dopamine system (Sullivan et al., 2008). Most of the addictive substances are plant-derived, including cocaine, caffeine, morphine, ephedrine, nicotine, and so on, and from an evolutionary perspective, the natural function of these plant alkaloids evolved to deter consumption, which is incompatible with the mesolimbic dopamine hypothesis of drug reward and reinforcement—an incompatibility that has been termed "the paradox of drug reward" (Sullivan et al., 2008).

A number of observations have led to renewed questions of the dopamine hypothesis. For example, first-time users of cannabis, or tobacco and other recreational drugs, usually have unpleasant responses with nausea and vomiting. It is also now recognized that these abused substances selectively activate specific pathways, so that while nicotine binds with cholinergic receptors, cannabinoids and opiates bind to cannabinoid and opioid receptors, respectively, and not dopaminergic receptors. It is therefore timely that there is accumulating evidence indicating a central role for the endocannabinoid system (ECS) in the regulation of the rewarding effects of abused substances. Such recent studies have shown that this endocannabinoid system is involved in the common neurobiological mechanism underlying drug addiction (De Vries & Schoffelmeer, 2005; Fattore et al., 2007; Maldonado, Valverde, & Berrendero, 2006; Parolaro, Vigano, & Rubino, 2005), and see Table 21.2. Thus, an endocannabinoid hypothesis of drug reward is postulated from data from our studies and those of others. Endocannabinoids mediate retrograde signaling in neuronal tissues and are involved in the regulation of synaptic transmission, to suppress neurotransmitter release by the presynaptic cannabinoid receptors (CB-Rs). This powerful modulatory action on synaptic transmission has significant functional implications and interactions with the effects of abused substances. Additional support for the endocannabinoid hypothesis of drug reward is derived from the action of cannabinoids or marijuana use on brain reward pathways that is similar to other abused substances. Furthermore, administration of cannabinoids or the use of marijuana exerts numerous pharmacological effects through their interactions with various neurotransmitters and neuromodulators (Table 21.2).

In our preliminary studies to test the endocannabinoid hypothesis of drug reward, we investigated the interaction between vanilloid and cannabinoid agonists and antagonists in the mouse model of aversion using the elevated plus-maze test. The vanilloid agonist used is a natural product, capsaicin, the active ingredient in hot chili peppers that is known to be habit forming. In a follow-up study, we determined the effect of the CB1 antagonist, rimonabant, on withdrawal aversions from chronic treatment with abused drugs. Our

Table 21.2
Framework for an Endocannabinoid Hypothesis of Drug Reward

- The existence of an endocannabinoid physiological control system (EPCS) with a central role in the regulation of the rewarding effects of abused substances.
- The EPCS is intricately involved in almost all the biological processes of the human body and brain.
- The EPCS appears to exert a powerful modulatory action on retrograde signaling associated with cannabinoid inhibition of synaptic transmission.
- The retrograde signaling appears to be involved in the modulation of neurotransmitter release by cannabinoids and endocannabinoids.
- The abundant distribution of the cannabinoid receptors in the brain provides the EPCS limitless signaling capabilities of cross-talk within, and possibly between, receptor families.
- A missense mutation in human fatty acid amide hydrolase may be associated with problem drug use in vulnerable individuals.
- Cannabinoids induce alterations in brain disposition and pharmacological actions of drugs of abuse.
- Changes in endocannabinoid contents in the brain of rats chronically exposed to nicotine, ethanol, or cocaine.
- "Runners high," the sense of euphoric well-being that comes with vigorous exercise such as running, stimulates the release and elevated levels of endocannabinoids.
- The mechanisms of dependence to different substances appear to be different in terms of their impact on the EPCS.
- The endocannabinoid transmission is a component of the brain reward system and appears to play a role in dependence/withdrawal to abused substances.
- Reduced sensitivity to reward in CB1 knockout mice. But mice that cannot make dopamine (mice lacking tyrosine hydroxylase) respond to rewarding stimuli, indicating reward without dopamine.
- Overeating, alcohol and sucrose consumption is decreased in CB1 receptor deleted mice.
- Involvement of endocannabinoid system in the neural circuitry regulating alcohol consumption and motivation to consume alcohol.
- Evidence for the existence of a functional link between the cannabinoid and opioid receptor systems in the control of alcohol intake and motivation to consume alcohol.
- Decreased alcohol self-administration and increased alcohol sensitivity and withdrawal in CB1 receptor knockout mice.
- Endocannabinoid system modulates opioid rewarding and addictive effects by cross-talk between endogenous opioid and endocannabinoid systems in drug reward.
- Involvement of endocannabinoid and glutamate neurotransmission in brain circuits linked to reward and mnemonic processes. Abolition of LTP in mice lacking mGluR5 receptors and enhanced LTP and memory in mice lacking cannabinoid CB1 receptors.
- Endocannabinoid system in memory-related plasticity may be a common mechanism in the control of conditioned drug seeking by cannabinoids.

results suggest that the endocannabinoid physiological control system may be important natural regulatory mechanisms for reward.

ENDOCANNABINOID PHYSIOLOGICAL CONTROL SYSTEM (EPCS) AND REWARD, DRUG ABUSE, AND ADDICTIONS

Cannabinoids are the constituents of the cannabis plant, and endocannabinoids are the marijuana-like substances produced on demand by the human body (Onaivi, Sugiura, & Di Marzo, 2006). Currently, there are two well-characterized CB-Rs with known splice variants, CB1-Rs and CB2-Rs (Onaivi et al., 2006), that are known to mediate the effects of marijuana use and those of the endocannabinoids. 2-Arachidonyl glycerol has emerged as one of the endocannabinoids that acts as a full agonist at CB-Rs. Anandamide, the first endocannabinoid isolated, is a partial agonist at CB-Rs and a full agonist at the vanilloid receptor. CB1-Rs are known to be expressed in the brain and in peripheral tissues. Although CB2-Rs was once believed to be restricted to immune cells, we and others have demonstrated that it is also functionally expressed in neurons, albeit at lower levels than CB1-Rs (Onaivi, Ishiguro, et al., 2006; Van Sickle et al., 2005). These cannabinoid receptors are G-protein coupled receptors with seven transmembrane domains.

Many studies now show that the endocannabinoid system is involved as the major player, and most likely, the common neurobiological mechanism underlying drug reward. There is substantial evidence supporting a role for the endocannabinoid system as a modulator of dopaminergic activity in the basal ganglia (Giuffrida & Piomelli, 2000). The endocannabinoid system therefore participates in the primary rewarding effects of alcohol, opioids, nicotine, cocaine, amphetamine, cannabinoids, and benzodiazepines through the release of endocannabinoids that act as retrograde messengers to inhibit classical transmitters, including dopamine, serotonin, GABA, glutamate, acetylcholine, and norepinephrine (Onaivi, Sugiura, et al., 2006). Furthermore, the endocannabinoid system is intricately involved in the common mechanisms underlying relapse to drug-seeking behavior by mediating the motivational effects of drug-related environmental stimuli and drug reexposure (Maldonado et al., 2006). Therefore, substantial data now point to a role of the endocannabinoid system in triggering and/or preventing reinstatement of drug-seeking behavior (Fattore et al., 2007). It appears that the effects of perturbation of the endocannabinoid system by drugs of abuse can be ameliorated by restoring the perturbed system using cannabinoid ligands.

It is not surprising that preliminary studies with cannabinoid antagonists are showing promise in the reduction of drug use, in smoking cessation, and reduction in alcohol consumption and, of course, rimonabant has been approved in Europe for treating obesity. It is hoped that these encouraging positive results will lead to new therapeutic agents in the treatment of drug dependency. The promiscuous action and distribution of cannabinoid receptors in most relevant biological systems provides the EPCS limitless signaling capabilities of cross-talk within, and possible between, receptor families that may explain the myriad behavioral effects associated with smoking marijuana. The EPCS, therefore, appears to play a central role in regulating the neural substrate underlying many aspects of drug addiction, including craving and relapse (Yamamoto, Anggadiredja, & Hiranita, 2004). The findings that the EPCS is involved in the reinstatement model provided evidence of the EPCS in the neural machinery underlying relapse. Relapse, the resumption of drug taking following a period of drug abstinence, is considered the main hurdle in treating drug addiction, and pharmacological modulation of the endocannabinoid tone with rimonabant gave positive results in human trials. A summary of data from recent studies of the efficacies of cannabinoid antagonist and mutant mice have recently been reviewed (Parolaro et al., 2005). As the usefulness of the pharmacotherapy of substance abuse has been limited, there is sufficient preclinical evidence for clinical trials to evaluate the efficacy of cannabinoid-based drugs in the treatment of drug dependency.

INTERACTION BETWEEN CB1 AND CB2 RECEPTORS IN DRUG ABUSE AND ADDICTION

The expression of CB1 cannabinoid receptors (CB1-Rs) in the brain and periphery has been well studied, but the brain neuronal expression of CB2-Rs had been ambiguous and controversial and its role in substance abuse is unknown. There is now ample evidence for the functional presence of CB2-Rs in mammalian brain neurons (Gong et al., 2006; Onaivi, 2006; Van Sickle et al., 2005). We have investigated the involvement of CB2-Rs in alcohol preference in mice and alcoholism in humans (Ishiguro et al., 2007). So we tested if CB2-Rs in the brain play a role in alcohol abuse/dependence in animal model and then examined an association between the CB2 gene polymorphism and alcoholism in a Japanese population. There is an association between the Q63R polymorphism of the CB2 gene and alcoholism in the Japanese population. Our data therefore revealed that CB2-Rs are functionally expressed in brain neurons and play a role in substance abuse and dependency (Gong et al., 2006; Ishiguro et al., 2007; Onaivi, 2006). The next question is now that we know that CB2-Rs are present in the brain, what is the nature of and contribution to the known effects of CB1-Rs in the rewarding effects of drug abuse? With the recent definitive demonstration of neuronal CB2-Rs in the brain, one possible explanation may be that CB2-Rs and CB1-Rs work independently and/or cooperatively in different neuronal populations to regulate a number of physiological activities influenced by drugs of abuse, cannabinoids, endocannabinoids, and marijuana use. Nevertheless, our studies and those of others demonstrate the functional expression of CB2-Rs in the brain that may provide novel targets for the effects of cannabinoids in substance abuse disorders beyond neuro-immunocannabinoid activity.

NEW PERSPECTIVES IN STUDYING THE INVOLVEMENT OF THE ENDOCANNABINOID SYSTEM IN REWARD PROCESSES

We used the elevated plus-maze test—a validated method to measure the performance of rodents that are nocturnal in nature and to obtain an index of anxiety when control and experimental animals are exposed to the maze. The plus-maze consists of two open arms and two enclosed arms linked by a central platform and arranged in a plus sign (+). The elevated plus-maze system was used to study withdrawal anxiogenesis from selected drugs with abuse potential, including cocaine, diazepam, and ethanol. The synthetic methanandamide was included in the study. Adult C57Bl/6 mice were evaluated in the elevated plus-maze test of anxiety following abrupt cessation from chronic treatment with selected doses of cocaine, diazepam, ethanol, 8%w/v, and methanandamide. In a separate group of these mice, the ability of the CB1 cannabinoid antagonist, rimonabant, to block the withdrawal aversions of mice from alcohol and selected drugs with abuse potential was determined. The in-vivo pharmacological interaction was evaluated by the co-administration of cannabinoids and vanilloid ligands. Capsaicin known to activate CB-Rs and vanilloid receptors (VR1-Rs) in the central nervous system (CNS) was used to study the involvement of the ECS in the habit-forming properties of capsaicin using mice. The interaction between the vanilloid and cannabinoid system was performed using selected agonists and antagonists. The ability of the antagonist drug to block agonist drug effect was also evaluated in this paradigm.

INTERACTION OF CANNABINOIDS AND VANILLOIDS: A BIOLOGICAL BASIS OF WHY SOME LIKE IT HOT AND OTHERS DO NOT

We tested the hypothesis that the endocannabinoid physiological control system (ECS) may play a role in the habit-forming properties of capsaicin and may also be involved in the rewarding effects of abused substances. In the first set of studies, the cross-talk between cannabinoids and vanilloids was determined by evaluating the interactions of capsaicin, a vanilloid receptor 1 agonist, and WIN5512-2, a cannabinoid agonist. The effect of the vanilloid receptor antagonist, capsazepine, and the cannabinoid antagonist, rimonabant, in the actions of capsaicin and the WIN55212-2 were determined. The aversive behavior induced in mice following treatment with capsaicin, which was dependent on gender and strain of mice used, was enhanced by pretreatment with WIN55212-2. While the 30 minutes with WIN55212-2 enhanced aversions induced by capsaicin, capsazepine or rimonabant blocked the aversions induced by capsaicin and WIN55212-2. The effect of capsaicin on the performance of mice in the plus-maze test was dependent on the gender and mouse strain, with C57BL/J male mice being more susceptible to the behavioral aversions induced by capsaicin.

ANTAGONISM OF WITHDRAWAL REACTION FROM ALCOHOL AND DRUG ABUSE BY CB1 RECEPTOR ANTAGONISM IN THE PLUS-MAZE TEST

The effects of rimonabant on the withdrawal aversions from cessation with chronic treatment of mice with the selected addictive drugs were evaluated. Cannabinoid CB1 receptor antagonism reduced behavioral aversions following withdrawal from alcohol, cocaine, and diazepam. It is important to note that rimonabant, the CB1-R antagonist alone, produced variable effects characterized by reduced aversion at low dose and increased aversions to the open arms of the maze at higher doses.

THE ENDOCANNABINOID SYSTEM IN REWARD PROCESSES

The major goal of the study is to understand the role of endocannabinoids (the marijuana-like substances produced by the human body) in drug reward and addiction. Cannabinoids, the constituents in marijuana, mediate their effects by acting on the endocannabinoids and their receptors (CB-Rs), while capsaicin, the pungent chemical in hot chili peppers, a habit-forming food substance, activates the vanilloid type 1 (VR1) receptors to produce its effects. Marijuana and capsaicin enhance appetite, taste, and perhaps addiction and habit-forming properties through CB-Rs and VR1 receptors. The data obtained reveal differential sensitivities of capsaicin in mice that were gender- and strain-dependent that may indicate why some like hot chili peppers and others do not. Mice naturally do not like capsaicin, and these data are supported by the finding that genetically modified mice lacking the VR1 receptor no longer avoid spicy peppers (Caterina et al., 2000). This may be due to the interaction between the cannabinoid and vanilloid systems. This is because both capsazepine and rimonabant (antagonists at vanilloid and cannabinoid receptors) blocked the aversions induced by WIN55212–2 and capsaicin, indicating a cross-talk between cannabinoid and vanilloid systems. Although the interaction between the EPCS and the vanilloid system is not well established and studied, the results from the investigation on whether the interaction between endocannabinoid and endovanilloid systems induced by the natural ligands could be a basis why some like hot chili peppers and others do not is intriguing. Therefore, it is tempting to speculate and extend the known regulation of the neural substrates altered by abused substances to an interaction or a cross-talk between the EPCS and the endovanilloid (VR1) system. The existence and involvement of the EPCS in this in-vivo model is presented as additional evidence that manipulating the EPCS could be exploited in reducing the behavioral consequences of withdrawal from drug dependency.

Finally, we tested the hypothesis that the EPCS is an integral component of the reward circuit using in-vivo tests. We determined the influence of CB-R antagonism on withdrawal anxiogenesis from chronic alcohol, cocaine, and diazepam treatment in vivo using the mouse plus-maze test. The CB1-R antagonist rimonabant blocked the behavioral aversions to the open arms of the plus-maze, which was precipitated from withdrawal from cocaine, diazepam, and alcohol. Similar to the withdrawal aversions in the plus-maze test, conditioned place preference (CPP) paradigm has been used to investigate the rewarding effects of cannabinoids. Rimonabant has been shown to counteract the CPP supported by classical reinforcers, including food, cocaine, and morphine (Chaperon, Soubrie, Puech, & Thiebot, 1998). This is in agreement with data that demonstrate the antagonistic activity of rimonabant against disruption of cognition or reward-enhancing properties of morphine, amphetamine, and cocaine (Poncelet, Barnouin, Breliere, Le Fur, & Soubrie, 1999), which we have extended to ethanol and diazepam. The blockade of the behavioral aversions by cannabinoid antagonist following chronic administration with alcohol, cocaine, and diazepam is in agreement with data obtained during cannabinoid-induced alterations in brain dispositions of drugs of abuse that correlated with behavioral alterations in mice (Reid & Bornheim, 2001). These results taken together suggest that in the CNS, the EPCS may be a directly important natural regulatory mechanism for reward in the brain and also contribute to reduction in aversive consequences of abused substances. Thus, the data presented, along with those of others, not only support the existence of the EPCS but also an endocannabinoid hypothesis of drug reward and addiction that may last beyond the dopamine hypothesis of drug reward.

CONCLUSIONS

The preliminary data on the association between activation of cannabinoid and vanilloid receptors show that the interaction of abused substances with the endocannabinoid system is pivotal in habit forming and a neural basis of drug abuse and dependency. Cannabinoids therefore appear to be involved in adding to the rewarding effects of addictive substances, including cocaine, alcohol, and benzodiazepines. Again, these results taken together suggest that in the CNS the EPCS may be a directly important natural regulatory mechanism for reward in the brain and also contribute to reduction in aversive consequences of abused substances. The existence and involvement of an endocannabinoid physiological control system in this in-vivo model is presented as additional evidence that manipulating the EPCS could be exploited in reducing the behavioral consequences of withdrawal from alcohol and drug dependency. It is a good thing that controversy is one of the fuels of science. Thus, there is a lot more research to be done to better understand the nature and the neurobiology of the endocannabinoid physiological control system in health and disease. In the end, the eternal bliss may not be dopamine but endocannabinoids—the brain and body's marijuana and beyond (Onaivi, Sugiura, et al., 2006).

ACKNOWLEDGMENTS

This work would not have been possible without the support, in part, by William Paterson University, Center for Research, the Dean College of Science and Health, Dr. DeYoung Student Worker Fund for maintenance of research animals, and the Provost Office for release time. I thank my colleagues in the Biology Department, and especially the Chairperson, Dr. Gardner, and Norman Schanz in the mouse laboratory. I acknowledge the assistance and support of Dr. Patricia Tagliaferro and my collaborators, including Drs. Hiroki Ishiguro, B. Emmanuel Akinshola, and Sanika Chirwa. I wish to thank past and present students for technical assistance in working with me, especially, Zoila Mora, Alex Perchuk, Danielle Colas, and Chiara Brandoni for direct involvement with some part of these studies. I would also like to thank Drs. John McPartland, Richard Rothman, Mike Baumann, and William Freed for constructive comments. I am indebted to Dr. George Uhl, the Chief of Molecular Neurobiology Branch at NIDA-NIH, where I am a Guest Scientist.

REFERENCES

Cannon, M. C., & Palmiter, R. D. (2003). Reward without dopamine. *J. Neuroscience*, 23, 10827–10831.

Caterina, M. J., Leffler, A., Malmberg, A. B., Martin, W. J., Traffon, J., & Petersen-Zeitz, K. R. (2000). Impaired nociception and pain sensation in mice lacking the capsaicin receptor. *Science, 288*, 306–313.

Chaperon, F., Soubrie, P., Puech, A. J., & Thiebot, M. H. (1998). Involvement of central cannabinoid (CB1) in the establishment of place conditioning in rats. *Psychopharmacology, 135*, 324–332.

De Vries, T. J., & Schoffelmeer, A. N. M. (2005). Cannabinoid CB1 receptors control conditioned drug seeking. *Trends Pharmacol Sci., 26*, 420–426.

Fattore, L., Spano, M. S., Deiana, S., Melis, V., Cossu, G., Fadda, P., et al. (2007). An endocannabinoid mechanism in relapse to drug seeking: A review of animal studies and clinical perspectives. *Brain Res Rev, 53*, 1–16.

Giuffrida, A. & Piomelli, D. (2000). The endocannabinoid system: A physiological perspective on its role in psychomotor control. *Chem Phys Lipids, 108*, 151–158.

Gong, J. P., Onaivi, E. S., Ishiguro, H., Liu, Q.-R., Tagliaferro, P. A., & Brusco, A. (2006). Cannabinoid CB2 receptors: Immunohistochemical localization in rat brain. *Brain Res, 1071*, 10–23.

Ishiguro, H., I., Iwasaki, S., Teasenfitz, L., Higuchi, S., Horiuchi, T., Saito, T., et al. (2007). Involvement of cannabinoid CB2 receptor in alcohol preference in mice and alcoholism in humans. *Pharmacogenomics J., 7*, 380–385.

Hnasko, T. S., Sotak, B. N., & Palmiter, R. D. (2005). Morphine reward in dopamine-deficient mice. *Nature, 438*, 854–857.

Horvitz, J. C. (2000). Mesolimbocortical and nigrostriatal dopamine responses to salient non-reward events. *Neuroscience, 96*, 651–656.

Koob, G. F., & Le Moal, M. (1997). Drug abuse: Hedonic homeostatic dysregulation. *Science, 278*, 52–58.

Maldonado, R., Valverde, O., & Berrendero, F. (2006). Involvement of the endocannabinoid system in drug addiction. *Trends Neurosci., 29*, 225–232.

Onaivi, E. S. (2006). Neuropsychobiological evidence for the functional presence and expression of cannabinoid CB2 receptors in the brain. *Neuropsychobiology, 54*, 231–246.

Onaivi, E. S., Ishiguro, H., Gong, J. P., Patel, S., Perchuk, A., Meozzi, P. A., et al. (2006). Discovery of the presence and functional expression of cannabinoid CB2 receptors in brain. *Ann N Y Acad Sci, 1074*, 514–536.

Onaivi, E. S., Sugiura, T., & Di Marzo, V. (Eds.). (2006). *The brain and body's marijuana and beyond*. Boca Raton, FL: CRC Taylor and Francis.

Parolaro, D., Vigano, D., & Rubino, T. (2005). Endocannabinoid and drug dependence. *Curr Drug Target—CNS Neurol Disorders, 4*, 643–655.

Patil, S. T., Zhang, L. U., Martenyi, F., Lowe, S. I., Jackson, K. A., Andrew, B. V., et al. (2007). Activation of MGlu2/3 receptor as a new approach to treat schizophrenia: A randomized phase 2 clinical trial. *Nature Medicine, 13,* 1102–1107.

Poncelet, M., Barnouin, M. C., Breliere, J. C., Le Fur, G., & Soubrie, P. (1999). Blockade of CB1 receptors by SR141716 selectively antagonizes drug-induced reinstatement of exploratory behavior in gerbils. *Psychopharmacology, 144,* 144–150.

Reid, M. J., & Bornheim, L. M. (2001). Cannabinoid-induced alterations in brain disposition of drugs of abuse. *Biochem. Pharmacol., 61,* 1357–1367.

Roll, E. T. (2005). *Emotion explained.* New York: Oxford University Press.

Salamone, J. D., Correa, M., Mingote, S. M., & Weber, S. M. (2005). Beyond the reward hypothesis: Alternative functions of nucleus accumbens dopamine. (2005). *Curr Opin Pharmacol. 5,* 34–41.

Solinas, M., Goldberg, S. R., & Piomelli, D. (2008). The endocannabinoid system in brain reward processes. *Br. J. Pharmacol, 154,* 369–383

Spanagel, R., & Weiss, F. (1999). The dopamine hypothesis of reward: Past and current status. *Trends Neurosci., 22,* 521–527.

Sullivan, R. J., Hagen, E. H., & Hammerstein, P. (2008). Revealing the paradox of drug reward in human evolution. *Proc. R. Soc. B, 275,* 1231–1241.

Van Sickle, M. D., Duncan, M., Kingsley, P. J., Mouihate, A., Urbani, P., Mackie, K., et al. (2005). Identification and functional characterization of brainstem cannabinoid CB2 receptors. *Science, 310,* 329–332.

Yamamoto, T., Anggadiredja, K., & Hiranita, T. (2004). New perspectives in the studies on endocannabinoid and cannabis: A role for the endocannabinoid-arachidonic acid pathway in drug reward and long-lasting relapse to drug taking. *J Pharmacol Sci., 96,* 382–388.

Chapter 22

Regulation of μ-Opioid Receptor Desensitization in Sensory Neurons

Cui-Wei Xie, MD, PhD

A common property of G protein-coupled-receptors (GPCRs) is desensitization, loss of signaling after repeated or continued stimulation of the receptor. Desensitization of the μ-opioid receptor, which is the primary target of clinical analgesia and drugs of abuse, has been a subject of intense investigation because of its potential role in the development of opiate tolerance and dependence. Recent studies examining μ-opioid desensitization in dorsal root ganglion (DRG) sensory neurons have revealed multiple mechanisms that regulate signaling and trafficking of the μ receptor, its interactions with other GPCRs, and G protein-effector interactions during acute and chronic opioid exposure. Several protein kinase systems, including phosphoinositide 3-kinase (PI3K), Akt, extracellular signal-regulated kinases (ErK) and p38 mitogen-activated protein kinase (p38 MAPK), have been shown to play important roles in these mechanisms. Adding another layer of complexity, emerging evidence indicates that formation of hetero-oligomers between the μ receptor and other GPCRs permits cross regulation of receptor signaling and trafficking, which in some cases leads to the development of cross desensitization. Further understanding of these dynamic processes could provide insight into the adaptive changes at cellular levels that initiate the complex behavioral changes in opiate tolerance and dependence.

DIFFERENT FORMS OF μ-OPIOID DESENSITIZATION IN DRG NEURONS

Primary cultures of rodent DRG neurons have been extensively used to study opioid regulation of voltage-gated Ca^{2+} channels (VGCCs). It is well documented that opioid receptors couple with Ca^{2+} channels through Gi and Go proteins. Activation of μ-opioid receptors significantly reduces multiple components of VGCC currents, predominantly N- and P/Q-type currents, through a mechanism involving direct interactions between G-protein βγ subunits (Gβγ) and the α_1 subunit of Ca^{2+} channels (Ikeda, 1996). The μ receptor-mediated VGCC inhibition contributes directly to the analgesic action of opiate drugs and has been demonstrated at multiple levels of the pain-processing pathways, including thalamic and periaqueductal grey neurons (Connor & Christie, 1998; Formenti et al., 1995) and peripheral sensory neurons (Nomura, Reuveny, & Narahashi, 1994; Taddese, Nah, & McCleskey, 1995). DRG sensory neurons in cultures express all major types of opioid receptors and VGCCs, providing a convenient model system to study opioid signaling and desensitization with regard to ion channel regulation. Notably, DRG cultures consist of a mixed population of neurons of various sizes. Expression of μ receptors in these neurons appears to be developmentally regulated with the highest level expressed in cells of all sizes during the first postnatal week. The expression then gradually declines in larger cells and is confined to small and medium cells by postnatal day 21 (Beland & Fitzgerald, 2001). Consistent with this expression pattern, only a subset of DRG neurons are sensitive to the effect of a selective μ agonist [D-Ala², N-MePhe⁴, Gly-ol⁵]-enkephalin (DAMGO) in cultures derived from adult animals (Schroeder & McCleskey, 1993), whereas the majority of DRG neurons (~90%) respond to DAMGO in cultures derived from early postnatal mice (Tan et al., 2003). The latter can therefore be readily used for the study of μ opioid desensitization.

Desensitization, defined as a loss of cell responsiveness to the agonist, can be mediated by a number of cellular regulatory events. At the receptor level, opioid desensitization has been associated with agonist-induced rapid receptor uncoupling with G proteins, reduction in cell surface receptors, or downregulation of total receptors (Connor, Osborne, & Christie, 2004; Johnson, Christie, & Connor, 2005; Marie, Aguila, & Allouche, 2006). Postreceptor changes that affect Gi/Go proteins, downstream signaling pathways, and the final effector such as ion channels can also contribute to desensitization of opioid signaling (Tan et al., 2003). Two relevant terms often mentioned in this context are the *homologous* and *heterologous* desensitization. Homologous desensitization refers to the process in which only the activated receptor reduces its responsiveness. Heterologous desensitization, however, reduces signaling of other receptors not activated by the agonist. Another way to define opioid desensitization is based on its time course. With regard to VGCC modulation, acute or rapid desensitization can occur within minutes of agonist exposure, whereas chronic desensitization often develops gradually over several hours. In DRG cultures, both acute and chronic μ opioid desensitization have been observed following DAMGO treatment (Nomura et al., 1994; Samoriski & Gross, 2000; Tan et al., 2003). The acute desensitization has rapid onset within one to five minutes, causes incomplete loss of opioid responses, and is often insensitive to the modulators of major protein kinases. In contrast, chronic desensitization has a much slower time course, leads to complete loss of opioid responses in 24 hours, and is heavily regulated by several protein kinase systems (Nomura et al., 1994; Tan et al., 2003). Acute and chronic μ opioid desensitization also differentially affect VGCC modulation by other Gi/Go-coupled receptors in DRG neurons. For example, γ-aminobutyric acid (GABA)$_B$ receptor-mediated VGCC inhibition can be heterologously reduced following acute but not chronic DAMGO desensitization. On the other hand, chronic DAMGO treatment induces heterologous desensitization to α2-adrenergic receptor-mediated VGCC inhibition (Samoriski & Gross, 2000; Tan et al., 2003). These findings suggest that acute and chronic desensitization are mechanistically different and may affect distinct components in the G protein-receptor-Ca^{2+} channel pathway.

How these different forms of desensitization are related to opioid tolerance in vivo remains an open question. Tolerance is defined as a decreased physiological response to the same dose of drug during repeated exposure. Compared to *in-vitro* desensitization, tolerance develops over a more extended period (hours to days) and involves complex changes not only at the cellular level but also in various neural networks. Many believe that cellular mechanisms of desensitization serve to initiate the cascade of events ultimately leading to opioid tolerance and dependence (Bailey & Connor, 2005; Borgland, 2001; Marie et al., 2006). However, the exact role of desensitization-related processes in the development of tolerance remains to be clarified. Studies have shown that such roles may vary in different experimental settings, depending upon the agonist applied, cell types, and the form of desensitization examined (Connor et al., 2004). As discussed below, prolonged desensitization coupled with poor receptor recycling is likely to promote tolerance. On the other hand, desensitization associated with rapid receptor internalization and recycling may in fact be a protective mechanism that prevents extended receptor signaling leading to tolerance (Martini & Whistler, 2007).

Protein Kinase Modulation of Desensitization

Two major groups of protein kinases have been implicated in GPCR desensitization observed in nonneuronal cells: members of G-protein receptor kinase (GRK) family and second messenger-activated protein kinases. Agonist-induced receptor phosphorylation by GRKs, followed by binding of β-arrestin and receptor uncoupling from G proteins, is considered a common mechanism for acute homologous desensitization. This process is often complemented by feedback phosphorylation via second messenger-activated kinases, such as protein kinase A (PKA), protein kinase C (PKC), and MAPK. These kinases can target both homologous and heterologous receptors (Chuang, Iacovelli, Sallese, & De Blasi, 1996) and affect postreceptor components, including G proteins (Fields & Casey, 1995) and effector ion channels (Hamid et al., 1999). Thus, GPCR desensitization could be mediated by multiple protein kinases with changes occurring at the receptor, G_i/G_o proteins, effectors, or their regulators.

Numerous studies have examined whether the above general mechanisms can apply to desensitization of μ opioid signaling. The μ-opioid receptor has various phosphorylation sites on Ser, Thr, and Tyr residues located on its three cytoplasmic loops and intracellular carboxyl terminal domain. Phosphorylation of these sites regulates signaling efficacy (McLaughlin & Chavkin, 2001) and receptor trafficking (El Kouhen et al., 2001). In cells expressing modified μ receptors with C-terminal truncation or point mutation at the putative phosphorylation sites, DAMGO- or morphine-induced desensitization is significantly attenuated or completely abolished (Deng et al., 2000; Pak, O'Dowd, & George, 1997; Schulz et al., 2004). These findings support the view that μ receptor phosphorylation may be a major contributor to opioid desensitization. It is particularly tempting to link acute desensitization with agonist-induced, rapid μ receptor phosphorylation because of their similar time courses. However, several issues remain to be addressed with this assumption. First, despite extensive investigation, the kinases responsible for μ receptor phosphorylation have not been firmly established. Overexpression of GRK2 in heterologous cells reportedly increases agonist-induced μ receptor phosphorylation (Schulz et al., 2004; Zhang et al., 1998), but evidence exists that activation of μ receptors fails to trigger accumulation of GRKs at the plasma membrane, indicating a weak interaction between the two (Schulz, Wehmeyer, & Schulz, 2002). Second, many relevant studies are conducted using heterologous expression systems, and so far, direct evidence is still lacking to confirm phosphorylation of the μ receptor by GRKs or other kinases in native neurons. Finally, as shown in DRG neurons (Nomura et al., 1994; Tan et al., 2003) and nonneuronal cells (Kaneko et al., 1997; Morikawa et al., 1998), acute desensitization of μ opioid regulation of VGCCs is not affected by altering the function of major protein kinases, including PKA, PKC, PI3K, Akt, and ErK, nor is it affected by nonspecific inhibitors of protein kinases or phosphatases such as H-8 and okadaic acid. These observations do not support a significant role of protein phosphorylation in this form of desensitization.

In contrast to the acute desensitization, our recent studies show that chronic desensitization in DRG neurons is regulated by a number of second messenger-activated protein kinases in the PI3K-Akt pathway and MAPK cascades (Tan et al., 2003). PI3K comprises a family of dual specificity enzymes with both lipid kinase and protein kinase activity, which can be directly activated by Gβγ dimmers upon activation of μ receptors. One of the key downstream targets of PI3K is Akt, a serine-threonine kinase. The activity of Akt is enhanced by the presence of phosphatidylinositol-3,4,5-P_3 (PIP_3), a lipid product of PI3K, but reduced by phosphates and tensin homolog (PTEN) that reduces the cellular level of PIP_3. In mouse DRG neurons, pharmacological blockade of PI3K activity during a four-hour DAMGO treatment significantly reduces the extent of chronic desensitization, whereas upregulation of cellular Akt levels in neurons lacking PTEN accelerates the desensitization in a PI3K-dependent manner. These findings clearly indicate a facilitating effect of the PI3K-Akt pathway on the chronic desensitization. Similarly, inhibition of the MAPK kinase (MEK)-Erk pathway with PD98059 attenuates DAMGO desensitization. Concurrent blockade of PI3K and Erk activity with selective inhibitors produces no additive relief of the desensitization, suggesting that the two kinases act in a serial manner. This is consistent with the finding in other cell types that μ agonists activate Erk through Gβγ- and PI3K-dependent mechanisms (Ai, Gong, & Yu, 1999). Further analyses demonstrate that chronic DAMGO exposure leads to loss of prepulse facilitation (PPF), a measure of voltage-dependent Gβγ-Ca^{2+} channel interactions, and that such a loss can be partially reversed by inhibition of PI3K or Erk activity. Thus, PI3K and Erk cascades may facilitate chronic desensitization through postreceptor modifications that weaken Gβγ-Ca^{2+} channel interactions. Interestingly, another component of the MAPK cascade, p38 MAPK, is also crucially involved in DAMGO desensitization but through different mechanisms. In HEK293 cells, p38 MAPK facilitates DAMGO-induced μ receptor internalization by enhancing the function of endocytic machinery regulated by the small GTPase Rab5 (Cavalli et al., 2001; Mace, Miaczynska, Zerial, & Nebreda, 2005). Blocking p38 MAPK activity attenuates both desensitization and internalization of the μ receptor in chronic DAMGO-treated DRG neurons. On the other hand, inhibition of p38 MAPK does not affect desensitization induced by morphine, a μ agonist triggering little receptor internalization. It is thus likely that involvement of p38 MAPK in the desensitization is closely related to its ability to regulate μ receptor internalization (Tan, Evans, & Xie, 2007).

μ-Opioid Receptor Trafficking and Desensitization

The μ-opioid receptor undergoes agonist-induced endocytosis via clathrin coated-pits, a process regulated by receptor phosphorylation and association with nonvisual β-arrestins. The exact role of this process in regulating opioid signaling has been a subject of intense investigation (Connor et al., 2004; Marie et al., 2006; Martini & Whistler, 2007). Studies in primary neurons and AtT20 cells have indicated that receptor internalization does not contribute to acute desensitization of μ receptors coupled to VGCCs (Borgland, Connor, Osborne, Furness, & Christie, 2003; Walwyn et al., 2006) or inward rectifying potassium channels (Arttamangkul, Torrecilla, Kobayashi, Okano, & Williams, 2006). The relationship between chronic desensitization and μ receptor internalization, however, is more complex. The internalization induced by prolonged agonist treatment not only attenuates opioid responsiveness via physical removal of the receptor from the cell surface but also promotes receptor dephosphorylation and recycling (Qiu, Law, & Loh, 2003). The internalized GPCRs can return to the cell surface through at least two recycling pathways, a fast/early sorting pathway occurring within minutes and a slow/late sorting pathway taking several hours (Sheff, Daro, Hull, & Mellman, 1999). When rapid recycling occurs, the internalization serves as an important means for receptor resensitization, effectively reducing the extent of apparent desensitization (Koch et al., 1998; Qiu et al., 2003). Alternatively, if the internalized receptors are trapped in late endosomes, desensitization can be enhanced because of significant loss of surface receptors (Law et al., 2000). Extended or repeated opioid exposure can also target internalized receptor to lysosomes for degradation, causing receptor downregulation and more persistent signaling reduction. Thus the functional consequence of μ receptor internalization may vary in different model systems, depending upon the rate and extent of endocytosis as well as its coupling with distinct intracellular sorting pathways that determine the postendocytic fate of the receptor.

In mouse DRG neurons, DAMGO treatment induces substantial μ receptor endocytosis within 20 minutes and results in an approximately 40 percent loss in surface μ receptors after 4- to 24-hour treatments. The internalized receptors are found to colocalize with Rab4 and Rab11, the respective marker of the early and late endosomes, suggesting that both the fast and slow sorting pathways participate in μ receptor recycling in these neurons (Walwyn et al., 2006). Chronic DAMGO desensitization can be prevented or significantly reduced when receptor endocytosis is abolished with p38 MAPK inhibitors (Tan et al., 2007) or when the number of surface μ receptors increases dramatically through adenovirus-mediated overexpression (Walwyn et al., 2004). It is hence conceivable that chronic DAMGO-induced μ receptor internalization may be coupled with delayed recycling through the late sorting pathway, resulting in sustained loss of surface receptors and desensitization. Such a link between internalization and chronic desensitization appears to be agonist selective. After a four-hour exposure to morphine, VGCC inhibition by morphine is significantly reduced but there is no evident μ receptor internalization (Tan et al., 2007). Interestingly, the effect of DAMGO remains relatively intact in chronic morphine-treated neurons (Walwyn et al., 2006). These findings indicate that morphine can induce desensitization through internalization-independent mechanisms, but such desensitization may be incomplete as revealed by testing with DAMGO, a more efficacious full agonist of the μ receptor. A possible interpretation here is that inability of morphine to stimulate endocytosis-related cellular processes, such as activation of p38 MAPK (Mace et al., 2005), may have prevented development of a full-fledged μ opioid desensitization in DRG neurons.

The differences in internalization efficacy of various opiate drugs have been linked with their distinct propensity in promoting tolerance and dependence. Full μ receptor agonists that stimulate internalization, such as etorphine and fentanyl, tend to produce less pronounced tolerance compared to morphine that is least effective in triggering internalization (Duttaroy & Yoburn, 1995). Expression in HEK293 cells of a chimeric receptor (μ/δ receptor), in which the C-terminus of the μ receptor is replaced with that of the δ opioid receptor, facilitates morphine-induced internalization and reduces cellular tolerance and cAMP superactivation, a cellular hallmark of opiate withdrawal (Finn & Whistler, 2001). More recent studies have provided *in-vivo* evidence that morphine tolerance and withdrawal are significantly reduced in a knockin mouse expressing a mutant μ receptor that internalizes in response to morphine (Kim et al., 2008). Thus, internalization could reduce the liability of opiate drugs for promoting tolerance and dependence, likely by limiting receptor signaling and downstream adaptive changes such as superactivation of the cAMP pathway.

Receptor Oligomerization and Desensitization

GPCRs interact with each other through formation of homo- or heteromeric receptor complexes. Such events have divergent impact on receptor binding, signaling or trafficking, and allow cross-regulation between different receptor systems (Bouvier, 2001; Devi, 2001). An increasing number of studies have shown that heterodimerization between the μ-opioid receptor and other GPCRs often reduces signaling of both receptors, promoting heterologous or cross-desensitization. In HEK293 cells expressing the heterodimer of μ and sst$_{2A}$ somatostatin receptors, exposure to the selective agonist of either receptor induces phosphorylation and desensitization of both receptors (Pfeiffer et al., 2002). Similarly, oligomerization of the μ receptor with the substance P receptor (NK1) facilitates agonist-induced cross-phosphorylation and cointernalization of μ and NK1 receptors in HEK293 cells (Pfeiffer et al., 2003). Another example is hetero-oligomerization of μ opioid and α$_{2A}$ adrenergic receptors. When both receptors are expressed in cell lines or transfected neurons, the heterocomplex formation enhances μ receptor signaling in response to morphine, but significantly reduces opioid responses following simultaneous application of morphine and the α$_{2A}$ agonist clonidine (Jordan, Gomes, Rios, Filipovska, & Devi, 2003). In DRG neurons, functional interactions between naturally existing μ and α$_{2A}$ receptors promote chronic cross-desensitization and cointernalization of the two receptors (Tan, 2005). An interesting common finding in these studies is modification of trafficking profiles of μ receptors in the presence of receptor oligomers. The observed cointernalization of the two interactive receptors in response to a single selective agonist may be explained by the "dragging" phenomenon in which the ligand-activated receptor can "drag" another receptor in the same complex to the endocytic pathway (He, Fong, von Zastrow, & Whistler, 2002). Formation of receptor complexes can also alter receptor interactions with β-arrestin, a key adaptor protein regulating receptor endocytosis and sorting, causing delayed receptor recycling and resensitization (Pfeiffer et al., 2003). As it often occurs between functionally related GPCRs, this type of heterodimeric interaction may serve as a negative feedback mechanism to suppress the activity of shared downstream signaling pathways during prolonged receptor stimulation.

While receptor cotrafficking may contribute significantly to the chronic cross-desensitization, direct inter-receptor communication within hetero-oligomers by conformational changes has been proposed for more rapid signaling regulation (Franco et al., 2005; George, O'Dowd, & Lee, 2002). Using fluorescence resonance energy transfer microscopy, a recent report demonstrates that μ and α$_{2A}$ receptors communicate with each other in the heterodimer through a cross-conformational switch that permits direct inhibition of one receptor by the other with subsecond kinetics (Vilardaga et al., 2008). It should also be noted that not all events of heteromerization lead to cross inactivation or desensitization. Formation of μ and δ opioid receptor heterodimers, for example, results in synergistic enhancement of receptor binding and signaling by μ and δ ligands (Gomes et al., 2000). Taken together, receptor oligomerization is a dynamic process regulated by different cellular mechanisms; further investigation is required to fully understand its molecular basis and functional consequence. Finally, most studies addressing this issue to date have been conducted in heterologous cells or in systems where receptors are overexpressed. This may lead to interactions nonexistent with endogenously expressed receptors. It is therefore necessary for future study to identify and characterize interactions between endogenous receptors in native neurons. Such knowledge could shed light on the control of opioid receptor signaling and treatment of opiate tolerance and dependence.

REFERENCES

Ai, W., Gong, J., & Yu, L. (1999). MAP kinase activation by mu opioid receptor involves phosphatidylinositol 3-kinase but not the cAMP/PKA pathway. *FEBS Lett., 456*, 196–200.

Arttamangkul, S., Torrecilla, M., Kobayashi, K., Okano, H., & Williams, J. T. (2006). Separation of mu-opioid receptor desensitization and internalization: Endogenous receptors in primary neuronal cultures. *J Neurosci, 26*, 4118–4125.

Bailey, C. P., & Connor, M. (2005). Opioids: Cellular mechanisms of tolerance and physical dependence. *Curr Opin Pharmacol, 5*, 60–68.

Beland, B., & Fitzgerald, M. (2001). Mu- and delta-opioid receptors are downregulated in the largest diameter primary sensory neurons during postnatal development in rats. *Pain, 90*, 143–150.

Borgland, S. L. (2001). Acute opioid receptor desensitization and tolerance: Is there a link? *Clin Exp Pharmacol Physiol, 28*, 147–154.

Borgland, S. L., Connor, M., Osborne, P. B., Furness, J. B., & Christie, M. J. (2003). Opioid agonists have different efficacy profiles for G protein activation, rapid desensitization, and endocytosis of mu-opioid receptors. *J Biol Chem, 278*, 18776–18784.

Bouvier, M. (2001). Oligomerization of G-protein-coupled transmitter receptors. *Nat Rev Neurosci, 2*, 274–286.

Cavalli, V., Vilbois, F., Corti, M., Marcote, M. J., Tamura, K., Karin, M., et al. (2001). The stress-induced MAP kinase p38 regulates endocytic trafficking via the GDI:Rab5 complex. *Mol Cell, 7*, 421–432.

Chuang, T. T., Iacovelli, L., Sallese, M., & De Blasi, A. (1996). G protein-coupled receptors: Heterologous regulation of homologous desensitization and its implications. *Trends Pharmacol Sci, 17*, 416–421.

Connor, M., & Christie, M. J. (1998). Modulation of Ca2+ channel currents of acutely dissociated rat periaqueductal grey neurons. *J Physiol, 509*, 47–58.

Connor, M., Osborne, P. B., & Christie, M. J. (2004). Mu-opioid receptor desensitization: Is morphine different? *Br J Pharmacol, 143*, 685–696.

Deng, H. B., Yu, Y., Pak, Y., O'Dowd, B. F., George, S. R., Surratt, C. K., et al. (2000). Role for the C-terminus in agonist-induced mu opioid receptor phosphorylation and desensitization. *Biochemistry, 39,* 5492–5499.

Devi, L. A. (2001). Heterodimerization of G-protein-coupled receptors: Pharmacology, signaling and trafficking. *Trends Pharmacol Sci, 22,* 532–537.

Duttaroy, A., & Yoburn, B. C. (1995). The effect of intrinsic efficacy on opioid tolerance. *Anesthesiology, 82,* 1226–1236.

El Kouhen, R., Burd, A. L., Erickson-Herbrandson, L. J., Chang, C. Y., Law, P. Y., & Loh, H. H. (2001). Phosphorylation of Ser363, Thr370, and Ser375 residues within the carboxyl tail differentially regulates mu-opioid receptor internalization. *J Biol Chem, 276,* 12774–12780.

Fields, T. A., & Casey, P. J. (1995). Phosphorylation of Gz alpha by protein kinase C blocks interaction with the beta gamma complex. *J Biol Chem, 270,* 23119–22325.

Finn, A. K., & Whistler, J. L. (2001). Endocytosis of the mu opioid receptor reduces tolerance and a cellular hallmark of opiate withdrawal. *Neuron, 32,* 829–839.

Formenti, A., Arrigoni, E., Martina, M., Taverna, S., Avanzini, G., & Mancia, M. (1995). Calcium influx in rat thalamic relay neurons through voltage-dependent calcium channels is inhibited by enkephalin. *Neurosci Lett, 201,* 21–24.

Franco, R., Casado, V., Mallol, J., Ferre, S., Fuxe, K., Cortes, A., et al. (2005). Dimer-based model for heptaspanning membrane receptors. *Trends Biochem Sci, 30,* 360–366.

George, S. R., O'Dowd, B. F., & Lee, S. P. (2002). G-protein-coupled receptor oligomerization and its potential for drug discovery. *Nat Rev Drug Discov, 1,* 808–820.

Gomes, I., Jordan, B. A., Gupta, A., Trapaidze, N., Nagy, V., & Devi, L. A. (2000). Heterodimerization of mu and delta opioid receptors: A role in opiate synergy. *J Neurosci, 20,* RC110.

Hamid, J., Nelson, D., Spaetgens, R., Dubel, S. J., Snutch, T. P., & Zamponi, G. W. (1999). Identification of an integration center for cross-talk between protein kinase C and G protein modulation of N-type calcium channels. *J Biol Chem, 274,* 6195–6202.

He, L., Fong, J., von Zastrow, M., & Whistler, J. L. (2002). Regulation of opioid receptor trafficking and morphine tolerance by receptor oligomerization. *Cell, 108,* 271–282.

Ikeda, S. R. (1996). Voltage-dependent modulation of N-type calcium channels by G-protein beta gamma subunits. *Nature, 380,* 255–258.

Johnson, E. E., Christie, M. J., & Connor, M. (2005). The role of opioid receptor phosphorylation and trafficking in adaptations to persistent opioid treatment. *Neurosignals, 14,* 290–302.

Jordan, B. A., Gomes, I., Rios, C., Filipovska, J., & Devi, L. A. (2003). Functional interactions between mu opioid and alpha 2A-adrenergic receptors. *Mol Pharmacol, 64,* 1317–1324.

Kaneko, S., Yada, N., Fukuda, K., Kikuwaka, M., Akaike, A., & Satoh, M. (1997). Inhibition of Ca2+ channel current by mu- and kappa-opioid receptors coexpressed in Xenopus oocytes: Desensitization dependence on Ca2+ channel alpha 1 sub-units. *Br J Pharmacol, 121,* 806–812.

Kim, J. A., Bartlett, S., He, L., Nielsen, C. K., Chang, A. M., Kharazia, V., et al. (2008). Morphine-induced receptor endocytosis in a novel knockin mouse reduces toler-ance and dependence. *Curr Biol, 18,* 129–135.

Koch, T., Schulz, S., Schroder, H., Wolf, R., Raulf, E., & Hollt, V. (1998). Carboxyl-terminal splicing of the rat mu opioid receptor modulates agonist-mediated inter-nalization and receptor resensitization. *J Biol Chem, 273,* 13652–13657.

Law, P. Y., Erickson, L. J., El-Kouhen, R., Dicker, L., Solberg, J., Wang, W., et al. (2000). Receptor density and recycling affect the rate of agonist-induced desensitization of mu-opioid receptor. *Mol Pharmacol, 58,* 388–398.

Mace, G., Miaczynska, M., Zerial, M., & Nebreda, A. R. (2005). Phosphorylation of EEA1 by p38 MAP kinase regulates mu opioid receptor endocytosis. *Embo J, 24,* 3235–3246.

Marie, N., Aguila, B., & Allouche, S. (2006). Tracking the opioid receptors on the way of desensitization. *Cell Signal, 18,* 1815–1833.

Martini, L., & Whistler, J. L. (2007). The role of mu opioid receptor desensitization and endocytosis in morphine tolerance and dependence. *Curr Opin Neurobiol, 17,* 556–564.

McLaughlin, J. P., & Chavkin, C. (2001). Tyrosine phosphorylation of the mu-opioid receptor regulates agonist intrinsic efficacy. *Mol Pharmacol, 59,* 1360–1368.

Morikawa, H., Fukuda, K., Mima, H., Shoda, T., Kato, S., & Mori, K. (1998). Desen-sitization and resensitization of delta-opioid receptor-mediated Ca2+ channel inhibition in NG108–15 cells. *Br J Pharmacol, 123,* 1111–1118.

Nomura, K., Reuveny, E., & Narahashi, T. (1994). Opioid inhibition and desensitiza-tion of calcium channel currents in rat dorsal root ganglion neurons. *J Pharmacol Exp Ther, 270,* 466–474.

Pak, Y., O'Dowd, B. F., & George, S. R. (1997). Agonist-induced desensitization of the mu opioid receptor is determined by threonine 394 preceded by acidic amino acids in the COOH-terminal tail. *J Biol Chem, 272,* 24961–24965.

Pfeiffer, M., Kirscht, S., Stumm, R., Koch, T., Wu, D., Laugsch, M., et al. (2003). Het-erodimerization of substance P and mu-opioid receptors regulates receptor traf-ficking and resensitization. *J Biol Chem, 278,* 51630–51637.

Pfeiffer, M., Koch, T., Schroder, H., Laugsch, M., Hollt, V., & Schulz, S. (2002). Het-erodimerization of somatostatin and opioid receptors cross-modulates phospho-rylation, internalization, and desensitization. *J Biol Chem, 277,* 19762–19772.

Qiu, Y., Law, P. Y., & Loh, H. H. (2003). Mu-opioid receptor desensitization: Role of receptor phosphorylation, internalization, and representation. *J Biol Chem, 278,* 36733–36739.

Samoriski, G. M., & Gross, R. A. (2000). Functional compartmentalization of opioid desensitization in primary sensory neurons. *J Pharmacol Exp Ther, 294,* 500–509.

Schroeder, J. E., & McCleskey, E. W. (1993). Inhibition of Ca2+ currents by a mu-opioid in a defined subset of rat sensory neurons. *J Neurosci, 13,* 867–873.

Schulz, R., Wehmeyer, A., & Schulz, K. (2002). Opioid receptor types selectively cointernalize with G protein-coupled receptor kinases 2 and 3. *J Pharmacol Exp Ther,* *300,* 376–384.

Schulz, S., Mayer, D., Pfeiffer, M., Stumm, R., Koch, T., & Hollt, V. (2004). Morphine induces terminal micro-opioid receptor desensitization by sustained phosphorylation of serine-375. *Embo J, 23,* 3282–3289.

Sheff, D. R., Daro, E. A., Hull, M., & Mellman, I. (1999). The receptor recycling pathway contains two distinct populations of early endosomes with different sorting functions. *J Cell Biol, 145,* 123–139.

Taddese, A., Nah, S. Y., & McCleskey, E. W. (1995). Selective opioid inhibition of small nociceptive neurons. *Science, 270,* 1366–1369.

Tan, M., Walwyn, W. M., Evans, C. J., Xie, C. W. (2009). p38 map kinase and beta-arrestin 2 mediate functional interactions between endogenous mu-opioid and alpha 2A-adrenergic receptors in neurons. *J Biol Chem.* Epub ahead of print, Jan 6, 2009, http://www.jbc.org/cgi/doi/10.1074/jbc.M806742200.

Tan, M., Groszer, M., Tan, A. M., Pandya, A., Liu, X., & Xie, C. W. (2003). Phosphoinositide 3-kinase cascade facilitates mu-opioid desensitization in sensory neurons by altering G-protein-effector interactions. *J Neurosci, 23,* 10292–10301.

Tan, M., & Xie, C. W. (2005). Interactions between mu-opioid and alpha 2A adrenergic receptors promote receptor internalization and desensitization. *Internat. Narc. Res. Conf. Abs,* M42.

Vilardaga, J. P., Nikolaev, V. O., Lorenz, K., Ferrandon, S., Zhuang, Z., & Lohse, M. J. (2008). Conformational cross-talk between alpha2A-adrenergic and mu-opioid receptors controls cell signaling. *Nat Chem Biol, 4,* 126–131.

Walwyn, W. M., Keith, D. E., Jr., Wei, W., Tan, A. M., Xie, C. W., Evans, C. J., et al. (2004). Functional coupling, desensitization and internalization of virally expressed mu opioid receptors in cultured dorsal root ganglion neurons from mu opioid receptor knockout mice. *Neuroscience, 123,* 111–121.

Walwyn, W. M., Wei, W., Xie, C. W., Chiu, K., Kieffer, B. L., Evans, C. J., et al. (2006). Mu opioid receptor-effector coupling and trafficking in dorsal root ganglia neurons. *Neuroscience, 142,* 493–503.

Zhang, J., Ferguson, S. S., Barak, L. S., Bodduluri, S. R., Laporte, S. A., Law, P. Y., et al. (1998). Role for G protein-coupled receptor kinase in agonist-specific regulation of mu-opioid receptor responsiveness. *Proc Natl Acad Sci U S A, 95,* 7157–7162.

Index

About the Editor and Contributors

EDITOR

Angela Browne-Miller, PhD, DSW, MPH, is the Set Editor of the *Praeger International Collection on Addictions* (2009), Director of Metaxis Institute for Personal, Social, and Systems Change, based in northern California, United States; Director of Browne and Associates Violence, Substance Abuse, and Trauma Treatment and Prevention Program, also in northern California; has been a keynote speaker at conferences around the world on addiction, violence, and behavior change; and is the author of numerous books, including *To Have and to Hurt: Seeing, Changing or Escaping Patterns of Abuse in Relationships* (2007) and *Rewiring Your Brain to Change Your Behavior* (2009). Dr. Browne-Miller earned two doctorates and two master's degrees at the University of California, Berkeley, where she lectured in three departments for 14 years, and has served as a National Institute of Mental Health Postdoctoral Fellow, a U.S. Department of Public Health Fellow, the public relations director for Californians for Drug Free Youth, the Research Education and Treatment Director for the Cokenders Alcohol and Drug Program, a member of the board of directors of the Employee Assistance Society of North America, an advisor to addiction treatment programs in the United States and several other countries, and project director on three California Department of Health violence prevention projects.

CONTRIBUTORS

Atul Ambekar, MD, is Assistant Professor at the National Drug Dependence Treatment Centre and Department of Psychiatry, All India Institute of Medical Sciences in New Delhi, Delhi, India. He earned his MD degree from All India Institute of Medical Sciences, a prestigious and internationally recognized institute in India. He worked as Senior Resident and later joined the United Nations Office on Drugs and Crime (UNODC), Regional Office for South Asia, New Delhi, as Research Officer. Subsequently, Dr. Ambekar joined the All India Institute of Medical Sciences as Assistant Professor. He is a resource person for trainings and research for various national and international organizations, such as UNODC, Joint United Nations Programme on HIV/AIDS (UNAIDS), and the government of India. He has several publications to his credit.

Charlotte A. Boettiger, PhD, is Assistant Professor of Psychology and Biomedical Research Imaging at the University of North Carolina Chapel Hill, in Chapel Hill, North Carolina, United States. She was formerly an Associate Investigator at the Ernest Gallo Clinic and Research Center and an Adjunct Assistant Professor in the University of California, San Francisco, Department of Neurology. She studied Biology as an undergraduate at the University of California Berkeley, and received her PhD in Neuroscience at UCSF, where she studied the cellular and synaptic mechanisms of vocal learning. She completed a postdoctoral fellowship with Dr. Mark D. Esposito at the Henry H. Wheeler, Jr., Brain Imaging Center in the Helen Wills Neuroscience Institute at UC Berkeley. Her research focuses on the cognitive neurobiology of addiction. Her experimental approach employs neuroimaging, behavioral techniques, genetics, and pharmacology studies in humans. Dr. Boettiger was awarded the Hugh O'Connor Memorial Fellowship by the Wheeler Center for the Neurobiology of Addiction in 2002.

Kathleen Bradbury-Golas, DNP, RN, APN, is Assistant Professor of Nursing at Richard Stockton College of New Jersey in Pomona, New Jersey, United States. She currently teaches across the nursing curriculum in both undergraduate and graduate nursing programs. She also practices part-time as a family nurse practitioner in southern New Jersey. Dr. Bradbury-Golas holds a Doctorate in Nursing Practice from Case Western Reserve University of Cleveland, Ohio, United States. She is certified as both a Family Nurse Practitioner, by the American Association of Nurse Practitioners, and an Adult Health Clinical Nurse Specialist, by the American Nurses' Credentialing Center. Dr. Bradbury-Golas completed her dissertation research studying health promotion practices and opiate-dependent users.

Giuseppe Carrà, MD, MSc, PhD, Consultant Psychiatrist and Research Fellow at University College London, England, studied Medicine at Milan University in Italy, and did his psychiatric training at Pavia University in Pavia, Italy. He has a PhD in Public Mental Health from the University of Pavia. Dr. Carrà did an MSc in Psychiatric Research at University College London. Since 1995, he has been a Consultant Psychiatrist at S. Paolo University Hospital Trust, Milan, though he worked for two years (2004–2006) in the Camden and Islington CMHTs. Since 2004, Dr. Carrà has been a Research Fellow at UCL. He is a Board Member of the International Society of Addiction. He claims the following governmental and institutional appointments: Member of the Guideline Development Group for Schizophrenia at the Italian National Institute of Health; Member of the Addiction Panel at the Italian Department of Health; Member of the panel of independent experts assisting the European Commission at Directorate General of Justice, Freedom and Security in the priority field "Prevent Drug Consumption and Inform the Public," July 2007–June 2010. Research interests include "dual diagnosis" of psychosis and substance misuse, psychoeducational interventions in schizophrenia, and adaptation and implementation of local guidelines.

Vicki W. Chanon, PhD, completed her PhD in the Cognitive Psychology Program at the University of North Carolina at Chapel Hill in 2007. Her dissertation focused on the neural correlates of varying types of attentional allocation (voluntary, reflexive, and social) in healthy adults using event-related potentials. As an undergraduate, Vicki earned her BA in Psychology and Philosophy at the University of Delaware. She is currently a postdoctoral researcher working with Dr. Charlotte Boettiger in the Behavioral Neuroscience Program at the University of North Carolina at Chapel Hill in Chapel Hill, North Carolina, United States. Her current research focuses on dysfunctional attentional processes in addictive disorders. Specifically, she is using behavioral, neuroimaging, and pharmacological methods to gain an understanding of the neurobiological underpinnings of attentional biases toward drug-related words and images in those suffering with addictive disorders.

Kyle M. Clayton, MS, is a Clinical Psychology graduate student at the University of Texas Tyler, in Tyler, Texas, United States. While at UT Tyler, he has been involved in research concerning neuropsychological testing for children with learning disabilities, correlations between olfaction and Alzheimer's disease, the impact of Lorazepam on neuropsychological measures in suspected dementia patients, the effect of exercise on cognition in women receiving adjuvant chemotherapy for breast cancer, and family-focused treatment of juvenile sex offenders. Mr. Clayton provides intervention for children and families as a counselor at a residential treatment center, a teacher/mentor for a youth center, and a caseworker for a foster care/adoption agency. Following the completion of his master's degree in May 2008, Mr. Clayton entered the doctoral program in clinical psychology at the University of Texas Southwestern Medical Center in Dallas.

Herbert C. Covey, PhD, of the Adams County Social Services Department, and the College of Continuing Education, University of Colorado Boulder in Boulder, Colorado, United States, and has taught juvenile delinquency for more than two decades. Dr. Covey received his PhD in Sociology from the University of Colorado at Boulder. He has published several articles on a wide array of subjects, including community corrections, disabilities, religion, street gangs, crime measurement, boomtown crime, research methods, determinant sentencing, violent mentally ill offenders, and social gerontology, among other topics. His current research involves substance abuse treatment and dietary practices of enslaved African Americans. He has also served as an academic journal reviewer for *Criminal Justice Review, Journal of Contemporary Criminal Justice, The Gerontologist, Journal of Applied Sociology,* and *Journal of Crime and Justice.* He is also a part-time instructor at the University of Colorado at Boulder. He has encountered many families and youth who have been involved with meth use and manufacture. He has authored or coauthored nine books and numerous academic articles. He is the editor of *The Meth Crisis* (2006), to which he contributed three chapters. He was a coauthor of the text *Youth Gangs* (2006) and sole author of *African American Slave Medicine: Herb and Non-Herbal Treatments* (2007). He coordinated four major symposiums on methamphetamine for judges, caseworkers, public health officers, law enforcement officers, child protection caseworkers, public administrators, ex-users, and other stakeholders.

Ann N. Dapice, PhD, is Director, Education and Research, of T. K. Wolf, Inc., a nonprofit Native American organization in Tulsa, Oklahoma, United States. With a PhD in Psychology, Sociology, and Philosophy from the University of Pennsylvania, she has served as professor and administrator at a number of universities, including the University of Pennsylvania, Widener University, Penn State University, and Goddard College, teaching Social Sciences and Native American Studies. Her cross-cultural research has been reported in professional journals, books, and academic presentations regionally, nationally, and internationally. Speaking engagements include topics related to addiction, stalking, and Native American issues. Dr. Dapice has served on the Elders Council for the American Indian Chamber of Commerce, is a Member of the Board of Directors of the Mental Health Association in Tulsa and the Tulsa Metropolitan Ministry/Domestic Violence Intervention Services Committee.

She consults with the University of Pennsylvania on Native American issues, where she is founder and Chair of the Association of Native Alumni.

Ted Goldberg, PhD, is Professor of Sociology in Stockholm, Sweden. He was awarded an undergraduate degree in Anthropology and Sociology from Uppsala University and a PhD in Sociology from the same university. Combining anthropological methodology with sociological theory, he has done extensive participant observation research on the drug scene in Stockholm. His main field of study is drug consumption and drug policy, and he has written numerous books and articles on these subjects. He has also written about modern Swedish society, the relevance of sociological theory for practical social work, migration, and alternative methods of teaching on the university level. For several decades, Dr. Goldberg has been one of the most outspoken critics of Swedish drug policy. He is currently teaching at the Department of Social Work at Stockholm University, and the Department of Caring Sciences and Sociology at the University of Gävle.

Dirk Hanson, MA, is a freelance science writer and novelist based in Ely, Minnesota, United States. Mr. Hanson has written extensively on technology, science, and medicine. He is the author of the books *The New Alchemists* and *The Incursion,* as well as a third, *Addiction: The Search for a Cure.* He maintains a blog, "Addiction Inbox," devoted to news and issues related to the science of substance abuse. He has also written for *California Magazine, Omni, CoEvolution Quarterly, Willamette Week, Whole Mind Newsletter,* and other magazines. He has worked as a business and technology reporter for the *Des Moines Register* and for numerous trade publications.

Mary F. Holley, MD, trained at Baylor College of Medicine in Houston, Texas. She is a licensed physician, formerly an obstetrician-gynecologist in northern Alabama, United States. She is founder and Director of Mothers Against Methamphetamine, a national nonprofit drug education organization. Dr. Holley is author of *Crystal Meth: They Call It Ice,* and has produced several educational videos for drug education and prevention. She serves on the Alabama Attorney General's Methamphetamine Task Force as Chairperson of the Education Committee. Her Web site can be seen at www.mamasite.net.

Olga Inozemtseva, PhD, obtained her PhD in the Behavioral Sciences (area of Neurosciences) at the Neuropsychology and Neurolinguistics Laboratory of the Institute of Neurosciences at the University of Guadalajara in Guadalajara, Jalisco, Mexico. Currently, Dr. Inozemtseva works in the same laboratory and gives courses concerning the structure and development of cognitive processes and executive functions. She directs theses and participates in tutoring committees at undergraduate, master's, and doctoral levels. She is the author of several publications (articles, book chapters, articles for dissemination). She has participated in projects in the area of infant neuropsychology that focus on development of children with genetic and hormonal alterations. At present, her professional interests are leading to neuropsychology of drug addiction, particularly, the neuropsychological consequences of substance abuse among addicted patients in a phase of abstinence. Dr. Inozemtseva is a member of the National System of Researchers, CONACyT, México.

Sonia Johnson, MSc, MRCPsych, DM, Professor in Social and Community Psychiatry, has studied Social and Political Sciences and Medicine at Cambridge and Oxford Universities, and then did an MSc in Social Psychology at the London School of Economics. She has a Doctorate in Medicine from the University of Oxford. Dr. Johnson did her psychiatric training in South London and was a Clinical Lecturer in Community Psychiatry at the Institute of Psychiatry. Since 1997, she has been a Senior Lecturer and Reader in Social and Community Psychiatry at University College London, in London, England. Since 2003, her clinical work has been in the Camden and Islington Early Intervention Service for young people with psychosis. Since 2001, Dr. Johnson has been course director for the MSc in Psychiatric Research, and has experience as a PhD supervisor. Her research interests include the evaluation of innovative service models, such as crisis resolution teams, crisis houses, and assertive outreach teams; epidemiology and treatment outcomes in early psychosis; women's mental health needs; "dual diagnosis" of psychosis and substance misuse; the development of the European Service Mapping Schedule (ESMS); and staff morale.

Jorge Juárez, PhD, obtained his master's degree in Psychobiology and his PhD in Biomedical Sciences at the Universidad Nacional Autónoma de México. Currently, he is Researcher and Professor at the Institute of Neurosciences at the University of Guadalajara in Guadalajara, Jalisco, Mexico. He has published numerous scientific articles and several chapters in scientific books and coordinated the edition of books. Dr. Juárez has been reviewer of scientific articles in journals of recognized prestige. Since 1988, his main area of research has focused on the neurophysiologic substratum of motivational aspects of behavior, primarily in relation to addictions. Dr. Juárez has imparted courses at the master's and doctorate levels and has directed undergraduate, master's and doctoral theses. He has been Coordinator of the Doctoral Program, Research Coordinator, and Member of the Ethics Committee, and the Editorial Council of the Institute of Neurosciences at the University of Guadalajara. Since 1990, has he belonged to the National System of Researchers, CONACyT, México.

Paula K. Lundberg-Love, PhD, is a Professor of Psychology at the University of Texas Tyler (UTT) in Tyler, Texas, United States, and the Ben R. Fisch

Endowed Professor in Humanitarian Affairs for 2001–2004. Her undergraduate degree was in Chemistry, and she worked as a chemist at a pharmaceutical company for five years prior to earning her Doctorate in Physiological Psychology with an emphasis in Psychopharmacology. After a three-year postdoctoral Fellowship in Nutrition and Behavior in the Department of Preventive Medicine at Washington University School of Medicine in St. Louis, she assumed her academic position at UTT where she teaches classes in psychopharmacology, behavioral neuroscience, physiological psychology, sexual victimization, and family violence. Subsequent to her academic appointment, Dr. Lundberg-Love pursued postgraduate training and is a licensed professional counselor. She is a member of Tyler Counseling and Assessment Center, where she provides therapeutic services for victims of sexual assault, child sexual abuse, and domestic violence. She has conducted a long-term research study on women who were victims of childhood incestuous abuse, constructed a therapeutic program for their recovery, and documented its effectiveness upon their recovery. She is the author of nearly 100 publications and presentations and is co-editor of *Violence and Sexual Abuse at Home: Current Issues in Spousal Battering and Child Maltreatment*. As a result of her training in psychopharmacology and child maltreatment, her expertise has been sought as a consultant on various death penalty appellate cases in the state of Texas.

Mark K. Mathews, LADC, BCCR, is currently pursuing a master's degree in Holistic Health Studies. Mr. Mathews works as a bio-counselor at Health Recovery Center in Minneapolis, Minnesota, United States. He is also the president of Bio-Recovery, a nutritional supplement company specializing in formulas to address addictions and mental illnesses.

Joan Mathews-Larson, PhD, LADC, holds a Doctorate in Nutrition and is the founder and Executive Director of the pioneering Health Recovery Center in Minneapolis, Minnesota, United States, an orthomolecular (psycho-biological) model for treating addiction and emotional disorders. This unique focus combines therapy with physiological intervention to repair biochemical damage that often manifests as impaired mental functioning and behavioral problems. Her work has received national recognition because of the high recovery rates this model produces. The loss of her 17-year-old son to suicide directly after he completed a treatment program fueled Dr. Mathews-Larson's ongoing search for more effective solutions. Her clinic has now successfully treated many thousands of people over three decades. Her published research in the *International Journal of Biosocial and Medical Research* in 1987 and 1991 describes this work. Her approach is outlined in the best-selling book *Seven Weeks to Sobriety* in 1992; followed by *Depression Free, Naturally,* in 2001. Her books have been reprinted in Finnish, Japanese, Icelandic, and Russian. Articles about her work have appeared in *Psychology Today, Let's Live, Alternative Medicine, Chicago Daily Herald, Harper's Bazaar, Prevention Magazine, Natural Health, Mpls, St. Paul Magazine, Minnesota Physician, Journal of Orthomolecular Medicine, San Francisco Chronicle, LA Times, New Orleans Times, Norway Times, Minneapolis Star Tribune,* and *Townsend Letter for Doctors.*

Scott E. McClure, PhD, is currently employed as a Senior Learning Skills Counselor with the University of California San Diego, Department of Psychiatry, Center for Criminality and Addiction Research, Training, and Application (CCARTA) in San Diego, California, United States. At CCARTA, he provides technology transfer of the most current evidence-based treatment procedures for substance use disorders to substance use treatment staff throughout the state of California. Dr. McClure has more than seven years of experience working with individuals who have co-occurring mental health and substance use issues across a broad scope of populations ranging from the severally mentally ill to university students. He has facilitated groups on post-traumatic stress disorder (seeking safety), adult attention deficit/hyperactivity disorder, dialectical behavior therapy, as well as implemented motivational interviewing and life skills groups while employed at the UCSD Co-occurring Disorder Outpatient Clinic. His clinical and research interests include criminality and addiction, trauma, ADHD, and multicultural issues.

Donald Omonge, BA, is pursuing his post-graduate degree (MA) in Disaster Management from the University of Nairobi in Nairobi, Kenya, and holds a Bachelor of Arts degree in sociology from Egerton University. He has six years of experience working with community-based organizations engaged in community development interventions, research, capacity building, and training. He is currently a training officer with SARAH (Substance Abuse Recovery And HIV/AIDS) Network, a Kenyan faith-based organization sponsored by the U.S. government for community-based HIV/AIDS and substance abuse prevention through behavior change interventions.

Emmanuel S. Onaivi, MSc, PhD, is Associate Professor in the Department of Biology at William Paterson University in Wayne, New Jersey, United States, and a Guest Scientist at U.S. National Institutes of Health. He received his MSc and PhD degrees from the University of Bradford, England. He conducted cannabinoid research as a Postdoctoral Fellow at MCV-VCU. He was an Instructor at LSU-Pennington Biomedical Research and a Visiting Research Scientist at Stanford University, before he was appointed to the faculty of Meharry Medical College, where his laboratory was the first to clone and sequence the mouse CB1 gene. At Vanderbilt University, his team reported racial and gender differences in the expression of CB1 cannabinoid receptors.

His current research is on cannabinoid genomics and proteomics on behavior and changes in anxiety and depression as a basis for addiction. Dr. Onaivi has published several papers, edited four books, including *The Biology of Marijuana from Gene to Behavior* (2002), supervised doctoral and postdoctoral fellows, and his student research was selected and presented on Capitol Hill in Washington, DC. He is a member of the Society for Neuroscience, IACM, and the newsletter editor for the International Drug Abuse Research Society. He received the William Paterson University Award for Excellence in Scholarship.

Meera Vaswani, PhD, earned her PhD degree from Delhi University, a leading university in India. She is a member of the National Drug Dependence Treatment Centre, Department of Psychiatry, All India Institute of Medical Sciences in New Delhi, Delhi, India, a prestigious and internationally recognized institute in India, where she was first a postdoctoral fellow, subsequently joined as a lecturer, and rose to be a professor. During this time, she was elected as Fellow of the Royal Society, London, and Member of the National Academy of Medical Sciences, India. She was selected for a United Nations fellowship, for which she worked in the University of Glasgow in the UK. She was one of the three scientists in the world selected for the Distinguished International Scientist Collaborative Award (DISCA) from the National Institute on Drug Abuse, National Institutes of Health, in 2007. Dr. Vaswani has completed several projects on addiction (alcohol and heroin addiction) and published many papers in both national and international journals. She has been a guest speaker in several national and international forums. She was the only delegate who was invited by Japan to represent India at the Asia Pacific Society of Biological Research in Alcoholism. Subsequently, she was elected to the Board of Directors for the Asia Pacific Society for Alcohol and Addiction Research (APSAAR).

Jace Waguspack, BS, received his BS in Psychology from Texas Christian University in May 2007. He is currently a master's level graduate student at the University of Texas Tyler in Tyler, Texas, United States. He is training in Clinical Psychology with an emphasis on Clinical Neuropsychology, and he intends to follow a PhD program in Neuropsychology upon attaining his master's degree. He hopes thereafter to become a licensed psychologist and assist in the assessment and rehabilitation of individuals that have received traumatic brain injury in a hospital setting. He has performed research in a neuroscience laboratory on the effects of neuro-immunological activation on learning in a mouse model. His current research interests include the study and use of neuropsychological assessment tools in populations with TBI and dementia.

Bethany L. Waits, BA, is a graduate student in Clinical Psychology at the University of Texas Tyler in Tyler, Texas, United States. She anticipates graduation in May 2010 and plans to pursue the licensed professional counselor designation upon completion of her degree. Ultimately, she would like to work as a therapist for a nonprofit community organization, such as a crisis center. In May 2007, she obtained her BA in Psychology from UT Tyler, graduating summa cum laude. Ms. Waits was accepted as a lifetime member of Psi Chi, the national honor society in psychology, and Alpha Chi, a national college honor society. While an undergraduate, she participated in a student panel addressing issues related to sexual assault on campus. Additionally, she has worked with several professors on various research projects.

Mary Theresa Webb, PhD, is founder and past Director of the Global Outreach for Addiction Leadership and Learning (GOAL) Project based in Aliquippa, Pennsylvania, United States. She was one of the founders of the International Substance Abuse and Addiction Coalition (ISAAC), based in the United Kingdom, and the OPORA Training Center in Moscow, Russia. (*Opora* is the Russian word for *support*. Moscow-based nongovernmental OPORA, which works with the Russian government to fight addiction, has trained more than 3,000 persons in addiction and Twelve-Step programs, and implemented 60 recovery groups in 31 cities in Russia.) As a global educator, she has personally and with others facilitated addiction trainings in the United States, Russia, Romania, Tajikistan, Bulgaria, Kenya, Tanzania, Honduras, and Egypt. Currently, Dr. Webb is the Project Director of the Kenya-based, USAIDS-funded Substance Abuse Rehabilitation and HIV/AIDS (SARAH) Network in Kenya. Dr. Webb holds a master's in Education from the University of Pittsburgh and a Doctor of Philosophy Degree in Family Systems/Addiction Intervention from the University of America. She is the author of *Tree of Renewed Life, Church Training Manual,* and coauthor of *Codependence in Family Systems.*

Kathryn M. Wells, MD, is Assistant Professor of Pediatrics and Pediatrician at the Kempe Center for the Prevention and Treatment of Child Abuse and Neglect at the University of Colorado Denver in Denver, Colorado, United States. She received her BA in Biology and Psychology with magna cum laude honors from Carroll College in Helena, Montana, and then attended medical school at Creighton University School of Medicine in Omaha, Nebraska. She received her MD in 1993. She received postgraduate training as a Pediatric Resident at Creighton University-Nebraska Universities Health Foundation Joint Pediatric Residency Program in Omaha. Dr. Wells has had fellowship training in Denver, Colorado, at the University of Colorado Health Sciences

Center, the Kempe Children's Center, and the Children's Hospital in the pediatric subspecialty field of Child Abuse and Neglect. She is often called on as an expert witness in child abuse and neglect cases as well as those involving substance abuse. She travels across the country as a medical expert on the effects of substance abuse on users and the children of users, especially methamphetamine. She is also actively involved in the Colorado Alliance for Drug Endangered Children and has made many presentations on the medical effects of methamphetamine use.

Cui-Wei Xie, MD, PhD, is a Professor in the Department of Psychiatry and Biobehavioral Sciences, David Geffen School of Medicine, and in the Semel Institute for Neuroscience and Human Behavior, at the University of California Los Angeles (UCLA), in Los Angeles, California, United States. She earned her doctoral degrees (MD, PhD) in 1984 from Peking University Health Science Center in Beijing, China. Her doctoral thesis work addressed opioid regulation of pain and cardiovascular function and received several awards from the National Ministry of Public Health in China. After receiving her degrees, Dr. Xie taught at Peking University and continued her research there as Associate Director of the Laboratory of Cardiopulmonary Endocrinology. She was named one of the 10 Outstanding Young Scientists by the Beijing Association of Science and Technology in 1986. Dr. Xie came to United States in 1987 as a visiting scholar at National Institutes of Health (NIH). She moved to Duke University two years later where she studied opioid regulation of hippocampal synaptic plasticity. Since joining UCLA faculty in 1995, Dr. Xie has continued her study on opioid receptor signaling and the cellular mechanisms underlying opioid desensitization and tolerance. She is the recipient of multiple research grants from NIH and has served on many review panels for the research grant programs of federal agencies and private foundations.